Women and Romance

Women and Romance

A Reader

EDITED BY

Susan Ostrov Weisser

New York University Press

NEW YORK AND LONDON

NEW YORK UNIVERSITY PRESS
New York and London

Library of Congress Cataloging-in-Publication Data

Women and romance : a reader / edited by Susan Ostrov Weisser.
p. cm.
Includes index.
ISBN 0-8147-9354-1 (alk. paper)—ISBN 0-8147-9355-X (pbk. : alk. paper)
1. Women. 2. Love. 3. Women in literature. 4. Love in literature. 5. Women and
literature. 6. Love stories—History and criticism. I. Weisser, Susan Ostrov.

HQ1386 .W65 2001
305.4—dc21   2001030493

New York University Press books are printed on acid-free paper,
and their binding materials are chosen for strength and durability.

Manufactured in the United States of America

10 9 8 7 6 5 4 3 2 1

For Madeline

Contents

Acknowledgments

A great many people kindly contributed their thoughts, knowledge, and practical suggestions to this book. I am particularly grateful to Ann Snitow for her initial enthusiasm, which jump-started the long process from idea to project. Niko Pfund, Eric Zinner, and Cecilia Feilla at New York University Press have been extremely encouraging; Cecilia in particular put up with the many questions and difficulties in the course of putting this reader together with exemplary patience and good humor. Despina Papazoglou Gimbel and Rachel Scharfman, also of New York University Press, and the copyeditor, Rosalie Morales Kearns, saw the book through the maze of production with superb professionalism and care.

Editing a reader can seem at times like a second full-time job; Laura Reitano, departmental secretary extraordinaire, helped me keep my first one, as well as my sanity. I would have been lost without her daily (sometimes extending to nightly) involvement.

I would like to thank Ruth Sternglantz, Shanna Willner, Robert Roth, and Mary Kay Blakely for their aid in smoothing the process of finding sources or authors. Barbara Crow was especially generous with her time and suggestions. Dora Keller contributed invaluable help transcribing Emma Goldman's difficult handwriting, and Alison Traweek did some of the footwork that brought this project to fruition. I am grateful to them, and to Cybèle Weisser, who did much-needed editing on a rough draft.

Finally, I would like to thank the many authors and publishers represented here who forfeited their usual fees because they thought the project was an important one. I hope this book rewards their generosity.

Introduction

Man's love is of man's life a thing apart,
'Tis woman's whole existence.

—Lord Byron

This is a book for anyone who is interested in understanding the conflicted but powerful female urge to experience the pleasure and endure the pain of romantic love. It may be especially interesting to women whose own desire for relationships with men is, vaguely or explicitly, in conflict with their feminist values of independence and self-assertion. Does romance weaken or empower women? Is it a debilitating illusion, a form of false consciousness, or the understandable expression of a universal human need, which women should pursue with less shame and greater self-assertion? Judging from the shelves of books advising women on love problems, there seems to be an ongoing difficulty in maintaining an *equal* and satisfying heterosexual romantic love relationship. What have feminists and antifeminists thought and written about this problem? Why do they frequently disagree, both with each other and among themselves?

I began this project because, as a feminist scholar and teacher who has long dealt with the literary expression of romantic love and its special relation to women, I have been frustrated that although there is an enormous body of scholarly, creative, and popular works of all sorts on romance, there appears to be no collection demonstrating the historical development of this subject as an *idea* specifically relating to women in Western society. Moreover, while there are volumes of literary and historical description of romance in print, and much philosophical and psychological musing about the nature of love as an individual expression of a timeless universal phenomenon, there has been shockingly little systematized thought regarding the ideology of romantic love as it is experienced by women since second-wave feminism in the 1970s. Self-help and pop-psychology books and magazine articles flood the market, but they all assume a reformist position in which the individual woman must take responsibility for "making the love she needs," without questioning the basic assumptions that inform the ideology of romantic love as an ideal. They appeal to women's anxieties without making them think. It is my ambition in this volume to provoke the reader to think more clearly and deeply about the ways women conceive of and behave in love.

Feminism has been largely successful in questioning traditional assumptions that women belong in the domestic realm rather than in the workplace, as well as in convincing educated women that they should be equals in their professional lives. Certainly a great deal of lip service is paid in the media to the new assertiveness of women, their independence, their courage in striking out in new directions. But, as Susan Douglas has shown in *Where the Girls Are* (1994), the feminist critique of standards for women's beauty has had minimal effect on the anxieties and consumer behavior of the ordinary woman who has internalized the necessity to be beautiful in the marketplace of love and success. Similarly, when women were told by first- and second-wave feminists that heterosexual relationships should be "equal" and that romantic love leaves them too vulnerable to exploitation by men, feminism itself ran headlong into the everyday resistance of women who see romantic love as a pleasure, a necessity, or even a biological imperative. My female students, almost without exception, value romantic love highly and see it as their "right." Their fear of losing it, or worse, never being valued enough to be among the chosen, often conflicts with or detracts from their interest in feminism.

The scholarship on the subject of love is not necessarily helpful in resolving this tension; it is both vast and contradictory as to whether romance is primarily biological or cultural in origin, universal or particular to social systems, embedded in the individual human psyche by evolution or another aspect of male-female social relations. Given the lack of a scholarly consensus on the subject, it is not surprising that feminists have also responded in strikingly different ways to its political import, as either champions, reformers, or revilers of romantic love for women. Feminist writers seem presently in conflict (not to say confusion) about the meaning and impact of romantic love as a subject that is not simply theoretical, but affects the lives of women everywhere in their everyday relations with men.

In this morass of opinion and behavior, nonheterosexual love represents a strong challenge to the assumptions of gender complementarity that often underlie the ethos of romance in the West. Some writers propose lesbian romance as a superior alternative or ideal version of passion because it is what Rita Mae Brown calls "woman-identified," celebrating its freedom from institutional norms and restrictions (see the essays by Rita Mae Brown and Suzanne Juhasz in this volume). Yet a number of the texts in this reader demonstrate that the strong romantic feeling that accompanies lesbian love relationships is not necessarily free of conflict: Emily Dickinson's letters to Sue, her beloved sister-in-law, are just as tortured as her letters to the unidentified but presumably male "Master," while Jane Rule and Lynne Harne look at problems of dependency, self-hatred, and conformity to hetero gender norms that are duplicated within lesbian relations.

With the patent failure of the second-wave feminists' denunciation of love, and the nineteenth-century dream of free love belied by the mixed effects of our century's supposed sexual liberation, contemporary feminists seem less willing to take on one of the experiences of pleasure seeming to unite men and women. Thus romance has once again become normal, "natural," and largely unquestioned, a formulation that is now increasingly applied to nonhetero romance as well in popular culture.

Perhaps romantic passion has attracted less attention in general than sexuality or marriage and motherhood because it is so accepted in Western society as self-expression and appears more a result of benign choice than sexual matters, on the one hand, and more individualized and "private" an experience than the institutional and legal rules associated with the family on the other. This leads to confusion, ambivalence, even a certain anxiety about how to "place" it. The diminution of organized feminist critical response since second-wave feminism (roughly from Simone de Beauvoir's *The Second Sex* to the late 1970s), however, is less understandable. It has been difficult in recent years to question the nature of romantic love, surely one of the pleasures (as well as structuring principles) of women's lives in Western societies.

Women's studies courses and the texts used in them would seem to be the natural locus for examining these very issues, yet a look at the contents of these commonly used readers reveals that most often there is little or no direct analysis of the role that romantic love plays in the life of the contemporary American woman. Typical divisions of topic in college textbooks might include "Women and Work," "Women and Health," "Women and Marriage," "Motherhood," and nearly always "Women and Sexuality." Oddly, given the ubiquitous importance of romantic love in popular culture and the focus of interest on it by young women so important as consumers of that culture, romantic love is always subsumed, if treated at all, under "Sex" or "Marriage and Family Life."

But of course it is exactly the experience and understanding of romantic love as a "normal" phenomenon of life that links sexuality and the institution of marriage/family for many young women, and determines a good deal about their choices and the course of their lives. As the presumed "emotionally literate" sex, the so-called relationship experts, women often talk of love as courtship (emotion leading to male commitment, marriage, family) in which the values of romantic love are opposed to pornography, cheap sex, promiscuity, and a low valuation of women. On the other hand, romantic passion is also seen as individual fulfillment, in which case it is more related to sexual pleasure for women and aligned with values of personal liberation, even rebellion. Romance bears a good deal of weight, some of it laden with tangles of meaning difficult to separate and see clearly.

It is my intention that this collection illustrate the various agendas of the cultural economy of romantic love in relation to women, rather than purport to solve the questions I have posed. I have deliberately confined the readings here to Western society, where romance has become ubiquitous in modern culture and of overwhelming importance in most women's lives. The special (though not exclusive) focus of this reader is on the divide between the feminist critique, not to say denunciation, of romantic love as a form of dependency and subordination to men, and the continuing popularity of the phenomenon among women, both in life and in popular genres such as romance movies and novels.

As we all know, Harlequin novels constitute a phenomenally successful industry, still growing, and still consumed overwhelmingly by women. Moreover, its explosion on the publishing scene exactly coincided with the rise of feminism as a form of politics in the 1960s. The context of the readings on popular romance in this volume is the conflict between competing ideologies in feminism and romance, and especially between the feminist suspicion of passion and the actual emotional life and behavior of the woman who desires romantic love.

Whether or not romantic love and its literary expression in popular romance are the most despicable forms of "dope for dupes," in Germaine Greer's famous formulation, or are subversive expressions of women's individual desire and subtly reflective of their ultimate power over men, seems a moot point to women who must deal with real problems of loneliness, the legitimacy of passion as an antidote to domestic burdens, or the imperatives of belonging to a couple for social status.

The real dilemma is that actual women, for the most part, want what is not supposed to be good for them. This is hardly surprising, given that romantic love is celebrated all over the media women are exposed to on a daily basis, that it is a traditional and unquestioned received category in Western society, and that, as some anthropologists and other social scientists argue, it is possibly a cultural universal (see the anthropologist W. R. Jankowiak's edited volume *Romantic Passion: A Universal Experience,* 1995) or part of our biological inheritance (Helen Fisher, *Anatomy of Love,* 1992). Female consumers of romance are understandably irritated by being told they should not desire what appears to be one of the few readily available joys sweetening alienated lives—or more likely, are unaware of the critique and debate at all, except for its reduction to the stereotypical antifeminist belief that "feminists don't like men."

This anthology attempts to contribute to this debate, one with an unusually important potential for affecting women's daily lives, by representing the varying viewpoints and vexed history of views on romance, beginning with historical selections that represent a variety of views of which modern readers are perhaps unaware. One of the difficulties of analyzing romantic love is that it is usually assumed, certainly in popular culture, to be an essential emotion, the same everywhere and at all times, a "thing" that one falls into or out of, with one person forever, or at least one person at a time. Whether or not there is truth in this idea, it gives romance a kind of invisibility in spite of (or because of) its ubiquity. The representation of a variety of views here seems to me to illustrate the ways a taken-for-granted, seemingly universal phenomenon can differ from era to era, from person to person, and even within the same person at different times. Of course, though lovers often feel themselves to be in a separate little cocoon of privacy, in fact the world is present all the time. Romantic love is never either just private or just public; one informs the other.

We are a specialist society, and like other aspects of human experience, love tends to be conceptualized and analyzed in parts: sociobiologists have one approach, clinical psychologists another, literary critics a third, and so on. For example, the psychologist may treat romance as if it were an individual adjustment to universal infantile desires; the neurobiologist as if it were chemical. The evolutionary psychologist views it as species-adaptive while the sociologist assumes it is socially adaptive; the anthropologist may be interested in its wide variations; the historian looks for ways that it is historically specific; the literary critic looks for patterns in the shape and thematics of the romance narrative. Meanwhile popular advice and self-help/pop-psychology books address a broader audience of women, as do magazines, songs, movies, TV, ads, and romance novels, as if romance were a universal yet intensely subjective experience of ideal meaning. This is the gap I would like to address. Why is there so little concordance between these views? What is at stake here for women?

Just as sexuality represents a double bind for women—to be seen as *just* an object of sexual desire is to be demeaned and not taken seriously, yet not to be seen as an object of sexual desire is to have no value at all—romantic desire in or for a woman cuts both ways also. The media tell women that being in love means adventure; liberation from normal bounds and everyday experience; opening up to vulnerability ("taking a chance") and bursting open inhibition; rebellion against prohibition; mutuality; support; perhaps a chance to be adored, the "star of one's own movie." Yet real-life experiences often expose power struggles and enormous disappointments (see Shere Hite, *Women and Love*, 1987).

In the current discourse about romance, men's and women's voices often conflict: thus the popularity of the Mars and Venus idea, which naturalizes this conflict of interest. For example, men might speak of their fear that women control men by sex, or that women's quest for commitment/secure attachment entails impossible promises and expectations. Men inherit a traditional narrative role in which they must assume a heroic stance, under pressure to appear as society expects them, constantly and infinitely sexual, not needy of love themselves. Meanwhile, women worry that being in love with a man gives him power over them, often leading to increased passivity or abuse in relationships, while not being loved leads to loneliness, social ostracism, and exploitation, sexual and otherwise. Then too, feminism has made women aware that they tend to define themselves in terms of men, emphasizing the need to learn independence, to emphasize work and friendship over being "adored." Whether seen as natural or historical, women's greater dependence on relationships leaves them vulnerable: a need for another often gives power to that other (Peplau, "Power in Dating Relationships," in *Women: A Feminist Perspective*, ed. Jo Freeman, 2d ed., 1979).

I have organized these selections in a way that I hope will help the reader compare and evaluate arguments about the vexed and varied relation of women to romantic love, see the historical direction they have taken, and grasp the complexity of issues most often addressed through the prism of one discipline or perspective alone. Part 1, which features historical essays, is followed by a selection of more personal documents, mainly letters by well-known authors, some of whom wrote the theory that appears elsewhere in the book. Other parts give a sampling of second-wave feminism, contemporary views, literary criticism, and analyses of popular romance in fiction, music, film, women's magazines, and comics. Because there is so much already collected on the topics of women's sexuality and marriage, I have generally tried to avoid selections that deal only or specifically with those topics, though they overlap inevitably with the practice of romantic love. I have also focused mainly on heterosexual experiences, not so much because they are normative as because they have represented a difficult political problem for women, though lesbianism has an interesting relation to these problems as either a proposed progressive solution to them (see Brown, Faderman, and Juhasz, this volume) or in duplicating them unintentionally (see Rule and Harne, this volume). The documents in parts 1 to 3 are arranged in roughly chronological order, whereas in parts 4 to 8 I have grouped them according to theme.

A perusal of these texts will disclose the difficulties of pinning down a simple or reliable definition of the term "romantic love." When we look at the historical documents, we can see that there is no one definition or characteristic feature of romantic love that has consistently persisted throughout Western history. Neither Capellanus nor Heloise, for example, sees romance as the first step toward marriage, whereas today the two are assumed to be inseparable in Western culture. To give another example, the nineteenth-century selections here, both by conservative advice book authors and radical feminists, presume a discontinuity between "holy and pure" romantic love and sexuality as we understand it today. Romance and domestic affection are often conflated in modern society, as we understand one to lead "naturally" to the other (if it doesn't, my students explain to me, it isn't "really" love after all, something Heloise would be surprised to hear).

Even the idea, so entrenched now, that women are more "suited" to romance than men by nature seems not to have been a universal belief in the Middle Ages. Certainly today there is a mass of contradictions in our popular conceptions of romantic love. For example, it is widely understood that love is the expected, ordinary experience—there is "the one" for everyone (or at least, as my students point out, everyone who is normal)—but it is also a glamorizing and glamorized experience, a taste of the sublime, the transcendent, sexual yet spiritual, and so forth. The most popular narrative in our culture is that women are hungry for relationships and try to trap men into them, yet men marry in far greater numbers after divorce than women do, and some studies seem to show that they fall in love more quickly. On the other hand, women report more euphoria in love, which does not necessarily translate as feeling it more. Women are supposed to be more sensitive, emotional, and nurturing in relationships, yet men (from Capellanus on) often perceive them as overly interested in material considerations, and in fact women rate professional status and material worth more highly in a romantic mate than men do (see Elaine Hatfield's review of psychological research literature in this volume).

In the midst of these confusing and often conflictual ideas, the cause of women's best interests can easily get lost. Ideally, I would like to help revive the debate about whether the practice of romantic love can be a justifiable pursuit under patriarchy or is always implicated in subordination, by showing the range of opinion on women, feminism, and romance. Though other issues of feminism—work, sexual harassment, rape, abortion, pornography, to name a few—have more concrete legal implications, surely romance affects a great many women's lives profoundly and enduringly. It is inconceivable to me to think of a feminism without a coherent critical understanding and evaluation of an experience many, if not most, women in the West think of (correctly or not) as universal and primary to their well-being, if not to the meaning of their lives. We need to read, talk, and think about these questions in a public arena if we are to find ways to resolve them.

Note to the reader: In the documents presented here I have omitted footnotes or parenthetical citations that were not pertinent to the excerpt. The notes that remain are by the original authors, except where I have indicated a different source.

Part I

Historical Views of Women and Romantic Love

It is impossible to provide the reader with more than a cursory glance at archival materials on the subject of women and romance, but it is possible to discern changes over time even in this abbreviated selection. We can see, for example, that before the eighteenth century there is a debate, not a consensus of opinion, on women's relation to emotion in general and to the experience of love in particular. Rousseau, publishing when a new evaluation of companionate marriage arose in the eighteenth century, wrote with confidence about the preoccupation of women with romance, and their greater suitability for it. Mary Wollstonecraft, by contrast, set the terms for much of the modern feminist contention over the validity of romantic experience for women. She strongly argued for the priority of reason over the claims of passion, which she viewed as a weakness, leading women into sexual error and subordination.

Victorian women, including most of the early suffragists, were frequently concerned with improving domestic relations while maintaining stable family ties, so that their discussion of romantic feeling appears mainly in their support for marriages motivated by "true," "pure," or "holy" love rather than by the economic dependence of the wife. At the beginning of the twentieth century, however, the American anarchist Emma Goldman (like the Russian revolutionary Alexandra Kollontai) denounced the tie between love and marriage as a form of enslavement for women, but rather than throw out the baby with the bathwater, advocated for "free love" without legal or economic bonds.

Interestingly, Rousseau's view that "love is a woman's whole life" is still very much with us in the twentieth century, as we see in the excerpt from William Robinson's 1917 book and the 1969 article by Barbara Bross and Jay Gilbey, all of whom describe the good effects that a "real" woman's love can have on a man.

Chapter One

From The Art of Courtly Love (c. 1185)

Andreas Capellanus

This excerpt is taken from an important medieval text instructing men and women on proper behavior in courtly love. The view that men are "weakened" by romantic passion while women are incapable of real love is in stark opposition to the conventional association of women with the nobility of love, romantic and maternal, in the modern period (see the selection by the historian Francesca Cancian in part 5).

By love men are weakened in three very logical ways: by the mere act of Venus, as the physiologists tell us, the powers of the body are very much lessened; love causes one to eat less and drink less, and so not unreasonably the body, being less nourished, has less strength; finally, love takes away a man's sleep and deprives him of all rest. But lack of sleep is followed in a man by bad digestion and great weakening of the body, as we can see from the rational physiological definition of the word sleep, for, as Johannicius[1] says, "Sleep is a rest of the animal powers with an intensification of the natural powers," and therefore lack of sleep is merely a wearying of the animal powers with weakening of the natural ones. In a fourth way, too, it may not unfittingly be said that the human body is weakened, for we believe that through sin all of God's gifts in a man are lessened and the span of man's life is shortened. Since, therefore, bodily strength is a great and especial gift to man, you will do wrong if you strive after things which can for any reason cause this particular gift to fail in you or to be in any way decreased. But from love come not only the things we have mentioned, but bodily sickness also; for a bad digestion upsets the humors within us, and so fevers and numberless illnesses arise. The loss of sleep also causes frequent alterations in the brain and in the mind, so that a man becomes raging mad. But too much brooding by day and by night, which all lovers indulge in, also brings on a certain weakness of the brain, and from this come many illnesses of the body. But I remember that I once found in certain medical books that because of the works of Venus men quickly grow old, and so I try by my entreaties to warn you not to love.

For yet another reason I urge you not to love: that is because in a wise man

From Andreas Capellanus, *The Art of Courtly Love,* ed. John Parry (New York: Columbia University Press, 1941), 199–202. © 1941 by Columbia University Press. Reprinted by permission of the publisher. Notes are by John Parry.

wisdom loses its function if he loves. No matter how full of wisdom any man may be, if he is seduced to the work of Venus he cannot be moderate or restrain by his wisdom the impulse of wantonness or keep from doing things that lead to death. Indeed, it is said that wise men become more wild with love and indulge more ardently in the pleasures of the flesh than those who have less knowledge to control them. But wise men, after they have sinned in love, are accustomed to despise the excesses of lust more than those who have little knowledge to support them. Who was filled with greater wisdom than Solomon, yet he sinned by wantoning beyond measure, and because of his love for women he did not fear to worship strange gods. And who was found greater or more famous for wisdom than David the Prophet, who, although he had innumerable concubines, lusted after the wife of Urias and dishonored her in adultery and like a perfidious homicide killed her husband?[2] What lover of women, then, can moderate his own desire if men so strong in the precepts of wisdom could make no use of it when the love of women was in question, and could not restrain their wantonness?

Again we confound lovers with another argument. The mutual love which you seek in women you cannot find, for no woman ever loved a man or could bind herself to a lover in the mutual bonds of love. For a woman's desire is to get rich through love, but not to give her lover the solaces that please him. Nobody ought to wonder at this, because it is natural. According to the nature of their sex all women are spotted with the vice of a grasping and avaricious disposition, and they are always alert and devoted to the search for money or profit. I have traveled through a great many parts of the world, and although I made careful inquiries I could never find a man who would say that he had discovered a woman who if a thing was not offered to her would not demand it insistently and would not hold off from falling in love unless she got rich gifts in one way or another. But even though you have given a woman innumerable presents, if she discovers that you are less attentive about giving her things than you used to be, or if she learns that you have lost your money, she will treat you like a perfect stranger who has come from some other country, and everything you do will bore her or annoy her. You cannot find a woman who will love you so much or be so constant to you that if somebody else comes to her and offers her presents she will be faithful to her love. Women have so much avarice that generous gifts break down all the barriers of their virtue. If you come with open hands, no women will let you go away without that which you seek; while if you don't promise to give them a great deal, you needn't come to them and ask for anything. Even if you are distinguished by royal honors, but bring no gifts with you, you will get absolutely nothing from them; you will be turned away from their doors in shame.[3] Because of their avarice all women are thieves, and we say they carry purses. You cannot find a woman of such lofty station or blessed with such honor or wealth that an offer of money will not break down her virtue, and there is no man, no matter how disgraceful and low-born he is, who cannot seduce her if he has great wealth. This is so because no woman ever has enough money—just as no drunkard ever thinks he has had enough to drink. Even if the whole earth and sea were turned to gold, they could hardly satisfy the avarice of a woman.

Furthermore, not only is every woman by nature a miser, but she is also envious and a slanderer of other women, greedy, a slave to her belly, inconstant, fickle in her speech, disobedient and impatient of restraint, spotted with the sin of pride and desirous of vainglory, a liar, a drunkard, a babbler, no keeper of secrets, too much given to wantonness, prone to every evil, and never loving any man in her heart.

Now woman is a miser, because there isn't a wickedness in the world that men can think of that she will not boldly indulge in for the sake of money, and, even if she has an abundance she will not help anyone who is in need. You can more easily scratch a diamond with your fingernail than you can by any human ingenuity get a woman to consent to giving you any of her savings. Just as Epicurus believed that the highest good lay in serving the belly, so a woman thinks that the only things worth while in this world are riches and holding on to what she has. You can't find any woman so simple and foolish that she is unable to look out for her own property with a greedy tenacity, and with great mental subtlety get hold of the possessions of someone else. Indeed, even a simple woman is more careful about selling a single hen than the wisest lawyer is in deeding away a great castle. Furthermore, no woman is ever so violently in love with a man that she will not devote all her efforts to using up his property. You will find that this rule never fails and admits of no exceptions.

NOTES

1. Honeïn-ben-Ishaq (809–873) wrote a sort of introduction to medicine, which developed into the much-read *Isagoge Iohannicii ad Artem Parvam Galeni*. According to Bossuat this passage is not found in Johannicius, but comes from Avicenna; Drouart la Vache's translation substitutes the name Avicenna for Johannicius in this passage.

2. II Kings (II Samuel), chap. 11.

3. Ovid *Art of Love* 11. 279–280.

Chapter Two

From The Worth of Women

Wherein Is Clearly Revealed Their Nobility and Their Superiority to Men (1600)

Moderata Fonte

In contrast to Capellanus's work, this Renaissance author, one of the very few females of the period to write directly on the relation of women to romantic love, presents women as victims of men due to women's inherently trusting, compassionate, and warmhearted nature.

"It may be seen from experience," added Cornelia, "that those few men who have loved truly have acted virtuously as well and have never been a cause of scandal to anyone. True love makes the proud humble, the ignorant learned, the timorous brave, the irascible gentle; it makes the foolish clever, and madmen wise. In brief, it can change men's nature, make the bad good and the good better. That's why love is often compared to fire: just as gold is refined in the fire, so man reaches a state of perfect refinement in the flame of true love. But, then, those who have none of the qualities we have just listed strive to appear what they are not, and, as I have said, they often succeed very well (much to our harm and peril), in concealing their falsity and ill intentions beneath an appearance of decency. So even if a man does seem, over a long period, to display that loyalty and true love that we have talked about, I should advise any woman who is sensible, well-respected, and virtuous to proceed cautiously, if she values her virtue and her reputation. Thus when some man sets himself to courting her, however sincere his courtship appears to be, she should never take him seriously in any way, and should neither allow herself to believe him, lest she find herself loving him in return, nor accept his messages or his favors, lest she find herself in his debt. In fact, right from the start, she should energetically defend and protect herself against these temptations (it should not be difficult for her), and she should behave this way with everyone who tries to lure her, rejecting each man's advances equally and refusing to listen to anyone, whether seriously or even in jest (in case she falls into the trap of those who feign sleep and finish up falling asleep in earnest). But above all things, even if she does feel some leaning toward a lover, she should on no account let this be understood: she should hide her feelings as much as possible and not give the man the least encouragement, in case he becomes arrogant and importunate, and dares to try and tempt her to something more serious. Because it can often happen that over time the pestering and the constant pleading of someone one loves and trusts are enough to move a heart, especially the heart of a tender, trusting, and impassioned woman—for, as the proverb says, even the hardest stones are worn away by drops of water."

"That would be fine," Leonora replied to this, "if it were something within our power to do. But we women are so trusting, so kind and sensitive by nature that we are quick to trust; and then, since we are also compassionate and warmhearted, we cannot help loving in return (though in a sincere and virtuous manner). For we assume that men are like us, both in truthfulness and in purity of motives; and this tendency to judge men by ourselves is the cause of our downfall."

"Tell me, my dear, sweet Corinna," said Helena. "Why is it that women, as Leonora says, are kinder and more innocent and trusting than men?"

"In my view," Corinna replied, "the explanation for this lies in women's natural disposition and complexion, which is, as all learned men agree, cold and phlegmatic.[1] This makes us calmer than men, weaker and more apprehensive by nature; more credulous and easily swayed, so that when some lovely prospect opens up before us, some enticing vista, we immediately drink in the image as though it were true, when it fact it is false. But despite all that, where our natural disposition is at fault, we should bring our intellect into play and use the torch of reason to light our way to recognizing these lovers' masks and protecting ourselves against them. In fact, we should pay about as much attention to them and give them about as much credence as the sensible little lamb gave to the wolf when it was imitating its mother's voice and begging it to open the gate."[2]

"That makes good sense to me," said Helena. "For women's nature is such that ferocity cannot dominate in it, since choler and blood make up a relatively minor part of our constitution. And that makes us kinder and gentler than men and less prone to carry out our desires, while men, by contrast, being of a hot and dry complexion, dominated by choler—all flame and fire—are more likely to go astray and can scarcely contain their tempestuous appetites. And that is the reason for the fierceness, waywardness, and fury of their anger, and the urgency and excessiveness of their burning, intemperate desires, carnal and otherwise. Desire in men is so powerful that their senses overpower their reason; and since that is the way in which men function (following their senses, without the controlling influence of reason), then you can hardly wonder if most of them have little time for virtuous deeds and give themselves up entirely to the pleasures and promptings of vice. For when the human spirit is joined to a body so constituted, the effects that follow can hardly be other than those that the nature and properties of the cause dictate. Isn't that the case?"

"Indeed," replied Corinna. "But by saying that, you are not refuting the claim that women are superior to men. On the contrary, you are rather lending further weight to it, because, in addition to what has already been said, you are now adding the fact that women's physical nature is superior to men's and that women act according to reason rather than appetite and thus refrain from evil and devote themselves to good. The same is not true of men, even though they certainly could be good and emend their nature if they wished to, considering the perfection of their intellect, resulting from the greater liveliness of spirit they are said to possess. But they do not care to use their intellect, nor to make the effort to contain their sensuality, and thus they go from bad to worse. So men are vicious both by nature and by will—and they try their best to corrupt us as well."

"So women's goodness derives from their nature rather than their will," said Helena. "Which means that since we are less naturally inclined to evil than men, if we abstain from it we hardly deserve much credit for it, while if we do succumb, our sin is a grave one—for, if the urgings of our nature are not strong, it implies a conscious decision to sin. Men, on the other hand, are almost forced into sin by their nature, as we have been saying; and when they succeed, through sheer moral strength, in controlling their urges, then their virtue must be recognized as outstanding and they deserve great credit for it."

"Aha!" said Corinna. "Even now, you are still having to admit that women are superior in nature to men; indeed, your whole argument rests on that assumption. And a consequence of that is that women are more perfect than men and of greater dignity. But you are wrong when you assert that for this reason men are more praiseworthy than us when they refrain from evil, because their urge to sin is greater and more powerful than ours. That is something I cannot concede, for it's easy to find any number of examples of women who have suffered the torments of sensuality more violently than many men. It may be that the inclination toward sensuality is stronger in men than in women, because their nature is more capacious and their will more imperious. But that does not mean that women are not just as fiercely assaulted as men by these natural forces and powers of the soul, or that women are not drawn toward sensual pleasures by as strong an urge of the will as their nature will allow. It's just as though there were two glasses, one large and one small: when both are filled with water, the large obviously contains a greater volume of water, but that does not change the fact that both glasses are full, brimming, and fully occupied with that volume of water which their maker designed them to hold. And thus we must conclude that women have fewer mental and physical resources for resisting temptation, but are still, within the limitations of their nature, as subject to the temptations of the senses as men—perhaps even more so, because of their yielding and unsuspecting nature, which lends them to be all the more easily carried away and overcome by natural passions. Yet women struggle to be good and resist their evil inclinations with a stout heart. And women do not simply face the obstacle of their own inclinations; they also need to summon enough strength to pit them-selves against men's corrupting influences. A double strength, then; and a kind of strength, you might say, that comes all the less easily to women because of their natural gentleness and kindness, which make them inclined, in all other areas of life, to put others' good and others' pleasures before their own. In this case, though, because they know that virtue must come above their own life and others', they accept the need to repress their desires and deny all pleasure both to themselves and the men they believe love them. But they do so at the cost of great violence to their hearts, and they deserve an infinite amount of credit for their victories."

"But even if I were to allow, for the sake of argument, that we women were less naturally inclined to error than men, then it must be taken into account that we are also less well equipped than they are to restrain ourselves; for if we want to claim that men are naturally more inclined to sensual desires, then they are also possessed of greater strength and judgment, so they can guard against those desires and rein them back. So when we women carry off our double victory, over our own desires and those of others (for that is, for the most part, what happens), then the honor we win for ourselves should be all the greater, just as a captain placed in charge of a well-manned fortress does not attain any particular glory when he defends it, for even when the attackers are many, he has many more in defense. The real praise goes, instead, to those who defend themselves with few supporters and succeed in defeating and beating off their enemies. It scarcely matters if those enemies—some of whom may lie within their own walls—are also few in number, for where there are few defenses, there is a real danger that the fierceness or length of the siege will bring the city to its knees. So we must conclude that women are more virtuous than men both by nature and through the exercise of their will."

"You are quite wrong, Corinna," Lucretia said. "In fact, would to God women were as steadfast as you make out, for then men would behave in a more reasonable way. What really happens is that men learn from experience that we are all too easy and yielding, and it is this that encourages them to try their luck with us. So they set themselves to tempting and pleading with such dedication that in the end they carry off the victory over some woman or other—something that would not happen if women behaved with true womanly dignity[3] and rejected them firmly right from the start, as they deserve. Because when a woman really sets her mind to it, she can dismiss any lover, however importunate and shameless he may be, with a single gesture."

"It is rather you who are in the wrong when you try to attack women in this way, Lucretia," Corinna retorted, "as though it were women who provided the opportunity for enterprising men to start laying traps for them. On the contrary, it is men who are the origin and source of all the evil, for women are like the flint in a tinderbox, which, though it encloses a potential flame within itself, does not issue that flame except when it is persistently struck by the steel. And, if men through their actions are the efficient cause and the prime movers in awakening women's senses (and we see the proof of this every day, watching the way they solicit women and molest them), then why should women bear the blame for something they do under duress? For a sin that arises from accidental causes and not from their own nature or from a clear act of will on their part? For something men have goaded them into? Women can hardly be expected under these circumstances to be colder than water or harder than iron; and even water and iron change their form when heated."

NOTES

1. The passage that follows rests on the theory, central to medieval and Renaissance thinking on medicine and psychology, that a person's psychosomatic makeup ("complexion") was determined by the combination in his or her body of the four essential bodily fluids or "humors" (blood, phlegm, yellow bile or choler, and black bile or melancholia), which in turn were combinations of the four essential properties ("qualities" or "contraries"), hot and cold, moist and dry. A dominance of blood (hot and moist) in the complexion made a person extrovert and "sanguine" (the word derives from the Latin for "blood"); while choler (hot and dry) made one quick-tempered ("choleric"); phlegm (cold and moist), dull and placid ("phlegmatic"); and melancholia (cold and dry), melancholic. The notion that women were by nature less hot than men (and thus, by implication, duller, more sedentary, and more timid) derives from Aristotle, whose views on sexual difference dominated medical thought on the subject throughout the Renaissance. This argument was frequently used to provide support for the thesis of women's inferiority to men. However, by the early sixteenth century, defenders of women had elaborated a set of strategies for responding to it, similar in some respects to those found here.

2. The reference is to a fable of Aesop.

3. The original *(se le donne fessero da donne)* puns on the etymology of the Italian word for "woman," *donna* (*domina*: "lady of the household," "woman of power and standing").

Chapter Three

From Émile (1762)

Jean-Jacques Rousseau

Rousseau had strong and influential opinions about love and the separate relation of male and female to its "laws": "Love is the realm of women," he declared elsewhere. "It is they who necessarily give the law in it." His views on the link between femininity and romance are most strongly stated in Émile, *excerpted here, part novel and part instruction manual for the ideal education of youth, in which two fictional characters, Émile and Sophy, are given directions by the narrator as to how to preserve love in marriage.*

A perfect man and a perfect woman should no more be alike in mind than in face, and perfection admits of neither less nor more.

In the union of the sexes each alike contributes to the common end, but in different ways. From this diversity springs the first difference which may be observed between man and woman in their moral relations. The man should be strong and active; the woman should be weak and passive; the one must have both the power and the will; it is enough that the other should offer little resistance.

When this principle is admitted, it follows that woman is specially made for man's delight. If man in his turn ought to be pleasing in her eyes, the necessity is less urgent, his virtue is in his strength, he pleases because he is strong. I grant you this is not the law of love, but it is the law of nature, which is older than love itself.

If woman is made to please and to be in subjection to man, she ought to make herself pleasing in his eyes and not provoke him to anger; her strength is in her charms, by their means she should compel him to discover and use his strength. The surest way of arousing this strength is to make it necessary by resistance. Thus pride comes to the help of desire and each exults in the other's victory. This is the origin of attack and defence, of the boldness of one sex and the timidity of the other, and even of the shame and modesty with which nature has armed the weak for the conquest of the strong.

Who can possibly suppose that nature has prescribed the same advances to the one sex as to the other, or that the first to feel desire should be the first to show it? What strange depravity of judgment! The consequences of the act being so different

From Jean-Jacques Rousseau, *Émile*, trans. Barbara Foxley (London: J. M. Dent and Sons; New York: E. P. Dutton, 1911), 322–24, 347, 354–55, 440–41. Note is by Barbara Foxley.

for the two sexes, is it natural that they should enter upon it with equal boldness? How can any one fail to see that when the share of each is so unequal, if the one were not controlled by modesty as the other is controlled by nature, the result would be the destruction of both, and the human race would perish through the very means ordained for its continuance?

Women so easily stir a man's senses and fan the ashes of a dying passion, that if philosophy ever succeeded in introducing this custom into any unlucky country, especially if it were a warm country where more women are born than men, the men, tyrannised over by the women, would at last become their victims, and would be dragged to their death without the least chance of escape.

Female animals are without this sense of shame, but what of that? Are their desires as boundless as those of women, which are curbed by this shame? The desires of the animals are the result of necessity, and when the need is satisfied, the desire ceases; they no longer make a feint of repulsing the male, they do it in earnest. Their seasons of complaisance are short and soon over. Impulse and restraint are alike the work of nature. But what would take the place of this negative instinct in women if you rob them of their modesty?

The Most High has designed to do honour to mankind; he has endowed man with boundless passions, together with a law to guide them, so that man may be alike free and self-controlled; though swayed by these passions man is endowed with reason by which to control them. Woman is also endowed with boundless passions; God has given her modesty to restrain them. Moreover, he has given to both a present reward for the right use of their powers. In the delight which springs from that right use of them, *i.e.*, the taste for right conduct established as the law of our behaviour. To my mind this is far higher than the instinct of the beasts.

Whether the woman shares the man's passion or not, whether she is willing or unwilling to satisfy it, she always repulses him and defends herself, though not always with the same vigour, and therefore not always with the same success. If the siege is to be successful, the besieged must permit or direct the attack. How skilfully can she stimulate the efforts of the aggressor. The freest and most delightful of activities does not permit of any real violence; reason and nature are alike against it; nature, in that she has given the weaker party strength enough to resist if she chooses; reason, in that actual violence is not only most brutal in itself, but it defeats its own ends, not only because the man thus declares war against his companion and thus gives her a right to defend her person and her liberty even at the cost of the enemy's life, but also because the woman alone is the judge of her condition, and a child would have no father if any man might usurp a father's rights.

Thus the different constitution of the two sexes leads us to a third conclusion, that the stronger party seems to be master, but is as a matter of fact dependent on the weaker, and that, not by any foolish custom of gallantry, nor yet by the magnanimity of the protector, but by an inexorable law of nature. For nature has endowed woman with a power of stimulating man's passions in excess of man's power of satisfying those passions, and has thus made him dependent on her goodwill, and compelled him in his turn to endeavour to please her, so that she may be willing to yield to his superior strength. Is it weakness which yields to force, or is it voluntary self-surrender? This uncertainty constitutes the chief charm of the man's victory, and the woman is usually cunning enough to leave him in doubt. In this respect the woman's mind exactly resembles her body; far from being ashamed of her weakness, she is proud of it; her soft muscles offer no resistance, she professes that she cannot lift the lightest weight; she would be ashamed to be strong. And why? Not only to gain an appearance of refinement; she is too clever for that; she is providing herself beforehand with excuses, with the right to be weak if she chooses . . .

See how we find ourselves led unconsciously from the physical to the moral constitution, how from the grosser union of the sexes spring the sweet laws of love. Woman reigns, not by the will of man, but by the decrees of nature herself; she had the power long before she showed it. That same Hercules who proposed to violate all the fifty daughters of Thespis was compelled to spin at the feet of Omphale, and Samson, the strong man, was less strong than Delilah. This power cannot be taken from woman; it is hers by right; she would have lost it long ago, were it possible. . . .

The same turn of mind which makes a woman of the world such an excellent hostess, enables a flirt to excel in the art of amusing a number of suitors. Coquetry, cleverly carried out, demands an even finer discernment than courtesy; provided a polite lady is civil to everybody, she has done fairly well in any case; but the flirt would soon lose her hold by such clumsy uniformity; if she tries to be pleasant to all her lovers alike, she will disgust them all. In ordinary social intercourse the manners adopted towards everybody are good enough for all; no question is asked as to private likes or dislikes provided all are alike well received. But in love, a favour shared with others is an insult. A man of feeling would rather be singled out for ill-treatment than be caressed with the crowd, and the worst that can befall him is to be treated like every one else. So a woman who wants to keep several lovers at her feet must persuade every one of them that she prefers him, and she must contrive to do this in the sight of all the rest, each of whom is equally convinced that he is her favourite.

If you want to see a man in a quandary, place him between two women with each of whom he has a secret understanding, and see what a fool he looks. But put a woman in similar circumstances between two men, and the results will be even more remarkable; you will be astonished at the skill with which she cheats them both, and makes them laugh at each other. Now if that woman were to show the same confidence in both, if she were to be equally familiar with both, how could they be deceived for a moment? If she treated them alike, would she not show that they both had the same claims upon her? Oh, she is far too clever for that; so far from treating them just alike, she makes a marked difference between them, and she does it so skilfully that the man she flatters thinks it is affection, and the man she ill uses thinks it is spite. So that each of them believes she is thinking of him, when she is thinking of no one but herself. . . .

I will go further and maintain that virtue is no less favourable to love than to other rights of nature, and that it adds as much to the power of the beloved as to that of the wife or mother. There is no real love without enthusiasm, and no enthusiasm without an object of perfection real or supposed, but always present in the imagination. What is there to kindle the hearts of lovers for whom this perfection is nothing, for whom the loved one is merely the means of sensual pleasure? Nay, not thus is the heart kindled, not thus does it abandon itself to those sublime transports which form the rapture of lovers and the charm of love. Love is an illusion, I grant you, but its reality consists in the feelings it awakes, in the love of true beauty which it inspires. That beauty is not to be found in the object of our affections, it is the creation of our illusions. What matter! do we not still sacrifice all those baser feelings to the imaginary model? and we still feed our hearts on the virtues we attribute to the beloved, we still withdraw ourselves from the baseness of human nature. What lover is there who would not give his life for his mistress? What gross and sensual passion is there in a man who is willing to die? We scoff at the knights of old; they knew the meaning of love; we know nothing but debauchery. When the teachings of romance began to seem ridiculous, it was not so much the work of reason as of immorality.

Natural relations remain the same throughout the centuries, their good or evil effects are unchanged; prejudices, masquerading as reason, can but change their outward seeming; self-mastery, even at the behest of fantastic opinions, will not cease to be great and good. And the true motives of honour will not fail to appeal to the heart of every woman who is able to seek happiness in life in her woman's duties. To a high-souled woman chastity above all must be a delightful virtue. She sees all the kingdoms of the world before her and she triumphs over herself and them; she sits enthroned in her own soul and all men do her homage; a few passing struggles are crowned with perpetual glory; she secures the affection, or it may be the envy, she secures in any case the esteem of both sexes and the universal respect of her own. The loss is fleeting, the gain is permanent. What a joy for a noble heart—the pride of virtue combined with beauty. Let her be a heroine of romance; she will taste delights more exquisite than those of Lais and Cleopatra; and when her beauty is fled, her glory and her joys remain; she alone can enjoy the past. . . .

"I have often thought that if the happiness of love could continue in marriage, we should find a Paradise upon earth. So far this has never been. But if it were not quite impossible, you two are quite worthy to set an example you have not received, an example which few married couples could follow. My children, shall I tell you what I think is the way, and the only way, to do it?"

They look at one another and smile at my simplicity. Emile thanks me curtly for my prescription, saying that he thinks Sophy has a better, at any rate it is good enough for him. Sophy agrees with him and seems just as certain. Yet in spite of her mockery, I think I see a trace of curiosity. I study Emile; his eager eyes are fixed upon his wife's beauty; he has no curiosity for anything else; and he pays little heed to what I say. It is my turn to smile, and I say to myself, "I will soon get your attention."

The almost imperceptible difference between these two hidden impulses is characteristic of a real difference between the two sexes; it is that men are generally less constant than women, and are sooner weary of success in love. A woman foresees man's future inconstancy, and is anxious; it is this which makes her more jealous.[1]

When his passion begins to cool she is compelled to pay him the attentions he used to bestow on her for her pleasure; she weeps, it is her turn to humiliate herself, and she is rarely successful. Affection and kind deeds rarely win hearts, and they hardly ever win them back. I return to my prescription against the cooling of love in marriage.

"It is plain and simple," I continue. "It consists in remaining lovers when you are husband and wife."

"Indeed," said Emile, laughing at my secret, "we shall not find that hard."

"Perhaps you will find it harder than you think. Pray give me time to explain.

"Cords too tightly stretched are soon broken. This is what happens when the marriage bond is subjected to too great a strain. The fidelity imposed by it upon husband and wife is the most sacred of all rights; but it gives to each too great a power over the other. Constraint and love do not agree together, and pleasure is not to be had for the asking. Do not blush, Sophy, and do not try to run away. God forbid that I should offend your modesty! But your fate for life is at stake. For so great a cause, permit a conversation between your husband and your father which you would not permit elsewhere.

"It is not so much possession as mastery of which people tire, and affection is often more prolonged with regard to a mistress than a wife. How can people make a duty of the tenderest caresses, and a right of the sweetest pledges of love? It is mutual desire which gives the right, and nature knows no other. The law may restrict this right, it cannot extend it. The pleasure is so sweet in itself! Should it owe to sad constraint the power which it cannot gain from its own charms? No, my children, in marriage the hearts are bound, but the bodies are not enslaved. You owe one another fidelity, but not complaisance. Neither of you may give yourself to another, but neither of you belongs to the other except at your own will.

"If it is true, dear Emile, that you would always be your wife's lover, that she should always be your mistress and her own, be a happy but respectful lover; obtain all from love and nothing from duty, and let the slightest favours never be of right but of grace. I know that modesty shuns formal confessions and requires to be overcome; but with delicacy and true love, will the lover ever be mistaken as to the real will? Will not he know when heart and eyes grant what the lips refuse? Let both for ever be master of their person and their caresses, let them have the right to bestow them only at their own will. Remember that even in marriage this pleasure is only lawful when the desire is mutual. Do not be afraid, my children, that this law will keep you apart; on the contrary, it will make both more eager to please, and will prevent satiety. True to one another, nature and love will draw you to each other."

Emile is angry and cries out against these and similar suggestions. Sophy is ashamed, she hides her face behind her fan and says nothing. Perhaps while she is saying nothing, she is the most annoyed. Yet I insist, without mercy; I make Emile blush for his lack of delicacy; I undertake to be surety for Sophy that she will undertake her share of the treaty. I incite her to speak, you may guess she will not dare to say I am mistaken. Emile anxiously consults the eyes of his young wife; he beholds them, through all her confusion, filled with a voluptuous anxiety which reassures him against the dangers of trusting her. He flings himself at her feet, kisses with rapture the hand extended to him, and swears that beyond the fidelity he has already promised, he will renounce all other rights over her. "My dear wife," said he, "be the arbiter of my pleasures as you are already the arbiter of my life and fate. Should your cruelty cost me life itself I would yield to you my most cherished rights. I will owe nothing to your complaisance, but all to your heart."

NOTE

1. In France it is the wives who first emancipate themselves; and necessarily so, for having very little heart, and only desiring attention, when a husband ceases to pay them attention they care very little for himself. In other countries it is not so; it is the husband who first emancipates himself; and necessarily so, for women, faithful, but foolish, importune men with their desires and only disgust them. There may be plenty of exceptions to these general truths; but I still think they are truths.

Chapter Four

From A Vindication of the Rights of Woman (1792)

Mary Wollstonecraft

Wollstonecraft was a teacher and writer who knew some of the most famous radicals of her day, including Thomas Paine and William Godwin, all of whom gathered in London to discuss the philosophy of rights that accompanied the American and French revolutions. Wollstonecraft's book is the first systematic social and political explanation of women's inferior position, in an age when women's characters were seen as biological givens. In response, she was called a "hyena in petticoats" by the writer Horace Walpole. Her view of romantic love is that social expectations misled young women into a foolish view of marriage, which should be more reasonably based on good judgment than the illusions of romance.

Pope has said, in the name of the whole male sex:

> Yet ne'er so sure our passion to create,
> As when she touch'd the brink of all we hate.

In what light this sally places men and women I shall leave to the judicious to determine. Meanwhile, I shall content myself with observing, that I cannot discover why, unless they are mortal, females should always be degraded by being made subservient to love or lust.

To speak disrespectfully of love is, I know, high treason against sentiment and fine feelings; but I wish to speak the simple language of truth, and rather to address the head than the heart. To endeavour to reason love out of the world would be to out-Quixote Cervantes, and equally offend against common sense; but an endeavour to restrain this tumultuous passion, and to prove that it should not be allowed to dethrone superior powers, or to usurp the sceptre which the understanding should ever coolly wield, appears less wild.

Youth is the season for love in both sexes; but in those days of thoughtless enjoyment provision should be made for the more important years of life, when reflection takes place of sensation. But Rousseau, and most of the male writers who

From Mary Wollstonecraft, *A Vindication of the Rights of Woman* (1792; London: Walter Scott, 1891), 25–27, 31–35, 95–98.

have followed his steps, have warmly indicated that the whole tendency of female education ought to be directed to one point—to render them pleasing.

Let me reason with the supporters of this opinion who have any knowledge of human nature. Do they imagine that marriage can eradicate the habitude of life? The woman who has only been taught to please will soon find that her charms are oblique sunbeams, and that they cannot have much effect on her husband's heart when they are seen every day, when the summer is passed and gone. Will she then have sufficient native energy to look into herself for comfort, and cultivate her dormant faculties? or is it not more rational to expect that she will try to please other men, and, in the emotions raised by the experience of new conquests, endeavour to forget the mortification her love or pride has received? When the husband ceases to be a lover, and the time will inevitably come, her desire of pleasing will then grow languid, or become a spring of bitterness; and love, perhaps, the most evanescent of all passions, gives place to jealousy or vanity.

I now speak of women who are restrained by principle or prejudice. Such women, though they would shrink from an intrigue with real abhorrence, yet, nevertheless, wish to be convinced by the homage of gallantry that they are cruelly neglected by their husbands; or, days and weeks are spent in dreaming of the happiness enjoyed by congenial souls, till their health is undermined and their spirits broken by discontent. How then can the great art of pleasing be such a necessary study? it is only useful to a mistress. The chaste wife and serious mother should only consider her power to please as the polish of her virtues, and the affection of her husband as one of the comforts that render her task less difficult, and her life happier. But, whether she be loved or neglected, her first wish should be to make herself respectable, and not to rely for all her happiness on a being subject to like infirmities with herself. . . .

Supposing, for a moment, that the soul is not immortal, and that man was only created for the present scene,—I think we should have reason to complain that love, infantine fondness, ever grew insipid and palled upon the sense. Let us eat, drink, and love, for tomorrow we die, would be, in fact, the language of reason, the morality of life; and who but a fool would part with a reality for a fleeting shadow? But, if awed by observing the improbable powers of the mind, we disdain to confine our wishes or thoughts to such a comparatively mean field of action, that only appears grand and important, as it is connected with a boundless prospect and sublime hopes, what necessity is there for falsehood in conduct, and why must the sacred majesty of truth be violated to detain a deceitful good that saps the very foundation of virtue? Why must the female mind be tainted by coquettish arts to gratify the sensualist, and prevent love from subsiding into friendship, or compassionate tenderness, when there are not qualities on which friendship can be built? Let the honest heart show itself, and *reason* teach passion to submit to necessity; or, let the dignified pursuit of virtue and knowledge raise the mind above those emotions which rather embitter than sweeten the cup of life, when they are not restrained within due bounds.

I do not mean to allude to the romantic passion, which is the concomitant of genius. Who can clip its wing? But that grand passion not proportioned to the puny enjoyments of life, is only true to the sentiment, and feeds on itself. The passions which have been celebrated for their durability have always been unfortunate. They have acquired strength by absence and constitutional melancholy. The fancy has hovered round a form of beauty dimly seen; but familiarity might have turned admiration into disgust, or, at least, into indifference, and allowed the imagination leisure to start fresh game. With perfect propriety, according to this view of things, does Rousseau make the mistress of his soul, Eloisa, love St. Preux, when life was fading before her; but this is no proof of the immortality of the passion.

Of the same complexion is Dr. Gregory's advice respecting delicacy of sentiment, which he advises a woman not to acquire, if she have determined to marry. This determination, however, perfectly consistent with his former advice, he calls *indelicate,* and earnestly persuades his daughters to conceal it, though it may govern their conduct, as if it were indelicate to have the common appetites of human nature.

Noble morality! and consistent with the cautious prudence of a little soul that cannot extend its views beyond the present minute division of existence. If all the faculties of woman's mind are only to be cultivated as they respect her dependence on man; if, when a husband be obtained, she have arrived at her goal, and meanly proud, rests satisfied with such a paltry crown, let her grovel contentedly, scarcely raised by her employments above the animal kingdom; but, if struggling for the prize of her high calling, she look beyond the present scene, let her cultivate her understanding without stopping to consider what character the husband may have whom she is destined to marry. Let her only determine, without being too anxious about present happiness, to acquire the qualities that ennoble a rational being, and a rough inelegant husband may shock her taste without destroying her peace of mind. She will not model her soul to suit the frailties of her companion, but to bear with them; his character may be a trial, but not an impediment to virtue.

If Dr. Gregory confined his remark to romantic expectations of constant love and congenial feelings, he should have recollected that experience will banish what advice can never make us cease to wish for, when the imagination is kept alive at the expense of reason.

I own it frequently happens, that women who have fostered a romantic unnatural delicacy of feeling, waste their[1] lives in *imagining* how happy they should have been with a husband who could love them with a fervid increasing affection every day, and all day. But they might as well pine married as single, and would not be a jot more unhappy with a bad husband than longing for a good one. That a proper education, or, to speak with more precision, a well-stored mind, would enable a woman to support a single life with dignity, I grant; but that she should avoid cultivating her taste, lest her husband should occasionally shock it, is quitting a substance for a shadow. To say the truth, I do not know of what use is an improved taste, if the individual be not rendered more independent of the casualties of life; if new sources of enjoyment, only dependent on the solitary operations of the mind, are not opened. People of taste, married or single, without distinction, will ever be disgusted by various things that touch not less observing minds. On this conclusion the argument must not be allowed to hinge; but in the whole sum of enjoyment is taste to be denominated a blessing?

The question is, whether it procures most pain or pleasure? The answer will decide the propriety of Dr. Gregory's advice, and show how absurd and tyrannic it is thus to lay down a system of slavery, or to attempt to educate moral beings by any other rules than those deduced from pure reason, which apply to the whole species.

Gentleness of manners, forbearance and long suffering, are such amiable Godlike qualities, that in sublime poetic strains the Deity has been invested with them; and, perhaps, no representation of His goodness so strongly fastens on the human affections as those that represent Him abundant in mercy and willing to pardon. Gentleness, considered in this point of view, bears on its front all the characteristics of grandeur, combined with the winning graces of condescension; but what a different aspect it assumes when it is the submissive demeanour of dependence, the support of weakness that loves, because it wants protection; and is forbearing, because it must silently endure injuries; smiling under the lash at which it dare not snarl. Abject as this picture appears, it is the portrait of an accomplished woman, according to the received opinion of female excellence, separated by specious reasoners from human excellence. Or, they[2] kindly restore the rib, and make one moral being of a man and woman; not forgetting to give her all the "submissive charms."

How women are to exist in that state where there is neither to be marrying nor giving in marriage, we are not told. For though moralists have agreed that the tenor of life seems to prove that *man* is prepared by various circumstances for a future state, they constantly concur in advising *woman* only to provide for the present. Gentleness, docility, and a spaniel-like affection are, on this ground, consistently recommended as the cardinal virtues of the sex; and, disregarding the arbitrary economy of nature, one writer has declared that it is masculine for a woman to be melancholy. She was created to be the toy of man, his rattle, and it must jingle in his ears whenever, dismissing reason, he chooses to be amused. . . .

Love, considered as an animal appetite, cannot long feed on itself without expiring. And this extinction in its own flame may be termed the violent death of love. But the wife, who has thus been rendered licentious, will probably endeavour to fill the void left by the loss of her husband's attentions; for she cannot contentedly become merely an upper servant after having been treated like a goddess. She is still handsome, and, instead of transferring her fondness to her children, she only dreams of enjoying the sunshine of life. Besides, there are many husbands so devoid of sense and parental affection that, during the first effervescence of voluptuous fondness, they refuse to let their wives suckle their children. They are only to dress and live to please them, and love, even innocent love, soon sinks into lasciviousness when the exercise of a duty is sacrificed to its indulgence.

Personal attachment is a very happy foundation for friendship; yet, when even two virtuous young people marry, it would perhaps be happy if some circumstances checked their passion; if the recollection of some prior attachment, or disappointed affection, made it on one side, at least, rather a match founded on esteem. In that case they would look beyond the present moment, and try to render the whole of life respectable, by forming a plan to regulate a friendship which only death ought to dissolve.

Friendship is a serious affection; the most sublime of all affections, because it is founded on principle, and cemented by time. The very reverse may be said of love. In a great degree, love and friendship cannot subsist in the same bosom; even when inspired by different objects they weaken or destroy each other, and for the same object can only be felt in succession. The vain fears and fond jealousies, the winds which fan the flame of love, when judiciously or artfully tempered, are both incompatible with the tender confidence and sincere respect of friendship.

Love, such as the glowing pen of genius has traced, exists not on earth, or only resides in those exalted, fervid imaginations that have sketched such dangerous pictures. Dangerous, because they not only afford a plausible excuse to the voluptuary, who disguises sheer sensuality under a sentimental veil; but as they spread affection, and take from the dignity of virtue. Virtue, as the very word imports, should have an appearance of seriousness, if not of austerity; and to endeavour to trick her out in the garb of pleasure, because the epithet has been used as another name for beauty, is to exalt her on a quicksand; a most insidious attempt to hasten her fall by apparent respect. Virtue and pleasure are not, in fact, so nearly allied in this life as some eloquent writers have laboured to prove. Pleasure prepares the fading wreath, and mixes the intoxicating cup; the fruit which virtue gives is the recompense of toil, and, gradually seen as it ripens, only affords calm satisfaction; nay, appearing to be the result of the natural tendency of things, it is scarcely observed. Bread, the common food of life, seldom thought of as a blessing, supports the constitution and preserves health; still feasts delight the heart of man, though disease and even death lurk in the cup or dainty that elevates the spirits or tickles the palate. They lively heated imagination likewise, to apply the comparison, draws the picture of love, as it draws every other picture, with those glowing colours, which the daring hand will steal from the rainbow, that is directed by a mind, condemned in a world like this, to prove its noble origin by panting after unattainable perfection, ever pursuing what it acknowledges to be a fleeting dream. An imagination of this vigorous cast can give existence to insubstantial forms, and stability to the shadowy reveries which the mind naturally falls into when realities are found vapid. It can then depict love with celestial charms, and dote on the grand ideal object—it can imagine a degree of mutual affection that shall refine the soul, and not expire when it has served as a "scale to heavenly," and, like devotion, make it absorb every meaner affection and desire. In each other's arms, as in a temple, with its summit lost in the clouds, the world is to be shut out, and every thought and wish that do not nurture pure affection and permanent virtue. Permanent virtue! alas! Rousseau, respectable visionary! thy paradise would soon be violated by the entrance of some unexpected guest. Like Milton's it would only contain angels, or men sunk below the dignity of rational creatures. Happiness is not material, it cannot be seen or felt! Yet the eager pursuit of the good, which everyone shapes to his own fancy, proclaims man the lord of this lower world, and to be an intelligential creature, who is not to receive but acquire happiness. They, therefore, who complain of the delusions of passion, do not recollect that they are exclaiming against a strong proof of the immortality of the soul.

But leaving superior minds to correct themselves, and pay dearly for their experience, it is necessary to observe, that it is not against strong, preserving passions, but romantic wavering feelings, that I wish to guard the female heart by exercising the understanding: for these paradisiacal reveries are oftener the effects of idleness than of a lively fancy.

NOTES

1. For example, the herd of Novelists.
2. *Vide* Rousseau and Swedenborg.

Chapter Five

From Editorial in the *Lily* (1852)

Elizabeth Cady Stanton

One of the mothers of women's rights in America, Stanton writes in the feminist newspaper the Lily *about the emptiness of romantic promises as a substitute for "self-dependence" for women. Conventionally for her time, she believed that women were "organized" (constituted) so as to have more self-control than men, presumably over sexual passion, so that women should be responsible for the "pure and holy" quality of love in marriage.*

If you could guarantee to every woman, for the whole of her natural life, the love of a great heart, the protection of a manly arm, the resource of an exhaustless purse, then might we in peace loll on in our luxurious homes, calmly contemplate the moon and stars, instead of anxiously watching the changing scenes of life, dream of fairy lands, scenes of enchantment, golden streets and cloudless skies, instead of dark realities, grim want; bloated vice, crushed innocence and outraged humanity,—talk of tournaments, knight errantry, woman's beauty, and man's chivalry, and all the romance of an imaginary existence, instead of the fact of woman's individuality, her true position on the footstool—that of self-supporter, self-protector, and self-defender, compelled to stand or fall, to live or die, alone.

Yes, teach woman self-dependance, and you end the vice of prostitution. She is driven to this commerce in nine cases out of ten from her necessities. Thank God, the true woman in her organization is too refined and spiritual, to be the victim of an overpowering passion. With her, the holy love of one alone, sanctifies the act of a visible union. Teach woman self-dependance, and you end the wholesale degradation of the sacred institution of marriage. We should then have no more of these ill-assorted matches, no marrying for a home, a support, a position, a head, a protector, a defender, &c., marrying to escape the horrors of a single life of inactivity and vacuity, the odious cognomen of *old maid*. Alas! how many a woman has wrecked her frail bark on this deceitful rock. Could not fame, distinction, the love of science, of literature, a highly cultivated taste in the arts, the editor's or professor's chair, authorship or philanthropy as fully satisfy the soul of woman, as does the inferior position she now looks to as the summun bonum of all happiness? as the submissive

From Elizabeth Cady Stanton, Editorial, *Lily*, vol. 4, no. 5 (May 1852): 40.

wife weary, exhausted, care-worn mother, the patient drudge, the pattern house-keeper, whose head, heart and hands are forever full of the necessities and comforts of the animal? Marriage is not necessary for all, and only right where two souls are knit together in a pure and holy love.

In my mind the very pivot of all reforms turns on the true view of the marriage relation. To a true and heaven appointed marriage several things are necessary. 1st. A perfect physical condition.—How strange it is that man in the discovery of great principles, so readily applys them to improvements in the arts and sciences, to all nature about him, animate and inanimate, but never to himself. Let him apply the same physiological laws to his own species, that he does in seeking the improvement of the inferior animals, and the result would be as striking in the one case as the other. No one should ever transmit the spark of immortality, except through a healthy channel in its highest condition. And this responsibility I throw on woman; for God has given her more self-control than man, and spirit must govern matter. By the aid of the sciences, and her own best and holiest instincts, let the well-developed, noble minded woman in her selection of a partner for life, marry no man for his fortune, his great connexions, or high sounding name. No matter what his surroundings may be—if his animal nature predominates over his moral and intellectual—if he finds his chief pleasures in eating, drinking, smoking, chewing tobacco, idly lounging about discussing theology and politics—for you will find plenty of these educated animals in high places—let him not be the father of thy children.

Chapter Six

From The Young Lady's Counsellor

Or, Outlines and Illustrations of the Sphere, the Duties, and the Dangers of Young Women (1855)

Daniel Wise

This American clergyman, writing a "guide to true happiness," decries the modern tendency on the part of young women to ideas "romantic, impassioned, immodest, derived from impure novels and impurer fancies." His book, consisting equally of description, advice, and warning, is typical of works aimed at young women of the mid-nineteenth century, attempting to control behavior by describing the immutable and universal laws of male and female "natures." As mass media grew in the nineteenth century, the availability to young women of romantic fiction and visual images in magazines increased greatly, leading to much alarmed writing on the consequences of such stimulation.

Marriage, properly viewed, is a union of kindred minds,—a blending of two souls in mutual, holy affection,—and not merely or chiefly a union of persons. Its physical aspects, pure and necessary as they are, are its lowest and least to be desired ones; indeed, they derive all their sanctity from the spiritual affinity existing between the parties. So emphatically is this the fact, that marriage without mutual affection is defilement and sin. Virtuous love alone can give dignity and innocency to the relation. Hence, the holy Scriptures enjoin husbands to "love their wives," and wives to "reverence their husbands," with the same authoritative voice as that with which they enjoin marriage itself.

These are the only views of this subject, young lady, that you can innocently entertain; and, in this light, it will not harm you in the least to reflect upon it. There are ideas, romantic, impassioned, immodest, derived from impure novels and impurer fancies, which you must prayerfully exclude from the chambers of your soul, or they will prepare you for the tempter, and lead you captive into an untimely marriage, if not into still deeper wretchedness. But those loftier conceptions of it will only stimulate you to cultivate those mental and moral qualities which will fit you to

From Daniel Wise, *The Young Lady's Counsellor, or, Outlines and Illustrations of the Sphere, the Duties, and the Dangers of Young Women* (New York: Carlton and Phillips, 1855, 1856), 234–37.

enjoy the state, and to the exercise of a calm judgment in the disposal of your affections.

Many young ladies indulge in very nonsensical opinions, or, I should rather say, notions, concerning love. They foolishly fancy themselves bound to be "smitten," to "fall in love," to be "love-sick," with almost every silly idler who wears a fashionable coat, is tolerably good-looking, and pays them particular attention. Reason, judgment, deliberation, according to their fancies, have nothing to do with love. Hence, they yield to their feelings, and give their company to young men, regardless of warning advice or entreaty. A father's sadness, a mother's tears, are treated with contempt, and often with bitter retorts. Their lovers use flattering words, and, like silly moths fluttering round the fatal lamp, they allow themselves to be charmed into certain misery. Reader, beware of such examples; eschew such false notions! Learn that your affections are under your own control; that pure affection is founded upon esteem; that estimable qualities in a man can alone secure the continuance of connubial love; that if these are not in him, your love has no foundation, it is unreal, and will fall, a wilted flower, as soon as the excitement of youthful passion is overpast. Restrain your affections, therefore, with vigor; it will cost you far less pain to stifle them in their birth, than to languish through the years of woe which are inseparable from an unsuitable marriage.

If I am correct in my statements concerning love and marriage, the true idea of courtship is already obvious. What is it in its beginning, but an opportunity for the parties to ascertain their fitness for each other? What, in its progress, but a means of forming and strengthening that genuine affection, which is the true basis of marriage? With every young lady the paramount question concerning him who offers her particular attentions, ought to be, "Is he worthy of my love?" Her first aim should be to decide it. She should observe him well and thoughtfully,—study his character as it may be expressed in his countenance, his words, spirit, and actions. Through her parents she should inquire into his previous history, and learn especially IF HE HAS BEEN A DUTIFUL SON AND AN AFFECTIONATE BROTHER.

Chapter Seven

From A Woman's Thoughts about Women (1858)

Dinah Maria Mulock Craik

The British writer Dinah Craik is representative of a common Victorian conjunction of views, on the one hand a protofeminist championing of sisterhood and work for women, on the other hand a denunciation of equality between men and women and the advocacy of Christian sacrifice on the part of women as a solution to the "woman problem." Her view of romantic love is that girls are given "nothing to do but fall in love," and thus are led down the road to discontented and useless lives. Although she does not question the relatively new association of romantic love with marriage, she believes that single women should pursue practical ends until marriage and lead dignified and serious lives of domestic usefulness if they do not marry.

I premise that these thoughts do not concern married women, for whom there are always plenty to think, and who have generally quite enough to think of for themselves and those belonging to them. They have cast their lot for good or ill, have realised in greater or less degree the natural destiny of our sex. They must find out its comforts, cares, and responsibilities, and make the best of all. It is the single women, belonging to those supernumerary ranks, which political economists tell us, are yearly increasing, who most need thinking about.

First, in their early estate, when they have so much in their possession—youth, bloom, and health giving them that temporary influence over the other sex which may result, and is meant to result, in a permanent one. Secondly, when this sovereignty is passing away, the chance of marriage lessening, or wholly ended, or voluntarily set aside, and the individual making up her mind to that which respect for Grandfather Adam and Grandmother Eve must compel us to admit, is an unnatural condition of being.

Why this undue proportion of single women should almost always result from over-civilisation, and whether, since society's advance is usually indicated by the advance, morally and intellectually, of its women—this progress, by raising women's ideal standard of the "holy estate," will not necessarily cause a decline in the very *un*holy estate which it is most frequently made—are questions too wide to be entered

From Dinah Maria Mulock Craik, *A Woman's Thoughts about Women* (New York: Rudd and Carleton, 1858), 9–26.

upon here. We have only to deal with facts—with a certain acknowledged state of things, perhaps incapable of remedy, but by no means incapable of amelioration.

But, granted these facts, and leaving to wiser heads the explanation of them—if indeed there be any—it seems advisable, or at least allowable, that any woman who has thought a good deal about the matter, should not fear to express in word—or deed, which is better,—any conclusions, which out of her own observation and experience she may have arrived at. And looking around upon the middle classes, which form the staple stock of the community, it appears to me that the chief canker at the root of women's lives is the want of something to do.

Herein I refer, as this chapter must be understood especially to refer, not to those whom ill or good fortune—*query, is it not often the latter?*—has forced to earn their bread; but "to young ladies," who have never been brought up to do anything. Tom, Dick, and Harry, their brothers, has each had it knocked into him from schooldays that he is to do something, to be somebody. Counting-house, shop, or college, afford him a clear future on which to concentrate all his energies and aims. He has got the grand *pabulum* of the human soul—occupation. If any inherent want in his character, any unlucky combination of circumstances, nullifies this, what a poor creature the man becomes!—what a dawdling, moping, sitting-over-the-fire, thumb-twiddling, lazy, ill-tempered animal! And why? "Oh, poor fellow! 'tis because he has got nothing to do!"

Yet this is precisely the condition of women for a third, a half, often the whole of their existence.

That Providence ordained it so—made men to work, and women to be idle—is a doctrine that few will be bold enough to assert openly. Tacitly they do, when they preach up lovely uselessness, fascinating frivolity, delicious helplessness—all those polite impertinences and poetical degradations to which the foolish, lazy, or selfish of our sex are prone to incline an ear, but which any woman of common sense must repudiate as insulting not only her womanhood but her Creator.

Equally blasphemous, and perhaps even more harmful, is the outcry about "the equality of the sexes;" the frantic attempt to force women, many of whom are either ignorant of or unequal for their own duties—into the position and duties of men. A pretty state of matters would ensue! Who that ever listened for two hours to the verbose confused inanities of a ladies' committee, would immediately go and give his vote for a female House of Commons? or who, on the receipt of a lady's letter of business—I speak of the average—would henceforth desire to have our courts of justice stocked with matronly lawyers, and our colleges thronged by

"Sweet girl-graduates with their golden hair?"

As for finance, in its various branches—if you pause to consider the extreme difficulty there always is in balancing Mrs. Smith's housekeeping-book, or Miss Smith's quarterly allowance, I think, my dear Paternal Smith, you need not be much afraid lest this loud acclaim for "women's rights" should ever end in pushing you from your stools, in counting-house, college, or elsewhere.

No; equality of the sexes is not in the nature of things. Man and woman were made for, and not like one another. One only "right" we have to assert in common with mankind—and that is as much in our own hands as theirs—the right of having something to do.

That both sexes were meant to labour, one "by the sweat of his brow," the other "in sorrow to bring forth"—and bring up—"children"—cannot, I fancy, be questioned. Nor, when the gradual changes of the civilised world, or some special destiny, chosen or compelled, have prevented that first, highest, and in earlier times almost universal lot, does this accidental fate in any way abrogate the necessity, moral, physical, and mental, for a woman to have occupation in other forms.

But how few parents ever consider this? Tom, Dick, and Harry, aforesaid, leave school and plunge into life; "the girls" likewise finish their education, come home, and stay at home. That is enough. Nobody thinks it needful to waste a care upon them. Bless them, pretty dears, how sweet they are! papa's nosegay of beauty to adorn his drawing-room. He delights to give them all they can desire—clothes, amusements, society; he and mamma together take every domestic care off their hands; they have abundance of time and nothing to occupy it; plenty of money, and little use for it; pleasure without end, but not one definite object of interest or employment; flattery and flummery enough, but no solid food whatever to satisfy mind or heart—if they happen to possess either—at the very emptiest and most craving season of both. They have literally nothing whatever to do, except to fall in love; which they accordingly do, the most of them, as fast as ever they can.

"Many think they are in love, when in fact they are only idle"—is one of the truest sayings of that great wise bore, Imlac, in *Rasselas,* and it has been proved by many a shipwrecked life, of girls especially. This "falling in love" being usually a mere delusion of the fancy, and not the real thing at all, the object is generally unattainable or unworthy. Papa is displeased, mamma somewhat shocked and scandalised; it is a "foolish affair," and no matrimonial results ensue. There only ensues—what?

A long, dreary season, of pain, real or imaginary, yet not the less real because it is imaginary; of anger and mortification, of impotent struggle—against unjust parents, the girl believes, or, if romantically inclined, against cruel destiny. Gradually this mood wears out; she learns to regard "love" as folly, and turns her whole hope and aim to—matrimony! Matrimony in the abstract; not *the* man, but any man—any person who will snatch her out of the dulness of her life, and give her something really to live for, something to fill up the hopeless blank of idleness into which her days are gradually sinking.

Well, the man may come, or he may not. If the latter melancholy result occurs, the poor girl passes into her third stage of young-ladyhood, fritters or mopes away her existence, sullenly bears it, or dashes herself blindfold against its restrictions; is unhappy, and makes her family unhappy; perhaps herself cruelly conscious of all this, yet unable to find the true root of bitterness in her heart: not knowing exactly what she wants, yet aware of a morbid, perpetual want of something? What is it?

Alas! the boys only have had the benefit of that well-known juvenile apophthegm, that

> "Satan finds some mischief still
> For idle hands to do:"

it has never crossed the parents' minds that the rhyme could apply to the delicate digital extremities of the daughters.

And so their whole energies are devoted to the massacre of old Time. They prick him to death with crochet and embroidery needles; strum him deaf with piano and harp playing—*not* music; cut him up with morning-visitors, or leave his carcass in ten-minute parcels at every "friend's" house they can think of. Finally, they dance him defunct at all sort of unnatural hours; and then, rejoicing in the excellent excuse, smother him in sleep for a third of the following day. Thus he dies, a slow, inoffensive, perfectly natural death; and they will never recognise his murder till, on the confines of this world, or from the unknown shores of the next, the question meets them: "What have you done with Time?"—Time, the only mortal gift bestowed equally on every living soul, and excepting the soul, the only mortal loss which is totally irretrievable.

Yet this great sin, this irredeemable loss, in many women arises from pure ignorance. Men are taught as a matter of business to recognise the value of time, to apportion and employ it: women rarely or never. The most of them have no definite appreciation of the article as a tangible divisible commodity at all. They would laugh at a mantua-maker who cut up a dress-length into trimmings, and then expected to make out of two yards of silk a full skirt. Yet that the same laws of proportion should apply to time and its measurements—that you cannot dawdle away a whole forenoon, and then attempt to cram into the afternoon the entire business of the day—that every minute's unpunctuality constitutes a debt or a theft (lucky, indeed, if you yourself are the only party robbed or made creditor thereof!): these slight facts rarely seem to cross the feminine imagination.

It is not their fault; they have never been "accustomed to business." They hear that with men "time is money;" but it never strikes them that the same commodity, equally theirs, is to them not money, perhaps, but *life*—life in its highest form and noblest uses—life bestowed upon every human being, distinctly and individually, without reference to any other being, and for which every one of us, married or unmarried, woman as well as man, will assuredly be held accountable before God.

My young-lady friends, of from seventeen upwards, your time and the use of it is as essential to you as to any father or brother of you all. You are accountable for it just as much as he is. If you waste it, you waste not only your substance, but your very souls—not that which is your own, but your Maker's.

Ay, there the core of the matter lies. From the hour that honest Adam and Eve were put into the garden, not—as I once heard some sensible preacher observe—"not to be idle in it, but to dress it and to keep it," the Father of all has never put one man or one woman into this world without giving each something to do there, in it and for it: some visible, tangible work, to be left behind them when they die.

Young ladies, 'tis worth a grave thought—what, if called away at eighteen, twenty, or thirty, the most of you would leave behind you when you die? Much embroidery, doubtless; various pleasant, kindly, illegible letters; a moderate store of good deeds; and a cart-load of good intentions. Nothing else—save your name on a tombstone, or lingering for a few more years in family or friendly memory. "Poor dear ———!

what a nice lively girl she was!" For any benefit accruing through you to your generation, you might as well never have lived at all.

But "what am I to do with my life?" as once asked me one girl out of the numbers who begin to feel aware that, whether marrying or not, each possesses an individual life, to spend, to use, or to lose. And herein lies the momentous question.

The difference between man's vocation and woman's seems naturally to be this— one is abroad, the other at home: one external, the other internal: one active, the other passive. He has to go and seek out his path; hers usually lies close under her feet. Yet each is as distinct, as honourable, as difficult; and whatever custom may urge to the contrary—if the life is meant to be a worthy or a happy one—each must resolutely and unshrinkingly be trod. But—*how?*

A definite answer to this question is simply impossible. So diverse are characters, tastes, capabilities, and circumstances, that to lay down a distinct line of occupation for any six women of one's own acquaintance, would be the merest absurdity.

"Herein the patient must minister to herself."

To few is the choice so easy, the field of duty so wide, that she need puzzle very long over what she ought to do. Generally—and this is the best and safest guide—she will find her work lying very near at hand: some desultory tastes to condense into regular studies, some faulty household quietly to remodel, some child to teach, or parent to watch over. All these being needless or unattainable, she may extend her service out of the home into the world, which perhaps never at any time so much needed the help of us women. And hardly one of its charities and duties can be done so thoroughly as by a wise and tender woman's hand. . . .

Let the superstructure of life be enjoyment, but let its foundation be in solid work—daily, regular, conscientious work: in its essence and results as distinct as any "business" of men. What they expend for wealth and ambition, shall not we offer for duty and love—the love of our fellow-creatures, or, far higher, the love of God? "Labour is worship," says the proverb: also—ay, necessarily so—labour is happiness. Only let us turn from the dreary, colorless lives of the women, old and young, who have nothing to do, to those of their sisters who are always busy doing something; who, believing and accepting the universal law, that pleasure is the mere accident of our being, and work its natural and most holy necessity, have set themselves steadily to seek out and fulfill theirs.

These are they who are little spoken of in the world at large. I do not include among them those whose labour should spring from an irresistible impulse, and become an absolute vocation, or it is not worth following at all—namely, the professional women, writers, painters, musicians, and the like. I mean those women who lead active, intelligent, industrious lives: lives complete in themselves, and therefore not giving half the trouble to their friends that the idle and foolish virgins do—no, not even in love-affairs. If love comes to them accidentally, (or rather providentially,) and happily, so much the better!—they will not make the worse wives for having been busy maidens. But the "tender passion" is not to them the one grand necessity that it is to aimless lives; they are in no haste to wed: their time is duly filled up; and if never married, still the habitual faculty of usefulness gives them in themselves and with others that obvious value, that fixed standing in society, which will for ever prevent their being drifted away, like most old maids, down the current of the new generation, even as dead May-flies down a stream.

They have made for themselves a place in the world: the harsh, practical, yet not ill-meaning world, where all find their level soon or late, and where a frivolous young maid sunk into a helpless old one, can no more expect to keep her pristine position than a last year's leaf to flutter upon a spring bough. But an old maid who deserves well of this same world, by her ceaseless work therein, having won her position, keeps it to the end.

Not an ill position either, or unkindly; often higher and more honourable than that of many a mother of ten sons. In households, where "Auntie" is the universal referee, nurse, playmate, comforter, and counsellor: in society, where "that nice Miss So-and-so," though neither clever, handsome, nor young, is yet such a person as can neither be omitted nor overlooked: in charitable works, where she is "such a practical body—always knows exactly what to do, and how to do it:" or perhaps, in her own house, solitary indeed, as every single woman's home must be, yet neither dull nor unhappy in itself, and the nucleus of cheerfulness and happiness to many another home besides.

She has not married. Under Heaven, her home, her life, her lot, are all of her own making. Bitter or sweet they may have been—it is not ours to meddle with them, but we can any day see their results. Wide or narrow as her circle of influence appears, she has exercised her power to the uttermost, and for good. Whether great or small her talents, she has not let one of them rust for want of use. Whatever the current of her existence may have been, and in whatever circumstances it has placed her, she has voluntarily wasted no portion of it—not a year, not a month, not a day.

Published or unpublished, this woman's life is a goodly chronicle, the title-page of which you may read in her quiet countenance; her manner, settled, cheerful, and at ease; her unfailing interest in all things and all people. You will rarely find she thinks much about herself; she has never had time for it. And this her life-chronicle, which, out of its very fulness, has taught her that the more one does, the more one finds to do—she will never flourish in your face, or the face of Heaven, as something uncommonly virtuous and extraordinary. She knows that, after all, she has simply done what it was her duty to do.

But—and when her place is vacant on earth, this will be said of her assuredly, both here and Other-where—*"She hath done what she could."*

Chapter Eight

From The Principles of Social Freedom (1871)

Victoria Woodhull

It would be a mistake to believe that there was a uniform opinion on romantic love and its relation to sexuality in the nineteenth century. The infamous radical "free love" proponent Woodhull represents the other extreme from Mulock and Wise. Woodhull had a fascinating life: she was first a mesmerist, then the first female stockbroker in America, later a journalist, speaker, and publisher, and an early admirer and publisher of Karl Marx. Her views on free love were considered scandalous; in this selection she defends herself against the popular charge of promiscuity and casual sex, defining the doctrine of free love as the idea that sexual love should be liberated from the legal obligation of marriage, in which women "do not own their own sexual organs." The principles of free love, she argues, should be applied equally to both men and women.

All the relations between the sexes that are recognized as *legitimate* are denominated marriage. *But of what does marriage consist?* This very pertinent question requires settlement before any real progress can be made as to what Social Freedom and Prostitution mean. It is admitted by everybody that marriage is a union of the opposites in sex, but is it a principle of nature outside of all law, or is it a law outside of all nature? Where is the point before reaching which it is not marriage, but having reached which it is marriage? Is it where two meet and realize that the love elements of their nature are harmonious, and that they blend into and make *one* purpose of life? or is it where a *soulless form* is pronounced over two who know *no* commingling of life's hopes? Or are *both* these processes required—first, the marriage union *without* the law, to be afterward solemnized *by* the law? If *both* terms are required, does the marriage continue after the *first* departs? or if the *restrictions* of the law are removed and the *love* continues, does *marriage* continue? or if the law unite two who *hate* each other, is that marriage? Thus are presented all the possible aspects of the case.

The *courts* hold if the law solemnly pronounce two married, *that they are* married, whether love is present or not. But is this really such a marriage as this enlightened age should demand? No! It is a stupidly arbitrary law, which can find no analogies

From Victoria Woodhull, *The Principles of Social Freedom* (New York: Woodhull, Claflin and Company, 1871), 13–14, 21–26.

in nature. Nature proclaims in *broadest terms,* and all her subjects re-echo the same *grand* truth, that sexual unions, which result in reproduction, are marriage. And sex exists wherever there is reproduction.

By analogy, the same law ascends into the sphere of and applies among men and women; for are not they a part and parcel of nature in which this law exists as a principle? This law of nature by which men and women are united by love is God's marriage law, the enactments of men to the contrary notwithstanding. And the precise results of this marriage will be determined by the character of those united; all the experiences evolved from the marriage being the legitimate sequences thereof.

Marriage must consist either of love or of law, since it *may* exist in form with either term absent; that is to say, people may be married by *law* and all love be lacking; and they may also be married by *love* and lack all sanction of law. True marriage must in reality consist entirely either of law or love, since there can be *no* compromise between the law of nature and *statute* law by which the former shall yield to the latter.

Law cannot change what nature has already determined. Neither will love obey if law command. Law cannot compel two to love. It has nothing to do either *with* love or with its absence. Love is superior to all law, and so also is hate, indifference, disgust and all other human sentiments which are evoked in the relations of the sexes. It legitimately and logically follows, if *love* have *anything* to do with marriage, that *law* has *nothing* to do with it. And on the contrary, if *law* have anything to do with marriage, that *love* has nothing to do with it. And there is no escaping the deduction. . . .

I assume, in the first place, when there is not mutual love there is no union to continue and nothing to justify, and it has already been determined that, as marriage should have love as a basis, if love depart marriage also departs. But laying this aside, see if there can any real good or happiness possibly result from an enforced contin-uance of marriage upon the part of one party thereto. Let all persons take this question home to their own souls, and there determine if they could find happiness in holding unwilling hearts in bondage. It is *against* the *nature of things* that *any* satisfaction can result from such a state of things except it be the satisfaction of knowing that you have succeeded in virtually imprisoning the person whom you *profess* to love, and that would be demoniacal.

Again. It must be remembered that the individual affairs of two persons are not the subject of interference by any third party, and if one of them choose to separate, there is no power outside of the two which can rightly interfere to prevent. Beside, who is to determine whether there will be more happiness sacrificed by a *continuation* or a *separation*. If a person is *fully* determined to separate, it is proof positive that another feeling *stronger* than all his or her sentiments of duty determine it. And here, again, *who* but the individual is to determine which course will secure the most good? Suppose that a separation is desired because one of the two loves and is loved elsewhere. In this case, if the union be maintained by force, at least *two* of three, and, probably, *all three* persons will be made unhappy thereby; whereas if separation come and the other union be consummated, there will be but one, unhappy. So even here, if the greatest good of the greatest number is to rule, separation is not only legitimate, *but* desirable. In all other things except marriage it is always held to be the right thing to do to *break* a *bad bargain* or *promise* just as soon as possible, and I hold that of *all things* in which this rule should apply, it should *first* apply to marriages.

Now, let me ask, would it not rather be the *Christian* way, in such cases, to say to the disaffected party: "Since you no longer love me, go your way and be happy, and make those to whom you go happy also." I know of no higher, holier love than that described, and of no more beautiful expression of it than was given in the columns of the *Woman's Journal*, of Boston, whose conductors have felt called upon to endeavor to convince the people that it has no affiliation with those who hold to no more radical doctrine of Free Love than they proclaim as follows:

"The love that I cannot command is not mine; let me not disturb myself about it, nor attempt to filch it from its rightful owner. A heart that I supposed mine has drifted and gone. Shall I go in pursuit? Shall I forcibly capture the truant and transfix it with the barb of my selfish affections, pin it to the wall of my chamber? God forbid! Rather let me leave my doors and windows open, intent only on living so nobly that the best cannot fail to be drawn to me by an irresistible attraction."

To me it is impossible to frame words into sentences *more holy, pure* and true than are these. I would ever carry them in my soul as my guide and guard, feeling that in *living* by them happiness would certainly be mine. To the loving wife who mourns a lost heart, let me recommend them as a panacea. To the loving husband whose soul is desolate, let me offer these as words of healing balm. They will live in history, to make their writer the *loved* and *revered* of unborn generations.

The tenth commandment of the Decalogue says: "Thou shalt not covet thy neighbor's wife." And Jesus, in the beautiful parable of the Samaritan who fell among thieves, asks: "Who is thy neighbor?" and answers his own question in a way to lift the conception wholly out of the category of mere local proximity into a sublime spiritual conception. In other words, he spiritualizes the word and sublimates the morality of the commandment. In the same spirit I ask now, Who is a *wife*? And I answer, not the woman who, ignorant of her own feelings, or with lying lips, has promised, in hollow ceremonial, and before the law, to love, but *she who really loves most,* and *most truly,* the man who commands her affections, and who in turn loves her, with or without the ceremony of marriage; and the man who holds the heart of such a woman in such a relation is "thy *neighbor,*" and *that woman is "thy neighbor's wife" meant in the commandment*; and whosoever, though he should have been a hundred times married to her by the law, shall claim, or *covet* even, the possession of that woman as against her true lover and husband in the spirit, sins against the commandment.

We know positively that Jesus would have answered in that way. He has defined for us "the neighbor," not in the paltry and commonplace sense, but spiritually. He has said: "He that looketh on a woman to lust after her hath committed adultery with her already in his heart." So, therefore, he spiritualized the idea of adultery. In the kingdom of heaven, to be prayed for daily, to come on earth, there is to be no "marrying or giving in marriage;" that is to say, formally and legally; but spiritual marriage must always exist, and had Jesus been called on to define a wife, can anybody doubt that he would, in the same spirit, the spiritualizing tendency and character of all his doctrine, have spiritualized the marriage relation as absolutely as he did the breach of it? that he would, in other words, have said in meaning precisely what I now say? And when Christian ministers are no longer afraid or ashamed *to be Christians* they will embrace this doctrine. Free Love will be an integral part of the religion of the future.

It can now be asked: What is the legitimate sequence of Social Freedom? To which I unhesitatingly reply: Free Love, or freedom of the affections. "And are you a Free Lover?" is the almost incredulous query.

I repeat a frequent reply: "I am; and I can honestly, in the fullness of my soul, raise my voice to my Maker, and thank Him that *I am,* and that I have had the strength and the devotion to truth to stand before this traducing and vilifying community in a manner representative of that which shall come with healing on its wings for the bruised hearts and crushed affections of humanity."

And to those who denounce me for this I reply: "Yes, I am a Free Lover. I have an *inalienable, constitutional* and *natural* right to love whom I may, to love as *long* or as *short* a period as I can; to *change* that love *every day* if I please, and with *that* right neither *you* nor any *law* you can frame have *any* right to interfere. And I have the *further* right to demand a free and unrestricted exercise of that right, and it is *your duty* not only to *accord* it, but, as a community, to see that I am protected in it. I trust that I am fully understood, for I mean *just* that, and nothing less!

To speak thus plainly and pointedly is a *duty I owe* to myself. The press have stigmatized me to the world as an advocate, theoretically and practically, of the doctrine of Free Love, upon which they have placed their stamp of moral deformity; the vulgar and inconsequent definition which they hold makes the theory an abomination. And though this conclusion is a no more legitimate and reasonable one than that would be which should call the Golden Rule a general license to all sorts of debauch, since Free Love bears the *same* relations to the moral deformities of which it stands accused as does the Golden Rule to the Law of the Despot, yet it obtains among many intelligent people. But they claim, in the language of one of these exponents, that "Words belong to the people; they are the common property of the mob. Now the common use, among the mob, of the term Free Love, is a synonym for promiscuity." Against this absurd proposition I oppose the assertion that words *do not* belong to the mob, but to that which they represent. Words are the exponents and interpretations of ideas. If I use a word which exactly interprets and represents what I would be understood to mean, shall I go to the *mob* and *ask of them* what interpretation *they* choose to place upon it? If lexicographers, when they prepare their dictionaries, were to go to the mob for the rendition of words, what kind of language would we have?

I claim that freedom means *to be free,* let the mob claim to the contrary as strenuously as they may. And I claim that love means an exhibition of the affections, let the mob claim what they may. And therefore, in compounding these words into Free Love, I claim that united they mean, and should be used to convey, their united definitions, the mob to the contrary notwithstanding. And when the term Free Love finds a place in dictionaries, it will prove my claim to have been correct, and that the mob have not received the attention of the lexicographers, since it will not be set down to signify sexual debauchery, and that only, or in any governing sense.

It is not only usual but also just, when people adopt a new theory, or promulgate a new doctrine, that they give it a name significant of its character. There are, however, exceptional cases to be found in all ages. The Jews coined the name of Christians, and, with withering contempt, hurled it upon the early followers of Christ. It was the most opprobrious epithet they could invent to express their detestation of those humble but honest and brave people. That name has now come to be considered as a synonym of all that is good, true and beautiful in the highest departments of our natures, and is revered in all civilized nations.

In precisely the same manner the Pharisees of to-day, who hold themselves to be representative of all there is that is good and pure, as did the Pharisees of old, have coined the word Free-Love, and flung it upon all who believe not alone in Religious and Political Freedom, but in that larger Freedom, which includes both these, Social Freedom.

For my part, I am extremely obliged to our thoughtful Pharisaical neighbors for the kindness shown us in the invention of so appropriate a name. If there is a more beautiful word in the English language than *love*, that word is *freedom*, and that *these two* words, which, with us, attach or belong to *everything* that is pure and good, should have been *joined* by our enemies, and *handed* over to us *already* coined, is certainly a high consideration, for which we should never cease to be thankful. And when we shall be accused of all sorts of wickedness and vileness by our enemies, who in this have been so just, may I not hope that, remembering how much they have done for us, we may be able to say, "Father, forgive them, for they know not what they do," and to forgive them ourselves with our whole hearts.

Of the love that says: "Bless *me*, darling;" of the love so called, which is nothing but selfishness, the appropriation of another soul as the means of one's own happiness merely, there is abundance in the world; and the still more animal, the mere desire for temporary gratification, with little worthy the name of love, also abounds. Even these are best left free, since as evils they will thus be best cured; but of that celestial love which says: "Bless *you*, darling," and which strives continually to confer blessings; of that genuine love whose office it is to bless others or another, there cannot be too much in the world, and when it shall be fully understood that this is the love which we mean and commend there will be no objection to the term Free Love, and none to the thing signified.

We not only *accept* our name, but we contend that *none* other could so well signify the *real* character of that which it designates—to be free and to love. But our enemies must be reminded that the fact of the existence and advocacy of such a doctrine cannot immediately elevate to high condition the great number who have been kept in degradation and misery by previous false systems. They must *not expect* at this early day of the new doctrine, that all debauchery has been cleansed out of men and women. In the haunts where it retreats, the benign influence of its magic presence has not yet penetrated. They must *not expect* that brutish men and debased women have as yet been touched by its wand of hope, and that they have already obeyed the bidding to come up higher. They must *not expect* that ignorance and fleshly lust have already been lifted to the region of intellect and moral purity. They must *not expect* that Free Love, before it is more than barely announced to the world, can perform what Christianity in eighteen hundred years has failed to do.

Chapter Nine

What Women Like in Men (1901)

Rafford Pyke

In this turn-of-the-century picture of what the "typical" woman looks for in a man she loves, the reader is informed that "her love will have in it that element of the maternal without which no true woman's love is ever quite complete." The contrast with the late-twentieth-century journalism in the last part of this book is striking and informative, though the idea that women's love includes or should include an element of maternal caretaking is still very much with us, as Elayne Rapping's selection shows (see part 7).

A very acute foreign observer of American life has lately published some interesting observations on the subject of American women. The most significant of his conclusions is found in what he says about the effect which advanced education has had upon the attitude of American women toward American men. Marriage, he thinks, is becoming less attractive to our American girls, because the development of their intelligence has wrought in them a sort of disillusionment, a comparative indifference toward the other sex. The discovery is early made by them that men are, after all, rather dull and commonplace; or still worse, that they are coarse and therefore unable to appeal to the finer needs of a woman's nature. Hence, the American girl is outgrowing the old traditional romantic desire for love and marriage for their own sake. "The ideal German girl thinks that she will marry only the man who will make her happy; the ideal American girl thinks that she can marry only the man without whom she will be unhappy."

There is a great deal of truth in this if we understand it as referring to women who have really attained to womanhood, and if we do not regard it as said of the very young girl. The very young girl is what she always has been and probably always will be. Theoretically, she is an interesting creature moving along through the early years of imperfect maturity, in maiden meditation, fancy-free, with no thought of men until she happens to meet *the* man who lays siege to her virgin heart and writes his name on the unsullied page of her imagination. Of course, this is not true. In reality, the typical young girl is concerned about nothing half so much as about men. It is an innocent concern, but it is, none the less, absorbing and intense. Everything in life centers in her mind about the potential Man, and in almost every casual male

Rafford Pyke, "What Women Like in Men," Cosmopolitan, vol. 31 (May–October 1901): 303-7.

she thinks she sees him. She has as yet not the slightest discrimination, for she has not yet had the slightest experience; and so the approach of any one in trousers is delightfully disquieting to her. She flutters and blushes, she is perpetually self-conscious, she catches at every conversational straw that seems to indicate some special interest or attention, she holds sage converse with her dearest friend upon the subject, and unless good fortune or an experienced mother watches over her, she falls headlong into love with the first fool who takes the trouble to flatter her simple vanity.

But the very young girl does not really count; and when we speak of the American woman we mean her who is in reality a woman, with all a woman's fine perception and with an intelligence trained by reading, by study, and above all, by observation and experience. And it is quite true that in these days, American women of this type are becoming every year more difficult, more discriminating, less willing to accept in any serious way the men who cross their paths in life. They do not love upon an impulse; they do not marry just for the sake of being styled "Mrs." instead of "Miss." They must be satisfied all through; or, as the foreign critic puts it, they want only the man who can make them feel that without him they will be unhappy. The best proof of this change of attitude in our women is to be found in the gradual disuse among us of the term "old maid." There was a time when to be called an "old maid" drove an envenomed shaft deep into a woman's soul. It was the most opprobrious epithet, save one, that could be applied to her. It meant that she was unmarried because no man would have her, and its ultimate implication was that not to marry some man— any man at a pinch—was almost disgraceful to a woman. Nowadays, the term has fallen out of use; for if at the present time a woman is not married, it means merely that she does not care to be: that she is not waiting eagerly for a man, but contentedly for *the* man; and if he never comes, then she prefers to keep her self-respect and remain unwedded.

Yet after all, while this great change with everything that it implies has surely taken place, womanhood itself has not changed in the slightest nor will it ever do so. In essentials, woman is what she always has been and what she always will be. Her nature is as fundamentally emotional as ever. She feels the need of love as much as ever. Passion and self-abandonment and the joy of life have not been extinguished in her. It is only that her intelligence and feeling have become keener and finer, and no longer respond to every casual appeal. She has more, far more, to give than she had in the past, and in consequence she demands far more from him to whom she gives it all. But to the man who can successfully appeal to her, she is as ever a creature of fire and air, a creature of infinite tenderness of beautiful unselfishness, of exquisite submission. What, then, are the qualities and attributes which, if a man possess them, will make him such that after she has known him, she cannot let him pass out of her life unloved; and loving whom she knows that he holds in his possession the power to read her very heartstrings? To do the subject any kind of justice and to follow out its hidden subtleties, one ought to write a book; yet I shall attempt as carefully as possible in this brief space to show just what it is that a woman of intelligence and knowledge and sentiment and fineness—*la femme de trente ans*—likes best in man.

First of all—to consider the most superficial phases of our subject—is the question of a man's appearance. Good looks in a man, as a very celebrated woman once remarked, are superfluous. A handsome man attracts attention, and so he has a certain preliminary advantage over a rival who is plain; yet this counts for very little in the end. John Wilkes, who was more than ugly, knew women well when he said: "Give me half an hour's start, and I am not afraid of the handsomest man in England." What woman do like very much is an air of distinction, a touch of breeding, an indescribable something in bearing and in manner that marks a man out as apart from the common, and makes others recognize instinctively that place must be made for him and deference shown him. But it is sufficient that a man look like a gentleman, and that there be nothing about him to excite unfavorable comment and especially ridicule. The same thing is true of his dress. Women despise a man who gives much thought to clothes; yet on the other hand, they wish him to be well set-up, neat, wholesome, trim and well-groomed, as every man should be, not as a matter of conscious effort, but by an instinctive sense of fitness and good taste. Women will pardon slovenliness in a genius, but they will never like it; and in one who is not a genius they will very justly infer from it the presence of something *louche* in habits or in character. All these facts serve as the illustration of a general truth: that a woman always prefers a man whom other women will approve of and admire; for the earlier promptings of a woman's love are due quite as much to vanity—or let us call it emulation—as to sentiment. They like the man whom other women would be sure to like, and they are prone to turn away from one whom others do not look at seriously.

The casual every-day accomplishments of a man have much to do with women's liking; and first of all comes *sarior faire.* He may or may not be what is rather vulgarly described as "a society man," yet he must understand and be familiar with the myriad little usages that form society's unwritten law. To be at ease in any set, to be equal to emergencies, to carry off an awkward situation with urbanity and perfect self-possession—this faculty wins unstinted admiration from a woman. And then there are the things that go with this—knowledge of the proper thing to do, the little courtesies, the delicate and tactful attentions that mean everything and nothing, the ability to order a dinner properly, to make things go off smoothly, to carry out a plan without a blunder or a jar, the carriage ready at the proper moment, the flowers specially arranged, the right seats at the theater, everything foreseen, every possible occurrence provided for, every want anticipated, every *contretemps* avoided. These are all unimportant in themselves, yet in the mass they never fail to create a strong impression in a woman; for a woman hates blunders and will trust a man in great things if she sees that he has a genius for making small things go off well.

Such a man is likely to understand a woman, and every woman adores the man who can do that. Illimitable fun has been poked at the troubles of the *femme incomprise,* but it has been quite unjust to her and very unintelligent. To be really understood, to say what she likes, to utter her innermost thoughts in her own way, to cast aside the traditional conventions that gall her and repress her, to have some one near her with whom she can be quite frank, and yet to know that not a syllable of what she says will be misinterpreted or mistaken, but rather *felt* just as she feels it all—how wonderfully sweet is this to every woman, and how few men are there who can give it to her! But the man who has the gift of intimacy can give it, and in giving it he can bind her to him as by links of steel. Who shall describe that wonderful gift of intimacy, that miracle in human intercourse, that rare blending of subtle intelligence, of exquisite tact, of wonderful sympathy? There are men who have it; and when a woman's acquaintance with such a man is only half an hour old, she will be telling him of things that she has never told to brother or sister or mother or husband or even to her nearest woman friend; and she will tell them—these intimate personal things—with absolute unconsciousness, so natural, so simple is it to give her confidence to this stranger who has laid his naked mind to hers, whose every word is a supreme expression of complete intelligence, anticipating and illumining her hidden thought, and answering each mood and each emotion as though he were her second self. Afterward, when they have parted, it comes over her with a sudden shock that she has violated every one of the conventions, that she has laid bare her secret soul, that she has been reckless, unwomanly—almost immodest. She is in an agony of doubt as to what he must be thinking of her, and she dreads to meet him for a second time. But she always does meet him, and in a moment the spell is again upon her; and her doubts and questionings melt from out her mind at the sound of that voice which thrills her so profoundly, that voice which has the quality of a violin, penetrating, tender, and with a lingering caress somewhere within its tones. She hesitates no more; for she has met the man who understands, the man whom women never can forget. There lives no woman who could not make the words of Emerson her creed: "When I meet a man whose mind is like my own but stronger, then I become his very slave."

But women like a man of whom the world has heard, who has done something that has made him known outside the sphere of private life, whose name stands for achievement and creation. A man like this bears with him always a passport to a woman's favor. First of all, his interest in her, if he shows such interest, gratifies her vanity, her emulation. She loves to think that one whom many seek has sought her out. She triumphs in the thought. But afterward, if he really enters into her inner life, her feeling is a nobler one than this. If she loves him, her love will have in it that element of the maternal without which no true woman's love is ever quite complete. He is hers; and she thrills with his success, and tries to comfort him in his defeats. She hates his enemies vindictively. She longs to help him, to be his inspiration. And if he can make her feel that she has so entered into his life as to be a part of it, that it is from her and from her love that he draws his hope, his strength, his courage— then he has given her a draught of flattery so delicious, so exquisite, that she could die from the very joy of it. But almost sweeter still are those moments when perhaps he is depressed and ill or half-disheartened, this man who faces the world and is strong to all besides herself; for then he makes the one supreme appeal to her very deepest, tenderest feelings; and there come over her a great wave of maternal tenderness, a passion of self-devotion, and as she mothers him, her whole woman's nature is stirred to its very depths.

Women like liberality in men, a largeness of view, a contempt of the petty, a certain splendid carelessness about the small things that do not count. A touch of irresponsibility, even, appeals to the feminine imagination, perhaps because responsibility is so much insisted on for women that they admire when they see it trampled on by men. Minute exactness, "fussing," too much system, insistence on the unimportant, are all traits that women despise when men exhibit them. They like a man who has a merry way of throwing aside the little cares of life and laughing at them, who doesn't bother his head over small affairs, who is magnificent in his neglect of rules and regulations. Women in their secret heart think that a man—the right sort of man—is entitled to do just what he pleases, and when they find him doing it in defiance of everybody and everything, having his own way in a kind of triumphant lawlessness, they may deplore it in their speech, but it delights their fancy all the same. It is so utterly unlike their way of doing things, so unlike their little indirections, their tortuous fashion of arriving at results, their small hypocrisies. They do not wholly understand it; and perhaps that is one more reason why it so appeals to them. Parsimony, stinginess, numbering pennies, and counting the cost—these things are perhaps of all the most obnoxious to a woman. She can love a prodigal, but she cannot take the slightest interest in a miser. Naturally penurious herself, or at least penurious in many things, she revels in a generous nature that enjoys profusion, and she loves to bask like a cat in an atmosphere of luxurious plenty. Ostentation does not please her, but rather that fondness for the good things of life which insists on having them, which accepts them like the air we breathe and the sunshine that warms us, simply and as a matter of course.

Gentleness always charms a woman, if it be the gentleness of strength and not of weakness. She loves to think that one who may be rough and hard to all the rest, can be to her as tender as another woman. It is, she thinks, the miracle of love. Yet she must always be made to feel that the gentleness is not immutable, but that back of it there lie the harsher qualities of man. It is a hard saying but it is true that the men whom women love the most are men who are quite capable of cruelty—not lightly nor without reason, yet beyond all doubt. When a woman feels that if she makes mistakes, if she assumes too much, or if she goes too far in her caprices, the gentleness will shrivel away and in its place will rise a terrifying harshness, then she will have the very real happiness that comes to the true woman when she knows that she has found her master.

A man should never let a woman be wholly sure of him, nor feel that she completely knows him. She really loves him all the better if she feels that he is in the last analysis inscrutable, that there is always something in his nature that she can never fully understand, and that even in his moments of supreme tenderness, there is still one hidden sanctuary where it is not permitted her to enter. This, and the feeling that she never can be wholly sure of him, are the things that keep a woman faithful to a man forever.

It is obvious enough that the man who can unite the qualities that have been here imperfectly defined can never be a very young man. The knowledge of life comes only with the lapse of years; the poise, the self-control, the achievement, the sympathy, are all the gifts of time. What is the golden age of manhood? There is that subtle and profoundly melancholy utterance of French genius—*Ah, si la jeunesse sarait, si la vieillese pouvait!* It seems to imply that power goes as wisdom comes; that what maturity gains, it pays for in the coin of youth; that as revelation enters the mind, capacity deserts the body. Yet this is only true in part. To every man there comes the period of perfection, the two splendid lustrums in which mind and body alike are ripened and matured; and when, if he have the gifts from nature, the world is at his feet. Ambition, achievement, creation, love—these are for him who at the age of thirty-five has learned life's lessons well; and for ten glorious years at least, he may enjoy them to the full. Experience has taught him everything that she can teach. His powers of body are still unimpaired. The fire runs through his veins. His mind is clear and sure. He has acquired a sense of true proportion. He does not waste his energies on what is worthless. He knows the best. He will accept no less. He reaches out his hand and all is his. He is as a god, knowing both good and evil. He is enlightened, and can enjoy each pleasure while avoiding every penalty which to the uninitiated lurks in every joy. Men listen to him and do his will. He is at home with young and old alike, for he stands between them with one hand outstretched to each. He looks back upon the past without regret, for it has taught him all he knows, has given all that he possesses. He looks forward to the future without disquietude, knowing that when the sunlight fades and grayness settles down upon his path, he will still be comforted by the assurance that he has enjoyed life to the full, and has taken from it all it has to give. The man of forty is the man for whom there are no mysteries and no impossibilities. And the heart of woman is the symbol of his absolute supremacy.

Such are the traits and qualities that women like in men: and when they are combined, they make the perfect lover: The mind that leads, the sympathy that charms, the strength that dominates, the gentleness that soothes, the mystery that fascinates.

The woman of the present day with her more sensitive organization, her more vivid imagination, her superior intelligence and her warmer temperament, can feel these things the more because she can understand them better than the half-developed woman of the past. Mediocrity is not for her: but when at last she finds and knows her mate, she is sublime in her self-abandonment. Having put away so many of the conventions of other days, the ones that still exist have little power over her. The teaching of her early years, the traditions of her sex, the fears, the doubts, the hesitancies—all these she tramples underfoot; and, seeking out the one man of her life, she stands before him in that splendid shamelessness which is the finest thing in perfect love. Mind, heart, and soul all cry out irresistibly within her; and, stirred with infinite emotion, shaken with passion, and thrilling with the ecstasy that comes but once in any life, she knows that there can be no joy for her so over-whelming as to die in adoration at his feet.

Chapter Ten

Marriage and Love (1914)

Emma Goldman

Goldman's famous essay presents marriage as the prostitution of "free" love for women. This classic text, separating romantic love and marriage as an institution, does not introduce a completely new idea; there is a subversive tradition in the West of separating marriage from love, including Charles Fourier, the French philosopher, and radical communities such as the Oneida community in New York state, though these were not necessarily oriented to the interests of women. Like the Russian feminist Alexandra Kollontai, who wrote about the "ideal of free love drawn by the hungry imagination of women fighting for their emancipation" at about the same time, Goldman linked romantic and sexual freedom, including the freedom from marriage and family, specifically to women's rights. Her analysis is a more specifically political enlargement of Victoria Woodhull's ideas.

The popular notion about marriage and love is that they are synonymous, that they spring from the same motives, and cover the same human needs. Like most popular notions this also rests not on actual facts, but on superstition.

Marriage and love have nothing in common; they are as far apart as the poles; are, in fact, antagonistic to each other. No doubt some marriages have been the result of love. Not, however, because love could assert itself only in marriage; much rather is it because few people can completely outgrow a convention. There are to-day large numbers of men and women to whom marriage is naught but a farce, but who submit to it for the sake of public opinion. At any rate, while it is true that some marriages are based on love, and while it is equally true that in some cases love continues in married life, I maintain that it does so regardless of marriage, and not because of it.

On the other hand, it is utterly false that love results from marriage. On rare occasions one does hear of a miraculous case of a married couple falling in love after marriage, but on close examination it will be found that it is a mere adjustment to the inevitable. Certainly the growing-used to each other is far away from the spon-

Emma Goldman, "Marriage and Love," in *Anarchism and Other Essays* (New York: Mother Earth Publishing House, 1911, 1914), 158–67.

taneity, the intensity, and beauty of love, without which the intimacy of marriage must prove degrading to both the woman and the man.

Marriage is primarily an economic arrangement, an insurance pact. It differs from the ordinary life insurance agreement only in that it is more binding, more exacting. Its returns are insignificantly small compared with the investments. In taking out an insurance policy one pays for it in dollars and cents, always at liberty to discontinue payments. If, however, woman's premium is a husband, she pays for it with her name, her privacy, her self-respect, her very life, "until death doth part." Moreover, the marriage insurance condemns her to life-long dependency, to parasitism, to complete uselessness, individual as well as social. Man, too, pays his toll, but as his sphere is wider, marriage does not limit him as much as woman. He feels his chains more in an economic sense.

Thus Dante's motto over Inferno applies with equal force to marriage: "Ye who enter here leave all hope behind."

That marriage is a failure none but the very stupid will deny. One has but to glance over the statistics of divorce to realize how bitter a failure marriage really is. Nor will the stereotyped Philistine argument that the laxity of divorce laws and the growing looseness of woman account for the fact that: first, every twelfth marriage ends in divorce; second, that since 1870 divorces have increased from 28 to 73 for every hundred thousand population; third, that adultery, since 1867, as ground for divorce, has increased 270.8 per cent; fourth, that desertion increased 369.8 per cent.

Added to these startling figures is a vast amount of material, dramatic and literary, further elucidating this subject. Robert Herrick, in *Together;* Pinero, in *Mid-Channel;* Eugene Walter, in *Paid in Full,* and scores of other writers are discussing the barrenness, the monotony, the sordidness, the inadequacy of marriage as a factor for harmony and understanding.

The thoughtful social student will not content himself with the popular superficial excuse for this phenomenon. He will have to dig down deeper into the very life of the sexes to know why marriage proves so disastrous.

Edward Carpenter says that behind every marriage stands the life-long environment of the two sexes; an environment so different from each other that man and woman must remain strangers. Separated by an insurmountable wall of superstition, custom, and habit, marriage has not the potentiality of developing knowledge of, and respect for, each other, without which every union is doomed to failure.

Henrik Ibsen, the hater of all social shams, was probably the first to realize this great truth. Nora leaves her husband, not—as the stupid critic would have it—because she is tired of her responsibilities or feels the need of woman's rights, but because she has come to know that for eight years she had lived with a stranger and borne him children. Can there be anything more humiliating, more degrading than a life-long proximity between two strangers? No need for the woman to know anything of the man, save his income. As to the knowledge of the woman—what is there to know except that she has a pleasing appearance? We have not yet outgrown the theologic myth that woman has no soul, that she is a mere appendix to man, made out of his rib just for the convenience of the gentleman who was so strong that he was afraid of his own shadow.

Perchance the poor quality of the material whence woman comes is responsible for her inferiority. At any rate, woman has no soul—what is there to know about her? Besides, the less soul a woman has the greater her asset as a wife, the more readily will she absorb herself in her husband. It is this slavish acquiescence to man's superiority that has kept the marriage institution seemingly intact for so long a period. Now that woman is coming into her own, now that she is actually growing aware of herself as a being outside of the master's grace, the sacred institution of marriage is gradually being undermined, and no amount of sentimental lamentation can stay it.

From infancy, almost, the average girl is told that marriage is her ultimate goal; therefore her training and education must be directed towards that end. Like the mute beast fattened for slaughter, she is prepared for that. Yet, strange to say, she is allowed to know much less about her function as wife and mother than the ordinary artisan of his trade. It is indecent and filthy for a respectable girl to know anything of the marital relation. Oh, for the inconsistency of respectability, that needs the marriage vow to turn something which is filthy into the purest and most sacred arrangement that none dare question or criticize. Yet that is exactly the attitude of the average upholder of marriage. The prospective wife and mother is kept in complete ignorance of her only asset in the competitive field—sex. Thus she enters into life-long relations with a man only to find herself shocked, repelled, outraged beyond measure by the most natural and healthy instinct, sex. It is safe to say that a large percentage of the unhappiness, misery, distress, and physical suffering of matrimony is due to the criminal ignorance in sex matters that is being extolled as a great virtue. Nor is it at all an exaggeration when I say that more than one home has been broken up because of this deplorable fact.

If, however, woman is free and big enough to learn the mystery of sex without the sanction of State or Church, she will stand condemned as utterly unfit to become the wife of a "good" man, his goodness consisting of an empty head and plenty of money. Can there be anything more outrageous than the idea that a healthy, grown woman, full of life and passion, must deny nature's demand, must subdue her most intense craving, undermine her health and break her spirit, must stunt her vision, abstain from the depth and glory of sex experience until a "good" man comes along to take her unto himself as a wife? That is precisely what marriage means. How can such an arrangement end except in failure? This is one, though not the least important, factor of marriage, which differentiates it from love.

Ours is a practical age. The time when Romeo and Juliet risked the wrath of their fathers for love, when Gretchen exposed herself to the gossip of her neighbors for love, is no more. If, on rare occasions, young people allow themselves the luxury of romance, they are taken in care by the elders, drilled and pounded until they become "sensible."

The moral lesson instilled in the girl is not whether the man has aroused her love, but rather is it, "How much?" The important and only God of practical American life: Can the man make a living? Can he support a wife? That is the only thing that justifies marriage. Gradually this saturates every thought of the girl; her dreams are not of moonlight and kisses, of laughter and tears; she dreams of shopping tours and bargain counters. This soul-poverty and sordidness are the elements inherent in the marriage institution. The State and the Church approve of no other ideal, simply because it is the one that necessitates the State and Church control of men and women.

Doubtless there are people who continue to consider love above dollars and cents. Particularly is this true of that class whom economic necessity has forced to become self-supporting. The tremendous change in woman's position, wrought by that mighty factor, is indeed phenomenal when we reflect that it is but a short time since she has entered the industrial arena. Six million women wage-earners; six million women, who have the equal right with men to be exploited, to be robbed, to go on strike; aye, to starve even. Anything more, my lord? Yes, six million wage-workers in every walk of life, from the highest brain work to the most difficult menial labor in the mines and on the railroad tracks; yes, even detectives and policemen. Surely the emancipation is complete.

Yet with all that, but a very small number of the vast army of women wage-workers look upon work as a permanent issue, in the same light as does man. No matter how decrepit the latter, he has been taught to be independent, self-supporting. Oh, I know that no one is really independent in our economic treadmill; still, the poorest specimen of a man hates to be a parasite; to be known as such, at any rate.

The woman considers her position as worker transitory, to be thrown aside for the first bidder. That is why it is infinitely harder to organize women than men. "Why should I join a union? I am going to get married, to have a home." Has she not been taught from infancy to look upon that as her ultimate calling? She learns soon enough that the home, though not so large a prison as the factory, has more solid doors and bars. It has a keeper so faithful that naught can escape him. The most tragic part, however, is that the home no longer frees her from wage-slavery; it only increases her task.

According to the latest statistics submitted before a Committee "on labor and wages, and congestion of population," ten per cent of the wage-workers in New York City alone are married, yet they must continue to work at the most poorly paid labor in the world. Add to this horrible aspect the drudgery of housework, and what remains of the protection and glory of the home? As a matter of fact, even the middle-class girl in marriage can not speak of her home, since it is the man who creates her sphere. It is not important whether the husband is a brute or a darling. What I wish to prove is that marriage guarantees woman a home only by the grace of her husband. There she moves about in *his* home, year after year, until her aspect of life and human affairs becomes as flat, narrow, and drab as her surroundings. Small wonder if she becomes a nag, petty, quarrelsome, gossipy, unbearable, thus driving the man from the house. She could not go, if she wanted to; there is no place to go. Besides, a short period of married life, of complete surrender of all faculties, absolutely incapacitates the average woman for the outside world. She becomes reckless in appearance, clumsy in her movements, dependent in her decisions, cowardly in her judgment, a weight and a bore, which most men grow to hate and despise. Wonderfully inspiring atmosphere for the bearing of life, is it not?

But the child, how is it to be protected, if not for marriage? After all, is not that the most important consideration? The sham, the hypocrisy of it! Marriage protecting the child, yet thousands of children destitute and homeless. Marriage protecting the child, yet orphan asylums and reformatories overcrowded, the Society for the Prevention of Cruelty to Children keeping busy in rescuing the little victims from "loving" parents, to place them under more loving care, the Gerry Society. Oh, the mockery of it!

Marriage may have the power to "bring the horse to water," but has it ever made him drink? The law will place the father under arrest, and put him in convict's clothes; but has that ever stilled the hunger of the child? If the parent has no work, or if he hides his identity, what does marriage do then? It invokes the law to bring the man to "justice," to put him safely behind closed doors; his labor, however, goes not to the child, but to the State. The child receives but a blighted memory of its father's stripes.

As to the protection of the woman—therein lies the curse of marriage. Not that it really protects her, but the very idea is so revolting, such an outrage and insult on life, so degrading to human dignity, as to forever condemn this parasitic institution.

It is like that other paternal arrangement—capitalism. It robs man of his birthright, stunts his growth, poisons his body, keeps him in ignorance, in poverty and dependence, and then institutes charities that thrive on the last vestige of man's self-respect.

The institution of marriage makes a parasite of woman, an absolute dependent. It incapacitates her for life's struggle, annihilates her social consciousness, paralyzes her imagination, and then imposes its gracious protection, which is in reality a snare, a travesty on human character.

If motherhood is the highest fulfillment of woman's nature, what other protection does it need save love and freedom? Marriage but defiles, outrages, and corrupts her fulfillment. Does it not say to woman, Only when you follow me shall you bring forth life? Does it not condemn her to the block, does it not degrade and shame her if she refuses to buy her right to motherhood by selling herself? Does not marriage only sanction motherhood, even though conceived in hatred, in compulsion? Yet, if motherhood be of free choice, of love, of ecstasy, of defiant passion, does it not place a crown of thorns upon an innocent head and carve in letters of blood the hideous epithet, Bastard? Were marriage to contain all the virtues claimed for it, its crimes against motherhood would exclude it forever from the realm of love.

Love, the strongest and deepest element in all life, the harbinger of hope, of joy, of ecstasy; love, the defier of all laws, of all conventions; love, the freest, the most powerful moulder of human destiny; how can such an all-compelling force be synonymous with that poor little State- and Church-begotten weed, marriage?

Free love? As if love is anything but free! Man has bought brains, but all the millions in the world have failed to buy love. Man has subdued bodies, but all the power on earth has been unable to subdue love. Man has conquered whole nations, but all his armies could not conquer love. Man has chained and fettered the spirit, but he has been utterly helpless before love. High on a throne, with all the splendor and pomp his gold can command, man is yet poor and desolate, if love passes him by. And if it stays, the poorest hovel is radiant with warmth, with life and color. Thus love has the magic power to make of a beggar a king. Yes, love is free;

it can dwell in no other atmosphere. In freedom it gives itself unreservedly, abundantly, completely. All the laws on the statutes, all the courts in the universe, cannot tear it from the soil, once love has taken root. If, however, the soil is sterile, how can marriage make it bear fruit? It is like the last desperate struggle of fleeting life against death.

Love needs no protection; it is its own protection. So long as love begets life no child is deserted, or hungry, or famished for the want of affection. I know this to be true. I know women who became mothers in freedom by the men they loved. Few children in wedlock enjoy the care, the protection, the devotion free motherhood is capable of bestowing.

The defenders of authority dread the advent of a free motherhood, lest it will rob them of their prey. Who would fight wars? Who would create wealth? Who would make the policeman, the jailer, if woman were to refuse the indiscriminate breeding of children? The race, the race! shouts the king, the president, the capitalist, the priest. The race must be preserved, though woman be degraded to a mere machine— and the marriage institution is our only safety valve against the pernicious sex-awakening of woman. But in vain these frantic efforts to maintain a state of bondage. In vain, too, the edicts of the Church, the mad attacks of rulers, in vain even the arm of the law. Woman no longer wants to be a party to the production of a race of sickly, feeble, decrepit, wretched human beings, who have neither the strength nor moral courage to throw off the yoke of poverty and slavery. Instead she desires fewer and better children, begotten and reared in love and through free choice; not by compulsion, as marriage imposes. Our pseudo-moralists have yet to learn the deep sense of responsibility toward the child, that love in freedom has awakened in the breast of woman. Rather would she forego forever the glory of motherhood than bring forth life in an atmosphere that breathes only destruction and death. And if she does become a mother, it is to give to the child the deepest and best her being can yield. To grow with the child is her motto; she knows that in that manner alone can she help build true manhood and womanhood.

Ibsen must have had a vision of a free mother, when, with a master stroke, he portrayed Mrs. Alving. She was the ideal mother because she had outgrown marriage and all its horrors, because she had broken her chains, and set her spirit free to soar until it returned a personality, regenerated and strong. Alas, it was too late to rescue her life's joy, her Oswald; but not too late to realize that love in freedom is the only condition of a beautiful life. Those who, like Mrs. Alving, have paid with blood and tears for their spiritual awakening, repudiate marriage as an imposition, a shallow, empty mockery. They know, whether love last but one brief span of time or for eternity, it is the only creative, inspiring, elevating basis for a new race, a new world.

In our present pygmy state love is indeed a stranger to most people. Misunderstood and shunned, it rarely takes root; or if it does, it soon withers and dies. Its delicate fiber can not endure the stress and strain of the daily grind. Its soul is too complex to adjust itself to the slimy woof of our social fabric. It weeps and moans and suffers with those who have need of it, yet lack the capacity to rise to love's summit.

Some day, some day men and women will rise, they will reach the mountain peak, they will meet big and strong and free, ready to receive, to partake, and to bask in the golden rays of love. What fancy, what imagination, what poetic genius can foresee even approximately the potentialities of such a force in the life of men and women. If the world is ever to give birth to true companionship and oneness, not marriage, but love will be the parent.

Chapter Eleven

From Woman
Her Sex and Love Life (1917)

William J. Robinson

Robinson, a popular author of sex manuals and observations on women's gynecology, marriage, and love relations, typifies the extremely popular view expressed by Rousseau that is still extant and debated: that women are "made for love," while love is subordinate to achievement in a man's life. Clearly reacting to changing views by and about women in the first decades of the twentieth century, Robinson traces this disparity in love to physical differences between men and women, which "modern" women, those who want to deny difference, cannot understand. His attempt to provide a scientific basis for gender differences in love relations interestingly anticipates modern sociobiology and evolutionary psychology, which often purport to do the same.

> Man's love is of man's life a thing apart,
> 'Tis woman's whole existence.

Yes, love is a woman's whole life.

Some modern women might object to this. They might say that this was true of the woman of the past, who was excluded from all other avenues of human activity. The woman of the present day has other interests besides those of Love. But I claim that this is true of only a small percentage of women; and in even this small minority of women, social, scientific and artistic activities cannot take the place of love; no matter how busy and successful these women may be, they will tell you if you enjoy their confidence that they are unhappy, if their love life is unsatisfactory. Nothing, nothing can fill the void made by the lack of love. The various activities may help to cover up the void, to protect it from strange eyes, they cannot fill it. For essentially woman is made for love. Not exclusively, but essentially, and a woman who has had no love in her life has been a failure. The few exceptions that may be mentioned only emphasize the rule. . . .

From William J. Robinson, *Woman: Her Sex and Love Life,* 6th ed. (New York: Critic and Guide Company, 1917), 28, 318–24.

In reading books or listening to lectures on sex, you will meet with statements which will seem to you contradictory. One time you will read or hear that the sex instinct is much more powerfully developed in man than it is in woman; next time you will come across the statement that sex plays a much more important rôle in women than it does in men. One time you will hear that men are oversexed, that they are by nature polygamous and promiscuous, while woman is monogamous and as a rule sexually frigid; the next time you will be assured that without love a woman's life is nothing, and you will be confronted with Byron's well-known and oft quoted two lines: Man's love is of man's life a thing apart, 'Tis woman's whole existence.

These contradictions are only apparent and result from two facts: first, that the words sex or sexual instinct and love are used indiscriminately and interchangeably as if they were synonymous terms, which they are not; second, there is failure to bear in mind the essential differences in the natures and manifestations of the sexual instincts in the male and the female. If these differences are made clear, the apparent contradictions will disappear. The outstanding fact to bear in mind is that in man the sex instinct bears a more sensual, a more physical, a coarser and grosser character, if you have no objection to these adjectives, than it does in woman. In women it is finer, more spiritual, more platonic, to use this stereotyped and incorrect term. In men the sex manifestations are more centralized, more local, more concentrated in the sex organs; in women they are more diffused throughout the body. In a boy of fifteen the libido sexualis may be fully developed, he may have powerful erections and a strong desire for normal sexual relations; in a girl of fifteen there may not be a trace of any purely sexual desire; and this *lack* of desire for *physical* sex relations may manifest itself in women up to the age of twenty or twenty-five (something that we *never* see in normal men); in fact, women of twenty-five and even older, who have not been stimulated and whose curiosity has not been aroused by novels, pictures, and tales of their married companions, may not experience any sexual desire until several months after marriage. But while their desire for actual sexual relations awakens much later than it does in men, their desire for love, for caresses, for hugging, for close friendship, for love letters, awakens much earlier than in men, and occupies a greater part in their life; they think of love more during their waking hours, and they dream of it more than men do.

A man—always bear in mind that when speaking of men and women I always speak of the average; exceptions in either direction will be found in both sexes—a man, I say, will generally tire of paying attentions to a woman if he feels that they will not eventually lead to the biologic goal—sexual relations. A woman can keep up with a man for years without any sexual intercourse, being fully satisfied or more or less satisfied with the sexual substitutes—embraces and kisses.

And here is as good a place as any to refer to the notion so assiduously inculcated in the minds of young women, that a persistent refusal of man's demands is a sure way of keeping a man's affections; that as soon as man has satisfied his desires, he has no further use for the girl. This may be the case with the lowest dregs—morally—of the male sex; it is the opposite of true of the male sex as a whole. And I believe that Marcel Prevost was the first one to point it out (in his *Le Jardin Secret*). Nothing will hold a man's affections so surely as normal sex relations. And the cause of this is not, as might be surmised, merely a moral one, the man considering himself in honor and duty bound to stick to the woman whose body he possessed. No, there is a much stronger and surer reason: the reason is of a physiological character. There is born a strong physical attraction which in the man's subconsciousness plays a stronger rôle than honor and duty. Excesses of course must be avoided, for excesses lead to satiety, and satiety is just as inimical to love as is excitement without any satisfaction.

Choice between Physical and Spiritual Love

But to return to our thesis: the difference between man's and woman's sex and love life. If a man had to make his *choice* between physical love, i.e., actual sex relations and spiritual love, i.e., love making, kisses, love letters, etc., he would generally choose the former. If a woman had to *choose,* she would generally choose the latter. The man and the woman would prefer both at the same time: physical and spiritual love. But that is not the question. The question is: if it came to a *choice;* and then the results would be as I have just indicated. The correctness of my statements will be corroborated by anybody having some knowledge of human sexuality. A man can fully enjoy sexual intercourse without any preliminaries; with a woman the preliminaries are of the utmost importance, and when these are lacking she is often incapable of experiencing any pleasure. Nay, the feeling of pleasure is not infrequently replaced by a feeling of dissatisfaction and even disgust. A man cares more for the physical and less for the mental and spiritual attributes of his sexual partner; with the woman just the opposite is the case. I am leaving out of consideration sexual impotence, because this is a real disability, and a man suffering with it only irritates the woman without satisfying her. For this she will not stand. But where the man is sexually potent—he may be aged and homely—his other physical attributes play but a small rôle with woman; his mental and spiritual qualities count with her for a good deal more. While a woman may be able to give a man perfect sexual satisfaction, and she may have an angelic character, if her body is not all that could be desired, the man will be dissatisfied and unhappy.

Love in Man Occupies Subordinate Place

Try as we may, we cannot get away from the fact that in man's life love occupies a subordinate place. I am speaking now of love, and not of "being in love." Being in love . . . is a distinctly pathological phenomenon, akin to insanity, and when a man is in love it may engross every fiber of him, it may preoccupy every minute of his waking hours, he may neglect all his work and shirk all his duties, in fact he is apt to make a much bigger fool of himself than a woman is under similar circumstances. He is less patient, he has less control over himself, he is less able to suffer, he is less capable of self-sacrifice. But this, as I said, all refers to "being in love," which is an entirely different thing from loving. A man may love ever so deeply, and if his love is reciprocated he will go on with his work in a smooth, unruffled manner. He will do better work for it—love is a wonderful stimulus—but he will be perfectly satisfied if he sees his love for an hour or two every day, or even once or twice a week. And if he has important and interesting work to do, he can part with his love for three months or six months without his heart breaking. Not so with woman. A woman who loves considers every day on which she does not see her lover a day lost. And she is apt to be unhappy and inefficient in her work on such days, and she bears separation with much greater difficulty than does man. I do not think that this is due to the fact that a woman's love is always more intense than a man's; no. But he usually has other interests which occupy his thoughts and emotions are centered on the man they love. When a woman loves, she could and would spend all her time with the man she loves. She would never tire of love making (I am not referring here to sex relations), or merely of being in the man's proximity. To woman love is a cloyless thing. Man distinctly does tire. No matter how much he may love a woman, too much lovemaking becomes cloying to him, and he wants to get away. Even mere proximity, if too prolonged, becomes irksome to him, and he begins to fret and fidget, and pull at his chains, even if the chains are but of gossamer. Woman should know these facts and act accordingly.

Chapter Twelve

From How to Love Like a Real Woman (1969)

Barbara Bross and Jay Gilbey

This excerpt from an advice book published in the 1960s by a pseudonymous gynecologist embodies a Victorian idea: "A woman's strength lies in her ability to give without taking. ... Far from taking advantage of her, [the man she loves] will become transformed." That this is asserted defensively in a very popular magazine for women in the midst of second-wave feminism makes this an important adjunct to the writings by radical feminists in part 3.

Why a Woman "Gives"

A woman gives herself without asking anything in return. She knows that the act of giving bears its own reward in the pleasure it gives the donor. If the recipient feels pleasure too, so much the better. But that is not the object. The object is the pleasure of *giving*. A woman asks as little of her man as she asks of her children. She devotes her entire life to a child, then sends it into the world—into the arms of another woman; or, in the case of a daughter, into the arms of a man.

I see sexual intercourse for women as a process of giving without asking, of giving without expecting anything in return. These are not idle speculations. They are the basis of marital happiness for women.

I say that a woman must give and give and give again—not because man is her master; nor because she believes that he has any God-given right to receive; nor because she places any value in the "rights" and "privileges" which our society gives him. Women must give and give and give again because it is their one and only way to obtain happiness for *themselves*; because the alternative—the daily making up of accounts (I give you a good time in bed and you give me a diamond ring)—is tantamount to prostitution. Nothing makes a woman unhappier than any attempt to estimate what her man should do for her and what she "owes" him in exchange. The moment she begins to think in these terms, she might as well consider the marriage or the affair as finished.

The most important rule to keep in mind is that there are no rules in lovemak-

From Barbara Bross and Jay Gilbey, "How to Love Like a Real Woman," *Cosmopolitan* vol. 166, no. 6 (June 1969): 85.

ing. If you just strive for a reasonable degree of spontaneity and variety, you can't go wrong.

Loving Like a Real Woman

A woman's strength lies in her ability to give without taking. She gives men rest and strength and tranquility because she gives them an antidote to the dog-eats-dog world in which they earn their living. For, when they come home, they can stop thinking in terms of what's-in-it-for-me. And—miracle of miracles—she will find how even the most selfish man is magically cleansed of his selfishness if he lives with a woman who is wholly unselfish. Far from taking advantage of her, he will become transformed into a human being who can also give without asking for anything in return.

This is far harder for a man to do than for a woman, because it simply is not in man's nature. If he is to survive, he *must* accept the rules of combat in a competitive society. But he is a human being too, and if he has a wife who asks nothing of him he will become far more decent, far kinder, and far less selfish than if she considers herself in daily competition with him.

Woman is man's intermediary between himself and nature. He considers her as part of nature, though he will never say so, but that is what he *feels*. Her periods echo the rhythm of nature. Her ability to give birth makes her part of nature. She is the mother. She is the earth. She *senses* where he can only *think* or *act*. Woman *is,* man *does*. That is the strength *and* weakness of *both* sexes. Do not ruin your marriage, or your love affair, by trying to compete with your man on his own masculine terms. You can only lose. And by that I do not mean that you may lose an argument; I mean that you may lose your dignity, your stature, your strength as a woman.

Every day of her married life, every day of any affair that she may be having before, during, or after marriage will bring her the same temptation: to talk back at him, to cut him down to size, to laugh at him, to show him who's boss. If she gives in to such temptations, a woman is the major loser.

The moment she starts to argue with him, fight with him, to balance accounts, she becomes *weak,* not strong. The rules of the struggle, the rules of the argument, are male. To argue is a male activity. To fight is a male activity. I say to women: Don't become a man in skirts. Don't fight. Don't argue. You are the stronger sex because he feels he must constantly prove his superiority. Whereas you need not prove anything. It is enough that you *are* . . . that you are there . . . quiet . . . unshakable . . . always ready to give. That is your strength.

Part II

Letters and Personal Writing

The contradictions of romantic love are not simply theoretical: they are most rawly exposed in the heat and suffering of personal lives. This part offers a small sample of personal writing, mainly letters from women about love or to their lovers. In several cases, the most passionate longing is reserved for lovers who are unavailable or have rejected them for a number of reasons, including their married status; this is a commentary on the idea that for women, love is inevitably connected to courtship and marriage.

In several cases (Wollstonecraft, Eliot, Goldman, de Beauvoir) there is an interesting contrast between theories of love and the practice of it; in others there is a passionate loss of selfhood or a sweep of euphoria, longing, or frustration that complicates the more abstract views of women in the didactic essays. A caveat to the reader: the personal material is not meant to detract from the political notions of the writers here, but to add fullness to them. As feminists have said, the personal *is* the political. No one was more conscious of this than Emma Goldman, who felt enslaved by her love affair while confident of her theoretical views on free love.

Chapter Thirteen

Letter to Abelard (12th century)

Heloise

The letters of the famous medieval nun (later abbess) Heloise, writing from a convent to the increasingly distant Abelard, a celebrated scholar and her former lover, are among the most famous of women's love letters. The lovers had undergone dramatic hardships: the scholar and teacher Abelard had been hired to tutor Heloise, the young niece of a wealthy man, and had been attacked and castrated by the uncle in revenge for his love affair with her. After the disaster, Heloise, at the age of nineteen, had consented under pressure from Abelard to become a nun, though as she admits, with no sense of religious vocation, while Abelard entered the Abbey of St. Denis, hundreds of miles away. Heloise presents a marked contrast to modern stereotypes of medieval women as constrained and repressed creatures with no life outside marriage. It is astonishing to read her own description of a passion so intense that she preferred to be Abelard's mistress rather than his wife.

How many grave treatises in the teaching, or in the exhortation, or for the comfort of holy women the holy Fathers composed, and with what diligence they composed them, thine excellence knows better than our humility. Wherefore to no little amazement thine oblivion moves the tender beginnings of our conversion, that neither by reverence for God, nor by love of us, nor by the examples of the holy Fathers hast thou been admonished to attempt to comfort me, as I waver and am already crushed by prolonged grief, either by speech in thy presence or by a letter in thine absence. And yet thou knowest thyself to be bound to me by a debt so much greater in that thou art tied to me more closely by the pact of the nuptial sacrament; and that thou art the more beholden to me in that I ever, as is known to all, embraced thee with an unbounded love. Thou knowest, dearest, all men know what I have lost in thee, and in how wretched a case that supreme and notorious betrayal took me myself also from me with thee, and that my grief is immeasurably greater from the manner in which I lost thee than from the loss of thee.

And the greater the cause of grief, the greater the remedies of comfort to be

From Peter Abelard and Heloise, *The Letters of Abelard and Heloise,* trans. C. K. Scott Moncrieff (New York: Random House, 1926, 1942), 56–61. Copyright © 1926 renewed 1954 by Alfred A. Knopf, a division of Random House, Inc. Reprinted by permission.

applied. Not, however, by another, but by thee thyself, that thou who art alone in the cause of my grief may be alone in the grace of my comfort. For it is thou alone that canst make me sad, canst make me joyful or canst comfort me. And it is thou alone that owest me this great debt, and for this reason above all that I have at once performed all things that thou didst order, till that when I could not offend thee in anything I had the strength to lose myself at thy behest. And what is more, and strange it is to relate, to such madness did my love turn that what alone it sought it cast from itself without hope of recovery when, straightway obeying thy command, I changed both my habit and my heart, that I might shew thee to be the one possessor both of my body and of my mind. Nothing have I ever (God wot) required of thee save thyself, desiring thee purely, not what was thine. Not for the pledge of matrimony, nor for any dowry did I look, nor my own passions or wishes but thine (as thou thyself knowest) was I zealous to gratify.

And if the name of wife appears more sacred and more valid, sweeter to me is ever the word friend, or, if thou be not ashamed, concubine or whore. To wit that the more I humbled myself before thee the fuller grace I might obtain from thee, and so also damage less the fame of thine excellence. And thou thyself wert not wholly unmindful of that kindness in the letter of which I have spoken, written to thy friend for his comfort. Wherein thou hast not disdained to set forth sundry reasons by which I tried to dissuade thee from our marriage, from an ill-starred bed; but wert silent as to many, in which I preferred love to wedlock, freedom to a bond. I call God to witness, if *Augustus,* ruling over the whole world, were to deem me worthy of the honour of marriage, and to confirm the whole world to me, to be ruled by me for ever, dearer to me and of greater dignity would it seem to be called thy strumpet than his empress.

For it is not by being richer or more powerful that a man becomes better; one is a matter of fortune, the other of virtue. Nor should she deem herself other than venal who weds a rich man rather than a poor, and desires more things in her husband than himself. Assuredly, whomsoever this concupiscence leads into marriage deserves payment rather than affection; for it is evident that she goes after his wealth and not the man, and is willing to prostitute herself, if she can, to a richer. As the argument advanced (in *Aeschines*) by the wise *Aspasia* to *Xenophon* and his wife plainly convinces us. When the wise woman aforesaid had propounded this argument for their reconciliation, she concluded as follows: "For when ye have understood this, that there is not a better man nor a happier woman on the face of the earth; then ye will ever and above all things seek that which ye think the best; thou to be the husband of so excellent a wife, and she to be married to so excellent a husband." A blessed sentiment, assuredly, and more than philosophic, expressing wisdom itself rather than philosophy. A holy error and a blessed fallacy among the married, that a perfect love should preserve their bond of matrimony unbroken, not so much by the continence of their bodies as by the purity of their hearts. But what error shews to the rest of women the truth has made manifest to me. Since what they thought of their husbands, that I, that the entire world not so much believed as knew of thee. So that the more genuine my love was for thee, the further it was removed from error.

For who among kings or philosophers could equal thee in fame? What kingdom or city or village did not burn to see thee? Who, I ask, did not hasten to gaze upon thee when thou appearedst in public, nor on thy departure with straining neck and fixed eye follow thee? What wife, what maiden did not yearn for thee in thine absence, nor burn in thy presence? What queen or powerful lady did not envy me my joys and my bed? There were two things, I confess, in thee especially, wherewith thou couldst at once captivate the heart of any woman; namely the arts of making songs and of singing them. Which we know that other philosophers have seldom followed. Wherewith as with a game, refreshing the labour of philosophic exercise, thou hast left many songs composed in amatory measure or rhythm, which for the suavity both of words and of tune being oft repeated, have kept thy name without ceasing on the lips of all; since even illiterates the sweetness of thy melodies did not allow to forget thee. It was on this account chiefly that women sighed for love of thee. And as the greater part of thy songs descanted of our love, they spread my fame in a short time through many lands, and inflamed the jealousy of many women against me. For what excellence of mind or body did not adorn thy youth? What woman who envied me then does not my calamity now compel to pity one deprived of such delights? What man or woman, albeit an enemy at first, is not now softened by the compassion due to me?

And, though exceeding guilty, I am, as thou knowest, exceeding innocent. For it is not the deed but the intention that makes the crime. It is not what is done but the spirit in which it is done that equity considers. And in what state of mind I have ever been towards thee, only thou, who hast knowledge of it, canst judge. To they consideration I commit all, I yield in all things to thy testimony. Tell me one thing only, if thou canst, why, after our conversion, which thou alone didst decree, I am fallen into such neglect and oblivion with thee that I am neither refreshed by thy speech and presence nor comforted by a letter in thine absence. Tell me, one thing only, if thou canst, or let me tell thee what I feel, nay what all suspect. Concupiscence joined thee to me rather than affection, the ardour of desire rather than love. When therefore what thou desiredst ceased, all that thou hadst exhibited at the same time failed. This, most beloved, is not mine only but the conjecture of all, not peculiar but common, not private but public. Would that it seemed thus to me only, and thy love found others to excuse it, by whom my grief might be a little quieted. Would that I could invent reasons by which in excusing thee I might cover in some measure my own vileness.

Give thy attention, I beseech thee, to what I demand; and thou wilt see this to be a small matter and most easy for thee. While I am cheated of thy presence, at least by written words, whereof thou hast an abundance, present to me the sweetness of thine image. In vain may I expect thee to be liberal in things if I must endure thee niggardly in words. Until now I believed that I deserved more from thee when I had done all things for thee, persevering still in obedience to thee. Who indeed as a girl was allured to the asperity of monastic conversion not by religious devotion but by thy command alone. Wherein if I deserve nought from thee, thou mayest judge my labour to have been vain. No reward for this may I expect from God, for the love of Whom it is well known that I did not anything. When thou hastenedst to God, I followed thee in the habit, nay preceded thee. For as though mindful of the wife of *Lot,* who looked back from behind him, thou deliveredst me first to the sacred garments and monastic profession before thou gavest thyself to God. And for that in this one thing thou shouldst have had little trust in me I vehemently grieved and was ashamed. For I (God wot) would without hesitation precede or follow thee to the Vulcanian fires according to thy word. For not with me was my heart, but with thee. But now, more than ever, if it be not with thee, it is nowhere. For without thee it cannot anywhere exist. But so act that it may be well with thee, I beseech thee. And well with thee will it be if it find thee propitious, if thou give love for love, little for much, words for deeds. Would that thy love, beloved, had less trust in me, that it might be more anxious! But the more confident I have made thee in the past, the more neglectful now I find thee. Remember, I beseech thee, what I have done, and pay heed to what thou owest me. While with thee I enjoyed carnal pleasures, many were uncertain whether I did so from love or from desire. But now the end shews in what spirit I began. I have forbidden myself all pleasures that I might obey thy will. I have reserved nothing for myself, save this, to be now entirely thine. Consider therefore how great is thine injustice, if to me who deserve more thou payest less, nay nothing at all, especially when it is a small thing that is demanded of thee, and right easy for thee to perform.

And so in His Name to whom thou hast offered thyself, before God I beseech thee that in whatsoever way thou canst thou restore to me thy presence, to wit by writing me some word of comfort. To this end alone that, thus refreshed, I may give myself with more alacrity to the service of God. When in time past thou soughtest me out for temporal pleasures, thou visitedst me with endless letters, and by frequent songs didst set thy *Heloise* on the lips of all men. With me every public place, each house resounded. How more rightly shouldst thou excite me now towards God, whom thou excitedst then to desire. Consider, I beseech thee, what thou owest me, pay heed to what I demand; and my long letter with a brief ending I conclude. Farewell, my all.

Chapter Fourteen

From Letters of Love and Gallantry Written by Ladies (1694)

This seventeenth-century letter reproaching a lover who debauched and then abandoned the author is unusually interesting because it was probably a "model" letter describing an already conventional situation and an ideal response to it. It anticipates the many reproaches for cruelty, neglect, or abandonment by real authors, including feminists, to follow.

From a Lady to a Gentleman, Who Promising Her Marriage, Debauched Her, and Then Left Her, Taking a Journey beyond the Sea

Cruelest of all your Sex.

I write not now that I'd remind you of your forsaken vows, for sure you need not these as a reproach to your past crimes, which always will remain in you as an opprobrious object to your future reflections, that you have brought an unhappy wretch to ruin; one, who unskilled in mankind's falsehood, had this in her fate, that she was too loving; whence comes the cause of all my misfortunes. My tender heart unwarily ran out and lodged itself with you, which, rifled of all its treasure, you have sent home bleeding, and full of wounds, which your unkindness made, and left it nothing but the experiment. How wretched have you made me. Ah! Could you have returned me all, how many sighs and tears would you have saved me? But Oh! 'tis out of Nature's reach, and as I was then forsaken by my good angels, I am likewise left by you forever.

Yet as you are going, I will not trouble you with my sorrows, nor any farther make known to you how miserable love has made me. Let my ——— go, and with him go all the kind stars, no matter what becomes of me; of whom you have no farther use then only to remember as an example how you may ruin more. Go then, and if in all your travels you meet a wretch so frail and so unfortunate as I, think with a relenting thought of me again, and save the fond believer from the ruin I am in, who, though undone by you, yet cannot help, subscribing myself,

Yours forever.

From Letters of Love and Gallantry Written by Ladies, in *English Women's Voices, 1540–1700*, ed. Charlotte Otten (Miami: Florida International University Press, 1992), 139–40. © 1992 by the Board of Regents of the State of Florida.

Chapter Fifteen

Letters to Gilbert Imlay (1793–95) and William Godwin (1796–97)

Mary Wollstonecraft

Wollstonecraft, considered by many the first feminist philosopher, is the author of, among other works, A Vindication of the Rights of Woman *(1792). Wollstonecraft's love letters are extraordinary reading. Her anguished protests to her lover, the American Gilbert Imlay, who left her alone with their infant in Paris to live with another mistress ("Reading what you have written relative to the desertion of women, I have often wondered how theory and practice could be so different"), may be contrasted with her letters during her successful but very brief marriage to the philosopher William Godwin: "I wish you, from my soul, to be rivetted in my heart; but I do not desire to have you always at my elbow." Her letters to Imlay refer to an unsuccessful suicide attempt made after she learned of his desertion. She died in 1797 after giving birth to her second child, the future novelist Mary Shelley.*

To Gilbert Imlay

[Neuilly-sur-Seine] Past Twelve o'Clock Monday night [c. August 1793]

I obey an emotion of my heart, which made me think of wishing thee, my love, good-night! before I go to rest, with more tenderness than I can to-morrow, when writing a hasty line or two under Colonel ———'s eye. You can scarcely imagine with what pleasure I anticipate the day, when we are to begin almost to live together; and you would smile to hear how many plans of employment I have in my head, now that I am confident my heart has found peace in your bosom.—Cherish me with that dignified tenderness, which I have only found in you; and your own dear girl will try to keep under a quickness of feeling, that has sometimes given you pain—Yes, I will be *good*, that I may deserve to be happy; and whilst you love me, I cannot again fall into the miserable state, which rendered life a burden almost too heavy to be borne.

But good-night!—God bless you! Sterne says, that is equal to a kiss—yet I would rather

From Mary Wollstonecraft, with prefatory memoir by C. Kegan Paul, *Letters to Imlay* (London: C. Kegan Paul, 1879), 2–3, 30–31, 96–99, 119–24, 146–51, 176–89. Note and information in square brackets are by C. Kegan Paul. *And from* Ralph M. Wardle, ed., *Godwin and Mary: Letters of William Godwin and Mary Wollstonecraft* (Lawrence: University of Kansas Press, 1966), 20–21, 33, 82–83. © 1966 by University of Kansas Press. Reprinted by permission of the publisher. Notes are by Ralph M. Wardle.

give you the kiss into the bargain, glowing with gratitude to Heaven, and affection to you. I like the word affection, because it signifies something habitual; and we are soon to meet, to try whether we have mind enough to keep our hearts warm.

Mary

•

[Paris] Wednesday Morning [January 8, 1794]

I will never, if I am not entirely cured of quarrelling, begin to encourage "quick-coming fancies," when we are separated. Yesterday, my love, I could not open your letter for some time; and, though it was not half as severe as I merited, it threw me into such a fit of trembling, as seriously alarmed me. I did not, as you may suppose, care for a little pain on my own account; but all the fears which I have had for a few days past, returned with fresh force. This morning I am better; will you not be glad to hear it? You perceive that sorrow has almost made a child of me, and that I want to be soothed to peace.

One thing you mistake in my character, and imagine that to be coldness which is just the contrary. For, when I am hurt by the person most dear to me, I must let out a whole torrent of emotions, in which tenderness would be uppermost, or stifle them altogether; and it appears to me almost a duty to stifle them, when I imagine *that I am treated with coldness.*

I am afraid that I have vexed you, my own ———. I know the quickness of your feelings— and let me, in the sincerity of my heart, assure you, there is nothing I would not suffer to make you happy. My own happiness wholly depends on you—and, knowing you, when my reason is not clouded, I look forward to a rational prospect of as much felicity as the earth affords—with a little dash of rapture into the bargain, if you will look at me, when we meet again, as you have sometimes greeted, your humbled, yet most affectionate

Mary

•

[Paris] February 9 [1795]

The melancholy presentiment has for some time hung on my spirits, that we were parted for ever; and the letters I received this day, by Mr. ———, convince me that it was not without foundation. You allude to some other letters, which I suppose have miscarried; for most of those I have got, were only a few hasty lines, calculated to wound the tenderness the sight of the superscriptions excited.

I mean not however to complain; yet so many feelings are struggling for utterance, and agitating a heart almost bursting with anguish, that I find it very difficult to write with any degree of coherence.

You left me indisposed, though you have taken no notice of it; and the most fatiguing journey I ever had, contributed to continue you. However, I recovered my health; but a neglected cold, and continual inquietude during the last two months, have reduced me to a state of weakness I never before experienced. Those who did not know that the canker-worm was at work at the core, cautioned me about suckling my child too long.—God preserve this poor child, and render her happier than her mother!

But I am wandering from my subject: indeed my head turns giddy, when I think that all the confidence I have had in the affection of others is come to this.—I did not expect this blow from you. I have done my duty to you and my child; and if I am not to have any return of affection to reward me, I have the sad consolation of knowing that I deserved a better fate. My soul is weary—I am sick at heart; and, but for this little darling, I would cease to care about a life, which is now stripped of every charm.

You see how stupid I am, uttering declamation, when I meant simply to tell you, that I consider your requesting me to come to you, as merely dictated by honour.—Indeed I scarcely understand you.—You request me to come, and then tell me, that you have not given up all thoughts of returning to this place.

When I determined to live with you, I was only governed by affection.—I would share poverty with you, but I turn with affright from the sea of trouble on which you are entering.— I have certain principles of action: I know what I look for to found my happiness on.—It is not money.—With you I wished for sufficient to procure the comforts of life—as it is, less will do.—I can still exert myself to obtain the necessaries of life for my child, and she does not want more at present.—I have two or three plans in my head to earn our subsistence; for do not suppose that, neglected by you, I will lie under obligations of a pecuniary kind to you!—No; I would sooner submit to menial service.—I wanted the support of your affection—that gone, all is over!—I did not think, when I complained of ———'s contemptible avidity to accumulate money, that he would have dragged you into his schemes.

I cannot write.—I inclose a fragment of a letter, written soon after your departure, and another which tenderness made me keep back when it was written.—You will see then the sentiments of a calmer, though not a more determined, moment.—Do not insult me by saying that "our being together is paramount to every other consideration!" Were it, you would not be running after a bubble, at the expence of my peace of mind.

Perhaps this is the last letter you will ever receive from me.

Mary

•

[Hull] Friday, June 12 [1795]

I have just received yours dated the 9th, which I suppose was a mistake, for it could scarcely have loitered so long on the road. The general observations which apply to the state of your own mind, appear to me just, as far as they go; and I shall always consider it as one of the most serious misfortunes of my life, that I did not meet you, before satiety had rendered your senses so fastidious, as almost to close up every tender avenue of sentiment and affection that leads to your sympathetic heart. You have a heart, my friend, yet, hurried away by the impetuosity of inferior feelings, you have sought in vulgar excesses, for that gratification which only the heart can bestow.

The common run of men, I know, with strong health and gross appetites, must have variety to banish *ennui*, because the imagination never lends its magic wand, to convert appetite into love, cemented by according reason.—Ah! my friend, you know not the ineffable delight, the exquisite pleasure, which arises from a unison of affection and desire, when the whole soul and senses are abandoned to a lively imagination, that renders every emotion delicate and rapturous. Yes; these are emotions, over which satiety has no power, and the recollection of which, even disappointment cannot disenchant; but they do not exist without self-denial. These emotions, more or less strong, appear to me to be the distinctive characteristic of genius, the foundation of taste, and of that exquisite relish for the beauties of nature, of which the common herd of eaters and drinkers and *child-begeters,* certainly have no idea. You will smile at an observation that has just occurred to me:—I consider those minds as the most strong and original, whose imagination acts as the stimulus to their senses.

Well! you will ask, what is the result of all this reasoning? Why I cannot help thinking that it is possible for you, having great strength of mind, to return to nature, and regain a sanity of constitution, and purity of feeling—which would open your heart to me.—I would fain rest there!

Yet, convinced more than ever of the sincerity and tenderness of my attachment to you, the involuntary hopes, which a determination to live has revived, are not sufficiently strong to dissipate the cloud, that despair has spread over futurity. I have looked at the sea, and at my child, hardly daring to own to myself the secret wish, that it might become our tomb; and that the heart, still so alive to anguish, might there be quieted by death. At this moment ten thousand complicated sentiments press for utterance, weigh on my heart, and obscure my sight.

Are we ever to meet again? and will you endeavour to render that meeting happier than the last? Will you endeavour to restrain your caprices, in order to give vigour to affection, and to give play to the checked sentiments that nature intended should expand your heart? I cannot indeed, without agony, think of your bosom's being continually contaminated; and bitter are the tears which exhaust my eyes, when I recollect why my child and I are forced to stray from the asylum, in which, after so many storms, I had hoped to rest, smiling at angry fate.—These are not common sorrows; nor can you perhaps conceive, how much active fortitude it requires to labour perpetually to blunt the shafts of disappointment.

Examine now yourself, and ascertain whether you can live in something like a settled stile. Let our confidence in future be unbounded; consider whether you find it necessary to sacrifice me to what you term "the zest of life;" and, when you have once a clear view of your own motives, of your own incentive to action, do not deceive me!

The train of thoughts which the writing of this epistle awoke, makes me so wretched, that I must take a walk, to rouse and calm my mind. But first, let me tell you, that, if you really wish to promote my happiness, you will endeavour to give me as much as you can of yourself. You have great mental energy; and your judgment seems to me so just, that it is only the dupe of your inclination in discussing one subject.

The post does not go out to-day. To-morrow I may write more tranquilly. I cannot yet say when the vessel will sail in which I have determined to depart.

Saturday Morning.

Your second letter reached me about an hour ago. You were certainly wrong, in supposing that I did not mention you with respect; though, without my being conscious of it, some sparks of resentment may have animated the gloom of despair—Yes; with less affection, I should have been more respectful. However the regard which I have for you, is so unequivocal to myself, I imagine that it must be sufficiently obvious to every body else. Besides, the only letter I intended for the public eye was to ———, and that I destroyed from delicacy before you saw them, because it was only written (of course warmly in your praise) to prevent any odium being thrown on you.[1]

I am harrassed by your embarrassments, and shall certainly use all my efforts, to make the business terminate to your satisfaction in which I am engaged.

My friend—my dearest friend—I feel my fate united to yours by the most sacred principles of my soul, and the yearns of—yes, I will say it—a true, unsophisticated heart.

Yours most truly
Mary

•

[Sweden] July 1 [1795]

I labour in vain to calm my mind—my soul has been overwhelmed by sorrow and disappointment. Every thing fatigues me—this is a life that cannot last long. It is you who must determine with respect to futurity—and, when you have, I will act accordingly—I mean, we must either resolve to live together, or part for ever, I cannot bear these continual struggles—But I wish you to examine carefully your own heart and mind; and, if you perceive the least chance of being happier without me than with me, or if your inclination leans capriciously to that side, do not dissemble; but tell me frankly that you will never see me more. I will then adopt the plan I mentioned to you—for we must either live together, or I will be entirely independent.

My heart is so oppressed, I cannot write with precision—You know however that what I so imperfectly express, are not the crude sentiments of the moment—You can only contribute to my comfort (it is the consolation I am in need of) by being with me—and, if the tenderest friendship is of any value, why will you not look to me for a degree of satisfaction that heartless affection cannot bestow?

Tell me then, will you determine to meet me at Basle?—I shall, I should imagine, be at ———— before the close of August; and after you settle your affairs at Paris, could we not meet there?

God bless you!

Yours truly
Mary

•

[Sweden] July 3 [1795]

There was a gloominess diffused through your last letter, the impression of which still rests on my mind—though, recollecting how quickly you throw off the forcible feelings of the moment, I flatter myself it has long since given place to your usual cheerfulness.

Believe me (and my eyes fill with tears of tenderness as I assure you) there is nothing I would not endure in the way of privation, rather than disturb your tranquility.—If I am fated to be unhappy, I will labour to hide my sorrows in my own bosom; and you shall always find me a faithful, affectionate friend.

I grow more and more attached to my little girl—and I cherish this affection without fear, because it must be a long time before it can become bitterness of soul.—She is an interesting creature.—On ship-board, how often as I gazed at the sea, have I longed to bury my troubled bosom in the less troubled deep; asserting with Brutus, "that the virtue I had followed too far, was merely an empty name!" and nothing but the sight of her—her playful smiles, which seemed to cling and twine round my heart—could have stopped me.

What peculiar misery has fallen to my share! To act up to my principles, I have laid the strictest restraint on my very thoughts.—yes; not to sully the delicacy of my feelings, I have reined in my imagination; and started with affright from every sensation, (I allude to ————) that stealing with balmy sweetness into my soul, led me to scent from afar the fragrance of reviving nature.

My friend, I have dearly paid for one conviction.—Love, in some minds, is an affair of sentiment, arising from the same delicacy of perception (or taste) as renders them alive to the beauties of nature, poetry, &c, alive to the charms of those evanescent graces that are, as it were, impalpable—they must be felt, they cannot be described.

Love is a want of my heart. I have examined myself lately with more care than formerly, and find, that to deaden is not to calm the mind—Aiming at tranquility, I have almost destroyed all the energy of my soul—almost rooted out what renders it estimable—Yes, I have damped that enthusiasm of character, which converts the grossest materials into a fuel, that imperceptibly feeds hopes, which aspire above common enjoyment. Despair, since the birth of my child, has rendered me stupid—soul and body seemed to be fading away before the withering touch of disappointment.

I am now endeavouring to recover myself—and such is the elasticity of my constitution, and the purity of the atmosphere here, that health unsought for, begins to reanimate my countenance.

I have the sincerest esteem and affection for you—but the desire of regaining peace, (do you understand me?) has made me forget the respect due to my own emotions—sacred emotions, that are the sure harbingers of the delights I was formed to enjoy—and shall enjoy, for nothing can extinguish the heavenly spark.

Still, when we meet again, I will not torment you, I promise you. I blush when I recollect my former conduct—and will not in future confound myself with the beings whom I feel to be my inferiors.—I will listen to delicacy, or pride.

[Unsigned]

•

[Hamburg] September 25 [1795]

I have just finished a letter, to be given in charge to captain ———. In that I complained of your silence, and expressed my surprise that three mails should have arrived without bringing a line for me. Since I closed it, I hear of another, and still no letter.—I am labouring to write calmly—this silence is a refinement on cruelty. Had captain ——— remained a few days longer, I would have returned with him to England. What have I to do here? I have repeatedly written to you fully. Do you do the same—and quickly. Do not leave me in suspense. I have not deserved this of you. I cannot write, my mind is so distressed. Adieu!

Mary

•

[Hamburg] September 27 [1795]

When you receive this, I shall either have landed, or be hovering on the British coast— your letter of the 18th decided me.

By what criterion of principle or affection, you term my questions extraordinary and unnecessary, I cannot determine.—You desire me to decide—I had decided. You must have had long ago two letters of mine, from———, to the same purport, to consider.—In these, God knows! there was but too much affection, and the agonies of a distracted mind were but too faithfully pourtrayed!—What more then had I to say?—The negative was to come from you.—You had perpetually recurred to your promise of meeting me in the autumn—Was it extraordinary that I should demand a yes, or no?—Your letter is written with extreme harshness, coldness I am accustomed to, in it I find not a trace of the tenderness of humanity, much less of friendship.—I only see a desire to heave a load off your shoulders.

I am above disputing about words.—It matters not in what terms you decide.

The tremendous power who formed this heart, must have foreseen that, in a world in which self-interest, in various shapes, is the principal mobile, I had little chance of escaping misery.—To the fiat of fate I submit.—I am content to be wretched; but I will not be contemptible.—Of me you have no cause to complain, but for having had too much regard for you—for having expected a degree of permanent happiness, when you only sought for a momentary gratification.

I am strangely deficient in sagacity.—Uniting myself to you, your tenderness seemed to make me amends for all my former misfortunes.—On this tenderness and affection with that confidence did I rest!—but I leaned on a spear, that has pierced me to the heart.—You have thrown off a faithful friend, to pursue the caprices of the moment.—We certainly are differently organized; for even now, when conviction has been stamped on my soul by sorrow, I can scarcely believe it possible. It depends at present on you, whether you will see me or not.—I shall take no step, till I see or hear from you.

Preparing myself for the worst—I have determined, if your next letter be like the last, to write to Mr. ——— to procure me an obscure lodging, and not to inform any body of my arrival.—There I will endeavour in a few months to obtain the sum necessary to take me to

France—from you I will not receive any more.—I am not yet sufficiently humbled to depend on your beneficence.

Some people, whom my unhappiness has interested, though they know not the extent of it, will assist me to attain the object I have in view, the independence of my child. Should a peace take place, ready money will go a great way in France—and I will borrow a sum, which my industry *shall* enable me to pay at my leisure, to purchase a small estate for my girl.— The assistance I shall find necessary to complete her education, I can get at an easy rate at Paris—I can introduce her to such society as she will like—and thus, securing for her all the chance for happiness, which depends on me, I shall die in peace, persuaded that the felicity which has hitherto cheated my expectation, will not always elude my grasp. No poor tempest-tossed mariner ever more earnestly longed to arrive at his port.

Mary

I shall not come up in the vessel all the way, because I have no place to go to. Captain——— —will inform you where I am. It is needless to add, that I am not in a state of mind to bear suspense—and that I wish to see you, though it be for the last time.

•

[Dover] Sunday, October 4 [1795]

I wrote to you by the packet, to inform you, that your letter of the 18th of last month, had determined me to set out with captain ———; but, as we sailed very quick, I take it for granted, that you have not yet received it.

You say, I must decide for myself.—I had decided, that it was most for the interest of my little girl, and for my own comfort, little as I expect, for us to live together; and I even thought that you would be glad, some years hence, when the tumult of business was over, to repose in the society of an affectionate friend, and mark the progress of our interesting child, whilst endeavouring to be of use in the circle you at last resolved to rest in; for you cannot run about for ever.

From the tenour of your last letter however, I am led to imagine, that you have formed some new attachment.—If it be so, let me earnestly request you to see me once more, and immediately. This is the only proof I require of the friendship you profess for me. I will then decide, since you boggle about a mere form.

I am labouring to write with calmness—but the extreme anguish I feel, at landing without having any friend to receive me, and even to be conscious that the friend whom I most wish to see, will feel a disagreeable sensation at being informed of my arrival, does not come under the description of common misery. Every emotion yields to an overwhelming flood of sorrow—and the playfulness of my child distresses me.—On her account, I wished to remain a few days here, comfortless as is my situation.—Besides, I did not wish to surprise you. You have told me, that you would make any sacrifice to promote my happiness—and, even in your last unkind letter, you talk of the ties which bind you to me and my child.—Tell me that you wish it, and I will cut this Gordian knot.

I now most earnestly intreat you to write to me, without fail, by the return of the post. Direct your letter to be left at the post-office, and tell me whether you will come to me here, or where you will meet me. I can receive your letter on Wednesday morning.

Do not keep me in suspense.—I expect nothing from you, or any human being: my die is cast!—I have fortitude enough to determine to do my duty; yet I cannot raise my depressed spirits, or calm my trembling heart.—That being who moulded it thus, knows that I am unable to tear up by the roots the propensity to affection which has been the torment of my life—but life will have an end!

Should you come here (a few months ago I could not have doubted it) you will find me at———. If you prefer meeting me on the road, tell me where.

Yours affectionately

Mary

•

[London, c. October 10, 1795]

I write you now on my knees; imploring you to send my child and the maid with ———, to Paris, to be consigned to the care of Madame ———, rue———, section de ———. Should they be removed, ——— can give their direction.

Let the maid have all my clothes, without distinction.

Pray pay the cook her wages, and do not mention the confession which I forced from her— a little sooner or later is of no consequence. Nothing but my extreme stupidity could have rendered me blind so long. Yet, whilst you assured me that you had no attachment, I thought we might still have lived together.

I shall make no comments on your conduct; or any appeal to the world. Let my wrongs sleep with me! Soon, very soon, shall I be at peace. When you receive this, my burning head will be cold.

I would encounter a thousand deaths, rather than a night like the last. Your treatment has thrown my mind into a state of chaos; yet I am serene. I go to find comfort, and my only fear is, that my poor body will be insulted by an endeavour to recal my hated existence. But I shall plunge into the Thames where there is the least chance of my being snatched from the death I seek.

God bless you! May you never know by experience what you have made me endure. Should your sensibility ever awake, remorse will find its way to your heart; and, in the midst of business and sensual pleasure, I shall appear before you, the victim of your deviation from rectitude.

Mary

•

[London] Sunday Morning [c. November 1795]

I have only to lament, that, when the bitterness of death was past, I was inhumanly brought back to life and misery. But a fixed determination is not to be baffled by disappointment; nor will I allow that to be a frantic attempt, which was one of the calmest acts of reason. In this respect, I am only accountable to myself. Did I care for what is termed reputation, it is by other circumstances that I should be dishonoured.

You say, "that you know not how to extricate ourselves out of the wretchedness into which we have been plunged." You are extricated long since.—But I forbear to comment.—If I am condemned to live longer, it is a living death.

It appears to me that you lay much more stress on delicacy than on principle; for I am unable to discover what sentiment of delicacy would have been violated by your visiting a wretched friend, if indeed you have any friendship for me. But since your new attachment is the only sacred thing in your eyes, I am silent—Be happy! My complaints shall never more damp your enjoyment; perhaps I am mistaken in supposing that even my death could, for more than a moment. This is what you call magnanimity. It is happy for yourself, that you possess this quality in the highest degree.

Your continually asserting that you will do all in your power to contribute to my comfort, when you only allude to pecuniary assistance, appears to me a flagrant breach of delicacy. I want not such vulgar comfort, nor will I accept it. I never wanted but your heart—That gone, you have nothing more to give. Had I only poverty to fear, I should not shrink from life. Forgive me then, if I say, that I shall consider any direct or indirect attempt to supply my necessities, as an insult which I have not merited, and as rather done out of tenderness for your own reputation, than for me. Do not mistake me; I do not think that you value money, therefore I will not accept what you do not care for, though I do much less, because certain privations are not painful to me. When I am dead, respect for yourself will make you take care of the child.

I write with difficulty—probably I shall never write to you again. Adieu!

God bless you!

To William Godwin

[August 19, 1796]

As I was walking with Fanny this morning, before breakfast, I found a pretty little fable,[2] directly in my path; and, now I have finished my review, I will transcribe it for thee.

A poor Sycamore growing up amidst a cluster of Evergreens, every time the wind beat through her slender branches, envied her neighbours the foliage which sheltered them from each cutting blast. And the only comfort this poor trembling shrub could find in her mind (as mind is *proved* to be only thought, let it be taken for granted that she had a mind, if not a soul) was to say, Well; spring will come soon, and I too shall have leaves. But so impatient was this silly plant that the sun could not glisten on the snow, without her asking, of her more experienced neighbours, if this was not spring? At length the snow began to melt away, the snow-drops appeared, and the crocus did not lag long behind, the hepaticas next ventured forth, and the mezereon began to bloom.

The sun was warm—balsamic as May's own beams. Now said the sycamore, her sap mounting, as she spoke, I am sure this is spring.

Wait only for such another day, said a fading Laurel; and a whether-beaten Pine nodded, to enforce the remonstrance.

The Sycamore was not headstrong, and promised, at least to wait for the morrow, before she burst her rind.

What a to morrow came! The sun darted forth with redoubled ardour; the winds were hushed. A gentle breeze fluttered the trees; it was the sweet southern gale, which Willy Shakespeare felt, and came to rouse the violets; whilst every genial zephyr gave birth to a primrose.

The Sycamore no longer regarded admonition. She felt that it was spring; and her buds, fostered by the kindest beams immediately came forth to revel in existence.

Alas! Poor Sycamore! The morrow a hoar frost covered the trees, and shrivelled up thy unfolding leaves, changing, in a moment the colour of the living green—a brown, melancholy hue succeeded—and the Sycamore drooped, abashed; whilst a taunting neighbour whispered to her, bidding her, in future, learn to distinguish february from April.—

Whether the buds recovered, and expanded, when the spring actually arrived—The Fable sayeth not—

•

[September 13, 1796]

You tell me, William, that you augur nothing good, when the paper has not a note, or, at least, Fanny to wish you a good morning—

Now by these presents let me assure you that you are not only in my heart, but my veins, this morning. I turn from you half abashed—yet you haunt me, and some look, word or touch thrills through my whole frame—yes, at the very moment when I am labouring to think of something, if not somebody, else. Get ye gone Intruder! though I am forced to add dear—which is a call back—

When the heart and reason accord there is no flying from voluptuous sensations, I find, do what a woman can—Can a philosopher do more?

Mary

•

[Tuesday, June 6, 1797]

It was so kind and considerate in you to write sooner than I expected that I cannot help hoping you would be disappointed at not receiving a greeting from me on your arrival at Etruria. If your heart was in your mouth, as I felt, just now, at the sight of your hand, you may kiss or shake hands with the letter and imagine with what affection it was written—If not—stand off, profane one!

I was not quite well the day after you left me; but it is past, and I am well and tranquil, expecting the disturbance produced by Master William's joy, who took it into his head to frisk a little at being informed of your remembrance. I begin to love this little creature, and to anticipate his birth as a fresh twist to a knot, which I do not wish to untie. Men are spoilt by frankness, I believe, yet I must tell you that I love you better than I supposed I did, when I promised to love you for ever—and I will add what will gratify your benevolence, if not your heart, that on the whole I may be termed happy. You are a tender, affectionate creature; and I feel it thrilling through my frame giving and promising pleasure.

Fanny wanted to know "what you are gone for," and endeavours to pronounce Etruria. Poor papa is her word of kindness—She has been turning your letter on all sides, and has promised to play with Bobby till I have finished my answer.

I find you can write the kind of letter a friend ought to write, and give an account of your movements. I hailed the sunshine, and moon-light and travelled with you scenting the fragrant gale—Enable me still to be your company, and I will allow you to peep over my shoulder, and see me under the shade of my green blind, thinking of you, and all I am to hear, and feel when you return—you may read my heart—if you will. . . .

I am not fatigued with solitude—yet I have not relished my solitary dinner. A husband is a convenient part of the furniture of a house, unless he be a clumsy fixture. I wish you, from my soul, to be rivetted in my heart; but I do not desire to have you always at my elbow—though at this moment I did not care if you were. Yours truly and tenderly,

Mary

NOTES

1. "This passage refers to letters written under a purpose of suicide, and not intended to be opened till after the catastrophe" (Godwin's note).

2. Mary probably meant her fable to tell allegorically the story of her recent recovery from grief at Imlay's abandonment—and her fear that Godwin might treat her in similar fashion.

Chapter Sixteen

From A Girl's Life Eighty Years Ago (1800)

Eliza Southgate Bowne

This letter by an ordinary young American woman at the turn of the nineteenth century is a thoughtful, unsentimental perspective on the relation between romance and marriage in her time. Though the "natural" connection between love and marriage was becoming a more and more popular notion, the writer observes that in fact it is less clear as a practice: "Not one woman in a hundred marries for love . . . Gratitude [for choosing us as a wife] is undoubtedly the foundation of the esteem we commonly feel for a husband." Eliza Southgate wrote this letter to her cousin in 1800 and married three years later, a union she described as "of equal affection."

c. October 1800

To Moses Porter.

My most charming Cousin! Most kind and condescending friend—teach me how I may express the grateful sense I have of the obligations I owe you; your many and long letters have chased away the spleen, they have rendered me cheerful and happy, and I almost forgot I was so far from home.—O shame on you! Moses, you know I hate this formality among friends, you know how gladly I would throw all these fashionable forms from our correspondence; but you still oppose me, you adhere to them with as much scrupulosity as to the ten commandments, and for aught I know you believe them equally essential to the salvation of your soul. But, Eliza, you have not answered my last letter! True, and if I had not have answered it, would you never have written me again—and I confess that I believe you would not—yet I am mortified and displeased that you value my letters so little, that the exertions to continue the correspondence must all come from me, that if I relax my zeal in the smallest degree it may drop to the ground without your helping hand to raise it. I do think you are a charming fellow,—would not write because I am in debt, well, be it so, my ceremonious friend,—I submit, and though I transgress by sending a half sheet more than you ever did, yet I assure you 'twas to convince you of the violence of my anger which could *induce* me to forget the rules of politeness. I am at Wiscassett. I have seen Rebecca every day, she is handsome as ever, and we both of us were in constant expectation of seeing you for 2 or 3 days, you did not come and we were disappointed.

From Eliza Southgate Bowne, *A Girl's Life Eighty Years Ago: Selections from the Letters* (New York: Scribner's 1887) 35–41.

I leave here for Bath next week. I have had a ranting time, and if I did not feel so offended, I would tell you more about it.

As I look around me I am surprised at the happiness which is so generally enjoyed in families, and that marriages which have not love for a foundation on more than one side at most, should produce so much apparent harmony. I may be censured for declaring it as my opinion that not one woman in a hundred marries for love. A woman of taste and sentiment will surely see but a very few whom she could love, and it is altogether uncertain whether either of them will particularly distinguish her. If they should, surely she is very fortunate, but it would be one of fortune's random favors and such as we have no right to expect. The female mind I believe is of a very pliable texture; if it were not we should be wretched indeed. Admitting as a known truth that few women marry those whom they would prefer to all the world if they could be viewed by them with equal affection, or rather that there are often others whom they could have preferred if they had felt that affection for them which would have induced them to offer themselves,—admitting this as a truth not to be disputed,—is it not a subject of astonishment that happiness is not almost banished from this connexion? Gratitude is undoubtedly the foundation of the esteem we commonly feel for a husband. One that has preferred us to all the world, one that has thought us possessed of every quality to render him happy, surely merits our gratitude. If his character is good—if he is not displeasing in his person or manners—what objection can we make that will not be thought frivolous by the greater part of the world?—yet I think there are many other things necessary for happiness, and the world should never compel me to marry a man because I could not give satisfactory reasons for not liking him. I do not esteem marriage absolutely essential to happiness, and that it does not always bring happiness we must every day witness in our acquaintance. A single life is considered too generally as a reproach; but let me ask you, which is the most despicable—she who marries a man she scarcely thinks *well* of—to avoid the reputation of an old maid—or she, who with more delicacy, than marry one she could not highly esteem, preferred to live single all her life, and had wisdom enough to despise so mean a sacrifice, to the opinion of the rabble, as the woman who marries a man she has not much love for—must make. I wish not to alter the laws of nature—neither will I quarrel with the rules which custom has established and rendered indispensably necessary to the harmony of society. But every being who has contemplated human nature on a large scale will certainly justify me when I declare that the inequality of privilege between the sexes is very sensibly felt by us females, and in no instance is it greater than in the liberty of choosing a partner in marriage; true, we have the liberty of refusing those we don't like, but not of selecting those we do. This is undoubtedly as it should be. But let me ask you, what must be that love which is altogether voluntary, which we can withhold or give, which sleeps in dulness and apathy till it is requested to brighten into life? Is it not a cold, lifeless dictate of the head,—do we not weigh all the conveniences and inconveniences which will attend it? And after a long calculation, in which the heart never was consulted, we determine whether it is most prudent to love or not.

How I should despise a soul so sordid, so mean! How I abhor the heart which is regulated by mechanical rules, which can say "thus far will I go and no farther," whose feelings can keep pace with their convenience, and be awakened at stated periods,—a mere piece of clockwork which always moves right! How far less valuable than that being who has a soul to govern her actions, and though she may not always be coldly prudent, yet she will sometimes be generous and noble, and that the other never can be. After all, I must own that a woman of delicacy never will suffer her esteem to ripen into love unless she is convinced of a return. Though our first approaches to love may be involuntary, yet I should be sorry if we had no power of controlling them if occasion required. There is a happy conformity or pliability in the female mind which seems to have been a gift of nature to enable them to be happy with so few privileges,—and another thing, they have more gratitude in their dispositions than men, and there is a something particularly gratifying to the heart in being beloved, if the object is worthy; it produces a something like, and "Pity melts the heart to love." Added to these there is a self-love which does more than all the rest. Our vanity ('tis an ugly word but I can't find a better) is gratified by the distinguished preference given us. There must be an essential difference in the dispositions of men and women. I am astonished when I think of it—yet—But I have written myself into sunshine—'tis always my way when anything oppresses me, when any chain of thoughts particularly occupies my mind, and I feel dissatisfied at anything which I have not the power to alter,—to sit down and unburthen them on paper; it never fails to alleviate me, and I generally give full scope to the feelings of the moment, and as I write all disagreeable thoughts evaporate, and I end contented that things shall remain as they are. When I began this it absolutely appeared to me that no woman, or rather not one in a hundred, married the man she should prefer to all the world—not that I ever could suppose that at the time she married him she did not prefer him to all others,—but that she would have preferred another if he had professed to love her as well as the one she married. Indeed, I believe no woman of delicacy suffers herself to think she could love any one before she had discovered an affection for her. For my part I should never ask the question of myself—do I love such a one, if I had reason to think he loved me—and I believe there are many who love that never confessed it to themselves. My Pride, my delicacy, would all be hurt if I discovered such *unasked* for love, even in my own bosom. I would strain every nerve and rouse every faculty to quell the first appearance of it. There is no danger, however. I could never love without being beloved, and I am confident in my own mind that no person whom I could love would ever think me sufficiently worthy to love me. But I congratulate myself that I am at liberty to refuse those I don't like, and that I have firmness enough to brave the sneers of the world and live an old maid, if I never find one I can love.

Chapter Seventeen

Letters to Ellen Nussey (1840) and Constantine Héger (1845)

Charlotte Bronte

Charlotte Bronte is one of the great Victorian novelists who wrote about women and love, notably in Jane Eyre, *which had the paradigmatic happy ending, and* Villette, *which did not. In* Jane Eyre *the heroine leaves her lover as soon as she discovers he is already married, but they remain in love and she is able to marry him later. Bronte's letters to the married schoolmaster who showed no interest in her are among the most moving and passionate of love letters. In 1840, at age twenty-four, she had written to her friend Ellen Nussey, who was anticipating a proposal from a suitor, that "no young lady should fall in love till the offer has been made, accepted, the marriage ceremony performed, and the first half-year of wedded life passed away . . . [then] very coolly, very moderately, very rationally. . . . [or] she is a fool." Yet in 1845 she was writing in desperation to her unattainable beloved, "To forbid me to write to you, to refuse to answer me, would be to tear from me my only joy on earth." As is so often the case, Bronte's theory and practice of love did not coincide.*

To Ellen Nussey

November 20, 1840.

My dearest Nell,—That last letter of thine treated of matters so high and important I cannot delay answering it for a day. Now I am about to write thee a discourse, and a piece of advice which thou must take as if it came from thy grandmother. But in the first place, before I begin with thee, I have a word to whisper in the ear of Mr. Vincent, and I wish it could reach him. In the name of St. Chrysostom, St. Simon, and St. Jude, why does not that amiable young gentleman come forward like a man and say all that he has to say personally, instead of trifling with kinsmen and kinswomen? "Mr. Vincent," I say, "go personally, and say: 'Miss ———, I want to speak to you.' Miss ——— will of course civilly answer, 'I am at your service, Mr. Vincent.' And then, when the room is cleared of all but yourself and herself, just take a chair nearer. Insist upon her laying down that silly . . . work, and listening to you.

From Clement King Shorter, *Charlotte Bronte and Her Circle* (London: Hodder and Stoughton, 1896; reprint, Westport, CT: Greenwood Press, 1970), 304–6. *And from* Charlotte Bronte, "The Love Letters of Charlotte Bronte to Constantin Héger," trans. M. H. Spielmann, first printed *London Times*, July 29, 1913.

Then begin, in a clear, distinct, deferential, but determined voice: 'Miss ———, I have a question to put to you—a very important question, Will you take me as your husband, for better, for worse. I am not a rich man, but I have sufficient to support us. I am not a great man, but I love you honestly and truly. Miss ———, if you knew the world better you would see that this is an offer not to be despised—a kind attached heart and a moderate competency.' Do this, Mr. Vincent, and you may succeed. Go on writing sentimental and love-sick letters to ———, and I would not give sixpence for your suit." So much for Mr. Vincent. Now Miss ———'s turn comes to swallow the black bolus, called a friend's advice. Say to her: "Is the man a fool? is he a knave? a humbug, a hypocrite, a ninny, a noodle? If he is any or all of these, of course there is no sense in trifling with him. Cut him short at once—blast his hopes with lightning rapidity and keenness. Is he something better than this? has he at least common sense, a good disposition, a manageable temper? Then consider the matter." Say further: "You feel a disgust towards him now—an utter repugnance. Very likely, but be so good as to remember you don't know him; you have only had three or four days' acquaintance with him. Longer and closer intimacy might reconcile you to a wonderful extent. And now I'll tell you a word of truth, at which you may be offended or not as you like." Say to her: "From what I know of your character, and I think I know it pretty well, I should say you will never love before marriage. After that ceremony is over, and after you have had some months to settle down, and to get accustomed to the creature you have taken for your worse half, you will probably make a most affectionate and happy wife; even if the individual should not prove all you could wish, you will be indulgent towards his little follies and foibles, and will not feel much annoyance at them. This will especially be the case if he should have sense sufficient to allow you to guide him in important matters." Say also: "I hope you will not have the romantic folly to wait for what the French call 'une grande passion.' My good girl, 'une grande passion' is 'une grande folie.' Mediocrity in all things is wisdom; mediocrity in the sensations is superlative wisdom." Say to her: "When you are as old as I am (I am sixty at least, being your grandmother), you will find that the majority of those worldly precepts, whose seeming coldness shocks and repels us in youth, are founded in wisdom."

No girl should fall in love till the offer is actually made. This maxim is just. I will even extend and confirm it: No young lady should fall in love till the offer has been made, accepted, the marriage ceremony performed, and the first half-year of wedded life has passed away. A woman may then begin to love, but with great precaution, very coolly, very moderately, very rationally. If she ever loves so much that a harsh word or a cold look cuts her to the heart she is a fool. If she ever loves so much that her husband's will is her law, and that she has got into a habit of watching his looks in order that she may anticipate his wishes, she will soon be a neglected fool.

To Constantine Héger

November 18th, 1845

Monsieur,

The six months of silence have run their course. It is now the 18th of Novr.; my last letter was dated (I think) the 18th of May. I may therefore write to you without failing in my promise.

The summer and autumn seemed very long to me; truth to tell, it has needed painful efforts on my part to bear hitherto the self-denial which I have imposed on myself. You, Monsieur, you cannot conceive what it means; but suppose for a moment that one of your children was separated from you, 160 leagues away, and that you had to remain six months without writing to him, without receiving news of him, without hearing him spoken of, without knowing aught of his health, then you would understand easily all the harshness of such an obligation.

I tell you frankly that I have tried meanwhile to forget you, for the remembrance of a person whom one thinks never to see again, and whom, nevertheless, one greatly esteems, frets too much the mind; and when one has suffered that kind of anxiety for a year or two, one is ready to do anything to find peace once more. I have done everything; I have sought occupations; I have denied myself absolutely the pleasure of speaking about you—even to Emily; but I have been able to conquer neither my regrets or my impatience. That, indeed, is humiliating—to be unable to control one's own thoughts, to be the slave of a regret, of a memory, the slave of a fixed and dominant idea which lords it over the mind. Why cannot I have just as much friendship for you, as you for me—neither more nor less? Then should I be so tranquil, so free—I could keep silence then for ten years without an effort.

My father is well but his sight is almost gone. He can neither read nor write. Yet the doctors advise waiting a few months more before attempting an operation. The winter will be a long night for him. He rarely complains; I admire his patience. If Providence wills the same calamity for me, may He at least vouchsafe me as much patience with which to bear it! It seems to me, Monsieur, that there is nothing more galling in great physical misfortunes than to be compelled to make all those about us share in our sufferings. The ills of the soul one can hide, but those which attack the body and destroy the faculties cannot be concealed. My father allows me now to read to him and write for him; he shows me, too, more confidence than he has ever shown before, and that is a great consolation.

Monsieur, I have a favour to ask of you: when you reply to this letter, speak to me a little of yourself, not of me; for I know that if you speak of me it will be to scold me, and this time I would see your kindly side. Speak to me therefore of your children. Never was your brow severe when Louise and Claire and Prosper were by your side. Tell me also something of the School, of the pupils, of the Governesses. Are Mesdemoiselles Blanche, Sophie, and Justine still at Brussels? Tell me where you travelled during the holidays—did you go to the Rhine? Did you not visit Cologne or Coblentz? Tell me, in short, my master, what you will, but tell me something. To write to an ex-assistant governess (No! I refuse to remember my employment as assistant governess—I repudiate it)—anyhow, to write to an old pupil cannot be a very interesting occupation for you, I know; but for me it is life.

Your last letter was stay and prop to me—nourishment for half a year. Now I need another and you will give it me; not because you bear me friendship—you cannot have much—but because you are compassionate of soul and you would condemn no one to prolonged suffering to save yourself a few moments' trouble. To forbid me to write to you, to refuse to answer me, would be to tear from me my only joy on earth, to deprive me of my last privilege—a privilege I never shall consent willingly to surrender. Believe me, my master, in writing to me it is a good deed that you will do. So long as I believe you are pleased with me, so long as I have hope of receiving news from you, I can be at rest and not too sad. But when a prolonged and gloomy silence seems to threaten me with the estrangement of my master—when day by day I await a letter, and when day by day disappointment comes to fling me back into overwhelming sorrow, and the sweet delight of seeing your handwriting and reading your counsel escapes me as a vision that is vain, then fever claims me—I lose appetite and sleep—I pine away.

May I write to you again next May: I would rather wait a year, but it is impossible—it is too long.

I must say one word to you in English. I wish I could write to you more cheerful letters, for when I read this over I find it to be somewhat gloomy—but forgive me, my dear master—do not be irritated at my sadness—according to the words of the Bible: "Out of the fulness of the heart, the mouth speaketh," and truly I find it difficult to be cheerful so long as I think I shall never see you more. You will perceive by the defects in this letter than *[sic]* I am forgetting the French language—yet I read all the French books I can get, and learn daily a portion by heart—but I have never heard French spoken but once since I left Brussels—and then it sounded like music in my ears—every word was most precious to me because it reminded me of you—I love French for your sake with all my heart and soul.

Farewell, my dear Master—may God protect you with special care and crown you with peculiar blessings.

C. B.

Chapter Eighteen

Letter to Herbert Spencer (1852)

George Eliot

The British novelist George Eliot's letter to the famous philosopher, who had rejected her, is filled with open passion ("If you become attached to some one else, then I must die"), but also something more: an assertion of her own right to feeling ("I am not ashamed of it") and self-respect ("in the light of reason and true refinement I am worthy of your respect and tenderness"), both conventionally denied to women who openly declared their love. She later had an enduring and successful liaison with the critic George Henry Lewes, who was unable to marry her because he could not obtain a divorce from his wife.

[Broadstairs, 16? July 1852][1]

I know this letter will make you very angry with me, but wait a little, and don't say anything to me while you are angry. I promise not to sin any more in the same way.

My ill health is caused by the hopeless wretchedness which weighs upon me. I do not say this to pain you, but because it is the simple truth which you must know in order to understand why I am obliged to seek relief.

I want to know if you can assure me that you will not forsake me, that you will always be with me as much as you can and share your thoughts and feelings with me. If you become attached to some one else, then I must die, but until then I could gather courage to work and make life valuable, if only I had you near me. I do not ask you to sacrifice anything—I would be very good and cheerful and never annoy you. But I find it impossible to contemplate life under any other conditions. If I had your assurance, I could trust that and live upon it. I have struggled—indeed I have—to renounce everything and be entirely unselfish, but I find myself utterly unequal to it. Those who have known me best have always said, that if ever I loved any one thoroughly my whole life must turn upon that feeling, and I find they said truly. You curse the destiny which has made the feeling concentrate itself on you—but if you will only have patience with me you shall not curse it long. You will find that I can be satisfied with very little, if I am delivered from the dread of losing it.

I suppose no woman ever before wrote such a letter as this—but I am not ashamed of it, for I am conscious that in the light of reason and true refinement I am worthy of your respect and tenderness, whatever gross men or vulgar-minded women might think of me

From George Eliot, *The George Eliot Letters*, ed. Gordon S. Haight, vol. 8 (New Haven: Yale University Press, 1954), 56–57. © 1954 by Yale University Press. Reprinted by permission of the publisher. Note is by Gordon S. Haight.

NOTE

1. It is impossible to date this letter with certainty. As I reconstruct the episode Spencer came to Broadstairs on Saturday, 10 July, and after his rejection of her love, G E handed this letter to him. It has no salutation and ends without a period.

Chapter Nineteen

Letters to "Master" (c. 1861) and Susan Gilbert Dickinson (1852, 1855)

Emily Dickinson

No one knows the identity of the man (?) to whom the poet Emily Dickinson addressed these letters, which were discovered and printed long after her death. It is in fact uncertain that they were ever sent. Not surprisingly, given that they were by Emily Dickinson, they are written in language unlike any other love letters: "Master—open your life wide, and take me in forever. . . . and all that Heaven will be will disappoint me." Dickinson's own corrections are given in brackets.

Dickinson also wrote many, many letters of devotion and longing to her sister-in-law, Susan Gilbert Dickinson, both before and after Susan's marriage to Dickinson's brother. Scholars disagree as to what extent the intensity of language used in these letters can be attributed to romantic love or to "romantic friendship" of the sort Lillian Faderman writes about in part 5.

To "Master"

Master.

If you saw a bullet hit a Bird—and he told you he was'nt shot—you might weep at his courtesy, but you would certainly doubt his word.

One drop more from the gash that stains your Daisy's bosom—then would you *believe?* Thomas' faith in Anatomy, was stronger than his faith in faith. God made me—*[Sir]* Master— I did'nt be—myself. I dont know how it was done. He built the heart in me. Bye and bye it outgrew me—and like the little mother—with the big child—I got tired holding him. I heard of a thing called "Redemption"—which rested men and women. You remember I asked you for it—you gave me something else. I forgot the Redemption *[in the Redeemed. I did'nt tell you for a long time, but I knew you had altered me—I]* and was tired—no more—* *[so dear did this stranger become that were it, or my breath—the Alternative—I had tossed the fellow away with a smile.]* I am older—tonight, Master—but the love is the same—so are the moon and the crescent. If it had been God's will that I might breathe where you

From Millicent Todd Bingham, *Emily Dickinson's Home* (New York: Harper and Brothers, 1955), 422, 430–31. *And from Open Me Carefully: Emily Dickinson's Intimate Letters to Susan Huntington Dickinson,* ed. Ellen L. Hart and Martha N. Smith (Amherst: Paris Press, 1998), 13, 54. © 1998 by Ellen L. Hart and Martha N. Smith.

breathed—and find the place—myself—at night—if I can never forget that I am not with you, and that sorrow and frost are nearer than I—if I wish with a might I cannot repress— that mine were the Queen's place—the love of the Plantagenet is my only Apology. To come nearer than presbyteries—and nearer than the new Coat—that the Tailor made—the prank of the Heart at play on the Heart—in holy Holiday—is forbidden me. You make me say it over. I fear you laugh—when I do not see—*[but]* "Chillon" is not funny. Have you the Heart in your breast—Sir—is it set like mine—a little to the left—has it the misgiving—if it wake in the night—perchance—itself to it—a timbrel is it—itself to it a tune?

These things are *[reverent]* holy, Sir, I touch them *[reverently]* hallowed, but persons who pray—dare remark *[our]* "Father"! You say I do not tell you all. Daisy confessed, and denied not.

Vesuvius dont talk—Etna—dont—*[thy]* one of them said a syllable, a thousand years ago, and Pompeii heard it, and hid forever. She could'nt look the world in the face, afterward—I suppose. Bashful Pompeii! "Tell you of the want"—you know what a leech[?] is, dont you—and *[remember that]* Daisy's Arm is small. And you have felt the Horizon, hav'nt you—and did the sea—never come so close as to make you dance?

I dont know what you can do for it—thank you—Master—but if I had the Beard on my cheek—like you, and you—had Daisy's petals—and you cared so for me—what would become of you? Could you forget me in fight, or flight, or the foreign land? Could'nt Carlo, and you and I walk in the meadows an hour—and nobody care but the Bobolink, and *his*— a *silver* scruple? I used to think when I died—I could see you—so I died as fast as I could— but the "Corporation" are going Heaven too so *[Eternity]* wont be sequestered—now *[at all]*. Say I may wait for you—say I need go with no stranger to the to me—untried *[country]* fold. I waited a long time—Master—but I can wait more—wait till my hazel hair is dappled— and you carry the cane—then I can look at my watch—and if the Day is too far declined— we can take the chances *[of]* for Heaven. What would you do with me if I came "in white"? Have you the little chest to put the Alive—in?

I want to see you more—Sir—than all I wish for in this world—and the wish—altered a little—will be my only one—for the skies.

Could you come to New England, *[this summer—could]* would you come to Amherst— Would you like to come—Master?

[Would it do harm—yet we both fear God—] Would Daisy disappoint you—no—she would'nt—Sir—it were comfort forever—just to look in your face, while you looked in mine—then I could play in the woods till Dark—till you take me where sundown cannot find us—and the true keep coming—till the town is full. *[Will you tell me if you will?]*

I did'nt think to tell you, you did'nt come to me "in white", nor ever told me why.

> *No Rose, yet felt myself a'bloom,
> No Bird—yet rode in Ether.

•

[No heading]

Oh! did I offend it—*[Did'nt it want me to tell it the truth]* Daisy—Daisy—offend it—who bends her smaller life to his (its), meeker (lower) every day—who only asks—a taste—*[who]* something to do for love of it—some little way she cannot guess to make that master glad.

A love so big it scares her, rushing among her small heart—pushing aside the blood and leaving her faint and white in the gust's arm. Daisy—who never flinched thro' that awful parting, but held her life so tight he should not see the wound—who would have sheltered him in her childish bosom (Heart)—only it was'nt big eno' for a Guest so large—*this* Daisy—grieve her Lord—and yet she (it) often blundered. Perhaps she grieved (grazed) his taste—perhaps her odd—Backwoodsman ways teased *[life troubled]* his finer sense (nature).

Daisy *[fea]* knows all that—but must she go unpardoned—teach her grace, preceptor, teach her majesty. Slow (Dull) at patrician things—even the wren upon her nest learns (knows) more than Daisy dares.

Low at the knee that bore her once with *[royal]* wordless rest *[now]* Daisy *[stoops]* kneels! a culprit—tell her her *[offence]* fault—Master—if it is *[not so]* small eno to cancel with *her life, [Daisy]* she is satisfied—but punish—do not *[dont]* banish her—Shut her in prison, Sir—only pledge that you will forgive—sometime—before the grave, and Daisy will not mind—she will awake in your likeness.

Wonder stings me more than the Bee—who did never sting me—but made gay music with his might wherever I *[may] [should]* did go. Wonder wastes my pound, you said I had no size to spare.

You send the water over the Dam in my brown eyes.

Iv'e got a cough as big as a thimble—but I dont care for that. Iv'e got a Tomahawk in my side but that dont hurt me much. *[If you]* Her master stabs her more.

Wont he come to her—or will he let her seek him, never minding *[whatere]* so long wandering if *[out]* to him at last.

Oh how the sailor strains, when his boat is filling—Oh how the dying tug, till the angel comes. Master—open your life wide, and take me in forever. I will never be tired—I will never be noisy when you want me to be still. I will be *[glad as the]* your best little girl—nobody else will see me, but you—but that is enough—I shall not want any more—and all that Heaven will be will disappoint me, only because it's not so dear

To Susan Gilbert Dickinson

February 1852

It's a sorrowful morning Susie—the wind blows and it rains; "into each life some rain must fall," and I hardly know which falls fastest, the rain without, or within—Oh Susie, I would nestle close to your warm heart, and never hear the wind blow, or the storm beat, again. Is there any room there for me, or shall I wander away all homeless and alone? Thank you for loving me, darling, and *will* you "love me more if ever you come home" *!* it is enough, dear Susie, I know I shall be satisfied. But what can I do towards you?—*dearer* you *cannot* be, for I love you so already, that it almost breaks my heart—perhaps I can love you *anew*, every day of my life, every morning and evening—Oh if you will let me, how happy I shall be!

•

January 1855

I am sick today, dear Susie, and have not been to church. There has been a pleasant quiet, in which to think of you, and I have not been sick eno' that I cannot write to you. I love you as dearly, Susie, as when love first began, on the step at the front door, and under the Evergreens, and it breaks my heart sometimes, because I do not hear from you. I wrote you many days ago—I wont say many weeks, because it will look sadder so, and then I cannot write—but Susie, it troubles me.

I miss you, mourn for you, and walk the Streets alone—often at night, beside, I fall asleep in tears, for your dear face, yet not one word comes back to me from that silent West. If it is finished, tell me, and I will raise the lid to my box of Phantoms, and lay one more love in; but if it lives and beats still, still lives and beats for me, then say me so, and I will strike the strings to one more strain of happiness before I die.

Chapter Twenty

Letters to Houghton Gilman (1898)

Charlotte Perkins Gilman

These extremely passionate letters by the American feminist Charlotte Perkins Gilman, author of the much-anthologized short story "The Yellow Wallpaper," show her hungry for love of many kinds ("the sweet big brotherly interest; the excusing mother and father love; the approving friendship. I am very greedy. I want all kinds of love and lots of it") but also placing a high value on intellectual companionship and the relative importance of shared political views ("A man might come much nearer to my work, my thought, that is true. I do not feel you near nor particularly sympathetic there"). She married the man to whom they are addressed, Houghton Gilman, in 1900. Charlotte Perkins Gilman was best known in her lifetime for her book Women and Economics, *which theorized that the basis of women's inferior social status was their economic dependence on men, and advocated communal housekeeping and child rearing.*

9.23 A.M.
Tues. May 16th. 1898

Goldsboro N.C. . . .

How good it is to have some one to turn to every day—to touch hearts with for a few moments even when hands and lips cannot meet. And you do care—don't you? You are interested? You care about this little lonely (lonely, *not* lovely!) woman who blows about the world in such queer ways, wishes so much and does so little. I don't mean just to *want* me; but the big sweet brotherly interest; the excusing mother and father love; the approving friendship. I am very greedy. I want all kinds of love and lots of it. And all the time there stands implacable behind it the feeling that it is not for me! . . .

. . . Last night I lectured again—first of series. 'Twas in the courthouse. Good audience in size; super excellent in quality. Professed itself pleased. I didn't enjoy it so well as last time. . . .

•

From Charlotte Perkins Gilman, A Journey from Within: The Love Letters of Charlotte Perkins Gilman, *1897–1900,* ed. and annotated by Mary A. Hill (London: Associated University Press, 1995), 139–40. © 1995 by Associated University Presses. From Charlotte Perkins Gilman Papers, Schlesinger Library, Radcliffe Institute, Harvard University. Reprinted by permission of the Schlesinger Library.

About 10.45 A.M.
Wed. May 18th '98

Goldsboro N.C...

I've been wondering a bit lately whether my "numbness" of sensation even to love and joy, is not due to my rigid training in voluntary numbness toward pain. Where one has spent years in denying a sensation—refusing to "answer the bell"—carefully withdrawing all consciousness from the affected part and pursuing other business, I should think it might very naturally affect one's power to feel anything. Now I am going to stop bothering about it. To accept gratefully the little trickling streams and occasional big rushing currents of love that I feel; and when I do not feel any, to rest assured that it is there—just as my pain is there though I refuse to feel it. . . .

Further, on the same lines, I am beginning to recognize that a life capable of such wide and varied interests as mine; and such a long steady unfailing "set" in the direction of what I believe to be the right, need not expect at the same time to be able to maintain a keen and steady interest in "daily duties"; with the constant change of focus that goes therewith.

I must be more humble—not expect to do everything. If I keep my mind open to see things as it should; and speak when I can—write when I can—why that is my "stint" and I should not resent the comparative vagueness and lack of adjustment in so many of my days. I suppose it is the old woman's temperament, with its exacting routine of hourly and momently duties; failing to adapt its conscience to the eccentric orbit of the work I am set to do. I'd better begin to apply some of my wisdom to my own life and become a more agreeable member of society. . . .

O this is such a good letter! But it is sinfully long, dear boy. You mustn't waste so much of your precious time on me. . . . Why there are about 1800 words in this letter! . . .

Dear Love—Dear dear Love—I do not think you need fear my ever loving any one else better. Of course no one can swear to the future, but I cannot imagine any man on earth catching up after the start you've got. . . . No one else on earth touches my early life as you do. And when I think of all I have been through, and of what it has cost me to tell even you about it; and how, in honor, I should have to tell it all again to another man if I came to love him—why I just want to bury my face in your neck—to feel you wrap me all up in your arms and hold me tight—never *never* to stir away from you. Our friendship, comradeship, cheery intimacy, means so much to me. The games and jokes and fun—that is like my brother and the pleasures of my childhood. . . .

A man might come much nearer to my work, my thought, that is true. I do not feel you near nor particularly sympathetic there. You are sympathetic with *me*—with my intentions; and you are as helpful as you can be to the external work; but we don't think in the same lines by nature. But, bless me! If I find a co-thinker, man or woman, there is nothing to prevent our co-thinking that I know of! I don't have to marry 'em! My one grave doubt has been deliciously settled; I know now that we are fitted to one another in the most important things. . . .

Disappointed in you? I? Why I don't expect anything of you except to be what you are—and I shan't be disappointed in that. . . . You understand to the full that I am a world-worker and must be—that I simply give you the part that stays at home, and that I shall go right on thinking, writing, lecturing, and travelling when I must. Of course I should give up a few years of the travelling in case certain contingencies arose. (Can't you see 'em arising!)

Chapter Twenty-one

Letters to Ben Reitman (1909, 1919);
Living My Life (1934)

Emma Goldman

Goldman's enormous ardor for Ben Reitman, her much younger lover whose nickname for her was "Mommy," was evident in her letters. Their affair had a painful ending with mutual recrimination. The abyss between them, by her account, was that though he was entirely devoted to her, her own devotion to anarchist ideals was deeper than his. The torment in these letters is evident and startling to read after the confident assertions of essays such as "Marriage and Love" (see part 1). Yet years later she wrote in her autobiography, Living My Life, *that she was able after years had passed to feel a "new friendliness and a clearer appreciation of what the man had given me," and "was no longer afraid to meet" him and his wife: "It was the same old Ben. . . . No change in him nor understanding for mine." Reitman was only one of several important romantic relationships in Goldman's life, many of them a painful struggle for her, at a time when she was writing fiery speeches such as "Marriage and Love."*

To Ben Reitman

December 13, 1909

You have made yourself perfectly plain, Ben dear. You have substantiated what I knew long ago, what I told you many times, namely love is an unknown thing to you. What you call love is an insatiable monster, that saps love's blood and then kicks it into the cold. Your love excludes giving, excludes concern for the wellbeing of the love object. Your love takes and takes and when it can take no more, it thrusts love aside in a manner so cold, so brutal, so inhuman, as if love had never existed.

Please do not think I scold or upbraid or blame you. . . . Can I blame the blind if he does not see, can I blame the deaf if he does not hear? Why Ben should I blame you? Besides, it is not a question of blame, it is a question of coming face to face with a terrible fact. Last Thursday, on that most terrible day of my life, the day of my greatest humiliation, I came face to face with a cruel fact. I saw that what you called love was only a caprice to satisfy your

From Letters by Emma Goldman to Ben Reitman, in Ben L. Reitman Papers, Special Collections, University Library, University of Illinois at Chicago. Reprinted by permission. Information in square brackets is by Susan Ostrov Weisser. *And from* Emma Goldman, *Living My Life* (1931; reprint, New York: AMS Press, 1934), 694–95.

every whim, no matter at what expense. I saw too that unless I continue to submit to that whim, I will have no place in your life, no place in your humanity, no place in your esteem.

Well, I do not blame you, I do not censure you, I do not condemn you. I only know I can never again put myself in a position that should give you the right to treat me, as you have on that black day in Boston.

I can never again place my soul at your heel to be kicked and bruised until it is sore beyond endurance. . . .

You are the first human being who has ever accused me of money considerations, and if you were not so utterly swallowed up by your own childish desires, you would know that I deserve no such accusation. If it were not so pathetic it would be funny. . . .

It's too bad we did not meet when propaganda meant more to me than everything else in the world, when I had no personal interest in people or things, when I could use everything and everybody for the sake of the cause. That time is past, much to the disadvantage of my life.

Meetings, free speech, are nothing to me now, if my love, my life, my peace, my very soul is to be mutilated. Work with you, so long as I had faith in your love, meant the greatest sweetest joy in life. That may account for my utter abandonment, my utter dissolution to my love for you. That may also account, why I the woman who has been treated with respect by friend and foe, could crouch on her knees and beg and plead with you. Yes, I believed in your love, or rather I believed too much in the power of my love to teach you, to make you see the beauty, the force, the greatness of love. I believe in it no longer, I have no faith in your love, and with it the joy of work with you is gone. I have no right to bring a message to people when there is no message in my soul. I have no right to speak of freedom when I myself became an abject slave in my love. I have no right to talk of the beauty of love with that hideous Thursday before me. . . .

I see I have already said too much. I hope you will be as happy as you can. I shall always be your friend, I am sure always be interested in your life. It is not a question of whether I love you well enough to stand your moods, or whether I want you. I know I shall never again endure what I have endured last Thursday. Never again.

Emma

•

December 14 or 15, 1909

I appreciate the intensity of feelings that prompted your letter, dear. I know you meant every word, indeed I have never doubted the sincerity of your love. . . . Angry with you? No, dear, I am not. I wish I were still in that youthful stage when I could be angry with those dear to me for anything they have done. That happy period is gone and with it all peace in life. How can I be angry with you? Don't I know you give as much as you can. Would to goodness I could content myself with that, and crave no more. Perhaps if my love for you had not so completely taken hold of me, if it had not swept me off my feet, if it had not excluded everyone and everything, I should have been less exacting. I have never received half the love I gave, but I never missed it particularly. You came into my life with such a terrific force, you gripped my soul, my nerves, my thoughts, my flesh, until all was blotted out, all else was silenced.

Theories, considerations, principles, consistency, friends, nay even pride and self-respect, only one thing remained, a terrible hunger for your love, an insatiable thirst for it. That explains my clinging, my holding on to you, I who never clung to anyone. That explains my agony when every woman would possess you at the exclusion of myself. Oh please, don't give me your assurances, I do not believe in them. Did you not forget my existence on that night when you stood out in the rain for 1 ½ [hours] trying to get the woman of your obsession. She spoiled your mood, you wrote. Yes, I know she did not yield. That always spoils your mood. I could name any amount of instances when some fool obsession blotted out my image. The consciousness of it, fear of it, made me cling to you even more, made me humiliate myself, made me follow you like a dog. Well, the outcome was inevitable. If love goes into dust, it deserves to be spat upon, if it crouches on its knees, it deserves to be kicked.

•

December 16, 1909

You ask if I love you. As if I did not love you, if I could say, no! no! no! I should be a happier woman, happier because I would find peace. You told me to make myself free, never to entangle myself with you again. If only I could do it. But what is space or time when one is madly, irrevocably in love, when one's whole being screams out, I love him, I love him! I love you, Ben, with all the concentrated subtle passion of a woman of my temperament. I shall probably never again know such a love, or feel anything for any other man. The tragedy is, that I love you so much, too deeply, too madly, and yet, and yet, when I think of that hideous day a week ago, of that cruel brutal day that turned you into stone, I feel that I must crush my love and never see you again. There have been many terrible days and nights this last year, days that dragged me into the gutter, days of doubt and despair. But there never has been such a day as the one last Thursday.

•

December 23, 1909

Precious lover mine,

After all, I am right in my belief in the power of love. Two weeks ago today, I was the poorest, most dejected creature on earth. All life, hope, faith were gone. I was simply stranded. Indeed, I was so terribly poor that I even lacked strength to end it all. To throw myself in front of the train, though my brain urged me to do it. All was dead and still in me, like in a graveyard. Today, I feel regenerated, reborn, new. What has performed the miracle? Why love, only love. If I did not love you so fervently, so completely, so absolutely, I could not have survived the shock of two weeks ago. I could not feel today as I do, full of hope and faith. I could not long with all my soul for you. Yes, love is great, is wonderful.

Dearest, I want to come to you, I am sorry it cannot be soon enough, but I must prepare and attend to everything. I will come though about the 7th or 8th. . . .

Your letter intoxicates me, sweetheart. You say you wish you could tell me how you love me, but you do, you do. And I hope with all my being you will also let me feel it. If I have your love, I have all that life can give, *I want nothing else.* Give myself to anyone? No, dear, I could not do that, not even in despair, not so long as I love you. It never even entered my mind for a moment, it couldn't dear because I have not stopped to crave you for one second. . . . I hope you may find some joy this Christmas. Think of me lover, just a little and remember, I want you my honey, yes I do.

With deep intense love,
Mommy

•

December 12, 1919

. . . I was glad to have been in Chicago and to see you again, dearest Molio. I never realized quite so well how far apart we have travelled. And nothing you have done since you left me, nothing you do can take away the ten wonderful years with you. If it is true that the power of endurance is the greatest test of love, then Molio mine, I have loved you much but I have been rewarded not only in great joy—in ecstasy—in all that makes life full and rich and sparkling. I really owe much to you during our years together. I have done my best and most valuable work, the continuance of M E [Mother Earth] during all the years. I owe them to you. Your devotion, your untiring work, and your tremendous energy. If I owe also much heart-ache, much soul searing misery to you, what of it. Nothing great in life can be achieved without great pain. I am glad to have paid the price. I only hope I too have given you something worth whatever price you have paid for your love I shall feel proud and glad.

From Living My Life

Stella grew uneasy on hearing that on our way east I intended to stop off in Chicago, where Ben was living. She implored me to give up the idea. "You will only lose the peace you have gained through months of struggle to free yourself from Ben," she pleaded. There was no need for anxiety, I assured her. In the isolation and loneliness of the cell one finds the courage to face the nakedness of one's soul. If one survives the ordeal, one is less hurt by the nakedness of other souls. I had worked my way through much anguish and travail to a better understanding of my relation with Ben. I had dreamed of having ecstatic love without the pettiness and jarring conditioned in it. But I learned to see that the great and the small, the beautiful and the mean, that had made up our life were inseparable springs from the same source, flowing to a common outlet. In my clarified perception the fine things in Ben now stood out in bolder relief, and the little no longer mattered. One so primitive as he, who was always moved by his emotions, could not do things half-way. He gave without measure or restraint. His best years, his tremendous zest for work, he had devoted to me. It is not unusual for woman to do as much for the man she loves. Thousands of my sex had sacrificed their own talents and ambitions for the sake of the man. But few men have done so for women. Ben was one of the few; he had dedicated himself completely to my interests. Emotionalism had guided his passion as it had his life. But, like nature unleashed, he would destroy with one hand the lavish gifts of the other. I had revelled in the beauty and strength of his giving, and I had recoiled from and struggled against the self-centred egotism which ignored and annihilated obstacles in the soul of the loved one. Erotically Ben and I were of the same earth, but in a cultural sense we were separated by centuries of time. With him social impulses, sympathy with mankind, ideas, and ideals were moods of the moment, and as fleeting. He had no means of sensing basic verities or inner need to convert them into his own.

My life was linked with that of the race. Its spiritual heritage was mine, and its values were transmuted into my being. The eternal struggle of man was rooted within me. That made the abyss between us.

In the solitude of prison I had lived away from the disturbing presence of Ben. Often my heart had called for him, but I had silenced its cry. I had promised myself after our last break never to see him again until I should have made order out of my emotional chaos. I had fulfilled my pledge; nothing was now left of the conflict that had lasted so many years. Neither love nor hate. Only a new friendliness and a clearer appreciation of what the man had given me. I was no longer afraid to meet Ben.

In Chicago he called, bringing a large bouquet of flowers. It was the same old

Ben, instinctively reaching out and his eyes opening wide in wonder at meeting no response. No change in him nor understanding for mine. He wanted to give me a party at his home. Would I come, he asked. "Of course," I said, "I will come to meet your wife and your child." I went. The dead had buried their dead, and I felt serene.

Chapter Twenty-two

Letters to Leonard Woolf (1912) and Vita Sackville-West (1929)

Virginia Woolf

Woolf, whose novels question the seemingly inevitable link between romance and marriage, presents an unusual view of love in her letter dated 1912: "I go from being half in love with you, and wanting you to be with me always, and know everything about me, to the extreme of wildness and aloofness," she wrote to Leonard Woolf before their marriage. "I feel no physical attraction in you." Her marital relations with Leonard Woolf seem to have been devoted but sexless. Another exchange from 1929 with the writer Vita Sackville-West shows by contrast a more playfully romantic relation.

To Leonard Woolf

Asheham [*Rodmell, Sussex*]

May 1st [1912]

Dearest Leonard,

To deal with the facts first (my fingers are so cold I can hardly write) I shall be back about 7 tomorrow, so there will be time to discuss—but what does it mean? You can't take the leave, I suppose if you are going to resign certainly at the end of it. Anyhow, it shows what a career you're ruining!

Well then, as to all the rest. It seems to me that I am giving you a great deal of pain—some in the most casual way—and therefore I ought to be as plain with you as I can, because half the time I suspect, you're in a fog which I don't see at all. Of course I can't explain what I feel—these are some of the things that strike me. The obvious advantages of marriage stand in my way. I say to myself. Anyhow, you'll be quite happy with him; and he will give you companionship, children, and a busy life—then I say By God, I will not look upon marriage as a profession. The only people who know of it, all think it suitable; and that makes me scrutinise my own motives all the more. Then, of course, I feel angry sometimes at the strength of your desire. Possibly, your being a Jew comes in also at this point. You seem so foreign. And then I am fearfully unstable. I pass from hot to cold in an instant, without any reason; except that I believe sheer physical effort and exhaustion influence me. All I can say is that in spite of these feelings which go chasing each other all day long when I am with you, there is some feeling which is permanent, and growing. You want to know of course whether it will ever make me marry you. How can I say? I think it will, because there seems no reason why it shouldn't—But I don't know what the future will bring. I'm half afraid of myself. I sometimes feel that no one ever has or ever can share something—Its the thing that makes you call me like a hill, or a rock. Again, I want everything—love, children, adventure, intimacy, work. (Can you make any sense out of this ramble? I am putting down one thing after another). So I go from being half in love with you, and wanting you to be with me always, and know everything about me, to the extreme of wildness and aloofness. I sometimes think that if I married you, I could have everything—and then—is it the sexual side of it that comes between us? As I told you brutally the other day, I feel no physical attraction in you. There are moments—when you kissed me the other day was one—when I feel no more than a rock. And yet your caring for me as you do almost overwhelms me. It is so real, and so strange. Why should you? What am I really except a pleasant attractive creature? But its just because you care so much that I feel I've got to care before I marry you. I feel I must give you everything; and that if I can't, well, marriage would only be second-best for you as well as for me. If you can still go on, as before, letting me find my own way, as that is what would please me best; and then we must both take the risks. But you have made me very happy too. We both of us want a marriage that is a tremendous living thing, always alive, always hot, not dead and easy in parts as most marriages are. We ask a great deal of life, don't we? Perhaps we shall get it; then, how splendid!

One doesn't get much said in a letter does one? I haven't touched upon the enormous variety of things that have been happening here—but they can wait.

D'you like this photograph?—rather too noble, I think. Here's another.

Yrs.
V S

To Vita Sackville-West

Monks House, Rodmell [*Sussex*]

5th April [1929]

"Not many women possess such great versatility as the Hon. V. Sackville-West . . . she has also the rare gift of enjoying solitude . . ." . . .

But listen. Hugh Walpole was coming; and I've put him off, and said I'm going to Kew with you. I mayn't be able to go to Kew, though, because I have had a dose or two of Chloral; and L. thinks it is walking that makes me sleep badly; I dont; never mind: we can sit and talk.

I cant be sure about dinner; I had to ask Hugh. Will you come? Only he mayn't come. Settle what you like when you come. Only don't be late this time.

Leonard's been having the rheumatism too. Its bitter, bitter. We missed the fine days—still the garden, the terrace, the view, even black and white in shower and wind make me wish—I'm not sure what—to write poetry; perhaps, and not an essay upon fiction.

Do you want a flat in Gordon Sqre [Vanessa's] very cheap?

Do you love me?

If you give me so much as a tuppenny mug from Woolworths, I never speak to you again.

I told Nessa the story of our passion in a chemists shop the other day. But do you really like going to bed with women she said—taking her change. "And how d'you do it?" and so she bought her pills to take abroad, talking as loud as a parrot.

A mongoose has just run into the bathroom. Nelly is terrified.

Virginia

Chapter Twenty-three

Letters to Jean-Paul Sartre (1938)

Simone de Beauvoir

"I love you, with a touch of tragedy and quite madly," the great feminist philosopher de Beauvoir wrote to her lover Sartre in 1938. That same summer she also wrote to him, "Something extremely agreeable has happened to me, . . . I slept with Little Bost three days ago. It was I who propositioned him, of course." Clearly, the author of The Second Sex *had an unusual love relation with Sartre, one that endured for many decades and has received much publicity, but is best judged by the letters themselves. We can see here both passion and an attempt to live without the conventions of romantic love and marriage.*

Hôtel de la gare
Albertville (Savoie)

Albertville, Wednesday [27 July 1938]

Dear little being,

I'm not going to write you a long letter, though I've hundreds of things to tell you, because I prefer to tell you them in person on Saturday. You should know, however:

1. First, that I love you dearly—I'm quite overcome at the thought that I'll see you disembarking from the train on Saturday, carrying your suitcase and my red hatbox—I can already picture us ensconced on our deckchairs overlooking a lovely blue sea and talking nineteen to the dozen—and I feel a great sense of well-being.[1]

2. You've been very sweet to write me such long letters. I'm hoping for another this evening at Annecy. You tell me countless pleasing little items of news, but the most pleasing of all is that you've found your subject. The big page looks extremely fine with that title, just the perverse kind you like: *Lucifer*—I can find no fault with it.[2]

3. Something extremely agreeable has happened to me, which I didn't at all expect when I left—I slept with Little Bost three days ago. It was I who propositioned him, of course. Both of us had been wanting it: we'd have serious conversations during the day, and the evenings would be unbearably oppressive. One rainy evening at Tignes, in a barn, lying face down a few inches away from one another, we gazed at each other for an hour finding various pretexts

to put off the moment of going to sleep, he babbling frantically, I racking my brains vainly for the casual, appropriate words I couldn't manage to articulate—I'll tell you it all properly later. In the end I laughed foolishly and looked at him, so he said: "Why are you laughing?" and I said: "I'm trying to picture your face if I propositioned you to sleep with me" and he said: "I was thinking that you were thinking that I wanted to kiss you but didn't dare." After that we floundered on for another quarter of an hour before he made up his mind to kiss me. He was tremendously astonished when I told him I'd always had a soft spot for him—and he ended up telling me yesterday evening that he'd loved me for ages. I'm very fond of him. We spend idyllic days, and nights of passion. But have no fear of finding me sullen or disoriented or ill at ease on Saturday; it's something precious to me, something intense, but also light and easy and properly in its place in my life, simply a happy blossoming of relations that I'd always found very agreeable. It strikes me as funny, on the other hand, to think that I'm now going to spend two days with Bienenfeld.

Goodbye, dear little being—I'll be on the platform on Saturday, or at the buffet if you don't see me on the platform. I'd like to spend long weeks alone with you. A big kiss.

Your Beaver

•

[Marseilles]

Saturday [September 1938]

Your own self, my love,

My beloved, I have your wire—so we're leaving. I'm amazed, since I understood things were going very badly. Summon me back at once if things do become worrying, I beg of you. It doesn't seem at all the same as when I was with you. When I'm with you, nothing seems terrible to me, not even leaving you. But away from you, the slightest fear is unbearable. I love you passionately—I'm empty and miserable without you. K. has been very sweet, and the first evening I was touched by seeing her again—but already she bores and rather irritates me, and her presence at this moment strikes me as absurd. Write to me immediately at the addresses provided. I love you, with a touch of tragedy and quite madly.

Your Beaver

NOTES

1. They were about to embark for Morocco.
2. The work in question was to become *Les Chemins de la Liberté* (The Roads to Freedom).

Chapter Twenty-four

A Letter to Larry (1989)

Mary Moore

Mary Moore is a writer living in New York City. This open letter to a lover who has a wife or another lover, which appeared in an alternative New York magazine, And Then, *is frank about the problems for a woman in loving a man who keeps her a secret from the rest of the world. The author views her own passion quite dispassionately and rationally, which makes for interesting reading.*

Dear Larry,

I spent the last two days stewing after reading *The New Other Woman: Contemporary Single Women in Affairs with Married Men,* a pop sociology book by Laurel Richardson. As you'd expect, it's pretty bad, but it did goad me into taking a closer and harder look at some things that have been nagging at me in a sort of inchoate way. I mean things about my involvement with you. About what I'm doing by getting involved with you now.

I'll spare you the moralizing aspect; you can fill in that part as well as I can.

In fact, I'd be less than honest if I didn't tell you that the chapter of Richardson's book that got to me wasn't "The Wife" but rather "Feeling Bad." Also "Endings."

But first, some Prehistory: As I've told you, I took a real emotional battering a few years ago when the man I'd been in a relationship with suddenly announced that he was leaving me for Another Woman (first variation). Till now, I've felt too vulnerable to risk any real involvement with a man. Instead, I've sought out encounters that would restore my sense of myself as desirable and attractive without the risk of making myself genuinely available. My fantasy was to have a stable of lovers, none of whom would live in New York; I would spend romantic but self-contained weekends with each of them in rotation; none of them would be indispensable and none would become entwined with my "real life."

In this frame of mind, seeing you every now and then suited me just fine. I could feel desirable and *in control.* These were very important positive feelings countering negative feelings spawned by the previous Traumatic Ending (second variation). But they were premised on distancing. I think this is what you intuited when you said I was "controlling" (sexist word) in sex.

So, The Script: I play the sexually liberated, emotionally independent, professionally successful, feminist woman. Not *just* a role, of course; I really am these things, but in a more complex and three-dimensional way.

However, there is also a Subtext. Unlike other men I've gone out with during this period, I *really* like you. I really liked you from the beginning. I sort of knew, but didn't really want to know, that I could, under the right circumstances, really like you. There was a part of me, then, that was always waiting to see whether something else might happen.

I told you recently, when we were discussing your problems, that the wish to be in control was utterly utopian. I was also talking about me.

Complication: Now I find myself more emotionally involved with you, more emotionally attached to you than I bargained for. Control is out of the question. At one level, this is all to the good. It signifies healing, willingness to risk, to be open to love. All other things being equal, I'd say good riddance to control.

But all other things are not equal. Your unavailability, the very thing that made you safe before, makes you dangerous now. You are not just an ordinary risk but a very high-risk risk.

"Feeling Bad." I already sense glimmers of ways in which I am/would be disempowered if we went on in this way. 1) It is the constraints of your situation, your schedule, that determine when we can see each other, speak to each other. I have to adjust, to wait for you. Classic feminine one-down position. Yech. 2) Structurally, the situation sets up a competition between two women over a man. So when I see Anita's picture on your wall or when you insinuate that she is "depressive" and "out of control," I compare myself to her and gauge the outcome in terms of "winning" or "losing." Classic scenario of male dominance. Yech. 3) Situation fosters distrust and jealousy, prompting rhetorical questions like: You're cheating on Anita, so why wouldn't you cheat on me? Do you have Other "Other Women"? What precisely is the nature of your interest in Carole Wotija? Etc. I even find myself shaken by what (I realize) may be false, unfounded, misleading and ideological rumors about your "history of philandering." No matter that we have no claims on each other, that I am seeing Other Men, that I don't even necessarily believe in monogamy. The structural pressures (triangular asymmetry on top of standard gender power asymmetry) are overwhelming. More classic gender-political issues. More yech. Hard in the best of times, but especially daunting for me now, when recent past makes Trust (major motif) so problematic.

Interior monologue: Do I need this? What would I be doing to myself, and saying about myself, if I put up with this? Very basic question about self-esteem.

Meta-critique: The preceding description is cast in terms that are not above suspicion. Perhaps I make myself too much the victim, the overdetermined pawn in a preprogrammed cultural script. Perhaps I foreclose the possibility of understanding what *you* are experiencing. Perhaps I capitulate too quickly to the dominant cultural interpretive framework and miss the chance to find another, more empowering, less deterministic description. Or are these worries really a desperate, pathetic, last-ditch stab at denial, rationalization, self-deception? Whichever, these *are* the dominant interpretive frames. How can I, a solitary, isolated, culturally stigmatized Other Woman, hold out against them?

Now, to "Endings" (Major recurrent theme): Richardson says the fantasized Happy Ending (he leaves his wife and marries the Other Woman; they live happily ever after) hardly ever happens. More frequently, he either stays with his wife or he leaves her but ends up with some third woman. In either case, the Affair does eventually end. The question is: How? Humanely or cruelly? Cleanly or messily?

The question of the Ending looms large for both of us now. For you, in the context of working out some resolution with Anita. For me, given that I have suffered horribly as a result of having been denied any agency, any participation, in the construction of the previous Ending. In fact, I suspect that some of my own behavior and thinking about the situation between the two of us is simultaneously a reworking of that previous experience; I am trying to construct a different kind of ending for me.

Reluctant But Ineluctable Conclusion: We should stop this now before it gets really murky, messy, painful. Before we lose respect for each other and for ourselves.

I don't know what exactly all this has meant for you, but I'm sure that it must be very different from what it has meant for me. I do know that there have been several points at which you were prepared simply to let it end (if not to end it) but at which I kept it alive by taking some initiative. I suppose it is appropriate in many ways for me to take the initiative again now.

(Good, empowering alternative to dependent waiting. Plus reclaiming the higher moral ground, upholding sisterhood, etc. Or perhaps: another bid for control? fleeing intimacy? doing it to them before they do it to me?)

The Future? Here I don't know what to say. Except that I feel very close to you and it's very important to me that we find some way to be in meaningful contact. Do you think we could figure out a way to become good friends and to continue to share our work with each other?

I can't deny that, even as I write about friendship, I still fantasize about love. Perhaps someday, later, when we're both free . . .

Love,
Mary

Part III

Second-Wave Feminist Theory

The second-wave feminist movement brought romantic love back to public discourses on feminism, beginning with Simone de Beauvoir's classic in 1952 and continuing to the mid-1970s. Rather than call for a more "pure love" with sexuality under women's control, or for "free love," feminist writers questioned or radically denounced romantic love itself as "dope for dupes" (Greer). Like Wollstonecraft's, Simone de Beauvoir's influential view employs antithetical poles of reason and intellectual work on the one hand, and the desire to submit oneself to passion on the other. The issues of the nineteenth and early twentieth centuries, such as the connection between a desirable feminine passivity and women's desire for romance, or the separation of "free love" from the institution of marriage, were rejected in the consciousness of new, radical demands for autonomy and power. As a whole, second-wave feminists of the 1970s were more cynical about the possibility of love being "free," in *or* out of marriage, than the first feminists. Instead, most urged women to renounce love wholesale as a form of false consciousness leading to inevitable domination, or else championed romantic lesbian love as a healthier alternative to the heterosexual dilemma (e.g., Rita Mae Brown). Yet some (e.g., Redstockings) see "real" love as a woman's "right," the fulfillment of a need presently subverted by men that must be reclaimed in the future. For these feminist authors, love was a topic as important as sexuality or marriage; not since the mid-1970s has there been such a focused examination of love as a political issue.

Chapter Twenty-five

From The Second Sex (1949)

Simone de Beauvoir

De Beauvoir's classic work is the definitive statement of second-wave feminism on romantic love; she turned the truism that "Love is woman's religion" into a political criticism, going a radical step beyond Goldman in giving women responsibility for their own love lives and providing the theoretical basis for late-twentieth-century feminism's discussion about romance as an important source of the psychological dependence and consequent subordination of women.

The word *love* has by no means the same sense for both sexes, and this is one cause of the serious misunderstandings that divide them. Byron well said: "Man's love is of man's life a thing apart; 'Tis woman's whole existence." Nietzsche expresses the same idea in *The Gay Science:*

> The single word love in fact signifies two different things for man and woman. What woman understands by love is clear enough: it is not only devotion, it is a total gift of body and soul, without reservation, without regard for anything whatever. This unconditional nature of her love is what makes it a *faith,*[1] the only one she has. As for man, if he loves a woman, what he *wants*[1] is that love from her; he is in consequence far from postulating the same sentiment for himself as for woman; if there should be men who also felt that desire for complete abandonment, upon my word, they would not be men.

Men have found it possible to be passionate lovers at certain times in their lives, but there is not one of them who could be called "a great lover";[2] in their most violent transports, they never abdicate completely; even on their knees before a mistress, what they still want is to take possession of her; at the very heart of their lives they remain sovereign subjects; the beloved woman is only one value among others; they wish to integrate her into their existence and not to squander it entirely on her. For woman, on the contrary, to love is to relinquish everything for the benefit of a master. As Cécile Sauvage puts it: "Woman must forget her own personality when she is in love. It is a law of nature. A woman is nonexistent without a master. Without a master, she is a scattered bouquet."

The fact is that we have nothing to do here with laws of nature. It is the difference in their situations that is reflected in the difference men and women show in their conceptions of love. The individual who is a subject, who is himself, if he has the courageous inclination toward transcendence, endeavors to extend his grasp on the world: he is ambitious, he acts. But an inessential creature is incapable of sensing the absolute at the heart of her subjectivity; a being doomed to immanence cannot find self-realization in acts. Shut up in the sphere of the relative, destined to the male from childhood, habituated to seeing in him a superb being whom she cannot possibly equal, the woman who has not repressed her claim to humanity will dream of transcending her being toward one of these superior beings, of amalgamating herself with the sovereign subject. There is no other way out for her than to lose herself, body and soul, in him who is represented to her as the absolute, as the essential. Since she is anyway doomed to dependence, she will prefer to serve a god rather than obey tyrants—parents, husband, or protector. She chooses to desire her enslavement so ardently that it will seem to her the expression of her liberty; she will try to rise above her situation as inessential object by fully accepting it; through her flesh, her feelings, her behavior, she will enthrone him as supreme value and reality: she will humble herself to nothingness before him. Love becomes for her a religion.

As we have seen, the adolescent girl wishes at first to identify herself with males; when she gives that up, she then seeks to share in their masculinity by having one of them in love with her; it is not the individuality of this one or that one which attracts her; she is in love with man in general. "And you, the men I shall love, how I await you!" writes Irène Reweliotty. "How I rejoice to think I shall know you soon: especially You, the first." Of course the male is to belong to the same class and race as hers, for sexual privilege is in play only within this frame. If man is to be a demigod, he must first of all be a human being, and to the colonial officer's daughter the native is not a man. If the young girl gives herself to an "inferior," it is for the reason that she wishes to degrade herself because she believes she is unworthy of love; but normally she is looking for a man who represents male superiority. She is soon to ascertain that many individuals of the favored sex are sadly contingent and earthbound, but at first her presumption is favorable to them; they are called on less to prove their worth than to avoid too gross a disproof of it—which accounts for many mistakes, some of them serious. A naïve young girl is caught by the gleam of virility, and in her eyes male worth is shown, according to circumstances, by physical strength, distinction of manner, wealth, cultivation, intelligence, authority, social status, a military uniform; but what she always wants is for her lover to represent the essence of manhood.

Familiarity is often sufficient to destroy his prestige; it may collapse at the first kiss, or in daily association, or during the wedding night. Love at a distance, however, is only a fantasy, not a real experience. The desire for love becomes a passionate love only when it is carnally realized. Inversely, love can arise as a result of physical intercourse; in this case the sexually dominated woman acquires an exalted view of a man who at first seemed to her quite insignificant.

But it often happens that a woman succeeds in deifying none of the men she knows. Love has a smaller place in woman's life than has often been supposed. Husband, children, home, amusements, social duties, vanity, sexuality, career, are much more important. Most women dream of a *grand amour,* a soul-searing love. They have known substitutes, they have been close to it; it has come to them in partial, bruised, ridiculous, imperfect, mendacious forms; but very few have truly dedicated their lives to it. The *grandes amoureuses* are most often women who have not frittered themselves away in juvenile affairs; they have first accepted the traditional feminine destiny: husband, home, children; or they have known pitiless solitude; or they have banked on some enterprise that has been more or less of a failure. And when they glimpse the opportunity to salvage a disappointing life by dedicating it to some superior person, they desperately give themselves up to this hope. Mlle Aïssé, Juliette Drouet, and Mme d'Agoult were almost thirty when their love-life began, Julie de Lespinasse not far from forty. No other aim in life which seemed worth while was open to them, love was their only way out.

Even if they choose independence, this road seems the most attractive to a majority of women: it is agonizing for a woman to assume responsibility for her life. Even the male, when adolescent, is quite willing to turn to older women for guidance, education, mothering; but customary attitudes, the boy's training, and his own inner imperatives forbid him to content himself in the end with the easy solution of abdication; to him such affairs with older women are only a stage through which he passes. It is man's good fortune—in adulthood as in early childhood—to be obliged to take the most arduous roads, but the surest; it is woman's misfortune to be surrounded by almost irresistible temptations; everything incites her to follow the easy slopes; instead of being invited to fight her own way up, she is told that she has only to let herself slide and she will attain paradises of enchantment. When she perceives that she has been duped by a mirage, it is too late; her strength has been exhausted in a losing venture.

The psychoanalysts are wont to assert that woman seeks the father image in her lover; but it is because he is a man, not because he is a father, that he dazzles the girl child, and every man shares in this magical power. Woman does not long to reincarnate one individual in another, but to reconstruct a situation: that which she experienced as a little girl, under adult protection. She was deeply integrated with home and family, she knew the peace of quasi-passivity. Love will give her back her mother as well as her father, it will give her back her childhood. What she wants to recover is a roof over her head, walls that prevent her from feeling her abandonment in the wide world, authority that protects her against her liberty. This childish drama haunts the love of many women; they are happy to be called "my little girl, my dear child"; men know that the words: "you're just like a little girl," are among those that most surely touch a woman's heart. We have seen that many women suffer in becoming adults; and so a great number remain obstinately "babyish," prolonging their childhood indefinitely in manner and dress. To become like a child again in a man's arms fills their cup with joy. The hackneyed theme: "To feel so little in your arms, my love," recurs again and again in amorous dialogue and in love letters. "Baby mine," croons the lover, the woman calls herself "your little one," and so on. A young woman will write: "When will he come, he who can dominate me?" And when he comes, she will love to sense his manly superiority. A neurotic studied by Janet illustrates this attitude quite clearly:

> All my foolish acts and all the good things I have done have the same cause: an aspiration for a perfect and ideal love in which I can give myself completely, entrust my being to another, God, man, or woman, so superior to me that I will no longer need to think what to do in life or to watch over myself. . . . Someone to obey blindly and with confidence . . . who will bear me up and lead me gently and lovingly toward perfection. How I envy the ideal love of Mary Magdalen and Jesus: to be the ardent disciple of an adored and worthy master; to live and die for him, my idol, to win at last the victory of the Angel over the beast, to rest in his protecting arms, so small, so lost in his loving care, so wholly his that I exist no longer.

Many examples have already shown us that this dream of annihilation is in fact an avid will to exist. In all religions the adoration of God is combined with the devotee's concern with personal salvation; when woman gives herself completely to her idol, she hopes that he will give her at once possession of herself and of the universe he represents. In most cases she asks her lover first of all for the justification, the exaltation, of her ego. Many women do not abandon themselves to love unless they are loved in return; and sometimes the love shown them is enough to arouse their love. The young girl dreamed of herself as seen through men's eyes, and it is in men's eyes that the woman believes she has finally found herself. Cécile Sauvage writes:

> To walk by your side, to step forward with my little feet that you love, to feel them so tiny in their high-heeled shoes with felt tops, makes me love all the love you throw around me. The least movements of my hands in my muff, of my arms, of my face, the tones of my voice, fill me with happiness.

The woman in love feels endowed with a high and undeniable value; she is at last allowed to idolize herself through the love she inspires. She is overjoyed to find in her lover a witness. This is what Colette's *Vagabonde* declares:

> I admit I yielded, in permitting this man to come back the next day, to the desire to keep in him not a lover, not a friend, but an eager spectator of my life and my person. . . . One must be terribly old, Margot said to me one day, to renounce the vanity of living under someone's gaze.

In one of her letters to Middleton Murry, Katherine Mansfield wrote that she had just bought a ravishing mauve corset; she at once added: "Too bad there is no one to *see* it!" There is nothing more bitter than to feel oneself but the flower, the perfume, the treasure, which is the object of no desire: what kind of wealth is it that does not enrich myself and the gift of which no one wants? Love is the developer that brings out in clear, positive detail the dim negative, otherwise as useless as a blank exposure. Through love, woman's face, the curves of her body, her childhood memories, her former tears, her gowns, her accustomed ways, her universe, everything she is, all that belongs to her, escape contingency and become essential: she is a wondrous offering at the foot of the altar of her god.

This transforming power of love explains why it is that men of prestige who know how to flatter feminine vanity will arouse passionate attachments even if they are quite lacking in physical charm. Because of their lofty positions they embody the Law and the Truth: their perceptive powers disclose an unquestionable reality. The woman who finds favor in their sight feels herself transformed into a priceless treasure. D'Annunzio's success was due to this, as Isadora Duncan explains in the introduction to *My Life:*

> When D'Annunzio loves a woman, he lifts her spirit from this earth to the divine region where Beatrice moves and shines. In turn he transforms each woman to a part of the divine essence, he carries her aloft until she believes herself really with Beatrice. . . . He flung over each favorite in turn a shining veil. She rose above the heads of ordinary mortals and walked surrounded by a strange radiance. But when the caprice of the poet ended, this veil vanished, the radiance was eclipsed, and the woman turned again to common clay. . . . To hear oneself praised with that magic peculiar to D'Annunzio is, I imagine, something like the experience of Eve when she heard the voice of the serpent in Paradise. D'Annunzio can make any woman feel that she is the centre of the universe.

Only in love can woman harmoniously reconcile her eroticism and her narcissism; we have seen that these sentiments are opposed in such a manner that it very difficult for a woman to adapt herself to her sexual destiny. To make herself a carnal object, the prey of another, is in contradiction to her self-worship: it seems to her that embraces blight and sully her body or degrade her soul. Thus it is that some women take refuge in frigidity, thinking that in this way they can preserve the integrity of the ego. Others dissociate animal pleasure and lofty sentiment. In one of Stekel's cases the patient was frigid with her respected and eminent husband and, after his death, with an equally superior man, a great musician, whom she sincerely loved. But in an almost casual encounter with a rough, brutal forester she found complete physical satisfaction, "a wild intoxication followed by indescribable disgust" when she thought of her lover. Stekel remarks that "for many women a descent into animality is the necessary condition for orgasm." Such women see in physical love a debasement incompatible with esteem and affection.

But for other women, on the contrary, only the esteem, affection, and admiration of the man can eliminate the sense of abasement. They will not yield to a man unless they believe they are deeply loved. A woman must have a considerable amount of cynicism, indifference, or pride to regard physical relations as an exchange of pleasure by which each partner benefits equally. As much as woman—and perhaps more— man revolts against anyone who attempts to exploit him sexually;[3] but it is woman who generally feels that her partner is using her as an instrument. Nothing but high admiration can compensate for the humiliation of an act that she considers a defeat.

We have seen that the act of love requires of woman profound self-abandonment; she bathes in a passive languor; with closed eyes, anonymous, lost, she feels as if borne by waves, swept away in a storm, shrouded in darkness: darkness of the flesh, of the womb, of the grave. Annihilated, she becomes one with the Whole, her ego is abolished. But when the man moves from her, she finds herself back on earth, on a bed, in the light; she again has a name, a face: she is one vanquished, prey, object.

This is the moment when love becomes a necessity. As when the child, after weaning, seeks the reassuring gaze of its parents, so must a woman feel, through the man's loving contemplation, that she is, after all, still at one with the Whole from which her flesh is now painfully detached. She is seldom wholly satisfied even if she has felt the orgasm, she is not set completely free from the spell of her flesh; her desire continues in the form of affection. In giving her pleasure, the man increases her attachment, he does not liberate her. As for him, he no longer desires her; but she will not pardon this momentary indifference unless he has dedicated to her a timeless and absolute emotion. Then the immanence of the moment is transcended; hot memories are no regret, but a treasured delight; ebbing pleasure becomes hope and promise; enjoyment is justified; woman can gloriously accept her sexuality because she transcends it; excitement, pleasure, desire are no longer a state, but a benefaction; her body is no longer an object: it is a hymn, a flame.

Then she can yield with passion to the magic of eroticism; darkness becomes light; the loving woman can open her eyes, can look upon the man who loves her and whose gaze glorifies her; through him nothingness becomes fullness of being, and being is transmuted into worth; she no longer sinks in a sea of shadows, but is borne up on wings, exalted to the skies. Abandon becomes sacred ecstasy. When she *receives* her beloved, woman is dwelt in, visited, as was the Virgin by the Holy Ghost, as is the believer by the Host. This is what explains the obscene resemblance between pious hymns and erotic songs; it is not that mystical love always has a sexual character, but that the sexuality of the woman in love is tinged with mysticism. " 'My God, my adored one, my lord and master"—the same words fall from the lips of the saint on her knees and the loving woman on her bed; the one offers her flesh to the thunderbolt of Christ, she stretches out her hands to receive the stigmata of the Cross, she calls for the burning presence of divine Love; the other, also, offers and awaits: thunderbolt, dart, arrow, are incarnated in the male sex organ. In both women there is the same dream, the childhood dream, the mystic dream, the dream of love: to attain supreme existence through losing oneself in the other.

NOTES

1. Nietzsche's italics.

2. In the sense that a woman may sometimes be called *"une grande amoureuse."*—Tr.

3. Lawrence, for example, in *Lady Chatterley's Lover,* expresses through Mellors his aversion for women who make a man an instrument of pleasure.

Chapter Twenty-six

From The Dialectic of Sex (1970)

Shulamith Firestone

Firestone's was the most influential of the radical feminist views in the 1970s that "men can't love," and that an entire change in male-female relations (the sex-class system) would have to occur before men and women could have real love. Unequal partners could not love in any valid way, she argued in The Dialectic of Sex.

A book on radical feminism that did not deal with love would be a political failure. For love, perhaps even more than childbearing, is the pivot of women's oppression today. I realize this has frightening implications: Do we want to get rid of love?

The panic felt at any threat to love is a good clue to its political significance. Another sign that love is central to any analysis of women or sex psychology is its omission from culture itself, its relegation to "personal life." (And whoever heard of logic in the bedroom?) Yes, it is portrayed in novels, even metaphysics, but in them it is described, or better, recreated, not analyzed. Love has never been *understood*, though it may have been fully *experienced*, and that experience communicated.

There is reason for this absence of analysis: *Women and Love are underpinnings. Examine them and you threaten the very structure of culture.*

The tired question "What were women doing while men created masterpieces?" deserves more than the obvious reply: Women were barred from culture, exploited in their role of mother. Or its reverse: Women had no need for paintings since they created children. Love is tied to culture in much deeper ways than that. Men were thinking, writing, and creating, because women were pouring their energy into those men; women are not creating culture because they are preoccupied with love.

That women live for love and men for work is a truism. Freud was the first to attempt to ground this dichotomy in the individual psyche: the male child, sexually rejected by the first person in his attention, his mother, "sublimates" his "libido"— his reservoir of sexual (life) energies—into long term projects, in the hope of gaining love in a more generalized form; thus he displaces his need for love into a need for recognition. This process does not occur as much in the female: most women never stop seeking direct warmth and approval.

There is also much truth in the clichés that "behind every man there is a woman," and that "women are the power behind [read: voltage in] the throne." (Male) culture was built on the love of women, and at their expense. Women provided the substance of those male masterpieces; and for millennia they have done the work, and suffered the costs, of one-way emotional relationships the benefits of which went to men and to the work of men. So if women are a parasitical class living off, and at the margins of, the male economy, the reverse too is true: *(Male) culture was (and is) parasitical, feeding on the emotional strength of women without reciprocity.*

Moreover, we tend to forget that this culture is not universal, but rather sectarian, presenting only half the spectrum. The very structure of culture itself, as we shall see, is saturated with the sexual polarity, as well as being in every degree run by, for, and in the interests of male society. But while the male half is termed all of culture, men have not forgotten there is a female "emotional" half: They live it on the sly. As the result of their battle to reject the female in themselves (the Oedipus Complex as we have explained it) they are unable to take love seriously as a cultural matter; but they can't do without it altogether. Love is the underbelly of (male) culture just as love is the weak spot of every man, bent on proving his virility in that large male world of "travel and adventure." Women have always known how men need love, and how they deny this need. Perhaps this explains the peculiar contempt women so universally feel for men ("men are so dumb"), for they can see their men are posturing in the outside world.

How does this phenomenon "love" operate? Contrary to popular opinion, love is not altruistic. The initial attraction is based on curious admiration (more often today, envy and resentment) for the self-possession, the integrated unity, of the other and a wish to become part of this Self in some way (today, read: intrude or take over), to become important to that psychic balance. The self-containment of the other creates desire (read: a challenge); admiration (envy) of the other becomes a wish to incorporate (possess) its qualities. A clash of selves follows in which the individual attempts to fight off the growing hold over him of the other. Love is the final opening up to (or, surrender to the dominion of) the other. The lover demonstrates to the beloved how he himself would like to be treated. ("I tried so hard to make him fall in love with me that I fell in love with him myself.") Thus love is the height of selfishness: the self attempts to enrich itself through the absorption of another being. Love is being psychically wide-open to another. It is a situation of total emotional vulnerability. Therefore it must be not only the incorporation of the other, but an *exchange* of selves. Anything short of a mutual exchange will hurt one or the other party.

There is nothing inherently destructive about this process. A little healthy selfishness would be a refreshing change. Love between two equals would be an enrichment, each enlarging himself through the other: instead of being one, locked in the cell of himself with only his own experience and view, he could participate in the existence of another—an extra window on the world. This accounts for the bliss that successful lovers experience: Lovers are temporarily freed from the burden of isolation that every individual bears.

But bliss in love is seldom the case: For every successful contemporary love experience, for every short period of enrichment, there are ten destructive love experiences, post-love "downs" of much longer duration—often resulting in the destruction of the individual, or at least an emotional cynicism that makes it difficult or impossible ever to love again. Why should this be so, if it is not actually inherent in the love process itself? . . .

I submit that love is essentially a much simpler phenomenon—it becomes complicated, corrupted, or obstructed by *an unequal balance of power.* We have seen that love demands a mutual vulnerability or it turns destructive: the destructive effects of love occur only in a context of inequality. But because sexual inequality has remained a constant—however its *degree* may have varied—the corruption "romantic" love became characteristic of love between the sexes. . . .

Romantic idealization is partially responsible, at least on the part of men, for a peculiar characteristic of "falling" in love: the change takes place in the lover almost independently of the character of the love object. Occasionally the lover, though beside himself, sees with another rational part of his faculties that, objectively speaking, the one he loves isn't worth all this blind devotion; but he is helpless to act on this, "a slave to love." More often he fools himself entirely. But others can see what is happening ("How on earth he could love her is beyond me!"). This idealization occurs much less frequently on the part of women, as is borne out by Reik's clinical studies. A man must idealize one woman over the rest in order to justify his descent to a lower caste. Women have no such reason to idealize men—in fact, when one's life depends on one's ability to "psych" men out, such idealization may actually be dangerous—though a fear of male power in general may carry over into relationships with individual men, appearing to be the same phenomenon. But though women know to be inauthentic this male "falling in love," all women, in one way or another, require proof of it from men before they can allow themselves to love (genuinely, in their case) in return. For this idealization process acts to artificially equalize the two parties, a minimum precondition for the development of an uncorrupted love—we have seen that love requires a mutual vulnerability that is impossible to achieve in an unequal power situation. *Thus "falling in love" is no more than the process of alteration of male vision—through idealization, mystification, glorification—that renders void the woman's class inferiority.*

However, the woman knows that this idealization, which she works so hard to produce, is a lie, and that it is only a matter of time before he "sees through her." Her life is a hell, vacillating between an all-consuming need for male love and approval to raise her from her class subjection, to persistent feelings of inauthenticity when she does achieve his love. Thus her whole identity hangs in the balance of her love life. She is allowed to love herself only if a man finds her worthy of love.

But if we could eliminate the political context of love between the sexes, would we not have some degree of idealization remaining in the love process itself? I think so. For the process occurs in the same manner whoever the love choice: the lover "opens up" to the other. Because of this fusion of egos, in which each sees and cares about the other as a new self, the beauty/character of the beloved, perhaps hidden to outsiders under layers of defenses, is revealed. "I wonder what she sees in him," then, means not only, "She is a fool, blinded with romanticism," but, "Her love has lent her x-ray vision. Perhaps we are missing something." (Note that this phrase is most commonly used about women. The equivalent phrase about *men's* slavery to love is more often something like, "She has him wrapped around her finger," she has him so "snowed" that he is the last one to see through her.) Increased sensitivity to the real, if hidden, values in the other, however, is not "blindness" or "idealization" but is, in fact, deeper vision. It is only the *false* idealization we have described above that is responsible for the destruction. Thus it is not the process of love itself that is at fault, but its *political,* i.e., unequal *power* context: the who, why, when and where of it is what makes it now such a holocaust. . . .

Simone de Beauvoir said it: "The word love has by no means the same sense for both sexes, and this is one cause of the serious misunderstandings which divide them." Above I have illustrated some of the traditional differences between men and women in love that come up so frequently in parlor discussions of the "double standard," where it is generally agreed: That women are monogamous, better at loving, possessive, "clinging," more interested in (highly involved) "relationships" than in sex per se, and they confuse affection with sexual desire. That men are interested in nothing but a screw (Wham, bam, thank you M'am!), or else romanticize the woman ridiculously; that once sure of her, they become notorious philanderers, never satisfied; that they mistake sex for emotion. All this bears out what we have discussed—the difference in the psychosexual organizations of the two sexes, determined by the first relationship to the mother.

I draw three conclusions based on these differences:

1) That men can't love. (Male hormones? Women traditionally expect and accept an emotional invalidism in men that they would find intolerable in a woman.)

2) That women's "clinging" behavior is necessitated by their objective social situation.

3) That this situation has not changed significantly from what it ever was.

Chapter Twenty-seven

From The Female Eunuch (1971)

Germaine Greer

Greer opposes the false consciousness of romantic love to an authentic eroticism for women. Her ideas about women's obsession with love and the humiliations they suffer as a result of its "cheap ideology" were not new, but her vivid writing style and the enormous popularity of her book The Female Eunuch *brought them to a wider public for the first time.*

In love, as *in* pain, *in* shock, *in* trouble.

Thus love is a state, presumably a temporary state, an aberration from the norm.

The outward symptoms of this state are sleeplessness, distraction, loss of appetite, alternations of euphoria and depression, as well as starry eyes (as in fever), and agitation.

The principal explanation of the distraction, which leads to the mislaying of possessions, confusion, forgetfulness and irresponsibility, is the overriding obsession with the love object, which may only have been seen from a distance on one occasion. The love object occupies the thoughts of the person diagnosed "in love" all the time despite the probability that very little is actually known about it. To it are ascribed all qualities considered by the obsessed as good, regardless of whether the object in question possesses those qualities in any degree. Expectations are set up which no human being could fulfill. Thus the object chosen plays a special role in relation to the ego of the obsessed, who decided that he or she is the *right* or the *only* person for him. In the case of a male this notion may sanction a degree of directly aggressive behavior either in pursuing the object or driving off competition. In the case of a female, no aggressive behavior can be undertaken and the result is more likely to be brooding, inexplicable bad temper, a dependence upon the telephone and gossip with other women about the love object, or even acts of apparent rejection and scorn to bring herself to the object's attention.

Formerly this condition was believed to afflict the individual acutely from the first contact with the object:

Whoever loved that loved not at first sight?[1]

However, the sudden and acute nature of the affliction seems to have been a characteristic of the illicit form, and since obsession has been made the basis of marriage, more gradual chronic states have also been recognized. The cause of the malady was supposed to have been the infective glance from the eyes of the love object, which was commonly referred to metaphorically as Cupid's arrow striking the beholder to the heart and leaving a wound which rankled and would not heal. In more extreme cases of destructive passion even more farfetched pseudoexplanations were invented, like Phaedra's belief that she was being specifically tormented by Venus:

> Ce n'est plus qu'une ardeur dans mes veines cachée:
> C'est Vénus toute entière a sa proie attachée.[2]

Such imagery makes great use of images of burning, implying both the heat of lust and the chafing of frustration. Ironically it was supposed that any attempt to control this condition, either by avoiding the object which caused it or seeking to exert the will over the passions, has the effect of banking a fire, which is to increase it so that eventually it leaps forth more violently than before. "Love will find a way. Love laughs at Locksmiths." Thus to "fall in love" was a terrible misfortune, which inevitably involved the break-up of any stable menage and self-immolation in irrational ardor. Racine used a French equivalent to describe love, both as an evil and an illness, by calling it *un mal.* The belief that love is a disease, or at least as haphazard and damaging as disease, survives in terms like *lovesick,* and in the imagery of popular corn.

Some of the longest lived popular song themes make direct use of the traditional imagery. The Muzak which dulls the apprehensions of tea-drinkers in fashionable hotels and thrills through the pump-rooms in faded resorts is still based upon the staple of the great songs of the thirties and forties. The words may be less well-known than the tunes, especially as Irving Berlin and his ilk are understandably loth to allow them to be quoted; nevertheless it is a rare tea-drinker or spa visitor who cannot croon absently along about moon and June. These "classics" are as overstuffed with references to hearts going thumpety-thump, eyes dazzled with starlight, blinded with the smoke and fumes from the furnace of passion which is the heart, as any of the extravagant poems of the quattrocento-secentisti. Lovers don't slip, they aren't pushed, they fall, hopefully if pathetically, right into the middle of a warm caress. They feel very strange but nice, afflicted it would seem by a pleasant ache, or even rubbed down with a velvet glove. They sigh, they sorrow and they get dizzy spells, or perhaps they do not, but then they just love to look in their beloved's eyes.

The supreme irony must be when the bored housewife whiles away her duller tasks, half-consciously intoning the otherwise very forgettable words of some pulp lovesong. How many of them stop to assess the real consequences of the fact that "all who love are blind" or just how much they have to blame that "something here inside" for? What songs do you sing, one wonders when your heart is no longer on fire and smoke no longer mercifully blinds you to the banal realities of your situation? (But of course there are no songs for that.)

Another song ironically denies that the singer is in love because he does not sigh or sorrow, or get dizzy spells. Are we so very far after all from Romeo's description of his conventionalized passion for a woman he did not know, who was utterly indifferent to his advances?

> Love is a smoke rais'd with the fume of sighs;
> Being purg'd a fire sparkling in lovers' eyes;
> Being vex'd, a sea nourish'd with lovers' tears.
> What is it else? a madness most discreet,
> A choking gall, and a preserving sweet.[3]

This attitude, which is an eminently consistent way of regarding adulterous passion, survives in the imagery of the state of "in love" as the proper one for spouses. It is still ironically maintained for example that love is blind, just as Cupid was represented in the courtly love tradition as blindfolded. However, this blindness is usually taken to mean only the refusal of the lover to see his beloved in any way realistically, and especially to discern his faults.

The impotence of will and rationality to deal with this mania is recognized in the common terms "madly," "wildly," "deliriously," "head-over-heels" in love, while it would be oxymoronic to claim to be gently, reliably or sensibly in love. There is some disagreement about the self-immunizing propensities of the disease, for some claim that one is only ever really in love once in a lifetime, others that it is better the second time around, others that the first time is the only genuine manifestation, still others that they fall in love every week or even every day.

> Sex is a momentary itch,
> Love never lets you go.[4]

It is an essential quality of the disease that it is incurable; this has meant that in cases where young people in love must be weaned of each other because they are too young or ill-assorted the only method is to deny that they are so afflicted. The "love" must be proved to be false on the grounds, say, that it cannot happen to people so young . . .

I can remember Nat King Cole topping the charts (sometime during my unspeakably dreary teens) with a heart-rendingly bland number about a couple surrounded by enemies forever trying to tell them they were too young to reallee bee in luv, because love was only a word that they had heard (like all the other concepts that they knew). The argument of the killjoys was manifestly invalid, for if they were to try the truth of the notion of love by experience, then presumably they would have to go ahead and love. However invalid the argument, the counter-conclusion of the song, that their love will last though years may go, hardly seems to constitute relevant refutation.

As love cannot actually be demonstrated to be present, so it cannot be demonstrated to be genuine. The advantage of denying its existence in a particular case is that the denial cannot be refuted, although, as the song insinuates, it is likely to give rise to an enduring pose of young love persecuted by the world, an Aucassin and Nicolette fantasy which endures chiefly to refute the critics.

Methods of diagnosis of this condition vary. External observers will base a judgment upon observation of agitation, impairment of concentration and efficiency, or an undue preoccupation with the love object expressed in curiosity or speculation. However, it must be noticed that such observers have a vested interest in the detection of love affairs because of the particular voyeurist pleasures they afford, and often precipitate such situations. "All the world loves a lover." The sufferer may diagnose himself as having contracted the disease because of the intensity of his reactions when the love object is expected or in sight or fails to make an anticipated appearance. He will also suffer the omnipresence of a mental image of the beloved in dreams, at meals, during completely irrelevant discussions. If the love remains unrequited the symptoms either fade gradually or become transferred to a new object or intensify until they become agonizing. Which of these alternatives ensues is largely dependent upon the attitude of the sufferer to his affliction. The greater the degree of masochism and the inherent doubt of competence in actually prosecuting a love-affair, the more he will resign himself to isolation and barren suffering. The unconscious love object then has to bear the brunt of responsibility for his self-induced condition and may be accused of cruelty or trifling with a good person's heart. If the lover enacts some outrage upon the object to revenge himself for its cruelty, he will find that it is treated with special consideration by the lawmakers who allow a special status to those who are "in love," especially if the object be considered unworthy. If his passion is denied this privilege, it will be justified by refusing it the status of "love" and relegating it to mere vengeful lust or some such.

Generally it is considered proper for women not to arrive in this state of obsession unless induced thereto by a man. Unfortunately the presentation of the state of being in love as a desirable and indeed consummate human experience is so powerful that adolescent girls seem to spend much more time in its throes than their male counterparts. However, the social fiction is kept up by the popular imagery of girls responding to male wooing and the contagion of love. The acid test of the experience is the astonishingly potent kiss. "It was my first kiss, and it filled me with such wild thundering rapture. I had been crazy about Mark so long, and now, with our kiss, I knew that he loved me too!"[5]

Love is *being crazy about someone* (Oh Ah'm jes' wil' about Harree!) and the extraordinary effects of the contact of the lip with lip and tongue with tongue bring on wild thundering rapture. However, in the case quoted the love was spurious although its symptoms were identical with the genuine ones: Betsy has just been kissed by Mark, "the best athlete in school and the wealthiest boy in town! Gosh, I am lucky," but she has a better friend in Hugh, the boy-next-door, who warns her about Mark and his fast, arrogant ways. In the second encounter Hugh plucks up courage to make a declaration and sweeps Betsy into his arms. . . . "His kiss set my heart to pounding and a feeling swept over me that I couldn't name . . . a feeling that brought a carpet of clouds under my feet . . ." This, it appears, is the real thing, or so the conclusion tells us: "I had made a mistake and had that for comparison! Love is not always what it seems, and kisses can be false!"[6]

The sensations caused by the two kisses are not genuinely distinguishable. Both are described in terms more appropriate to the abnormal experiences of the organism under drugs—pounding of the heart, roaring in the ears, and cottony legs; in fact *love* is also the drug which makes sexuality palatable in popular mythology. Sex without love is considered a crude animal evacuation: with love it becomes ecstatic and transcendental. Obviously it is meant to perform an autosuggestive function in affecting cortical sexual responses, and it probably does. The fact still remains that Betsy can only distinguish between the two kisses on some kind of political ground: it is in fact desirable for Betsy to marry into her own class, and one would not object if the policy were openly stated instead of cloaked in the mumbo-jumbo of the comparison between two identical kisses. In both cases the terms of reference are more apt to hallucination than to motivation for marriage; the emphasis is all on egotistic response, not at all on communication between the persons indulging in such osculation.

This confusion typifies all literature on the diagnosis of true love. Sentimental bias militates against the subjugating of love to any rational or willful control, while anarchic passion is regarded with deep suspicion. Generally, as in the above sample, the most appropriate match must be transmogrified into the most gratifying. The real difference between true and false love, which are both compounds of lust and fantasy, is that true love leads to marriage. Provided it does that, a significant downgrade in the level of excitement is tolerated but not admitted. Adultery and fornication are still more exciting than marriage, but our culture is committed to maintaining the contrary. We are actually committed to the belief that this mania is an essential precondition to marriage.... IS IT A SIN TO MARRY BEFORE FALLING IN LOVE? was the banner of an advertisement for Taylor Caldwell's *Let Love Come Last.*[7] Paradoxically love sanctifies both marriage and illicit encounters. "Love conquers all."

The irrationality of love is fondly celebrated in those pulp stories of women who gave up cold career and ambition for the warmth of a husband's pressing love. Efficient career woman X holds out against junior buyer Y's love for her for months until he acts cold and she gets jealous, or until he has an accident and she rides in the ambulance with him. After all "When love calls—who can really deny it?"[8]

Love is here either compared to a necessary human function (*cf.* Nature calls!) or to a person summoning to a pleasant duty, another survival of older forms of analogue. Nevertheless the crises in such a story were aimed to reveal to the unconscious sufferer that she was in fact in love, just as the leper finds out by pouring boiling water over his numb feet. Some such testing is allowable, and even prescribed for those who doubt that they are really truly in love. "Love is never really love until it is reality-tested." Trial separations can be useful in proving the durability of an obsession. Some experts in this kind of homeopathy have devised questionnaires which the patient must apply for himself, a fairly unreliable procedure at best. The questions may range from "If he left you, could you bear to go on living?" to "Do you find his breath unpleasant?" A more common procedure is to advise the lovelorn, a term which has sinister connotations if only anyone ever understood it, what love is *not,* which is no guide to what it *is.*

Love is not mere thrill or passing pleasure. It is not escape from loneliness or boredom, nor is it a comfortable adjustment for practical convenience or mutual benefit. It is not a one-way feeling, and it can't be made two-way by wishing or willing it so.

The adolescent lover following this rule of thumb may be excused for feeling a little confusion. Certainly, many poets and others have burnt with one-way love; the establishment of parity in love is quite impossible. It is impossible to know if pleasure is passing before it is past, and if it is not an escape from loneliness and boredom, or a comfortable mutual arrangement, there would seem to be little point in setting it up as a desideratum at all. The positive description supplied by the same author is not less daunting:

Love is many things. It's a little child's satisfied response to attention and tenderness and it's also the older child's affectionate curiosity. It's the playfulness of adolescents and their romantic flight of imagination. Then again it is the earnest, mature devotion of mature marriage . . .

Love is delicate, elusive and above all spontaneous. It thrives on honesty and sincerity and naturalness combined with mutual responsibleness and concern. At the beginning it just "happens" but to flourish and endure it requires the full capacity for giving of the open heart and soul.[9]

This is one man's attempt to counteract the dangerous mythology of falling in love as a basis for marriage, but it is not convincing. Such a vague but deeply committed view never inspired a single love poem. The lure of the psychedelic experience of love which makes the world a beautiful place, puts stars in your eyes, sweeps you off your feet, thumps you in the breast with Cupid's bird-bolt is not lessened by such bad prose. The magical mania still persists as a powerful compulsion in our imagination. "Was he very much in love with her?" the second wife asks of her dead rival. "He was crazy about her," they say of the man who killed his faithless wife, and the jury recommends mercy. "I knew he was a murderer but I was in love with him," says the lady who married the man in the condemned cell. Love, love, love—all the wretched cant of it, masking egotism, lust, masochism, fantasy under a mythology of sentimental postures, a welter of self-induced miseries and joys, blinding and masking the essential personalities in the frozen gestures of courtship, in the kissing and the dating and the desire, the compliments and the quarrels which vivify its barrenness. "We were not made to idolize one another, yet the whole strain of courtship is little more than rank idolatry."[10] It may seem that young men no longer court with the elaborate servilities that Mary Astell, the seventeenth-century feminist, was talking about, but the mystic madness of love provides the same spurious halo, and builds up the same expectations which dissipate as soon as the new wife becomes capable of "calmly considering her Condition." In the twentieth century a feminist like Ti-Grace Atkinson makes a similar point more crudely: "Love is the victim's response to the rapist."[11]

Not all love is comprehended in such a description, but the sickening obsession which thrills the nervous frames of the heroines of great love affairs whether in cheap "romance" comic-papers or in hardback novels of passionate wooing is just that. Women must recognize in the cheap ideology of *being in love* the essential persuasion to take an irrational and self-destructive step. Such obsession has nothing to do with love, for love is not swoon, possession or mania, but "a cognitive act, indeed the only way to grasp the innermost core of personality."[12]

NOTES

1. Christopher Marlowe, *Hero and Leander,* 1. 178.

2. Jean Racine, *Phèdre,* I, iii, 11, 151–2.

3. William Shakespeare, *Romeo and Juliet,* I, i, 11. 196–200.

4. Kingsley Amis, "An Ever-fixed Mark," *Erotic Poetry,* ed. William Cole (New York, 1963), p. 444.

5. *Sweethearts,* Vol. II, No. 57, December, 1960, "Kisses Can Be False."

6. *Ibid.*

7. Quoted in Albert Ellis, *The Folklore of Sex* (New York, 1961), p. 209.

8. *Sweethearts* (*loc. cit.*), "When Love Calls."

9. *Datebook's Complete Guide to Dating,* edited by Art Unger (New Jersey, 1960), p. 89.

10. Mary Astell, *An Essay in Defence of the Female Sex* (London, 1721), p. 55.

11. Ti-Grace Atkinson, *vide infra* "Rebellion," quoted from an article by Irma Kurtz in the *Sunday Times Magazine,* September 14, 1969.

12. O. Schwarz, *The Psychology of Sex* (London, 1957), p. 20.

Chapter Twenty-eight

In Favor of True Love over Settling (1975);
Going for What We Really Want (1975)

Colette Price ("Joyce O'Brien"); Kathie Sarachild

Unlike Firestone, the Redstockings, an important radical feminist group active in the 1970s, did not reject love between men and women; on the contrary, they saw love as "going for what we want, our own true desires," analogous to the importance of validating women's sexuality.

In Favor of True Love over Settling

Joyce O'Brien

Two years ago, married and with a young child, I fell in love with another man. Within a very short space of time I knew I had to leave my husband; the relationship with him had suddenly become intolerable. I also knew the love affair was about to come to an end. Things happened very quickly. I have never been more directly, precisely, absolutely in touch with my feelings and I acted on every one of them. Since, I have been trying to figure out what happened—but first let me tell you about my mother.

My mother and I were never really close. We liked each other, sort of had a basic understanding. I had been liking her better though since I joined Women's Liberation and she seemed to be responding to the liking. I was in a really bad state after fully executing the above mentioned instant upheaval. I was genuinely in despair but I also had this other, more complicated feeling of growing strength, first because I felt absolutely justified about everything I had done—I felt I did what I had to do; second, because I was free, I was starting all over again. Anyway, she called, my mother. I hadn't planned on telling her anything, or not much anyhow. This required

Colette Price [Joyce O'Brien, pseud.], "In Favor of True Love over Settling," in Redstockings, *Feminist Revolution* (New Paltz, NY: Redstockings, 1975), 110–12. Kathie Sarachild, "Going for What We Really Want," in Redstockings, *Feminist Revolution*, 145–47. Sarachild's article was first presented as a speech at the Women's Strike March, August 26, 1971. Both pieces, as well as writings from the 1960s rebirth years of feminism and by current women's liberation organizers, are available from Redstockings Women's Liberation Archives for Action, P.O. Box 2625, Gainesville, FL 32602-2625. Redstockings' catalog is available online at www.afn.org/~redstock.

some tact, budding friendship or not. More, I'm afraid, than I could muster up at that moment.

"Ma," I found myself saying; "men stink."

"What's the matter, Joyce?" she asked, kindly enough.

"Oh, I don't know," I said hesitating—my mind really too muddled to carry off any pretenses. "I left Paul," I said. "I fell in love with someone else and left Paul."

"Oh no, Joyce," she began. "Are you sure that's what you want . . . ?"

"That's not all." I interrupted. "The someone else . . . he left me. I feel rotten, Ma. I really loved the guy." There was a silence.

"Well, Joyce," she said rather warmly, "you know sometimes these things just don't work out. I was very much in love with someone once and that didn't work out either."

"You were?" I said, actually rather shocked. I told her all the bad news—at once—and she's telling me she was in love once and she's not talking about my father. "With whom?" I asked, suddenly overwhelmed with curiosity by the story of my mother's love affair.

"Oh, it was a long time ago," she said. "I was 25. He was a lawyer, a brilliant, up and coming lawyer. I fell in love with him almost immediately."

"It sounds familiar," I said.

"We went together nearly five years."

"What happened?" I asked.

"I don't really know," she said. "He had a very sick mother, he never seemed quite ready . . . willing . . . to make the necessary moves."

"It lasted five years?"

"Yes, nearly."

"Did you sleep with him?" I asked, carried away with the openness of the conversation.

"Joyce, of course not," she said, reverting for a second to her middle-American Catholic tone. "Oh, Joyce, did you . . . ?"

"Of course I did," I said, feeling rather confident that the change in sexual mores from her generation to mine was certainly a change for the better.

"Well, maybe that's why it didn't work out," she suddenly offered, beginning a familiar speech about how men don't respect women they can have too easily.

"Ma," I interrupted to remind her, "you didn't and I did and neither of us got the man."

"Yes, I guess that's true," she said thoughtfully. "You know, Joyce," she continued in the same thoughtful tone, "he never married, to this day he never married. I just couldn't wait for him any longer," she said, almost apologetically. "I was 30 years old, which was even harder to be then than it is now. I met your father; he was nice, ambitious. I didn't love him, it's true, but there was a future—I grew to love him."

Was my mother telling me she didn't love my father? She was in love once, it didn't seem possible, so she settled for my father. Was she admitting to me that she settled for my father? Wow!

You know, I don't know why I left my husband. I mean I know why I left, it's just that when I think about it, it doesn't seem to make sense. My marriage was not in bad shape. Well, I didn't think about it much, but had I, I never would have said we were headed for trouble. I do remember that disturbing conversation I had with Carol, though. God, it must have been three years ago now. "Why did you marry your husband?" she asked in the course of talking about something or other.

"Oh, I don't know," I said casually, "I was young, there was a strong attraction, but if I had to do it over again things would certainly be different." I never understood what made me say that—for weeks I remained in disbelief that I really did say it. I had never verbalized that my marriage involved any sort of compromise before, much less that things could be done differently. Like my mother. Had she told anyone before what she told me?

But Paul and I were going along as we always had. If there was trouble brewing wouldn't I have known about it? Wouldn't he? You know, I left him painlessly. I felt nothing, really nothing—with the slight exception of a few brief moments when, with all his things packed, he moved toward the door and walked out. I responded to the physical act of his leaving. The presence of a body—now the absence of a body. You're a cold, empty, shallow person he told me. I couldn't sympathize, not even when I repeated it myself a few weeks later to my now departing lover. Was I in a daze for five years? No, my mother said it: "settling". She forced me to admit it. I was settling. If my mother had told me what she had at any other time I don't think I'd have understood. I think I might have felt sorry for her. I might have condescendingly felt badly that my mother was forced to settle. At the moment I am more than appreciative for that bit of truth—it allows me to look at my own settlings. My mother fell in love and, finding it impossible, moved toward settling. I came from settling, fell in love, and found it incredible that it was even possible for the brief time it was possible. I remember the sensation—all my old, long-forgotten desires swarming back to me, all my hopes and dreams and ideals about what relationships could encompass. Did I really stop believing in the possibility of love? I believed in it once, I remember.

Things seemed so hard when I was younger. They seem hard now, too, but I understand them better and that helps. All the pressures. I never said I felt pressured to date, but I did. I never said I felt pressured to marry but I did. Dating was just such a burden. My dating ratio was 50 to 1. For every one exciting escapade I had, I had to sit through 50 boring, smiling, lovely times. "Good night," I would say, "I had a lovely time," and run through the front door.

Dating boys who were at times hard to tolerate was one thing; feeling obliged to marry some of them because you went too far was something else. Sex was a *big* problem. Periodically I would get heavily entangled, as we used to call it, with some guy and then feel obliged to marry him. It's not that these guys were proposing, mind you, it's just that I felt obliged—it was probably my way of working off the guilt of the escapades, although I do remember some guys who felt I should feel obliged.

I would make up lists during these times of heavy entanglement. In one column— Reasons Why I Feel Obliged to Marry; in the other—Reasons Why I Feel I Have the Right to Live My Own Life. Once when I really felt trapped and it looked like the inevitable might come to pass, I planned a series of activities which I hoped might possibly keep me busy for the rest of my life. At least, I thought, I won't be bored. That marriage never came to pass, but my best friend wasn't so lucky. She wound up quitting school at 16 to marry the guy she went too far with.

There may not be many good things left to say about the "free love" era after men got through defining it, but it still remains a better alternative than enforced marriage. It's true I settled for Paul, but, somehow, at the time, it seemed like a lot less settling than I had been doing—and probably was. Did I believe that love was possible then, with all of that? I'm not sure now—did I stop believing it or just get tired? Either way, though, you stop fighting, stop struggling. I remember feeling I just wanted to get this love thing over with; I was anxious to get on with life.

So, in fact, I didn't leave Paul for another man, or rather just because of another man; I knew the love affair was over with before the separation was even proposed. I was settled with Paul. I left because I fell in love. Because somehow I got back in touch with what I really wanted. If love was possible, why not put up a fight to try and get it? It's powerful stuff, this love thing.

I wonder if I can really give the credit to my lover, though. True, he put me in touch with it, but he turned out not to be such a firm believer himself. He had the convictions, but lacked the courage. I should credit Women's Liberation.

My own consciousness had been changing in the movement over the last five years. It allowed me to look more honestly at my situation—my group did anyhow, so I could see clearly what I had and what I didn't have, what I wanted and what I didn't want. Clearly if a women's revolution is possible, why not love?

I connected when my mother acknowledged her compromise. To get back in touch with what you really want, first you have to admit you don't have it. The conflict which came from that admission now seemed less draining than the compromise. No, not just less draining—invigorating because you could go out and search for it. Suddenly it just made absolute sense that faced with the alternatives of fighting for what you really want, a fight you might lose or you might win, or settling for something you don't really want, a situation in which there can be no winning, it was a lot smarter to pick the fight.

It's been awhile now since I got back in touch with what I really want. And clearly knowing what you really want and trying to get it are two entirely separate dilemmas. I'm doing my share of settling. I want to remain alive long enough to continue the fight. I have to live my life *now,* and I want to do it in the best way possible with the most I can get from life. But I'm holding onto my dreams, too. I'm staying in touch with what I really want so I'll be sure to recognize it when it comes along. My settlings now are different, they're done with my full awareness, they're done always in comparison to how this measures up to my dreams. I keep my eye on the target though I might shuffle around it. You don't feel guilty about these settlings. You know they're a matter of survival.

I think my mother has trouble with that sometimes. She seems to put up with a lot more from my father at times than I calculate she has to. I wonder if she feels guilty for not having loved him and therefore tries to make up for it in these little ways. Well, maybe it's a way out idea; they've been married for a long time now. But it's an interesting thought if not overly sentimental to think that someone so understands what a precious exchange love is, that if it were lacking, they would feel obliged to try very hard in other ways to make up for it.

I just had a thought. Marriages are breaking up like crazy these days. There was a certain sector of the movement at one time that encouraged women to break the chains of that oppressive union because love between men and women was impossible. Wouldn't it be ironic if, among those women now leaving their marriages, it turned out to be because they now saw love as possible, not impossible, and they decided to go out after it?

Going for What We Really Want

Kathie Sarachild

There's a lot of talk about the different sections of the women's movement, and some people say that the major division in the movement is between those who want to work inside the system and those who want to work outside the system, that this is what distinguishes the radicals in the women's movement from what they call reformist groups like the National Organization for Women (N.O.W.) or the newly formed Women's Political Caucus. But the real question is not working from inside or outside the present economic and political system, the real question is what are you working for? What are your final goals, both personal and political?

It's not a question of working inside or outside the system . . . it's a question of whether we want to finally go after what we really want, our own true desires, or whether we are toning down our desires, lying about them, even to ourselves, in order to get favors from men who have power. It's a question of knowing what our true desires are and working wherever we are, in whatever way we are able to, to achieve the power over our lives that we need.

It's a question of going after what we really want in our work lives and in our love lives—and, as women really know, the two are very related—and only having power will get us what we really want in both. It will get us the kind of jobs we want *and* the kind of love relationships. When we have power, men will finally begin to give *us* love rather than the other way around, the real love we've all been longing for all these years, and this will change our relationships with women, too.

It's a question of whether some of us are out to get a few favors from men under male supremacy or whether we're out to eliminate male supremacy once and for all. If we're out for the same goals—and I think most women are, that most women want to go all the way, or else not bother with the fight at all—if we're out for the same goals, to tell the whole truth, to expose male supremacy everywhere, leaving no corner still dirty, and win full power over our lives, then it doesn't necessarily matter whether we work inside or outside the system. We're going to have to do both and we're going to have to use every means at our disposal to do it. Being true to what we really want, knowing what we really want, gives us power.

Now a lot of women have felt that they had to tone themselves down in order to "reach most women." And they spend a lot of time counseling others to tone themselves down. All I can say is that in my experience, you don't reach most women by toning yourself down, by lying about your needs and desires. That's the kind of deceit you use against people you really consider your enemies or your inferiors. It doesn't work with the people who are on your side, not with your own people. You don't reach most women with lies, you reach them with the truth. You reach out to people with the truth, and something in them either responds to it or doesn't. The truth arouses people's imagination, stirs the imagination. Lies are boring, lies are what women have heard a million times before. The truth is new and the truth is powerful. And in my experience, more and more women in all walks of life want to hear it. They want to tell it; and they're only interested in talk and action that goes right to the heart of what women's problems are. And the course that the women's movement has taken demonstrates, reflects, what I myself have experienced.

I remember back in the days of New York Radical Women there were some women who counseled us that using the term women's liberation was too radical; and yet women's liberation was a term that inspired powerful excitement and feeling in some of us, that expressed the spirit of what we really wanted and so we used it anyway, even though people counseled us it might be too radical and turn women off. And, as we all know, it has become the term to describe the whole movement.

I am not saying that women should pretend to be *more* radical than they really are, either, in order to "reach women." I think we women have suffered too long from worrying about what other people think. . . . whether it's about what men think or about what other women think. Toning ourselves up—like toning ourselves down—is just another form of *not* being radical, of not being authentic. We have to do that, of course, in order to survive in our daily lives . . . but our movement should be dealing with what we really want and how we're going to get it.

People think they have to tone themselves down to win support from women . . . that women aren't radical. They asked for abortion law reform instead of repeal, when large numbers of women, myself included, would only rally for repeal. People worried that all-female groups would be too anti-male and turn women off, whereas women all around the country rallied to these groups. It is the radical language of the movement which has spread like wildfire. Sisterhood is powerful, women's liberation, consciousness-raising, male chauvinism—even male chauvinist pig.

Now we were also counseled that to oppose abortion reforms, to press for abortion repeal—total repeal of all abortion laws—was asking too much, would turn people off. But we just knew that we didn't want to fight at all if it wasn't for what we really want—that abortion reform was just more insult and humiliation for women—and so we decided not only to fight for repeal but to oppose more reforms in the abortion law. We busted up a reform hearing and demanded repeal instead. Woman after woman got up and testified how the reforms being proposed would not have helped her through her terrible illegal abortion one bit. It was the demand for repeal that rallied all the people to the march, that rallied all the people who worked on the court case, that created all the pressure which got us the most liberal abortion law in the nation. It didn't get us what we really wanted, but at least we fought for what we really wanted . . . we let them know what we really wanted and that we're not going to stop fighting for women's liberation 'til we get it, and a lot else, too. And by doing this we actually won some real relief in our lives, much more than we would have ever gotten if we had lied about our desires and supported reform. In my experience, toning things down—lying about ourselves—turns women off, it doesn't turn women on.

I was visiting in a consciousness-raising group on Long Island of mostly so-called middle class, suburban, married women, and they were mad at the Women's Political Caucus for not being radical enough when the caucus kept saying we're not going to be like men, we're going to be non-violent. I heard about a speech Martha Shelley gave once which she opened by asking, "Who says women are non-violent?," and then she pulled out a rolling pin and held it over her head. And I was talking to the neighbor of a friend of mine in another suburb—upstate New York this time. My friend's neighbor was the wife of one of the neighborhood policemen. Well, when she heard I was in Redstockings, a radical women's liberation group, she got very excited and started telling me about many of her ideas and dreams, one of which was that all the secretaries of New York were to go out on strike. You see, women all over the country have a sense of the fantastic power women could have to change our situation . . . and that policeman's wife was not just talking about the power of the ballot . . . elections . . . she was talking about something that would bring New York City to a halt—and not just for more money, but for political demands—for a whole new way of life, because that's what feminism is about; it's basically the demand for a whole new way of life. That kind of strike is what revolutionaries call a political strike and they consider it a much more advanced form of action than simply an economic strike.

Okay, so what are the women who want to go all the way, after what we really want and after the power to get it, going to do inside and outside the system to unify our work . . . to make all our individual struggles, however small or on however specific an issue, still be part of the whole fight for freedom for women and the elimination of male supremacy across the board? How can we get to the point where large numbers of us understand what we want clearly enough to be able to unite around it?

One way many of us hoped this could be done was in consciousness-raising groups, that in consciousness-raising groups we would be able to stay in touch with what we really wanted even as we had to make compromises in our daily lives and even in some of our political battles. We also thought of consciousness-raising groups as a way we would all stay in touch with all the issues of feminism even though we might be doing our concrete political work on only one issue.

Of course, writing is another way of doing this. And this, of course, is what we hoped *Woman's World* newspaper could do. *Woman's World* and the writing in it would be a means of keeping what we really want in sight . . . in our own sight and visible to the whole world . . . even as we might have to accept certain short-term compromises in our actions. We hoped that *Woman's World* could help the feminist movement do the theoretical work that every woman must do at all times if we women are ever to achieve full liberation.

We needed a means of keeping what we really want in sight, constantly defining and developing it. To do this we have to:

1. Know exactly what it is we want, what we really want, dare to express it, be able to express it, and, therefore, define it.

2. Know how far you—we—are from what it is we want, be able to analyze this at all times as exactly as possible. In other words, we must figure out what the obstacles are to our true goals, and be able to spot them as they are ever changing, ever being turned into new forms.

3. We have to know what exactly it is that has gotten us our improvements, reforms, changes when they do occur.

4. And we need tactics, which, among other things come from knowing all the above. We must devise the most effective tactics for overcoming the obstacles, and these tactics will include strategic advances or strategic retreats. The question was how to do this.

What gains we have made recently—and there have definitely been some already, affecting the lives of masses of women—we've only made because there is now a movement, and it is essential that all women know this if we are to continue to make gains. Until we've gone all the way and defeated male supremacy, until we women have won full and equal power for ourselves and can begin to relax, there will have to continue to be a militant feminist movement here at all times.

And in order to stay alive, the movement must grow; it has to keep growing, reaching more and more women and therefore more and more corners of male supremacy. But women aren't going to keep on joining the movement, women aren't going to stay in the movement, unless it expresses our true desires, unless it tells the truth and fights for the truth.

For instance, most women wouldn't join a movement that called for "free love" when some women in the movement were saying that it is okay for men to sleep around and to sleep with a woman and leave her the next day, because they know that isn't either freedom (for women) or love (for women). They would know it is a lie. And they also aren't going to join a movement that doesn't say anything about men, that skirts the problems with men and talks about women's "identity" all the time, even about freeing *men* from nagging wives and various other alleged female monsters. We *are* the nagging wives and we know we only nag in an effort to get what is our due . . . and when we escalate our tactics beyond nagging, men—and women—who complained about nagging are going to wish we had gone back to nagging.

Chapter Twenty-nine

Radical Feminism and Love (1974)

Ti-Grace Atkinson

Another important and influential voice in radical feminism, Atkinson attempts in this essay to define love within the philosophy of radical feminism. "I propose that the phenomenon of love is the psychological pivot in the persecution of women," she states baldly. In this piece Atkinson tries to define women as a class marked by the internalization of oppression, the deepest form of which is women's psychological attachment to romantic love.

Radical feminism is a new political concept.[1] It evolved in response to the concern of many feminists that there has never been even the beginnings of a feminist analysis of the persecution of women. Until there is such an analysis, no coherent, effective program can be designed to solve the problem. The October 17th Movement[2] was the first radical feminist group, and it has spent a great deal of its first five months working out the structure and details of a causal class analysis.

The analysis begins with the feminist *raison d'être* that women are a class, that this class is political in nature, and that this political class is oppressed. From this point on, radical feminism separates from traditional feminism.

The class of women is one-half of a dichotomized class definition of society by sex. The class of women is formed by positing another class in opposition: the class of men, or the male role. Women exist as the corollaries of men, and exist as human beings only insofar as they are those corollaries.

Without women, men would be limited only as to reproduction, not as to human existence itself. Similarly as women to men, nonwhites could not exist as human beings without the positing of whites. Of course, both the terms "men" and "whites" are role definitions, but that is, after all, what political definitions are all about.[3]

Oppression is an ongoing activity. If women are a political class and women are being oppressed, it must be that some other political class is oppressing the class of women. Since the very definition of women entails that only one other class could be relevant to it, only one other class could possibly be oppressing women: the class of men.

Since it is clear that men oppress women, and since this oppression is an ongoing process, it was clear to radical feminists that women must understand the *dynamics* of their oppression. Men are the *agents* of the oppression of individual women, and these agents use various means to achieve the subordination of their counterclass.

But over thousands of years, men have created and maintained an enclosure of institutionalized oppression to fortify their domination of women by using many institutions and values as *vehicles* of oppression, e.g., marriage, family, sexual intercourse, love, religion, prostitution. Women are the *victims* of this oppression.

The class of women[4] has several peculiar political characteristics:

(1) the class of women, or the female role, is generally agreed to be the largest single political class in history
(2) the oppression of the class of women *qua* women is stable historically and similar geographically
(3) the political class of women, or the female role, is generally agreed to be the earliest political class in history, therefore all known cultures are constructed with the oppression of women as the major foundational ingredient (i.e., the class of women is the key functional unit in all of our social, economic, and political institutions and values)
(4) the class of women has been dispersed over time, thereby further suppressing it, throughout later class systems: e.g., chronological, familial, religious, racial, economic.

These special characteristics of the class of women affect the radical feminist analysis in two major directions. First, it is clear that the male and female roles do not comprise a simple class confrontation. While class confrontation, with the consequence of mutually exclusive interests qua male and female role interests, is an important element in the dynamics of the oppression of women, it is complicated by the institutions and values, created by men to consolidate their roles as Oppressors. These institutions form unnatural alliances or contracts between men and women against the interests of the victims' basic class identification.

It is in the interests of the Oppressor to "unite" with the Oppressed; the key to maintaining the Oppressor role is to *prevent the Oppressed from uniting.* As long as the Oppressor has some kind of "contract," be it "marriage" or "love," with the Oppressed, he can bring pressure within that private or individual contract, in which he has unequal power because of his political class identification, to keep his subordinate "partner" subordinate. A woman can only change her political definition by organizing with other women to change the definition of the female role, eventually eliminating it, thereby freeing herself to be human.

These cross-sexual alliances, because they are definitively inequitable, and because they thus necessarily alienate women from their natural class interest, are antifeminist. The tension created by the male/female role confrontation and the pseudo-alliances across these role interests has the structural appearance of a web of boxes with a single woman trapped in each one. The tension between these two conflicting interests has frustrated the natural consequence of confrontation (the annihilation of the role system) and maintained the oppression of women as stable.

Second, because the class of women is slightly larger than its oppressor class, and because the oppression of women has not been changed significantly either over time or place, it follows that either

(1) women are biologically subhuman and feel, therefore, that they are not oppressed but naturally assume a subordinate role (this explanation is outside any possible feminist interpretation), or that

(2) a large part of the policing of the oppression of women has to be internalized not only into the female role but into the female as well. There has to be a blurring between the biological class of females (a human being with the *capacity* to bear children, *period*) and the sociological class of women (a human being who *must* bear children, should rear them, et cetera, the rest of the female role follows from the first point).[5]

Since radical feminists assume that the source of the necessity within the female to maintain the female role lies within the male in his political role as Oppressor, it must be that the internal coercion within the female to maintain the female role is not essentially biological in nature but psychological.

I propose that the phenomenon of love is the psychological pivot in the persecution of women. Because the internalization of coercion must play such a key functional part in the oppression of women due to their numbers alone, and because of the striking grotesqueness of the one-to-one political units "pairing" the Oppressor and the Oppressed, the hostile and the powerless, and thereby severing the Oppressed from any kind of political aid, it is not difficult to conclude that women by definition must exist in a special psychopathological state of fantasy both in reference to themselves and to their manner of relating to their counterclass. This pathological condition, considered the most desirable state for any woman to find herself in, is what we know as the phenomenon of love.

Because radical feminists consider the dynamics of their oppression the focal point of their analysis, it was obvious that some theory of "attraction" would be needed. Why do women, even feminists, consort with the enemy? For sex? Very few women ever say that; that's the male-role reason. What nearly all women mutter in response to this is: "for love."

I distinguish between "friendship" and "love." "Friendship" is a rational relationship which requires the participation of two parties to the mutual satisfaction of both parties. "Love" can be felt by one party; it is unilateral by nature, and, combined with its relational character, it is thus rendered contradictory and irrational.

There has been very little analytic work done on the notion of "love." This is remarkable, considering the importance of it in ethics and political philosophy. Philosophers usually skirt it or brush it aside by claiming it's "irreducible," or "irrational." Or they smile and claim it's the *"sine qua non."* All these things may be true and are clues to the political significance of "love": it's basic; it's against individual human interest; a great deal rests upon it.

Any theory of attraction could begin with the definition of the verb "to attract": the exertion of a force such as magnetism to draw a person or thing, and susceptibility in the thing drawn. Magnetism is caused by friction or conflict, and the primary relationship between men and women of class confrontation or conflict certainly suffices for the cause of magnetism. Usually the magnetized moves toward the magnet in response to the magnet's power; otherwise the magnetized is immobile.

The woman is drawn to $\longrightarrow$ attracted by $\longrightarrow$ desirous of $\longrightarrow$ in love with $\longrightarrow$ the man. She is power*less*, he is power*ful*.

The woman is instinctively trying to recoup her definitional and political losses by fusing with the enemy. "Love" is the woman's pitiful deluded attempt to attain the human: by fusing, she hopes to blur the male/female role dichotomy, and that a new division of the human class might prove more equitable. She counts on the illusion she has spun out of herself in order to be able to accept the fusion, to be transferred to the whole and, thus, that the new man will be garbed now equally in her original illusion.

Unfortunately, magnetism depends upon inequity. As long as the inequity stands, the fusion may hold (everything else relevant remaining the same). If the inequity changes, the fusion and the magnetism fall with the inequity.

A woman can unite with a man as long as she is a woman, i.e., subordinate, and no longer. There's no such thing as a "loving" way out of the feminist dilemma: that it is as a *woman* that women are oppressed, and that in order to be free she must shed what keeps her secure.

The October 17th Movement recently devoted one of its meetings to a discussion of "love" and tried to analyze together how this phenomenon operated. The main difficulty was, and was left at, understanding the shift from the woman desiring an alliance with the power*ful* to the woman being *in love with* the man.

It's clear that love has to do with some transitional or relational factor. But from what to what? It is a psychological state the woman feels she must enter into. But why, exactly?

She is going from the political, the power*less* identification, to the individual, one-to-one unit. She is disarming herself to go into the enemy camp.

Is love a kind of hysterical state, a *mind*less state therefore a *pain*less state, into which women retreat when the contradiction between the last shreds of their human survival and the everyday contingencies of being a woman becomes most acute?

Is love a kind of frenzy, or something like a Buddhist immolation, to unite with the One? The love women feel for men is most akin to religious love.

But hysteria might be a more useful paradigm for us since it's limited almost exclusively to women (the word "hysterical" derives from the Greek word for "uterus") and the condition is marked by certain characteristics strikingly similar to those of "love": anxiety converted into functional symptoms of illness, amnesia, fugue, multiple personality.

NOTES

1. [April 12, 1969; I was asked to write something special for a feminist issue of the Barnard College newspaper. I have long understood that the only way to reach people on feminism is to go for that aspect that is *their* jugular.

In *Juniata I,* pp. 25–39, I sketch out the problem of reaching women under the age or situation of the major female institutions: marriage, motherhood, prostitution. However, college women are approaching that twilight zone just prior to these major traps: they are about to fall in love. Or they are at least looking to do so.

Voila! Love. The feminist jugular for the college "girl."]

2. [Later renamed The Feminists.]

3. The situation is not improved by substituting the biologically functional term "female" for the sociologically functional "woman"—both terms serve essentially political functions.

4. I distinguish between the "class of women" and the "woman class." The "woman class" refers to what might be called the sex-class or the "s-class": society dichotomized by sex. The class of women, or one half of the s-class, is primarily defined by the s-class.

The class of men is further dichotomized in important political ways, e.g., by color, economics, and so forth.*

An oppressed individual is assigned its role through its primary class dichotomy, thus, from the "s-class" to the "woman class." An oppressed individual also transfers its individual identity to its dichotomy in the context of other class systems, as in the case of the woman class and the black class.

The "class of women" refers to the class of individual women within the s-class. It is this sense of class that women must deal with first.

*[See my development of class divisions within both the male and female classes in *Juniata II: The Equality Issue,* pp. 65–75.

I distinguish between "identification" classes (within the female class) and "power" classes (within the male class).]

5. [Reference again as in *Abortion: Paper Number II,* pp. 1–3, and *The Institution of Sexual Intercourse,* pp. 13–23, to the capacity/function distinction.]

Chapter Thirty

From It's All Dixie Cups to Me (1976)

Rita Mae Brown

Brown, one of the important representatives of lesbian feminism in the 1970s, holds a view altogether different from Firestone and Atkinson's. "Love is the enemy of unequal social structure," she claims, arguing that women can use love to return to the "root self" that contains unexplored desires. Brown believes that women should be "woman-identified" in order to begin the process of discovering themselves and loving freely.

Americans have the Dixie-cup mentality—if you don't like someone, then crumple them up and throw them away. Auto graveyards, prisons and mental institutions share one thing in common: all contain society's cast-offs. The truly remarkable aspect of the Dixie-cup mentality is not that Americans throw people and things away but that we assume we can always get another. Cars are replaceable. People are replaceable. All you have to do is look the market over and select the one best suited to your needs.

To complete the cycle of conspicuous abundance and waste we thought we could replace ourselves. And what could be more American? Everyone is out for the best self they can get. Mother called it, "Turning over a new leaf." Religious folk call it, "Rebirth." Madison Avenue sells it as a "New You." Psychology gravely refers to it as an "Identity Crisis." It's all Dixie-cups to me.

Bad as our used car lot attitude toward other people may be, our attitude toward ourselves is even more treacherous. We throw away parts of ourselves we consider unpleasant. Consequently, we suffer head-on collisions with the ghosts of our former selves driving down a twisting road that turns in on itself before we can hit the brakes. The need for conscious identity is a manufactured item. The fact that so many people are dismantling and refurbishing themselves turns this phenomena into a bizarre assembly line.

The moment a person dissociates herself from her self, she becomes a spectator to her own life. She becomes schizophrenic. Reality retreats under screening room scrutiny. The self is then once removed from experience. If you aren't your self then, for you, no one else can be a self either. You'll be too busy looking for your self to see other human beings. You'll catch narcissistic paralysis.

There is another self beneath the social self. Social self is self consciousness through comparison. What makes the bedrock self, the root self, so difficult to define is that we owned our self before the moment of comparison. . . .

Identity within the Movement

The Movement was and is correct in stating that women's collective past bled a river of pain. The Movement tried to call out what is strong in women. We tried to find examples from the past. It's hard for many women to grant that strength to a living woman in their midst. Woman-hatred again, dead women are more lovable than living women. Identifying with other women proved rocky at first but over time it became easier.

Recognizing that our collective past was as painful as our individual pasts, the Movement sought a solution to all that pain and desolation. Toss away your hateful past and as for a collective past, dip into the mists of matriarchy, at least life was better then. With the help of your sisters you too can build a new and stronger self. When in doubt pray to the Great Mother in the Skies or Isis or Sappho.

And here is where we hurt ourselves, intellectually and organizationally. How are we to reach others if we deny our past, personal or collective? We must remember our old, oppressed selves. We must resolve the pain of our mothers. We can't blot out that past by ignoring the thousands of years of male supremacy and nodding out in the haze of pre-recorded history—matriarchy. We need to unearth that matriarchal past but it is of the utmost importance that we don't forget for one minute what came between us today and matriarchy. We need to understand our past and use it for the future. One of the earmarks of humanness is a conception of the past and a possibility of the future.

Identity, selfhood, cannot be bought, sought or given. A lover, a therapist, the Women's Movement will not make a "new" you. A certain degree of re-evaluation will provide insights into why you did what you did, possibly even helping you see patterns in your behavior. But even that won't tell you who you are. The chilling point is: Why ask? You are you when you "forget" you. Not reject you, not throw your self away like a living Dixie-cup or a worn out Studebaker. Stop looking for a car when you're driving one.

Earlier, I noted that we suffer head-on collisions with the ghosts of our former selves. There's a difference between inspecting your self/past and discarding your self/past. Another way to look at it is to think of your past and the collective past as a boomerang. Throw it away, turn your head and watch out, the boomerang will come back at you. For instance: suppose before you became a feminist you were a dogmatic Lutheran. Now after feminism you are a dogmatic Lesbian. You won't see this repeating pattern because you think you threw the Dixie-cup away. Your friends may see the pattern. Any mention on their part will probably be resented because you thought you'd cut the thread to your oppressed past and your former behavior.

Only by telling who we were and where we came from can another woman know the truth of our journey. Only then can she trust us for we've given her a roadmap.

Feminism, the root self, isn't one magic moment of understanding then life becomes easy. Feminism begins a process that brings us closer and closer to you/our goal. You'll come home. Home to your root self. Home to the self before social consciousness of self.

The root self, for me, develops from two bases: Emotion and Work. Emotion is the toughest to pin down especially when writing in English. We're told that there is a whole orchestra of emotions. True enough, but I think all emotions spring from two sources: Love and Fear. Fear in its purest stage is a response to physical or mental danger. Fear is reactive. Love is active. Love is the root emotion.

To return to root self we must return to love, a difficult journey in a country that hates women. That is why women-identification, women loving other women, putting women first, putting themselves first is so crucial to our finding our root selves and to us finding the power of our movement.

Love's reality is that it eats away at social structure, at control, so it must be suppressed. Think of the furor over black-white couples. Love threatened a necessary part of racism, that the races remain separate. Or what about cross-class friendships. These are frowned upon, "Stay with your own kind," because in essence, the emotion disrupts oppression.

Love is the enemy of unequal social structure. When people really love they become disobedient. And by love I don't just mean sex because that's a tiny fraction of the love we are capable of. Sex has been used to confine love because it serves male supremacy to limit love to a biological function which keeps us in our place.

After woman-identification, people usually return to some activity they discarded because it was discouraged, Dixie-cupped by parents, teachers, the old gang of psychological thugs. Reinforced by other women and by increasing feelings of strength a woman returns to earlier, lost interests. Re-discovering a happy part of childhood is one more step toward the self before social consciousness of self.

Through my observation, this re-discovery is linked to some form of work. Just as a knowledge of past and future mark us off as human so does the need for fulfilling work, for purpose. A squirrel buries her nuts by instinct. She is born knowing what to do and how to do it. We have to learn. What we learn depends on sex, class and race. Before we suffered consciousness of categorization most of us expressed some preferences about what we liked doing. We liked music or we took clocks apart or whatever. Those pre-school desires, I believe, are close to the root self. An adult going back to that early desire may or may not be able to make a career of it but she'll be getting closer to her self. That renewed strength helps her face a hostile world. It also means she is not going to be content with oppression. She will no longer settle for less. If a woman can make a living from her early work drive she is in an enviable position. She will be especially able to help her sisters since her time won't be divided into earning a wage vs. doing what she wants.

The amazing thing about work is that the more you enjoy your work the harder you work and the less self-conscious you are. You get very close to that root self.

Returning to the root self under male supremacy is a tremendous battle for we must fight the entire Western world as we know it. Under male supremacy love for other humans is labeled irrational, frivolous and so on unless love is within the context of marriage and family where love is one-sided. Once a woman makes the great breakthrough to woman-identification, to discovery of worth, the road becomes smoother although it isn't always safe. We still don't know exactly how a woman becomes woman-identified although we do know the more contact she has with strong, positive women the more likely this will happen.

The Women's Movement, for all our mistakes, is right to hold a mirror up to our faces. By clearly seeing ourselves we can use the jolt of self awareness as an oppressed person to lead us back to our past and simultaneously to our future. By identifying with other women, with ourselves, we gain a definite goal: Freedom. Our self is linked with other selves. The ultimate act of humanness, identifying with others, guides us. Slowly, heightened self-consciousness fades as we connect, understand, love and breathe the lives of our sisters. By identifying with other women some of them begin to identify with us, giving us the love and faith to pursue our work. Within the goal of women's freedom we find our more personal goals.

And one day, in good time, you'll glance in your mirror and discover it's a window. Welcome, Sister, you've come home at last.

Part IV

Contemporary Feminist Theory

The concerns of feminist writers after the second wave have been varied: the discussion of whether lesbianism is more progressive as a romantic choice than heterosexuality (Harne); a recognition that love is not the same for all women (Lorde, Collins), or for the same woman at different points in her life; in general, a call for a wider, more complex understanding of both the rewards and dangers of romance than was available in second-wave feminism (Goodison, Delphy, Thompson).

Chapter Thirty-one

From Scratching the Surface
Some Notes on Barriers to Women and Loving (1978)

Audre Lorde

The lesbian poet and essayist Audre Lorde wrote this early piece asking black women to recognize the "right to . . . love where we choose." Homophobia, she argues, should not separate women any more than rivalry over men should.

Racism: *The belief in the inherent superiority of one race over all others and thereby the right to dominance.*

Sexism: *The belief in the inherent superiority of one sex and thereby the right to dominance.*

Heterosexism: *The belief in the inherent superiority of one pattern of loving and thereby its right to dominance.*

Homophobia: *The fear of feelings of love for members of one's own sex and therefore the hatred of those feelings in others.*

The above forms of human blindness stem from the same root—the inability to recognize or tolerate the notion of difference as a beneficial and dynamic human force, and one which is enriching rather than threatening to the defined self.

To a large degree, at least verbally, the black community has moved beyond the "two steps behind her man" mode of sexual relations sometimes mouthed as desirable during the sixties. This was a time when the myth of the black matriarchy as a social disease was being presented by racist forces for an excuse or diversion, to redirect our attentions away from the real sources of black oppression.

For black women as well as black men, it is axiomatic that if we do not define ourselves for ourselves, we will be defined by others—for their use and to our

From Audre Lorde, "Scratching the Surface: Some Notes on Barriers to Women and Loving," *Black Scholar*, vol. 9, no. 7 (April 1978): 31–35. © 1978 by *The Black Scholar*. Reprinted by permission of *The Black Scholar*.

detriment. The development of self-defined black women, ready to explore and pursue our power and interests within our communities, is a vital component in the war for black liberation. The image of the Angolan woman with a baby on one arm and a gun in the other is neither romantic nor fanciful. Black women in this country coming together to examine our sources of strength and support, and to recognize our common social, cultural, emotional, and political interests, is a development which can only contribute to the power of the black community as a whole. For it is only through the coming together of self-actualized individuals, female and male, that any real advances can be made. The old sexual power-relationships based on a dominant/subordinate model between unequals have not served us as a people, nor as individuals.

Black women who define ourselves and our goals beyond the sphere of a sexual relationship can bring to any endeavor the realized focus of a completed and therefore empowered individual. Black women and black men who recognize that the development of their particular strengths and interests does not diminish the other, do not diffuse their energies fighting for control over each other. We focus our attentions against the real economic, political and social forces at the heart of this society which are ripping ourselves and our children and our worlds apart. . . .

Today, the red herring of homophobia and lesbian-baiting is being used in the black community to obscure the true double face of racism/sexism. Black women sharing close ties with each other, politically or emotionally, are not the enemies of black men. Too frequently, however, an attempt to rule by fear tactics is practiced by some black men against those black women who are more ally than enemy. These tactics are sometimes expressed as threats of emotional rejection: "Their poetry wasn't too bad but I couldn't take all those lezzies (lesbians)." The man who says this is warning every black woman present who is interested in a relationship with men—and most black women are—that (1) if she wishes to have her work considered she must eschew any other allegiance except to him and (2) any woman who wishes his friendship and/or support had better not be "tainted" by woman-identified interests.

If such threats of labelling, vilification and/or emotional isolation are not enough to bring black women docilely into camp as followers, or persuade them to avoid each other as political or emotional support for each other, then the rule by terror can be expressed physically, as on the campus of a New York college recently, where black women sought to come together around feminist concerns. Violently threatening phone calls were made to those black women who dared to explore the possibilities of a feminist connection with non-black women. Some of these women, intimidated by these threats and the withdrawal of male approval, did turn against their sisters. When threats did not prevent the attempted coalition of black feminists, the resulting hysteria left some black women beaten and raped. Whether the threats by black men actually led to these assaults, or merely encouraged the climate of hostility within which they could occur, the results upon the women attacked were the same.

Wars and jails have decimated the ranks of black males of marriageable age. The fury of many black heterosexual women against white women who date black men is rooted in this unequal sexual equation, since whatever threatens to widen that equation is deeply and articulately resented. But this is essentially unconstructive resentment because it extends sideways, and can never result in true progress on the issue, because it does not question the vertical lines of power or authority, nor the sexist assumptions which dictate the terms of the competition. And the racism of white women can be better addressed where it is less complicated by their own sexual oppression. In this situation it is not the non-black woman who calls the tune, but rather the black man who turns away from himself in his sisters, or who, through a fear borrowed from white men, reads her strength not as a resource but as challenge.

All too often the message comes loud and clear to black women from black men: "I am the prize and there are not too many of me and remember I can always go elsewhere. So if you want me you'd better stay in your place which is away from each other, or I will call you lesbian and wipe you away." Black women are programmed to define themselves within this male attention and to compete with each other for it, rather than to recognize their common interests. . . .

Instead of keeping our attentions focused upon the real enemies, enormous energy is being wasted in the black community today by both black men and heterosexual black women, in anti-lesbian hysteria. Yet women-identified women—those who sought their own destinies and attempted to execute them in the absence of male support—have been around in all of our communities for a long time. As Yvonne Flowers of York College pointed out in a recent discussion, the unmarried aunt, childless or otherwise, whose home and resources were often a welcome haven for different members of the family, was a familiar figure in many of our childhoods. And within the homes of our black communities today, it is not the black lesbian who is battering and raping our under-age girl-children, out of displaced and sickening frustration.

The black lesbian has come under increasing attack from both black men and heterosexual black women. In the same way that the existence of the self-defined black woman is no threat to the self-defined black man, the black lesbian is an emotional threat only to those black women who are unsure of, or unable to, express their feelings of kinship and love for other black women, in any meaningful way. For so long, we have been encouraged to view each other with suspicion, as eternal competitors, or as the visible face of our own self-rejection.

But traditionally, black women have always bonded together in support of each other, however uneasily and in the face of whatever other allegiances which militated against that bonding. We have banded together with each other for wisdom and strength and support, even when it was only in relationship to one man. We need only look at the close—although highly complex and involved—relationship between African co-wives; or at the Amazon warriors of ancient Dahomey, who fought together as the Kings' main and most ferocious bodyguard. We need only look at the more promising power wielded by the West African Market Women Associations of today, and those governments which have risen and fallen at their pleasure.

In a verbatim retelling of her life, a 92-year-old Efik-Ibibio woman of Nigeria recalls her love for another woman:

I had a woman friend to whom I revealed my secrets. She was very fond of keeping secrets to herself. We acted as husband and wife. We always moved hand in glove and my husband and hers knew about our relationship. The villagers nicknamed us twin sisters. When I was out of gear with my husband, she would be the one to restore peace. I often sent my children to go and work for her in return for her kindnesses to me. My husband being more fortunate to get more pieces of land than her husband, allowed some to her, even though she was not my co-wife.[1]

The Fon of Dahomey still have 12 different kinds of marriage, one of which is known as "giving the goat to the buck," where a woman of independent means marries another woman who then may or may not bear children, all of whom will belong to the blood line of the other woman.[2] Some marriages of this kind are arranged to provide heirs for women of means who wish to remain "free," and some are homosexual relationships. Marriages of this kind occur throughout Africa, in several different places among different peoples.[3]

In all of these cases, the women involved are recognized parts of their communities, evaluated not by their sexuality but by their respective places within the community.

While a piece of each black woman remembers the old ways of another place and time, when we enjoyed each other in a sisterhood of work and play and power, other pieces of us, less functional, eye each other with suspicion as we have been programmed to do. In the interests of separation, and to keep us out of touch with our own power, black women have been taught to view each other as always suspect, heartless competitors for the scarce male, the all-important prize that will legitimize our existence. This becomes an ultimate and dehumanizing denial of self, no less lethal than that dehumanization of racism which is so closely allied to it.

If the recent hysterical rejection of lesbians in the black community is based solely upon an aversion to the idea of sexual contact between members of the same sex (a contact existing for ages in most of the female compounds across the African continent, from reports) why then is the idea of sexual contact between black men so much more easily accepted, or unremarked? Is the reality of the imagined threat the existence of a self-motivated, self-defined black woman who will not fear nor suffer some terrible retribution from the gods because she does not necessarily seek her face in a man's eyes, even if he has fathered her children? Female-headed households in the black community are not always situations by default.

The distortion of relationship which says "I disagree with you, or I do not share your lifestyle, so I must destroy you" leaves black people with basically uncreative victories, defeated in any common struggle. That is jugular vein psychology, based on a fallacy which holds that your assertion or affirmation of your self must mean an attack upon my self—or that my defining myself will somehow prevent or retard your self-definition. The supposition that one sex needs the other's acquiescence in order to exist prevents both from moving together as self-defined persons toward a common goal.

This is a prevalent mistake among oppressed peoples, and is based upon the false notion that there is only a limited and particular amount of freedom that must be divided up between us, with the largest and juiciest pieces going as spoils to the victor or the stronger. So instead of joining together to fight for more, we quarrel between ourselves for a larger slice of the one pie. Black women fight between ourselves over men instead of pursuing and using who we are and our strengths; black women and men fight between ourselves over who has more of a right to freedom, instead of seeing each other's struggles as part of our own; black and white women fight between ourselves over who is the more oppressed, instead of seeing those areas in which our causes are the same. (Of course, this last separation is worsened by the intransigent racism that white women too often fail to, or cannot, address in themselves.)

As black women we have the right and responsibility to define ourselves, and to seek our allies in common cause with black men against racism, and with white women against sexism. But most of all as black women we have a right to recognize each other without fear and to love where we choose, for both homosexual and heterosexual black women today share a history of bonding and strength that our particular sexual preferences should not blind us to.

NOTES

1. Andreski, Iris. *Old Wives Tales: Life-Stories of African Women.* Schocken Books. New York. 1970. p. 131.

2. Herskovits, Melville. *Dahomey.* Northwestern Univ. Press. Evanston. 1967. 2 volumes. i, pp. 320–321.

3. Ibid., i, p. 322.

Chapter Thirty-two

From Close to Home
A Materialist Analysis of Women's Oppression (1984)

Christine Delphy

Delphy is an important theorist of materialist feminism, one of the few who have written directly about romantic love. Rejecting "idealist and naturalist" views about the possibility of equality in love, such as we saw represented in part 1 of this volume, she examines the material context of romance and concludes that there are concrete reasons why "the association of a woman with a man does not have the same objective meaning for him as it has for her."

The interpersonal relationship of a man and a woman is not an island, contrary to what our friends would have us believe. Even if a husband and wife or two lovers do not work together, their respective situations in the labour market, as members of differently treated groups in this market, are part of their overall situation—and therefore of their relationship, even though the latter appears to have nothing to do with labour or the market. The involuntary benefits the man in a couple derives from his group membership on the "occupational" scene, are not absent from the loving, relational, conjugal scene, whatever you call it. They are part of the objective resources which he brings to it, whether he wants to or not, simply in bringing his person. The non-benefits of the woman in the couple are also part of what she does, or does not, bring into the relationship. An individual man does not need to lift a finger to have an advantage over women in the labour market; but nor can he help being so advantaged, nor can he renounce this advantage. In the same way, he may not necessarily take active advantage of his institutional privileges in marriage, but he still has them.

Even accepting that a man may not seek to take full advantage of his benefits at all levels, and of the disadvantages at all levels of the woman he has in front of him; and accepting that he wants to set the relationship up as egalitarian, what does this mean? At most that he does not pursue his advantage voluntarily, that is to say, that he does not voluntarily use his *initial advantage* to obtain *others*. But he cannot renounce this initial advantage because he cannot suppress it single-handedly. He cannot destroy what is not of his making. And for the same reason he cannot suppress the institutional disadvantages of "his" woman.

Benefits and advantages tied to group membership (to one's "sex") do not play their most important role in one's heterosexual relationships directly. Rather they are factors which make the more immediate power relationships possible, because there is, institutionally, no symmetry between the "partners" in any conjugal or paraconjugal relationship (and every "love relationship" between a man and a woman comes into this category). The directly economic constraints and the general social constraints in such an association are infinitely stronger for women than for men, and the penalties attached to refusing such relationships are infinitely worse for them. Thus the association of a woman with a man does not have the same objective meaning for him as it has for her, which reflects the ideological norm that marriage and "human relations" are women's affair, and that they are a "real woman's" major preoccupation; which in turn reflects the different subjectivities of men and women (the importance of love and the emotions in general in women's consciousness). Arguably discrimination in the labour market exists only to turn and return women to marriage, precisely in so far as marriage constitutes their objectively most profitable, or least bad, "career" (ideologically: their "destiny," their "whole existence").

This asymmetry manifests itself on the occasion of *a* marriage, within a given union, because of the interpersonal tensions which then emerge, but it is not caused by this union. The asymmetry pre-exists the union: it is the reason for its unequal and eventually conflictual *form*. But above all it is the reason for the very existence of the union: for "heterosexuality" in Adrienne Rich's usage.

In short, not only is it not necessary for a man to be a voluntary oppressor for a woman to be oppressed in heterosexual relationships, but the general oppression which precedes any particular relationship itself determines the very existence of the relationship. The particular individual man does not play a personal role in this general oppression, which occurs before his appearance on the scene: but, reciprocally, no personal initiative on his part can undo or mitigate what exists before and outside his entrance.

Only a view of human relationships which involves splitting individuals from society, which considers them as two distinct, albeit linked, orders, which sees a split between what goes on inside and outside people's heads, and inside and outside particular relationships, and between the "political" and the "personal", could postulate that interpersonal relationships are a matter of choice and "emotions". Only such a view could suggest that any of these choices and emotions are asocial in nature, and that they are not all affected by social determinants. Only such a view, which is idealist or indeed naturalist, could produce the belief that asocial islets of egalitarian personal relations can exist inside an oppressive structure.

It is not surprising that we frequently come across such idealist and individualistic arguments, since these are the dominant ideologies of our society. Idealism impregnates our whole lives and all our most everyday concepts.

What *is* surprising is that many of our male friends who produce them are left intellectuals—self-styled marxists and materialists—yet they use idealist arguments about women's oppression. Why should they abandon materialism there?

Perhaps it is because they cannot participate in the production of new materialist explanations—not being part of the political movement which is fighting for women's liberation, and not occupying that social position which has an objective interest in unmasking the ideology, i.e. not being victims of the oppression. On the other hand, this does not explain why they do not adopt the points of view produced *by* the victims. Perhaps we need to resort to a more cynical explanation for our friends' abandonment of materialism; to look to the fact that, under the circumstances, materialist thought is in contradiction with their objective class interests, and to recognize that it certainly serves men's interests to apply ideological thought to women.

It then becomes interesting to note the ways in which these objective interests are translated: the various ways in which our friends think about women, and what this reveals (betrays) about their attachment to their own class interests, since what they say and do often contradicts (betrays) their avowed political purpose. Time and time again they affirm support for the *women's* movement, yet they do not support *all* women, and indeed they seek to divide women against each other.

Chapter Thirty-three

Really Being in Love Means Wanting to Live in a Different World (1983)

Lucy Goodison

As opposed to many of the radical feminists of the 1970s in the previous part, Goodison, a British feminist, sees falling in love as a "healthy response to a crazy world," full of risk but also possibility for growth and even radical change. She directly addresses the problematic relation of feminism to romance, weighing the pros and cons of love experiences in women's lives.

So reads a situationist leaflet lying on my bedroom floor.[1] Since 1968 the Left and the women's movement have given "falling in love" a very bad press. Women have pointed to the way it tends to make us feel helpless, passive, uncomprehending, dependent, immobilised: the very feelings we are struggling to leave behind. From a socialist and feminist viewpoint we have been reminded how "falling in love" is individualistic, objectifying, linked to escapist notions of romantic love, exploited by advertisements to encourage consumerism, and tied firmly at the far end to the great institution of marriage which helps to keep the cogs of society ticking over. All in all we can see that it is clearly "incorrect," and one reaction has been to ignore it.[2]

And yet falling in love does not go away. We all do it. It is gripping, exciting. We long for it. It makes other more politically "correct" areas of our life pale by comparison. It keeps cropping up. Its power is unquestionable.

Perhaps somewhere between the traditional view of accepting it as an inevitable part of human nature, and the tendency to dismiss it as a capitalist con, there is a third path: one which involves looking at the experience in detail and grappling with its process. In this way we might gain more access to using its power rather than becoming its victim. This has not been done. As a subject it has largely remained untouchable. Perhaps we secretly like having an area of our lives that we cannot explain and are not expected to.

As with a religious experience, no one can contradict our feelings.[3] We are sent

Lucy Goodison, "Really Being in Love Means Wanting to Live in a Different World," in *Sex and Love*, ed. S. Cartledge and J. Ryan (London: Women's Press, 1983), 48–66. Reprinted by permission of the Women's Press.

reeling into talk about "wonderful feelings" which "just happen." We seem to fear that if we look too hard its magic will vanish. We can however try to chart unknown seas, not in order to plunder them, or cut them down to size, but the better to explore and travel them. We are not trying to reduce the excitement in our lives, but to increase our ability to choose and direct that excitement.

So what is falling in love like? How does it happen? What are the steps, the progressions? It is not one unitary or primary experience, but rather a number of experiences bound up together, different feelings present in different people in different proportions. It may vary as widely as one orgasm from another. However, there are certain common experiences, and before investigating the "whys" and "wherefores" I shall briefly sketch what these seem to be. From women's accounts, some common threads seem to recur whether the object of our passion is a man or a woman, so I shall describe both together as different aspects of the same process. I shall use women's novels, poems and personal accounts, as well as some of the media clichés which have influenced us so strongly and which remain the backdrop of our efforts to create a new language for our experience.

Over the years I have done extensive field work on this subject. I am not describing a place where I have not been, though I have never written about it before. My account feels very tentative, like early maps of uncharted territories, and much of it is written in blood.

Step one, you find someone to love. It often happens through "love at first sight," the impact of a first encounter:

> Who is this stick of corn? or is she a lion?
> she's doing yoga on the lawn
> brown body bending like a snake
> her face is miles wide; she is open
> eyes welcome . . . have I really known her
> somewhere before? was I born with her?[4]

A bell rings, something beckons far beyond words. Yet often the reason for the attraction is not obvious. The objects of our passion often lack traditional "qualities" like money or looks. They may also be too old, too young. They may be different from us, unsuitable or unavailable. But the line is cast, the bait is taken, and we are hooked.

What happens next? One friend compared falling in love to LSD in the way it changes reality. Another woman writes that it is as if the world has been stopped and started again.[5] We often hear about a general sensation of disorientation, a feeling that the cosmos has moved in its tracks, the concrete and the clay beneath our feet have crumbled. And this shifting world is permeated by a terrible wanting. Marge Piercy, in her novel *Small Changes,* describes how Miriam experiences the power and relentlessness of this yearning:

> Where so much had been, plans and projects and curiosities and relationships and speculations and histories, was now everything and nothing in one: this painful hollow wanting, this fierce turbulence, this centering about him white hot and icy, cold and dark and bright.[6]

Miriam lies on her bed in embryo position curled round her obsession and feels as if her self and identity are dissolving. Her ability to operate in the world is seriously impaired. "I can't do my homework and I can't think straight," sang Connie Francis in my teens. Miriam has a more grown-up version of the same problem:

> When she did her work at all, she did it perfunctorily . . . she would resent the trivial chatter about programming languages that made her for a moment unable to loose her whole energies on her obsession. . . . She seemed to have nothing left for anyone else, anything else. She was stupefied in general and in that one touch point intensely burning like a laser.[7]

Though the overwhelming feeling is of emotion or intensity, it is very localised and there can be a narrowing of vision, a deadening of other areas of life. Stored aggression erupts as violence; stored love, too, seems able to break out with an edge as cutting as a knife.

It is this laser-like cutting quality which can give being in love an active, rebellious, even political flavour. Sometimes there can be anger contained in that ferocious energy: a schoolteacher angry at the reactionary staff falls in love with a sixth-former; a teenager falls in love with someone who will shock her parents. It can be a way of cocking a snook at authority, of striking a blow at society. Traditionally falling in love is a great defier of convention, breaking barriers imposed by class, race and prejudice: the lady of the manor who falls in love with the gypsy, the Capulet who falls for the Montague. It can act as the beam of light which cuts through the crap, which reveals the mediocrity, hypocrisy and banality of so much in our society. As the libertarian magazine *Ink* pointed out in their "In Love" issue:

> The experience . . . gives us a glimpse of the exuberance and energy which might be set free when our relations with one another are liberated from the system that perverts them. . . . Being in love shatters . . . constraints. We give presents instead of buying and selling, we touch instead of avoiding one another's eyes.[8]

Amidst alienation it makes us feel inexorably connected; amidst deceit its sheer impact makes us feel that something is real; in muddy waters of pain and compromise it can feel like a lifetime. Though it can obliterate the rest of the world, sometimes it can also make the whole world come alive. Sometimes its light, rather than turning inwards, can turn outwards to infuse the whole range of vision. Something in it tells us it could be a revolutionary force: "They never wanted us to feel like this. Killers beware! With love like this we can move mountains and break your prisons down. It is no dope to help us to forget, oh no. This love is dangerous."[9]

Another contradiction with falling in love is that although we may feel vanished and drained into the loved one, we may also at some level feel ourselves more intensely. We are super-conscious of something important happening to us. We step into the limelight in our own lives. There can even be an unwonted narcissism or relish in our experience. The strength of our feelings imparts a new self-confidence and meaning to life.[10] Though we are not in control of it, we are undoubtedly the carriers of some huge power:

> I have a feeling, a strange feeling:
> she seems to potentiate me. I am expanding: will I burst
> like a star on the world?[11]

Or as Marge Piercy describes it: "Much of the time she felt lucky, chosen, exalted. Her life seemed infused with intensity, a plenum, shining and holy. She was never bored. Her previous life seemed vacuous by comparison."[12]

How does this whole experience connect with romantic love? Romantic fantasies (about moonlit nights, wedding bells, true love to the death against all opposition, and so on) may be an important element, but from all accounts they are rarely central. They may be the preformed moulds which society offers us to pour our love into: but they are not its source. These fantasies are pretty, while the central drive of falling in love seems to be more of a blood-and-guts affair. It is not just glamorous and appealing. More than wanting to cosset the beloved, we may feel we want to eat them alive. We may idealise the loved one, but that may slip away like a mask to reveal ferocious hatred and rage if things go wrong. Romantic feelings and fantasies may be the blossoms produced by being in love, but its roots lie deeper in the earth. The power it feeds on is not essentially romantic, but one that tears at the innards.

So what is this strange and physically overwhelming power? Is it primarily sexual? Here comes another irony. In some of the most passionate accounts of "being in love," the sexual experience itself is not totally satisfactory. Erica Jong writes in an autobiographical novel about a woman who leaves a very compatible sexual relationship with her husband for a love-affair in which at first she finds it very hard to reach orgasm:

> He fucked as if he wanted to get back inside the womb. My heart was beating so hard I couldn't come. . . . Josh felt like kin to me, my long-lost brother. . . . I went right to the edge of orgasm and wasn't able to come. This had happened the night before. . . . And the oddest part of it was: I didn't care. . . .
>
> We locked together like two pieces of a puzzle. . . . What other point was there in bringing a man and woman together *except* to stretch the soul and expand the imagination, except to tear things apart and put them back together in new ways?. . . . The mere rubbing that sooner or later results in orgasm was not all one looked for. A vibrator could do that.[13]

Here is another woman's experience:

> The sex was wonderful, overwhelming, not because it worked particularly well in itself, but because it was with him. One of my most most precious memories is of a night when I simply lay sleepless and blissed-out in his arms. What was most powerful was not the sex but the *intimacy* I felt with him.[14]

We hear accounts of passionate love where sex "works" perfectly, or relationships which centre on the strong bonding of sex, but there are also accounts of sexual difficulties and incompatibilities which are dwarfed by the power of being in love. Some intense bonding seems to occur which may channel through sexuality, but is not subsumed in it. Pure lust is generally recognised as a different experience. It is possible to feel a magnificent lust for a person, to connect with her or him intensely and magically through sex, without ever feeling "in love." Sexual feelings may be an important factor in falling in love, but it is as if those feelings are informed from another source, from some other connection between the two people.

Finally, I need to mention how falling in love can end. Sometimes it endures, developing into a long-term relationship. What is then retained or lost of the original impetus is part of a wider discussion about long-term sexual relationships. Does the intensity of the passion fade, endure, transmute? Is it compatible with daily life, living together, children? What is the difference between "falling in love," "being in love," and "loving" someone in a steadier and more whole way? These issues fall outside the scope of this piece. But perhaps more common than the happy-ever-after ending is for a relationship to die young. Apart from cases where circumstances tear lovers apart, this generally happens through one person "falling out of love."

Like falling in love, falling out of love can happen suddenly. You may wake up one morning and feel different. It can be as if a dream has passed to be replaced by reality. The person suddenly looks very ordinary. What did I see in her/him? Sometimes there is a sensation of relief at the return to "normality". Sometimes there is a vague sense of loss at the inexplicable passing of passion:

> Where are the sons of summer now?
> The winter has come
> And you don't know how to turn your dreams into coal . . .
> And I can't help but get a little bit blue
> Thinking about the precious nothing we once knew.
>
> (Carly Simon)

A few nostalgic grains of stardust are left in the hand, and life goes on as normal.

Alternatively, it happens the other way round. Some loves are unrequited from the start, or the other person may start to give you a hard time or fall out of love with you. Then comes more than a vague sense of loss. That is when the heartaches really begin. In *Small Changes* Miriam feels her strength and identity slip away:

> She waited. She waited two hours, while anger and resentment wound her tighter and tighter. She tried to fight her tension. . . . Why must she sit like—like a woman was supposed to, stewing? Her anxiety stripped away her sense of herself as a strong person moving through things in her own style. She became dependent woman. She became scared woman. This waiting had teeth.[15]

Very recognisable is the process whereby Miriam becomes more and more desperate to regain the love that is slipping away from her. Our efforts to recover, to rebuild our power in ourselves, are continually dogged by referral to that other person who remains the magical standard by which everything is measured, the philosopher's stone without which nothing can be gold.

What is so excruciating about this state is its closeness to the worst stereotypes of how women are meant to be: dependent, empty, passive, waiting, pleading. However hard we fight it consciously, we can feel drawn to wallow in the "rich stew of masochism."[16] It hurts so *good*. We feel "right," we feel in character, as if the pain is part of our birthright as women, so intimate and close that it almost becomes precious to us, as Marge Piercy writes of Janis Joplin:

You embodied the pain hugged to the breasts like a baby.
You embodied the beautiful blowsy gum of passivity . . .
That willingness to hang on the meathook and call it love,
That need for loving like a screaming hollow in the soul.[17]

When the beloved is completely and irrevocably lost, the immensity of love's joy can turn its flipside to reveal an immensity of pain. The craziness of happiness can come perilously near real craziness and self-hatred, as one woman writes:

The same waves that crested in the elation of BE HERE NOW and ALL IS ONE sucked me back under and I was CRAZY as never before. I lost control. I suffered disbelief and an excruciating desire not to BE ME that allowed me to touch bottom in some amorphous way . . . and declare "I am bankrupt."[18]

This love that can be like a meathook, this love that can drive us crazy, where does its power come from? I have described the terrain, the superficial process, but what are the force fields at work under the earth? Like many major experiences, falling in love is perhaps over-determined and can be explained on a number of different levels. I shall mention some of these, and describe some of the factors which may conspire to send us hurtling over the abyss. I shall also mention various theoretical frameworks which may throw light on the process, drawing mainly but not exclusively on psychological models placed within the social context of capitalism. Knowing whether the same factors would be present or relevant in another culture or another period of history would illuminate our political understanding of falling in love, and our sense of how that experience could be transformed; but this question would need a separate article to do it justice, and here I can only bear it in mind.

One precipitating factor seems to be immediate life-circumstances, which often include some kind of "rebound" situation, or a reaction to suppression. People often seem to fall in love as a reaction from another relationship. The original relationship may be deteriorating, or there may be unexpressed resentment in it, perhaps due to infidelity, neglect, or subtle domination by one partner. A certain level of need or tension has accumulated. Strong feelings are present but they are blocked or stuck. Then suddenly an outburst of passion shoots, not into hurt or anger in that relationship, but into overwhelming love for a different person. The new relationship allows a release of feeling and expression which had been blocked in the first relationship. The connection of the new passion to the original person is rarely felt; often s/he appears to be completely wiped off the map. Thus Erica Jong's heroine reacts with total blankness to the husband she has just left: "Couldn't he hear in my voice that I didn't miss him at all, that he had never even existed, that he was a ghost, a shadow? I suppose not."[19] This view of falling in love presents it as a substitution, its fierce energy partly fuelled by the need to escape from an existing situation.

Sometimes that situation does not involve another person. Sometimes it is simply a long period in an emotional desert, a long period without joy or sexual satisfaction or physical affection or expression or intensity in any relationship or activity, which builds up until there is a "charge" of need which will eventually spark across to make contact with another person. Is this level of repression, in relationships and outside them, a feature specific to capitalism? *Ink* suggested that even in a Utopia we might need "release in concentrated bursts of energy. Would communal, ecstatic, religious, spiritual, sexual experiences be a feasible alternative?"[20] However the charge builds up, that charge and the readiness to fall in love lie in the subject. She may even make a false start and have a short-lived infatuation with one person before falling deeply in love with another: a kind of practice run. Her antennae are out. Falling in love is what she needs. The timing is hers.

But how do we choose the object of so much unstinting affection? What qualifies them for the job? One theory proposed by various schools of psychology is that they fill gaps in ourselves, resonating with qualities which are absent or not fully realised in our own personality. This means we love not the whole, but only that part of the person which we need to complete us. As Fritz Perls of the Gestalt school of therapy put it:

> We don't usually love a *person*. That's very, very rare. We love a certain *property* in that person, which is either identical with our behaviour or supplementing our behaviour, usually something that is a supplement to us. We think we are in love with the total person, and actually we are disgusted with other aspects of this person.[21]

So what kind of properties do we love in the beloved? Often it is something which is forbidden in ourselves, perhaps something quite different or alien, and this is why the chosen one may at first sight appear very unsuitable. S/he expresses qualities we have buried in ourselves, whether they are painfully unacceptable or idealised.[22] According to humanistic astrology, someone with too much "earth" in their chart might seek a person with "fire" qualities of intuition, creativity, vitality and adventure.[23] The chosen individual, who carries what we most fear or desire, becomes essential to our wholeness. To be complete we need to possess her. That obsessive feeling of wanting to eat the beloved alive is perhaps partly fuelled by the yearning to be whole.

The irony of projection is that while the lover experiences all the focus and meaning of her life as being with the beloved, in fact the beloved is an (often unwitting) actor in the lover's own internal drama. The beloved is chosen for the behaviour and feelings she catalyses in the lover, the qualities she draws to the surface, the buttons she happens to push. What is so magical about the person is that s/he illuminates the *lover's* internal landscape. As Raymond Durgnat writes of the role Jeanne Moreau plays in the film *Les Amants*: "although she is seduced, in the sense that he lures her to follow him through the magical landscape, the landscape is herself, her own desires. His role is little more than that of a *porteur* in a romantic ballet."[24] The power, the joy, is actually our own, but we rarely feel it as such. We need another to find ourselves, while we think we are finding them.

Ultimately, this can appear a rather sordid view of falling in love: we limp along appropriating others to fill gaps in ourselves, we latch onto them like vampires. Our own vitality and power in creating the situation remain unrecognised. Is it peculiar to patriarchy and capitalism that people have such large gaps that need filling? As people with more psychic scars, more unused potential, fewer outlets for self-realisation, are women in our society perhaps particularly prone to construct fantasies and seek completeness in another through these means?

However, we can also recognise that projection is a way of growing. It is possible to re-own, to reclaim what you are hooked onto the other person for. This process can be carried out quite explicitly in the therapy relationship, where the patient is sometimes encouraged to transfer feelings (which may be quite passionate) onto the therapist. In this case, as Perls points out:

> The therapist is supposed to have all the properties which are missing in this person. So, first the therapist provides the person with the opportunity to discover what he [she] needs—the missing parts that he [she] has alienated and given up to the world. Then the therapist must provide the opportunity, the situation in which the person can grow. And the means is that we frustrate the patient in such a way that he [she] is forced to develop his [her] own potential (my parentheses).[25]

Even in a personal love relationship, it is possible to recognise those magnetic, coveted qualities as one's own, and to work to express them more oneself.

Perhaps one way of understanding falling out of love is that the projection, which is often inaccurate, suddenly falls through. When the images which have been projected onto the beloved shatter, the person feels betrayed, "as if 'part of myself' had been taken away; and it has, but only because that part of myself, that image of self, was given to the other in the first place."[26] Using another person as a symbol of our own potential can probably never stand the test of exposure to real life and actual contact for a great length of time. When the power given to a symbol is reclaimed, or recognised as inappropriate, the scales fall and we are left with just an ordinary-seeming person again.

In the meantime, however, the individual in love may have undergone enormous psychological and physical changes: the impact of such a powerful process of projection allows a suspension of normal beliefs, tensions and behaviour patterns, making space for new patterns to form. In the Seth books about the nature of human consciousness, Jane Roberts suggests that major problems can be shifted by any form of "conversion":

> Under that general term I include strong emotional arousal and fresh emotional involvement, affiliation, or sense of belonging. This may involve religion, politics, art, or simply falling in love.
>
> In all of these areas the problem, whatever its nature or cause, is . . . "magically" transferred to another facet of activity, projected away from the self. Huge energy blocks are moved. . . .
>
> Love, as it is often experienced, allows an individual to take his [her] sense of self-worth from another for a time, and to at least momentarily let the other's belief in his [her] goodness supersede his [her] own beliefs in lack of worth. Again, I make a distinction between this and a greater love in which two individuals, knowing their own worth, are able to give and to receive.[27]

The upheaval associated with falling in love may, then, be a signal or catalyst of major personal change. In societies which offer more structures to mark such changes (whether through politics, art, religion, rituals or rites of passage), we may wonder whether falling in love looms as large as in our own. A key element in the process seems to be the ability temporarily to transcend personal limitations and boundaries. The Psychosynthesis school of therapy suggests that an external ideal or figure can be a link to the higher Self which is reflected and symbolised in that figure.[28] You lose yourself temporarily in that figure in order to re-form. The psychological shake-up opens the way to a regrouping of the personality in a more coherent and unified form. In traditional language, the person "drowns," "dissolves," or is "consumed" by the "fires" of passion: again we find the implication of love as an agent of transformation.

Another angle on understanding falling in love has been to compare it to the overwhelming experience of childhood love for the mother, and to see it as some kind of regression to that early situation. This link is at the core of much traditional language about love, from the endearment "baby," to the descriptive language about the loss of identity, the melting or dissolving, the all-consuming wanting, the return to an irrational or pre-rational state, the deep yearning and nostalgia as if for something which has been irrevocably lost. A woman in love can feel as totally vulnerable, as deeply intimate, as passionately identified with another, as a newborn baby with her mother. Perhaps it is some unanswered need for that time, or the premature loss of that childlike aspect of ourselves as we learnt the adult female role of caring, coping and servicing, which leaves a part of our being still crying out with open mouth for mother-love, and desperate to recreate it. As Melanie Klein puts it: "However gratifying it is in later life to express thoughts and feelings to a congenial person, there remains an unsatisfied longing for an understanding without words— ultimately for the earliest relation with the mother."[29]

If this need is part of the power behind falling in love, it might explain why intimacy and skin contact are sometimes more central to it than the act of sex itself. The yearning is perhaps not so much for orgasm as for symbiosis. This view would explain why the joy of falling in love is often very close to pain. Given the conditions of mothering in our society, few of us had a completely satisfactory early relationship with our mother, or were able to grow away from it in our own time. Recreating the same deep bond, it is hard for us to believe that the closeness will not turn sour or be withdrawn as happened with our original mother; perhaps we even unconsciously choose people who will fail us in exactly the same way that our mother did. This may be why the pain seems in some way precious. Perhaps we continually recreate the same scenario, hoping always that we can in this way free ourselves from it, that we can make a new ending.

Jane Rule argues that a relationship based on dependent mother-love is degrading and doomed to failure. She comments:

> I am always nervous about the suggestion that, as lesbians, we should mother each other, though I understand that the image comes from our first source of love. Our mothers are also the first source of rejecting power against whom we screamed our dependent rage. As adults, if we cry out for that mother-love, the dependent rage inevitably follows, and what is even more disconcerting is that, given total attention and sympathy, we are soon restless to be free, for we aren't any longer children.[30]

In this gripping re-run of our early emotional lives, it seems that men can stand in for our mummies, or women represent our daddies. What is riveting is the *internal* dynamic, the replay of the tragic drama. As Miriam tells Jackson in *Small Changes:*

> I wasn't a loved child, and I have those mechanisms of the woman who gets hooked on trying to make someone love her. You become the father I was never pretty enough to please. You become the mother who never found my best good enough.[31]

In her book, *Room to Breathe,* Jenny James states that for her the endless re-enactment is of winning not her mother's, but her father's love. She describes how, in one relationship after another, an inaccessible and desired person becomes unwanted as soon as they are won over and thus cease to recreate the right degree of childhood pain.[32]

But what is it that makes certain people "right" to stand in for our mothers and fathers in this way? Is it, as some believe, the recognition of a twin soul reincarnated from the passion of a past life?[33] Or is that they are in the right place at the right time and imagination does the rest? There may be superficial parallels in personality and behaviour, but sometimes more invisible connections seem to be at work.

Here it seems relevant to examine how falling in love is experienced in the body. It is often associated with acute physical sensations, such as stomach churning, warm glows, tingles down the spine, and so on. However, these sensations are rarely investigated or correlated to our emotional experience.[34] Our ignorance of the body is so immense that I can only mention certain aspects of our experience which need to be discussed and understood at much greater depth.

Though I have said the experience may not be primarily a sexual one, it is certainly physical. We are to a certain extent aware of how the five senses are involved. Eyes are often the magnet for attraction, as in "love at first sight." The voice of the beloved is often important: in fairy stories a person may fall in love with the sound of another's singing. Taste and smell are perhaps more important than we consciously recognise. Techniques apparently now exist for odour "fingerprinting" of human bodies: perhaps some people carry a smell which reaches us very effectively or echoes the irresistible smell of mother. The implication of recognising the role of sight, hearing and smell may be that we can be physically sensitive to a person before there is any contact. Our bodies may respond to a stranger in far more ways than we are consciously aware of. Touch is also important. Here a woman recounts a common experience: "When I first met J., I was sitting next to her in a chair. My hand accidently brushed against hers and I felt a charge between us like electricity, as if there was a current between our two hands."[35]

Here we have to stop and reconsider. Another vocabulary is entering the accounts. Why is it that one person's touch, given it is equally smooth or gentle or hot or cold, feels so different from another's and can galvanise us, or not? Why is it that one person's eyes say "Hello," while another's reach into the soul and draw it magnetically? Here we are moving beyond the generally recognised powers of the five senses. What do we believe the eyes do when they "mesmerise"? What do the eyes and voice do when they "hypnotise"? The language of Alison Buckley's poem is illuminating:

> In the first splash of meeting, first half-second
> I looked; I saw she was open like a radar-scanner
> picking up every prickly tingle from me. Smiles zoomed out
> undulating quanta of warmth, racing each other
> penetrating, and bursting inside my eyes
> travelling light years inside my head.

Radar, electricity. A contact which zooms, races, penetrates, undulates like radio waves. This is precisely the kind of language used by esoteric anatomy to describe the phenomenon of the "energy body" which is thought to interpenetrate and surround our physical body.

The theory is that each person has an energy-field similar to, but not identical with, an electromagnetic energy-field.[36] This "electromagnetic" energy runs through the body along channels and radiates outwards from it. An inner layer of radiation close to the skin surface has been recorded photographically by Kirlian aura photography[37] which shows variations in the aura depending on the health, temper and state of mind of the person. The theory also suggests that people's energy-fields interact with each other. We can respond unconsciously to the energy emitted by another, and may be attracted or repelled by conflicts or resonances in the energy-fields.

This theory has some resonances in our everyday experience. There is the language of "good vibes" and "bad vibes" and of being "drawn" to or getting a "buzz" from someone. There are the metaphors of electricity from the accounts I have quoted, and many people will recognise the experience of feeling "drained" by spending time with a depressed person. Some people may have experienced the movement of "energy" in their body during yoga exercises, or may have met it as "body energy" in bioenergetic massage or therapy; others may relate it to the "meridians" of acupuncture.

This language could be used to give expression to the powerful rushes of feeling between lovers. One way of describing falling in love could be as a bonding between two people who have a particularly acute and needed exchange of energy to make with one another. This might explain the intense feelings of separation and difference combined with feelings of kinship: like two pieces of a jigsaw puzzle, each has what the other needs to make her whole. This "fine" energy contact has been described as a sixth sense which imbues and informs the contact made through the other five. It sums up the feeling of wordless connection as a movement of energy between two people. It could account for the sense of undercutting normal ways of relating, as well as the sense of being physically potentiated, experiencing intimacy and close contact, without sex necessarily being the prime mover.

I am suggesting this approach as another of the theoretical frameworks which we could use for understanding the process of falling in love. It is not a popular approach, but it interests me personally as it provides a language for certain aspects of the experience which other theories ignore. We do not have to "believe" in it, any more than we have to "believe" in projection, but we can explore the usefulness of each framework. Nor do I see any of the theories described in this (personal and certainly incomplete) survey as incompatible or mutually exclusive alternatives. To say that two people have mutually interlocking energy-fields may be another way of saying that one has been building up tension which the other can release; or that one smells like the other's mother; or that they are formed so that it is easy for each to project onto the other; or that they fill holes in each other's personality. The same process can be understood on a number of different levels. To talk about "energy" does not exclude looking at things in psychological and social terms, although we need to develop a more subtle framework to combine these understandings.

As an ineffable, intense and other-worldly experience, being in love has been compared to religious ecstasy. It has also been suggested that sexual relationships more often have spiritual overtones for women than for men. Béla Grunberger writes: "As man's sexual life is focused on immediate instinctual relief, woman's love is also located in time, but she dreams of eternity."[38] Socially we can explain this male/female difference, if it exists, as a result of our upbringing and conditioning around sexuality and relationships; but what is being referred to may be the greater facility women experience in tuning in to fine energy. Alexander Lowen defines the soul as "the sense or feeling in a person of being part of a larger or universal order,"[39] and sees it as the result of our body energy interacting with the energy around us in the world and in the universe, which gives the feeling of being part of something bigger than yourself. Perhaps the strong link which occurs when we fall in love can open us up to these wider connections. Perhaps it is an experience which opens the "lines" between ourselves and the world.[40] In a culture which denies spirituality outside the confines of established religion, falling in love may have become unusually important as one of our few routes to an experience of the transcendent. It has been understood as a distortion of a deep urge to love the world which through social pressures gets funnelled into one person.

In this, falling in love typifies the contradictory nature of our experiences under capitalism and patriarchy, our efforts to be human in a world organised along inhuman lines. The positive is so entwined with the negative. Falling in loves makes us feel strong, but it also makes us feel weak. It is liberating, but it is also obsessive. It tunes us in to our love and warmth, but also to our gaping need and vulnerability. It reaches out, yet it is highly individualistic. Even the much-vaunted melting and closeness has been open to challenge. Though spiritual disciplines may suggest that "Love is the recognition of the same consciousness in another as in oneself,"[41] others assert that true contact involves a recognition of separateness and differences.[42] From the perspective of political activity, falling in love has been seen as regressive, self-indulgent, privatised, time-wasting.

So how should we deal with it from a perspective of feminism? Should we struggle against these tendencies and feelings in ourselves as counter-productive? I don't think so. Rather, I feel we should take that power and vitality and work with them. If we were not damaged and empty, if our life-experiences had been different, perhaps our loving would not be shot through with need, pain and obsession. But we are as we are, and we have to start from there. Rather than denigrating falling in love, we could see it as a healthy response to a crazy world and perhaps one of the stratagems our organism uses to survive. Perhaps it gives a release where a release is badly needed. On many levels it seems to be a vehicle for the expression of the suppressed. We could see it as a distorted expression of real needs, but in some ways it may be a healthy choice for us: a lifeline enabling us to give and receive love in a way we usually cannot. The idea of love may have been misused, but to deny that we want and need intimacy with others is to avoid the whole issue.[43] We probably need both symbiosis with and separateness from other people, and what is important is for us to develop access to both, to open the channels so that we can move easily into each as we need, instead of lurching in juddering spasms from one to the other, out of control.[44] Instead of attempting to censor or dismiss these passionate feelings, we could work creatively with them. Perhaps the question is not why we have these "incorrect" and humiliating experiences and how we can stop having them, but rather why that intensity and vitality of contact is confined to such a localised area; and how we can gain more access to experiencing and directing that vitality in other areas of our lives.

How can we do this? The first and crucial step seems to be owning our own power in the situation. We use the term "falling" in love which disguises the fact that we have chosen to leap and have abdicated responsibility for our experience. The feelings, fantasies and sensations that possess us are in fact our own. We say that another "makes" us feel unbelievable excitement, but actually the excitement is ours.[45] If we can feel it in one situation, we can feel it in another. We need to cease thinking of others as the source or reference point for our feelings, and recognise our own role more clearly.

One way of doing this is to become more conscious of the stages and details of the process of falling in love. It is time to stop muddying our experience by talking about things which "mysteriously happened" to us. What exactly *did* happen? Where did I feel it in my body? When have I experienced similar sensations? Who or what triggered it? What did they do? What did I do? What happens if I do something different? Gradually we can learn the paths into all these experiences for ourselves.[46] One area to clarify is the link for each of us with sexuality. What turns us on sexually? What makes us fall in love? What is the difference? We need to get more familiar with the body's language. As Jane Rule comments:

> Sex is not so much an identity as a language which we have for so long been forbidden to speak that most of us learn only the crudest of its vocabulary and grammar. If we are to get past the pattern of dominance and submission, of possessive greed, we must outgrow love as fever, as "the tragic necessity of human life," and speak in tongues that set us free to be loving equals.[47]

Body awareness seems crucial. How can we retain a sense of our own power when we are draining out of our bodies to identify with another? One woman reports realising that "the most important thing was not to make him love me but for me to love aliveness."[48] Our experience of aliveness is in and through our body's sensations and processes: this is our ground, our sustenance, our inner richness, and we lose our power if we abandon it.

There are other aspects of the process with which we can get more familiar. What if I start a relationship with a slow burner rather than a flash in the pan? What do I gain or lose? If falling in love is a reaction to suppression, what exactly do I need to release: anger? sexual desire? grief? political energy? What other ways do I have of breaking out, of expressing what is held in? If projection is involved, we can ask: What *are* my "fancies" about this person I fancy? When have I had similar fantasies? How do they connect to fantasies I have about myself? What does this person have that I need or believe that I lack? How can I bring those qualities into my life independently of them?[49] What does this person potentiate in me, and how could I potentiate it in myself? We might also ask: Is this person like my mother/father? In what ways does s/he love or fail me like my mother/father did? Do I want to change that and make a new ending?

If falling in love makes us feel spiritual, what else has the same effect? If we feel something similar when massaging or meditating or gardening or listening to music, we can watch those experiences. What are the situations, the ingredients, the states of mind that predispose us to feel that way? Thus we can learn how to choose certain experiences and not others. Falling in love is not unfathomable: the fathoms are ours, and we can learn to swim in our own depths without diminishing their power and beauty.

Another step we can take is consciously to broaden the scope of our loving feelings. Part of this may be to realise that we "fall in love" in situations far from the socially recognised romantic or sexual ones. Because our culture does not validate such feelings, we tend to dismiss them ourselves. In accordance with prevailing economic and social pressures, we envision a hierarchy of relationships with the perfect couple at the top, while "chance encounters with . . . children, old people, gas fitters, kite-flyers, just don't have a look in."[50] Here a woman describes a situation which would never normally be graced with the title of "being in love":

> "Oh Johnny, it's you!" When my granny was dying, my brother looked after her and they developed a love relationship. When he visited her in hospital after an operation, she greeted him as she would a lover. There was an intimacy and excitement and interest and tenderness between them which looked to me like two people who are in love.[51]

We hear of non-sexual relationships between women which carry passion, fascination, delight and a peculiar resonance for the two friends involved. Mothers describe being "in love" with their babies, intimately bonded by a magic line as strong as an umbilical cord. And it does not stop with people. A teenager may claim to be "in love" with a horse. And what about moments of work which we can suddenly connect to, or the love-affair with a particular career or activity which may last stormily over many years? Or the times when ideas seize us and obsess us? Or the feeling of uplift on a mass demonstration when we feel intensely towards every other human being there? We can "fall in love" with ourselves, or with a country, or with a movement. Perhaps recognising and nurturing those experiences can be one way of diffusing the passionate intimacy and contact of "falling in love" into wider areas of our lives. Enormous power and vitality is involved: imagine what we could do with it. As *Ink* pointed out:

> Puritans should note what while . . . resistance can take the form of the worker's absolute need for food and shelter, it is also manifested in the desire for excitement instead

of boredom, love instead of politeness. The desire for love, conscious of itself and what opposes it, would become a determination to transform the whole of human behaviour and its economic roots.[52]

I would like to believe that it could. The first step may be to accept and know our own experience better, and to move outwards from there. We may be able to make the first step towards transforming our love from a bewildering passion for one person to a deep-rooted lust for all of life. We can at least try.

NOTES

1. The leaflet, headed "Everything tends to reduce lovers to objects," is marked BIB 2, bubble CPP—bm.

2. This lack of discussion of the subject is pointed out by Daphne Davis, "Falling in love again," *Red Rag, A Magazine of Women's Liberation*, no. 13, p. 12. Elizabeth Wilson also notes with regret the way that socialism and feminism have neglected romance, in "Fruits of Passion," *City Limits*, No. 74, March, 1983.

3. This point is expressed more fully by Davis, *op. cit.*, pp. 12, 13.

4. From Alison Buckley, "For Tasha," in *Art and Feminism*, Laurieston Hall, 1977.

5. Rosie Boycott, "Falling in love again," *Honey*, IPC Magazines, 1982. The article is a detailed personal account of the start of an intense love affair.

6. Marge Piercy, *Small Changes*, Fawcett Publications, Greenwich, Conn., 1974, p. 193.

7. *ibid.*, pp. 194, 195.

8. *Ink in Love: Exploding the Romantic Myth*, Ink No. 29, 21 February 1972, p. 12.

9. This is one of a number of personal accounts by women which for reasons of privacy I am leaving anonymous. I am indebted to a number of other women who have discussed their experiences with me, have read this piece and expressed encouragement and valuable dis-agreements, as well as giving helpful contributions and suggestions about changes. In partic-ular I would like to thank Sue Cartledge, Inga Czudnochowski, Marie Maguire, Jo Ryan and Stef Pixner.

10. Again, this point is made by Davis, *op. cit.*, p. 13.

11. Buckley, *op. cit.*

12. Piercy, *op. cit.*, p. 195.

13. Erica Jong, *How to Save Your Own Life*, Panther Books, London, 1977, pp. 203, 204, 207, 208.

14. See note 9, above.

15. Piercy, *op. cit.*, p. 197.

16. Piercy, "Burying blues for Janis," in Lucille Iverson and Kathryn Ruby (eds), *We Become New: Poems by Contemporary American Women*, Bantam Books, 1975, pp. 4–5.

17. *ibid.*

18. Slim, "If I loved me half as much as I love you," in *Country Women*, issue 24, pp. 18–20.

19. Jong, *op. cit.*, p. 207.

20. *Ink in Love, op. cit.*, p. 8.

21. Frederick S. Perls, *Gestalt Therapy Verbatim*, Bantam Books, London, 1971, p. 10.

22. This point is made in Ralph Metzner, *Maps of Consciousness*, Collier Macmillan, London, 1971, p. 152. Showing that projection is not unique to this century, Stendhal discusses

the same process under the term "crystalisation." See Stendhal, *Love*, trans. by Gilbert and Suzanne Sale, Penguin, Harmondsworth, 1975.

23. See Liz Greene, *Relating: An Astrological Guide to Living with others on a small Planet*, Coventure, London, 1976, pp. 149–150.

24. Raymond Durgnat, *Eros in the Cinema*, Marion Boyars, 1966.

25. Perls, *op. cit.*, p. 40.

26. Metzner, *op. cit.*, p. 152.

27. Jane Roberts, *The Nature of Personal Reality: A Seth Book*, Prentice-Hall, New Jersey, 1974, p. 382.

28. See Roberto Assagioli, *Psychosynthesis*, Turnstone Books, 1975, pp. 25–6.

29. Melanie Klein, *Envy and Gratitude and Other Works 1946–63*, Hogarth Press, 1963, p. 100.

30. Jane Rule, "Homophobia and romantic love," in *Outlander: Stories and Essays*, The Naiad Press, Florida, 1981, p. 184.

31. Piercy, *Small Changes*, p. 211.

32. Jenny James, *Room to Breathe*, Coventure, London, 1975, p. 151.

33. See, for example, Dion Fortune, *The Esoteric Philosophy of Love and Marriage*, The Aquarian Press, Wellingborough, 1974, pp. 60–2.

34. Davis in *Red Rag, op. cit.*, p. 13, makes this point and suggests that we may imagine we are in love when all we are feeling are sexual desires or hunger pangs.

35. See note 9, above.

36. For a fuller account of this theory, see David V. Tansley, *Radionics and the Subtle Anatomy of Man*, Health Science Press, Devon, 1972.

37. For a brief account of this method, see Brian and Marita Snellgrove, *The Unseen Self*, Kirlian Aura Diagnosis, Carshalton, Surrey, 1979.

38. Bela Grunberger, "Narcissism in female sexuality," in Janine Chasseguet-Smirgel, (ed), *Female Sexuality: New Psychoanalytic Views*, Virago, London, 1981, p. 71.

39. Alexander Lowen, *Bioenergetics*, Coventure, London, 1976, p. 67.

40. This term comes from the books of Carlos Castaneda. See, for example, the incident where Castaneda "sees" the "lines," in *Journey to Ixtlan*, Penguin, Harmondsworth, 1974, p. 267.

41. This idea is suggested by the Arica spiritual teachings.

42. Perls, for example, distinguishes "confluence" from real contact which consists of the appreciation of differences. See *Gestalt Therapy Verbatim*, pp. 271–2.

43. As Davis points out in *Red Rag, op. cit.*, p. 12.

44. For many of the ideas in this passage, and particularly here, I am indebted to the therapeutic work of Jenner Roth in her sexuality workshops and in her individual therapy practice in London.

45. See note 44.

46. See note 44.

47. Rule, *op. cit.*, p. 185.

48. Slim, *op. cit.*, p. 20.

49. Gestalt therapy offers some simple and useful techniques for owning fantasies and projections by role-playing. See Sheila Ernst and Lucy Goodison, *In Our Own Hands*, The Women's Press, London, 1981, chs. 3, 6.

50. *Ink in Love, op. cit.*, p. 9.

51. See note 9, above.

52. *Ink in Love, op. cit.*, p. 12.

Chapter Thirty-four

Black Men and the Love and Trouble Tradition (1990)

Patricia Hill Collins

This American feminist theorist comments on the double message of African American women's writing and singing in the blues tradition: men are strongly loved but they are also troublesome, if not abusive. She connects this "love and trouble tradition" to gender ideologies of femininity and masculinity in the West, in conjunction with the unique historical role of racial oppression informing black male and female relations.

In her ground-breaking essay, "On the Issue of Roles," Toni Cade Bambara remarks, "now it doesn't take any particular expertise to observe that one of the most characteristic features of our community is the antagonism between our men and our women" (Bambara 1970a, 106). Exploring the tensions between African-American men and women has been a long-standing theme in Black feminist thought. In an 1833 speech, Maria Stewart boldly challenged what she saw as Black men's lackluster response to racism: "Talk, without effort, is nothing; you are abundantly capable, gentlemen, of making yourselves men of distinction; and this gross neglect, on your part, causes my blood to boil within me" (Richardson 1987, 58). Ma Rainey, Bessie Smith, and other classic Black women blues singers offer rich advice to Black women on how to deal with unfaithful and unreliable men (Harrison 1978, 1988; Lieb 1981; Russell 1982). More recently, Black women's troubles with Black men have generated anger and, from that anger, self-reflection: "We have been and are angry sometimes," suggests Bonnie Daniels, "not for what men have done, but for what we've allowed ourselves to become, again and again in my past, in my mother's past, in my centuries of womanhood passed over, for the 'sake' of men, whose manhood we've helped undermine" (1979, 62).

Another long-standing theme in Black feminist thought is the great love Black women feel for Black men. African-American slave narratives contain countless examples of newly emancipated slaves who spent years trying to locate their lost loved ones (Gutman 1976). Love poems written to Black men characterize much of Black women's poetry (Stetson 1981). Black women's music is similarly replete with love songs. Whether the playful voice of Alberta Hunter proclaiming that her "man is a handy man," the mournful cries of Billie Holiday singing "My Man," the sadness Nina Simone evokes in "I Loves You Porgy" at being forced to leave her man, or the powerful voice of Jennifer Holliday, who cries out, "you're gonna love me," Black vocalists identify Black women's relationships with Black men as a source of strength, support, and sustenance (Harrison 1978, 1988; Russell 1982). Black activist Fannie Lou Hamer succinctly captures what a good relationship between a Black woman and man can be: "You know, I'm not hung up on this about liberating myself from the black man, I'm not going to try that thing. I got a black husband, six feet three, two hundred and forty pounds, with a 14 shoe, that I don't *want* to be liberated from" (Lerner 1972, 612).

African-American women have long commented on this "love and trouble" tradition in Black women's relationships with Black men. Novelist Gayl Jones explains: "The relationships between the men and the women I'm dealing with are blues relationships. So they're out of a tradition of 'love and trouble.' . . . Blues talks about the simultaneity of good and bad, as feeling, as something felt. . . . Blues acknowledges all different kinds of feelings at once" (Harper 1979, 360). Both the tensions between African-American women and men and the strong attachment that we feel for one another represent the both/and conceptual stance in Black feminist thought.

Understanding this love and trouble tradition requires assessing the influence of Eurocentric gender ideology—particularly its emphasis on oppositional dichotomous sex roles—on the work and family experiences of African-Americans. Definitions of appropriate gender behavior for Black women, Black men, white women, and white men not only affect social institutions such as schools and labor markets, they also simultaneously shape daily interactions among and within each group. Analyses claiming that African-Americans would be "just like whites" if offered comparable opportunities implicitly support the prevailing sex/gender hierarchy and offer the allegedly "normal" gender ideology of white male and female sex roles as alternatives for putatively "deviant" Afrocentric ones. Similarly, those proclaiming that Black men experience more severe oppression than Black women and that Black women must unquestioningly support Black male sexism rarely challenge the overarching gender ideology that confines both whites and Blacks (see, e.g., Staples 1979). As Audre Lorde queries, "if society ascribes roles to black men which they are not allowed to fulfill, is it black women who must bend and alter our lives to compensate, or is it society that needs changing?" (1984, 61). Bonnie Daniels provides an answer: "I've learned . . . that being less than what I am capable of being to boost someone else's ego *does not help either of us* for real" (1979, 61).

Black women intellectuals directly challenge not only that portion of Eurocentric gender ideology applied to African-Americans—for example, the controlling images of mammy, the matriarch, the welfare mother, and Jezebel—but often base this rejection on a more general critique of Eurocentric gender ideology itself. Sojourner Truth's 1851 query, "I could work as much and eat as much as a man—when I could get it—and bear the lash as well! And ain't I a woman?" confronts the premises of the cult of true womanhood that "real" women were fragile and ornamental. Toni Cade Bambara contends that Eurocentric sex roles are not only troublesome for African-Americans but damaging: "I have always, I think, opposed the stereotypical definitions of 'masculine' and 'feminine,' . . . because I always found the either/or implicit in those definitions antithetical to what I was all about—and what revolution for self is all about—the whole person" (Bambara 1970, 101). Black activist Frances Beale echoes Bambara by identifying the negative effects that sexism within the Black community had on Black political activism in the 1960s:

> Unfortunately, there seems to be some confusion in the Movement today as to who has been oppressing whom. Since the advent of Black power, the Black male has exerted a more prominent leadership role in our struggle for justice in this country. He sees the system for what it really is for the most part, but where he rejects its values and mores on many issues, when it comes to women, he seems to take his guidelines from the pages of the *Ladies' Home Journal*. (Beale 1970, 92)

While some African-American women criticize Eurocentric gender ideology, even fewer have directly challenged Black men who accept externally defined notions of both Black and white masculinity (Sizemore 1973; Wallace 1978). The blues tradition provides the most consistent and long-standing text of Black women who demand that Black men reject stereotypical sex roles and "change their ways." Songs often encourage Black men to define new types of relationships. In "Do Right Woman— Do Right Man," when Aretha Franklin (1967) sings that a woman is only human and is not a plaything but is flesh and blood just like a man, she echoes Sojourner Truth's claim that women and men are equally human. Aretha sings about knowing that she's living in a "man's world" but she encourages her man not to "prove" that he's a man by using or abusing her. As long as she and her man are together, she wants him to show some "respect" for her. Her position is clear—if he wants a "do right, all night woman," he's got to be a "do right, all night man." Aretha challenges African-American men to reject Eurocentric gender ideology that posits "it's a man's world" in order to be a "do right man." By showing Black women respect and being an "all night" man—one who is faithful, financially reliable, and sexually expressive— Black men can have a relationship with a "do right woman."

REFERENCES

(Bambara), Toni Cade. 1970. "On the Issue of Roles." In *The Black Woman: An Anthology*, edited by Toni Cade (Bambara), 101–10. New York: Signet.

Beale, Frances. 1970. "Double Jeopardy: To Be Black and Female." In *The Black Woman: An Anthology*, edited by Toni Cade (Bambara), 90–100. New York: Signet.

Daniels, Bonnie. 1979. "For Colored Girls . . . A Catharsis." *Black Scholar* 10(8–9): 61–62.

Franklin, Aretha. 1967. *I Never Loved a Man the Way I Love You*. Atlantic Recording Corp.

Gutman, Herbert. 1976. *The Black Family in Slavery and Freedom, 1750–1925*. New York: Random House.

Harper, Michael S. 1979. "Gayl Jones: An Interview." In *Chant of Saints: A Gathering of Afro-American Literature, Art, and Scholarship*, edited by Michael S. Harper and Robert B. Stepto, 352–75. Urbana: University of Illinois Press.

Harrison, Daphne Duval. 1978. "Black Women in the Blues Tradition." In *The Afro-American Woman: Struggles and Images,* edited by Sharon Harley and Rosalyn Terborg-Penn, 58–73. Port Washington, NY: Kennikat Press.

———. 1988. *Black Pearls: Blues Queens of the 1920s.* New Brunswick, NJ. Rutgers University Press.

Lerner, Gerda, ed. 1972. *Black Women in White America: A Documentary History.* New York: Vintage.

Lieb, Sandra. 1981. *Mother of the Blues: A Study of Ma Rainey.* Amherst: University of Massachusetts Press.

Lorde, Audre. 1984. *Sister Outsider.* Trumansburg, NY: The Crossing Press.

Richardson, Marilyn, ed. 1987. *Maria W. Stewart, America's First Black Women Political Writer.* Bloomington: Indiana University Press.

Russell, Michele. 1982. "Slave Codes and Liner Notes." *In But Some of Us Are Brave,* edited by Gloria T. Hull, Patricia Bell Scott, and Barbara Smith, 129–40. Old Westbury, NY: Feminist Press.

Sizemore, Barbara A. 1973. "Sexism and the Black Male." *Black Scholar* 4(6–7): 2–11.

Staples, Robert. 1979. "The Myth of Black Macho: A Response to Angry Black Feminists." *Black Scholar* 10(6): 24–33.

Stetson, Erlene, ed. 1981. *Black Sister: Poetry by Black American Women, 1746–1980.* Bloomington: Indiana University Press.

Wallace, Michele. 1978. *Black Macho and the Myth of the Superwoman.* New York: Dial Press.

Chapter Thirty-five

From Beyond Sex and Romance?
Lesbian Relationships in Contemporary Fiction (1998)

Lynne Harne

The author argues that contemporary politics pushes lesbians into monogamous romance and coupledom, after the model of heterosexual relations. She decries the easy acceptance of this hetero romantic paradigm and calls for a challenge to it within lesbianism.

I have been reading lesbian feminist contemporary fiction on and off since the early days of the women's movement in the 1970s. For me as for many other lesbian feminists, such fiction provides not only enjoyment but also at times affirmation of lesbian feminist identity, and on occasion it has reflected and contributed to debates about lesbian feminist politics. With some notable exceptions, however, I have found representations of lesbian feminist personal relationships in such fiction problematic. They are often imitative of heterosexual literature and present images of lesbian intimate relationships that are either highly romanticised or from the libertarian end of the spectrum, pornographic and objectifying of women, with some novels utilising both types of representation. Moreover, representations of friendship between lesbians which are not sexual and other types of important relationships that lesbians may have, such as political and work relationships, are infrequently foregrounded as the subject matter of lesbian novels.

As such we are left with ideological messages about lesbian identity and politics which can be profoundly reactionary. Such messages convey the impression that in order to be a lesbian you have to be in a romantic and sexual relationship and that the fundamental goal of all lesbians is long-term domestic coupledom. Lesbians who are not in such relationships are viewed as "sad and lonely" or sexually and emotionally "unfulfilled." Long-term coupledom is also seen as the only means of providing real security and safety for lesbians. The ideologies of "falling in love" and / or sexual desire and attraction are viewed as unquestionable and unchallengeable emotions. These may be presented from an essentialist perspective as "natural" feelings or from

From Lynne Harne, "Beyond Sex and Romance? Lesbian Relationships in Contemporary Fiction," in *Beyond Sex and Romance? The Politics of Contemporary Lesbian Fiction,* ed. Elaine Hutton (London: Women's Press, 1998), 124–28. Reprinted by permission of the Women's Press Ltd.

poststructuralist and psychoanalytic perspectives as being so deeply embedded within our psyches that they are out of our control.[1] Lesbians who are not in a sexual and emotional relationship are regarded as constantly being on the look-out for such a relationship or recovering from the last one. Perhaps such representations in what purports to be lesbian feminist fiction are not surprising, given the current paucity of political debate and discussion around lesbian personal relationships.

While lesbian feminists have highlighted the institution of heterosexuality as one of the cornerstones of patriarchal control of women, the ideologies of romantic love and of long-term "monogamy" have been only spasmodically challenged and although issues such as autonomy and inequality have been addressed *within* lover relationships, the powerful discourse of coupledom, and a recognition that this can work against women's autonomy and the sustaining of feminist movements, has not been seriously critiqued in recent years. Julie Bindel and Joan Scanlon (1996) suggest that there has been a retreat into unquestioning coupledom by lesbian feminists as a response to the sexual exploitation and objectification of women represented in the sexual libertarian and S & M debates of the 1980s, and that there is an assumption that "couple-structured relationships" are the only (moral) alternative to "SM culture." This retreat has been increased by material considerations such as fears of economic insecurity as the welfare state has diminished and by the professionalisation of feminist politics whereby the public and private worlds have once again become politically separated. This gap between the public and private has to a large extent been filled by therapy, which has not only depoliticised lesbian personal relationships to such a degree that it is almost impossible not to talk about them in psychological terms[2] but has also had a profoundly negative effect on questioning the benefits of the couple relationship.

Much therapy for lesbians appears to be oriented towards reinforcing couple relationships: examples include couple counselling for relationships that are on the rocks; therapy to spice up your sex life when so called "lesbian bed death" occurs (perhaps they just found something better to do); therapy for lesbians who love too much (what about the ideology of romance here); and therapy to "recover" so that you can move on to the next relationship. Perhaps most insidiously the therapist becomes a synthetic substitute friend, a friend who will provide a sympathetic listening ear but who won't challenge you politically about your life.

The assimilationist politics of the lesgay movement, which has dispensed with feminist analysis, has also had an impact. This movement is campaigning for the legal recognition of lesbian and gay marriages and for lesbian and gay couples to have the same social rights as heterosexual couples, rather than challenging the assumptions of dependency involved in such policies and the ideology that it is desirable that everyone should live in couple relationships. The widespread adoption of the term "partner," which tends to sound like a business arrangement, is an outcome of this type of politics.

On a more positive note, there do appear to be the beginnings of renewed theoretical debate on the politics of lesbians' personal relationships among lesbian feminists, including questioning the practice of prioritising and valuing the sexual couple relationship over and above other kinds of relationships, such as close friendships between women. Janice Raymond's ground-breaking book *A Passion for Friends* (1986) was one of the first to theorise the importance of *discerning* friendship in sustaining and building feminist movement, arguing that it is as much hetero-*relations* as hetero-*sexuality* that sustains hetero-patriarchy.

Going beyond the debates on "non-monogamy" in the 1970s and early 1980s among lesbian feminists, where the issue was seen mainly in sexual terms, Becky Rosa (1994, pp 107–8) defines monogamy as "the ideology that as adults we should primarily bond with one person, meeting most of our [socially constructed] needs from them (sexual, emotional, physical etc.)." We might also add to this list political, social and intellectual needs. Bindel and Scanlon stress that the concept of monogamy was developed by men to prescribe sexual fidelity for women, and was not ever meant to apply to men. They argue that it is the enforcing of "emotional monogamy" through the practice of couplism that is damaging to the development of intimate friendships and to sustaining lesbian feminist political networks.

Rosa also questions whether the very real feelings of insecurity that lesbians experience actually diminish in exclusive couple relationships. While such relationships may for a time provide a sense of safety from a patriarchal heterosexual world, the impossible demands often put on such relationships to make up for all kinds of insecurities invariably fail and result in relationship break-up. Friends are then turned to for emotional and social support, until a new relationship starts and the friend(s) may once again become less important than the new lover. She argues that so much time may be taken up in developing and sustaining a couple relationship that this allows little time for building feminist community and political activism.

Some lesbian feminists do attempt to practice their personal relationships in a different way, but, as Bindel and Scanlon emphasise, this is difficult to do in the current political and cultural vacuum where any questioning of romance and couple-dom can appear "unreasonable or judgemental." In the early days of second-wave feminism, the ideology of romance was challenged far more than it is today, when any sexual relationship between lesbians is often now referred to uncritically as a "romantic relationship," to distinguish it from and give it more value than (non-sexual) friendships.

Lesbian feminists have also problematised the male-defined concepts and language of personal relationships as applied to women, arguing that in the twentieth century a false dichotomy between sexual intimacy and friendship has been created, where only the former is supposed to carry with it close feelings of intimacy (Rosa, 1994). But there is also a danger in attempting to turn the clock back and romanticising friendships. Raymond warned against sentimentalising or assuming any natural capacity for women to be friends with each other, as happened in the early days of the movement. It cannot be assumed that we can be friends with all women, or that "politics and friendship" always go together. Friendship can operate in many different ways and on different levels; nevertheless, many women experience friendships which are important in organising for political change and / or have considerable impact on their lives.

The confines of male-defined language remain. While lesbian feminists have attempted to replace the romantic connotations of the word *love* with others to describe all different kinds of close relationships and friendships between women, such attempts have so far been unsuccessful. Words such as affection[3] seem hopelessly sentimental for the beginning of the twenty-first century, and we are left with inadequate terms to describe the different kinds of personal relationships that lesbian feminists may have with each other but that do not fit into the prescribed categories discussed above.

NOTES

1. The psychoanalytic "out of control" perspective is reflected in the novels of Sarah Schulman, which I do not propose discussing in this chapter as I do not consider them feminist.

2. See, for example, Celia Kitzinger and Rachel Perkins, *Changing Our Minds: Lesbian Feminism and Psychology,* Onlywomen Press, London, 1993.

3. Raymond (1986) refers to "gyn/affection," but this is not a term which has been widely adopted by lesbian feminists.

REFERENCES

Bindel, Julie and Joan Scanlon, "Barking Back", *Trouble and Strife,* 33 (Summer 1996), pp 68–72

Raymond, Janice, *A Passion for Friends: Toward a Philosophy of Female Affection,* The Women's Press, London, 1986

Rosa, Becky, "Anti-monogamy: A Radical Challenge to Compulsory Heterosexuality?", in Gabriele Griffin, Marianne Hester, Shirin Rai and Sasha Roseneil, eds, *Stirring It: Challenges for Feminism,* Taylor and Francis, London, 1994

Chapter Thirty-six

From Search for Tomorrow
On Feminism and the Reconstruction of Teen Romance (1984)

Sharon Thompson

Thompson, a writer and activist, focuses on the mixed messages contemporary society gives teenage girls about empowerment in relation to sex and romance. She calls for feminism to be more responsive to the pull of the pleasures of romance to teenage girls, as well as its dangers for them.

From a feminist perspective, the efforts of teenage girls to shape their sexual lives are striking in the degree to which they involve an attempt to exercise sexual power, particularly given how poor a bargaining position many feel they are in and how desperately they want to make the bargain of sex for love. But there are clearly problems here, both for teenage girls and for feminism.

At the least, many teenage girls seem in dire need of some of the basics of feminist advice. The pain and frustration that many heterosexual teenage girls feel stems, largely, from the futility of trying to blindly strike the old bargain of sex for love under changed material and social conditions. They need to know that it is not because there is something wrong with them that the old bargain no longer works. They need to know what some possible terms of new bargains might be and have some broader understanding of the different ways in which adolescent sexual experience might be—or has been—shaped and explicated. They need to know more about pleasure—that they have a right to pleasure and how to get it. They need to have a more objective understanding of what is going on in male sexual decision-making.

Feminism has not very effectively communicated its understanding of the sexual and romantic dialectic to teenage girls, although it has had liberating and clarifying significance for the lives of teenage girls in its defense of teenage sexual and reproductive freedom and its support of teenage girls' right to know the facts about their bodies and about sexuality. Those who have dispensed feminist advice to teenagers in the recent past have fallen, with notable, mostly health-oriented exceptions, into the traps of protectionism and euphemism. One wing of the feminist movement talks solely in terms of rape, incest, molestation, and exploitation. There is unquestionably a place in feminism for this work. But in not acknowledging the limits of a politics that deals with only sexual violence and not with other sexual and romantic themes, and in conflating violence with sexuality, this work often fails to describe, or leave space for, the breadth of teenage girls' experience. The feminist relationship to romance has also taken a toll. Feminism has generally derogated romance. The rationalist tradition that feminism is heir to viewed romance as a variety of superstition that would vanish in the light of reason and free love, and nineteenth- and twentieth-century feminists alike have distrusted romance as one of the chief ways that woman "do it" to themselves, that is, dupe and enchain themselves. Romance, we have said, is a trap too charged with misogyny and domination for women to risk. But can a field so magnetized with Oedipal material be simply written off? And if not, how much can it be moved around, played with, redesigned, resocialized, so that it enriches but does not kill. At the least, there are strategic reasons not to defer to romance but to acknowledge its power.[1]

In contrast to the angry tone of the work that equates sex with violence, another strain of the discourse has been cheerful, characterized by such guidelines as "just be yourself" or "do what you want to do, what will make you happy," notions that rest on some of the most prevalent assumptions of the 1960s;[2] for example, that feelings are simple, linear, trustworthy, and unambiguous; that they are a natural base for morality and spring forth of their own spontaneous energy after the removal of restraints, conventions, and coercion. There are other simplicities here as well. In place of romance, this work has urged healthy peer sex and/or masturbation. The belief that peer sex is naturally pure and equal is naive at best. The emphasis on masturbation is important for its emphasis on the pedagogy of orgasm and for the extent to which it has represented an opposition to the taboo on female sexual autonomy. But the enthusiasm for masturbation as a replacement for other forms of sexual experience raises some questions as well. Is it, perhaps, a way of keeping sex clean, out of the mess of passion and exudation? A way of encouraging girls to turn, as usual, inward? Other pieces of this literature advertise feminism as a solution to the problem of contemporary relationship. Teenage girls are cynical about this material, because it makes light of their experience and it does not work. There are few panaceas for romantic and sexual problems. Feminism can offer a diagnosis regarding the sources of these problems in gender socialization and inequity and a number of long-term strategies for change. It can suggest the path of autonomy, but we have no magic words, no love potions. In the most recent past, a conservative hue about "too much, too soon" has arisen in some feminist quarters, which argue for rulemaking.[3] This position misdiagnoses the key structural problem. Teenage girls are not having too much, too soon. They have too little—too little pleasure, too few options, not enough sexual power. Even if rulemaking were an effective parental option, it would not be so for feminism. Only a return to the primal rule—the shotgun connection of sex, reproduction, and marriage—can make the old bargain of sex for permanent love work. Unless we are prepared to rule out feminism, we must look to a different strategy. We can no more run backwards to the taboos of the past because we see that change brings disorientation and suffering than revolutionaries could voluntarily reinstate a tyrant.

The feminist task in regard to adolescent sexuality is limited and strategic. Feminism can not make romance simple, easy, painless. "There is," as Ellen Willis said, "an irreducible risk in loving," and there are risks in freedom as well.[4] For feminism the chief goal is not finally to protect young girls from the sexual reality but to protect and expand the possibilities for women's liberation—that is, for equalizing the genders and expanding women's opportunities for knowledge, pleasure, and work—for lives rich with personal and collective meaning. We cannot retreat from alienation into the illusory shelter of the past. "There is only one way left to escape the alienation of present day society," as Barthes suggested, *"to retreat ahead of it,"* toward a more supple and various integration of sex, romance, love, and work, the collective and the individual, the shared and the personal.[5]

In regard to theory, there are many open questions. We need to reconsider, for example, the psychoanalytic discourse about latency and separation in connection with sexual experience, and we need to think about ways to enhance patterns of socialization that would lead to a more probable integration of sex and work for girls. The divergence in gender socialization for peer sexual relations also raises some thorny questions. While the gender gap has lessened in some respects, in others it seems to be dangerously widening, as some teenage girls flee to motherhood and boys to anomie. The monogamization of teenage sex also raises serious questions. Is this an expansion of possibility and experience or a reduction?[6]

The feminist relationship to romance also calls for reconsideration. Effective feminist work with teenagers must speak to the magnetism and concerns of sex and romance not dismiss them. Feminism, like romance, must be a dance as well as a march, must admit the pull of the body and of fantasy as well as of conscience, must be a seduction as well as an obligation, appeasement as well as demand, must be a struggle not only for justice and equality, but for the accommodation of these with the web of promise and possibility that winds back through the centuries and will lead toward the future. In practice, this means that feminists must defend the sexual autonomy without which no new culture of adolescent sex and romance can take shape. We must also protect teenagers' reproductive health. These are givens, but in addition feminists must take up again the task of connecting with personal experience. Consciousness raising at puberty could be very important to young girls coming of age sexually because it is precisely at this point that many take on femininity like stigma. Projects focusing on romantic disappointment could speak directly to the concerns of teenage girls (a Heartbreak Hotline? Romantics Anonymous?). We must acknowledge and explicate the difficulty of transforming the relation between the genders and speak to why that transformation is worth the pain of change. We must level with teenage girls and give them an opening to level with feminism—so that feminism becomes theirs as it has been ours. There is no rationale here for false optimism, condescending dogmatism. Adolescents have a notoriously keen distaste for hypocrisy, patronage, condescension, and autocratic invasions of privacy and freedom. Finally, because in the throes of romance, many girls drop out of school or fall behind in their work, feminists must struggle to ensure that those programs that permit students to catch up educationally or return to school after an absence are not cut out of existence as they are currently being, but rather expanded.

In the long run, a strategy consonant with feminism—that is, consonant with the equality of women—must work toward increasing pleasure and decreasing frustration; disentangling sex, intimacy, and romance at least sufficiently so that their difference becomes perceptible; narrowing the distance between the genders; integrating growth, separation, and sensuality; and transforming sexual and reproductive freedom for women into what it has been traditionally—if mythically—for men: a source of comfort, pleasure, and excitement, a sequence, as the quest-romance depicts it, of "marvelous adventures."[7]

But we cannot pretend that sexual and romantic life is a series of marvelous adventures for most teenage girls today. To construct the future, we must acknowledge the painful realities of the present as well as its advantages (which are also, it is important to recall, tangible and significant). We must do this not solely because we want to organize teenagers in defense of feminism, as necessary as that is, but also because if we do not, we leave teenage girls out on the jagged cutting edge created by the separation of sex from reproduction. We leave adolescence for girls, in other words, in perhaps a worse condition than we found it when we were ourselves taken with the fervor of feminism, and that is a grave betrayal not only of feminism, but of women.

NOTES

1. In comparison, the popular forms that appeal to teenage girls—soap operas and romances, for example—seem profoundly, if opportunistically, relevant to teenage experience. Romances go straight to the point: they tantalize with the brass ring of true love; they play out the Oedipal drama. In the end, they proffer a happy Freudian resolution (not frigid but not precisely separated either); but at least the genre makes it clear. The happy ending is fiction. Soap operas touch on separation, on the connection between male and female, on the problem of continuity itself. The lure of the soaps is not happiness but suspense. Like a rigid sex and gender system, they guarantee tomorrow. For discussions of nineteenth-century feminist ideas regarding rationality, sex, and romance, see, for example, William Leach, *True Love and Perfect Union: The Feminist Reform of Sex and Society*, New York, Basic, 1980, and Linda Gordon's review of that volume, "The Women's Dream of Perfect Harmony," *In These Times*, April 8–14, 1981, p. 20. For another discussion of romance, see Shulamith Firestone, *The Dialectic of Sex: The Case for Feminist Revolution*, New York: Bantam, 1970, pp. 146–55.

2. The best-known example is Andrea Eagan's *Why am I so Miserable If These Are the Best Years of My Life?*, New York, Pyramid, 1977, a book whose easy optimism belies its title; see Chapter 1, pp. 19–31, and p. 109. It is important to acknowledge that Eagan was one of the first to recognize that time was separating teenagers and feminists and to attempt to talk feminism and sex to teenage girls. Within the limitations of its terms and genre, the book does its best to have a bearing on real life. Unfortunately, real life turns out to be more complicated and difficult than the genre can reflect.

3. *Ms.*, July 1983, cover and pp. 37–43.

4. Ellen Willis, *Beginning to See the Light*, New York, Random House, 1981, p. 145.

5. Roland Barthes, *The Pleasure of the Text*, New York, Hill & Wang, 1975, p. 40.

6. My instinct here is that strategies that emphasize pressuring boys into the adolescent equivalent of companionate marriage are doomed to failure, and they are not necessarily good for girls. Although there are important cultural differences in these matters, it seems generally the case that boys currently flee the more, the greater the pressure toward intimacy. Adolescence may be at once too soon and too late to resolve the problem of male socialization. Engaging boys in nurturant activities may be a good idea, but irrevocable nuclearity is another issue. And while romantic affirmation may be a tonic for many girls, and while some girls find in pregnancy and early marriage a reason to save their own lives, this may also constitute another way of being "swallowed up by the family."

7. Northrop Frye, *Anatomy of Criticism,* New York: Atheneum, 1966, p. 192.

Part V

Explaining Romance
Feminist History, Sociology, and Psychology

Historians have played an important role in undermining the presumption that romantic love is the same everywhere for everyone. Francesca Cancian and Lillian Faderman, two of the most important historians who have written directly about women and romantic feelings, trace changes in the conceptualization of romance that are important commentaries on the presumed universality of romance. Feminist psychologists and sociologists have attempted a more objective analysis of the phenomenon of romantic love as it has shaped women's lives, while providing a perspective many feminists believe to be lacking in Freudian and other traditionally male explanations of women's psyches. Each author has her own approach to the problem of love for women. For example, Jessica Benjamin emphasizes the eroticized power relations of childhood, which lead to masochistic desires in women's romantic fantasies, while Elaine Hatfield finds that there are few real measurable gender differences in romantic expectations. The British sociologist Stevi Jackson believes that "rehabilitating romance" is not good for women, since it always echoes the conditions of social and economic life.

Chapter Thirty-seven

The Feminization of Love (1986)

Francesca M. Cancian

According to Cancian, a historian, the idea that women's "sphere" is based on romantic love is the "cause of our current social organization of love." We believe, she argues, that women need love more than men and are better at emotional relationships because love itself has become "feminized," particularly in American history. For a more extended treatment of this subject, see her book, Love in America *(1987).*

A feminized and incomplete perspective on love predominates in the United States. We identify love with emotional expression and talking about feelings, aspects of love that women prefer and in which women tend to be more skilled than men. At the same time we often ignore the instrumental and physical aspects of love that men prefer, such as providing help, sharing activities, and sex. This feminized perspective leads us to believe that women are much more capable of love than men and that the way to make relationships more loving is for men to become more like women.[1] This paper proposes an alternative, androgynous perspective on love, one based on the premise that love is both instrumental and expressive.[2] From this perspective, the way to make relationships more loving is for women and men to reject polarized gender roles and integrate "masculine" and "feminine" styles of love.

The Two Perspectives

"Love is active, doing something for your good even if it bothers me" says a fundamentalist Christian. "Love is sharing, the real sharing of feelings" says a divorced secretary who is in love again. In ancient Greece, the ideal love was the adoration of a man for a beautiful young boy who was his lover. In the thirteenth century, the exemplar of love was the chaste devotion of a knight for another man's wife. In Puritan New England, love between husband and wife was the ideal, and in Victorian times, the asexual devotion of a mother for her child seemed the essence

Francesca M. Cancian, "The Feminization of Love," *Signs,* vol. 11, no. 4 (summer 1986): 692–709.

of love.[3] My purpose is to focus on one kind of love: long-term heterosexual love in the contemporary United States.

What is a useful definition of enduring love between a woman and a man? One guideline for a definition comes from the prototypes of enduring love—the relations between committed lovers, husband and wife, parent and child. These relationships combine care and assistance with physical and emotional closeness. Studies of attachment between infants and their mothers emphasize the importance of being protected and fed as well as touched and held. In marriage, according to most family sociologists, both practical help and affection are part of enduring love, or "the affection we feel for those with whom our lives are deeply intertwined."[4] Our own informal observations often point in the same direction: if we consider the relationships that are the prototypes of enduring love, it seems that what we really mean by love is some combination of instrumental and expressive qualities.

Historical studies provide a second guideline for defining enduring love, specifically between a woman and a man.[5] In precapitalist America, such love was a complex whole that included work and feelings. Then it was split into feminine and masculine fragments by the separation of home and workplace. This historical analysis implies that affection, material help, and routine cooperation all are parts of enduring love.

Consistent with these guidelines, my working definition of enduring love between adults is a relationship wherein a small number of people are affectionate and emotionally committed to each other, define their collective well-being as a major goal, and feel obliged to provide care and practical assistance for each other. People who love each other also usually share physical contact; they communicate with each other frequently and cooperate in some routine tasks of daily life. My discussion is of enduring heterosexual love only; I will for the sake of simplicity refer to it as "love."

In contrast to this broad definition of love, the narrower, feminized definition dominates both contemporary scholarship and public opinion. Most scholars who study love, intimacy, or close friendship focus on qualities that are stereotypically feminine, such as talking about feelings.[6] For example, Abraham Maslow defines love as "a feeling of tenderness and affection with great enjoyment, happiness, satisfaction, elation and even ecstasy." Among healthy individuals, he says, "there is a growing intimacy and honesty and self-expression."[7] Zick Rubin's "Love Scale," designed to measure the degree of passionate love as opposed to liking, includes questions about confiding in each other, longing to be together, and sexual attraction as well as caring for each other. Studies of friendship usually distinguish close friends from acquaintances on the basis of how much personal information is disclosed, and many recent studies of married couples and lovers emphasize communication and self-disclosure. A recent book on marital love by Lillian Rubin focuses on intimacy, which she defines as "reciprocal expression of feeling and thought, not out of fear or dependent need, but out of a wish to know another's inner life and to be able to share one's own."[8] She argues that intimacy is distinct from nurturance or caretaking and that men are usually unable to be intimate.

Among the general public, love is also defined primarily as expressing feelings and verbal disclosure, not as instrumental help. This is especially true among the more affluent; poorer people are more likely than they to see practical help and financial assistance as a sign of love.[9] In a study conducted in 1980, 130 adults from a wide range of social classes and ethnic backgrounds were interviewed about the qualities that make a good love relationship. The most frequent response referred to honest and open communication. Being caring and supportive and being tolerant and understanding were the other qualities most often mentioned.[10] Similar results were reported from Ann Swidler's study of an affluent suburb: the dominant conception of love stressed communicating feelings, working on the relationship, and self-development.[11] Finally, a contemporary dictionary defines love as "strong affection for another arising out of kinship or personal ties" and as attraction based on sexual desire, affection, and tenderness.[12]

These contemporary definitions of love clearly focus on qualities that are seen as feminine in our culture. A study of gender roles in 1968 found that warmth, expressiveness, and talkativeness were seen as appropriate for women and not for men. In 1978 the core features of gender stereotypes were unchanged although fewer qualities were seen as appropriate for only one sex. Expressing tender feelings, being gentle, and being aware of the feelings of others were still ideal qualities for women and not for men. The desirable qualities for men and not for women included being independent, unemotional, and interested in sex.[13] The only component perceived as masculine in popular definitions of love is interest in sex.

The two approaches to defining love—one broad, encompassing instrumental and affective qualities, one narrow, including only the affective qualities—inform the two different perspectives on love. According to the androgynous perspective, both gender roles contain elements of love. The feminine role does not include all of the major ways of loving; some aspects of love come from the masculine role, such as sex and providing material help, and some, such as cooperating in daily tasks, are associated with neither gender role. In contrast, the feminized perspective on love implies that all of the elements of love are included in the feminine role. The capacity to love is divided by gender. Women can love and men cannot.

Some Feminist Interpretations

Feminist scholars are divided on the question of love and gender. Supporters of the feminized perspective seem most influential at present. Nancy Chodorow's psychoanalytic theory has been especially influential in promoting a feminized perspective on love among social scientists studying close relationships. Chodorow's argument—in greatly simplified form—is that as infants, both boys and girls have strong identification and intimate attachments with their mothers. Since boys grow up to be men, they must repress this early identification, and in the process they repress their capacity for intimacy. Girls retain their early identification since they will grow up to be women, and throughout their lives females see themselves as connected to others. As a result of this process, Chodorow argues, "girls come to define and experience themselves as continuous with others; . . . boys come to define themselves as more separate and distinct."[14] This theory implies that love is feminine—women are more open to love than men—and that this gender difference will remain as long as women are the primary caretakers of infants.

Scholars have used Chodorow's theory to develop the idea that love and attachment are fundamental parts of women's personalities but not of men's. Carol Gilligan's influential book on female personality development asserts that women define their identity "by a standard of responsibility and care." The predominant female image is "a network of connection, a web of relationships that is sustained by a process of communication." In contrast, males favor a "hierarchical ordering, with its imagery of winning and losing and the potential for violence which it contains." "Although the world of the self that men describe at times includes 'people' and 'deep attachments,' no particular person or relationship is mentioned. . . . Thus the male 'I' is defined in separation."[15]

A feminized conception of love can be supported by other theories as well. In past decades, for example, such a conception developed from Talcott Parsons's theory of the benefits to the nuclear family of women's specializing in expressive action and men's specializing in instrumental action. Among contemporary social scientists, the strongest support for the feminized perspective comes from such psychological theories as Chodorow's.[16]

On the other hand, feminist historians have developed an incisive critique of the feminized perspective on love. Mary Ryan and other social historians have analyzed how the separation of home and workplace in the nineteenth century polarized gender roles and feminized love.[17] Their argument, in simplified form, begins with the observation that in the colonial era the family household was the arena for economic production, affection, and social welfare. The integration of activities in the family produced a certain integration of expressive and instrumental traits in the personalities of men and women. Both women and men were expected to be hard working, modest, and loving toward their spouses and children, and the concept of love included instrumental cooperation as well as expression of feelings. In Ryan's words, "When early Americans spoke of love they were not withdrawing into a female byway of human experience. Domestic affection, like sex and economics, was not segregated into male and female spheres." There was a "reciprocal ideal of conjugal love" that "grew out of the day-to-day cooperation, sharing, and closeness of the diversified home economy."[18]

Economic production gradually moved out of the home and became separated from personal relationships as capitalism expanded. Husbands increasingly worked for wages in factories and shops while wives stayed at home to care for the family. This division of labor gave women more experience with close relationships and intensified women's economic dependence on men. As the daily activities of men and women grew further apart, a new worldview emerged that exaggerated the differences between the personal, loving, feminine sphere of the home and the impersonal, powerful, masculine sphere of the workplace. Work became identified with what men do for money while love became identified with women's activities at home. As a result, the conception of love shifted toward emphasizing tenderness, powerlessness, and the expression of emotion.[19]

This partial and feminized conception of love persisted into the twentieth century as the division of labor remained stable: the workplace remained impersonal and separated from the home, and married women continued to be excluded from paid employment. According to this historical explanation, one might expect a change in the conception of love since the 1940s, as growing numbers of wives took jobs. However, women's persistent responsibility for child care and housework, and their lower wages, might explain a continued feminized conception of love.[20]

Like the historical critiques, some psychological studies of gender also imply that our current conception of love is distorted and needs to be integrated with qualities associated with the masculine role. For example, Jean Baker Miller argues that women's ways of loving—their need to be attached to a man and to serve others—result from women's powerlessness, and that a better way of loving would integrate power with women's style of love.[21] The importance of combining activities and personality traits that have been split apart by gender is also a frequent theme in the human potential movement.[22] These historical and psychological works emphasize the flexibility of gender roles and the inadequacy of a concept of love that includes only the feminine half of human qualities. In contrast, theories like Chodorow's emphasize the rigidity of gender differences after childhood and define love in terms of feminine qualities. The two theoretical approaches are not as inconsistent as my simplified sketches may suggest, and many scholars combine them;[23] however, the two approaches have different implications for empirical research.

Evidence on Women's "Superiority" in Love

A large number of studies show that women are more interested and more skilled in love than men. However, most of these studies use biased measures based on feminine styles of loving, such as verbal self-disclosure, emotional expression, and willingness to report that one has close relationships. When less biased measures are used, the differences between women and men are often small.

Women have a greater number of close relationships than men. At all stages of the life cycle, women see their relatives more often. Men and women report closer relations with their mothers than with their fathers and are generally closer to female kin. Thus an average Yale man in the 1970s talked about himself more with his mother than with his father and was more satisfied with his relationship with his mother. His most frequent grievance against his father was that his father gave too little of himself and was cold and uninvolved; his grievance against his mother was that she gave too much of herself and was alternately overprotective and punitive.[24]

Throughout their lives, women are more likely to have a confidant—a person to whom one discloses personal experiences and feelings. Girls prefer to be with one friend or a small group, while boys usually play competitive games in large groups. Men usually get together with friends to play sports or do some other activity, while women get together explicitly to talk and to be together.[25]

Men seem isolated given their weak ties with their families and friends. Among blue-collar couples interviewed in 1950, 64 percent of the husbands had no confidants other than their spouses, compared to 24 percent of the wives.[26] The predominantly upper-middle-class men interviewed by Daniel Levinson in the 1970s were no less isolated. Levinson concludes that "close friendship with a man or a woman is rarely experienced by American men."[27] Apparently, most men have no loving relationships besides those with wife or lover; and given the estrangement that often occurs in marriages, many men may have no loving relationship at all.

Several psychologists have suggested that there is a natural reversal of these roles in middle age, as men become more concerned with relationships and women turn toward independence and achievement; but there seems to be no evidence showing that men's relationships become more numerous or more intimate after middle age, and some evidence to the contrary.[28]

Women are also more skilled than men in talking about relationships. Whether working class or middle class, women value talking about feelings and relationships and disclose more than men about personal experiences. Men who deviate and talk a lot about their personal experiences are commonly defined as feminine and maladjusted.[29] Working-class wives prefer to talk about themselves, their close relationships with family and friends, and their homes, while their husbands prefer to talk about cars, sports, work, and politics. The same gender-specific preferences are expressed by college students.[30]

Men do talk more about one area of personal experience: their victories and achievements; but talking about success is associated with power, not intimacy. Women say more about their fears and disappointments, and it is disclosure of such weaknesses that usually is interpreted as a sign of intimacy.[31] Women are also more accepting of the expression of intense feelings, including love, sadness, and fear, and they are more skilled in interpreting other people's emotions.[32]

Finally, in their leisure time women are drawn to topics of love and human entanglements while men are drawn to competition among men. Women's preferences in television viewing run to daytime soap operas, or if they are more educated, the high-brow soap operas on educational channels, while most men like to watch competitive and often aggressive sports. Reading tastes show the same pattern. Women read novels and magazine articles about love, while men's magazines feature stories about men's adventures and encounters with death.[33]

However, this evidence on women's greater involvement and skill in love is not as strong as it appears. Part of the reason that men seem so much less loving than women is that their behavior is measured with a feminine ruler. Much of this research considers only the kinds of loving behavior that are associated with the feminine role and rarely compares women and men in terms of qualities associated with the masculine role. When less biased measures are used, the behavior of men and women is often quite similar. For example, in a careful study of kinship relations among young adults in a southern city, Bert Adams found that women were much more likely than men to say that their parents and relatives were very important to their lives (58 percent of women and 37 percent of men). In measures of actual contact with relatives, though, there were much smaller differences: 88 percent of women and 81 percent of men whose parents lived in the same city saw their parents weekly. Adams concluded that "differences between males and females in relations with parents are discernible primarily in the subjective sphere; contact frequencies are quite similar."[34]

The differences between the sexes can be small even when biased measures are used. For example, Marjorie Lowenthal and Clayton Haven reported the finding, later widely quoted, that elderly women were more likely than elderly men to have a friend with whom they could talk about their personal troubles—clearly a measure of a traditionally feminine behavior. The figures revealed that 81 percent of the married women and 74 percent of the married men had confidants—not a sizable difference.[35] On the other hand, whatever the measure, virtually all such studies find that women are more involved in close relationships than men, even if the difference is small.

In sum, women are only moderately superior to men in love: they have more close relationships and care more about them, and they seem to be more skilled at love, especially those aspects of love that involve expressing feelings and being vulnerable. This does not mean that men are separate and unconcerned with close relationships, however. When national surveys ask people what is most important in their lives, women tend to put family bonds first while men put family bonds first or second, along with work.[36] For both sexes, love is clearly very important.

Evidence on the Masculine Style of Love

Men tend to have a distinctive style of love that focuses on practical help, shared physical activities, spending time together, and sex.[37] The major elements of the masculine style of love emerged in Margaret Reedy's study of 102 married couples in the late 1970s. She showed individuals statements describing aspects of love and asked them to rate how well the statements described their marriages. On the whole, husband and wife had similar views of their marriage, but several sex differences emerged. Practical help and spending time together were more important to men. The men were more likely to give high ratings to such statements as: "When she needs help I help her," and "She would rather spend her time with me than with anyone else." Men also described themselves more often as sexually attracted and endorsed such statements as: "I get physically excited and aroused just thinking about her." In addition, emotional security was less important to men than to women, and men were less likely to describe the relationship as secure, safe, and comforting.[38] Another study in the late 1970s showed a similar pattern among young, highly educated couples. The husbands gave greater emphasis to feeling responsible for the partner's well-being and putting the spouse's needs first, as well as to spending time together. The wives gave greater importance to emotional involvement and verbal self-disclosure but also were more concerned than the men about maintaining their separate activities and their independence.[39]

The difference between men and women in their views of the significance of practical help was demonstrated in a study in which seven couples recorded their interactions for several days. They noted how pleasant their relations were and counted how often the spouse did a helpful chore, such as cooking a good meal or repairing a faucet, and how often the spouse expressed acceptance or affection. The social scientists doing the study used a feminized definition of love. They labeled practical help as "instrumental behavior" and expressions of acceptance or affection as "affectionate behavior," thereby denying the affectionate aspect of practical help. The wives seemed to be using the same scheme; they thought their marital relations were pleasant that day if their husbands had directed a lot of affectionate behavior to them, regardless of their husbands' positive instrumental behavior. The husbands' enjoyment of their marital relations, on the other hand, depended on their wives' instrumental actions, not on their expressions of affection. The men actually saw instrumental actions as affection.[40] One husband who was told by the researchers to increase his affectionate behavior toward his wife decided to wash her car and was surprised when neither his wife nor the researchers accepted that as an "affectionate" act.

The masculine view of instrumental help as loving behavior is clearly expressed by a husband discussing his wife's complaints about his lack of communication: "What does she want? Proof? She's got it, hasn't she? Would I be knocking myself out to get things for her—like to keep up this house—if I didn't love her? Why does a man do things like that if not because he loves his wife and kids? I swear, I can't figure what she wants." His wife, who has a feminine orientation to love, says something very different: "It is not enough that he supports us and takes care of us. I appreciate that, but I want him to share things with me. I need for him to tell me his feelings."[41] Many working-class women agree with men that a man's job is something he does out of love for his family,[42] but middle-class women and social scientists rarely recognize men's practical help as a form of love. (Indeed, among upper-middle-class men whose jobs offer a great deal of intrinsic gratification, their belief that they are "doing it for the family" may seem somewhat self-serving.)

Other differences between men's and women's styles of love involve sex. Men seem to separate sex and love while women connect them,[43] but, paradoxically, sexual intercourse seems to be the most meaningful way of giving and receiving love for many men. A twenty-nine-year-old carpenter who had been married for three years said that, after sex, "I feel so close to her and the kids. We feel like a real family then. I don't talk to her very often, I guess, but somehow I feel we have really communicated after we have made love."[44]

Because sexual intimacy is the only recognized "masculine" way of expressing love, the recent trend toward viewing sex as a way for men and women to express mutual intimacy is an important challenge to the feminization of love. However, the connection between sexuality and love is undermined both by the "sexual revolution" definition of sex as a form of casual recreation and by the view of male sexuality as a weapon—as in rape—with which men dominate and punish women.[45]

Another paradoxical feature of men's style of love is that men have a more romantic attitude toward their partners than do women. In Reedy's study, men were more likely to select statements like "we are perfect for each other."[46] In a survey of college students, 65 percent of the men but only 24 percent of the women said that, even if a relationship had all of the other qualities they desired, they would not marry unless they were in love.[47] The common view of this phenomenon focuses on women.

The view is that women marry for money and status and so see marriage as instrumentally, rather than emotionally, desirable. This of course is at odds with women's greater concern with self-disclosure and emotional intimacy and lesser concern with instrumental help. A better way to explain men's greater romanticism might be to focus on men. One such possible explanation is that men do not feel responsible for "working on" the emotional aspects of a relationship, and therefore see love as magically and perfectly present or absent. This is consistent with men's relative lack of concern with affective interaction and greater concern with instrumental help.

In sum, there is a masculine style of love. Except for romanticism, men's style fits the popularly conceived masculine role of being the powerful provider.[48] From the androgynous perspective, the practical help and physical activities included in this role are as much a part of love as the expression of feelings. The feminized perspective cannot account for this masculine style of love; nor can it explain why women and men are so close in the degrees to which they are loving.

Negative Consequences of the Feminization of Love

The division of gender roles in our society that contributes to the two separate styles of love is reinforced by the feminized perspective and leads to political and moral problems that would be mitigated with a more androgynous approach to love. The feminized perspective works against some of the key values and goals of feminists and humanists by contributing to the devaluation and exploitation of women.

It is especially striking how the differences between men's and women's styles of love reinforce men's power over women. Men's style involves giving women important resources, such as money and protection that men control and women believe they need, and ignoring the resources that women control and men need. Thus men's dependency on women remains covert and repressed, while women's dependency on men is overt and exaggerated; and it is overt dependency that creates power, according to social exchange theory.[49] The feminized perspective on love reinforces this power differential by leading to the belief that women need love more than do men, which is implied in the association of love with the feminine role. The effect of this belief is to intensify the asymmetrical dependency of women on men.[50] In fact, however, evidence on the high death rates of unmarried men suggests that men need love at least as much as do women.[51]

Sexual relations also can reinforce male dominance insofar as the man takes the initiative and intercourse is defined either as his "taking" pleasure or as his being skilled at "giving" pleasure, either way giving him control. The man's power advantage is further strengthened if the couple assumes that the man's sexual needs can be filled by any attractive woman while the woman's sexual needs can be filled only by the man she loves.[52]

On the other hand, women's preferred ways of loving seem incompatible with control. They involve admitting dependency and sharing or losing control, and being emotionally intense. Further, the intimate talk about personal troubles that appeals to women requires of a couple a mutual vulnerability, a willingness to see oneself as weak and in need of support. It is true that a woman, like a man, can gain some power by providing her partner with services, such as understanding, sex, or cooking; but this power is largely unrecognized because the man's dependency on such services is not overt. The couple may even see these services as her duty or as her response to his requests (or demands).

The identification of love with expressing feelings also contributes to the lack of recognition of women's power by obscuring the instrumental, active component of women's love just as it obscures the loving aspect of men's work. In a culture that glorifies instrumental achievement, this identification devalues both women and love.[53] In reality, a major way by which women are loving is in the clearly instrumental activities associated with caring for others, such as preparing meals, washing clothes, and providing care during illness; but because of our focus on the expressive side of love, this caring work of women is either ignored or redefined as expressing feelings. Thus, from the feminized perspective on love, child care is a subtle communication of attitudes, not work. A wife washing her husband's shirt is seen as expressing love, even though a husband washing his wife's car is seen as doing a job.

Gilligan, in her critique of theories of human development, shows the way in which devaluing love is linked to devaluing women. Basic to most psychological theories of development is the idea that a healthy person develops from a dependent child to an autonomous, independent adult. As Gilligan comments, "Development itself comes to be identified with separation, and attachments appear to be developmental impediments."[54] Thus women, who emphasize attachment, are judged to be developmentally retarded or insufficiently individuated.

The pervasiveness of this image was documented in a well-known study of mental health professionals who were asked to describe mental health, femininity, and masculinity. They associated both mental health and masculinity with independence, rationality, and dominance. Qualities concerning attachment, such as being tactful, gentle, or aware of the feelings of others, they associated with femininity but not with mental health.[55]

Another negative consequence of a feminized perspective on love is that it legitimates impersonal, exploitive relations in the workplace and the community. The ideology of separate spheres that developed in the nineteenth century contrasted the harsh, immoral marketplace with the warm and loving home and implied that this contrast is acceptable.[56] Defining love as expressive, feminine, and divorced from productive activity maintains this ideology. If personal relationships and love are reserved for women and the home, then it is acceptable for a manager to underpay workers or for a community to ignore a needy family. Such behavior is not unloving; it is businesslike or shows a respect for privacy. The ideology of separate spheres also implies that men are properly judged by their instrumental and economic achievements and that poor or unsuccessful men are failures who may deserve a hard life. Levinson presents a conception of masculine development itself as centering on achieving an occupational dream.[57]

Finally, the feminization of love intensifies the conflicts over intimacy between women and men in close relationships. One of the most common conflicts is that the woman wants more closeness and verbal contact while the man withdraws and wants less pressure.[58] Her need for more closeness is partly the result of the feminization of love, which encourages her to be more emotionally dependent on him. Because love is feminine, he in turn may feel controlled during intimate contact. Intimacy is her "turf," an area where she sets the rules and expectations. Talking about the relationship, as she wants, may well feel to him like taking a test that she made up and that he will fail. He is likely to react by withdrawing, causing her to intensify her efforts to get closer. The feminization of love thus can lead to a vicious cycle of conflict where neither partner feels in control or gets what she or he wants.

Conclusion

The values of improving the status of women and humanizing the public sphere are shared by many of the scholars who support a feminized conception of love; and they, too, explain the conflicts in close relationships in terms of polarized gender roles. Nancy Chodorow, Lillian Rubin, and Carol Gilligan have addressed these issues in detail and with great insight. However, by arguing that women's identity is based on attachment while men's identity is based on separation, they reinforce the distinction between feminine expressiveness and masculine instrumentality, revive the ideology of separate spheres, and legitimate the popular idea that only women know the right way to love. They also suggest that there is no way to overcome the rigidity of gender roles other than by pursuing the goal of men and women becoming equally involved in infant care. In contrast, an androgynous perspective on love challenges the identification of women and love with being expressive, powerless, and nonproductive and the identification of men with being instrumental, powerful, and productive. It rejects the ideology of separate spheres and validates masculine as well as feminine styles of love. This viewpoint suggests that progress could be made by means of a variety of social changes, including men doing child care, relations at work becoming more personal and nurturant, and cultural conceptions of love and gender becoming more androgynous. Changes that equalize power within close relationships by equalizing the economic and emotional dependency between men and women may be especially important in moving toward androgynous love.

The validity of an androgynous definition of love cannot be "proven"; the view that informs the androgynous perspective is that both the feminine style of love (characterized by emotional closeness and verbal self-disclosure) and the masculine style of love (characterized by instrumental help and sex) represent necessary parts of a good love relationship. Who is more loving: a couple who confide most of their experiences to each other but rarely cooperate or give each other practical help, or a couple who help each other through many crises and cooperate in running a household but rarely discuss their personal experiences? Both relationships are limited. Most people would probably choose a combination: a relationship that integrates feminine and masculine styles of loving, an androgynous love.

NOTES

I am indebted to Frank Cancian, Steven Gordon, Lillian Rubin, and Scott Swain for helpful comments and discussions.

1. The term "feminization" of love is derived from Ann Douglas, *The Feminization of Culture* (New York: Alfred A. Knopf, 1977).

2. The term "androgyny" is problematic. It assumes rather than questions sex-role stereotypes (aggression is masculine, e.g.); it can lead to a utopian view that underestimates the social causes of sexism; and it suggests the complete absence of differences between men and women, which is biologically impossible. Nonetheless, I use the term because it best conveys my meaning: a combination of masculine and feminine styles of love. The negative and positive aspects of the concept "androgyny" are analyzed in a special issue of *Women's Studies* (vol. 2, no. 2 [1974]), edited by Cynthia Secor. Also see Sandra Bem, "Gender Schema Theory and Its Implications for Child Development: Raising Gender-aschematic Children in a Gender-schematic Society," *Signs: Journal of Women in Culture and Society* 8, no. 4 (1983): 598–616.

3. The quotations are from a study by Ann Swidler, "Ideologies of Love in Middle Class America" (paper presented at the annual meeting of the Pacific Sociological Association, San Diego, 1982). For useful reviews of the history of love, see Morton Hunt, *The Natural History of Love* (New York: Alfred A. Knopf, 1959); and Bernard Murstein, *Love, Sex and Marriage through the Ages* (New York: Springer, 1974).

4. See John Bowlby, *Attachment and Loss* (New York: Basic Books, 1969), on mother-infant attachment. The quotation is from Elaine Walster and G. William Walster, *A New Look at Love* (Reading, Mass.: Addison-Wesley Publishing Co., 1978), 9. Conceptions of love and adjustment used by family sociologists are reviewed in Robert Lewis and Graham Spanier, "Theorizing about the Quality and Stability of Marriage," in *Contemporary Theories about the Family*, ed. W. Burr, R. Hill, F. Nye, and I. Reiss (New York: Free Press, 1979), 268–94.

5. Mary Ryan, *Womanhood in America*, 2d ed. (New York: New Viewpoints, 1979), and *The Cradle of the Middle Class: The Family in Oneida County, N.Y., 1790–1865* (New York: Cambridge University Press, 1981); Barbara Ehrenreich and Deirdre English, *For Her Own Good: 150 Years of Experts' Advice to Women* (New York: Anchor Books, 1978); Barbara Welter, "The Cult of True Womanhood: 1820–1860," *American Quarterly* 18, no. 2 (1966): 151–74; Carl N. Degler, *At Odds* (New York: Oxford University Press, 1980).

6. Alternative definitions of love are reviewed in Walster and Walster; Clyde Hendrick and Susan Hendrick, *Liking, Loving and Relating* (Belmont, Calif.: Wadsworth Publishing Co., 1983); Ira Reiss, *Family Systems in America*, 3d ed. (New York: Holt, Rinehart & Winston, 1980), 113–41; Margaret Reedy, "Age and Sex Differences in Personal Needs and the Nature of Love" (Ph. D. diss., University of Southern California, 1977).

7. Abraham Maslow, *Motivation and Personality*, 2d ed. (New York: Harper & Row, 1970), 182–83.

8. Zick Rubin's scale is described in his article "Measurement of Romantic Love," *Journal of Personality and Social Psychology* 16, no. 2 (1970): 265–73; Lillian Rubin's book on marriage is *Intimate Strangers* (New York: Harper & Row, 1983), quote on 90.

9. The emphasis on mutual aid and instrumental love among poor people is described in Lillian Rubin, *Worlds of Pain* (New York: Basic Books, 1976); Rayna Rapp, "Family and Class in Contemporary America," in *Rethinking the Family*, ed. Barrie Thorne (New York: Longman, Inc., 1982), 168–87; S. M. Miller and F. Riessman, "The Working-Class Subculture," in *Blue-Collar World*, ed. A. Shostak and W. Greenberg (Englewood Cliffs, N.J.: Prentice-Hall, Inc., 1964), 24–36.

10. Francesca Cancian, Clynta Jackson, and Ann Wysocki, "A Survey of Close Relationships" (University of California, Irvine, School of Social Sciences, 1982, typescript).

11. Swidler.

12. *Webster's New Collegiate Dictionary* (Springfield, Mass.: G. C. Merriam Co., 1977).

13. Paul Rosencrantz, Helen Bee, Susan Vogel, Inge Broverman, and Donald Broverman, "Sex Role Stereotypes and Self-Concepts in College Students," *Journal of Consulting and Clinical Psychology* 32, no. 3 (1968): 287–95; Paul Rosencrantz, "Rosencrantz Discusses Changes in Stereotypes about Men and Women," *Second Century Radcliffe News* (Cambridge, Mass., June 1982), 5–6.

14. Nancy Chodorow, *The Reproduction of Mothering* (Berkeley: University of California Press, 1978), 169. Dorothy Dinnerstein presents a similar theory in *The Mermaid and the Minotaur: Sexual Arrangements and Human Malaise* (New York: Harper & Row, 1976). Freudian and biological dispositional theories about women's nurturance are surveyed in Jean Stockard and Miriam Johnson, *Sex Roles* (Englewood Cliffs, N.J.: Prentice-Hall, Inc., 1980).

15. Carol Gilligan, *In a Different Voice* (Cambridge, Mass.: Harvard University Press, 1982), 32, 159–61; see also L. Rubin, *Intimate Strangers*.

16. Talcott Parsons and Robert F. Bales, *Family, Socialization and Interaction* (Glencoe, Ill.: Free Press, 1955). For a critical review of family sociology from a feminist perspective, see Arlene Skolnick, *The Intimate Environment* (Boston: Little, Brown & Co., 1978). Radical feminist theories also support the feminized conception of love, but they have been less influential in social science; see, e.g., Mary Daly, *Gyn/Ecology: The Metaethics of Radical Feminism* (Boston: Beacon Press, 1979).

17. I have drawn most heavily on Ryan, *Womanhood* (n. 5 above); Ryan, *Cradle* (n. 5 above); Ehrenreich and English (n. 5 above); Welter (n. 5 above).

18. Ryan, *Womanhood*. 24–25.

19. Similar changes occurred when culture and religion were feminized, according to Douglas (n. 1 above). Conceptions of God's love shifted toward an image of a sweet and tender parent, a "submissive, meek and forgiving" Christ (149).

20. On the persistence of women's wage inequality and responsibility for housework, see Stockard and Johnson (n. 14 above).

21. Jean Baker Miller, *Toward a New Psychology of Women* (Boston: Beacon Press, 1976). There are, of course, many exceptions of Miller's generalization, e.g., women who need to be independent or who need an attachment with a woman.

22. In psychology, the work of Carl Jung, David Bakan, and Bem are especially relevant. See Carl Jung, "Anima and Animus," in *Two Essays on Analytical Psychology: Collected Works of C. G. Jung* (New York: Bollinger Foundation, 1953), 7: 186–209; David Bakan, *The Duality of Human Existence* (Chicago: Rand McNally & Co., 1966). They are discussed in Bem's paper, "Beyond Androgyny," in *Family in Transition*, 2d ed., ed. A Skolnick and J. Skolnick (Boston: Little, Brown & Co., 1977), 204–21. Carl Rogers exemplifies the human potential theme of self-development through the search for wholeness. See Carl Rogers, *On Becoming a Person* (Boston: Houghton Mifflin Co., 1961).

23. Chodorow (n. 14 above) refers to the effects of the division of labor and to power differences between men and women, and the special effects of women's being the primary parents are widely acknowledged among historians.

24. The data on Yale men are from Mirra Komarovsky, *Dilemma of Masculinity* (New York: W. W. Norton & Co., 1976). Angus Campbell reports that children are closer to their mothers than to their fathers, and daughters feel closer to their parents than do sons, on the basis of large national surveys, in *The Sense of Well-Being in America* (New York: McGraw-Hill Book Co., 1981), 96. However, the tendency of people to criticize their mothers more

than their fathers seems to contradict these findings; e.g., see Donald Payne and Paul Mussen, "Parent-Child Relations and Father Identification among Adolescent Boys," *Journal of Abnormal and Social Psychology* 52 (1956): 358–62. Being "closer" to one's mother may refer mostly to spending more time together and knowing more about each other rather than to feeling more comfortable together.

25. Studies of differences in friendship by gender are reviewed in Wenda Dickens and Daniel Perlman, "Friendship over the Life Cycle," in *Personal Relationships,* vol. 2, ed. Steve Duck and Robin Gilmour (London: Academic Press, 1981), 91–122; and Beth Hess, "Friendship and Gender Roles over the Life Course," in *Single Life,* ed. Peter Stein (New York: St. Martin's Press, 1981), 104–15. While almost all studies show that women have more close friends, Lionel Tiger argues that there is a unique bond between male friends in *Men in Groups* (London: Thomas Nelson, 1969).

26. Komarovsky, *Blue-Collar Marriage* (New York: Random House, 1962), 13.

27. Daniel Levinson, *The Seasons of a Man's Life* (New York: Alfred A. Knopf, 1978), 335.

28. The argument about the middle-age switch was presented in the popular book *Passages,* by Gail Sheehy (New York: E. P. Dutton, 1976), and in more scholarly works, such as Levinson's. These studies are reviewed in Alice Rossi, "Life-Span Theories and Women's Lives," *Signs* 6, no. 1 (1980): 4–32. However, a survey by Claude Fischer and S. Oliker reports an increasing tendency for women to have more close friends than men beginning in middle age, in "Friendship, Gender and the Life Cycle," Working Paper no. 318 (Berkeley: University of California, Berkeley, Institute of Urban and Regional Development, 1980).

29. Studies on gender differences in self-disclosure are reviewed in Letitia Peplau and Steven Gordon, "Women and Men in Love: Sex Differences in Close Relationships," in *Women, Gender and Social Psychology,* ed. V. O'Leary, R. Unger, and B. Wallston (Hillsdale, N.J.: Lawrence Erlbaum Associates, 1985), 257–91. Also see Zick Rubin, Charles Hill, Letitia Peplau, and Christine Dunkel-Schetter, "Self-Disclosure in Dating Couples," *Journal of Marriage and the Family* 42, no. 2 (1980): 305–18.

30. Working-class patterns are described in Komarovsky, *Blue Collar Marriage.* Middle-class patterns are reported by Lynne Davidson and Lucille Duberman, "Friendship: Communication and Interactional Patterns in Same-Sex Dyads," *Sex Roles* 8, no. 8 (1982): 809–22. Similar findings are reported in Robert Lewis, "Emotional Intimacy among Men," *Journal of Social Issues* 34, no. 1 (1978): 108–21.

31. Rubin et al., "Self-Disclosure."

32. These studies, cited below, are based on the self-reports of men and women college students and may reflect norms more than behavior. The findings are that women feel and express affective and bodily emotional reactions more often than do men, except for hostile feelings. See also Jon Allen and Dorothy Haccoun, "Sex Differences in Emotionality," *Human Relations* 29, no. 8 (1976): 711–22; and Jack Balswick and Christine Avertt, "Gender, Interpersonal Orientation and Perceived Parental Expressiveness," *Journal of Marriage and the Family* 39, no. 1 (1977): 121–28. Gender differences in interaction styles are analyzed in Nancy Henley, *Body Politics: Power, Sex and Non-verbal Communication* (Englewood Cliffs, N.J.: Prentice-Hall, Inc., 1977). Also see Paula Fishman, "Interaction: The Work Women Do," *Social Problems* 25, no. 4 (1978): 397–406.

33. Gender differences in leisure are described in L. Rubin. *Worlds of Pain* (n. 9 above), 10. Also see Margaret Davis, "Sex Role Ideology as Portrayed in Men's and Women's Magazines" (Stanford University, typescript).

34. Bert Adams, *Kinship in an Urban Setting* (Chicago: Markham Publishing Co., 1968), 169.

35. Marjorie Lowenthal and Clayton Haven, "Interaction and Adaptation: Intimacy as a Critical Variable," *American Sociological Review* 33, no. 4 (1968): 20–30.

36. Joseph Pleck argues that family ties are the primary concern for many men, in *The Myth of Masculinity* (Cambridge, Mass.: MIT Press, 1981).

37. Gender-specific characteristics also are seen in same-sex relationships. See M. Caldwell and Letitia Peplau, "Sex Differences in Same Sex Friendship," *Sex Roles* 8, no. 7 (1982): 721–32; see also Davidson and Duberman (n. 30 above), 809–22. Part of the reason for the differences in friendship may be men's fear of homosexuality and of losing status with other men. An exploratory study found that men were most likely to express feelings of closeness if they were engaged in some activity such as sports that validated their masculinity (Scott Swain, "Male Intimacy in Same-Sex Friendships: The Impact of Gender-validating Activities" [paper presented at annual meeting of the American Sociological Association, August 1984]). For discussions of men's homophobia and fear of losing power, see Robert Brannon, "The Male Sex Role," in *The Forty-nine Percent Majority*, ed. Deborah David and Robert Brannon (Reading, Mass.: Addison-Wesley Publishing Co., 1976), 1–48. I am focusing on heterosexual relations, but similar gender-specific differences may characterize homosexual relations. Some studies find that, compared with homosexual men, lesbians place a higher value on tenderness and verbal self-disclosure and engage in sex less frequently. See, e.g., Alan Bell and Martin Weinberg, *Homosexualities* (New York: Simon & Schuster, 1978).

38. Unlike most studies, Reedy (n. 6 above) did not find that women emphasized communication more than men. Her subjects were upper-middle-class couples who seemed to be very much in love.

39. Sara Allison Parelman, "Dimensions of Emotional Intimacy in Marriage" (Ph. D. diss., University of California, Los Angeles, 1980).

40. Both spouses thought their interaction was unpleasant if the other engaged in negative or displeasurable instrumental or affectional actions. Thomas Wills, Robert Weiss, and Gerald Patterson, "A Behavioral Analysis of the Determinants of Marital Satisfaction," *Journal of Consulting and Clinical Psychology* 42, no. 6 (1974): 802–11.

41. L. Rubin, *Worlds of Pain* (n. 9 above), 147.

42. See L. Rubin, *Worlds of Pain;* also see Richard Sennett and Jonathan Cobb, *Hidden Injuries of Class* (New York: Vintage, 1973).

43. For evidence on this point, see Morton Hunt, *Sexual Behavior in the 1970s* (Chicago: Playboy Press, 1974), 231; and Alexander Clark and Paul Wallin, "Women's Sexual Responsiveness and the Duration and Quality of Their Marriage," *American Journal of Sociology* 21, no. 2 (1965): 187–96.

44. Interview by Cynthia Garlich, "Interviews of Married Couples" (University of California, Irvine, School of Social Sciences, 1982).

45. For example, see Catharine MacKinnon, "Feminism, Marxism, Method, and the States: An Agenda for Theory," *Signs* 7, no. 3 (1982): 515–44. For a thoughtful discussion of this issue from a historical perspective, see Linda Gordon and Ellen Dubois, "Seeking Ecstacy on the Battlefield: Danger and Pleasure in Nineteenth Century Feminist Thought," *Feminist Review* 13, no. 1 (1983): 42–54.

46. Reedy (n. 6 above).

47. William Kephart, "Some Correlates of Romantic Love," *Journal of Marriage and the Family* 29, no. 3 (1967): 470–74. See Peplau and Gordon (n. 29 above) for an analysis of research on gender and romanticism.

48. Daniel Yankelovich, *The New Morality* (New York: McGraw-Hill Book Co., 1974), 98.

49. The link between love and power is explored in Francesca Cancian, "Gender Politics:

Love and Power in the Private and Public Spheres," in *Gender and the Life Course,* ed. Alice S. Rossi (New York: Aldine Publishing Co., 1984), 253–64.

50. See Jane Flax, "The Family in Contemporary Feminist Thought," in *The Family in Political Thought,* ed. Jean B. Elshtain (Princeton, N.J.: Princeton University Press, 1981), 223–53.

51. Walter Gove, "Sex, Marital Status and Mortality," *American Journal of Sociology* 79, no. 1 (1973): 45–67.

52. This follows from the social exchange theory of power, which argues that person A will have a power advantage over B if A has more alternative sources for the gratifications she or he gets from B than B has for those from A. See Peter Blau, *Exchange and Power in Social Life* (New York: John Wiley & Sons, 1964), 117–18.

53. For a discussion of the devaluation of women's activities, see Michelle Rosaldo, "Woman, Culture and Society: A Theoretical Overview," in *Woman, Culture and Society,* ed. Michelle Rosaldo and Louise Lamphere (Stanford, Calif.: Stanford University Press, 1973), 17–42.

54. Gilligan (n. 15 above), 12–13.

55. Inge Broverman, Frank Clarkson, Paul Rosenkrantz, and Susan Vogel, "Sex-Role Stereotypes and Clinical Judgments of Mental Health," *Journal of Consulting Psychology* 34, no. 1 (1970): 1–7.

56. Welter (n. 5 above).

57. Levinson (n. 27 above).

58. L. Rubin, *Intimate Strangers* (n. 8 above); Harold Rausch, William Barry, Richard Hertel, and Mary Ann Swain, *Communication, Conflict and Marriage* (San Francisco Jossey-Bass, Inc., 1974). This conflict is analyzed in Francesca Cancian, "Marital Conflict over Intimacy," in *The Psychosocial Interior of the Family,* 3d ed., ed. Gerald Handel (New York: Aldine Publishing Co., 1985), 277–92.

Chapter Thirty-eight

From Surpassing the Love of Men (1981)

Lillian Faderman

Faderman's important work traces the prevailing concept of "romantic friendship" between women in American history, particularly in the nineteenth century, as a significant alternative to heterosexual love and marriage in a typical woman's life.

Passionate romantic friendship between women was a widely recognized, tolerated social institution before our century. Women were, in fact, expected to seek out kindred spirits and form strong bonds. It was socially acknowledged that while a woman could not trust men outside her family, she could look to another female for emotional sustenance and not fear betrayal. . . . But her relationship to another female went beyond . . . affectionate exchanges. It was not unusual for a woman to seek in her romantic friendship the center of her life, quite apart from the demands of marriage and family if not in lieu of them. When women's role in society began to change, however—when what women did needed to be taken more seriously because they were achieving some of the powers that would make them adult persons—society's view of romantic friendship changed.

Love between women—relationships which were *emotionally* in no way different from the romantic friendships of earlier eras—became evil or morbid. It was not simply that men now saw the female sexual drive more realistically. Many of the relationships that they condemned had little to do with sexual expression. It was rather that love between women, coupled with their emerging freedom, might conceivably bring about the overthrow of heterosexuality—which has meant not only sex between men and women but patriarchal culture, male dominance, and female subservience. Learning their society's view of love between women, females were compelled to suppress natural emotion; they were taught to see women only as rivals and men as their only possible love objects, or they were compelled to view themselves as "lesbian," which meant "twisted" either morally or emotionally. What was lovely and nurturing in love between women, what women of other centuries clearly understood, became one of the best-guarded secrets of the patriarchy.

In the sophisticated twentieth century women who chose to love women could no longer see themselves as romantic friends, unless they enveloped themselves in a phenomenal amount of naïveté and were oblivious to modern psychology, literature, and dirty jokes. If they persisted in same-sex love past adolescence, they would at least have to take into account what society thought of lesbians, and they would have to decide to what extent they would internalize those social views. If they were unusually strong or had a strong support group, they might escape regarding themselves as sick sinners. For many of them, without models to show that love between women was not intrinsically wrong or unhealthy, the experts' pronouncements about lesbianism worked as a self-fulfilling prophecy. They became as confused and tormented as they were supposed to be. But it was only during this brief era in history that tragedy and sickness were so strongly attributed to (and probably for that reason so frequently found in) love between women.

This changed with the rise of the second wave of feminism. Having made a general challenge to patriarchal culture, many feminists in the last decade began to challenge its taboos on love between women too. They saw it as their job to divest themselves of all the prejudices that had been inculcated in them by their male-dominated society, to reexamine everything regarding women, and finally to reclaim the meaning of love between women. Having learned to question both the social order which made women the second sex and the meaning behind the taboos on love between women, they determined to live their lives through new definitions they would create. They called themselves women-identified-women, or they consciously attempted to lift the stigma from the term "lesbian" and called themselves lesbian-feminists, by which they meant that they would put women first in their lives because men had proven, if not on a personal scale then on a cultural scale, that they were not to be trusted. Lesbian-feminists see men and women as being at odds in their whole approach to the world: men, as a rule, are authoritarian, violent, cold, and women are the opposite. Like romantic friends before them, lesbian-feminists choose women, kindred spirits, for their love objects. Unlike most romantic friends, however, they understand through feminist doctrine the sociopolitical meaning of their choice.

Lesbian-feminists differ from romantic friends in a number of ways. Most significantly, the earlier women generally had no hope of actually spending their lives together despite often reiterated fantasies that they might; but also romantic friends did not have an articulated doctrine which would help them explain why they could feel closer to women than to men. And the primary difference which affected their relationship to the world is that romantic friends, unlike lesbian-feminists, seldom had reason to believe that society saw them as outlaws—even when they eloped together like the Ladies of Llangollen did. Lesbian-feminists understand, even when they are comfortable within a large support group, that the world outside views them as criminal and reduces their love to a pejorative term. Whatever anger they began with as feminists is multiplied innumerable times as lesbian-feminists as soon as they experience, either in reality or by observation, society's hostility to what is both logical and beautiful to them. Even if they do not suffer personally—if they do not lose their children in court or if they are not fired from their jobs or turned out by their families because of their political-sexual commitments—lesbian-feminists are furious, knowing that such possibilities exist and that many women do suffer for choosing to love other women. Romantic friends never learned to be angry through their love.

There is a good deal on which lesbian-feminists disagree, such as issues concerning class, whether or not to form monogamous relationships, the virtues of communal living, whether separatism is necessary in order to live as a lesbian-feminist, the nature of social action that is efficacious, etc. But they all agree that men have waged constant battle against women, committed atrocities or at best injustices against them, reduced them to grown-up children, and that a feminist ought not to sleep in the enemy camp. They all agree that being a lesbian is, whether consciously or unconsciously perceived, a political act, a refusal to fulfill the male image of woman-hood or to bow to male supremacy. Perhaps for romantic friends of other eras their relationship was also a political act, although much more covert: With each other they could escape from many of the externally imposed demands of femininity that were especially stringent throughout much of the eighteenth and nineteenth centu-ries. They could view themselves as human beings and prime rather than as the second sex. But they did not hope that through their relationship they might change the social structure. Lesbian-feminists do.

They see their lesbian-feminism not just as a personal choice regarding life-style, even though it is certainly a most personal choice. But it is also a political choice which challenges sexism and heterosexism. It is a choice which has been made often in the context of the feminist movement and with an awareness of the ideology behind it. It has seemed the only possible choice for many women who believe that the personal is political, that to reject male supremacy in the abstract but to enter into a heterosexual relationship in which the female is usually subservient makes no sense. Contemporary lesbianism, on the other hand, makes a great deal of sense. It is a combination of the natural love between women, so encouraged in the days of romantic friendships, with the twentieth-century women's freedom that feminism has made possible.

While romantic friends had considerable latitude in their show of physical affec-tion toward each other, it is probable that, in an era when women were not supposed to be sexual, the sexual possibilities of their relationship were seldom entertained. Contemporary women can have no such innocence. But the sexual aspect of their lesbian-feminist relationships generally have less significance than the emotional sustenance and the freedom they have to define themselves. While many lesbian-feminist relationships can and do continue long after the sexual component has worn off, they cannot continue without emotional sustenance and freedom of self-definition. Romantic friends of other eras would probably have felt entirely comfort-able in many lesbian-feminist relationships had the contemporary label and stigma been removed.

But many women today continue to be frightened by love between women because the pejorative connotation of the contemporary label and the stigma are still very real for them. Such fear is bound to vanish in the future as people continue to reject strict orthodoxy in sexual relationships: Women will be less and less scared off by the idea of same-sex love without examining what it entails beyond "sexual abnormality." The notion of lesbianism will be neutralized. As females are raised to be more independent, they will not assume that heterosexual marriage is necessary for survival or fulfillment; nor will they accept male definitions of womanhood or non-woman-hood. They will have no need to repress natural feelings of affection toward other women. Love between women will become as common as romantic friendship was in other eras. The twentieth-century combination of romantic friendship and female independence will continue to yield lesbian-feminism.

In an ideal world lesbian-feminism, which militantly excludes relationships with men, would not exist. And, of course, the romantic friendships such as women were permitted to conduct in other centuries—in which they might be almost everything to each other but in which a male protector was generally needed in order for them to survive—would not exist either. Instead, in a utopia men would not claim supremacy either in social or personal relationships, and women would not feel that they must give up a part of themselves in order to relate to men. Women with ambition and strength and a sense of themselves would have no reason to see men as the enemy out to conquer and subdue them. Nor would there be any attempt to indoctrinate the female with the notion that to be normal she must transfer the early love she felt for her mother first to her father and then to a father substitute—a man who is more than she is in all ways: older, taller, better educated, smarter, stronger. Women as well as men would not select their love objects on the basis of sexual politics, in surrender or in reaction to an arbitrary heterosexual ideology. They would choose to love another only in reference to the individual needs of their own personalities, which ideally had been allowed to develop untrammelled and free of sex-role stereotyping. Potential or actual bisexuality, which is today looked on by lesbian-feminists as a political betrayal and by heterosexuals as an instability, would be normal, both emotionally and statistically. But until men stop giving women cause to see them as the enemy and until there ceases to be coercion to step into prescribed roles without reference to individual needs and desires, lesbian-feminists will continue to view their choice as the only logical one possible for a woman who desires to be her own adult person.

Chapter Thirty-nine

From The Overvaluation of Love
A Study of a Common Present-Day Feminine Type (1934)

Karen Horney

Karen Horney was an eminent psychoanalytic theorist as well as practitioner who broke from Freud's analysis of femininity. Horney's groundbreaking essay bravely contradicts the assumption of her day (see Robinson in part 1) that women were biologically "meant" to live for love and marriage: "Those who maintain this point of view [the patriarchal ideal of womanhood] mistakenly infer from external behavior the existence of an innate instinctual disposition." She concludes that women, rather than being repressed sexually, are not taught to value themselves and their lives and so tend to "compulsively overvalue" men.

Women's efforts to achieve independence and an enlargement of her field of interest and activities are continually met with a skepticism whose burden is that such efforts are impelled merely by the pressure of economic necessity, and that they run counter, besides, to her inherent character and her natural tendencies. Accordingly, all efforts of this sort are said to be without any vital significance for woman, whose every thought, in point of fact, centers exclusively upon the male or upon motherhood, in much the manner expressed in Marlene Dietrich's famous song, "I know only love, and nothing else."

Various sociological considerations immediately suggest themselves in this connection, of too familiar and obvious a character, however, to require time spent upon them. This attitude towards woman, whatever its basis and however it may be assessed, represents the patriarchal ideal of womanhood, of woman as one whose only longing it is to love a man and be loved by him, to admire him and serve him, and even to pattern herself after him. Those who maintain this point of view mistakenly infer from external behavior the existence of an innate instinctual disposition thereto; whereas, in reality, the latter cannot be recognized as such, for the reason that biological factors never manifest themselves in pure and undisguised

From Karen Horney, "The Overvaluation of Love: A Study of a Common Present-Day Feminine Type," *Psychoanalytic Quarterly*, vol. 3 (1934): 605–11. © 1964 by the *Psychoanalytic Quarterly*. Reprinted by permission of Other Press, LLC, and the Estate of Karen Horney.

form, but always as modified by tradition and environment. As Briffault has recently pointed out in some detail in *The Mothers*, the modifying influence of "inherited tradition," not only upon ideals and beliefs but also upon emotional attitudes and so called instincts, cannot possibly be overestimated.[1] Inherited tradition means for woman, however, a compressing of her originally probably very considerable participation in general tasks into the narrower sphere of eroticism and motherhood. The adherence to inherited tradition fulfills certain day-to-day functions for both society and the individual; of their social aspect we shall not speak here, and, considered from the standpoint of the psychology of the individual, it need only be mentioned that this mental construction is for the male at times a matter of great inconvenience, yet on the other hand constitutes for him a source from which his self-esteem can always derive support. For woman, conversely, with her lowered self-esteem of centuries' duration, it constitutes a haven of peace in which she is spared the exertions and anxieties associated with the cultivation of other abilities and of self-assertion in the face of criticism and rivalry. It is comprehensible, therefore—speaking solely from the sociological standpoint—that women who nowadays obey the impulse to the independent development of their abilities are able to do so only at the cost of a struggle against both external opposition and such resistances within themselves as are created by an intensification of the traditional ideal of the exclusively sexual function of woman.

It would not be going too far to assert that at the present time this conflict confronts every woman who ventures upon a career of her own and who is at the same time unwilling to pay for her daring with the renunciation of her femininity. The conflict in question is thus one which is conditioned by the altered position of woman and which is confined to those women who enter upon or follow a vocation, who pursue special interests, or who aspire in general to an independent development of their personality.

Sociological insight makes one fully cognizant of the existence of conflicts of this kind, of their inevitability, and, in broad outline, of many of the forms in which they are manifested and of their more remote effects. It enables one—to give but a single instance—to understand how there result attitudes which vary from the one extreme of a complete repudiation of femininity on the one hand to the opposite extreme of a total rejection of intellectual or vocational activities on the other.

The boundaries of this field of inquiry are marked off by such questions as the following: Why is it that in a given case the conflict takes the particular form it does, or its solution is reached in just the manner it is? Why do some women fall ill in consequence of this conflict, or suffer a considerable impairment in the development of their potentialities? What predisposing factors on the part of the individual are necessary to such a result? And what types of outcome are possible? In a word, at the point where the problem of the fate of the individual emerges, one enters the domain of individual psychology, in fact of psychoanalysis.

As a matter of fact, the observation upon a certain type of woman about to be presented do not proceed from a sociological interest, but arise out of certain definite difficulties encountered in the analysis of a number of women which compelled a consideration of the specific factors responsible for these difficulties. The present report is based upon seven analyses of my own, and upon a number of additional cases familiar to me through analytic conferences. The majority of these patients had no prominent symptoms, in the main; two had a tendency to not at all typical depression and occasional hypochondriacal anxiety; two had infrequent attacks which had been diagnosed as epileptic. But in every case the symptoms, so far as they were present at all, were overshadowed by certain difficulties connected in each instance with the patient's relations to men and to work. As so often happens, their difficulties as such were more or less clearly sensed by the patients as arising out of their own personalities.

But it was by no means a simple matter to grasp the actual problem involved. The first impression did not yield much more than the fact that for these women their relation to men was of great importance to them, but that they had never succeeded in establishing a satisfactory relationship of any duration. Either attempts to form a relationship had failed outright, or there had been a series of merely evanescent relationships, broken off either by the man in question or the patient—relationships which moreover often showed a certain lack of selectivity. Or if a relationship of greater duration and deeper significance were entered into, it invariably foundered in the end on the rocks of some attitude or behavior on the part of the woman.

There was at the same time in all these cases an inhibition in the sphere of work and accomplishment and a more or less well marked impoverishment of interests. To some extent these difficulties were conscious and immediately evident, but in part the patients were unaware of them as such until the analysis brought them to light.

It was only after somewhat prolonged analytic work that I recognized in certain gross examples that the central problem here consisted not in an inhibition respecting love but in an entirely too exclusive concentration upon men. These women were as though possessed by the single thought, "I must have a man"—obsessed with an idea overvalued to the point of absorbing every other thought, so that by comparison all the rest of life seemed stale, flat and unprofitable. The capabilities and interests which most of them possessed either had no meaning at all for them or had lost it all. In other words, conflicts affecting their relations to men were present and could be to a considerable extent relieved, but the actual problem lay not in too little but in too much emphasis upon their love life.

In some instances inhibitions respecting work first appeared in the course of analysis and increased, while simultaneously the relation to men improved through the analysis of the anxieties associated with sexuality. By the patient and her associates this change was variously evaluated. On the one hand it was regarded in the light of progress—as in the case of the father who expressed his pleasure in the fact that his daughter had become so feminine as a result of her analysis that she now wanted to get married and had lost all interest in study. On the other hand, in the course of consultations I repeatedly encountered complaints that this or that patient had attained to a better relationship with men through the analysis, but had lost her previous efficiency, ability and pleasure in work and was now exclusively occupied with the desire for male companionship. This was food for thought. Evidently such a picture might also represent an artefact of analysis, a miscarriage of treatment. Still, this was the outcome only in the case of certain women, and not in others. What were the predisposing factors that determined the one outcome or the other? Was there something in the total problem of these women which had been overlooked?

Finally, another trait characterized all these patients in more or less striking degree—*a fear of not being normal.* This anxiety appeared in the sphere of erotism, in relation to work, or in a more abstract and diffuse form as a general feeling of being different and inferior which they attributed to an inherent and hence unalterable predisposition.

There are two reasons why this problem only gradually became clarified. On the one hand, the picture represents to a great extent our traditional conception of the truly feminine woman, who has no other aim in life than to lavish devotion upon a man. The second difficulty lies in the analyst himself, who, convinced of the importance of the love life, is consequently disposed to regard the removal of disturbances in this domain as his prime task. He will, therefore, be glad to follow patients who emphasize of their own accord the importance of this sphere into the problems of this kind which they present. If a patient were to tell him that the great ambition of his life was to take a trip to the South Sea Islands and that he expected the analysis to resolve the inner conflicts which stood in the way of the fulfillment of this wish, the analyst would naturally put the question, "Tell me, why is this trip of such vital importance to you?" The comparison is of course inadequate, because sexuality is really of greater importance than a journey to the South Seas; but it serves to show that our discernment, quite right and proper in itself, of the importance of heterosexual experience can on occasion blind us to a neurotic overevaluation of and overemphasis upon this sphere.

Seen from this standpoint, these patients present a discrepancy of a double sort. Their feeling for a man is in reality so complicated—I should like to say descriptively, so loose—that their estimate of a heterosexual relationship as the only valuable thing in life is undoubtedly a compulsive overvaluation. On the other hand, their gifts, abilities and interests, and, as I should like at once to add, their ambition and the corresponding possibilities of achievement and satisfaction, are very much greater than they assume. We are dealing, therefore, with a displacement of emphasis from attainment or the struggle for achievement to sex; indeed, so far as one may speak of objective facts in the field of values, what we have here is an objective falsification of values. For although in the last analysis sex is a tremendously important, perhaps the most important, source of satisfaction, it is certainly not the only one, nor the most trustworthy. . . .

As in life too, the relation to men is pushed into the foreground, and this with conspicuous frequency in the form of acting out. Often one man after another plays a part, ranging from mere approaches to sexual relations; while accounts of what he has done or not done, whether he loves or disappoints them, and of how they have reacted to him, take up at times the greater part of the hour and are tirelessly spun out to the smallest detail. The fact that this represents an acting out and that this acting out subserved the resistance was not always immediately evident. At times it was veiled because of the patient's endeavor to demonstrate that a satisfactory relation with a man, perhaps even one of vital significance, was getting under way—

an endeavor which accorded with a similarly directed wish on the part of the analyst. In retrospect I can say, however, that with a more exact knowledge of the specific problem of these patients and of their specific transference reaction, it is possible as a rule to see through this game and thus considerably to limit their acting out. . . .

NOTE

1. Briffault, R.: *The Mothers,* London, 1927; vol. II, p. 253: "The sexual division of labour upon which social development had been founded in primitive societies was abolished in the great economic revolution brought about by agriculture. Woman, instead of being the chief producer, became economically unproductive, destitute, and dependent. . . . One economic value alone was left to woman, her sex."

Chapter Forty

From The Alienation of Desire
Women's Masochism and Ideal Love (1986)

Jessica Benjamin

In this important and widely cited analysis, the contemporary theorist and psychoanalyst Jessica Benjamin explains women's romantic idealization of men as a kind of masochism based on the worship of the unattainable father's power. Her book-length study of this idea is The Bonds of Love: Psychoanalysis, Feminism, and the Problem of Domination *(1988).*

All my foolish acts and all the good things I have done have the same cause: an aspiration for a perfect and ideal love in which I can give myself completely, entrust my being to another . . . How I envy the ideal love of Mary Magdalene and Jesus: to be the ardent disciple of an adored and worthy master; to live and die for him, my idol . . . (Janet's patient, cited in de Beauvoir, 1952, p. 716–17).

The analysis I have offered to the roots of ideal love in the identification with the rapprochement father of separation affords the possibility of reconstructing and reintegrating theories of masochism and femininity. The failure to appreciate the importance of ideal love in the father-daughter tie and its parallelism with many aspects of the father-son tie has led to many psychoanalytic misunderstandings of women. The boy's early psychic structure is seen as derivative of both mother and father bonds; the girl's psychic structure, whether derived from the maternal identification or organized by penis envy is seen as strangely detached from the father. The current emphasis on maternal identification may ignore the problem that the mother is not articulated as a sexual subject and the crucial role played by the father as a figure of identification. In Freud's understanding of women, the gap in the girl's subjectivity left by the missing father appeared as "the lack" and the theory of penis envy emerged to fill it. The conclusion was drawn that the girl's masculinity complex was an obstacle to femininity and that feminine sexual self-esteem could be drawn from the passive oedipal relation to the father. More recently, Blum (1977) has argued that penis envy should be seen as the organizer not of femininity but of "female masculinity" which may actually impede the development of femininity. Here the danger of accepting the notion of primary feminine identity and rejecting bisexuality becomes apparent. I believe, rather, that this envy represents a desire for important elements of selfhood associated with masculinity: independence, self-esteem, excitement, and agency. What is desirable is the integration of those elements through the girl's integration of maternal and paternal identifications. It is the failure to achieve this integration and the accompanying withdrawal from autonomy and agency, especially sexual agency, that fosters conflict with femininity and, ultimately, masochism.

A full delineation of the failure of this integration is still the gap in our theory. "In this culture there may be a basic contradiction between sexual liberation and personal liberation (or autonomy) for women isofar as sexuality as constructed expressed dependent or masochistic trends," wrote Person (1980). The psychological beginnings of this contradiction may be seen in the girl's struggle at rapprochement— a struggle vastly complicated by the prevalent denial of women's subjectivity. The frustration, or absence, of an ideal identificatory love relationship with someone who represents desire and excitement can be seen to damage any child's sense of agency. But even with successful paternal identification in the early father-daughter tie, conflict may arise between the preoedipal and oedipal love for the father, that is, between identification with the object and love for him. Once genital love has entered the picture, in the oedipal phase or in adolescence, the situation becomes more complicated and conflictual for all parties. While these further developments demand a great deal more exploration, some gross patterns deriving from the gender division are obvious: difficulty in integrating agency and love may arise both from the father's ultimate refusal to accept a feminine equal to the mother's inability to model autonomy. A succinct statement of the problem was made by Doris Bernstein (1983):

> Analytic literature says little about the relationships of fathers and daughters: primarily the focus is on the father as libidinal object, as protector and rescuer from the mother. Fathers do not seem able to offer themselves as objects of identification to girls as they do to their sons—with few exceptions. To the extent that the father's individuation rests on the biological base of difference from mother, to the extent that he mobilized, or continues to mobilize the "no, I am unlike" to maintain his autonomy, the more *unable* he is to permit or welcome his daughter's identification with him as he is his son's. Repeatedly, women have complained that their fathers encouraged intellectual development and education but only up to a certain point [p. 196].

The point is that paternal identification is not merely defensive, but reflects positive strivings that must be fostered through identification and parental recognition. Although it is preferable, under the present gender constellation, that fathers should be as available to their daughters as to their sons, this solution is not without conflict for the girl. In the girl's inner world, the obstacles to paternal identification are reflected in injury to the grandiose self, to narcissistic self-esteem, and to the sense of agency, and in inability to separate from the primary object. This means that loving the father will often be associated either with one's own castration, since father's lover must relinquish agency and competition, or with the guilt of castrating him (Chasseguet-Smirgel, 1970). As long as the sexual division persists—the mother representing the primary attachment object, who holds and soothes, and the father representing the separation object identified with the outside world of freedom and excitement—the father will be important to girls as well as to boys in the effort to differentiate and recognize themselves in another subject of desire. The difficulties that attend this paternal identification, as well as its absence altogether, is the basis for adult versions of ideal love.

Ideal love may characterize a whole spectrum of relationships, including those of covert submission and idealization, those featuring persisting unrequited longings in the face of abandonment and rejection, and those that openly erupt into sadomaso-chistic practices. Most of the issues of separation and recognition, the narcissistic pathology associated with masochism, can be contextualized in terms of rapproche-ment issues in general and difficulties in consolidating father-daughter identification in particular. Women are often drawn into relationships of submission because they seek a second chance for ideal love, a chance to reconstitute father-daughter identi-fication in which their own desire and subjectivity can finally be recognized. Even in those relationships that involve annihilation of the self, one can often discern the fantasy of resolving the conflict between activity and passivity. As de Beauvoir (1952) wrote, "This dream of annihilation is in fact an avid will to exist . . . when woman gives herself completely to her idol, she hopes that he will give her at once possession of herself and of the universe he represents" (p. 717).

Woman's ideal love, the submission to or adulation of the idealized other in whom one hopes to recognize oneself, parallels the identificatory love of the boy's rapprochement complex. The masculine orientation that Freud (1919) noted in women's beating fantasies—the fact that they were the boy being beaten—may now be seen as modeled on the homoerotic, identificatory nature of the boy's love of the father in this phase. In fantasy, the girl is portraying herself as the boy that is in love with his father; but finally she is punished, castrated, denied that vital link of identity and equality with the father.

Although ideal love is often charged with oedipal fears and guilt and is combined with genital object love for the father, it can also exist by itself as the legacy of the girl's rapprochement complex. The replay of identificatory love for the father is best seen not as regression into masculinity but as a revival of unresolved conflicts and aspirations that attended this earlier phase. In the boy's ideal love he seeks to protect his omnipotence and grandiosity, to establish separateness through identification with someone who is already separate, to recognize his desire in the father's desire and be recognized in return. These aims can also be found as primary motives in woman's ideal love. Perhaps what most distinguishes our approach from Freud's is the notion that these aspirations are legitimate and may hold the key to active femininity, once they are disentangled from the helpless envy and disavowal of womanhood that have filled the lack of her own desire and agency.

By way of illustrating the roots of ideal love in the identificatory love of rapproche-ment, I shall briefly sketch a case. Elaine was a young woman writer who could not get over her preoccupation with a man who had left her. This man represented the idealized father with whom she wanted to identify in order to disidentify from her mother. Elaine explicity saw her lover as her ideal, a person like herself as she wished to be: he was magical, outrageous, creative, imaginative, unconventional. He alone understood her, her eccentricity, her outrageousness, her wild and free spirit, her refusal to be a conventional female. After his departure, she began work on a mystery novel in which he was the incestuously loved older brother and she was the tomboy-ish sidekick whom he took everywhere. She rejected the trappings of femininity, dressed as a boy, performed feats of physical courage and mechanical ingenuity. When her hero deserts her, the heroine struggles to carry on, still living in the shadow of her brother's charismatic abilities. She tries to prove herself to him, to live up to the independence she thinks he embodies, in the hope that he will finally acknowledge her. The story parallels Elaine's actual ideal love affair, which was largely fueled by the need to have a person highly different from her mother who would recognize her. It bore all the features of longing for a homoerotic, narcissistic love affair with the father and the world. Her lover was so vital and attractive to her because of "something to do with freedom." She often said he was "the only one who recognized my true self; he made me feel alive."

Elaine perceives her ambitions to have been thwarted by both parents in a sex-stereotypical way. Her mother, who had many children, was weak and ineffectual, wholly without aspirations for herself or her children, and especially paralyzed when it came to helping them with "anything we did *outside*." Her father had never given her the recognition she wanted. He had been too outside—distant, angry, judgmen-tal, and impatient with his children and wife, involved in his own work and failure, and frequently criticizing her for being stupid or timid when she did not meet his expectations. Elaine believes that her mother was valuable as a source of comfort and soothing to her babies and children when they were little, but that she was devoid and discouraging of any excitement or spark—all that is important in life. When Elaine identifies with her mother or sisters, she feels paralyzed, sick, weak. Moreover she is terrified of the depths of submission and self-annihilation her sister reached in her terrible desire to please her father. As a result Elaine refuses to invest the therapist with the power to help her and suffers because of what she terms her inability to have "faith," which she readily admits reflects her fear of devotion to an idol. At the same time, she expresses contempt for any soothing or comfort, although her agita-tion and inability to self-soothe is flagrant; fearing the debilitating sympathy her mother offered, she must remain separate from her at all costs.

Elaine's memories confirm that the mother withdrew the moment her children began to crawl away from her, returning when a child was injured and required her ministrations. The withdrawal of the holding environment in the face of the child's separation is the commonly cited environmental failure underlying ego pathology of this kind (e.g., Masterson, 1981). The crisis of separation has occurred in a context where all separation is experienced as a threat to attachment, and so the object is both inconstant and potentially engulfing. Elaine became one of the many children who, by rapprochement, are clinging and fearful in mood, making occasional dan-gerous and disastrous forays out of the mother's orbit. The masochistic ideal love is a simultaneous expression of this helplessness and separation anxiety even while it is an attempt to overcome it by borrowing the other's cohesiveness. On one hand, Elaine is seeking a heroic sadist, one who represents the liberating father rather than the engulfing mother. On the other hand, what she really needs is someone who supplies not only the missing excitement but also the holding environment. Such containment is acceptable only in its most masculine form because it would otherwise threaten to pull her back into the fusion with the helpless, engulfing mother.

The ideal love is chosen to solve the problem posed by frustration of desire and agency and the ensuing rage at nonrecognition—an avenue of escape through a figure of identification. In this sense, it is defensive. But the creation of this father figure, seen in terms of the normal splitting of the rapprochement also entails a wish. This wish should not become invisible to us merely because it appears in the more disturbed version fueled by rage and frustration. Successful treatment involves both aspects. In escaping her mother, Elaine hopes to escape her own tremendous rage at her for failing to withstand her daughter's attack. Unleashed activity and aggression would destroy whatever remains of the good mother within. Thus she regards her anger and desire as highly driven, even monstrous, and can unleash them safely only in the hands of a man who is more powerful, in control, and does not depend on her for his strength. Only when such destruction is permitted can she find her own creativity, she maintains. Here ideal love, sustaining the idealized phallic father image, combines two sets of needs: (1) to achieve what boys get from their fathers in the normal course of rapprochement, a vehicle of solving that conflict between separation and dependency that preserves grandiosity and omnipotence, salvaging self-esteem and independent will and desire; (2) to put her desire finally in another's hands, make him the manager of the highly disturbing and driven need for freedom and self-expression that is permeated with rage and so can be contained only by a figure of supreme independence and power. On one hand, the father's unavailability for identificatory love has led to the effort to recreate it in a masochistic relationship. On the other hand, the inadequacy of the mother as a figure for identification has intensified that longing for identificatory love and combined it with the search for an object that can withstand aggression and separation. The ideal love seeks the never attained synthesis by imbuing the loved man with features of both the ideal mother and the ideal father, containment and excitement.

The need for an object who is truly outside, who does survive destruction in Winnicott's (1971) sense, is crucial to the fantasy of the ideal love. The man who does not depend on her can be truly outside, and it is this fact—not merely the propensity for suffering—that so often makes only the unreliable abandoning figure a safe or attractive one. The ideal lover seems to offer the boundedness and limits within which one can experience abandonment and creativity. The analysis of masochistic fantasy repeatedly shows that in the control of the other, the masochist seeks the freedom of releasing her own desire, as well as the recognition of her deepest self (Benjamin, 1983). Elaine has also described such experience in reference to her teachers, saying that they provide you with the freedom to turn inward and explore, understanding when you have "got it." The element of containment and boundedness that informs this fantasy underscores the important role played by failure of the holding environment in the etiology of masochism. This is the failure of the ideal mother, the containing, holding mother who can support excitement and outside exploration, who can withstand and limit aggression, who can give permission to separate and can recognize the child's independent accomplishments. Her direct recognition is as crucial to the child as the indirect recognition achieved through identification with the ideal father.

In Elaine's history and treatment it is apparent that the need to escape a weak, engulfing mother is at war with the need to turn back to the mother and engage in the struggle for that recognition—the struggle to death for the life of the self. Simply, we are talking about the mother's ability to provide a structure for the child's aggression that makes it possible to integrate that aggression with its close relatives: activity, will, and desire. It is not merely the recognizing response of the exuberant father that ignites the child's own sense of activity and desire. As discussions of the psychoanalytic situation as a holding environment suggest, the function of containment is also important. Or, as Elaine described the good teacher, the need is for an other whose presence does not violate but permits and helps to recognize the experience of one's own *inner* desire.

Behind the ideal love we have seen the early father identification. But this identification is part of a whole complex that includes the ambivalence toward the mother, the struggle to reconcile independence and dependency, the need for recognition from a mother who survives that struggle. In the actual analysis of masochism, returning to the struggle with the mother is as crucial as reexperiencing the disappointment with the ideal father. The problem of woman's desire must finally be situated in the difficulties with mother and father in the rapprochement complex. These difficulties stem from the gender division: the mother is not the active subject of desire for the child, and the father is that subject. For the daughter, the constellation of a mother who is lacking subjectivity and a father who does possess it presents a difficult choice. Particularly if she fails to receive that recognition from her father, but even if she does so, her active subjectivity and her sense of femininity must be in conflict. A frustrated identification with the father is one primary motif in the masochistic relationship. But even a "successful" identification can create conflicts with feminine identity as long as the girl is confronted with the mother's own lack. Usually, this means that she will find herself faced with a conflict between her sexuality and her sense of autonomous self, because the longing for ideal love exerts the greatest pull on her sexuality, if not on her activity in the world. The sense that female sexuality is an active creative force ultimately depends as much, therefore, on the mother's actual realization of subjectivity as on the father.

While the ego and self pathology that underly masochism can readily be traced to failures in the holding environment and the internalization of a containing mother, the gender content of masochism, its association with femininity, involves the dynamic relationship of mother and father in our present gender system. The structural conditions of gender that now exist do not allow for reconciliation of agency and desire with femininity. Although they often fit the common reality of our gender arrangements, we have criticized the theoretical assumptions about early female development that make feminine submission seem inevitable: that mothers cannot be a figure of separation for both children, that fathers cannot offer their daughters what they offer their sons. We must challenge the structure of heterosexuality in which the father supplies the missing excitement and the way out of the dyad, functions defensively to "beat back the maternal power" (Chasseguet-Smirgel, 1976), and denies the mother's subjectivity as too threatening (Dinnerstein, 1976). The normative image of motherhood that psychoanalysis has long adumbrated must be revised: the ideal of a mother who provides symbiosis and then separation "on demand" must be replaced by the mother who also moves under her own steam. The mother's own integration of separateness and agency must be the profound source from which her recognition of the child's autonomy proceeds. Ideally, the adult woman's sense of agency and separateness should mitigate her sense of having to *be* the all-perfect mother of infantile fantasy, and so should help disconfirm the child's fantasy of maternal power and paternal defense.

The drawbacks of the constellation of idealized masculinity as a protection from primitive maternal power have been pointed out by many feminists: the defensive repudiation of the mother by the boy may further his separation but does not help him to resolve intimacy and independence (Miller, 1973; Gilligan, 1982; Chodorow, 1978, 1979). I believe that the idealization of the father resulting from the conventional gender role and parenting constellation is never fully counteracted. Even when reality contradicts this paternal ideal, it remains active inside as a longing, a fallback position whenever real agency and recognition fail. The father remains the figure who stands for subjectivity and desire, so that, culturally speaking, woman's desire must always contend with this monopoly. Both sexes can therefore continue to comply in ideal love the prevalent form of domination and submission in erotic life. The association of femininity with masochism, the submission to an idealized other, derives above all from the early idealization of the father, an idealization charged with the urgency of resolving the crisis of separation and establishing the self. The other side of this idealization is the derogation of femininity and motherhood and the consequent difficulty in reconciling maternal identification with an active sense of self, preventing the emergence of woman's desire.

In the analysis of ideal love an inverse relationship emerges between desire and recognition on one hand and submission on the other. To oversimplify: the more agency and recognition, the less submission. But this does not necessarily mean that the opportunity to exercise agency—as some feminists imply—will reverse the tendency toward submission once it is firmly in place as an internal object relation-ship that compensates and eroticizes the loss of self. Once the relationship of identi-fication in which the child recognizes her own desire has been marked by failure with the appropriate parent at the appropriate phase, the search for a powerful ideal figure who represents the desiring self begins to replace it. Agency and recognition are achieved vicariously by submitting to this ideal lover, often in conventionally acceptable forms of wifely self-sacrifice. When identification such as that between toddler and father occurs at the appropriate phase with the pleasure of mutual recognition, then identification serves as a vehicle of development. But when identi-fication emerges later in ideal love, it becomes an impediment, a vicarious substitute. Thus ideal love becomes a perversion of identification, an extension of early identi-ficatory love into a substitute form of embodying one's own desire. Ultimately, we can agree with Freud that woman's masochism is linked to the retreat from active sexuality; however, this retreat begins not with resignation to anatomical imperatives but with failures in early individuation. And we see in masochism, especially the variant of ideal love, woman's alienated search for her own desire.

REFERENCES

Beauvoir, S. de (1952). *The Second Sex.* New York: Knopf.

Benjamin, J. (1983). Master and slave: The fantasy of erotic domination. In: *Powers of Desire,* ed. A Snitow, C. Stansell, & S. Thompson. New York: Monthly Review Press, pp. 280–299.

Bernstein, D. (1983). The female superego: a different perspective. *Internat. J. Psycho-Anal.* 64: 187–202.

Blum, H. (1977). Masochism, the ego ideal, and the psychology of women. In: *Female Psychology,* ed. H. Blum. New York: International Universities Press, pp. 157–192.

Chasseguet-Smirgel, J. (1970). Feminine guilt and the Oedipus complex. In: *Female Sexuality,* ed. J. Chasseguet-Smirgel. Ann Arbor: Michigan University Press, pp. 94–134.

———— (1976). Freud and female sexuality. *Internat. J. Psycho-Anal.,* 57:275–286.

Chodorow, N. (1978). *The Reproduction of Mothering.* Berkeley: University of California Press.

———— (1979). Difference, relation and gender in psychoanalytic perspective. *Socialist Rev.* 9(4):51–70. Also published as: Gender, relation, and difference in psychoanalytic perspectives in *The Future of Difference,* ed. H. Eisenstein & A. Jardine. New Brunswick, NJ: Rutgers University Press, 1985.

Dinnerstein, D. (1976). *The Mermaid and the Minotaur.* New York: Harper & Row.

Freud, S. (1919). A child is being beaten. *Standard Edition,* 17:179–204. London: Hogarth Press, 1955.

Gilligan, C. (1982). *In a Different Voice.* Cambridge, MA: Harvard University Press.

Masterson, J. F. (1981). *The Narcissistic and Borderline Disorders.* New York: Brunner/Mazel.

Miller, J. B. (1973). New issues, new approaches. In: *Psychoanalysis and Women,* ed. J. B. Miller. Baltimore: Penguin, pp. 375–406.

Person, E. S. (1980). Sexuality as the mainstay of identity: Psychoanalytic perspectives. *Signs,* 5:605–630.

Winnicott, D. W. (1971). The use of an object and relating through identifications. In: *Playing and Reality.* Harmondsworth, Middlesex, Eng: Penguin, pp. 101–111.

Chapter Forty-one

From What Do Women and Men Want from Love and Sex? (1983)

Elaine Hatfield

Hatfield reviews the research on gender differences in romantic love and concludes that, contrary to sociobiological explanations, men and women want much the same thing in romantic relations (passion, companionship, and so on). While she finds evidence for only slight differences in areas of power, control, and dominance, some research indicates that women are more willing to sacrifice their well-being for love. On the whole, however, her study of the literature shows that male and female are more alike than they are different in relation to romantic love.

Love has not been protected from ravages of the battle between the sexes. From time immemorial, men and women have been accusing one another of being incapable of feeling or returning love; for example, "Men can't love" (Firestone, 1971, p. 152) and "Men love women; women merely love love" (Anonymous).

The controversy is far from over. Recently, a woman posed an intriguing question in my human sexuality class: "Why are love affairs generally such disasters?" She had decided it was hopeless—"Men and women just want different things." Her bitter feelings sparked an intense debate.

Most of the students said they believed that men and women were really very much alike. They might talk about things differently, but in truth they both cared about the same kinds of things.

"Not so," said an indignant minority. Students then suggested a bewildering list of ways in which they thought men and women differed:

"Women care about love. They have to trust their partners if they're to have good sex."

"What men care about is sex; they want to have a lot of sex, with a lot of partners, in a lot of ways." ("Yeah! Yeah!" came a rowdy chorus.)

"Men claim to be egalitarian, but they all want to marry virgins; women want someone who is sexually experienced."

"Women are capable of intimacy. Men aren't. They won't talk about their feelings."

"Women want commitment; men don't want to be pinned down."

"Women say they want intimacy, but just let a man express a little weakness, and they really give it to him."

What an array of sexual stereotypes! Is there any truth in them?

Review of the Research Literature

I reviewed the research literature in order to find the answer to two questions: (1) What do men and women want out of their intimate relationships—the same things or markedly different things? and (2) What specifically, is the nature of these differences?

Most theorists seemed to agree that—in the main—men and women hope for very similar things from their intimate relationships. There are, however, probably *some* significant differences in the things they desire.

Sociobiologists contend that men and women are *genetically* programmed to desire different things from their intimate relations (see Hagen, 1979; Symons, 1979; and Wilson, 1975). Symons (1979) argues that gender differences are probably the most powerful determinant of how people behave sexually. Symons's sociobiological argument proceeds as follows: According to evolutionary biology, animals inherit those characteristics that ensure that they will transmit as many of their genes to the next generation as possible. It is to men and women's advantage to produce as many surviving children as possible. But men and women differ in one critical respect—in order to produce a child, men need only to invest a trivial amount of energy; a single man can conceivably father an almost unlimited number of children. On the other hand, a woman can conceive only a limited number of children. It is to a woman's advantage to ensure the survival of the children she does conceive. Symons observes, "The enormous sex differences in minimum parental investment and in reproductive opportunities and constraints explain why *Homo sapiens,* a species with only moderate sex differences in structure, exhibits profound sex differences in psyche" (p. 27).

What are the gender differences Symons insists are "wired in"? According to Symons,

1. Men desire a variety of sex partners; women do not.
2. Men are inclined to be polygamous (possessing many wives); women are more malleable in this respect; they are equally satisfied in polygamous, monogamous, or polyandrous marriages (possessing many husbands).
3. Men are sexually jealous. Women are more malleable in this respect; they are concerned with security—not fidelity.

4. Men are sexually aroused by the sight of women and women's genitals; women are not aroused by men's appearance.

5. For men, "sexual attractiveness" equals "youth." For women, "sexual attractiveness" equals "political and economic power."

6. Men have every reason to pursue women actively. They are programmed to impregnate as many women as possible. Women have every reason to be "coy." It takes time to decide if a man is a good genetic risk—is likely to be nurturant and protective.

7. Men are intensely competitive with one another. Competition over women is the most frequent cause of violence. Women are far less competitive.

In contrast, social learning theorists insist that gender differences are learned. Men and women are very adaptable. A half century ago, Margaret Mead in *Sex and Temperament in Three Primitive Societies* (1969) discussed three cultures of New Guinea (now Papua New Guinea) and their gender-role standards. She described the Arapesh, a culture in which both genders had "feminine" traits; the Mundugamur, among whom both genders were "masculine"; and the Tchambuli, among whom the men were "feminine" and women were "masculine."

Thus, learning theorists argue, if men and women desire different things from intimate relationships, it's because they've been *taught* to desire different things (see Bernard, 1972; Byrne & Byrne, 1977; Firestone, 1971; Griffitt & Hatfield, in press; Hatfield & Walster, 1981; Safilios-Rothschild, 1977; and Tavris & Offir, 1977).

Learning theorists do not always agree about what men and women have been trained to want from intimate relationships. For example, some argue that men are quicker to love, and love more deeply, than do women (Hobart, 1958; Kanin, Davidson, & Scheck, 1970; Hill, Rubin, & Peplau, 1976). Others argue that women love more deeply (Firestone, 1971; Kanin, Davidson, & Sheck, 1970). Some think it is men who are most possessive and jealous; others think that women are (see Clanton & Smith, 1977).

What does research indicate? Are there gender differences in what men and women want out of their intimate love relationships? Theorists have speculated that male-female differences are probably most striking in four areas: (1) concern with love, (2) concern with sex, (3) desire for intimacy, and (4) desire for control.

Concern with Love

According to folklore, it is women who are most concerned with love. Theorists of every political persuasion have assumed that the cultural stereotype—women love; men work—has a ring of truth.

Aristotle argued that it could hardly be otherwise. He theorized that, by nature, men are superior in every respect to women; not only are they superior in body and mind, but even in the ability to live on via the next generation. Aristotle erroneously believed that semen transmitted the soul to the embryo. "Feminine secretions" transmitted only a temporary earthly body to the next generation. Thus, Aristotle argued that "because the wife is inferior to her husband, she ought to love him more than herself; algebraically, this would compensate for their inequality and result in a well-balanced relationship." For Aristotle, the "fact" that women are concerned with loving and being loved, while men care far less, is written in their genes (or rather, in their "semen" and "secretions").

Interestingly enough, modern feminists have tended to agree with Aristotle—they too assume that women are the more romantic of the two genders. For example, Dorothy Dinnerstein (1977, p. 70) writes,

> It has often been pointed out that women depend lopsidedly on love for emotional fulfillment because they are barred from absorbing activity in the public domain. This is true. But it is also true that men can depend lopsidedly on participation in the public domain because they are stymied by love.

Shulamith Firestone (1971) agrees. In *The Dialectic of Sex,* she observes, "Men can't love." She comments, "That women live for love and men live for work is a truism. . . . Men were thinking, writing, and creating, because women were pouring their energies into those men; women . . . are preoccupied with love" (pp. 126–127). Firestone does not argue that women should cease being lovers. She argues, instead, that men and women must become equals, so they *both* can love.

This commonsense view—that women are intensely concerned with love while men's feelings are more muted—has been echoed by a wide array of psychologists and sociologists (see, for example, Parsons, 1959; Langhorn & Secord, 1955; and Parsons & Bales, 1955). The theorists agree—but do the facts support the theorists?

Research suggests that the facts are more complicated than one might expect: Men and women seem to differ in what they mean by love. But who is defined as the "romantic" depends on your definition of love.

The Meaning of Love

What do we mean by "love"? Lee (1977) and Hatkoff and Lasswell (1979) argue that "love" means very different things to different people. Hatkoff and Lasswell (1979) have concluded that men and women differ in the way they conceptualize love. They interviewed 554 blacks, whites, and Asians as well as members of several other ethnic groups. The lovers' ages ranged from under 18 to 60. They conclude that men are more romantic and self-centered lovers. Women are more dependent, companionate, and practical. No one is very altruistic.

Research by other investigators suggests that their conclusions might have some validity. Let us consider the evidence regarding gender differences in the different kinds of love.

Romantic Love. Several theorists agree with Hatkoff and Lasswell's (1979) finding that men are more romantic than are women. In 1958, sociologist Charles Hobart asked 923 men and women to respond to a series of statements related to romanticism. . . .

Hobart (1958) found that men had a somewhat more romantic view of male-female relationships than did women. On the average, women agreed with about four of the romanticism items. Men agreed with about five of them.

Recently, social psychologists tried to replicate Hobart's work in an effort to determine if it is still men who are the real romantics. They found evidence to indicate that men may still be the more romantic sex (see Dion & Dion, 1973, 1979; and Knox & Sporakowski, 1968).

Other researchers support Hatkoff and Lasswell's findings that men—as the romantics—are more likely to fall in love at first sight, become deeply committed to a romantic dream, and suffer bitterly when their romantic fantasies fall apart. For example, Kanin, Davidson, and Scheck (1970) interviewed 700 young lovers. "How early," they asked, "did you become aware that you loved the other?" Of the men, 20 percent fell in love before the fourth date; only 15 percent of the women fell in love that early. At the other extreme, 30 percent of the men, compared to 43 percent of the women, were not sure if they were in love by the twentieth date. Men seemed willing to fall headlong into love; women were far more cautious about getting involved.

There is also some evidence that it is men who cling most tenaciously to an obviously stricken affair and who suffer most when it finally dies. A group of Harvard scientists (Hill, Rubin, & Peplau, 1976) charted the course of 231 Boston couples' affairs for two years. They found that usually it was the women who decided whether and when an affair should end; men seemed to stick it out to the bitter end. When an affair finally did flicker out, the men suffered most. The men felt most depressed, most lonely, least happy, and least free after a breakup. They found it extremely hard to accept the fact that they were no longer loved, that the affair was over and there was nothing they could do about it. They were plagued with the hope that if only they said the right thing or did the right thing everything would be as it was. Women were far more resigned, and thus were better able to pick up the pieces of their lives and move on. And the contention that it is men who suffer most when an affair flickers out, is consistent with the fact that three times as many men as women commit suicide after a disastrous love affair (Bernard, 1972).

Self-centered Love. Self-centered lovers see love as a pleasant pastime. Following the Roman poet Ovid's advice, they play the game of love for their own purposes. The rules of the game are to exploit a relationship to its fullest without getting deeply involved.

Few social psychologists have explored self-centered love, probably because most people don't consider it to be love at all. Hatkoff and Laswell (1979) do, and they found that men are far more likely to be self-centered lovers than women. Replicating their findings, Dion and Dion (1973) also found that men can be more exploitative in love relationships than women.

Dependent Love. A number of scientists have studied dependent love, although they have chosen to label this intense state as "passionate love" (the term we prefer), "puppy love," "infatuation," or "falling in love" (as opposed to "being in love").

Hatfield and Walster (1981, p. 9) defined passionate love as "A state of intense absorption in another. Sometimes lovers are those who long for their partners and for complete fulfillment. Sometimes lovers are those who are ecstatic at finally having attained their partners' love, and, momentarily, complete fulfillment. A state of intense psychological arousal." Tennov (1979) argues that passionate love has the following basic components:

1. Lovers find it impossible to work, to study, to do anything but think about the beloved.
2. They long to be loved in return.
3. Their mood fluctuates wildly; they are ecstatic when they hope they might be loved, despairing when they feel they're not.
4. They find it impossible to believe that they could ever love again.
5. They fantasize about how it would go if their partner declared his or her love for them.
6. They're shy in the other's presence.
7. When everything seems lost, their feelings are even more intense than usual.
8. They search for signs (a squeeze of the hand, a knee that doesn't move away, a gaze that lingers) that signify that the other desires them.
9. Their heart aches when they imagine they might lose the other.
10. They feel like walking on air when the other seems to care.
11. They care so desperately about the other that nothing else matters; they are willing to sacrifice anything for love.
12. Love *is* blind; lovers idealize one another.

Contrary to the evidence presented earlier that men tend to be more romantic, researchers have found that, while a relationship is at its highest pitch, women experience the euphoria and agony of romance more intensely than do men. Kanin, Davidson, and Scheck (1970) asked men and women to rate (on the following scale: 1 = none; 2 = slight; 3 = moderate; 4 = strong; 5 = very strong) how they felt when they were in love; that is, to what extent did they experience the following love reactions:

( ) Felt like I was floating on a cloud

( ) Felt like I wanted to run, jump, and scream

( ) Had trouble concentrating

( ) Felt giddy and carefree

( ) Had a general feeling of well-being

( ) Was nervous before dates

( ) Had physical sensations: cold hands, butterflies in the stomach, tingling spine, and so on

( ) Had insomnia

In this study, the women appeared to be the most passionate. They generally experienced the symptoms of passionate love with some intensity. Men did not, with one exception: men and women were both nervous before dates. The recent work of Tennov (1979) provides additional support for the contention that women feel more "symptoms" of love than do men.

Researchers have found only one exception to this conclusion. Traupmann and Hatfield (1981) interviewed men and women at all stages of life about their feelings for their partners. They interviewed 191 dating couples and 53 newlywed couples right after their marriages and then again a year later. They also interviewed 106 older women, but (unfortunately, for our purposes) they did not interview women's husbands. These people were asked how much passionate love they felt for their partners and how much love they thought their partners felt for them. Possible answers were (1) "None at all," (2) "Very little," (3) "Some," (4) "A great deal," and (5) "A tremendous amount." Unlike previous researchers, they found that during courtship and the early years of marriage, men and women felt equally passionate about one another. Both steady daters and newlywed men and women felt "a great deal" of passionate love for their partners. It was only in old age that men *may* begin to love their partners with slightly more passion than they are loved in return. Older women reported that their husbands loved them with "some" passion. They reported feeling slightly less passionate about their husbands. Whether or not their husbands agree with this assessment is unknown. In summary, women appear to love the most passionately, at least until old age.

Companionate and Practical Love. Women appear to *like* their partners more than their partners like them in return. Researchers have talked about this friendly kind of love as companionate love, practical love, or just plain love. For most people, this is the essence of love.

Hatfield and Walster (1981) agree that liking and companionate love have much in common. They define companionate love as "The affection we feel for those with whom our lives are deeply entwined" (p. 9). Rubin (1970) explored some of the components of love. He argued that love includes such elements as idealization of the other, tenderness, responsibility, the longing to aid and be aided by the loved one, intimacy, the desire to share emotions and experiences, sexual attraction, the exclusive and absorptive nature of the relationship, and finally, a relative lack of concern with social norms and constraints.

Again, researchers find that, from the first, women are the friendly lovers. Traup-mann and Hatfield (1981), also asked dating, newlywed, and older people how *companionately* they loved their partners and how much they thought they were loved in return. They found that from the dating period until very late in life, women admitted they loved their partners more companionately than they were loved in return. Both steady daters and newlyweds expressed a "great deal" to "tremendous amount" of companionate love for their partners. By age 50, most people still expressed "a great deal" of companionate love for their mates—even after many years of marriage. At each point in time women feel more companionate love than do men. It is only in the final years of life that men and women come to love one another companionately with equal intensity. With long experience, equal respect and love evidently comes.

For many women, the fact that they love more passionately and companionately than they are loved in return is deeply unsettling. They continue to long for love throughout their marriages.

My colleagues and I (Hatfield et al., 1981) interviewed casually dating and newly-wed couples in an attempt to determine what they wished from their sexual relations. Men and women's concern with love was assessed via such questions as "During sex, I wish my partner was . . ." (possible answers ranged from "Much more caring and considerate" to "Much less caring and considerate") and "I wish my partner would . . ." ("Talk lovingly much more during sex" to "Talk lovingly much less during sex"). Both dating and newlywed women said they wished their partners would be more affectionate during sexual intercourse; men thought the amount of affection they received was "just about right."

Altruistic Love. Altruism is a classical form of love—love that is patient, kind, that never demands reciprocity. All the great religions share this concept of love. For example, St. Paul, in his letters to the Corinthians, wrote that Christians have a duty to care about others, whether the others are deserving of their love or not.

The data on who is most altruistic—men or women—are confusing. Sociologist John Lee asked Americans, Canadians, and Britons about their love experiences. He didn't find anyone, man or woman, who was very altruistic. Lee (1974, p. 50) admits,

> I found no saints in my sample. I have yet to interview an unqualified example of [altruism], although a few respondents had brief [altruistic] episodes in relationships that were otherwise tinged with selfishness. For instance, one of my subjects, seeing that his lover was torn between him or another man, resolved to save her the pain of deciding; he bowed out gracefully. His action fell short of pure [altruism], however, because he continued to be interested in how well his beloved was doing, and was purely and selfishly delighted when she dropped the other man and returned to him.

Hatkoff and Lasswell (1979) interviewed blacks, whites, and Asians, ranging in age from 18 to 60, about their perceptions, memories, and experiences of love. In Hawaii, it was women (especially Asian women) who were most altruistic. In the mainland United States, men had higher altruism scores than women. Thus, cultural factors probably have an enormous influence on altruism.

Recently, however, other research suggests women may be willing to sacrifice more for love than are men. Psychologists have begun to study couples' implicit "marriage contracts"—men and women's unconscious understandings as to what sort of give-and-take is fair. In his book on marriage contracts, for example, Sager (1976, pp. 4–5) observes,

> The concept of . . . marriage contracts has proven extremely useful. . . . But what must be emphasized above all is the reciprocal aspect of the contract: What each partner expects to give and receive in exchange are crucial. Contracts deal with every conceivable aspect of family life: relationships with friends, achievements, power, sex, leisure time, money, children, etc.

And researchers have attempted to determine how fair men and women perceive their respective "contracts" to be (Hatfield, Walster, & Traupmann, 1979; Utne et al., in press; Traupmann & Hatfield, in press; Traupmann, Hatfield, & Sprecher, 1982). The researchers contacted dating couples, newlyweds, and elderly couples who had been married for up to 60 years, and asked them how fair they thought their relationships were.

Couples in this series of studies were asked to focus on four possible areas of concern:

1. *Personal concerns:* How attractive were they and their partners? How sociable? Intelligent?

2. *Emotional concerns:* How much love did they express for one another? How much liking, understanding, and acceptance? How much sexual pleasure did they give and get? Were they faithful? How committed to one another? Did they respect their partners' needs for freedom?

3. *Day-to-day concerns:* How much of the day-to-day maintenance of the house did they and their partners do? How about finances? Companionability? Conversation? Decision making? Remembering special occasions? Did they fit in with one another's friends and relatives?

4. *Opportunities gained and lost:* How much did they gain simply from going together or being married? (For example, how much did they appreciate the chance to be married? To be a parent or a grandparent? Having someone to grow old with?) How about opportunities forgone?

After considering all these things, men and women were asked how fair they thought their relationships were. Were they getting more than they felt they deserved? Just what they deserved? Or less than they thought they had coming from their relationships?

Researchers found that regardless of whether couples were dating, newlyweds, or long marrieds, both men and women agreed that the men were getting the best deal. Both men and women agreed that, in general, men contribute less to a marriage than women do and get more out of marriage than do women.

Bernard (1972) provides additional support for the notion that women sacrifice more for love than men do. In her review of the voluminous literature contrasting "his marriage" versus "her marriage," she observes a strange paradox. Women are generally thought to be more eager to marry (and marry anyone) than are men. Yet women are the "losers" in marriage. She notes that "being married is about twice as advantageous to men as to women in terms of continued survival" (p. 27). As compared to single men, married men's mental health is far better, their happiness is greater, their earning power is greater, after middle age their health is better, and they live longer. The *opposite* is true for married as compared to single women. For example, all symptoms of psychological distress show up more frequently than expected among married women: nervous breakdowns, nervousness, inertia, insomnia, trembling hands, nightmares, perspiring hands, fainting, headaches, dizziness, and heart palpitations. They show up much less frequently than expected among unmarried women.

These data, then, suggest that, like it or not, women sacrifice the most for love.

Perhaps for women, marriage should carry a warning label: "This relationship may be hazardous to your health."

Summary

The evidence, then, makes clear that there is no simple answer to the question "Who is most loving—men or women?" Men tend to have a more romantic view— and a more exploitative view—of love than do women.

When we turn to passionate love, it is women who are the great lovers. Women experience the euphoria and the agony of love more intensely than do men. Yet, for most people, it is probably companionate love that represents "true love" at its best. Here, the evidence is clear. Women love more than they are loved in return. It is unclear who loves most unselfishly, men or women. Most evidence suggests, once again, that it is women who are willing to sacrifice the most for love.

Concern with Sex

The second type of gender difference that scientists have investigated is in concern with sex. Traditionally, theorists have assumed that sex is far more important for men than for women. According to cultural stereotypes, men are eager for sexual activity; women set limits on such activity. Theorists from the sociobiological and cultural-contingency perspectives can agree with this observation. What they disagree about, is *why* such a gender difference exists.

A number of biological determinists, most notably Freud, have argued that biology is destiny, and that interest in sexual activities is determined primarily by genes, hormones, and anatomy. Sociobiologists contend that men and women are genetically programmed to be differentially interested in sexual experience and restraint (see Hagen, 1979; Symons, 1979; Wilson, 1975). They argue that men are genetically programmed to seek out sexual activity; women, to set limits on it.

At the other end of the spectrum are social learning theorists, who argue that sexual behavior is learned (see Bernard, 1972; Byrne & Byrne, 1977; Firestone, 1971; Foucault, 1973; Griffitt & Hatfield, in press; Hatfield & Walster, 1981; Rubin, 1973; Safilios-Rothschild, 1977; Tavris & Offir, 1977). These authors argue that the sociopolitical context determines who is allowed to be sexual and who is forbidden to be, who is punished for violating sexual rules and who is not, and even what kinds of foreplay and sexual positions are considered to be normal. Because this is a male-dominated society, they argue, existing sexual norms meet the needs of men. Men are encouraged to express themselves sexually; women are punished for doing so. The style of intercourse men prefer (for example, the "missionary" position) is considered normal; the activities that women prefer (such as cuddling and cunnilingus) are neglected. No wonder, then, that men find sex in its common forms more appealing than do women.

Regardless of theorists' debates as to *why* men and women may differ in their enthusiasm for sex, they generally agree that men and women *do* differ. But, as we have seen earlier, cultural stereotypes are not always correct. What does research indicate?

In the earliest sex research, scientists found fairly sizable gender differences. In more recent research, researchers find that although gender differences still exist, they are not always so strong as theorists have assumed. Gender differences have begun to narrow, or disappear.

Gender Differences in Liking for Erotica

Early research supported the traditional assumption that men, not women, are interested in erotica (Kinsey, et al., 1948, 1953). Recently, however, researchers have found that there are few, if any, gender differences in response to literary erotica (Veitch & Griffitt, 1980) or to audiotapes of sexual encounters (Heiman, 1977). . . .

Willingness to Initiate Sexual Activity

In Kinsey's day, a double standard existed. Men were allowed, if not encouraged, to get sex whenever and wherever they could. Women were supposed to save themselves for marriage. In light of the double standard, it was not surprising that both men and women agreed that men were more likely to initiate sex and that women were more likely to resist sexual advances (see Baker, 1974; Ehrmann, 1959; Kaats & Davis, 1970; Reiss, 1967; Schofield, 1965; Sorensen, 1973).

Recent evidence suggests that traditional standards, although changing, are not yet dead. Contemporary college students reject a sexual double standard (Hopkins, 1977; Komarovsky, 1976; Peplau, Rubin, & Hill, 1976). Yet, this new single standard does not seem to have changed the cultural stereotype of male as sexual initiator and female as limit setter. Even today, it is almost always the man who initiates sexual activity. In a recent study of unmarried students, the man was found to have more say than the woman about the type and frequency of sexual activity (Peplau, Rubin, & Hill, 1976) except when a dating couple had decided to abstain from coitus in which case the woman's veto was the major restraining influence (Peplau, Rubin, & Hill, 1977).

Gender Differences in Sexual Experience

There is compelling evidence that men and women are becoming very similar with regard to sexual experience, however.

In the classic studies of sexuality, researchers found that society's double standard influenced sexual experience. For example, Kinsey and his colleagues (1948, 1953) tried to assess how sexually active men were throughout their lives, compared to women. They found that (1) indeed, men did seem to engage in more sexual activity than did women, and (2) men and women had strikingly different sexual histories.

At 18, it was usually the man who pushed to have sex. Kinsey and his associates reported that most men were as sexually expressive at age 15 as they would ever be.

In fact, according to Masters and Johnson (1966, 1970) 25 percent of men are impotent by age 65; 50 percent are impotent by age 75.

Women's experience was markedly different. Most women were slow to begin sexual activity. At 15, most women are quite inactive. Sometime between the ages of 16 and 20, they slowly shed their inhibitions and begin to feel more enthusiastic about sexual exploration. They continue their high rates of sexual activity for fully two decades. Not until their late 40s does their sexual behavior begin to ebb.

In commenting on women's sexual histories, Kinsey and his colleagues (1953, pp. 353–354) observed,

> One of the tragedies which appears in a number of the marriages originates in the fact that the male may be most desirous of sexual contact in his early years, while the responses of the females are still underdeveloped and while she is still struggling to free herself from the acquired inhibitions which prevent her from participating freely in the marital activity. But over the years most females become less inhibited and develop an interest in sexual relations, which they may then maintain until they are in their fifties or even sixties. But by then the responses of the average male may have dropped so considerably that his interest in coitus, and especially in coitus with a wife who has previously objected to the frequencies of his requests, may have sharply declined.

Moreover, the age differential that is common in marriages (the men being older) may contribute to this problem.

Since Kinsey's day, researchers (DeLamater & MacCorquodale, 1979; Erhmann, 1959; Schofield, 1965; Reiss, 1967; Sorensen, 1973) continued to interview samples of young people about their sexual behavior: Had they ever necked? At what age did they begin? French kissed? Fondled their lover's breasts or genitals? Had their own genitals fondled? Had intercourse? Oral-genital sex? When responses from these studies are compared, we find that indeed, a sexual revolution *is* occurring. In the early studies, in general, men were far more experienced than were women. By the end of the 1970s, these differences had virtually disappeared. As DeLamater and MacCorquodale (1979) observe,

> There are virtually no differences in the incidence of each of the behaviors. Unlike most earlier studies which generally reported lower frequencies of more intimate activities among females, we find that women are as likely as men to have ever engaged in these behaviors. The only exception occurs with coitus, which women . . . are less likely to have experienced. (*Among students,* 75 percent of men and 60 percent of women had had intercourse. *Among nonstudents,* 79 percent of men and 72 percent of women had had intercourse.) [p. 58]

DeLamater and MacCorquodale continue:

> Thus, the gender differences in lifetime behavior which were consistently found in studies conducted in the 1950s and 1960s have narrowed considerably. This is also an important finding; it suggests that those models which have emphasized gender as an explanatory variable are no longer valid. [p. 58]

When men and women are together in a close, loving relationship, they seem equally likely to desire to engage in sexual activity. There is only one type of situation in which scientists find women are still more reserved than men: if men and women are offered a chance to participate in uncertain, unconventional, or downright bizarre sexual activities, men are more willing to take the risk than are women.

For example, in the Clark and Hatfield (1981) study, . . . college men and women were hired to approach Florida State University students of the other gender. If a woman requested a date, suggested that the man visit her apartment, or even go to bed with her, she was generally very successful in getting the stranger to agree. Men were generally at ease with such requests. They said such things as "Why do we have to wait until tonight?" or "I can't tonight, but tomorrow would be fine." When a man made such a request, however, he was much less successful. Although the majority of women would date a man who approached her, few would go to his apartment, and none would agree to go to bed with him. Typical responses to males were "You've got to be kidding" or "What's wrong with you? Leave me alone."

Sociobiologists such as Symons (1979) argue that the gender differences Clark and Hatfield describe are genetically "wired in"; that women are genetically programmed to desire one, deeply intimate, secure relationship, while men are programmed to desire anonymous, impersonal, casual sex. Other scientists have documented that, even today, men are more eager to have sex with a variety of partners, in a variety of ways, and so on. (Sociobiologists such as Symons, 1979, would argue that these gender differences too, are "wired in.") For example, Hatfield and her colleagues (in press) interviewed casually dating and newlywed couples about their sexual preferences. They assessed desire for variety via such questions as

1. "I wish my partner were . . ." (Answers range from "Much more unpredictable about *when* he or she wants to have sex," to "Much more predictable about *when* he or she wants to have sex.")
2. "I wish my partner would be . . ." (Answers range from "Much more experimental sexually" to "Much more conventional sexually.")
3. "I wish my partner were . . ." (Answers range from "Much more variable about *where* we have sex" to "Much more conventional about *where* we have sex.")
4. "I wish my partner were . . ." (Answers range from "Much more wild and sexy" to "Much less wild and sexy.")

The authors predicted that men would be more interested in exciting, diverse experiences than women would be. That is exactly what they found. The men wished their sex lives were a little more exciting. Women tended to be slightly more satisfied with the status quo.

In summary, then, recent evidence suggests that, although some gender differences remain in men and women's concern with sex, a sexual revolution *is* occurring. The gender differences we have described—in responsiveness to pornography, willingness to initiate sex, and sexual experience—are rapidly disappearing. Recent studies indicate that women and men are becoming increasingly similar in their sexual preferences and experiences.

Desire for Intimacy

The third way in which theorists agree men and women differ is in desire for intimacy. What is intimacy? Intimacy is not a static state, but a *process.* Intimacy may be defined as a process by which a couple—in the expression of thought, emotion, and behavior—attempts to move toward more complete communication on all levels. According to many clinicians, one of the major tasks people face is the achievement of a separate identity while, at the same time, achieving a deeply intimate relationship with others (Erikson, 1968a, 1968b; Kantor & Lehr, 1975; Kaplan, 1978). Both separateness and intimacy are generally considered to be basic human needs (see Freud, 1922; Maslow, 1954). Kaplan suggests that adults spend much of their lives resolving the dilemma between achieving a sense of self while at the same time establishing close nurturant relations with others.

According to family therapists, men have the easiest time achieving an independent identity; women have the easiest time achieving closeness with others. Napier (1977) describes two types of people who seem, with uncanny accuracy, to attract one another. Type I (usually a woman) is only minimally concerned with maintaining her independence. What she cares about is achieving emotional closeness. She seeks "fusion with the partner," "oneness" or "we-ness" in the marriage. She puts much energy into planning "togetherness" activities. Type I fears rejection and abandonment. She feels rejected when her partner chooses to spend an evening alone, or with other friends. Her feeling of rejection may even extend to times when her partner is engaged in necessarily exclusive activities—such as earning an income, studying for exams, or writing a manuscript.

Type I's partner, Type II (usually a man), is most concerned with maintaining his sense of self and personal freedom and autonomy. He feels a strong need to establish his territory within the common household: to have "my study," "my workshop," "my car." Similarly, he feels compelled to draw sharp lines around psychological space: "my night out," "my career," "my way of handling problems." What he fears is being "suffocated," "stifled," or "engulfed," or in some manner intruded on by his spouse.

Napier observes that men and women's efforts to reduce their anxieties make matters worse. Women (seeking more closeness) clasp their mates tightly, thereby contributing to the men's anxiety. The men (seeking more distance) retreat further, which increases their wives' panic, inducing further "clasping." Sociobiologists such as Symons (1979) argue that the gender difference Napier describes is genetically "wired in"; that women are genetically programmed to desire one, deeply intimate, secure relationship; men, to desire anonymous, impersonal, casual sex.

Theorists can agree, then, that women are far better at intimacy than are men. Family therapists take it for granted that the fact that women are very comfortable with intimate relationships and men are not is a common cause of marital friction. And there are literally dozens of books exhorting men to share their feelings. Therefore, it is startling that there has been so little research devoted to gender differences in intimacy. Worse yet, it is difficult to draw any conclusions from the research that does exist. If I were forced to guess what future research will reveal, I would guess as follows: Women's complaints that men just won't share their deepest feelings is a legitimate one. In general, women *are* more comfortable with intimacy than are men. But paradoxically, even though women complain about men's lack of intimacy in love relationships, male-female differences are *smallest* in a love affair. Women find it fairly easy to be intimate with their lovers, with men friends, with other women, and with children. Many men can be intimate only with their lovers. It is here that they reveal most of themselves—not as much as their lovers might like, but far more than they share with anyone else. It is most difficult for men to be close to other men.

These are broad conclusions—too broad, perhaps. What are the sparse data on which these overgeneralizations are based? A few social psychologists have explored gender differences in people's willingness to get close to others. Generally, they have defined intimacy as a willingness to disclose one's ideas, feelings, and day-to-day activities to lovers, friends, or strangers, and to listen to their disclosures in return.

Psychologist Sidney Jourard (1964) developed one of the most commonly used measures of intimacy, the Jourard Self-Disclosure Questionnaire (JSDQ). The JSDQ consists of 60 questions in all. It asks people to think about how much they typically disclose to others in six different areas of life . . .

Jourard calculates respondents' self-disclosure scores by adding up their scores in each of the six areas. What was your score? What was your partner's score? Were the differences between the two of you typical of those social psychologists find between men and women in general?

In self-disclosure research, four findings have consistently emerged. First, both men and women disclose far more about themselves in intimate than in casual relationships. In casual encounters, most people are willing to reveal only the sketchiest, most stereotyped information about themselves. The Renaissance French essayist Montaigne (quoted in Thomas, 1979) observed that everyone is complex, multifaceted:

> All contradictions may be found in me . . . bashful, insolent; chaste, lascivious; talkative, taciturn; tough, delicate; clever, stupid; surly, affable; lying, truthful; learned, ignorant; liberal, miserly and prodigal: all this I see in myself to some extent according to how I turn. . . . I have nothing to say about myself absolutely, simply and solidly, without confusion and without mixture, or in one word.

In intimate relationships, more of the complexities and contradictions are revealed. In deeply intimate relationships, friends and lovers feel free to reveal far more facets of themselves. As a consequence, intimates share profound information about one another's histories, values, strengths and weaknesses, idiosyncracies, hopes, and fears (Altman & Taylor, 1973; Huesmann & Levinger, 1976; Jourard, 1964; Worthy, Gary, & Kahn, 1969).

Second, in their deeply intimate relationships, men and women often differ little, if at all, in how much they are willing to reveal to one another. For example, Rubin and his colleagues (1980) asked dating couples via the Jourard Self-Disclosure Questionnaire how much they had revealed themselves to their partners. Did they talk about their current relationships? Previous opposite-sex affairs? Their feelings about their parents and friends? Their self-concepts and life views? Their attitudes and interests? Their day-to-day activities? The authors found that, overall, men and women did *not* differ in how much they were willing to confide in their partners.

There was a difference, however, in the *kind* of things men and women were willing to share with those they love. Men were more willing to share their views on politics and their pride in their strengths. Women were more likely to disclose their feelings about other people and their fears. Interestingly enough, Rubin and his colleagues found that the stereotyped form of communication is most common in traditional men and women.

Some authors have observed that neither men or women may be getting the exactly the amount of intimacy they would like. Women may want more intimacy than they are getting; men may want far less. There is evidence that couples tend to negotiate a level of self-disclosure that is bearable to both. In the words of the movie *My Fair Lady*, this ensures that "*neither* really gets what either really wants at all" (Chaikin & Derlega, 1975).

Third, in less intimate relationships, women disclose far more to others than do men (Jourard, 1971; Cozby, 1973). Rubin and his colleagues (1980, p. 306) point out that "The basis for such differences appears to be in socialization practices. Whereas women in our culture have traditionally been encouraged to show their feelings, men have been taught to hide their feelings and to avoid displays of weakness (Pleck & Sawyer, 1974). As Kate Millett (1975) has put it: "Women express, men repress." The authors argue that it is traditional men and women who differ most on emotional sharing. They discovered that more egalitarian couples were more likely to disclose themselves fully to one another.

Fourth, and last, women receive more disclosures than do men. This is not surprising in view of the fact that the amount of information people reveal to others has an enormous impact on the amount of information they receive in return (see Altman, 1973; Davis & Skinner, 1974; Jourard, 1964; Jourard & Friedman, 1970; Marlatt, 1971; Rubin, 1975; Worthy, Gary, & Kahn, 1969).

There does seem to be some evidence, then, that women feel slightly more comfortable with intense intimacy in their love relationships than do men, and are far more comfortable revealing themselves in more casual relationships than are men. Tradition dictates that women should be the "intimacy experts." And today, women *are* more comfortable sharing their ideas, feelings, and behavior than are men. But what happens if this situation changes? Rubin and his colleagues (1980) suggest that such changes have already begun.

The prognosis is mixed. Young women usually say they would be delighted if the men they love could be intimate. I'm a bit skeptical that it will be this easy. Change is always difficult. More than one man has complained that when he finally dared to reveal his weaker aspects to a woman, he soon discovered that she was shocked by his lack of "manliness." Family therapists such as Napier (1977) have warned us that the struggle to find individuality *and* closeness is a problem for everyone. As long as men were fleeing from intimacy, women could safely pursue them. Now that men are turning around to face them, women may well find themselves taking flight. In any case, the confrontation is likely to be exciting.

And the change should have real benefit. As Rubin and his colleagues (1980, p. 316) observe,

> Men and women should have the freedom to decide for themselves when they will reveal themselves—and when they will listen to another's revelations. "Full disclosure" need not be so full that it eliminates all areas of privacy, even within the most intimate relationships . . . [given that] we believe the ethic of openness is a desirable one. Especially when contemplating marriage, it is valuable for women and men to be able to share rather fully—and equally—their thoughts and feelings about themselves, each other, and their relationship. . . . It is encouraging to discover that a large majority of the college students we studied seem to have moved, even if incompletely, and sometimes uneasily, toward the ethic of openness.

There is one final way in which theorists have speculated that men and women may differ—in their desire to flow with the moment versus to dominate, to achieve.

Desire for Control

Traditionally, men are supposed to control themselves, other people, and the environment. The ideal man carefully controls his thoughts. He is objective, logical, and unemotional. He hides his feelings, or if he does express any feelings, he carefully telescopes the complex array of human feelings into a single emotion: anger. Men are supposed to be dominant; women, to be submissive. A "real man" is even supposed to control the environment by taming nature.

In contrast with the ideal man, the ideal woman is supposed to be emotional and responsive to other people and the environment. The ideal woman is expressive and warm. She shares herself openly with others but is, at the same time, highly vulnerable to their disapproval. Comfortable expressing a rainbow of feminine feelings— love, anxiety, joy, and depression—she is less in touch with anger. Tears and smiles come easily; anger is an alien emotion. A "real woman" is regarded as somewhat like a child; she is attractive and caring but not independent or competent.

There is considerable evidence that, even today, most men and women hold these stereotypes. Inge Broverman and her colleagues (1972) asked people what men and women *should be* like and what they really *are* like. The answer was clear: "Women are expressive and nurturant; men are in control and instrumental."

What is the purpose of all this male control? Achievement. Some people, usually men, view intimate relations—the one place where people can be themselves, totally relaxed, confident that they will be accepted no matter what, a place for exploring the possibilities of life—as yet another arena for achievement. In reviewing male sexual myths, Zilbergeld (1978) observed that, even in their most intimate relationships, men are more goal oriented than women. In summary, he concludes that "In sex, as elsewhere, it's performance that counts" (p. 35).

According to theorists, then, there are marked gender differences in three areas: (1) desire to be "in control"; (2) desire to dominate their partners or submit to them, and (3) desire to "achieve" in their love and sexual relations.

Unfortunately, although a great deal has been written about these topics, there is almost no research documenting that these differences do in fact exist. Let us review what scientists do know.

Desire to Be in Control

As I said in the previous section, it appears that even in love relationships, men are more concerned than women about possessing and expressing appropriate thoughts, feelings, and behaviors. It is especially difficult for men to acknowledge their weaknesses.

Desire to Dominate or Submit to Others

Sociobiologists have argued that gender differences in dominance-submission are genetically "wired in." Males can ensure the survival of their genes by dominating women; women, by submitting to one man.

There is little evidence, however, to support such a contention. The only study relevant to this issue examined gender differences in the desire for dominance-submission on couple's intimate sexual encounters (Hatfield et al., 1981). The study reviewed a number of reasons why men's and women's desires might differ.

Most men and women accept traditional roles. They believe that men and women ought to be very different: men "should" be dominant; women "should" be submissive (Broverman et al., 1972). In fact, however, men and women are surprisingly similar in dominance-submission (Maccoby & Jacklin, 1974). Thus, perhaps both men and women secretly fear they do not "measure up." Men may worry that they're not sufficiently "masculine"—they may feel compelled to exaggerate their "macho" image, to deny any hint of weakness. They want their partners to be as submissive as possible. Women, worried about their "femininity," may wish to deny any hint of strength; they may want their partners to be "real men," dominant and strong. If such a dynamic is operating, men might be expected to wish secretly that their partners would be more feminine, women, to wish their mates would be more dominant.

That's one possibility, but there is another. Gender roles are limiting. Modern men and women may secretly wish that they could express themselves more honestly, but they may be afraid to do so. Some men may want to express their submissive side, and some women may want to express their dominant side in sexual relations. Some theorists have argued that men, forced to be more dominant than they wish to be in their daily activities, are especially attracted to masochistic sexual experiences (Gibson, 1978; Green & Green, 1973; Kamiat, 1936; Krafft-Ebing, 1903). According to this same logic, we might expect women to find sadism equally appealing. Few theorists, however, have ever suggested that they do (Robertiello, 1970; for an exception to this statement, see Stoller, 1978). According to this reasoning, then, we might expect to find that *both* men and women wish their sexual repertoires could be expanded—men wishing their partners would sometimes take the lead, women wishing their partners would sometimes behave more submissively.

To determine which, if either, of these possibilities is true, I and my colleagues (Hatfield et al., 1981) asked dating and newlywed couples how they *wished* things were in their sexual relationships. We measured men and women's desire for dominance submission via such questions as

1. "During sex, I wish my partner would . . ." (Answers range from "Give many more instructions and requests" to "Give many less instructions and requests.")
2. "I wish my partner was . . ." (Answers range from "Much more willing to do what I want sexually" to "Much less willing to do what I want sexually.")
3. "I wish my partner would play . . ." (Answers range from "The dominant role in sex much more" to "The dominant role in sex much less.")
4. "I wish my partner would play . . ." (Answers range from "The submissive role in sex much more" to "The submissive role in sex much less.")

When we examined men and women's reactions to these items, a surprising result emerged: there is no evidence that couples wish men could be more dominant and women could be more submissive—nor any evidence that they wish they could be more androgynous in their sexual lives. What *do* the data show? Interviews suggested two surprising conclusions. First, as family therapists have noted, couples seem to have a communication problem. Both men and women wish *their partners* would be a little clearer about what they want sexually, but these same men and women are evidently reluctant to say what *they* want. Second, in general, if anything, *both* men and women wish their partners would be more assertive about what they want sexually. Of the two, men are the more eager for their partners to take an active role. Evidently, in spite of some therapists' concerns, women have not yet become so dominant and demanding that they frighten men away.

Desire to Achieve in Love and Sex

It is fascinating to speculate about the effects that such gender differences, if they exist, would have on love and sexual relations. Are most men so concerned about acquiring an impressive reputation that, if they had a choice between having a warm, wonderful, sexual encounter and having a reputation of being the world's greatest lover, they would choose the latter? Is women's definition of a "good lover" someone who is loving, tender, and intimate? Do the very men who are most eager to succeed at being "a great lover" focus on "achievements" that women care little about—the objective facts of a sexual encounter such as the size of their partners' breasts, length of their own penises, the number of their conquests, how long they last sexually, and the number of their orgasms? These are interesting speculations, but no one has conducted research on these questions.

In summary, men are more concerned than women about being in control, dominating others, and achieving at love according to the theorists. However, empirical research is needed to determine whether these theoretical speculations are accurate.

Conclusions

In this chapter, I have explored what is known about gender differences in four areas: love, sex, intimacy, and control. Many theorists have seen men and women as very different—to the point of almost being incompatible. A consideration of the evidence, however, indicates that nature has arranged things more sensibly. Men and women are surprisingly similar in what they want out of their most intimate relations. Everyone, male *and* female, wants love *and* sex, intimacy *and* control. Yet, if one is determined, one can detect some slight differences between the genders. Women may be slightly more concerned with love; men, with sex. Women may be somewhat more eager for a deeply intimate relationship than are men. Men may be a little more eager to be in control of things, perhaps to dominate their partners, to "achieve" at love than are women. This last contention is badly in need of research: the available research clearly indicates far greater similarities than differences in the feelings of men and women about sex and love.

REFERENCES

Altman, I. Reciprocity of interpersonal exchange. *Journal for the Theory of Social Behavior,* 1973, 3, 249–261.

Altman, I. & Taylor D. A. *Social penetration: The development of interpersonal relationships,* New York: Holt, Rinehart & Winston, 1973.

Baker, M. J., *The effects of inequity on heterosexual behavior: A test for compensation in inequitable relationships.* Unpublished manuscript, Department of Sociology, University of Wisconsin, 1974.

Bernard, J. *The future of marriage.* New York: Bantam Books, 1972.

Broverman, I., Vogel, S., Broverman, D., Clarkson, F., & Rosenkrantrz, P. Sex role stereotypes: A current appraisal. *Journal of Social Issues,* 1972, 28, 59–78.

Byrne, D., & Byrne, L. *Exploring human sexuality.* New York: Crowell, 1977.

Chaikin, A. L., & Derlega, V. J. *Sharing intimacy: What we reveal to others and why.* Englewood Cliffs, N.J.: Prentice-Hall, 1975.

Chesler, P. *Women and madness.* New York: Doubleday, 1972.

Clanton, G., & Smith, L. G. (Eds.). *Jealousy.* Englewood Cliffs, N.J.: Prentice-Hall, 1977.

Clark, R. D., III, & Hatfield, E. *Gender difference in receptivity to sexual offers.* Unpublished manuscript, 1981.

Cozby, P. C. Self-disclosure: A literature review. *Psychological Bulletin,* 1973, 79, 73–91.

Davis J. B., & Skinner, A. E. Reciprocity of self-disclosure in interviews: Modeling of social exchange. *Journal of Personality and Social Psychology,* 1974, 29, 779–784.

DeLamater, J., & MacCorquodale, P. *Premarital sexuality: Attitudes, relationships, behavior.* Madison: University of Wisconsin Press, 1979.

Dinnerstein, D. *The mermaid and the minotaur: Sexual arrangements in human malaise.* New York: Harper Colophon Books, 1977.

Dion, K. L., & Dion, K. K. Correlates of romantic love. *Journal of Consulting and Clinical Psychology,* 1973, 41, 51–56.

Dion, K. L., & Dion, K. K. Personality and behavioral correlates of romantic love. In M. Cook

& G. Wilson (Eds.), *Love and attraction: An international conference.* New York: Pergamon, 1979.

Ehrmann, W. *Premarital dating behavior.* New York: Holt, Rinehart & Winston, 1959.

Erikson, E. *Identity, youth and crisis.* New York: Norton, 1968a.

Erikson, E. *Childhood and society* (Rev. ed.). New York: Norton, 1968b.

Firestone, S. *The dialectic of sex.* New York: Bantam Morrow, 1971.

Foucault, M. *The order of things.* New York: Random House, 1973.

Freud, S. [Certain neurotic mechanisms in jealousy, paranoia and homosexuality.] In *Collected papers* (Vol. 2.), (J. Riviere & A. R. J. Strachey, trans.). London: Hogarth Press and Institute of Psychoanalysis, 1922.

Gibson, I. *The English vice: Beating sex and shame in Victorian England and after.* London: Duckworth, 1978.

Green, C., & Green, G. S.-M: *The last taboo.* New York: Grove Press, 1973.

Griffitt, W., & Hatfield, E. Gender identities and gender roles: Psychosocial determinants, in *Psychology of sexual behavior.* Glenview, Ill.: Scott, Foresman, in press.

Hagen, R. *The bio-sexual factor.* New York: Doubleday, 1979.

Hatfield, E., Traupmann, J., Sprecher, S., Greenberger, D., & Wexler, P. *Male/female differences in concern with intimacy, variety, and power in the sexual relationship.* Unpublished manuscript, 1981.

Hatfield, E., & Walster, G. W. *A new look at love.* Reading, Mass.: Addison-Wesley, 1981.

Hatfield, E., Walster, G. W., & Traupmann, J. Equity and premarital sex. In M. Cook & G. Wilson (Eds.), *Love and attraction: An international conference.* New York: Pergamon Press, 1979. (Reprinted from *Journal of Personality and Social Psychology,* 1978, 37, 82–92.)

Hatkoff, T. S., & Lasswell, T. E. Male-female similarities and differences in conceptualizing love. In M. Cook & G. Wilson (Eds.), *Love and attraction: An international conference.* New York: Pergamon Press, 1979.

Heiman, J. P. A psychophysiological exploration of sexual arousal patterns in females and males. *Psychophysiology,* 1977, 14, 266–274.

Hill, C. T., Rubin, Z., & Peplau, L. A. Breakups before marriage: The end of 103 affairs. *Journal of Social Issues,* 1976, 32, 147–168.

Hobart, C. W. The incidence of romanticism during courtship. *Social Forces,* 1958, 36, 362–367.

Hopkins, J. R. Sexual behavior in adolescence. *Journal of Social Issues,* 1977, 33, 67–85.

Huesmann, L. R., & Levinger, G. Incremental exchange theory: A formal model for progression in dyadic social interaction. In L. Berkowitz & E. Walster (Eds.), *Advances in Experimental Social Psychology* (Vol. 9). New York: Academic Press, 1976.

Jourard, S. M. *The transparent self.* Princeton, N.J.: D. Van Nostrand, 1964.

Jourard, S. *Self-disclosure: An experimental analysis of the transparent self.* New York: Wiley, 1971.

Jourard, S., & Friedman, R. Experimenter-subject distance in self-disclosure. *Journal of Personality and Social Psychology,* 1970, 15, 278–282.

Kaats, G. R., & Davis, K. E. The dynamics of sexual behavior of college students. *Journal of Marriage and the Family,* 1970, 32, 390–399.

Kamiat, A. H. Male masochism and culture. *Psychoanalytic Review,* 1936, 23, 84–91.

Kanin, E. J., Davidson, K. D., & Scheck, S. R. A research note on male/female differentials in the experience of heterosexual love. *The Journal of Sex Research,* 1970, 6, 64–72.

Kantor, D., & Lehr, W. *Inside the family.* San Francisco: Jossey-Bass, 1975.

Kaplan, L. J. *Oneness and separateness: From infant to individual.* New York: Simon & Schuster, 1978.

Kinsey, A. C., Pomeroy, W. B., & Martin, C. E. *Sexual behavior in the human male.* Philadelphia: Saunders, 1948.

Kinsey, A. C., Pomeroy, W. B., Martin, C. E., & Gebhard, P. H. *Sexual behavior in the human female.* Philadelphia: Saunders, 1953.

Knox, D. H., & Sporakowski, M. J. Attitudes of college students toward love. *Journal of Marriage and the Family,* 1968, *30,* 638–642.

Komarovsky, M. *Dilemmas of masculinity: A study of college youth.* New York: Norton, 1976.

Krafft-Ebing, R. von. [*Psychopathia sexualis: A medico-forensic study.*] New York: Pioneer, 1939. (Trans. of 12th edition, originally published, 1903.)

Langhorn, M. C., & Secord, P. Variations in martial needs with age, sex, marital status, and regional locations. *Journal of Social Psychology,* 1955, *41,* 19–37.

Lee, J. A. The styles of loving *Psychology Today,* 1974, *8,* 43–51.

Lee, J. A. *The colors of love.* New York: Bantam Books, 1977.

Maccoby, E. E., & Jacklin, C. N. *The psychology of sex differences.* Stanford, Calif.: Stanford University Press, 1974.

Marlatt, G. A. Exposure to a model and task ambiguity as determinants of verbal behavior in an interview. *Journal of Consulting and Clinical Psychology,* 1971, *36,* 268–276.

Maslow, A. H. *Motivation and personality.* New York: Harper, 1954.

Masters, W. H., & Johnson, V. E. *Human sexual response.* Boston: Little, Brown, 1966.

Masters, W. H., & Johnson, V. E. *Human sexual inadequacy.* Boston: Little, Brown, 1970.

Mead, M. *Sex and temperament in three primitive societies.* New York: Dell, 1969.

Millett, K. The shame is over. *Ms Magazine,* January 1975, pp. 26–29.

Napier, A. Y. *The rejection-intrusion pattern: A central family dynamic.* Unpublished manuscript, School of Family Resources, University of Wisconsin, Madison, 1977.

Parsons, T. The social structure of the family. In R. N. Anshen (Ed.), *The family: Its function and destiny.* New York: Harper, 1959.

Parsons, T., & Bales, R. F. *Family, socialization, and interaction process.* New York: The Free Press, 1955.

Peplau, L., Rubin, Z., & Hill, C. The sexual balance of power. *Psychology Today,* 1976, *10,* 142–147; 151.

Peplau, L. A., Rubin, Z., & Hill, C. T. Sexual intimacy in dating couples. *Journal of Social Issues,* 1977, *33,* 86–109.

Pleck, J. H., & Sawyer, J. (Eds.). *Men and masculinity.* Englewood Cliffs, N.J.: Prentice-Hall, 1974.

Reiss, I. L. *The social context of premarital sexual permissiveness.* New York: Holt, Rinehart & Winston, 1967.

Robertiello, R. C. Masochism and the female sexual role. *Journal of Sex Research,* 1970, *6,* 56–58.

Rubin, Z. Measurement of romantic love. *Journal of Personality and Social Psychology,* 1970, *16,* 265–273.

Rubin, Z. *Liking and loving: An invitation to social psychology.* New York: Holt, Rinehart & Winston, 1973.

Rubin, Z. Disclosing oneself to a stranger: Reciprocity and its limits. *Journal of Experimental Social Psychology,* 1975, *11,* 233–260.

Rubin, Z., Hill, C. T., Peplau, L. A., & Dunkel-Schetter, C. Self-disclosure in dating couples: Sex roles and the ethic of openness. *Journal of Marriage and the Family,* 1980, *42,* 305–317.

Safilios-Rothschild, C. *Love, sex, and sex roles.* Englewood Cliffs, N.J.: Prentice-Hall, Spectrum Books, 1977.

Sager, C. *Marriage contracts and couple therapy.* New York: Brunner/Mazel, 1976.

Schofield, M. *The sexual behavior of young people.* Boston: Little, Brown, 1965.

Sorensen, R. C. *Adolescent sexuality in contemporary America.* New York: World, 1973.

Stoller, R. J. *Sexual excitement.* New York: Pantheon Books, 1978.

Symons, D. *The evolution of human sexuality.* New York: Oxford University Press, 1979.

Tavris, C., & Offir, C. *The longest war: Sex differences in perspective.* New York: Harcourt Brace Jovanovich, 1977.

Tennov, D. *Love and limerence.* New York: Stein & Day, 1979.

Thomas, L. *The medusa and the snail.* New York: Bantam Books, 1979.

Traupmann, J., & Hatfield, E. Love: Its effects on mental and physical health. In J. March, S. Kiesler, R. Fogel, E. Hatfield, & E. Shanas (Eds.), *Aging: Stability and change in the family.* New York: Academic Press, 1981.

Traupmann, J. & Hatfield, E. How important is fairness over the lifespan? *International Journal of Aging and Human Development,* in press.

Traupmann, J., Hatfield, E., & Sprecher, S. *The importance of "fairness" for the material satisfaction of older women.* Unpublished manuscript, 1982.

Utne, M. K., Hatfield, E., Traupmann, J. & Greenberger, D. Equity, marital satisfaction and stability. *Basic and Applied Social Psychology,* in press.

Veitch, R., & Griffitt, W. The perception of erotic arousal in men and women by same- and opposite-sex peers. *Sex Roles,* 1980, 6, 723–733.

Wilson, E. O. *Sociobiology.* Cambridge, Mass.:Belknap Press, 1975.

Worthy, M. A., Gary, L., & Kahn, G. M. Self-disclosure as an exchange process. *Journal of Personality and Social Psychology,* 1969, 13, 63–69.

Zilbergeld, B. *Male sexuality: A guide to sexual fulfillment.* Boston: Little, Brown, 1978.

Chapter Forty-two

Male-Female Relations

How the Past Affects the Present (1988)

Audrey B. Chapman

Chapman offers a sociological view of the ways black women are affected in love relationships by difficult conditions, including "mate sharing" (that is, male infidelity) and economic hardship.

With all the recent media attention to the plight of the Black family, it would be hard to ignore the fact that great problems still exist between Black men and women. However, it is a mistake to view these problems in a vacuum. Any objective observer can see that family relations have changed throughout American society as a whole, not just within the Black community. Yet it is probably true that economics compounds the problems in the Black community more so than in the white community.

A thorough discussion of the future for Black family structure calls for an examination of the historical chasm between Black men and women. Powerful controlling myths surround the relationship between Black men and women, and those myths still influence Black thinking and behavior. It is baffling to contemplate how some of the myths that took hold during slavery still cripple us today.

Rodgers-Rose indicated in the book, *The Black Woman* (1980), how devastating the stereotypes of the shiftless Black male and the hostile woman have been to Blacks. Blacks internalize these feelings and bring them into their relationships. Many women say that Black men can't be counted upon, because they have met a few who can't give Black women the support they need. Another persistent and damaging myth is that of a controlling Black woman.

These stereotypes serve as two examples of myths from the past that continue to plague relationships today. Ideas like these have been perpetuated by society, and Black males and females collude in them, consciously and subconsciously. Thus, they continue to struggle with each other, instead of uniting against the external forces that keep them in turmoil. Some Blacks remain bent on merely surviving, rather than devoting their energies toward controlling their lives.

Since the 1960s, Blacks have experienced many external negative pressures, at a time when many Blacks expected to be doing better. Social changes that occur in the larger society filter out and affect the Black community, as well. The sexual revolution, a climbing divorce rate, and a return to conservatism and subtle racism have brought new challenges for many Black families. Although many Black families surmounted these pressures, many others still anguish in the hopelessness of the situation. Obviously, these factors greatly affect relationships. As Black Americans, we witness the fallout today.

Some 59 percent of all Black families will be female-headed households by 1990. With these larger responsibilities, women are bound to feel some anxiety and hostility toward men. And men are feeling confused and less involved. The latest statistic from the Children's Foundation reported 13.8 million children lived in poverty in 1983, an increase of more than four million since 1973. The plight of Black children and their families has worsened dramatically compared with whites since 1980. Black children are three times as likely to live in poverty or in female-headed households. Many of these children are born to unwed teenage mothers.

Americans are aware of how the economy has always played a central role in causing hardships for men and women. This has caused the divorce rate to double among Black couples since 1980. These results challenge the future of Black relationships more than ever before.

For those who have never married, the social arena has changed so that many women face a future without the prospect of marriage partners. Some blame this dynamic on the male shortage. In 1980 there were just under 30 million unmarried women within the total population, compared to 21.5 million single men. What prevails today is a large number of middle-class single men and women who need security but fear commitment. This fear of commitment dominates relationships, dating back to several decades of changing sex roles.

There is yet another group that has been affected also by the social change of the last 15–20 years—married couples. They now face tension because of competing career and roles, problems of remarriages, and stepchildren. These couples must meet many needs and demands, while having little time and energy for themselves.

What It's Like Today

Presently relationships seem in flux. Since the women's movement and the sexual revolution. Blacks have taken on a "yo-yo" or approach-avoidance mentality, in which two people interact briefly (often only physically), only to reunite several weeks later or never again. If married, some focus less on intimacy and more on superficiality.

Alvin Toffler in *Future Shock* (1970) attempted to prepare Americans for what he referred to as the "SuperIndustrial Revolution." In his book he suggests that this phase would place more of an emphasis upon "freedom" instead of commitment.

Whereas previous generations stayed in marriages because of societal expectations, today Americans witness a new attitude of "doing your own thing." The result has been an increase in the single population, serial monogamy with several marriages of short duration, and an increase in unwed mothers.

A recent *U.S. News and World Report* (February 1986) article indicated that among the baby boomers between ages 25 and 29, 39 percent of the men have delayed marriage, while 26 percent of the women remain single—substantial increases since 1970 for both sexes. More than 60 percent of those living alone are female. About half of this group earn middle-income salaries, while 44 percent earn under $10,000. It is estimated that there are 20.6 million single adults.

Economics has grave effects upon marital prospects for Blacks. There is an estimated excess of one million women in the Black population, resulting in a ratio of 90 males per 100 females. So there are many more Black females who are single, never married, or divorced than there are white counterparts. In 1985, there were 39.5 percent Black never-marrieds and 8.5 percent divorcees.

The shift from an industrial to high tech economy has pushed a great number of Black males into unemployment. Unemployment rates rose higher in 1982–83 for Black men than for women between 18 and 44 years of age. Job prospects have been decreasing for Black men in all age groups since 1955, while increasing for Black and white females. Black males between 35 and 44 years of age experienced a 14.2 percent rate of unemployment, compared to 10.1 percent for Black females during 1983 (U.S. Bureau of Labor Statistics, November 1983). This dismal fact leaves the Black women (with the exception of Black single mothers) miles ahead of Black men in the labor force, thus creating obvious social problems for both sexes.

The social rift between Black males and females begins at an early period of development. The same internal and external forces of family and society that encourage young Black females toward scholastic achievement discourage the young Black males from attaining this same goal. Society teaches Black males instead to prove their manhood through excelling in sports, music, and hustling. Therefore, some young Black men learn early in life how to gain status in a system hostile to them.

Black society loses its young men early in the educational system, which creates the imbalance in economic strata. The lack of competitive skills reduces access into the professional job market, where the real economic gains exist. In 1972, Blacks represented 12.7 percent of all 18-year-olds, 10.5 percent of all high school graduates, 8.7 percent of all college freshmen, and 6.5 percent of all graduates awarded bachelor's degrees. By 1979, Blacks represented only about 4 percent of all professional and doctoral degree recipients (Berryman, 1983).

Between 1976 and 1981, Black women increased their number of doctoral degrees by 29 percent and their number of first professional degrees by 71 percent over the six-year period. Doctoral degrees awarded to Black men decreased by 10 percent and first professional degrees by 12 percent during the same period of time, 1984.

An estimated 40 percent of the Black male population is functionally illiterate. Also, during adolescence, there is often an increase in homicide, suicide, incarceration, and substance abuse among Black men. The depressing news about these threatening statistics is that these circumstances leave a large number of Black women available in America without Black partners. What are the results? Black women focus more upon their education as a possible means of economic, social, and sexual independence, instead of their reliance upon a man. Black men, on the other hand, seem confused today about how to provide the needs for the "new Black woman" who seems so self-sufficient. Because the professional Black man is not available in large numbers, the ones who are risk rejection because they do not meet certain standards.

Some men who are desirable do not concern themselves with lacking partners and the other men avoid approaching women in order to avoid vulnerability.

Women then feel less powerful to assert themselves when they are in a relationship because the opportunity to find another one is not great.

Women feel more responsible for the outcome of relationships than do men. This applies equally to white women and Black women. They persevere in unsatisfying situations just to keep peace within the relationship, only to discover that behavior creates other dynamics—confusion. This reaction often creates rivalry, jealously, and competition among women, and hostility toward men.

Some men, on the other hand, approach stress in relationships with what may seem a cavalier attitude. Whereas many women tend to devote more attention toward maintaining relationships, men, who are in a more advantageous position, tend to end them more readily since they are, unlike women, always in demand.

But society seems to be in the throes of a period of a "throwaway" style of relating, with brief emotional ties. Women emerged from the women's movement feeling autonomous, with less need for permanent commitments. Sexual liaison sex became "in" and intimacy "out." This new way of relating left many feeling unfulfilled and lacking emotional connections. For Blacks not actively taking part in the movement, many took part by conveniently adopting various aspects of this new life-style. Many experts believe the imbalance between the sexes further aggravates this problem.

The status of relationships is of great importance today. Many people are concerned about the apparent chasm between men and women, and the resulting ill effects on the future of the family. The problem is that the society has been slow in adjusting to some very powerful social changes of the last few decades. The resulting confusion and tension for individuals and families is what Americans are witnessing today. Many men and women struggle without really understanding the underlying reasons for the new tensions between them. This lack of understanding makes change or improvement most difficult.

Where Are Blacks Heading

Perhaps the best place to begin exploring where relationships stand is with the current structure of the Black family in America. The family is changing because of certain external issues, causing the natural balance in relationships to be in flux. Households headed by females increased from 28 percent to 41 percent between 1970 and 1982. This is partially a result of a rise in the divorce rate and an increase in the numbers of unwed mothers. By 1982, only 49 percent of Black children lived with one parent, and 8 percent lived with neither parent. William Julius Wilson, University of Chicago, predicts that by the end of the century, 70 percent of Black men will be unemployed.

The New York Times reported in 1982 that the divorce rate had doubled for Black women. There are 257 divorces to every 1,000 Black women, a ratio that rose 104 percent since 1970. For Black males, *The New York Times* reported that there were 151 divorced to every 1,000 who were married, up from 62 in 1972. The difference in the rates for Black men was the fact that they marry sooner and at higher rates than do divorced Black women. Remarried on the census statistics is counted as a marriage.

The divorce rate counts as the second largest category for singles in this country. The first is the never married persons, who these days are forestalling marriage over longer periods. The 1986 U.S. Census indicates that there are now 39.5 percent more Black singles who never married in this country, compared to 54.6 percent for their white counterparts. This leaves more Black women single (divorced, widowed, or never married) than men, creating a sex ratio imbalance of 76 Black males per 100 Black females nationally. There is an estimated excess of one million women in the Black population. The other condition that creates a greater imbalance is the selection process that middle-class women use in selecting a potential mate. Many men are considered "unacceptable," if they are not good looking, professional, with an income of at least $90,000, well-bred, with degrees, and so on.

During the research effort on the book *Mansharing: Dilemma or Choice* (Chapman, 1986), 2,000 women were interviewed nationally on why mate selection was difficult. Over 75 percent (1,580) of them reported having fewer problems meeting men than identifying someone who would fulfill many of their needs. Most of the women answered to the survey by indicating, "It's not who he is, but what the possibilities are for him to gain access to power." Because of unequal economic factors, more Black men do not fit into these categories.

Aside from the economic unsuitability of Black men, other factors contribute to the shortage of available Black men. There is also a high mortality rate among Black men; many are incarcerated, in mental hospitals, drug addicts, in the military (overseas), or simply not interested in Black women. Most recently, the rate of Black homosexuality appears to be more visible in the Black community. All of these factors reduce the eligibility pool of Black men, creating more women who desire partners at an age when fewer exist.

The imbalance promotes an interesting social structure for Black men—a situation sometimes referred to as mate sharing. Mate sharing occurs in a situation in which two or more women may share one man. They may be married or single, aware or unaware of the status.

In 1982 a workshop was offered on man sharing for Washington, D.C. women. At the first session, 120 women attended in order to understand more fully man sharing. Others, however, attended because they had chosen to share men. These women usually ranged between the ages of 35 and 45 and were divorced or widowed. They were in search of companionship, not marriage. More often, these women viewed sharing as a dilemma and were in conflict and depressed about the lack of an exclusive relationship.

The interesting reaction was the difference in some women who were opposed to sharing, but who had information that they had shared many times.

Harriette McAdoo conducted a research study on single parent mothers in Washington to determine how they felt about sharing men. The study found that while these women reported having difficulty with sharing, there was a discrepancy in their behavior. Although only a small number agreed to a shared arrangement, almost four times that number reported that they had participated nonetheless.

Documented in the book *Too Many Women* (1983), Secord found whenever there has been an excess of females in society, there was a devaluing of marriage and monogamy. In 1986 a sexual survey was conducted by *New Women Magazine*, in which 65 percent of the men admitted they had been unfaithful to a wife or lover and 34 percent of the women had suggested that they had also been unfaithful. Given the statistical ratio between Black men and women, it creates an atmosphere in which many women unknowingly share a partner.

Robert Staples, in *The World of Black Singles* (1981), noted that because of the surplus of Black women, it's a "buyer's market" in the marital arena for Black men.

It is clear that the numbers affect the problems of stability in relationships, but that is not the entire issue. The other factor is that Black men and women, as well as whites, embraced the changing gender role issues with much anxiety.

Christopher Lasch suggests in his book *The Culture of Narcissism* (1979) that American men and women have taken flight from "feelings" and have entered an era of sexual warfare. It seems that relations between the sexes have become characterized by a greater investment in sexual freedom, but with diminishing emotional returns. Americans are into a period of living for the moment.

The appearance that everything that happens between a man and woman is okay, and that everything includes anything has become a tempting illusion for many, resulting in an escalating tension between men and women. Much of this tension stems from the collapse of "chivalry ethics." Lasch describes the outcome when men and women pursue sex for sex itself—"the efficient contraceptive, legalized abortion, and a realistic and healthy acceptance of the body have weakened the links that once tied sex to love, marriage and procreation. Men and women now pursue sexual pleasure as an end in itself, unmediated even by the conventional trappings of romance."

So both sexes, in order to survive in an era of detached unions, must work hard to manipulate their emotions to protect themselves against pain and rejection. That is why relationships appear so shaky that they cannot accommodate mutual demands or expectations—not to mention commitment and monogamy. Both sexes invest in playing it safe.

Informal interviews in counseling practice indicate that men and women feel lonely, sad, and scared about the lack of stable relationships with the opposite sex. This awareness usually occurs for both after many years on the social circuit. These individuals often begin to realize that developing loving bonds need not be such a scary undertaking. With that they can learn that positive relationships are at the root of strong families for Black people.

Some Black couples have always managed to avoid the "1970s–1980s" trend of relating. A closer investigation of how these Black couples are faring is essential in the development of a model for those still seeking a new way to interact emotionally with the opposite sex.

Those Who Are Making It Work

Many today struggle with the question of how they can maintain "good" relationships. Some believe that the importance of friendship supersedes the importance of sexual union, social commitments, and other short-term affairs. Love is a natural and basic need; every living object needs it.

Because greater numbers of men and women discover the importance of spiritual bonding, many newly experience what love and friendship really are. Some are aware that what was abandoned in the 1970s needs to be recouped for survival in today's world. Many realize that a good friendship forms the basis of strong, durable relationships.

Many couples take their relationships so seriously that they structure time for communication, relaxation, and spiritual union. They work very hard on fairness within the union. Some even have weekly meetings to keep tensions from mounting in the household. These couples relate spiritually as friends long after the glow is gone. For example, one couple who both maintained high-powered jobs and travelled extensively, decided to hold weekly family meetings just to keep communications open and conflict at a minimum in their household.

For married couples in the past, friendship was the basis of their commitment to each other. They learned how to understand each other's needs, likes, and dislikes. They learned the process of give and take and the ability to be less selfish. There was an acceptance of the total person that allowed patience and endurance during trying times. Black men and women need to relearn some of the "old ways." Single persons need to gain closeness in similar ways.

Many single women form support groups to further unite around a common concern or need. This allows them to share and not compete with other women over personal relationships. It allows them to know they're not alone in their experiences. Civic organizations, sororities, singles' associations, church groups, also provide a base for meeting and developing friendships. Developing cross-sex friendships is another way of extending one's self. Friendships will provide important support networks when families are often far away.

Cross-sex friendships can be difficult for some to formulate, mainly because few role models for doing so exist. Time was that many patterns of cross-sex friendships existed. For example, if a man was working in another town, a friend of his might oversee his household needs while he was away. Examples in the Black community of this type occur today, but the community needs many more.

Black men have formed several groups around the country addressing the need to support single heads of household. Concerned Black Men and Adopt A Family are but two organizations that address these needs in the community.

Another trend in relationships today for some Blacks is the new response to crossing the color line. According to the 1984 Census, of the total population of 46 million white males, 64,000 are married to Black women. And of the total population of 3.5 million Black couples, 100,000 Black men are married to white women.

In an informal interview with 350 Black single women, 205 stated that they had dated a white male and the others believed at some point that they would. When asked why they would consider this, they all said they "want more economic options and a chance at identifying a partner where (they believed) less hassles would exist."

Of Black men, according to Robert Staples's study, 85 percent had had at least one interracial experience. The report on the Educational Status of Black Americans, from the 1985 College Board Report, recorded even more interracial couples paired with white male/Black female. It is suspected that as more Black women attend higher education and move further up in status, they may move away from Black men. Thus the traditional Black family unit is at stake.

Blacks must be concerned about the educational and psychological status of Black men because of the implications for the survival of Black family life. If Black males continue to be an endangered species through social oppression while some Black females continue to succeed, there may be the potential for a tremendous gulf between the sexes. This wedge would affect Black people by creating a different life-style for future generations. It will promote other dynamics as well.

There will be unorthodox ways of relating—older women will be seeking younger men at greater rates; communal households of women and children (divorced and unwed) will join together for support; and the selection of mates from the cross-cultural pool of men will be more inviting.

Most fear provoking, though, is the possibility that the Black population may end up with the single, unwed women (adolescent or adult) as the only ones producing families, while the middle-class population postpones marriage as an alternative to careers or finding "Mr. or Ms. Right."

Blacks need to recognize that they still have choices. We need to challenge the awful myth that we cannot get along. The statistics don't have to be strong indicators of the future, unless Blacks allow them to be. Blacks must strive toward empowerment, making decisions that are based upon what's real in America, rather than what they would like to experience through false expectations from material gains. The middle class must reach back and invite those less fortunate to come along.

Blacks must become more comfortable with the fact that total dependence upon the system that oppresses the race will never set Blacks free. Blacks must also realize that they will survive more effectively if they have each other, regardless of the availability of men. Blacks must applaud those who are making professional strides, because they may have the clout to make the difference for the race as a whole. By this gain, everyone gains.

Black men and women must realize their joint responsibility for today's tensions in relationships and therefore strive to join together to create healthy connections. Values and ethics have been challenged in the past few years. Sexual health problems and the lack of closeness and intimacy cause many to reconsider the old style of relating. Even though these ways were not perfect, they did create relationships of substance. So if Blacks want successful relationships, they must be willing to take some risks. This may mean, even if the male shortage continues, that people will recommit themselves to mutually monogamous relationships. Conceptualizing relating on a more humanistic basis, friendship will become more vital as the basis for developing realistic love.

Love is the pulse of spirituality and bonding. No race of people has ever succeeded without it. Blacks have always gotten through difficult times through strong efforts of brotherhood and sisterhood.

Once Blacks accept total responsibility together, women can be relieved of bearing alone the social burdens and men can stop feeling undervalued and threatened. With this in mind, men and women must reexamine their own values and needs. Put simply, Black men and women must decide to structure their personal lives in more respectful and loving ways for the future of the race. The next generation's very existence depends upon this premise.

REFERENCES

Berryman, S. (1983) Who Will Do Science? New York: Rockefeller Foundation.

Chapman, A. B. (1986) Mansharing: Dilemma or Choice. New York: William Morrow.

Lasch, C. (1979) The Culture of Narcissism. New York: Warner Communications.

McAdoo, H. (1983) Extended Family Support of Black Single Mothers. DHSS Research Report #5701 MH32159, March. Washington, DC: Government Printing Office.

Rodgers-Rose, L. [ed.] (1980) The Black Woman. Beverly Hills, CA: Sage.

Secord, P. (1983) Too Many Women. Beverly Hills, CA: Sage.

Staples, R. (1981) The World of Black Singles. Westport, CT: Greenwood.

Toffler, A. (1970) Future Shock. New York: Random House.

U.S. News & World Report (1986) "Among baby boomer memories." Horizon Section, 4.

Williams, J. D. [ed.] (1984) The State of Black America. New York: National Urban League.

Chapter Forty-three

Love and Romance as Objects of Feminist Knowledge (1993)

Stevi Jackson

Jackson, a sociologist who has written a great deal on romantic love, traces the history of feminist analyses of love. She points out the naïveté in the belief of some earlier feminists that once women see through the illusion of romantic love, it will lose its hold on them. Rather, her view is that love is "emotional labor" mainly done by women in a specific historical and cultural context, and worries that "romance is being rehabilitated" by women anxious to please men.

In recent years feminists have had far more to say about romantic fiction than about romantic love as such. A satisfactory account of women's interest in romance, however, itself requires that we pay attention to the emotional resonances such fiction has for women, that we give greater consideration to romantic love as an emotion. I am not suggesting that there is something called "love" that exists outside society and culture. Emotions are cultural constructs, not pre-social essences: they are socially ordered, linguistically mediated and culturally specific (Jaggar, 1989; Hochschild, 1983; Rosaldo, 1984).

The critiques of love which emerged in the early years of second-wave feminism began to explore love as a socially constructed emotion, but these analyses have not been built upon substantially in recent feminist scholarship. I want to look again at this earlier work which, while limited by its particular historical context, offered insights which are worth recovering. I will then explore possible means of developing a theorization of romantic love drawing on more recent feminist perspectives on romance, subjectivity and sexuality.

Stevi Jackson, "Love and Romance as Objects of Feminist Knowledge," in *Making Connections: Women's Studies, Women's Movements, Women's Lives,* ed. Mary Kennedy, Cathy Lubelska, and Val Walsh (Washington, DC: Taylor and Francis, 1993), 39–50. Reprinted by permission, Copyright © 1993 selection and editorial arrangement by Cathy Lubelska and Val Walsh.

Early Feminist Critiques of Love

Feminist scepticism about love has a long history. First-wave feminists only rarely questioned the naturalness of love between men and women, but some tentatively began to explore the ways in which it was shaped by relations of dominance and subordination. For example, Cicely Hamilton, in *Marriage as a Trade*, first published in 1909, argued that since marriage was for most women an economic and social necessity, they could not afford to be wholeheartedly romantic (Hamilton, 1981, p. 28). In many respects Hamilton anticipates later feminist critiques of marriage and of compulsory heterosexuality—although she champions the cause of celibacy rather than lesbianism. In arguing that men are far more romantic than women, however, her analysis differs from that of second-wave feminists who tended to see love as the bait which trapped women into marriage.

An alternative perspective, closer to later socialist feminist analyses, is that of the Russian revolutionary Alexandra Kollontai. She argued that the extreme individualism of capitalism produces an "inescapable loneliness" which we try to remedy through love (1972, p. 4). In seeking this route to personal happiness we show little consideration for the one we love: rather we make absolute claims on them. This is exacerbated by the idea of possessing the partner, establishing ownership of the other's physical and emotional self, and excluding all others. Kollontai was well aware that double standards of sexual morality restricted women far more than men, that women became possessions on marriage in a way that men did not. She envisaged, however, a new morality arising from ideals of working-class solidarity which would undermine individualism, possessiveness and patriarchal values. Whereas Hamilton speculated that liberation from compulsion might lead to many women eschewing heterosexual relations altogether, Kollontai's vision is of "deeper and more joyful" relationships between women and men entered into in a spirit of freedom and equality (*ibid.*, p. 13).

The publication of de Beauvoir's *The Second Sex* in 1949 paved the way for second-wave feminist analyses which saw love as a means of gaining women's acquiescence to their submission. For de Beauvoir women's self-abnegation through love not only reinforced their subordination but resulted from a subjectivity constituted through that subordination.

> There is no other way out for her but to lose herself, body and soul, in him who is represented to her as absolute, as the essential. . . . She chooses to desire her enslavement so ardently that it will seem to her the expression of her liberty . . . she will humble herself to nothingness before him. Love becomes for her a religion. (de Beauvoir, 1972, p. 653)

Love and its discontents were on the agenda of second-wave feminism in its early years as an aspect of wider debates about the politics of sexuality.[1] Love was seen as an ideology which justified our exploitation by men and simultaneously ensnared us into oppressive relationships with them. As the slogan put it: "It starts when you sink into his arms and ends with your arms in his sink."

Love made women vulnerable not only to exploitation, but also to being hurt by men. As de Beauvoir said, "the word love has by no means the same meaning for both sexes" (1972, p. 652), a view endorsed by Firestone. Both of these theorists argued that women invest more in love and that they give more affection to men than they receive in return. Firestone asserted that "love, perhaps even more than childbearing, is the pivot of women's oppression today" (1972, p. 121). What was so dangerous about love was, as de Beauvoir had noted, women's tendency to immerse ourselves totally in it. Becoming so obsessed with love diverted energies from other possible achievements. Moreover, making one person the centre of one's emotional universe was taken as symptomatic of emotional impoverishment elsewhere—a point which Kollontai had also made. The exclusivity of love meant quantifying and confining our emotions. As Lee Comer expressed it: "Like so much butter, romantic love must be spread thickly on one slice of bread; to spread it over several is to spread it 'thinly' " (1974, p. 219). Hence we concentrate passion on one partner, taking jealousy as the proof of love rather than as "an excrescence on our emotions" (*ibid.*, p. 220). Similarly, Firestone asks: "Why has all the joy and excitement been concentrated, driven into one narrow, difficult-to-find human experience, and all the rest laid waste?" (1972, p. 147).

Underlying these critiques was a belief in the possibility of a less exclusive and possessive form of love, freed from power relationships and bourgeois institutions. Again we hear echoes of Kollontai's earlier utopian vision. Firestone argues for the rediffusion of "sexual joy and excitement . . . over . . . the spectrum of our lives" (*ibid.*, p. 147). For Comer romantic love is symptomatic of our fragmented emotional lives, but "In rare moments, when the external categories which fragment our emotions fall away, we do glimpse the possibilities of whole feelings" (Comer, 1974, p. 219). These "whole feelings" involve a plurality of loves directed towards a multiplicity of others.

Compared with more recent feminist analyses of subjectivity, much of this may sound naive. The very possibility of "whole feelings" now seems questionable, as does the notion of a "purer" love uncontaminated by cultural and social structures. These early feminist accounts recognized that romantic love was not a constant feature of human nature, but were over-optimistic about the possibility of change. The tone of much second-wave writing implied that, once the illusion of romantic love was "seen through," all we needed was an effort of will to break free from its shackles. This effectively precluded the possibility of confronting the potency of this emotion and seeking for an explanation of it. Once the oppressive nature of heterosexual love had been exposed, to try to explore it further seemed at best frivolous and at worst ideologically unsound.

Another shortcoming of the writings of this period was their unproblematized heterosexual focus. Some of the general points raised could apply to any exclusive romantic attachment, whether lesbian or heterosexual, but the heterosexual nature of love was taken as given. These analyses of love did, of course, contain within them an implicit critique of heterosexuality, but this was not their explicit object. By the time more telling critiques of heterosexuality emerged in the late seventies and early eighties (Rich, 1980; Wittig, 1992) love as such had ceased to be a matter of much concern.

In what follows I will be dealing primarily with heterosexual love and romance, but I hope to do so in a way which makes heterosexuality problematic. The discourses through which we make sense of love have, I would argue, largely been framed within a patriarchal and heterosexual context and impinge also on those who, in Wittig's (1992) terms, are fugitives from compulsory heterosexuality. In re-examining romantic love I am not discounting the contributions of earlier feminists. Although flawed, their accounts raised questions which deserve further consideration in the light of more recent theoretical development. Their central theme—that love serves to bind us to our subordination—is one that still needs to be pursued.

Love's Mysteries

Romantic convention tells us that love is in essence indefinable and mysterious: "fools give you reasons, wise men [sic] never try". Emotions, in the sense of what is subjectively felt by individuals, are obviously not immediately observable, but this does not place them beyond explanation. Alison Jaggar observes that we "have no access either to our own emotions or to those of others, independent of or unmediated by the discourse of our culture" (Jaggar, 1989, p. 148). There is thus no way of exploring love except through the ways in which it is talked and written about. Language, however, itself contributes to the cultural construction of emotions and is a means by which we participate in creating a shared sense of what emotions are. If the discourses of love and romance circulating within our culture help shape our experience and understanding of love, they can also be drawn upon in analyzing it.

I am particularly interested in the idea of being or falling "in love." The adjectives commonly used to describe this experience mark it as very different from other forms of love. Love for parents, children, siblings or friends is not usually thought of as mysterious, compelling, overwhelming, uncontrollable, inexplicable and ecstatic—nor even is love in long-term sexual relationships. A distinction is commonly made between loving someone and being in love with them. The latter is recognized as a more transient emotion, but the ideology of heterosexual romance tells us that falling in love is the prelude to a lasting, secure and stable conjugal union. This ideal, as Jacqueline Sarsby points out, is contradictory:

> Love is seen as the bolt from the blue against which one cannot struggle, the pre-ordained meeting of twin souls, the compulsion which allows one to break any of society's rules as long as one is faithful to the emotion itself. The extraordinary contradiction lies in the fact that love is the almost prescribed condition for marriage in most of Europe and the United States . . . millions of private, potentially socially disruptive, emotional dramas are virtually the only acceptable means of moving towards marriage. (1983, pp. 5–6)

There is a further contradiction here in the ideal of romantic love as the basis of an affectionate and caring relationship. Feminists from Kollontai to Firestone have suggested that romantic love is not really about caring for another, but is self-centred and individualistic. To be in love is to make another the centre of your universe, but it also demands the same in return: that we should be the "only one" for the other. Being "in love" is not a gentle feeling: it is often characterized as violent, even ruthless (Bertilsson, 1986). "More than wanting to cosset the beloved we may feel we want to eat them alive" (Goodison, 1983, pp. 51–2).

Within Western culture falling in love has often been described as a form of ecstasy akin to a mystical experience, as "comparable in force and in momentum to a religious conversion" (Bertilsson, 1986, p. 28). Even feminist accounts, otherwise firmly grounded in material reality, sometimes slide towards mysticism. Frigga Haug, for example, asserts that through love we retrieve the "buried and forgotten stirrings of the soul," that love reorganizes "the forces of the soul." (Haug *et al.*, 1987, pp. 278–9). Casting love in such terms is problematic in that it seems to accord it a special legitimacy, placing it on some higher plane inaccessible to reason or explanation. It does, however, suggest that love is experienced as a deeply felt inner transformation.

There appears to be something about romantic love as described in feminist, social scientific, psychoanalytic and literary writings which suggests that it is the product of restriction and unattainability. The excitement of being in love is fuelled by "compulsion and denial" and "gratification destroys the compulsion little by little" (Wilson, 1983, p. 42). The chronic insecurity so often suffered by lovers is not, I think, merely a result of romantic passion but is fundamental to its continuance: being "in love" appears to wear off once lovers feel secure with each other. Insecure and compulsive passion centred on a unique other can engender feelings of power-lessness, of being at the mercy of the beloved. It also, however, holds out the promise of power—of being the loved one, of ensnaring another into total psychic dependence. The attraction that love has for women may in part be because it is a means by which they can aspire to power over men. This is a central theme of romantic narrative (Modleski, 1984)—in both fairy-tales and romantic fiction love tames and transforms the beast.

The potency of romantic passion is not easily accounted for, yet it is patterned in ways which indicate that it is culturally constructed. It is also clearly deeply embedded in our subjectivities. It is an emotion to which both sceptics and romantics can succumb, which is felt by lesbians as well as by heterosexual women. It is much easier to refuse to participate in romantic rituals, to resist pressures towards conventional marriage, to be cynical about "happy ever after" endings than it is to avoid falling in love.

Desire and Psychoanalysis

Psychoanalytic theory is often invoked to explain aspects of our subjectivities which are irrational or inconsistent, especially where sexuality is concerned. Psychoanalysis challenges the idea of a rational, unitary human subject and in theorizing desire it might seem to offer an explanation of how and why we fall in love. Hence its attraction for many feminists seeking to explain the pleasures of romantic fiction (e.g. Kaplan, 1986; Light, 1984; Radway, 1987). This approach is, however, problematic.

Janice Radway (1987) uses Chodorow's (1978) work in attempting to explain the

appeal of romantic fiction to women, in particular to explain why women's emotional needs go unmet, leading them to seek vicarious satisfaction in romance. For
Chodorow the fact that women mother produces gender differentiation, in particular
women's nurturant capacities and men's inability to nurture. Femininity is developed
through a girl's identification with her mother, while masculinity requires boys to
break from the feminine and hence repress their nurturant capacities. In the process
men's sense of self becomes more autonomous, that of women relational (Chodorow,
1978). This account is quite intelligible without its psychoanalytic trappings, but
placed within the framework of psychoanalysis it becomes reductionist. All the
complexities of our subjectivities are reduced to the early experience of being moth-
ered. Such a perspective is also universalistic, assuming that this pattern occurs—
albeit with variations—in all societies. Importantly, in the present context, desire is
absent from Chodorow's analysis. It may explain women's need for warmth, affection
and attention and men's incapacity to give women what they want, but it does not
explain the force of being "in love" nor the tendency for passion to subside once the
lover feels secure. Radway is only able to apply Chodorow to her romance readers
because of her failure to confront the fact that what the women are reading is as
much about passion as it is about nurture (McRobbie, 1991).

The perspective deriving from the work of Lacan, which places desire at the centre
of its concerns, appears more promising in this respect (Mitchell and Rose, 1982).
Lacanians make a distinction between a need, which is capable of satisfaction, and
desire, which is not (Rose, 1982). The idea of desire as a yearning for unattainable
fulfilment does seem to accord with the various emotions and sensations experienced
when "in love." The compulsion to possess the other totally, to be made whole by
them, also finds a correspondence in the psychoanalytic theorization of desire constituted through lack. There are, however, a number of problems here. The lack
which underpins desire is held to be a consequence of the series of splits and losses
which accompany our entry into language and culture as language cuts us off for
ever from direct experience of the "real." Becoming speaking subjects also means
submitting to the Law (of the father/phallus) which comes between mother and child
and which forces us to take up positions as gendered subjects. Entering language
thus involves inevitable loss. The sequence of events through which desire is constituted is conceptualized in terms of entry into language and culture *per se,* not of
entering a specific culture. Desire, by implication, is an essential part of human social
nature. Lacanian psychoanalysis does not admit of the possibility of emotions being
structured differently in different cultural settings and thus imagines the whole world
to be beset by the same desire—an assumption that anthropologists would make us
wary of (Rosaldo, 1984; Errington and Gewertz, 1987).

I am not convinced, either, that the Lacanian account can deal with the specifics
of the ways in which language structures emotional and sexual experience even
within Western culture. Emotions are not simply "felt" as internal states provoked
by the unconscious sense of lost infantile satisfactions—they are actively structured
and understood through culturally specific discourses. These discourses differentiate
between love as nurture, being "in love," lust and sexual arousal—all of which are
conflated in the psychoanalytic concept of desire. While accounts of being "in love"

produced from within our culture are congruent with "desire" as something intrinsically incapable of satisfaction, such accounts also acknowledge levels of emotional and sexual feeling quite unlike this. For example "desire" as used in common-sense parlance can mean a form of sexual arousal which is perfectly satiable. It is questionable whether "desire" in any sense can be said to be constituted at the moment of our entry to language when we have barely begun to gain access to the discourses through which we make sense of emotion and sexuality (Jackson, 1983).

Lacanian psychoanalysis, while ostensibly an account of the cultural construction of emotion, locates "desire" as an inner state and thus precludes the possibility of linking the experience of "love" to specific cultural contexts and to the specific discourses and narratives which give shape to our emotions. Feminist accounts of the pleasures of romance reading within this type of psychoanalytic framework, for example Alison Light (1984) on *Rebecca* and Cora Kaplan (1986) on *The Thorn Birds*, seem to me to suggest that romantic fiction reflects, gives voice to or is constructed around a set of emotions which already exist. I would argue, on the contrary, that romantic narrative itself contributes to the cultural construction of love. I do not maintain, as some early critics of romance did, that it is simply a means of brainwashing women into subservience. Rather I am suggesting that this is but one of the resources from which we create a sense of what our emotions are. As Michelle Rosaldo argues, "feelings are not substances to be discovered in our blood, but social practices organised by stories that we both enact and tell. They are structured by our forms of understanding" (Rosaldo, 1984).

Tales of Love: Narratives of the Feminine Self

Our subjectivities, including that aspect of them we call emotions, are shaped by the social and cultural milieu we inhabit, through processes which involve our active engagement with sets of meanings available in our culture. We create for ourselves a sense of what our emotions are, of what being "in love" is, through learning scripts, positioning ourselves within discourses, constructing narratives of self. "The script for love has already been written and is being continually recycled in all the love songs and love stories of Western literature and contemporary media" (Brunt, 1988, p. 19).

When we fall in love it feels like "getting to star in your own movie" *(ibid.)*. What Ros Brunt is describing here is not a passive internalization of these scripts but an active locating of ourselves within them. We can identify with love stories not because they record some pre-existing emotion, but because our cultural tradition supplies us with narrative forms with which we begin to be familiarized in childhood and through which we learn what love is. Narratives are not only encountered in novels, plays and films—they are very much a part of everyday cultural competences. We constantly tell stories to ourselves and others and we continually construct and reconstruct our own biographies in narrative form. Hence subjectivity is in part constituted through narrative.

The narratives woven around love and romance are available to both women and men within our culture, but not equally so. Being constituted as feminine involves girls in discourses of feeling and emotion, and more specifically the culture of romance, from which boys are more often excluded or from which they exclude themselves in order to affirm their own maleness. It is through the idiom of sexual bravado and conquest, a discourse of sexual drives—and not the language of romance—that masculinity is asserted (Hollway, 1984; Wood, 1984).

Children learn the standard pattern of romance narrative very early in life from such sources as fairy-tales (see Davies, 1989). For girls this acculturation into romance is continued through reading matter marketed for their consumption. Through such sources, as well as through conversations with other girls and adult women, girls are learning nuances of meaning through which they make sense of emotions and relationships.[2] This is by no means a process of passive inculcation into romanticism, rather romance narrative is a resource girls use to make sense of their emotional and social world. As Christian-Smith (1991) found, young teenage readers may look to romance fiction as a means of learning about heterosexual relationships. This may be one of the few sources available to young women where sexual "knowledge" connects with feelings and desires (see also Gilbert and Taylor, 1991; Thomson and Scott, 1991). Romance is a fictional form which girls learn to manipulate, employing its narrative devices to construct their own private fantasies (Thompson, 1989).

We should not assume that the reduction in the space given to romantic fiction in teenage magazines noted by McRobbie (1991) heralds the decline of the culture of romance. The features in many of these magazines, especially those concerning the stars of popular music, may well be providing the material for personal romantic fantasies which girls find preferable to the stilted photo-stories they are offered (Thompson, 1989). Moreover, the decline in the romance content of magazines should be balanced against the growth of "teen fiction" formula romances noted in the American and Australian contexts (Christian-Smith, 1991); Gilbert and Taylor, 1991). The American versions are widely available in the UK and according to my younger students are avidly read and exchanged by girls in their early teens, along with Mills and Boon romances. Girls are certainly capable of being critical of romantic fiction (Frazer, 1987; Gilbert and Taylor, 1991), but its continued popularity makes it unwise to deny it any effectivity in the construction of feminine subjectivity.

What is being created and reproduced in these narratives as well as elsewhere in the feminine culture of girls and women is a certain form of emotional literacy which men rarely acquire. Women's dissatisfaction with men's emotional illiteracy is a noted source of dissatisfaction in heterosexual relationships (Hite, 1988; Mansfield and Collard, 1988), and is also central to Radway's (1987) account to the pleasures of reading romance. As well as satisfying unmet needs for nurturance, romance also redefines problematic aspects of masculinity: the emotionally cold "spectacularly masculine" hero ultimately reveals himself as a tender, caring lover. There is a danger here, however, of conflating the two forms of love which those who inhabit our Western culture habitually distinguish between—caring affectionate love and romantic passion.

The romances which Radway describes do not simply represent the heroine as the recipient of affection, but as the object of uncontrollable passion. Often the hero rapes the heroine. This is constructed not as an act of violence but as the result of overwhelming desire. Radway suggests that women are thus enabled to deal with real fears about male violence without questioning the patriarchal culture which sustains it. While recognizing that this is an accommodation to patriarchy, Radway does not explore the interconnections between this eroticization of male power and women's subordination. That women find pleasure and excitement in male sexual violence *is* problematic, and evidence of it is not confined to Radway's research. It is also a feature of Helen Taylor's (1989) study of *Gone With The Wind* fans, many of whom found the scene in which Rhett rapes Scarlett highly erotic. They do not, however, generally describe this scene as a rape: rather Rhett is seen as "driven mad" by his love for Scarlett and his actions are read as resulting from *her* power over him. The meaning of the quintessential male enactment of power over woman is thus reversed. Elizabeth Wilson comments that "the magic of dominance and submission is written into romantic tales just as much as it is written into pornography" (1983, p. 43). Insofar as romance helps to construct a form of femininity which finds pleasure in submission, this is a very good reason why we should retain our critical stance on it.

Some recent accounts of women's consumption of romance and other popular fictions give me the uneasy feeling that romance is being rehabilitated. In moving beyond the straightforward dismissal of romance as a means of co-opting women into heterosexual monogamy—and in offering new perspectives which take women's pleasure in romance seriously—feminists like Radway have produced more sophisticated accounts of women's readings of romance. At the same time, this shift of emphasis risks blunting the edge of feminist critique. Recognizing the pleasure gained from reading romance should not prevent our being critical of it. As Tania Modleski has recently written, "even the cultural analyst may sometimes be a 'cultural dupe' . . . we all exist inside ideology . . . we are all victims, down to the very depth of our psyches, of political and cultural domination (even though we are never *only* victims)" (Modleski, 1991, p. 45).

Conclusion: The Material and the Emotional

I have suggested that narratives of self are something we actively construct through accessing certain discourses and narrative structures existing within our culture, that subjectivity is discursively constructed. Despite my scepticism about psychoanalysis I would not wish to rule out the possibility that certain felt emotional needs and desires are constituted through our early experiences of nurture and through our entry into a particular culture, nor would I rule out the role of unconscious processes. However, I prefer an account which recognizes the historical and cultural specificity of these experiences and which does not regard our emotional needs as essentially fixed at some point in childhood. It is also important to keep in mind the material power differences between women and men. Women's economic dependence and the emotional and physical labour they perform for men underpin romantic narratives and our experience of romantic attachments.

One of the strengths of early feminist critiques of love lay in the linkage between the emotional and the material: that romance ends with your arms in his sink. This connection may have been articulated rather crudely, but we should not ignore the material contexts in which our subjectivities are forged. I am not suggesting that emotions can be linked to the material in any simple reductionist sense, but rather that connections do exist and should be noted. The emotional labour women perform, for example, clearly is linked to other forms of labour, and love is central to the justification of women's material exploitation. Women's emotional impoverishment in the economy of love (Langford, 1992) parallels their relative material poverty in terms of the distribution of family resources. Similarly emotional dependence is not unconnected with material dependence. I do not believe that these correspondences between emotional and economic relations are accidental or merely coincidental. Precisely how we theorize such interconnections, however, is a difficult issue to resolve.

NOTES

1. I have chosen to focus here on Lee Comer (1974) and Shulamith Firestone (1972)—a British socialist feminist and an American radical feminist—whose work gives a flavour of the range of views being discussed within the WLM in the early seventies.

2. This is certainly culturally specific. For a discussion of the gulf of understanding that separates a young Western woman from her counterpart in New Guinea see Errington and Gewertz, 1987, p. 128.

REFERENCES

Beauvoir, S. de (1972) *The Second Sex*, Harmondsworth, Penguin.

Bertilsson, M. (1986) "Love's Labour Lost? A sociological view," *Theory, Culture and Society*, 3, 1, pp. 19–35.

Brunt, R. (1988) "Love is in the Air," *Marxism Today*, February, pp. 18–21.

Chodorow, N. (1978) *The Reproduction of Mothering*, Berkeley, University of California Press.

Christian-Smith, L. (1991) *Becoming a Woman through Romance*, London, Routledge.

Comer, L. (1974) *Wedlocked Women*, Leeds, Feminist Books.

Davies, B. (1989) *Frogs and Snails and Feminist Tales*, Sydney, Allen and Unwin.

Errington, F. and Gewertz, D. (1987) *Cultural Alternatives and a Feminist Anthropology*, Cambridge, Cambridge University Press.

Firestone, S. (1972) *The Dialectic of Sex*, London, Paladin.

Frazer, E. (1987) "Teenage girls reading *Jackie*," *Media, Culture and Society*, 9, pp. 407–25.

Gilbert, P. and Taylor, S. (1991) *Fashioning the Feminine*, Sydney, Allen and Unwin.

Goodison, L. (1983) "Really Being In Love Means Wanting to Live in a Different World," in Cartledge, S. and Ryan, J. (Eds) *Sex and Love: New Thoughts on Old Contradictions*, London, Women's Press, pp. 48–66.

Hamilton, C. (1981) *Marriage as a Trade*, London. The Women's Press.

Haug, F. *et al.* (1987) *Female Sexualization*, London, Verso.

Hite, S. (1988) *Women and Love: A Cultural Revolution in Progress*, London, Viking.

Hochschild, A. (1983) *The Managed Heart*, Berkeley, University of California Press.

Hollway, W. (1984) "Gender Difference and the Production of Subjectivity," in Henriques, J., Hollway, W., Urwin, C., Venn, C. and Walkerdine, V. *Changing the Subject,* London, Methuen, pp. 227–63.

Jackson, S. (1983) "The Desire for Freud: Psychoanalysis and Feminism," *Trouble and Strife,* 1, pp. 32–41.

Jaggar, A. (1989) "Love and Knowledge: Emotion in Feminist Epistemology," in Jaggar, A. and Bordo, S. (Eds) *Gender/Body/Knowledge: Feminist Reconstructions of Being and Knowing,* New Brunswick, Rutgers University Press, pp. 145–71.

Kaplan, C. (1986) *Sea Changes,* London, Verso.

Kollontai, A. (1972) *Sexual Relations and the Class Struggle,* Bristol, Falling Wall Press.

Langford, W. (1992) "Gender, Power and Self-Esteem: Women's Poverty in the Economy of Love," The Women's Studies Network (UK) Conference.

Light, A. (1984) " 'Returning to Manderley'—Romance Fiction, Female Sexuality and Class," *Feminist Review,* 16, pp. 7–25.

Mansfield, P. and Collard, J. (1988) *The Beginning of the Rest of Your Life,* London, Macmillan.

McRobbie, A. (1991) *Feminism and Youth Culture,* London, Macmillan.

Mitchell, J. and Rose, J. (Eds) (1982) *Feminine Sexuality: Jacques Lacan and the* école freudienne, London, Macmillan.

Modleski, T. (1984) *Loving With a Vengeance,* London, Methuen.

Modleski, T. (1991) *Feminism Without Women,* New York, Routledge.

Radway, J. (1987) *Reading the Romance,* London, Verso.

Rich, A. (1980) "Compulsory Heterosexuality and Lesbian Existence," *Signs: Journal of Women in Culture and Society,* 5, 4, pp. 631–60.

Rosaldo, M. (1984) "Toward an Anthropology of Self and Feeling," in Shweder, R. A. and LeVine, R. A. (Eds) *Culture Theory,* Cambridge, Cambridge University Press, pp. 137–57.

Rose, J. (1982) "Introduction II," in Mitchell, J. and Rose, J. (Eds) *Feminine Sexuality: Jacques Lacan and the* école freudienne, London, Macmillan, pp. 27–57.

Sarsby, J. (1983) *Romantic Love and Society,* Harmondsworth, Penguin.

Taylor, H. (1989) *Scarlett's Women: Gone With The Wind and Its Female Fans,* London, Virago.

Thompson, S. (1989) "Search for Tomorrow: On Feminism and the Reconstruction of Teen Romance," in Vance, C. (Ed.) *Pleasure and Danger: Exploring Female Sexuality,* London, Pandora, pp. 350–84.

Thomson, R. and Scott, S. (1991) *Learning About Sex: Young Women and the Social Construction of Sexual Identity,* London, Tufnell Press.

Wilson, E. (1983) "A New Romanticism?" in Phillips, E. (Ed.) *The Left and the Erotic,* London, Lawrence and Wishart.

Wittig, M. (1992) *The Straight Mind and Other Essays,* Hemel Hempstead, Harvester Wheatsheaf.

Wood, J. (1984) "Groping Towards Sexism: Boy's Sex Talk," in McRobbie, A. and Nava, M. (Eds) *Gender and Generation,* London, Macmillan, pp. 54–84.

Part VI

Literary Criticism

Romance has been not only a perennial subject of literature, but also a frequent subject of comment by literary critics, most frequently in connection with the analysis of a specific work of poetry or fiction. The selections here cover a range of subjects: a modern critique of the way a traditional prefeminist writer, Jane Austen, used romantic love as a solution to the problems she addressed in her fiction (Poovey); considerations of black women's novels and lesbian romance as different from traditional white hetero fiction (Naylor and Juhasz); and Gornick's denunciation of romantic love in contemporary writing.

Chapter Forty-four

From Persuasion and the Promises of Love (1983)

Mary Poovey

Poovey is a literary critic who has written extensively on ideologies of gender in the nineteenth century. Poovey's influential essay analyzes the role of romantic love in the work of Jane Austen, who finds easy refuge from complex moral problems in "the promise of love."

Essentially, *Persuasion* advances the argument, proposed as early as *Pride and Prejudice*, that personal feeling can be a moral force within society. Whereas in the earlier novel the way of life eventually ratified by desire was that of the landed gentry, in *Persuasion* feeling is put in the service of—and is gratified by—the much less certain lifestyle of those who earn their social position by ongoing personal effort. And whereas in *Pride and Prejudice* the aggressive energy of Elizabeth Bennet had to be chastened into love by circumstances and Fitzwilliam Darcy, in the later novel Anne Elliot's persistent love prevails, finally triumphing over both the pride of her lover and the institutional inhibitors that would disguise or deny it altogether. But by using individual feeling to inaugurate moral reform and by rewarding that desire with the conventional prizes of bourgeois society—marriage and (implicitly) a family—Austen is finally reproducing an unresolved (and in these terms unresolvable) contradiction inherent in her culture's values. This contradiction centers in the promise which is invariably fused to the demands of propriety; it centers, that is, in the concept of romantic love.

In Austen's society as today, romantic love purports to be completely "outside" ideology. It claims to be an inexplicable, irresistible, and possibly even biological drive which, in choosing its object, flaunts the hierarchy, the priorities, the inequalities of class society. Romantic love seems to defy self-interest and calculation as merrily as it ignores income and rank; as a consequence, if it articulates (or can be educated to do so) an essentially unselfish, generous urge toward another person, it may serve as an agent of moral reform: Louisa Musgrove might become a more

From Mary Poovey, *"Persuasion* and the Promises of Love," in *The Representation of Women in Fiction: Selected Papers from the English Institute, 1981,* ed. C. Heilbrun and M. Higgonet (Baltimore: Johns Hopkins University Press, 1983), 171–77., Reprinted by permission. Copyright © 1983 by Johns Hopkins University Press.

serious person through loving Benwick, just as Henry Crawford seems launched on a significant course of moral improvement by his love for Fanny Price. But it is crucial to recognize that the moral regeneration ideally promised by romantic love is as individual and as private as its agent. In fact, the fundamental assumption of romantic love—and the reason it is so compatible with bourgeois society—is that the personal can be kept separate from the social, that one's "self" can be fulfilled in spite of—and in isolation from—the demands of the marketplace. Once one accepts this division of society into separate spheres, it is possible to argue that the gratification of personal desire will inaugurate social reform only if one assumes a social organization which structurally accommodates influence—at the smallest level, the nuclear family or, at a more general level, the patriarchal society modeled upon the family. If this concentric arrangement of "spheres" (which is, of course, actually a hierarchy of power) is disrupted or even seriously challenged—as it was during Jane Austen's lifetime—then the movement from individual fulfillment to social improvement becomes problematic. Ironically, even as the importance of imagining some program for social reform increases, the gap between the private and the public seems to widen and, completing the circle, the more necessary it becomes to believe that at least in the privacy of one's own home, the comfort of one's own family, and the personal gratification of one's own love, there can be deeply felt and hence "substantial" satisfaction.

In her realistic portrayal of the inevitable connections between the public and the private spheres and in her allusions to that complex society beyond the personal interests of her characters, Jane Austen exposes the fallacy of this claim for personal autonomy. Given the fact that living together in society necessarily requires dependence and compromise, the belief that one can withdraw or simply gratify oneself is morally irresponsible and, finally, practically untrue. Even Mrs. Smith has Nurse Rooke to connect her to the public world of Bath, and as Anne's prolonged and problematic courtship of Wentworth proves, even the most adamant personal desire must be defined within other social relations which are also configurations of power.

But in retaining the premises and promises of romantic love even as she makes this point, Jane Austen also perpetuates one of the fundamental myths of bourgeois society. For the model of private gratification which romantic love proposes is able to disguise the inescapable system of economic and political domination only by foregrounding those few relationships which flatter our desire for personal autonomy and power. But the notion that romantic relationships actually have the kind of social power this emotional prominence suggests is actually an illusion: in the absence of institutions that actually link the private and the public spheres, romantic relationships, by their very nature, cannot materially affect society. And even more distressing, they cannot even provide women more than the kind of temporary, imaginative consolation which serves to defuse criticism of the very institutions that make such consolation necessary. For by focusing on courtship, the myth of romantic love tends to freeze the relationship between a man and a woman at its moment of greatest intensity, when both partners are seen (and see themselves) in the most flattering light and, and perhaps most important, when women exercise their greatest power. Romantic love, in other words, seems to promise women in particular ongoing emotional intensity which ideally compensates for all the practical opportunities they are denied. But all it can actually yield is the immediate gratification of believing that this single moment of woman's power will endure, that the fact that a woman seems most desirable when she is most powerful will have an afterlife in marriage and in society. In Jane Austen's society, of course, romantic love did not alter the institutions of marriage or property or female dependence. And even the private gratification available in the domestic sphere could not live up to the intensity and power promised by romantic love, for as a wife and mother, a woman could at best act indirectly, through her children, through sacrifice, through duty. Romantic love, finally, had its most vital, most satisfying existence not in society but in art.

The problems these ideological contradictions generate in Jane Austen's novels are clear in *Persuasion*. In order to give individual feeling moral authority—in order, that is, to place romance in the service of propriety, social reform, and realism— Austen must posit the existence of separate spheres within her fiction. These separate spheres exist at the levels of content and form, and at each level the "private" sphere is theoretically linked to the "public" sphere by the influence bred of contiguity. But these private spheres are actually qualitatively different from the public spheres. Whereas the public spheres activate expectations generated by her readers' actual experiences in class society, whereas they are governed by psychological and social realism and the iron law of cause and effect, the private spheres open out onto romance: they activate and feed off expectations generated by reading other romantic novels; they arouse and satisfy desire. Each of Jane Austen's novels contains these special pockets of romance, not just in their most obtrusive form—those fairy-tale marriages that stop realism dead in its tracks—but in unexpected, out-of-the-way places as well. Thus in *Persuasion* Mrs. Smith remains miraculously, inexplicably cheerful against all the odds her social situation dictates—and even though in the same novel Elizabeth Elliot withers in much less barren soil. And in *Mansfield Park* Fanny and William Price keep domestic affection alive even though we see it atrophy and die in both squalid Portsmouth and immaculate Mansfield Park. At the level of form this division of the fiction into public and private spheres dictates the relegation of all the potentially subversive content to a marginal position or a carefully delimited arena. Paradoxically, the "private," romantic spheres of her novels—Marianne's passion for Willoughby, Darcy's love for Elizabeth, Fanny's yearning for Edmund, Emma's capacity to love, and Anne's fidelity to Wentworth—must all be rigorously contained, whether by the narrative distancing of *Sense and Sensibility*, the circum- stantial frustration of *Mansfield Park* and *Persuasion*, or the encrustation of other, less admirable traits, such as we see in *Pride and Prejudice* and *Emma*. This separation is essential to protect romance from the necessarily deflating power of reality. But it is also essential, finally, in order to ensure that the demands of reality will be taken seriously, not merely repressed or imaginatively escaped. For even though the private sphere is the location and source of the greatest fulfillment Austen can imagine, so, too, does this sphere nourish the very subjectivity which is potentially fatal to the claims of other people, to morality, and, implicitly, to society itself.

In the absence of institutional opportunities for power, then, Jane Austen can effect the aesthetic resolution she desires only by *asserting* that the private sphere of domestic relationships can remain autonomous yet retain a unique and powerful moral dimension. Such resolution is only symbolic, of course, and as we have seen, it can be achieved only by repressing or displacing those questions which might jeopardize it. The fact that Jane Austen's novels contain almost no examples of happy marriages despite their inevitable culmination in a happy marriage summarizes both the price of such symbolic resolution and its attractions. For, on the one hand, for Austen to move chronologically, realistically, from the suspended promise of romantic love to a dramatization of the power relations inherent in marriage (dynamics which she portrays elsewhere with such ruthless wit) would be to risk depriving romantic love of its capacity to engage our imaginations by offering us flattering images of socially acceptable (if unavailable) power. And even more damaging, it would be implicitly to call into question both the consoling assumption that the emotional gratification of love makes up for the absence of other forms of self-expression and the enabling belief that the self-denial which society demands can yield the fulfillment that every person desires. But, on the other hand, freezing the narratives precisely at the height of emotional intensity endorses the promises of romantic love and, in so doing, enjoins the reader to imitate the moral love which the hero and heroine promise to bring to fruition in society. And equally important, the model of female power inherent in the premises of romantic love provides Jane Austen the artist a legitimate paradigm for the self-assertion with which she not only expresses her own desires but works in the service of moral reform.

The division of society and morality into separate public and private spheres was a solution particularly attractive to women. Because bourgeois society defined women in terms of their relationships—specifically, their conjugal or familial relationships—because they were granted power within the "proper sphere" of the home, and because the theory of "influence" postulated a model for the dissemination of domestic virtues throughout society, women had a particular investment in conceptualizing their space as special and as containing special moral authority. More generally, however, we should remember that the cultural ideology of which romantic love was but a part had at its heart the same separation of spheres we see in Austen's novel. For bourgeois ideology held out the promise that every individual would have an equal opportunity to work for equal material rewards, a promise which the limitations of natural resources and the inherent inequalities of class society rendered patently false. The existence of a private sphere, replete with the resources of boundless love and uncritical sympathy, essentially promised a compensatory substitute for other kinds of unavailable gratification—for men as well as women. Not incidentally, of course, the home further reinforced bourgeois ideology through this very compensatory gratification, for it provided competitive labor both an end and a means—a goal to defend and, within the patriarchal family, a nursery for the habits of propriety and the promises of romantic love. To the extent that we still defend these goals and seek these promises, we are still anxious to acquiesce in those resolutions which make them seem not only right but possible.

Chapter Forty-five

From Love and Sex in the Afro-American Novel (1989)

Gloria Naylor

This essay by the well-known fiction writer, author of The Women of Brewster Place, *is unusual in that it directly addresses the accusation that female black authors focus on sexuality rather than romantic love, and speculates why this might appear to be so.*

Modern black women writers have not only stepped forward but stepped beyond the traditional restraints against females exploring their own sexuality. Gwendolyn Brooks, Nikki Giovanni, and Ntozake Shange are among the many poets who have led the way in tackling the taboos against writing about abortion, menstruation, and orgasm—the last a whole subject in and of itself. But in just confining ourselves to the novel, we see a wealth of exploration. Without apology or romanticism, Paule Marshall produced Merle Kibona, a beautiful black-skinned woman with a loud voice, flashing bracelets, and a passion for living so strong that she haunted the minds of her sexual partners—male and female, black and white. Toni Morrison gave us Sula, who outraged an entire town because she saw nothing wrong in taking pleasure from sleeping with other women's husbands without love or regret. But I believe Alice Walker is the most skilled and the most creative in portraying women characters who exult in and are sometimes victimized by their sexuality—Meridian, Celie, Shug Avery, and any female protagonist in *In Love and Trouble*.

But sex is sex, and love is something else again. Whenever the question arises about the alleged lack of love or affection in the Afro-American literary tradition, criticism is rarely directed toward the classics—*Native Son* or *Invisible Man*, or, for that matter, any novel by a male. While black men have written freely about female sexuality, depicting love seems to have been silently relegated to women. Just as the black woman's body was the battleground for "proving" the chastity of an entire race, now it is the black woman's novels that are held accountable for "proving" that the Afro-American community contains harmonious and loving couples. Having said that much by way of a preface, I want to address this particular criticism of the Afro-

From Gloria Naylor, "Love and Sex in the Afro-American Novel," *Yale Review* 78, no. 1 (1989): 25–31. Reprinted by permission.

American female novelist because I feel that it is not only fallacious but rooted in another—and more insidious—form of double consciousness.

Baldwin's narrator in *Beale Street* says: "I hope that nobody has ever had to look at anybody they love through glass." She is referring to the glass that is erected in the visiting rooms of prisons. Many of us are still prisoners. Du Bois's veil has been lifted for many middle-class professionals in the arts and in academia, some of whom were born into privilege, and some of whom are now power brokers. The veil has turned into glass, and that glass is a mirror in which we believe we are seeing our true selves. But we're actually seeing something else: we will wake up in the morning and notice that there are a pair of dark feet peeking out of our Bill Blass pajamas. Then we bathe, shave, comb our hair. And since there's been a civil rights movement, we've no reservation about fixing ourselves a bowl of gourmet grits for breakfast. We may even take the time to write out checks for the United Negro College Fund or Jesse Jackson's presidential campaign. A quick glance into the hall mirror before going out of the door to meet the world, and right there—behind the brown of our irises— there's a tiny little white man staring back at us. And these are the eyes that have read and judged whether or not there has been love in the Afro-American novel, not the eyes that should be turned inward to our own experiences.

The novels by contemporary black women are, indeed, reflective of our unique history and experience. Although the African and European lived and worked side by side, they were governed by radically different worldviews and adhered to a different set of mores in their respective communities as slave and master. And when Africans entered the broader stream of society as Afro-Americans they were able to survive in a hostile environment—and some even to succeed—due to a unique relationship between the sexes. Survival meant that black men and women had to define their roles differently. While William Wells Brown was cloning his female slaves in the image of the white cult of true womanhood, Harriet Jacobs was living the life of an enslaved mulatto; and her account of how she retained her dignity under sexual assault is vastly different from that of the fictionalized Clotell. By the time Jacobs had reached puberty she knew that she was soon going to be forced into a sexual liaison with her owner, who was much older than herself and married. So she deliberately entered into a relationship with another white man who was young and single, and she bore him two children. Jacobs understood the effect this brutally honest account would have on her northern liberal audiences, but she also understood that she existed within a different set of moral parameters. And it was within those boundaries that she carved a path of dignity for herself by her own definition of piety and purity:

> But, O, ye happy women, whose purity has been sheltered from childhood, who have been free to choose the objects of your affection, whose homes are protected by law, do not judge the poor desolate slave girl too severely. If slavery had been abolished, I, also, could have married the man of my choice, I could have had a home shielded by the laws . . . but all my prospects have been blighted by slavery . . . I tried hard to preserve my self-respect.

The Afro-American also inherited a different definition of domesticity. Slave women would live in trial marriages with a man, and it was only after conception that the arrangement would be finalized. And once finalized, it was normally adhered to until death or forced separation tore the couple apart. The security of most Euro-American marriages hinged on the bride bringing chastity to her new home, but for the slave Afro-American it was a demonstrated ability to conceive. The child was the true beginning of a family, and the family was the source of sanity in the slave community. Given the precariousness of their circumstances, slaves even created extended families that held the same import for them as the Euro-American nuclear family. So while a father figure might be absent in black women's literature, there is always a family. And that presence is central and often celebrated in all of its forms.

Finally, we need to speak of submissiveness. That was not in the cards for us. Black women have rightfully not depicted themselves as frail damsels given to fainting spells, or as the kind of silent, long-suffering middle-class housewives who have emerged in contemporary literature. Our history decreed that if we tried to pull something like a fainting spell, our heads would hit the floor. Whether in the cotton fields of the South or the factories of the North, black women worked side by side with their men to contribute to the welfare of the family. This did not mean that men were demeaned and unloved, but it did mean that black women had a voice about the destiny of their families. That independence and resiliency were admired because they aided in our collective survival when society made it difficult for black men to find work. But when we began to internalize Euro-American values, then black women were no longer "real" women—and of course only a real woman could love or be loved by a man.

Depictions of strong women who fought back with their hands or their mouths flow from our unique history, and it does not mean that there is an absence of affection between the sexes. Note carefully the timbre of this passage from Paule Marshall's *Praisesong for the Widow:*

> But she never left off telling him about himself—his no-'count, shiftless ways, his selfishness, his neglect of his own. Spending damn near your whole paycheck on some barfly and a bunch of good-timing niggers and your children's feet at the door. She sent her grievances echoing up and down the deserted street, and strumming along the power line to the trolley, telegraphing them from one end of Brooklyn to the other. She acquainted the sleeping houses with her sorrow. Her rage those dark mornings spoke not only for herself but for the thousands like her for blocks around, lying sleepless in the cold-water flats and one-room kitchenettes, the railroad apartments you could run a rat through and the firetraps above the stores on busy Fulton Street and Broadway; waiting, all of them, for some fool to come home with his sodden breath and half his pay envelope gone. Lying there enraged and vengeful, planning to put the chain on the door, change the lock first thing in the morning, have his clothes waiting out in the hall for him when he came lurching in at dawn. Or she'd be gone, her and the kids. She'd just take her babies and go! The place stripped of all sign of them when he got there. Vowing as she lay there straining to hear his unfocused step on the stairs and the key scratching blindly around the eye of the lock, that there would be no making up this time, no forgiving. This was one time he wasn't going to get around her with his pleas and apologies and talk, with his hands seeking out her breasts in the darkness. Not this morning! Nigger, you so much as put a finger on me this morning and you'll draw back a nub! Praying (Lord please!) that he wouldn't turn on the light and simply stand

there looking at her with his shamefaced self, his pain, until her love—or whatever it was she still felt for him—came down.

In the writings of Afro-American women, the test of love is what the black woman stays *through*. It is normally only death or desertion that tears her from the man. But critics only zero in on the trials in an attempt to show that this literature is pessimistic and hopeless. Margaret Atwood said, "People without hope do not write books." That is quite true. It is more than difficult to craft a work of art—at times it is inhumanly demanding. Bitterness and hatred are simply not powerful enough to keep you going. You cannot make those sacrifices year after year if you are not fueled by both love of your work and love of your subject matter.

Alice Walker's work has been distorted by many black critics through the very glass I've been discussing. People who attacked her recent novel, *The Color Purple*, blatantly misrepresented the entire context of that book. They only looked at the first third and disregarded the growth of all of her characters. The infamous Mister changes into a sensitive man (as most of the men have changed in her novels) and he actually becomes the spokesperson for Walker's definition of love:

> This is the first time I lived on earth as a natural man. It feels like a new experience. . . .
> Anyhow, he say, you know how it is. You ast yourself one question, it lead to fifteen. I start to wonder why us need love, why us suffer. Why us black. Why us men and women. . . .
> Why you think? I ast.
> I think us here to wonder, myself. To wonder. To ast. And that in wondering bout the big things and asting bout the big things, you learn about the little ones almost by accident. . . . The more I wonder, he say, the more I love.

In their novels black women writers have always wondered about our relationships to our men (sexual or not), and our relationships to each other (sexual or not). And I believe it is fair to say that we have not been met halfway. We already know about the classics, *Native Son* and *Invisible Man*. David Bradley's *The Chaneysville Incident* and Ernest J. Gaines's *A Gathering of Old Men* are classics in the making, and it is refreshing to read in the first of them a probing and sensitive treatment of male bonding. But, ironically, both novels have white women as the motivating force or channel for their narratives. It seems that for the most part black male writers have not used their creative energy to wonder about their relationships with *us*. And, since Baldwin, none have stepped forward even to explore the subject of relationships between black men.

It is not my intention here to castigate male writers or critics. On the contrary: I am putting out a call to the black men who are within reach of my voice. There is a whole unexplored territory in our literature—and in our experience—waiting for some man who is courageous enough to enter it. And it does take courage, given this society's definition of what it is to be a "man," for a male and especially a black male to say, yes, I am vulnerable enough to fear loving her or him; I fear hurting; I fear that the relationship just may not work, but I am willing to expose the whole process of wondering on paper. It would be a pity if, after wresting literacy and our very being out of this society, we as artists don't have the courage to define ourselves only by what we are. And it would also be a pity if we as critics wait for the outside world to view our work through its value systems and hail the pain, so we can jump in and hail the pain, too. Both ways we lose the message: *I am here.* That *I* contains myriad realities—not all of them pretty, but not all of them ugly, either:

> and somehow when you talk about home
> it never gets across how much you
> understood their feelings
> as the whole family attended meetings about Hollydale
> and even though you remember
> your biographers never understand
> your father's pain as he sells his stock
> and another dream goes
> And though you're poor it isn't poverty that
> concerns you
> and though they fought a lot
> it isn't your father's drinking that makes any difference
> but only that everybody is together and you
> and your sister have happy birthdays and very good
> Christmasses
> and I really hope no white person ever has cause
> to write about me
> because they never understand
> Black love is Black wealth and they'll
> probably talk about my hard childhood
> and never understand that
> all the while I was quite happy
>   (Nikki Giovanni, "Nikki-Rosa")

Chapter Forty-six

Lesbian Romance Fiction and the Plotting of Desire
Narrative Theory, Lesbian Identity, and Reading Practice (1998)

Suzanne Juhasz

Juhasz, a literary critic, looks at the way lesbian romances appealingly differ from heterosexual romance fictions in their "interplay of sameness and difference." She has also written about her own attraction to the romance genre in her book, Reading from the Heart: Women, Literature and the Search for True Love *(1994). It would be interesting to read this essay alongside Lynn Harne's in part 4.*

For years now it has been a feminist custom, a cliché really, to bash the romance plot. Boy meets girl, boy loses girl, boy gets girl—and in the process, girl gets destroyed. Read *Bride* magazine and you lose your NOW membership card. Feminist academic theory was once adamant about the fact that the romance plot in fiction was a patriarchal construction that not only told the tale of women's oppression but encoded and enforced it: "the romance plot," wrote Rachel Blau DuPlessis in *Writing Beyond the Ending: Narrative Strategies of Twentieth-Century Women Writers* (1985), "is a trope for the sex-gender system as a whole."[1]

At the same time, however, there were other feminist scholars who began to note that there might be a difference when the plot went "girl meets boy, girl loses boy, girl gets boy": that when women wrote the romance, narrative might serve as a form of resistance rather than co-optation.[2] have recently argued, for example, in *Reading from the Heart,* that women's romance fiction expresses a fantasy about love in which the hero is turned into a maternal figure, who offers both recognition and nurture to the heroine, so that loving and maturing are not two plots but one. The "happy ending" thus may be viewed as the achievement of self-identity through the process of loving, not the crushing of the heroine into the gender system, as represented by the institution of marriage. I thus bring together structural elements such as plot with psychodynamic ingredients such as "fantasy," "recognition," "nurture," "self-identity," "maturing," and, of course, "loving," to discuss how formulaic narrative

Suzanne Juhasz, "Lesbian Romance Fiction and the Plotting of Desire: Narrative Theory, Lesbian Identity, and Reading Practice," *Tulsa Studies in Women's Literature,* vol. 17, no. 1 (spring 1998): 65–82. © 1998 by the University of Tulsa. Reprinted by permission.

patterns might embody a psychodynamic content that does not replicate a patriarchal status quo.

The debate that began around heterosexual romance fiction has been rekindled around the lesbian romance. To the specter of the totalizing patriarchal plot has been added the power of the heterosexual plot. No matter that the story is now "girl meets girl, girl loses girl, girl gets girl"; for Julie Abraham in *Are Girls Necessary? Lesbian Writing and Modern Histories*, "plot" equals "heterosexual." "There could be no 'lesbian plot,' " she writes, "equivalent to the heterosexual plot, because the construction of heterosexuality is in modern culture the construction of heterosexuality as the norm, and because the function of literary conventions, like all conventions, is to normalize."[3] Even though the story is about romance between two women, Abraham insists that if they are narratively positioned as lovers, they must enact heterosexuality and heterosexual consequences: "The subject of the lesbian novel is always, in a sense, the problem of not-heterosexuality, which is to say, finally, that the subject of the lesbian novel remains, like the subject of all other novels about women, heterosexuality" (p. 4). In this thoughtful study, Abraham quickly shifts her focus to a discussion of "lesbian writing" as opposed to "lesbian novels," finding in history an alternative source of narrative convention available to lesbian writers in which the personal and the public can be merged "as a way of constructing narratives beyond the heterosexual limits of literary 'reality' "(p. 29).

Abraham's notion that *plot* equals *heterosexual* rests in a tradition of narrative theory that sees narration as a system of codes that replicate dominant social structures. In *Alice Doesn't* (1984), for example, Teresa de Lauretis exposed the inscription of gender hierarchy and heterosexuality in narrative codes, that is, the active and passive "positionalities of desire" described by Yuri Lotman, in which the active, mobile protagonist (male) confronts and overcomes the passive, immobile boundary space (female) in order to secure his identity.[4] Recently, Marilyn Farwell in *Heterosexual Plots and Lesbian Narratives* has summarized what happens when narrative is understood as a structure that replays social expectations and cultural codes:

> In the most important societal parallel, narrative is likened to society's institutions of romance and marriage. . . . this model invokes categories of subjectivity which privilege the male and assure the hierarchical placement of male and female in a heterosexual relationship. Those rules and institutions which ask all of us to marry, to have children, and to assume sexually oppositional positions become the ideologically inflected, abstract codes by which genres such as the *Bildungsroman* and the romance and marriage plots tell their tale. (p. 40)

Must plot necessarily replicate dominant social structures? Is there any way in which impulses that counter dominant ideology can find verbal expression? Theorizing women's writing, French feminists have proposed various versions of experimental stylistics, such as Julia Kristeva's concept of the semiotic or *l'écriture féminine* of Luce Irigaray and Hélène Cixous. Queer theory has given us ways to detect the presence of what is gay, lesbian, bisexual, or transgendered by reading against the literal grain, the "straight" plot. Terry Castle, for example, in her important essay, "The Apparitional Lesbian," decrying "that trend toward representational candor which one can detect in mainstream lesbian writing from *The Well of Loneliness* on," insists that we must look at "rather more ambitious and self-conscious literary works."[5]

Yet it is "mainstream" writing that is read by most readers in the world beyond the academy. Romance fiction is generally popular fiction, frequently formula fiction. Indeed, *Pride and Prejudice* is a romance, too. But one factor that distinguishes "literary fiction" from "pulp fiction" is the dependence in the latter on plot rather than style or language as the primary agent for the representation of meaning. In *Reading the Romance*, Janice Radway's interviewees (members of a romance readers' club) say that they like Jane Austen's heroines and find her stories intriguing, but that they do not particularly appreciate having to pay so much attention to her verbal structures. Radway comments,

> Words, phrases, and sentences do not themselves become the object of attention but exist as a channel or conduit through which the reader gains access to the truly important, the meanings that constitute the romantic story of the lovers. Romance writers and readers alike understand the purpose of the text to be the romantic tale itself, just as they conceive the activities of writing and reading as a *storytelling* cycle.[6]

Rather than proving that popular romances should therefore be banished from our academic view, this offers important information about how some readers read. Instead of throwing out the romance with the lesbian (as many lesbian theorists seem to want to do), I would rather try to think more carefully about plot itself and, in the process, take the abiding power and influence of the lesbian romance seriously, in the way that some feminist critics have done with the heterosexual romance. After all, there exist hundreds of lesbian romance novels, written by lesbians who do not seem to know they are fooling themselves when they think they are writing love stories about two women, even as there exist readers who apparently derive pleasure and satisfaction from reading stories about two women falling in love, having difficulties, and finally getting together in the end.

I have chosen as my case in point a Naiad romance. Naiad Press is the veritable godmother of lesbian small presses, a major source for the publication of lesbian formula fiction. My text is Sarah Aldridge's *Keep To Me, Stranger* (1989)[7] The author is a lesbian romance veteran, with many such novels to her credit. With a Naiad romance by Aldridge, then, we are in the heartland of lesbian romance territory. I chose this particular book, not because it represents all lesbian romances, but because it is as "mainstream" as they come.

I chose it for another reason as well: because I had read and enjoyed it in the process of my own coming out as a lesbian. My own "pleasure and satisfaction," along with the circumstances that occasioned these responses, lead me in this essay to focus on (1) the importance of thinking about readerly needs and desires and (2) the relationship between reading needs and writing forms. I am concerned, for example, with the common readerly desire to identify with literary plots and characters—to achieve the satisfaction and also the instruction that derive from the process of seeing oneself depicted in fiction.

The less this happens, the more it tends to matter. That is, in the case of the love that has no name, the love that does not exist, according to British law,[8] reading about it actually happening means a lot. When Castle looks at literary fiction, she discovers a pattern of ghosting in which lesbians come into the text as apparitions, as ghosts. "The spectral figure," writes Castle, "is a perfect vehicle for conveying what must be called—though without a doubt paradoxically—that 'recognition through negation' which has taken place with regard to female homosexuality in Western culture since the Enlightenment." She concludes: "the metaphor has functioned as the necessary psychological and rhetorical means for objectifying—and ultimately embracing—that which otherwise could not be acknowledged" (p. 60). Yet this very necessity for metaphor and suggestion points to a counter need: for literalness. Not to have to "read between the lines" but to encounter lines in which lesbians are there: *out* rather than *between*. When lesbians' stories are plotted before our very eyes, romances in which girl goes out and gets girl, we may be reading fantasy, but we are engaged in a real way with a story which we desire for ourselves. (Radway points out how important it is to the Smithton readers that the characters in romance fiction seem "real": just so the fantasy—they lived happily ever after—will be believable, possible, p. 203). This kind of narrative works to satisfy the need of readers—in this case, lesbians—to see ourselves in representational forms, to see that we do, indeed, exist and that our existence matters. These plots validate the sense of identity that readers have or seek and also show us something about what might constitute that identity. This is the continuing power of the lesbian romance, a power that finds its locus in the structures of plot.

"Plot" may be a function of narrative, but "needs" and "purposes" are aspects of psyche—not to mention impulses such as "fantasy" and "desire." In bringing together narrative and inter- and intra-psychic structures, I am viewing both writing and reading as psychodynamic as well as formalist or culturally materialist acts. When narrative is considered as a language act responding to needs and desires that do not reify cultural conventions, we can think about the possibility of its both reflecting and ringing changes on lived experience through the images it creates and the stories it tells—stories that serve to represent lesbian identity in a literal and, in contemporary fiction, affirmative manner. Narrative viewed from this perspective possesses the capability to do something other than "replicate dominant social structures": it can and does render alternative paradigms.

Yet to say that you are reading to find or create your "identity" is in some circles as laughable as saying that you are reading for the plot. Postmodernists tend to see both language and self-identity as constructed by the culture's dominant ideologies. Identity cannot arise from "inside" the individual. There is no inherent or true self. Identity functions as a fabrication, or perhaps a performance, which is socially, politically, and linguistically determined. However, to recognize the insights of social construction does not seem to some, myself included, to preclude the existence of identity or subjectivity per se. It is possible to acknowledge the forces of cultural construction, of historicity, and the critique of essentialism, without doing away with the idea of self-identity altogether—or with the need for it. Jane Flax helpfully posits a distinction between "unitary" and "core" concepts of self. A "core" self is one that, in the words of the psychologist D. W. Winnicott, possesses a sense of continuity or "going on being."[9] A core self can be fluid and multiply determined, "a shifting and always changing intersection of complex, contradictory, and unfinished processes." But this is a different matter altogether from the lack of any ability to sustain coherence.[10] As Flax points out, "those who celebrate or call for a 'decentered' self seem self-deceptively naive and unaware of the basic cohesion within themselves that makes the fragmentation of experiences something other than a terrifying slide into psychosis."[11]

For those of us who belong to a group that has been marginalized or pathologized by dominant ideologies, the insights of social constructionism can in fact be particularly valuable. The critique of the notion of an essentialist and universal model of "healthy" selfhood—rational, autonomous, and masterful—a self that looks a lot like the white middle- or upper-class European male, is apt and helpful. At the same time, however, members of marginalized groups have, I think rightfully, been suspicious of the thorough-going dismantling of identity—at the very time when their political struggles for recognition have gained ground. Identity goes on mattering, especially to people who have been denied the right to have one, or who have been asked to change or hide the identity we want to have.

Yet while academic theory has begun to explore the boundaries of gender and sexuality, no longer lumping them together as one biologically determined entity, both gender identity and sexual identity form a large part of how a person understands and portrays herself. And if identity responds to external forces, including narrative, in its formation, then it will respond to narratives that challenge cultural hegemony as well as those that reify it. It is no accident, for example, that lesbians who are in the process of coming out become avid Naiad readers (I was not unique in that proclivity), or that lesbians who are isolated from a lesbian community, like my good friend in Curtis, Nebraska, a town of 600, develop a predilection for lesbian detective novels. As the monster in Mary Shelley's novel *Frankenstein* cries, "I had never yet seen a being resembling me or who claimed any intercourse with me. What was I"?[12]

What is interesting or valuable or helpful or possibly radical about a lesbian romance? *Keep To Me, Stranger* tells the tale of Helena and Billie, who meet, fall in love, encounter great difficulties, but solve them and, we assume, live happily ever after. The plot of the novel can be summarized as follows. Helena has just been hired as a company manager by Rosenstein's, a classy New York women's department store. There she meets Billie, whose great-grandmother founded the store. Billie has no official job position, but she loves the store and works there, too. Both are closeted lesbians. They meet and fall in love.

Meanwhile, however, several of the male members of the store's board are plotting to sell this family-owned company to a conglomerate. They feel it is too old-fashioned in its present form and not central to the family finances, which have diversified into investment banking and other holdings. To this end Helena is wooed, literally as well as figuratively, by several men associated with the store. Billie, along with many of the women who work at the store, wants to continue in the protofeminist spirit of Old Leah, the woman who founded it. Helena is asked to advise the board on this crucial decision.

In the meantime, Helena and Billie encounter difficulties in their romantic relationship because (a) Helena likes to keep business and her personal life separate, and she is confused about being involved with a lover who is so implicated in the store, and (b) Billie's central relationship has heretofore been with her mother, who is jealous of any other relationship or activity for her daughter. What will happen to the store? Will Billie and Helena be able to continue their relationship? Will true love conquer all? The happy ending in this novel turns out to depend upon both the strength and the interconnections between women's relationships on all levels of experience, from the institutional level, the store, through that of friendship between women, to that of intimate relationship, represented by mother and daughter, lover and lover. In reading this story I found a narrative structure that problematizes the notion that there is no romance plot other than a heterosexual plot. Although *Keep To Me, Stranger* makes no claim to stylistic innovation—it is linear, incremental, and literal—it does problematize the notion that narrative form replicates normative societal practices and therefore, like them, institutionalizes heterosexuality. It also offers a structure that is different from the supposedly necessary exchange between two oppositional positionalities, a desirer and a desiree, the "masculine" and the "feminine."

In this novel the institution of heterosexuality turns out to be a veneer over another organizing cultural structure that I will call feminosociality. Maternal, sororal, and homoerotic relationships and institutions are both the grid that situates the plot and the network that produces it. The plot is organized so as to remove the heterosexual veneer in order to display this culture of feminosociality. It does so by tracing the love story of two women, two lovers, who both desire and are desired by each other, yet for whom desire as an active and energizing force is impeded by developmental issues that stem from their primary and formative relationship with their mothers. Neither can be "whole" at the start (that is, a person with a full and productive self-identity) because neither can integrate work and love—Helena, because she cannot acknowledge her need for love (a life of feeling and intimacy); Billie because she cannot acknowledge her need for work (a life of agency, authority, public action). The characters are thus both different and equal in their positionality.

That each is closeted as a lesbian is the symbol of her intrapsychic problems and of her initial co-optation by heterosexual institutions—the psychodynamic and the social are here reciprocally related to each other. The romance plot engages its heroines in the working through of these issues—it enables them to come out—by developing their relationship with each other, with other women, especially with their mothers, and with the homosocial culture that surrounds them. In the happy ending their individual, romantic, and social needs are fulfilled. Each has reached a truer and more complete identity, which means that both can work and love fully and openly. They are out to themselves and to the world.

This novel is based in an implicit theoretical perspective that foregrounds the importance of gender to women's identities and lives, and, in particular, the importance of gender to lesbian identity. It positions the mother-daughter relationship as central to female subjectivity, self-identity, and sexuality, as a source and model for all other relationships between women. Various feminist psychoanalytic theories have focused on the importance of the mother-daughter relationship. The French feminist theories of *l'écriture féminine*, for example, are based in the centrality of the mother to women's development. However, they have been attacked by many lesbians for their heterosexual bias. Although focused on the original bond between mother and daughter and presuming the power and authority of relationships among or between women, such theories by and large assume heterosexuality as the normative outcome for female desire and consequently deny lesbian sexuality. "In narrative terms, then," writes Farwell, "the lesbian exists only in the lyrical mode of the pre-Oedipal" (p. 52).[13] In *The Practice of Love: Lesbian Sexuality and Perverse Desire*, Teresa de Lauretis is more critical yet, noting how the maternal imaginary metaphorizes lesbianism into the sign of an implicitly heterosexual female resistance and desire.[14] In contrast, in her essay "The Space Between: Daughters and Lovers in *Anne Trister*," Lizzie Thynne looks at this Canadian romance film by Lea Poole in the light of the work of Irigaray to suggest connections between a girl's early unconscious desire for her mother and an adult lesbian affair. "Many lesbians," she writes,

> have resisted the notion that desire between women has anything to do with mother-love, apparently because the association has commonly been used to dismiss lesbianism as an immature and/or pathological sexuality. I am not proposing that there is any direct equivalence between the two, but that reconceptualizing this primary relationship of our early life is an important part of validating the choice of a female love-object in later life.[15]

In her paper Thynne shows how "echoes of a mother-daughter relationship" are mediated through the exchange of symbols in the film—painting, desert, sand—which "represent that link while also allowing them [mother and daughter] to establish boundaries and not merely mirror or merge with each other" (p. 107). Her point is that the earliest love between mother and infant, which sets the tone and the template for all subsequent love relationships (be they heterosexual or homosexual), is of great importance to the manner in which lesbian lovers play out their relationship.

Nearly everyone begins with a sensual and, I would argue, romantic relationship with a woman. These templates are in operation for men with women, for women with men, for women with women, and, for that matter, for men with men. As Nancy Chodorow writes in *Femininities, Masculinities, Sexualities*, "most girls seek to create in love relationships an internal emotional dialogue with the mother: to recreate directly the early infantile or oedipal connection; to reconcile, rescue, or repair; to attack, incorporate, or reject; to emancipate themselves or define themselves against her."[16] Because she is studying film, Thynne focuses on images and imagery, but her approach is suggestive and supports my own efforts in attempting to describe how an emphasis on the psychodynamic aspects of character and relationship are related to formal elements in artistic production, such as plot.

Keep To Me, Stranger understands character psychodynamically: early developmental experience and relationships influence adult characterological behavior. They do not cause the heroines' lesbianism, but they do contribute to the characters' ability or lack thereof to be active and comfortable with their identities. A heterosexual culture puts pressure on any lesbian to disavow or hide her sexuality. But how she deals with homophobia has much to do with "who" she is. "Who she is" has much to do, in turn, with "who" her mother is and what her mother's relation to sexual conventions is and has been.

Helena's adult life, for example, is clearly related to her childhood struggles. Her mother, divorced when her daughter was eight, had suffered from a sense of inadequacy and failure until she found another husband—no matter that he did not love her daughter. Helena experienced her mother's priority for her relationships with men as rejection. In turn, she herself rejected her mother—and the world that created her mother—for a business career and for liaisons with women, which her mother suspected but was never told about. Their present relationship is now false: "both of them aware that there lay a vast field of feelings, opinions, desires that neither of them could express" (p. 116). Mother and daughter still love each other deeply, even as they did when there were no husbands and fathers to come between them, but they have lost the way to feel intimacy.

Helena is the first woman to join the executive officers since the death of the founder twenty years before, but she has been hired because she is a management professional. Helena is a woman who has been trained to act like a man, which is why, of course, the male board members have chosen her. Not only does she understand modern business practices, but she bases her ideas about professionalism on male behavior. She despises the way traditional women cannot separate their emotional lives from the world of business and professional demands—"her friends who gave up careers to become wives and mothers" (p. 115). She prides herself on keeping her personal and work lives separate. Her personal life is private, indeed secret. The novel suggests that Helena's jealousy of her mother's need for men has made her reject a femininity that operates in such a fashion. Acting like a man is one way not to need men. So is loving women. Is Helena a lesbian because she loves her mother, because she hates men, because she just "is"? The novel is not about to answer these questions. What is clear, however, is that she has disavowed her femaleness because she feels that being a woman is the reason for her mother's rejection.

Billie's connection to her mother is even more pronounced because, rather than being cut off, it has continued into the daughter's adulthood as the primary relationship in her life. Billie, we remember, is the great-granddaughter of Old Leah. Although Billie does not actually hold a position at Rosenstein's, everybody agrees that Billie has inherited something from Old Leah, "some special gift for preserving the traditions of the store" (p. 13). But Billie does not work, not professionally, so dependent is she on her mother, Rosalie, who is Old Leah's only granddaughter. These three women form the matriarchal chain that should be controlling Rosenstein's. But Billie's mother, spoiled by Leah, has chosen to expend her energies on society and charity—and on her daughter, Billie. Billie, in her turn, controlled by her doting and possessive mother, plays at her involvement with Rosenstein's. Thus Billie, who cannot work professionally, is the opposite of Helena—except that she too is a lesbian and closeted, especially from her mother, a situation that has forced her to be "deceitful, wary, untruthful," producing "a pain she could not assuage" (p. 296).

Late in the novel, Helena learns from Billie's cousin (and first lover) Michelle that the source of Billie's passivity (which we can read as ultra-"femininity") is the hiding of her sexuality from her mother:

> All her natural instincts—her outgoingness, her initiative, her mental quickness—were sacrificed to hiding what she really is. . . . I thought she'd never find the woman who would really rouse her, for whom she would feel a strong enough love that she would break the barriers that held her prisoner. It turns out that you're the one. You're the only person who has ever sparked Billie into action. She adores you. Because of you, Billie's inner fire is bursting forth. (p. 243)

Indeed, Billie and Helena fall in love because each is sensitive to the true or "real self" of the other—the potential and lost, whole self: "There was a coming together of their spirits, as if they had known each other for a long time" (p. 100). "It was as if," thinks Helena after a night with Billie, "she were awakening from a dream in which she was the real, essential Helena, someone she had lost touch with since the far-off days of her little girlhood" (p. 108). However, this true self that each cherishes in the other is implicit, not explicit—not alive and well and functioning in the external world. A kind of closeted self, we could say.

But the story to be told in women's romance fiction is one of maturation as much as love, for love and self-development prove to be aspects of one another. The complications and difficulties that the relationship occasions provide as well the opportunity for self-development. Complications and difficulties there certainly are. Helena has gone and done it: become emotionally involved with someone from work—not a man, a woman. What will this do to her prized professionalism—her judgment, objectivity, skill? And Billie has fallen in love, jeopardizing her cherished but dishonest relationship with her mother. This is another place where the plot becomes important, for character and plot significantly inform one another. Each heroine's problems contribute to that part of the romance plot that places impediments in the way of the love affair's trajectory, so that it will not move in a direct line from A meets B to A gets B. This is true for all romances. For lesbian romances, sexual identity itself is usually the major problem or impediment. The plot functions to establish and then to solve these difficulties.

The plot of this novel is organized, as I have said, so as to display the existence of a culture of feminosociality and to engage the characters in this culture—a women's culture. Reading this novel, I was reminded of Adrienne Rich's infamous essay, "Compulsory Heterosexuality and Lesbian Existence," written by the lesbian feminist poet in 1980. This paper provoked a furor of controversy in its proclamation of a "lesbian continuum" in culture, a "range . . . of woman-identified experience, not simply the fact that a woman has had or consciously desired genital sexual experience with another woman."[17] Rich's aim in describing such a continuum was to recognize heterosexuality as a political institution and to challenge its dominance with the recognition of structures of "women-identification" actually in operation in modern culture. She asked us to "consider the possibility that all women—from the infant suckling at her mother's breast, to the grown woman experiencing orgasmic sensations while suckling her own child, perhaps recalling her mother's milk smell in her own, to two women, like Virginia Woolf's Chloe and Olivia, who share a laboratory, to the woman dying at ninety, touched and handled by women—exist on a lesbian continuum" (p. 54). Rich was trying not so much to whitewash or erase lesbian sexuality as to identify lesbian experience as an aspect of female experience, "with particular oppressions, meanings, and potentialities we cannot comprehend as long as we simply bracket it with other sexually stigmatized existences" (p. 53). Although Rich was attacked because, on the one hand, she threatened straight women by calling them lesbians and, on the other hand, she threatened lesbians by seeming to take away their difference from straight women, she showed in her essay that important similarities and affiliations exist between people who are gendered female, notwithstanding those differences that also exist between them due to class, race, ethnicity, and sexual orientation. Primary women-centered relationships are important to our understanding of female desire, whether it be expressed homoerotically or heterosexually. Against the institution of heterosexuality, *Keep To Me, Stranger* positions feminosocial bonding and culture.[18] There is a literal institution in this novel, which supplies both environment and theory for a women-centered culture: Rosenstein's is "matriarchal" in origin and in organization.

Rosenstein's was founded at the turn of the century, as I have mentioned, by "Old Leah," a working-class Jewish seamstress. Leah, a German-Jewish immigrant who had a child and a scholar husband to support, began by doing piecework as a seamstress; ultimately she started a shop, where other women and she could work, making fine clothing for wealthy women (her boss had been exploiting her and she discovered it). Although her male descendants (heirs to her fortune and her empire) liked to think of her as a proper wife and mother, in actuality she "always acted for herself," was quite open about being the owner of the business, and "told her sons what to do, even in public, as if she was the father and not the mother, the husband and not the wife" (p. 34). Consequently, even as the founder of the department store was a protofeminist, so, under her leadership, her store was originally organized as a female-centered institution in a normatively male-centered culture. But the store is now endangered because the women in the family, like Billie's mother, have abandoned it to the men, and the spirit of care, attention, and creativity (equated with Leah and with a female mode) has slipped away.

The plot of this novel is organized as a movement of discovery. Helena is, after all, a stranger—to Rosenstein's, to the Rosenstein family, to Billie (for all that Helena instinctively "recognizes" her). Helena needs to understand the store and its ways, and behind that the ways of the family that owns it, in order to make her decision about the store's future. She needs to understand her lover, Billie. Why does Billie drink so much? Why is Billie so passive and secretive? The novel follows Helena in her quest. What she discovers in her search is the weave of women that forms the fabric of the world that is Rosenstein's. There is Esther, secretary to the board, who tells Helena the store's history. There is Rachel, the head buyer, trained by Old Leah herself. Rachel teaches Helena more about the store, about clothing, and about Billie.

Rachel is almost a second mother to Billie, and, as it turns out, Rachel is also a lesbian. Yet another lesbian in the family is the notorious Michelle (notorious because she lives as a lesbian who is out), who also tells Helena about Billie.

As the women talk together, Helena slowly becomes a part of their world. Although the love scenes between Helena and Billie are the focus of emotional and sexual desire in the narrative, this energy radiates out to involve all the women, their presence motivating Helena's knowledge and development. Helena slowly changes, beginning to understand, for one thing, that her love for Billie affects her professional life—indeed, her understanding of professionalism itself. Always she had understood business as a world of men, its rules of behavior and styles of communication "based on . . . the support networks that men traditionally created in their competition with one another" (p. 43). But even as the world made by Old Leah is not a man's world, so Helena's love for Billie draws her into a situation where the neat dichotomy she has drawn between her two "selves" will not hold: "But where was she with Billie in all of this? Billie did not fit into the situation in which she found herself. Billie had become a part of her she could not excise. Billie was inextricably involved in her working life, yet Billie was outside it altogether" (p. 249). Helena, in other words, is becoming more of a "woman," more of her "self." It is her association with the women's culture that above all affects her personal and intrapsychic life.

Helena works so hard that she falls ill and thus provides the opportunity for the plot to reintroduce her mother, who comes to the city to care for her. Even as it is women talking to women that knits the weave forming the cultural grid, so Helena and her mother's conversations help reknit her personal life. Her mother begins to discover the truth about her daughter's emotional and sexual life and does not reject her. As her mother's plane departs, Helena thinks: "Was the link between herself and her mother, which she had thought to have faded in the last few years, proved still strong enough to convey the truth of her emotional life? A feeling, which grew stronger as she pondered, told her that this was the fact" (p. 213).

Finally, Helena makes her decision about Rosenstein's. Her solution is *not* to decide the fate of the store but to make two presentations, showing two trajectories: selling to the conglomerate, staying independent. She will leave it to the board to decide. Helena is right not to make the decision. It is Billie who must do it: Billie who "has her great grandmother's touch"; who "understands, right down to the ground, what Old Leah did and why she did it," as Rachel tells Helena (p. 72). But for Billie to create for herself a real and dominant role at Rosenstein's, she must come to terms with her mother and *their* relationship. Even as Helena, in the course of her section of the narrative, has had to effect a rapprochement with her mother for the purpose of self-maturation, so it is necessary that Billie face hers.

Thus the novel turns in its final chapter to Billie, who now sees that "the most intimate relationship she had ever had—with her mother" has turned into a prison, from which she must break out or "she would become a nothing. . . . In no other way could she ever win Helena" (p. 275). She must take the risk of breaking her powerful and cherished connection with her mother in order to make that connection real. There must be a confrontation with her mother, with, in other words, "the reality of her situation . . . with the need to establish the direction of her life" (p. 275).

Her mother (whose vote on the board will be the deciding one) holds the key to everything: to Billie's future, to the future of Rosenstein's. But then again, she thinks: "Or, really, could the key be in her own hands? Hadn't it always lain there in her own passive hands, whose fingers had been too nerveless to make use of it?" (p. 275). Billie does not want to stop loving her mother. But she does want Helena. She knows she must fight for what she wants—all of it.

"You bitch, you pervert, you dirty thing!" (p. 270), shrieks Billie's mother, Rosalie, to Helena, when Billie comes out to her mother at last. But Billie holds her ground, and Rosalie's prejudice about lesbianism turns out to be bound up in her fear that Billie will leave her. Marrying a man, or even being heterosexual, does not threaten the primary female bond as loving another woman does. Billie appeases her mother on both scores, by reassuring her that "Nobody has stolen me from you. I love you as I always have. You're my mother" (pp. 321–22), and by attacking homophobia:

> Mamma, those are the ideas of men. Those are the words men use. They want to keep women submissive. You're a woman, like me. There cannot be anything disgusting about loving a woman. Don't you realize: these are men's thoughts, what most men want women to believe. Men are afraid of women's bodies. That is why they beat us, rape us, kill us. That is why they invent these religious taboos about our bodies. Tell me, did you really feel unclean when you gave birth to me? (p. 322)

Rosalie's response turns the tide: "No of course not! That's nothing but superstition!" (p. 322).

Now Billie broaches the subject of the store. What's wrong, Rosalie says, is that it doesn't have anyone "looking after it" the way Old Leah did. Billie says firmly: "I can look after the store." "If I had the daughter I thought I had," says Rosalie, she would not think twice about voting to keep the store as it is (p. 328). Billie's response is that Rosalie can indeed keep her if she can accept Helena as Billie's love. Her point is that one relationship does not mean the end of the other. But if Rosalie cannot under-stand, then indeed, "I will not have a mother. You will not have a daughter. We'll live truncated lives—at your choice" (p. 329). Rosalie, in demanding an exclusive relationship with her daughter, has in fact contradicted the implicit ideology of the feminosocial system that calls for a continuum or network of relations.

Billie's anger and willingness to fight for her love (that is, her active behavior, the opposite of her lifelong passivity) have won, as we knew they would. She is a "real woman" now, even as Helena is likewise a "real woman" for recognizing her emo-tional side. As reward, Billie gets to keep Rosalie, she gets to love Helena, she gets a job, and the store is saved. As for Helena, she gets Billie and her own mother ("She said that she would never cut herself off from me, under any circumstances. . . . She would accept you," Helena tells Billie. "She likes you very much," p. 344). And she gets a woman partner to run Rosenstein's. "That's natural enough," says Billie. "It was a woman's creation" (pp. 359–60).

The plot of *Keep To Me, Stranger* uses a romance formula—girl meets girl, girl loses girl, girl gets girl—to develop a fantasy in which a world structured by feminosocial bonding will become normative rather than aberrant, central rather than marginal.

This world is formed in and emblematized by the mother-daughter relationship (even as the organizing paradigm for the alternative world is the father-son relationship). Homoeroticism between women is thus viewed as an extension and renegotiation of the original primary bond. The lesbian lovers, rather than being stigmatized, punished, or ghosted, are positioned as members of a feminosocial community with values, norms, and ideologies that can influence the culture at large. Rich's "lesbian continuum" is absolutely relevant here because, at least in this novel, gender is the dominant trope. Here lesbians are women who love women, and the erotic and sexual nature of this love is seen as a version of all the other kinds of love between women that create a women-centered culture.

Notwithstanding its simple language and formulaic structure, the novel suggests something powerfully revisionary: that the mother-daughter dynamic, because it is the first bond, the first experience of love, intimacy, and desire, serves as a template for later relationships. Not only does its original dynamic directly affect the subsequent relationships of each heroine, but it remains itself an important relationship in the present tense, as in each case it is renegotiated by two adult women. The plot is organized to create a "continuum" of relationships with women for each heroine, beginning with her relationship to her mother and moving on to all the rest, especially her sexual and romantic love for the other heroine.

In its emphasis on gender, this novel does not question the construction of gender, as does social constructionism, nor its boundaries, as does queer theory. But neither does it reify conventional gender arrangements that position "woman" as a relationship to "man." In narrative terms there are two heroines who both become more fully female. Thus "woman" is not passive to the male's active; nor is she emotional to the male's rational, private to the male's public, and so forth. Rather, "woman" is a person who is active and agential in both personal and public spheres. The heroines' similar achievement of womanhood through different paths is underscored by their lesbian sexuality. Lesbianism is understood as a relationship of woman to woman. In such ways the novel challenges conventional gender definitions even as it continues to affirm the primary significance of gender in lived experience.

The fantasies expressed in this romance novel are articulated and created through narrative patterns that reveal a world of feminosociality behind the veneer of the heterosocial. The plot functions to bring this "institution" from the background to the foreground. A narrative trajectory of discovery is plotted for both heroines that is both social and psychodynamic in nature, having as a goal the development of a full and mature identity for each. Even as social structures define the possibilities and limitations for identity, so psychodynamic structures, the network of desires and responses forming the mental world of each individual, affect how social experience is allotted meaning. Identity is at issue, lesbian identity, because the foremost fantasy explored by this text is that a person could *be* a lesbian in such a way as to function usefully and satisfiedly in the life that she lives.

Emphasizing the plot, as I do, is necessary because plot is what organizes this kind of writing: it is what, in mainstream fiction, enables the development of character. Character development is of crucial significance because a basic fantasy in most women's romance fiction is that love and maturation are aspects of one another. In lesbian romance fiction, the same expectation holds true, but it is complicated by the forbidden nature of this version of female sexuality. If for heterosexual women sexuality "goes without saying" because it is normative, for lesbians sexuality might all too well go without saying because it is taboo. A lesbian's status as a mature woman demands that she have full access to and employment of her sexuality: that she be out to herself and to the world. The existence of a women's "world" that is normative and encompassing supports the coming out process more readily; thus it also facilitates maturation. Plot and character intrinsically affect or inform one another. The happy ending in lesbian romance fiction is that girl gets girl. For the happy ending to be satisfying, it has to be believable; to be believable, it has to be realistic; to be realistic, there has to be a plot and a concomitant development of character that make possible and probable what, in the world outside the novel, is more usually suppressed and/or repressed. The very literalness of the writing, the very linearity of the narrative support the fantasy or wished-for elements that this plot introduces. Yet in this fashion the romance also disrupts rather than maintains dominant social structures: specifically, heterosexuality and phallocentrism.

The particular story told by *Keep To Me, Stranger,* suggestive as it is in many ways, is of course not in every detail the plot of all lesbian romances. But the ways in which this novel employs plot are, I think, typical of the narrative structure of much mainstream or popular writing. I have tried to demonstrate how this form of narrative can be disruptive to the dominance of conventional ideologies. In this way I am challenging the prevalence of theories maintaining either that (1) language is itself a cultural construction; culture is patriarchal and heterosexual; ergo, language cannot escape being an agent of the culture that constructs it—that is, patriarchal, heterosexist; or (2) experimental writing of one kind or another is the only possible hope for deconstructing the conventionality of language. What I would argue is that language as a system of signs is more neutral than these theories allow; it is language usage that determines how it is written and read and how it ultimately means. As Farwell writes, language systems are "the result of history, tradition, symbolic connections, and reader expectation" (p. 30). Thus the central issue seems to me to be not so much whether language or even subjectivity is "free" from culture or constructed by it, as whether that culture, the situation in which language users are embedded, includes the experience and vision of alterity and difference. People do imagine something other than the status quo, and they struggle in various ways to attain and to validate that difference. Practice as well as theory embodies that struggle. People use language as well as are used by it. (Indeed, theorists use the very language they condemn in order to express their critique of it.) Likewise, readers use texts and texts use readers in a process that is, for all of these practitioners, social change.

NOTES

1. Rachel Blau DuPlessis, *Writing Beyond the Ending: Narrative Strategies in Twentieth-Century Women Writers* (Bloomington: Indiana University Press, 1985), p. 5.

2. Rachel Brownstein in *Becoming A Heroine: Reading about Women in Novels* (New York: Viking Press, 1982), Janice Radway in *Reading the Romance: Women, Patriarchy and Popular Literature* (Chapel Hill: University of North Carolina Press, 1984), Tania Modleski in *Loving with a Vengeance: Mass-Produced Fantasies for Women* (New York: Methuen, 1982), Carol Thurston in *The Romance Revolution: Erotic Novels by Women and the Quest for a New Sexual Identity* (Urbana: University of Illinois Press, 1987), and Suzanne Juhasz in *Reading From the Heart: Women, Romance, and the Search for True Love* (New York: Viking Press, 1995) have affirmed from various perspectives both the difference and the significance of romance as a genre when it is written by women. In particular, Radway, Thurston, and I all point to the transformative quality of the female fantasy that is articulated in these novels, whereby heroes can be turned into the kind of lovers that women desire: at once nurturing and egalitarian. This is, in Radway's words, "the imaginative transformation of masculinity to conform with female standards" (p. 147); or, as Thurston puts it, "even if some or all of that is still a fantasy in their own lives rather than a reality, it is indicative of their aspirations" (p. 111).

3. Julie Abraham, *Are Girls Necessary? Lesbian Writing and Modern Histories* (New York: Routledge, 1996), p. 3. Subsequent references will be cited parenthetically in the text.

4. Teresa de Lauretis, *Alice Doesn't: Feminism, Semiotics, Cinema* (Bloomington: Indiana University Press, 1984), p. 118; quoted in Marilyn Farwell, *Heterosexual Plots and Lesbian Narratives* (New York: New York University Press, 1996), p. 31. Subsequent references to Farwell's study will be cited parenthetically in the text.

5. Terry Castle, *The Apparitional Lesbian: Female Homosexuality and Modern Culture* (New York: Columbia University Press, 1993), p. 55. Subsequent references will be cited parenthetically in the text.

6. Radway, pp. 197–98.

7. Sarah Aldridge, *Keep To Me, Stranger* (Tallahassee: Naiad Press, 1989). Subsequent references will be cited parenthetically in the text.

8. In her essay, "The Regulation of Lesbian Sexuality through Erasure: The Case of Jennifer Saunders," Anna Marie Smith points out that British law from 1533 to 1991 depicts criminal sexual practices as deriving from male homosexuality or, at most, heterosexual female prostitution, in *Lesbian Erotics*, ed. Karla Jay (New York: New York University Press, 1995), pp. 170–73.

9. Jane Flax, *Thinking Fragments: Psychoanalysis, Feminism and Postmodernism in the Contemporary West* (Berkeley: University of California Press, 1990), p. 218.

10. Flax, *Disputed Subjects: Essays on Psychoanalysis, Politics, and Philosophy* (New York: Routledge, 1993), pp. 108, 103.

11. Flax, *Thinking Fragments*, pp. 218–19.

12. Mary Shelley, *Frankenstein: Or, the Modern Prometheus* (New York: New American Library, 1965), p. 116. The quotation appeared at the close of a message that I recently received asking for more donations to the library of the Gay/Lesbian/Bisexual/Transgender Center at my university.

13. I challenge this idea, that the preoedipal exists somewhere outside of culture and thus its representations in language must be interventions from outside the symbolic, in "Adventures in the World of the Symbolic: Emily Dickinson and Metaphor," in *Feminist Measures: Soundings in Poetry and Theory*, ed. Cristanne Miller and Lynn Keller (Ann Arbor: University of Michigan Press, 1994), pp. 139–62.

14. De Lauretis, *The Practice of Love: Lesbian Sexuality and Perverse Desire* (Bloomington: Indiana University Press, 1994), p. 192.

15. Lizzie Thynne, "The Space Between: Daughters and Lovers in *Anne Trister*," in *Romance*

Revisited, ed. Lynne Pearce and Jackie Stacey (New York: New York University Press, 1995), p. 105. Subsequent references will be cited parenthetically in the text.

16. Nancy Chodorow, *Femininities, Masculinities, Sexualities: Freud and Beyond* (Lexington: University Press of Kentucky, 1994), p. 82.

17. Adrienne Rich, "Compulsory Heterosexuality and Lesbian Existence," in *Blood, Bread, and Poetry: Selected Prose 1979–1985* (New York: W. W. Norton, 1986), p. 51. Subsequent references will be cited parenthetically in the text.

18. In her study of male homosocial bonding, *Between Men: English Literature and Male Homosocial Desire* (New York: Columbia University Press, 1985), Eve Kosofsky Sedgwick specifically acknowledges the existence of "an intelligible continuum of aims, emotions, and valuations" that link "lesbianism with other forms of women's attention to women: the bond of mother and daughter, for instance, the bond of sister and sister, women's friendships, 'networking,' and the activities of feminism" (p. 2). (Her footnote is to Adrienne Rich.) Although she refers to the sense of women's "cultural resources of resistance, adaptation, revision, and survival" (p. 18), Sedgwick's emphasis is on the political power that causes female sexuality to be used for the maintenance of male bonding. "Better analyses," she notes, "are needed of the relations between female-homosocial and male-homosocial structures" (p. 18).

Chapter Forty-seven

The End of the Novel of Love (1997)

Vivian Gornick

Gornick is a powerful writer, and her argument that the "idea of love as a means of illumination—in literature as in life" is over is provocative and important, whether or not one agrees with it. Her point is that the world has changed so much, particularly in reference to the experience and understanding of women, that romantic love as a metaphor for transcendence and self-understanding is no longer credible.

When I was a girl the whole world believed in love. My mother, a communist and a romantic, said to me. "You're smart, make something of yourself, but always remember, love is the most important thing in a woman's life." Across the street Grace Levine's mother, a woman who lit candles on Friday night and was afraid of everything that moved, whispered to her daughter. "Don't do like I did. Marry a man you love." Around the corner Elise Goldberg's mother slipped her arms into a Persian lamb coat and shrugged, "It's just as easy to fall in love with a rich man as a poor man," and she meant it. Love was the operative word.

It was a working-class, immigrant neighborhood in the Bronx. Most of our homes were marked by an atmosphere of emotional indifference, if not open antagonism. I don't think I ever walked into a house where I felt the parents loved each other, or had once loved each other. I knew early that the people around me had married out of a set of necessities stronger than the absence of passion. Still, everyone believed in love. *Our* lives might be small and frightened, but in the ideal life, it was felt—the educated life, the brave life, the life out in the world—love would not only be pursued, it would be achieved: and once achieved transform existence: create a rich, deep, textured prose out of the ordinary reports of daily life. The promise of love alone would one day give us the courage to leave these caution-ridden precincts and turn our faces toward: experience. That was it, really. Love, we knew, would put us at the center of our own experience. In fact, only if we gave ourselves over to passion, without stint and without contractual assurance, would we *have* experience.

Oh yes, we in the Bronx knew that love was the supreme accomplishment. We knew it because we, too, had been reading *Anna Karenina* and *Madame Bovary* and

Vivian Gornick, "The End of the Novel of Love," *Chronicle of Higher Education*, vol. 43, no. 49 (August 15, 1997): B4–5. © 1997 by Vivian Gornick. Reprinted by permission.

The Age of Innocence all our lives, as well as the ten thousand middlebrow versions of those books, and the dime-store novels too. We knew it because we lived in a culture soaked through with the conviction that love had transforming powers: To know pass was to break the bonds of the frightened, ignorant self. There might, of course, be a price to pay. One might be risking the shelter of respectability if one fell in love with the wrong person, but in return for such loss one would be gaining the only knowledge worth having. The very meaning of human risk was embedded in the pursuit of love.

We in the Bronx believed as we did because for 150 years in the West the idea of romantic love had been emblematic of the search for self-understanding: an influence that touched every aspect of the world enterprise. In literature, good and great writers alike sounded depths of thought and emotion that made readers feel the life within themselves in the presence of words written to celebrate the powers of love.

I remember the first time—it wasn't so long ago—I turned the last page of a novel and it came over me that love as a metaphor was over. The book was Jane Smiley's *The Age of Grief*. I'd thought it a fine piece of work, resonant with years of observation about something profound, but it struck me as a small good thing, and I remember sitting with the book on my lap wondering. Why only a small good thing? Why am I not stirred to a sense of larger doings here? Almost immediately I answered myself with. Love is the problem here. It's the wrong catalyst. It doesn't complicate the issue, it reduces it. My own thought startled me. I'd never before considered that love might dilute the strength of a good novel rather than gather it in.

The situation in *The Age of Grief* is that of a couple in their thirties who've been together 10 or 12 years, living in some small city, the parents of three little girls. The narrating voice is that of the husband: grave, intelligent, trustworthy. One winter night, he tells us, driving home from a church concert in which the wife has performed—he at the wheel with one of the children beside him, she in back with the other two—he hears her say, "I'll never be happy again." He looks at her face in the rear-view mirror. Suddenly he knows that she is having an affair, and all he wants is that she not confess.

What follows then is a wonderfully told tale of the months of family life that pass as the husband hopes to avert open crisis, and the wife wanders about like a sick cat, trying to muddle silently through her own sadness and suppressed desire. The climax occurs when the entire family falls ill with the flu and the husband sees them through so beautifully, so decently, that you, the reader, could weep, reading his scrupulous recapitulation of the fever that has at last overtaken them all. The day after the last child recovers, the wife bolts. And then she returns.

The genius of the narrative lies in the desperate calm with which the husband charts the weeks and months of unhappy suspicion, all the while a piece of unwanted knowledge is collecting steadily in him. "I am 35 years old," he tells us in the middle of his story, "and it seems to me that I have arrived at the age of grief. Others arrive there sooner. Almost no one arrives much later. . . . It is not only that we know that love ends, children are stolen, parents die feeling that their lives have been meaning-less. . . . It is more that . . . after all that schooling, all that care . . . the cup must come around, cannot pass from you, and it is the same cup of pain that every mortal drinks from." There. He has said what he came to say, and said it quite clearly.

The final paragraph reads: "Shall I say I welcomed my wife back with great sadness, more sadness than I had felt at any other time? It seems to me that marriage is a small container, after all, barely large enough to hold some children. Two inner lives, two lifelong meditations of whatever complexity, burst out of it and out of it, cracking it, deforming it. Or maybe it is not a thing at all, nothing, something not present. I don't know, but I can't help thinking about it."

The situation is worthy of Tolstoy or Flaubert or Wharton—a pair of protagonists moving into the long littleness of life, falling into chaos when one of them jerks in the wind for a moment, refusing to accommodate the stasis ahead—and while Jane Smiley may not have the skills of the masters, her gifts are nonetheless considerable. Yet, for me, *The Age of Grief* failed to grow large. The story moved me to sadness and regret, but it could not persuade me to the tragic or the inevitable. I found myself arguing with its premises.

It was necessary that I believe the wife is driven to risk all for an experience that promises to give her back a self she has failed to achieve in her marriage; but the conviction that such knowledge would be hers if she went off with the man she was now burning for refused to exert power over me. As the novella progressed I saw that I was thinking. If this woman leaves her husband for her lover, in six months she'll be right back where she started. There isn't a reason in the world to believe she will know herself any better with the second man than she does with the first. This passion of hers is a quick fix, a soporific. We've all been through it a thousand times. She's foolish to think love will save her. I certainly don't.

And then again, I thought, If she *does* go off, what is she actually risking? When Emma Bovary was loosening her stays with a man other than her husband, or Anna Karenina running away from hers, or Newbold Archer agonizing over whether to leave New York with Ellen Olenska, people were indeed risking all for love. Bourgeois respectability had the power to make of these characters social pariahs. Strength would be needed to sustain exile. Out of such risk taking might come the force of suffering that brings clarity and insight. Today, there are no penalties to pay, no world of respectability to be excommunicated from. Bourgeois society as such is over. If the wife in *The Age of Grief* walks away from her marriage, she'll set up housekeeping on the other side of town with a man named Jerry instead of one named Dave, in ten minutes make a social life the equivalent of the one her first marriage had provided her, and in two years she and her new husband will find themselves at a dinner party that includes the ex-husband and his new wife: everyone chatting amiably. Two years after that, one morning in the kitchen or one night in the bedroom, she'll slip and call Jerry Dave, and they will both laugh.

For this character to be hungering for erotic passion at a crucial moment when she's up against all that she has, and has not, done with her life struck me as implausible. She *had* to know better. I thought. On the other hand, if blissing out was what the wife was up to, then the story could be made large only if the author of her being called her on it. But Jane Smiley wasn't calling her on it. She was using the illicit passion of the wife straight—as though she expected me, the reader, to accept erotic longing at face value, as an urgency compelling enough to bring into relief the shocking ordinariness of these stricken lives. But I did not accept it. I could not. I know too much about love. We *all* know too much. I could not accept as true that a love affair would bring the wife (and therefore me) to feel deeply the consequence of her original insufficient intentions. And that is why an otherwise excellent novella struck me as a small good thing. Embedded as it was in a convention, not a truth, the conceit itself prevented the writer from asking the questions necessary to deepen thought and action.

Only 40 years ago most of us occupied a world remarkably free of direct experience. We grew up expecting to repeat our parents' lives: certainly, we repeated their platitudes. However much some of us may have acted the girl or the boy of advanced ideas, we all (secretly or otherwise) subscribed to Aristophanes' fable: Somewhere out there was our fated "other half," the one true love that would rescue us from loneliness and drift. This expectation was central to our lives: what is otherwise known as a self-fulfilling prophecy.

When love-and-marriage failed to deliver us to the promised land within, we became sad, angry, confused. We thought we'd been cheated. We still believed in love but clearly: You could make a mistake. You could take Wrong for Right, and then marriage not only failed to rescue, it became existential hell.

There was, of course, always divorce, but 40 years ago nobody *we* knew got divorced. We'd also heard about psychoanalysis (from movies and novels), but in the Bronx such treatment was taken as proof of irredeemable defeat—hardly a legitimate search for relief from the confusion in which many of us were passing our lives. As yet, there was nothing for it but to endure. We became fond of responding to irony in novels of love as one would to a finger pressed against the flesh near an open sore.

Good writers, of course, had the boldness to deliver border reports from the country of married sadness and anger, and these reports were received with morbid excitement. In the '50s John Cheever's stories of marital disillusion seemed profound. That famous climactic moment in Cheever when the husband *realizes* his wife holds him in contempt, or the wife *knows* the husband is committing adultery, these moments delivered an electric charge. The knowledge encoded in them seemed literally stunning, leaving the characters riven, their lives destroyed. Who, after all, could go on after this? Then came the shocker—the thing that made the story large, awesome, terrible—they *did* go on like this. The reader came to the last sentence and sat staring into space, the void opening at her feet.

The world was changing but it was not yet changed; that's why Cheever's stories had such power. Great-love-and-lasting-marriage was still the expectation upon which lives were predicated; until the moment the expectation dissolved out, it seemed immutable. We were living Cheever's stories, but we did not know how to make any larger sense of things than he had made of them.

Then, within a generation, everything everywhere in the world conspired to *make* us know. Suddenly, there *was* divorce. And psychotherapy. And sex and feminism and drugs, as well as crime in the street. In short, it was the Fall of Rome. From one end of the city to the other. Even in the Bronx. Frightening, but exciting as well. We who had married for life were reprieved: at liberty to correct the mistake. We would fall in love again, and this time we'd do it right. *Now* we would discover ourselves, emerge into the fine, free creatures we had always known we could be. We got divorced, and we went into therapy. And this is what happened:

We loved once, and we loved badly. We loved again, and again we loved badly. We did it a third time, and we were no longer living in a world free of experience. We saw that love did not make us tender, wise, or compassionate. Under its influence we gave up neither our fears nor our angers. Within ourselves we remained unchanged. The development was an astonishment: not at all what had been expected. The atmosphere became charged with revelation, and it altered us permanently as a culture.

A couple of years ago, at dinner with a couple I've known for years—he is an academic, she a poet; he makes the money, she does not—I fell into some aimless exchange about marriage, in the middle of which the husband had occasion to announce casually. "Of course, it's a given that the one who does the supporting holds the one being supported in contempt." The wife stared at him. He stared back. Then she gasped, "Henry! I can hardly believe you've said what you've just said." He looked at her, unperturbed. "What is it?" he asked mildly. "Is this something we don't all know?" Silence fell on the company. She looked bleak, he remained impassive. A minute later she said the equivalent of Pass the salt. I remember thinking, If life was still a Cheever story this would have been the climactic moment, but as it is now 1995 it is only a break in the conversation.

Henry was speaking a hard, simple truth we have all absorbed. Love, this truth tells us, like food or air, is necessary but insufficient: It cannot do for us what we must do for ourselves. Certainly, it can no longer act as an organizing principle. Romantic love now seems a yearning to dive down into feeling and come up magically changed; when what is required for the making of a self is the deliberate pursuit of consciousness. Knowing *this* to be the larger truth, as many of us do, the idea of love as a means of illumination—in literature as in life—now comes as something of an anticlimax. If in a story (as in actuality) neither the characters nor the narrator realizes, *to begin with,* that love is not what it's all about, then the story will know at its conclusion only what it knows at the beginning. Such a tale may establish sorrow and sentimental regret, but it cannot achieve a sense of the tragic or the inevitable. The panic with which people discover that the life they are living is the only one they are able to make—this panic cannot be addressed if the major event in the story is going to be a new affair.

It is not that thousands of people aren't doing exactly what the husband and the wife in *The Age of Grief* are doing—of course they are, every hour on the hour. It is, rather, that their situation no longer signifies. It cannot provide insight, it can only repeat a view of things that today feels sadly tired and without the power to make one see anew. Somewhat like a going-nowhere analysis in which we recite again and again what we have repeatedly failed to act on. Such failure transforms insight into ritual. Ritual sustains the status quo. When a patient repeats an insight ritually he is living in bad faith: without intentionality, in thrall to passive longing. When a writer sits down to tell a tale based on experience that in effect has become "ritual," it is the equivalent of living in bad faith.

In great novels we always feel that the writer, at the time of the writing, knows as much as anyone around can know, and is struggling to make sense of what is perceived somewhere in the nerve endings if not yet in clarified consciousness. When a novel gives us *less* than many of us know—and is content with what is being given—we have middlebrow writing. Such writing—however intelligent its author, however excellent its prose—is closer to the sentimental than to the real. The reader senses that the work is sentimental because the metaphors are inaccurate: approximate, not exact. To get to those nerve endings a metaphor must be exact, not approximate. The exact metaphor is writer's gold.

A hundred years ago love provided such gold. When Lawrence, James, Stendhal were writing, readers felt themselves in the presence of men diving down into the depths. For these writers love was a snake pit, marriage a menacing drama. Their insights were penetrated through with anxiety, their stories accumulated dread. Love, then, provided the context within which an enormous amount could and did get said. The writing promised self-understanding—that alone which gives courage for life—and it delivered.

Even 50 years ago—when most of us occupied a world free of experience—it could still deliver, and at the hands of writers who were good, not great. In 1950, Rosamond Lehmann—in the 1930s she had been Jane Smiley's English counterpart— wrote a novel in which the central situation is that of a man who falls in love with a pair of sisters. He marries one, and within a few years begins sleeping with the other. This story, at the time of the writing, struck readers as bold, thrilling, dramatic. I picked the book up a few years ago, ready to experience a literary curiosity, but I found the novel strong and memorable. Lehmann had made of the situation a remarkable context for the weakness of human intensity, and had let her characters live long enough to see that each of their lives had taken shape around the weakness. A novelist formed in a time when love was everything had used love to explore fully a flash of true insight. I turned the last page feeling penetrated by the pitiableness of life.

Could this book have been written today? Never. Its power is wholly dependent on the static quality of the world against which its characters are struggling. Everything they learn and do and become takes place against that restraint. It is because they cannot get out that the intensity builds and they break the taboo. The broken taboo allows them into themselves. That is how the story deepens.

Put romantic love at the center of a novel today, and who could be persuaded that in its pursuit the characters are going to get to something large? That love is going to throw them up against themselves in such a way that we will all learn something important about how we got to be as we are, or how the time in which we live got to be as it is? No one, it seems to me. Today, I think, love as a metaphor is an act of nostalgia, not of discovery.

Part VII

The Popular Romance
Readers, Writers, Critics

Like Mary Wollstonecraft, George Eliot believed that the cause of women would never advance without serious intellectual effort, undermined by "silly" novels devoted exclusively to love. Between Eliot's condemnation and the rise of popular culture studies in the twentieth century, the enormous industry of mass-market popular romance such as the Harlequin novel was consolidated, and critics began to study the genre in earnest. Among the first to take this genre seriously enough to comment on, Ann Snitow found these forms to be retrogressive and antifeminist to the point of being a "pornography of the emotions." Later a famous study by the sociologist Janice Radway concluded that women use the narrative shape of romance to express a wish for reform in their intimate relations and to manage their private time away from domestic duties. From the point of view of a literary critic, Tania Modleski sees a great deal of anger as well as melting submission in the way literary heroines respond to the hero. Since then, feminist romance writers and readers have written their own urgent defenses of romance as a form of female power and adventure that is capable of transforming gender relations.

It is appropriate to examine other forms of media besides fictional writing, such as film, television, magazines, music, advertising and self-help books. All these have subsumed print fiction in their visibility, influence, and preoccupation with romance. Women probably form the majority of the audience for these social forms when their focus is romantic love, and the selections here analyze the ways the mass media construct masculinity and femininity in representing the ideal of romance.

Chapter Forty-eight

From Silly Novels by Lady Novelists (1856)

George Eliot

The association of women with "silly" romances has a long tradition, as we can see in this highly critical essay by one of the great novelists of the nineteenth century. The context in which Eliot wrote, midcentury England, was one in which female authors had a great deal of difficulty being taken seriously. For this reason Eliot wished to dissociate the nobility of purpose in the best writing from the frivolity of romantic writing by women.

Silly novels by Lady Novelists are a genus with many species, determined by the particular quality of silliness that predominates in them—the frothy, the prosy, the pious, or the pedantic. But it is a mixture of all these—a composite order of feminine fatuity, that produces the largest class of such novels, which we shall distinguish as the *mind-and-millinery* species. The heroine is usually an heiress, probably a peeress in her own right, with perhaps a vicious baronet, an amiable duke, and an irresistible younger son of a marquis as lovers in the foreground, a clergyman and a poet sighing for her in the middle distance, and a crowd of undefined adorers dimly indicated beyond. Her eyes and her wit are both dazzling; her nose and her morals are alike free from any tendency to irregularity; she has a superb *contralto* and a superb intellect; she is perfectly well-dressed and perfectly religious; she dances like a sylph, and reads the Bible in the original tongues. Or it may be that the heroine is not an heiress—that rank and wealth are the only things in which she is deficient; but she infallibly gets into high society, she has the triumph of refusing many matches and securing the best, and she wears some family jewels or other as a sort of crown of righteousness at the end. Rakish men either bite their lips in impotent confusion at her repartees, or are touched to penitence by her reproofs, which, on appropriate occasions, rise to a lofty strain of rhetoric; indeed, there is a general propensity in her to make speeches, and to rhapsodize at some length when she retires to her bedroom. In her recorded conversations she is amazingly eloquent, and in her unrecorded conversations, amazingly witty. She is understood to have a depth of insight that looks through and through the shallow theories of philosophers, and her

From George Eliot, "Silly Novels by Lady Novelists," *Westminster Review*, vol. 66 (October 1856): 442–61.

superior instincts are a sort of dial by which men have only to set their clocks and watches, and all will go well. The men play a very subordinate part by her side. You are consoled now and then by a hint that they have affairs, which keeps you in mind that the working-day business of the world is somehow being carried on, but ostensibly the final cause of their existence is that they may accompany the heroine on her "starring" expedition through life. They see her at a ball, and are dazzled; at a flower-show, and they are fascinated; on a riding excursion, and they are witched by her noble horsemanship; at church, and they are awed by the sweet solemnity of her demeanour. She is the ideal woman in feelings, faculties, and flounces. For all this, she as often as not marries the wrong person to begin with, and she suffers terribly from the plots and intrigues of the vicious baronet; but even death has a soft place in his heart for such a paragon, and remedies all mistakes for her just at the right moment. The vicious baronet is sure to be killed in a duel, and the tedious husband dies in his bed requesting his wife, as a particular favour to him, to marry the man she loves best, and having already dispatched a note to the lover informing him of the comfortable arrangement. Before matters arrive at this desirable issue our feelings are tried by seeing the noble, lovely, and gifted heroine pass through many *mauvais moments,* but we have the satisfaction of knowing that her sorrows are wept into embroidered pocket-handkerchiefs, that her fainting form reclines on the very best upholstery, and that whatever vicissitudes she may undergo, from being dashed out of her carriage to having her head shaved in a fever, she comes out of them all with a complexion more blooming and locks more redundant than ever.

We may remark, by the way, that we have been relieved from a serious scruple by discovering that silly novels by lady novelists rarely introduce us into any other than very lofty and fashionable society. We had imagined that destitute women turned novelists, as they turned governesses, because they had no other "lady-like" means of getting their bread. On this supposition, vacillating syntax and improbable incident had a certain pathos for us, like the extremely supererogatory pincushions and ill-devised nightcaps that are offered for sale by a blind man. We felt the commodity to be a nuisance, but we were glad to think that the money went to relieve the necessitous, and we pictured to ourselves lonely women struggling for a maintenance, or wives and daughters devoting themselves to the production of "copy" out of pure heroism,—perhaps to pay their husband's debts, or to purchase luxuries for a sick father. Under these impressions we shrank from criticising a lady's novel: her English might be faulty, but, we said to ourselves, her motives are irreproachable; her imagination may be uninventive, but her patience is untiring. Empty writing was excused by an empty stomach, and twaddle was consecrated by tears. But no! This theory of ours, like many other pretty theories, has had to give way before observation. Women's silly novels, we are now convinced, are written under totally different circumstances. The fair writers have evidently never talked to a tradesman except from a carriage window; they have no notion of the working-classes except as "dependents"; they think five hundred a-year a miserable pittance; Belgravia and "baronial halls" are their primary truths; and they have no idea of feeling interest in any man who is not at least a great landed proprietor, if not a prime minister. It is clear that they write in elegant boudoirs, with violet-coloured ink and a ruby pen;

that they must be entirely indifferent to publishers' accounts, and inexperienced in every form of poverty except poverty of brains. It is true that we are constantly struck with the want of verisimilitude in their representations of the high society in which they seem to live; but then they betray no closer acquaintance with any other form of life. If their and peers and peeresses are improbable, their literary men, tradespeople, and cottagers are impossible; and their intellect seems to have the peculiar impartiality of reproducing both what they *have* seen and heard, and what they have *not* seen and heard, with equal unfaithfulness.

There are few women, we suppose, who have not seen something of children under five years of age, yet in "Compensation," a recent novel of the mind-and-millinery species, which calls itself a "story of real life," we have a child of four and a half years old talking in this Ossianic fashion—

> "Oh, I am so happy, dear gran'mamma;—I have seen,—I have seen such a delightful person: he is like everything beautiful,—like the smell of sweet flowers, and the view from Ben Lomond;—or no, *better than that*—he is like what I think of and see when I am very, very happy; and he is really like mamma, too, when she sings; and his forehead is like *that distant sea*," she continued, pointing to the blue Mediterranean; "there seems no end—no end; or like the clusters of stars I like best to look at on a warm fine night. . . . Don't look so . . . your forehead is like Loch Lomond, when the wind is blowing and the sun is gone in; I like the sunshine best when the lake is smooth. . . . So now—I like it better than ever . . . it is more beautiful still from the dark cloud that has gone over it, *when the sun suddenly lights up all the colours of the forests and shining purple rocks, and it is all reflected in the waters below.*"

We are not surprised to learn that the mother of this infant phenomenon, who exhibits symptoms so alarmingly like those of adolescence repressed by gin, is herself a phœnix. We are assured, again and again, that she had a remarkably original mind, that she was a genius, and "conscious of her originality," and she was fortunate enough to have a lover who was also a genius, and a man of "most original mind."

This lover, we read, though "wonderfully similar" to her "in powers and capacity," was "infinitely superior to her in faith and development," and she saw in him the " 'Agape'—so rare to find—of which she had read and admired the meaning in her Greek Testament; having, *from her great facility in learning languages,* read the Scriptures in their original *tongues.*" Of course! Greek and Hebrew are mere play to a heroine; Sanscrit is no more than *a b c* to her; and she can talk with perfect correctness in any language except English. She is a polking polyglott, a Creuzer in crinoline. Poor men! There are so few of you who know even Hebrew; you think it something to boast of if, like Bolingbroke, you only "understand that sort of learning, and what is writ about it;" and you are perhaps adoring women who can think slightingly of you in all the Semitic languages successively. But, then, as we are almost invariably told, that a heroine has a "beautifully small head," and as her intellect has probably been early invigorated by an attention to costume and deportment, we may conclude that she can pick up the Oriental tongues, to say nothing of their dialects, with the same aërial facility that the butterfly sips nectar. Besides, there can be no difficulty in conceiving the depth of the heroine's erudition, when that of the authoress is so evident.

In "Laura Gay," another novel of the same school, the heroine seems less at home in Greek and Hebrew, but she makes up for the deficiency by a quite playful familiarity with the Latin classics—with the "dear old Virgil," "the graceful Horace, the humane Cicero, and the pleasant Livy;" indeed, it is such a matter of course with her to quote Latin, that she does it at a pic-nic in a very mixed company of ladies and gentlemen, having, we are told, "no conception that the nobler sex were capable of jealousy on this subject. And if, indeed," continues the biographer of Laura Gay, "the wisest and noblest portion of that sex were in the majority, no such sentiment would exist; but while Miss Wyndhams and Mr. Redfords abound, great sacrifices must be made to their existence." Such sacrifices, we presume, as abstaining from Latin quotations, of extremely moderate interest and applicability, which the wise and noble minority of the other sex would be quite as willing to dispense with as the foolish and ignoble majority. It is as little the custom of well-bred men as of well-bred women to quote Latin in mixed parties; they can contain their familiarity with "the humane Cicero" without allowing it to boil over in ordinary conversation, and even references to "the pleasant Livy" are not absolutely irrepressible. But Ciceronian Latin is the mildest form of Miss Gay's conversational power. Being on the Palatine with a party of sightseers, she falls into the following vein of well-rounded remark: "Truth can only be pure objectively, for even in the creeds where it predominates, being subjective, and parcelled out into portions, each of these necessarily receives a hue of idiosyncrasy, that is, a taint of superstition more or less strong; while in such creeds as the Roman Catholic, ignorance, interest, the bias of ancient idolatries, and the force of authority, have gradually accumulated on the pure truth, and trans-formed it, at last, into a mass of superstition for the majority of its votaries; and how few are there, alas! whose zeal, courage, and intellectual energy are equal to the analysis of this accumulation, and to the discovery of the pearl of great price which lies hidden beneath this heap of rubbish." We have often met with women much more novel and profound in their observations than Laura Gay, but rarely with any so inopportunely long winded. A clerical lord, who is half in love with her, is alarmed by the daring remarks just quoted, and begins to suspect that she is inclined to free-thinking. But he is mistaken; when in a moment of sorrow he delicately begs leave to "recal to her memory, a *depôt* of strength and consolation under affliction, which, until we are hard pressed by the trials of life, we are too apt to forget," we learn that she really has "recurrence to that sacred depôt," together with the tea-pot. There is a certain flavour of orthodoxy mixed with the parade of fortunes and fine carriages in "Laura Gay," but it is an orthodoxy mitigated by study of "the humane Cicero," and by an "intellectual disposition to analyse."

"Compensation" is much more heavily dosed with doctrine, but then it has a treble amount of snobbish worldliness and absurd incident to tickle the palate of pious frivolity. Linda, the heroine, is still more speculative and spiritual than Laura Gay, but she has been "presented," and has more, and far grander, lovers; very wicked and fascinating women are introduced—even a French *lionne;* and no ex-pense is spared to get up as exciting a story as you will find in the most immoral novels. In fact, it is a wonderful *pot pourri* of Almack's, Scotch second-sight, Mr. Rogers's breakfasts, Italian brigands, death-bed conversions, superior authoresses,

Italian mistresses, and attempts at poisoning old ladies, the whole served up with a garnish of talk about "faith and development," and "most original minds." Even Miss Susan Barton, the superior authoress, whose pen moves in a "quick decided manner when she is composing," declines the finest opportunities of marriage; and though old enough to be Linda's mother (since we are told that she refused Linda's father), has her hand sought by a young earl, the heroine's rejected lover. Of course, genius and morality must be backed by eligible offers, or they would seem rather a dull affair; and piety, like other things, in order to be *comme il faut*, must be in "society," and have admittance to the best circles.

"Rank and Beauty" is a more frothy and less religious variety of the mind-and-millinery species. The heroine, we are told, "if she inherited her father's pride of birth and her mother's beauty of person, had in herself a tone of enthusiastic feeling that perhaps belongs to her age even in the lowly born, but which is refined into the high spirit of wild romance only in the far descended, who feel that it is their best inheritance." This enthusiastic young lady, by dint of reading the newspaper to her father, falls in love with the *prime minister,* who, through the medium of leading articles and "the *resumé* of the debates," shines upon her imagination as a bright particular star, which has no parallax for her, living in the country as simple Miss Wyndham. But she forthwith becomes Baroness Umfraville in her own right, astonishes the world with her beauty and accomplishments when she bursts upon it from her mansion in Spring Gardens, and, as you foresee, will presently come into contact with the unseen *objet aimé.* Perhaps the words "prime minister" suggest to you a wrinkled or obese sexagenarian; but pray dismiss the image. Lord Rupert Conway has been "called while still almost a youth to the first situation which a subject can hold in the *universe,*" and even leading articles and a *resumé* of the debates have not conjured up a dream that surpasses the fact.

> The door opened again, and Lord Rupert Conway entered. Evelyn gave one glance. It was enough; she was not disappointed. It seemed as if a picture on which she had long gazed was suddenly instinct with life, and had stepped from its frame before her. His tall figure, the distinguished simplicity of his air—it was a living Vandyke, a cavalier, one of his noble cavalier ancestors, or one to whom her fancy had always likened him, who long of yore had, with an Umfraville, fought the Paynim far beyond sea. Was this reality?

Very little like it, certainly.

By-and-by, it becomes evident that the ministerial heart is touched. Lady Umfraville is on a visit to the Queen at Windsor, and,

> The last evening of her stay, when they returned from riding, Mr. Wyndham took her and a large party to the top of the Keep, to see the view. She was leaning on the battlements, gazing from that "stately height" at the prospect beneath her, when Lord Rupert was by her side. "What an unrivalled view!" exclaimed she.
>
> "Yes, it would have been wrong to go without having been up here. You are pleased with your visit?"
>
> "Enchanted! A Queen to live and die under, to live and die for!"
>
> "Ha!" cried he, with sudden emotion, and with a *eureka* expression of countenance, as if he had *indeed found a heart in unison with his own.*

The "*eureka* expression of countenance," you see at once to be prophetic of marriage at the end of the third volume; but before that desirable consummation, there are very complicated misunderstandings, arising chiefly from the vindictive plotting of Sir Luttrell Wycherley, who is a genius, a poet, and in every way a most remarkable character indeed. He is not only a romantic poet, but a hardened rake and a cynical wit; yet his deep passion for Lady Umfraville has so impoverished his epigrammatic talent, that he cuts an extremely poor figure in conversation. When she rejects him, he rushes into the shrubbery, and rolls himself in the dirt; and on recovering, devotes himself to the most diabolical and laborious schemes of vengeance, in the course of which he disguises himself as a quack physician, and enters into general practice, foreseeing that Evelyn will fall ill, and that he shall be called in to attend her. At last, when all his schemes are frustrated, he takes leave of her in a long letter, written, as you will perceive from the following passage, entirely in the style of an eminent literary man:

> "Oh, lady, nursed in pomp and pleasure, will you ever cast one thought upon the miserable being who addresses you? Will you ever, as your gilded galley is floating down the unruffled stream of prosperity, will you ever, while lulled by the sweetest music—thine own praises,—hear the far-off sigh from that world to which I am going?"

On the whole, however, frothy as it is, we rather prefer "Rank and Beauty" to the other two novels we have mentioned. The dialogue is more natural and spirited; there is some frank ignorance, and no pedantry; and you are allowed to take the heroine's astounding intellect upon trust, without being called on to read her conversational refutations of sceptics and philosophers, or her rhetorical solutions of the mysteries of the universe.

Chapter Forty-nine

Mass Market Romance

Pornography for Women Is Different (1979)

Ann Snitow

In this important feminist essay, Snitow analyzes romance fiction as a kind of "pornog-raphy for women," a glossing over of women's role in late capitalism. Until Snitow's work and that of another critic, Ann Douglas, who wrote about mass-media romance as "soft-porn culture" in 1980, there was no serious consideration of the genre, which was felt to be beneath the purview of literary or feminist criticism.

I

Last year 109 million romantic novels were sold under an imprint you will not see in the *New York Times* best-seller lists or advertised in its *Book Review*. The publisher is Harlequin Enterprises, Ltd., a Canadian company, and its success, a growth of 400 percent since 1976, is typical of the boom in romantic fiction marketed for women.[1]

At a bookstore or drugstore a Harlequin Romance costs 95¢, but the company does a large percentage of its business through the mail, sending 8 titles a month to 12 million subscribers in North America. Since a Harlequin is almost always 188 pages long (55,000–58,000 words), subscribers could be reading about three hundred and seventy-five pages a week. Reading is more private and more absorbing than televi-sion. A book requires stopping the housework, waiting for that lunch or coffee break at the office. "Your passport to a dream," say the television ads for Harlequins, which picture a weary secretary sinking gratefully into solitary reading on her lunch hour.

If one includes the large number of novels published by other companies but essentially keeping to the Harlequin formula—"clean, easy to read love stories about contemporary people, set in exciting foreign places"[2]—the number of books of this specific genre being sold has risen to several hundred million a year. This is a figure in another statistical universe from the sales of books we usually call "bestsellers." This article offers a series of hypotheses about the appeal Harlequin romances have for the women reading them.

Ann Snitow, "Mass Market Romance: Pornography for Women Is Different," *Radical History Review*, vol. 20 (spring–summer 1979): 141–61. Reprinted by permission.

II

To analyze Harlequin romances is not to make any literary claims for them. Nevertheless, it would be at best grossly incurious, and at worst sadly limited, for literary critics to ignore a genre that millions and millions of women read voraciously. Though I propose to do a literary analysis of Harlequin romances as a way to get at the nature and power of their appeal, they are not art but rather what Lillian Robinson has called "leisure activities that *take the place* of art."[3] This is to say that they fill a place left empty for most people. How do they fill it, and with what?

After a recent talk I gave about Harlequin romances, a member of the audience asked, "Would a reader of Harlequin romances be insulted by your lecture?" This is a disturbing question because the terms I use here to describe the Harlequin formula and its appeal *are* insulting, but to whom? In describing the sensibility of the Harlequin type of romance, I am not presuming to describe the sensibility of its readers. In matters of popular culture, we are not what we eat.

The old line about commercial popular culture, that it is soma for the masses produced by a cynical elite, has been replaced, and properly so, by a more complex idea of the relation between the consumers and sellers of mass culture: in this newer view, popularity is by definition considered a species of vitality. In other words, consumers are not seen merely as passive repositories, empty vessels into which debilitating ideologies are poured. This recognition of the force of popular forms, of their appeal to the depth structures in all our minds, is an important development in our critical thinking.[4]

Certainly the romantic novels for women I will discuss here reflect a complex relationship between readers and publishers. Who is manipulating whom? Each publisher is the prisoner of past successes, trying to find again the somewhat mysterious combination of elements that made a particular book hit the taste of the street. The way in which people experience mass cultural products in a heterogeneous society is erratic, subject to many forces. Harlequins, for example, are only one strain in the mass paperback market aimed primarily at women readers. There are also Gothics (now rather passé), spectaculars, historical romances, family sagas, fotonovelas, and true confessions.[5] Each one of these has its own species of appeal. Does each also have its own specific audience? The mass audience may be manipulated in some ways and may be controlling the market in others but it is also and always omnivorous, capable of digesting contradictory cultural impulses and at the same time resisting suggestion altogether.

In this essay I try to steer a careful course between critical extremes, neither assuming that romance novels are dope for catatonic secretaries, nor claiming for them a rebellious core of psychological vitality. I observe in these books neither an effective top-down propaganda effort against women's liberation, nor a covert flowering of female sexuality. Instead, I see them as accurate descriptions of certain *selected* elements of female consciousness. These novels are too pallid to shape consciousness but they feed certain regressive elements in the female experience. To observe that they express primal structures in our social relations is not to claim either a cathartic usefulness for them or a dangerous power to keep women in their place.

The books are interesting because they define a set of relations, feelings, and assumptions that do indeed permeate our minds. They are *mass* paperbacks not only because they are easy to read pablum but also because they reflect—sometimes more, sometimes less consciously, sometimes amazingly naively—commonly experienced psychological and social elements in the daily lives of women. That the books are unrealistic, distorted, and flat are all facts beside the point. (I am not concerned here with developing an admiration for their buried poetics.) Their particular sort of unreality points to what elements in social life women are encouraged to ignore; their distortions point to larger distortions culture-wide; their lack of richness merely bares what is hidden in more inclusive, more personally controlled works of art, the particular nature of the satisfactions we are all led to seek by the conditions of our culture.

III

What is the Harlequin romance formula? The novels have no plot in the usual sense. All tension and problems arise from the fact that the Harlequin world is inhabited by two species incapable of communicating with each other, male and female. In this sense these Pollyanna books have their own dream-like truth: our culture produces a pathological experience of sex difference. The sexes have different needs and interests, certainly different experiences. They find each other utterly mystifying.

Since all action in the novels is described from the female point of view, the reader identifies with the heroine's efforts to decode the erratic gestures of "dark, tall and gravely handsome"[6] men, all mysterious strangers or powerful bosses. In a sense the usual relationship is reversed: woman is subject, man, object. There are more descriptions of his body than of hers ("Dark trousers fitted closely to lean hips and long muscular legs...") though her clothes are always minutely observed. He is the unknowable other, a sexual icon whose magic is maleness. The books are permeated by phallic worship. Male is good, male is exciting, without further points of reference. Cruelty, callousness, coldness, menace, are all equated with maleness and treated as a necessary part of the package: "It was an arrogant remark, but Sara had long since admitted his arrogance as part of his attraction."[7] She, on the other hand, is the subject, the one whose thoughts the reader knows, whose constant reevaluation of male moods and actions make up the story line.

The heroine is not involved in any overt adventure beyond trying to respond appropriately to male energy without losing her virginity. Virginity is a given here; sex means marriage and marriage, promised at the end, means, finally, there can be sex.

While the heroine waits for the hero's next move, her time is filled by tourism and by descriptions of consumer items: furniture, clothes, and gourmet foods. In *Writers Market* (1977) Harlequin Enterprises stipulates: "Emphasis on travel." (The exception is the occasional hospital novel. Like foreign places, hospitals offer removal from the household, heightened emotional states, and a supply of strangers.) Several of the books have passages that probably come straight out of guide books, but the *particular* setting is not the point, only that it is exotic, a place elsewhere.[8]

More space is filled by the question of what to wear. "She rummaged in her cases, discarding item after item, and eventually brought out a pair of purple cotton jeans and a matching shift. They were not new. She had bought them a couple of years ago. But fortunately her figure had changed little, and apart from a slight shrinkage in the pants which made them rather tighter than she would have liked, they looked serviceable."[9] Several things are going on here: the effort to find the right clothes for the occasion, the problem of staying thin, the problem of piecing together outfits from things that are not new. Finally, there is that shrinkage, a signal to the experienced Harlequin reader that the heroine, innocent as her intent may be in putting on jeans that are a little too tight, is wearing something revealing and will certainly be seen and noted by the hero in this vulnerable, passive act of self-exposure. (More about the pornographic aspects later. In any other titillating novel one would suspect a pun when tight pants are "serviceable" but in the context of the absolutely flat Harlequin style one might well be wrong. More, too, about this style later on.)

Though clothes are the number one filler in Harlequins, food and furniture are also important and usually described in the language of women's magazines:[10] croissants are served hot and crispy and are "crusty brown,"[11] while snapper is "filleted, crumbed and fried in butter" and tomato soup is "topped with grated cheese and parsley"[12] (this last a useful, practical suggestion anyone could try).

Harlequins revitalize daily routines by insisting that a woman combing her hair, a woman reaching up to put a plate on a high shelf (so that her knees show beneath the hem, if only there were a viewer), a woman doing what women do all day, is in a constant state of potential sexuality. You never can tell when you may be seen and being seen is a precious opportunity. Harlequin romances alternate between scenes of the hero and heroine together in which she does a lot of social lying to save face, pretending to be unaffected by the hero's presence while her body melts or shivers, and scenes in which the heroine is essentially alone, living in a cloud of absorption, preparing mentally and physically for the next contact.

The heroine is alone. Sometimes there is another woman, a competitor who is often more overtly aware of her sexuality than the heroine, but she is a shadow on the horizon. Sometimes there are potentially friendly females living in the next bungalow or working with the patient in the next bed, but they, too, are shadowy, not important to the real story, which consists entirely of an emotionally isolated woman trying to keep her virginity and her head when the only person she ever really talks to is the hero, whose motives and feelings are unclear: "She saw his words as a warning and would have liked to know whether he meant [them] to be."[13]

The heroine gets her man at the end, first, because she is an old-fashioned girl (this is a code for no premarital sex) and, second, because the hero gets ample opportunity to see her perform well in a number of female helping roles. In the course of a Harlequin romance, most heroines demonstrate passionate motherliness, good cooking, patience in adversity, efficient planning, and a good clothes sense, though these are skills and emotional capacities produced in emergencies, and are not, as in real life, a part of an invisible, glamorless work routine.

Though the heroines are pliable (they are rarely given particularized character traits; they are all Everywoman and can fit in comfortably with the life-style of the strong-willed heroes be they doctors, lawyers, or marine biologists doing experiments on tropical islands), it is still amazing that these novels end in marriage. After one hundred and fifty pages of mystification, unreadable looks, "hints of cruelty"[14] and wordless coldness, the thirty-page denouement is powerless to dispel the earlier impression of menace. Why should this heroine marry this man? And, one can ask with equal reason, why should this hero marry this woman? These endings do not ring true, but no doubt this is precisely their strength. A taste for psychological or social realism is unlikely to provide a Harlequin reader with a sustaining fantasy of rescue, of glamour, or of change. The Harlequin ending offers the impossible. It is pleasing to think that appearances are deceptive, that male coldness, absence, boredom, are not what they seem. The hero *seems* to be a horrible roué; he *seems* to be a hopeless, moody cripple; he *seems* to be cruel and unkind; or he *seems* to be indifferent to the heroine and interested only in his work; but always, at the end a rational explanation of all this appears. In spite of his coldness or preoccupation, the hero really loves the heroine and wants to marry her.

In fact, the Harlequin formula glorifies the distance between the sexes. Distance becomes titillating. The heroine's sexual inexperience adds to this excitement. What is this thing that awaits her on the other side of distance and mystery? Not knowing may be more sexy than finding out. Or perhaps the heroes are really fathers—obscure, forbidden objects of desire. Whatever they are, it is more exciting to wonder about them than to know them. In romanticized sexuality the pleasure lies in the distance itself. Waiting, anticipation, anxiety—these represent the high point of sexual experience.

Perhaps there is pleasure, too, in returning again and again to that breathless, ambivalent, nervous state *before* certainty or satiety. Insofar as women's great adventure, the one they are socially sanctioned to seek, is romance, adventurousness takes women always back to the first phase in love. Unlike work, which holds out the possible pleasures of development, of the exercise of faculties, sometimes even of advancement, the Harlequin form of romance depends on the heroine's being in a state of passivity, of not knowing. Once the heroine knows the hero loves her, the story is over. Nothing interesting remains. Harlequin statements in *Writers Market* stress "upbeat ending essential here" (1977). Here at least is a reliable product that reproduces for women the most interesting phase in the love/marriage cycle and knows just when to stop.

IV

What is the world view implied by the Harlequin romance formula? What are its implicit values? The novels present no overt moral super-structure. Female virginity is certainly an ideal, but an ideal without a history, without parental figures to support it or religious convictions to give it a context. Nor can one say money is a value; rather it is a given, rarely mentioned. Travel and work, though glamorous, are not really goals for the heroine either. They are holding patterns while she awaits love.

Of course, the highest good is the couple. All outside events are subordinated to the psychodrama of its formation. But the heroine must struggle to form the couple without appearing to do so. Her most marketable virtue is her blandness. And she is always proud when she manages to keep a calm façade. She lies constantly to hide her desires, to protect her reputation. She tries to cover up all signs of sexual feeling, upset, any extreme of emotion. She values being an ordinary woman and acting like one. (Indeed, for women, being ordinary and being attractive are equated in these novels. Heroes are of course expected to have a little more dash and sometimes sport scars.) Finally, the heroine's value system includes the given that men are all right, that they will turn into husbands, despite appearances to the contrary.

The world of Harlequin novels has no past. (At most, occasionally the plot requires a flashback.) Old people hardly appear except as benevolent peripheral presences. Young women have no visible parents, no ties to a before. Everyone is young though the hero is always quite a bit older than the heroine. Is this why there are no parents, because the lover is really *in loco parentis?*

Harlequins make no reference to a specific ethnic group or religion. (In this they differ from a new popular mass form, the family saga, which is dense with ethnic detail, national identity, *roots.*) Harlequins are aggressively secular: Christmas is always the tinsel not the religious Christmas. One might expect to find romance linked, if only sentimentally, to nature, to universal categories, to first and last things. Harlequins assiduously avoid this particular shortcut to emotion (while of course exploiting others). They reduce awe of the unknown to a speculation on the intentions of the cold, mean stranger and generally strip romance of its spiritual, transcendent aspect.

At the other extreme from the transcendent, Harlequins also avoid all mention of local peculiarities beyond the merely scenic. They reduce the allure of difference, of travel, to a mere travelogue. The couple is alone. There is no society, no context, only surroundings. Is this what the nuclear family feels like to many women? Or is this, once again, a fantasy of safety and seclusion, while in actuality the family is being invaded continually and is under pressures it cannot control?

The denatured quality of Harlequins is convenient for building an audience: anyone can identify. Or, rather, anyone can identify with the fantasy that places all the characters in an upper-class, polite environment familiar not in experience but in the ladies' magazines and on television. The realities of class—workers in dull jobs, poverty, real productive relations, social divisions of labor—are all, of course, entirely foreign to the world of the Harlequin. There are servants in the novels lest the heroine, like the reader, be left to do all the housework, but they are always loyal and glad to help. Heroines have familiar service jobs—they are teachers, nurses, nursery-maids—but the formula finds a way around depicting the limitations of these jobs. The heroine can do the work ordinary women do while still seeming glamorous to the reader either because of *where* the heroine does her work or how she is rescued from doing it.

All fiction is a closed system in many respects, its language mainlining into areas of our conscious and subconscious selves by routes that by-pass many of the things we know or believe about the real world of our daily experience. This by-passing is a form of pleasure, one of art's pleasing tricks. As Fred Kerner, Harlequin's director of publishing, said when describing the formula to prospective authors in *The Writer*: "The fantasy must have the same appeal that all of us discovered when we were first exposed to fairy tales as children."[15] I do not wish to imply that I would like to remove a Harlequin romance from the hands of its readers to replace it with an improving novel that includes a realistically written catalogue of woman's griefs under capitalism and in the family. My purpose here is diagnostic. A description of the pared-down Harlequin formula raises the question: What is it about this *particular* formula that makes it so suggestive, so popular, with such a large female readership, all living under capitalism, most living—or yearning to live—in some form of the family?

Harlequins fill a vacuum created by social conditions. When women try to picture excitement, the society offers them one vision, romance. When women try to imagine companionship, the society offers them one vision, male, sexual companionship. When women try to fantasize about success, mastery, the society offers them one vision, the power to attract a man. When women try to fantasize about sex, the society offers them taboos on most of its imaginable expressions except those that deal directly with arousing and satisfying men. When women try to project a unique self, the society offers them very few attractive images. True completion for women is nearly always presented as social, domestic, sexual.

One of our culture's most intense myths, the ideal of an individual who is brave and complete in isolation, is for men only. Women are grounded, enmeshed in civilization, in social connection, in family, and in love (a condition a feminist culture might well define as desirable) while all our culture's rich myths of individualism are essentially closed to them. Their one socially acceptable moment of transcendence is romance. This involves a constant return in imagination to those short moments in the female life cycle, courtship. With the exception of the occasional gourmet meal, which the heroine is often too nervous to eat, all other potential sources of pleasure are rigidly excluded from Harlequin romances. They reinforce the prevailing cultural code: pleasure for women is men. The ideal of romance presented in these books is a hungry monster that has gobbled up and digested all sorts of human pleasures.

There is another way in which Harlequin romances gloss over and obscure complex social relations: they are a static representation of a quickly changing situation—women's role in late capitalism. They offer a comfortably fixed image of the exchange between men and women at the very moment when the social actuality is confusing, shifting, frightening. The average American marriage now lasts about five years. A rape takes place every twelve minutes. While the social ferment of the sixties gave rise to the Gothic form in cheap fiction—family dramas that were claustrophic and anti-erotic compensations for an explosion of mobility and sexuality—in the seventies we have the blander Harlequins, novels that are picaresque and titillating, written for people who have so entirely suffered and absorbed the disappearance of the ideal of home that they don't want to hear about it any more. They want instead to read about premarital hopefulness.

Harlequin romances make bridges between contradictions; they soothe ambivalence. A brutal male sexuality is magically converted to romance; the war between men and women who cannot communicate ends in truce. Stereotyped female roles are charged with an unlikely glamour, and women's daily routines are revitalized by the pretense that they hide an ongoing sexual drama.

In a fine piece about modern Gothic romances, Joanna Russ points out that in these novels, " 'Occupation: Housewife' is simultaneously avoided, glamorized, and vindicated."[16] Female skills are exalted: it is good to nurture, good to observe every change in expression of the people around you, important to worry about how you look. As Russ says, the feminine mystique is defended and women are promised all sorts of psychological rewards for remaining loyal to it. Though in other respects, Gothics are very different from Harlequins, they are the same in this: both pretend that nothing has happened to unsettle the old, conventional bargain between the sexes. Small surface concessions are made to a new female independence (several researchers, misreading I believe, claim that the new heroines are brave and more interested in jobs than families)[17] but the novels mention the new female feistiness only to finally reassure readers that *plus ça change, plus c'est la même chose.* Independence is always presented as a mere counter in the sexual game, like a hairdo or any other flirtatious gesture; sexual feeling utterly defeats its early stirrings.

In fact, in Harlequin romances, sexual feeling is probably the main point. Like sex itself, the novels are set in an eternal present in which the actual present, a time of disturbing disruptions between the sexes, is dissolved and only a comfortably timeless, universal battle remains. The hero wants sex; the heroine wants it, too, but can only enjoy it after the love promise has finally been made and the ring is on her finger.

V

Are Harlequin romances pornography?

> She had never felt so helpless or so completely at the mercy of another human being . . . a being who could snap the slender column of her body with one squeeze of a steel-clad arm.
>
> No trace of tenderness softened the harsh pressure of his mouth on hers . . . there was only a savagely punishing intentness of purpose that cut off her breath until her senses reeled and her body sagged against the granite hardness of his. He released her wrists, seeming to know that they would hang helplessly at her sides, and his hand moved to the small of her back to exert a pressure that crushed her soft outlines to the unyielding dominance of his and left her in no doubt as to the force of his masculinity.[18]

In an unpublished talk,[19] critic Peter Parisi has hypothesized that Harlequin romances are essentially pornography for people ashamed to read pornography. In his view, sex is these novels' real *raison d'être*, while the romance and the promised marriage are primarily salves to the conscience of readers brought up to believe that sex without love and marriage is wrong. Like me, Parisi sees the books as having some active allure. They are not just escape; they also offer release, as he sees it, specifically sexual release.

This is part of the reason why Harlequins, so utterly denatured in most respects, can powerfully command such a large audience. I want to elaborate here on Parisi's definition of *how* the books are pornography and, finally, to modify his definition of what women are looking for in a sex book.

Parisi sees Harlequins as a sort of poor woman's D. H. Lawrence. The body of the heroine is alive and singing in every fiber; she is overrun by a sexuality that wells up inside her and that she cannot control. ("The warmth of his body close to hers was like a charge of electricity, a stunning masculine assault on her senses that she was powerless to do anything about.")[20] The issue of control arises because, in Parisi's view, the reader's qualms are allayed when the novels invoke morals, then affirm a force, sexual feeling, strong enough to override those morals. He argues further that morals in a Harlequin are secular; what the heroine risks is a loss of social face, of reputation. The books uphold the values of their readers, who share this fear of breaking social codes, but behind these reassuringly familiar restraints they celebrate a wild, eager sexuality that flourishes and is finally affirmed in "marriage," which Parisi sees as mainly a code word for "fuck."

Parisi is right: *every* contact in a Harlequin romance is sexualized:

> Sara feared he was going to refuse the invitation and simply walk off. It seemed like an eternity before he inclined his head in a brief, abrupt acknowledgement of acceptance, then drew out her chair for her, his hard fingers brushing her arm for a second, and bringing an urgent flutter of reaction from her pulse.[21]

Those "hard fingers" are the penis; a glance is penetration; a voice can slide along the heroine's spine "like a sliver of ice." The heroine keeps struggling for control but is constantly swept away on a tide of feeling. Always, though, some intruder or some "nagging reminder" of the need to maintain appearances stops her. "His mouth parted her lips with bruising urgency and for a few delirious moments she yielded to her own wanton instincts." But the heroine insists on seeing these moments as out of character: She "had never thought herself capable of wantonness, but in Carlo's arms she seemed to have no inhibitions."[22] Parisi argues that the books' sexual formula allows both heroine and reader to feel wanton again and again while maintaining their sense of themselves as not that sort of women.

I agree with Parisi that the sexually charged atmosphere that bathes the Harlequin heroine is essentially pornographic (I use the word pornographic as neutrally as possible here, not as an automatic pejorative). But do Harlequins actually contain an affirmation of female sexuality? The heroine's condition of passive receptivity to male ego and male sexuality is exciting to readers, but this is not necessarily a free or deep expression of the female potential for sexual feeling. Parisi says the heroine is always trying to humanize the contact between herself and the apparently under-socialized hero, "trying to convert rape into love making." If this is so, then she is engaged on a social as well as a sexual odyssey. Indeed, in women, these two are often joined. Is the project of humanizing and domesticating male sexual feeling an erotic one? What is it about this situation that arouses the excitement of the anxiously vigilant heroine and of the readers who identify with her?

In the misogynistic culture in which we live, where violence toward women is a common motif, it is hard to say a neutral word about pornography either as a legitimate literary form or as a legitimate source of pleasure. Women are naturally overwhelmed by the woman-hating theme so that the more universal human expression sometimes contained by pornography tends to be obscured for them.

In recent debates, sex books that emphasize both male and female sexual feeling as a sensuality that can exist without violence are being called "erotica" to distinguish them from "pornography."[23] This distinction blurs more than it clarifies the complex mixture of elements that make up sexuality. Erotica is soft core, soft focus; it is gentler and tenderer sex than that depicted in pornography. Does this mean true sexuality is diffuse while only perverse sexuality is driven, power hungry, intense, and selfish? I cannot accept this particular dichotomy. It leaves out too much of what is infantile in sex—the reenactment of early feelings, the boundlessness and omnipotence of infant desire and its furious gusto. In pornography all things tend in one direction, a total immersion in one's own sense experience, for which one paradigm must certainly be infancy. For adults this totality, the total sexualization of everything, can only be a fantasy. But does the fact that it cannot be actually lived mean this fantasy must be discarded? It is a memory, a legitimate element in the human lexicon of feelings.

In pornography, the joys of passivity, of helpless abandon, of response without responsibility are all endlessly repeated, savored, minutely described. Again this is a fantasy often dismissed with the pejorative "masochistic" as if passivity were in no way a pleasant or a natural condition.

Yet another criticism of pornography is that it presents no recognizable, delineated characters. In a culture where women are routinely objectified it is natural and progressive to see as threatening any literary form that calls dehumanization sexual. Once again, however, there is another way to analyze this aspect of pornography. Like a lot of far more respectable twentieth-century art, pornography is not about personality but about the explosion of the boundaries of the self. It is a fantasy of an extreme state in which all social constraints are overwhelmed by a flood of sexual energy. Think, for example, of all the pornography about servants fucking mistresses, old men fucking young girls, guardians fucking wards. Class, age, custom—all are deliciously sacrificed, dissolved by sex.

Though pornography's critics are right—pornography is exploitation—it is exploitation of *everything*. Promiscuity by definition is a breakdown of barriers. Pornography is not only a reflector of social power imbalances and sexual pathologies; it is also all those imbalances run riot, run to excess, sometimes explored *ad absurdum*, exploded. Misogyny is one content of pornography; another content is the universal infant desire for complete, immediate gratification, to rule the world out of the very core of passive helplessness.

In a less sexist society, there might be a pornography that is exciting, expressive, interesting, even, perhaps, significant as a form of social rebellion, all traits that, in a sexist society, are obscured by pornography's present role as escape valve for hostility toward women, or as metaphor for fiercely guarded power hierarchies. Instead, in a sexist society, we have two pornographies, one for men, one for women. They both have, hiding within them, those basic human expressions of abandon I have described. The pornography for men enacts this abandon on women as objects. How different is the pornography for women, in which sex is bathed in romance, diffused, always implied rather than enacted at all. This pornography is the Harlequin romance.

I described above the oddly narrowed down, denatured world presented in harlequins. Looking at them as pornography obviously offers a number of alternative explanations for these same traits: the heroine's passivity becomes sexual receptivity and, though I complained earlier about her vapidity, in pornography no one need have a personality. Joanna Russ observed about the heroines of Gothic romances something true of Harlequin heroines as well: they are loved as babies are loved, simply because they exist.[24] They have no particular qualities, but pornography bypasses this limitation and reaches straight down to the infant layer where we all imagine ourselves the center of everything by birthright and are sexual beings without shame or need for excuse.

Seeing Harlequins as pornography modifies one's criticism of their selectivity, their know-nothing narrowness. Insofar as they are essentially pornographic in intent, their characters have no past, no context; they live only in the eternal present of sexual feeling, the absorbing interest in the erotic sex object. Insofar as the books are written to elicit sexual excitation, they can be completely closed, repetitive circuits always returning to the moment of arousal when the hero's voice sends "a velvet finger"[25] along the spine of the heroine. In pornography, sex is the whole content; there need be no serious other.

Read this way, Harlequins are benign if banal sex books, but sex books for women have several special characteristics not included in the usual definitions of the genre pornography. In fact, a suggestive, sexual atmosphere is not so easy to establish for women as it is for men. A number of conditions must be right.

In *The Mermaid and the Minotaur,* an extraordinary study of the asymmetry of male and female relationships in all societies where children are primarily raised by women, Dorothy Dinnerstein discusses the reasons why women are so much more dependent than men on deep personal feeling as an ingredient, sometimes a precondition, for sex. Beyond the obvious reasons, the seriousness of sex for the partner who can get pregnant, the seriousness of sex for the partner who is economically and socially dependent on her lover, Dinnerstein adds another, psychological reason for women's tendency to emotionalize sex. She argues that the double standard (male sexual freedom, female loyalty to one sexual tie) comes from the asymmetry in the way the sexes are raised from infancy. Her argument is too complex to be entirely recapitulated here but her conclusion seems crucial to our understanding of the mixture of sexual excitement and anti-erotic restraint that characterizes sexual feeling in Harlequin romances:

Anatomically, coitus offers a far less reliable guarantee of orgasm—or indeed of any intense direct local genital pleasure—to woman than to man. The first-hand coital pleasure of which she is capable more often requires conditions that must be purposefully sought out. Yet it is woman who has less liberty to conduct this kind of search . . . societal and psychological constraints . . . leave her less free than man to explore the erotic resources of a variety of partners, or even to affirm erotic impulse with any one partner. These constraints also make her less able to give way to simple physical delight without a sense of total self-surrender—a disability that further narrows her choice of partners, and makes her still more afraid of disrupting her rapport with any one partner by acting to intensify the delight, that is, by asserting her own sexual wishes. . . .

What the double standard hurts in women (to the extent that they genuinely, inwardly, bow to it) is the animal center of self-respect: the brute sense of bodily prerogative, of having a right to one's bodily feelings . . . Fromm made this point very clearly when he argued, in *Man for Himself,* that socially imposed shame about the body serves the function of keeping people submissive to societal authority by weakening in them some inner core of individual authority. . . . On the whole . . . the female burden of genital deprivation is carried meekly, invisibly. Sometimes it cripples real interest in sexual interaction, but often it does not: indeed, it can deepen a woman's need for the emotional rewards of carnal contact. What it most reliably cripples is human pride.[26]

This passage gives us the theoretical skeleton on which the titillations of the Harlequin formula are built. In fact, the Harlequin heroine cannot afford to be only a mass of responsive nerve endings. In order for her sexuality, and the sexuality of the novels' readers, to be released, a number of things must happen that have little to do directly with sex at all. Since she cannot seek out or instruct the man she wants, she must be in a state of constant passive readiness. Since only one man will do, she has the anxiety of deciding, "Is this *the* one?" Since an enormous amount of psychic energy is going to be mobilized in the direction of the man she loves, the man she sleeps with, she must feel sure of him. A one-night stand won't work; she is only just beginning to get her emotional generators going when he is already gone. And orgasm? It probably hasn't happened. She couldn't tell him she wanted it and couldn't tell him *how* she wanted it. If he is already gone, there is no way for her erotic feeling for him to take form, no way for her training of him as a satisfying lover to take place.

Hence the Harlequin heroine has a lot of things to worry about if she wants sexual satisfaction. Parisi has said that these worries are restraints there merely to be deliciously overridden, but they are so constant an accompaniment to the heroine's erotic feelings as to be, under present conditions, inseparable from them. She feels an urge toward deep emotion; she feels anxiety about the serious intentions of the hero; she role-plays constantly, presenting herself as a nurturant, passive, receptive figure; and all of this is part of sex to her. Certain social configurations feel safe and right and are real sexual cues for women. The romantic intensity of Harlequins— the waiting, fearing, speculating—are as much a part of their functioning as pornography for women as are the more overtly sexual scenes.

Nor is this just a neutral difference between men and women. In fact, as Dinnerstein suggests, the muting of spontaneous sexual feeling, the necessity that is socially forced on women of channeling their sexual desire, is in fact a great deprivation. In

The Mermaid and the Minotaur Dinnerstein argues that men have a number of reasons, social and psychological, for discomfort when confronted by the romantic feeling and the demand for security that so often accompany female sexuality. For them growing up and being male both mean cutting off the passionate attachment and dependence on woman, on mother. Women, potential mother figures themselves, have less need to make this absolute break. Men also need to pull away from that inferior category, Woman. Women are stuck in it and naturally romanticize the powerful creatures they can only come close to through emotional and physical ties.

The Harlequin formula perfectly reproduces these differences, these tensions, between the sexes. It depicts a heroine struggling, against the hero's resistance, to get the right combination of elements together so that, for her, orgasmic sex can at last take place. The shape of the Harlequin sexual fantasy is designed to deal women the winning hand they cannot hold in life: a man who is romantically interesting—hence, distant, even frightening—while at the same time he is willing to capitulate to her needs just enough so that she can sleep with him not once but often. His intractability is exciting to her, a proof of his membership in a superior class of beings but, finally, he must relent to some extent if her breathless anticipation, the foreplay of romance, is to lead to orgasm.

Clearly, getting romantic tension, domestic security, and sexual excitement together in the same fantasy in the right proportions is a delicate balancing act. Harlequins lack excellence by any other measure, but they are masterly in this one respect. In fact, the Harlequin heroine is in a constant fever of anti-erotic anxiety, trying to control the flow of sexual passion between herself and the hero until her surrender can be on her own terms. If the heroine's task is "converting rape into love making," she must somehow teach the hero to take time, to pay attention, to feel, while herself remaining passive, undemanding, unthreatening. This is yet another delicate miracle of balance that Harlequin romances manage quite well. How do they do it?

The underlying structure of the sexual story goes something like this:

1. The man is hard (a walking phallus).
2. The woman likes this hardness.
3. But, at the outset, this hardness is *too hard*. The man has an ideology that is anti-romantic, anti-marriage. In other words, he will not stay around long enough for her to come, too.
4. Her final release of sexual feeling depends on his changing his mind, but *not too much*. He must become softer (safer, less likely to leave altogether) but not too soft. For good sex, he must be hard, but this hardness must be *at the service of the woman*.

The following passage from Anne Mather's *Born Out of Love* is an example:

His skin was smooth, more roughly textured than hers, but sleek and flexible beneath her palms, his warmth and maleness enveloping her and making her overwhelmingly aware that only the thin material of the culotte suit separated them. He held her face between his hands, and his hardening mouth was echoed throughout the length and breadth of his body. She felt herself yielding weakly beneath him, and his hand slid from her shoulder, across her throat to find the zipper at the front of her suit, impelling it steadily downward.

"No, Logan," she breathed, but he pulled the hands with which she might have resisted him around him, arching her body so that he could observe her reaction to the thrusting aggression of his with sensual satisfaction.

"No?" he probed with gentle mockery, his mouth seeking the pointed fullness of her breasts now exposed to his gaze. "Why not? it's what we both want, don't deny it." . . .

Somehow Charlotte struggled up from the depth of a sexually-induced lethargy. It wasn't easy, when her whole body threatened to betray her, but his words were too similar to the words he had used to her once before, and she remembered only too well what had happened next. . . .

She sat up quickly, her fingers fumbling with the zipper, conscious all the while of Logan lying beside her, and the potent attraction of his lean body. God, she thought unsteadily, what am I doing here? And then, more wildly: Why am I leaving him? *I want him!* But not on his terms, the still small voice of sanity reminded her, and she struggled to her feet.[27]

In these romantic love stories, sex on a woman's terms is romanticized sex. Romantic sexual fantasies are contradictory. They include both the desire to be blindly ravished, to melt, and the desire to be spiritually adored, saved from the humiliation of dependence and sexual passivity through the agency of a protective male who will somehow make reparation to the woman he loves for her powerlessness.

Harlequins reveal and pander to this impossible fantasy life. Female sexuality, a rare subject in all but the most recent writing, is not doomed to be what the Harlequins describe. Nevertheless, some of the barriers that hold back female sexual feeling are acknowledged and finally circumvented quite sympathetically in these novels. They are sex books for people who have plenty of good reasons for worrying about sex.

While there is something wonderful in the heroine's insistence that sex is more exciting and more momentous when it includes deep feeling, she is fighting a losing battle as long as she can define deep feeling only as a mystified romantic longing on the one hand, and as marriage on the other. In Harlequins the price for needing emotional intimacy is that she must passively wait, must anxiously calculate. Without spontaneity and aggression, a whole set of sexual possibilities is lost to her just as, without emotional depth, a whole set of sexual possibilities is lost to men.

Though one may dislike the circuitous form of sexual expression in Harlequin heroines, a strength of the books is that they insist that good sex for women requires an emotional and social context that can free them from constraint. If one dislikes the kind of social norms the heroine seeks as her sexual preconditions, it is still interesting to see sex treated not primarily as a physical event at all but as a social drama, as a carefully modulated set of psychological possibilities between people. This is a mirror image of much writing more commonly labeled pornography. In fact one cannot resist speculating that equality between the sexes as child rearers and workers might well bring personal feeling and abandoned physicality together in wonderful combinations undreamed of in either male or female pornography as we know it.

The ubiquity of the books indicates a central truth: romance is a primary category of the female imagination. The women's movement has left this fact of female consciousness largely untouched. While most serious women *novelists* treat romance with irony and cynicism, most women do not. Harlequins may well be closer to describing women's hopes for love than the work of fine women novelists. Harlequins eschew irony; they take love straight. Harlequins eschew realism; they are serious about fantasy and escape. In spite of all the audience manipulations inherent in the Harlequin formula, the connection between writer and reader is tonally seamless; Harlequins are respectful, tactful, friendly toward their audience. The letters that pour in to their publishers speak above all of involvement, warmth, human values. The world that can make Harlequin romances appear warm is indeed a cold, cold place.

NOTES

1. Harlequin is 50 percent owned by the conglomerate controlling the *Toronto Star*. If you add to the Harlequin sales figures (variously reported from between 60 million to 109 million for 1978) the figures for similar novels by Barbara Cartland and those contemporary romances published by Popular Library, Fawcett, Ballantine, Avon, Pinnacle, Dell, Jove, Bantam, Pocket Books, and Warner, it is clear that hundreds of thousands of women are reading books of the Harlequin type.

2. Blurb in Harlequin Romance. Elizabeth Graham, *Mason's Ridge* (Toronto: Harlequin Books, 1978), and others. (Quotation cited from *Best Sellers*.)

3. Lillian S. Robinson, *Sex, Class, and Culture* (Bloomington: Indiana University Press, 1978). p. 77.

4. In her article "Integrating Marxist and Psychoanalytic Approaches to Feminist Film Criticism" (*Jump Cut*, Fall 1979), Ann Kaplan gives a useful survey of this shift in Left critical thinking about mass culture. See also Robinson, *Sex, Class, and Culture* and Stuart Ewen, *Captains of Consciousness* (New York: McGraw-Hill, 1976.)

5. Kate Ellis has explored the nature and history of Gothic romances: "Paradise Lost: The Limits of Domesticity in the Nineteenth-Century Novel," *Feminist Studies* 2, no. 2/3 (1975): 55–63; "Charlotte Smith's Subversive Gothic," *Feminist Studies* 3, no. 3/4 (Spring–Summer 1976); 51–55; and "Feminism, Fantasy, and Women's Popular Fiction," forthcoming. In "Women Read Romances that Fit Changing Times," *In These Times*, 7–13 February 1979, she gives a more general survey of the different kinds of mass market paperbacks available to women, each with its own particular appeal.

6. Rachel Lindsay, *Prescription for Love* (Toronto: Harlequin Books, 1977), p. 10.

7. Rebecca Stratton, *The Sign of the Ram* (Toronto: Harlequin Books, 1977), pp. 56, 147.

8. Here is an example of this sort of travelogue prose: "There was something to appeal to all age groups in the thousand-acre park in the heart of the city—golf for the energetic, lawn bowling for the more sedate, a zoo for the children's pleasure, and even secluded walks through giant cedars for lovers—but Cori thought of none of these things as Greg drove to a parking place bordering the Inlet." Graham, *Mason's Ridge*, p. 25.

9. Anne Mather, *Born Out of Love* (Toronto: Harlequin Books, 1977), p. 42.

10. See Joanna Russ, "Somebody's Trying to Kill Me and I Think It's My Husband: The Modern Gothic," *Journal of Popular Culture* 6, no. 4 (Spring 1973) 1: 666–91.

11. Mather, *Born Out of Love*, p. 42.

12. Daphne Clair, *A Streak of Gold* (Toronto: Harlequin Books, 1978), p. 118.

13. Lindsay, *Prescription for Love*, p. 13.

14. Stratton, *The Sign of the Ram*, p. 66. The adjectives "cruel" and "satanic" are commonly used for heroes.

15. May 1977, p. 18.

16. Russ, "Somebody's Trying to Kill Me," p. 675.

17. See for example, Josephine A. Ruggiero and Louise C. Weston, "Sex Role Characterizations of Women in Modern Gothic Novels," *Pacific Sociological Review* 20, no. 2 (April 1977): 279–300.

18. Graham, *Mason's Ridge*, p. 63.

19. Delivered April 6, 1978, Livingston College, Rutgers University.

20. Stratton, *The Sign of the Ram*, p. 132.

21. Ibid., p. 112.

22. Ibid., pp. 99, 102, and 139.

23. Gloria Steinem, "Erotica and Pornography: A Clear and Present Difference," *MS.* (November 1978), and other articles in this issue. An unpublished piece by Brigitte Frase, "From Pornography to Mind-Blowing" (MLA talk, 1978), strongly presents my own view that this debate is specious. See also Susan Sontag's "The Pornographic Imagination," in *Styles of Radical Will* (New York: Delta, 1978), and the Jean Paulhan preface to *Story of O*, "Happiness in Slavery" (New York: Grove Press, 1965).

24. Russ, "Somebody's Trying to Kill Me," p. 679.

25. Stratton, *The Sign of the Ram*, p. 115.

26. Dorothy Dinnerstein, *The Mermaid and the Minotaur: Sexual Arrangements and Human Malaise* (New York: Harper and Row, 1976), pp. 73–75.

27. Mather, *Born Out of Love*, pp. 70–72.

Chapter Fifty

Women Read the Romance
The Interaction of Text and Context (1983)

Janice A. Radway

Radway, a sociologist, produced the most well-known and influential study of popular romance so far, one that is still widely cited in scholarly literature. Her groundbreaking thesis, based on interviews with readers rather than textual analysis alone, is that women do not use romance for "escape" only, but revise its interpretation to suit their own psychological affirmations of empowerment. For a full-length treatment, see her book Reading the Romance *(1984).*

By now, the statistics are well known and the argument familiar. The Canadian publisher, Harlequin Enterprises, alone claims to have sold 168 million romances throughout the world in the single year of 1979.[1] In addition, at least twelve other paperback publishing houses currently issue from two to six romantic novels every month, nearly all of which are scooped up voraciously by an audience whose composition and size has yet to be accurately determined.[2] The absence of such data, however, has prevented neither journalists nor literary scholars from offering complex, often subtle interpretations of the meaning of the form's characteristic narrative development. Although these interpreters of the romance do not always concur about the particular ways in which the tale reinforces traditional expectations about female-male relationships, all agree that the stories perpetuate patriarchal attitudes and structures. They do so, these critics tell us, by continuing to maintain that a woman's journey to happiness and fulfillment must always be undertaken in the company of a protective man. In the words of Ann Snitow, romances "reinforce the prevailing cultural code" proclaiming that "pleasure for women is men."[3]

The acuity of interpretations such as those developed by Snitow, Ann Douglas, and Tania Modleski certainly cannot be denied.[4] Indeed, their very complexity lends credence to the secondary, often implicit claim made by these theorists of the romance that their proposed interpretations can also serve as an adequate explana-

Janice A. Radway, "Women Read the Romance: The Interaction of Text and Context," *Feminist Studies*, vol 9, no. 1 (spring 1983): 53–78. © 1983 by *Feminist Studies*, Inc. Reprinted by permission of *Feminist Studies*, Inc.

tion of the genre's extraordinary popularity. However, a recent ethnographic study of a group of regular romance readers clustered about a bookseller, who is recognized by authors and editors alike as an "expert" in the field, suggests that these explanations of reading choice and motivation are incomplete.[5] Because these interpreters do not take account of the actual, day-to-day context within which romance reading occurs, and because they ignore romance readers' own book choice and theories about why they read, they fail to detect the ways in which the activity may serve positive functions even as the novels celebrate patriarchal institutions. Consequently, they also fail to understand that some contemporary romances actually attempt to reconcile changing attitudes about gender behavior with more traditional sexual arrangements.

The particular weaknesses of these interpretations as *explanations* of reading behavior can be traced to the fact that they focus only on the texts in isolation. This reification of the literary text persists in much practical criticism today which continues to draw its force from the poetics of the New Criticism and its assertion that the text, as a more or less well-made artifact, contains a set of meanings that can be articulated adequately by a trained critic.[6] Interpretive reading is an unproblematic activity for these students of the romance because they too assume that the text has intrinsic power to coerce all cooperative readers into discovering the core of meaning that is undeniably *there* in the book. Moreover, because their analysis proceeds under the assumption that a literary work's objective reality remains unchanged despite differences among individual readers and in the attention they devote to the text, these critics understandably assume further that their own reading of a given literary form can stand as the representative of all adequate readings of it. Finally, they assume also that their particular reading can then become the object of further cultural analysis that seeks to explain the popularity of the form and its appeal to its audience. In the end, they produce their explanation merely by positing a desire in the reading audience for the specific meaning they have unearthed.

New theories of the literary text and the reading process have been advanced, however, the basic premises of which call for a modification of this standard explanatory procedure. Although the myriad forms of reader-theory and reader-response criticism are too diverse and too complicated to review in any depth here, all acknowledge, to a greater or lesser degree, that the reader is responsible for what is made of the literary text.[7] Despite their interest in the *making* of meaning, reader-theorists do not believe that literary texts exert no force at all on the meaning that is finally produced in a given reading. Rather, most argue that literary meaning is the result of a complex, temporally evolving interaction between a fixed verbal structure and a socially situated reader. That reader makes sense of the verbal structure by referring to previously learned aesthetic and cultural codes. Literary meaning, then, in the words of Stanley Fish, perhaps the most prominent of reader-theorists, is "the property neither of fixed and stable texts nor of free and independent readers but of interpretive communities that are responsible both for the shape of the reader's activities and for the texts those activities produce."[8]

Clearly, the reader-theory emphasis on the constitutive power and activity of the reader suggests, indeed almost demands, that the cultural critic who is interested in the "meaning" of a form and the causes of its popularity consider first whether she is a member of a different interpretive community than the readers who are her ostensible subjects. If she is, she may well produce and evaluate textual meaning in a manner fundamentally different from those whose behavior she seeks to explain. None of the early students of the romance have so foregrounded their own interpretive activities. Because of their resulting assumption of an identity between their own reading and that of regular romance readers, they have severed the form from the women who actually construct its meaning from within a particular context and on the basis of a specific constellation of attitudes and beliefs. This assumption has resulted, finally, in an incomplete account of the particular ideological power of this literary form, in that these critics have not successfully isolated the particular function performed through the act of romance reading which is crucially important to the readers themselves. In ignoring certain specific aspects of the romance readers' daily context, they have also failed to see how the women's selection and construction of their favorite novels addresses the problems and desires they deem to be characteristic of their lives.

To guard against the ever-present danger of advancing a theory about the meaning of a text for a given audience on the basis of a performance of that text, which no individual in the group would recognize, one must investigate exactly what the entire act of romance reading means to the women who buy the books. If the romance is to be cited as evidence testifying to the evolution or perpetuation of cultural beliefs about women's roles and the institution of marriage, it is first necessary to know what women actually understand themselves to be doing when they read a romance they like. A more complete cultural analysis of the contemporary romance might specify how actual readers interpret the actions of principal characters, how they comprehend the final significance of the narrative resolution and, perhaps most important, how the act of repetitively encountering this fantasy fits within the daily routine of their private lives. We need to know not what the romantic text objectively means—in fact, it never means in this way—but rather how the *event* of reading the text is interpreted by the women who engage in it.[9]

The interpretation of the romance's cultural significance offered here has been developed from a series of extensive ethnographic-like interviews with a group of compulsive romance readers in a predominantly urban, central midwestern state among the nation's top twenty in total population.[10] I discovered my principal informant and her customers with the aid of a senior editor at Doubleday whom I had been interviewing about the publication of romances. Sally Arteseros told me of a bookstore employee who had developed a regular clientele of fifty to seventy-five regular romance readers who relied on her for advice about the best romances to buy and those to avoid. When I wrote to Dot Evans, as I will now call her, to ask whether I might question her about how she interpreted, categorized, and evaluated romantic fiction, I had no idea that she had also begun to write a newsletter designed to enable bookstores to advise their customers about the quality of the romances published monthly. She has since copyrighted this newsletter and incorporated it as a business. Dot is so successful at serving the women who patronize her chain outlet that the central office of this major chain occasionally relies on her sales predictions to gauge romance distribution throughout the system. Her success has also brought her to the attention of both editors and writers for whom she now reads manuscripts and galleys.

My knowledge of Dot and her readers is based on roughly sixty hours of interviews conducted in June 1980, and February 1981. I have talked extensively with Dot about romances, reading, and her advising activities as well as observed her interactions with her customers at the bookstore. I have also conducted both group and individual interviews with sixteen of her regular customers and administered a lengthy questionnaire to forty-two of these women. Although not representative of all women who read romances, the group appears to be demographically similar to a sizable segment of that audience as it has been mapped by several rather secretive publishing houses.

Dorothy Evans lives and works in the community of Smithton, as do most of her regular customers. A city of about 112,000 inhabitants, Smithton is located five miles due east of the state's second largest city, in a metropolitan area with a total population of over 1 million. Dot was forty-eight years old at the time of the survey, the wife of a journeyman plumber, and the mother of three children in their twenties. She is extremely bright and articulate and, while not a proclaimed feminist, holds some beliefs about women that might be labeled as such. Although she did not work outside the home when her children were young and does not now believe that a woman needs a career to be fulfilled, she feels women should have the opportunity to work and be paid equally with men. Dot also believes that women should have the right to abortion, though she admits that her deep religious convictions would prevent her from seeking one herself. She is not disturbed by the Equal Rights Amendment and can and does converse eloquently about the oppression women have endured for years at the hands of men. Despite her opinions, however, she believes implicitly in the value of true romance and thoroughly enjoys discovering again and again that women can find men who will love them as they wish to be loved. Although most of her regular customers are more conservative than Dot in the sense that they do not advocate political measures to redress past grievances, they are quite aware that men commonly think themselves superior to women and often mistreat them as a result.

In general, Dot's customers are married, middle-class mothers with at least a high school education.[11] More than 60 percent of the women were between the ages of twenty-five and forty-four at the time of the study, a fact that duplicates fairly closely Harlequin's finding that the majority of its readers is between twenty-five and forty-nine.[12] Silhouette Books has also recently reported that 65 percent of the romance market is below the age of 40.[13] Exactly 50 percent of the Smithton women have high school diplomas, while 32 percent report completing at least some college work. Again, this seems to suggest that the interview group is fairly representative, for Silhouette also indicates that 45 percent of the romance market has attended at least some college. The employment status and family income of Dot's customers also seem to duplicate those of the audience mapped by the publishing houses. Forty-two percent of the Smithton women, for instance, work part-time outside the home. Harlequin claims that 49 percent of its audience is similarly employed. The Smithton women report slightly higher incomes than those of the average Harlequin reader (43 percent of the Smithton women have incomes of $15,000 to $24,999, 33 percent have incomes of $25,000 to $49,999—the average income of the Harlequin reader is $15,000 to $20,000), but the difference is not enough to change the general sociological status of the group.

In one respect, however, Dot and her customers may be unusual, although it is difficult to say for sure because corroborative data from other sources are sadly lacking. Although almost 70 percent of the women claim to read books other than romances, 37 percent nonetheless report reading from five to nine romances each week. Even though more than one-half read less (from one to four romances a week), when the figures are converted to monthly totals they indicate that one-half the Smithton women read between four and sixteen romances a month, while 40 percent read more than twenty. This particular group is obviously obsessed with romantic fiction. The most recent comprehensive survey of American book readers and their habits has discovered that romance readers tend to read more books within their favorite category than do other category readers, but these readers apparently read substantially fewer than the Smithton group. Yankelovich, Skelly, and White found in their 1978 study that 21 percent of the total book reading public had read *at least* one gothic or romance in the last six months.[14] The average number of romantic novels read by this group in the last six months was only nine. Thus, while it is probably true that romance readers are repetitive consumers, most apparently do not read as consistently or as constantly as Dot and her customers. Romances undoubtedly play a more significant role, then, in the lives of the Smithton women than they do in those of occasional romance readers. Nevertheless, even this latter group appears to demonstrate a marked desire for, if not dependency upon, the fantasy they offer.

When asked why they read romances, the Smithton women overwhelmingly cite escape or relaxation as their goal. They use the word "escape," however, both literally and figuratively. On the one hand, they value their romances highly because the act of reading them literally draws the women away from their present surroundings. Because they must produce the meaning of the story by attending closely to the words on the page, they find that their attention is withdrawn from concerns that plague them in reality. One woman remarked with a note of triumph in her voice: "My body may be in that room, but I'm not!" She and her sister readers see their romance reading as a legitimate way of denying a present reality that occasionally becomes too onerous to bear. This particular means of escape is better than television viewing for these women, because the cultural value attached to books permits them to overcome the guilt they feel about avoiding their responsibilities. They believe that reading of any kind is, by nature, educational.[15] They insist accordingly that they also read to learn.[16]

On the other hand, the Smithton readers are quite willing to acknowledge that the romances which so preoccupy them are little more than fantasies or fairy tales that always end happily. They readily admit in fact that the characters and events discovered in the pages of the typical romance do not resemble the people and occurrences they must deal with in their daily lives. On the basis of the following comments, made in response to a question about what romances "do" better than other novels available today, one can conclude that it is precisely the unreal, fantastic shape of the story that makes their literal escape even more complete and gratifying. Although these are only a few of the remarks given in response to the undirected question, they are representative of the group's general sentiment.

> Romances hold my interest and do not leave me depressed or up in the air at the end like many modern day books tend to do. Romances also just make me feel good reading them as I identify with the heroines.

> The kind of books I mainly read are very different from everyday living. That's why I read them. Newspapers, etc., I find boring because all you read is sad news. I can get enough of that on TV news. I like stories that take your mind off everyday matters.

> Different than everyday life.

> Everyone is always under so much pressure. They like books that let them escape.

> Because it is an escape, and we can dream. And pretend that it is our life.

> I'm able to escape the harsh world a few hours a day.

> It is a way of escaping from everyday living.

> They always seem an escape and they usually turn out the way you wish life really was.

> I enjoy reading because it offers me a small vacation from everyday life and an interesting and amusing way to pass the time.

These few comments all hint at a certain sadness that many of the Smithton women seem to share because life has not given them all that it once promised. A deep-seated sense of betrayal also lurks behind their deceptively simple expressions of a need to believe in a fairy tale. Although they have not elaborated in these comments, many of the women explained in the interviews that despite their disappointments, they feel refreshed and strengthened by their vicarious participation in a fantasy relationship where the heroine is frequently treated as they themselves would most like to be loved.

This conception of romance reading as an escape that is both literal and figurative implies flight from some situation in the real world which is either stifling or overwhelming, as well as a metaphoric transfer to another, more desirable universe where events are happily resolved. Unashamed to admit that they like to indulge in temporary escape, the Smithton women are also surprisingly candid about the circumstances that necessitate their desire. When asked to specify what they are fleeing from, they invariably mention the "pressures" and "tensions" they experience as wives and mothers. Although none of the women can cite the voluminous feminist literature about the psychological toll exacted by the constant demand to physically and emotionally nurture others, they are nonetheless eloquent about how draining and unrewarding their duties can be. [17] When first asked why women find it necessary to escape, Dot gave the following answer without once pausing to rest:

> As a mother, I have run 'em to the orthodontist, I have run 'em to the swimming pool. I have run 'em to baton twirling lessons. I have run up to school because they forgot their lunch. You know, I mean really. And you do it. And it isn't that you begrudge it. That isn't it. Then my husband would walk in the door and he'd say, "Well, what did you do today?" You know, it was like, "Well, tell me how you spent the last eight hours, because I've been out working." And I finally got to the point where I would say, "Well, I read four books, and I did the wash and got the meal on the table and the beds are all made and the house is tidy." And I would get defensive like, "So what do you call all this? Why should I have to tell you because I certainly don't ask you what you did for eight hours, step by step."
>
> But their husbands do do that. We've compared notes. They hit the house and it's like "Well, all right, I've been out earning a living. Now what have you been doin' with your time?" And you begin to be feeling, "Now, really, why is he questioning me?"

Romance reading, as Dot herself puts it, constitutes a temporary "declaration of independence" from the social roles of wife and mother. By placing the barrier of the book between themselves and their families, these women reserve a special space and time for themselves alone. As a consequence, they momentarily allow themselves to abandon the attitude of total self-abnegation in the interest of family welfare which they have so dutifully learned is the proper stance for a good wife and mother. Romance reading is both an assertion of deeply felt psychological needs and a means for satisfying those needs. Simply put, these needs arise because no other member of the family, as it is presently constituted in this still-patriarchal society, is yet charged with the affective and emotional reconstitution of a wife and mother. If she is depleted by her efforts to care for others, she is nonetheless expected to restore and sustain herself as well. As one of Dot's customers put it, "You always have to be a Mary Poppins. You can't be sad, you can't be mad, you have to keep everything bottled up inside."

Nancy Chodorow has recently discussed this structural peculiarity of the modern family and its impact on the emotional lives of women in her influential book, *The Reproduction of Mothering*,[18] a complex reformulation of the Freudian theory of female personality development. Chodorow maintains that women often continue to experience a desire for intense affective nurturance and relationality well into adulthood as a result of an unresolved separation from their primary caretaker. It is highly significant, she argues, that in patriarchal society this caretaker is almost inevitably a woman. The felt similarity between mother and daughter creates an unusually intimate connection between them which later makes it exceedingly difficult for the daughter to establish autonomy and independence. Chodorow maintains on the other hand, that because male children are also reared by women, they tend to separate more completely from their mothers by suppressing their own emotionality and capacities for tenderness which they associate with mothers and femininity. The resulting asymmetry in human personality, she concludes, leads to a situation where men typically cannot fulfill all of a woman's emotional needs. As a consequence, women turn to the act of mothering as a way of vicariously recovering that lost relationality and intensity.

My findings about Dot Evans and her customers suggest that the vicarious pleasure a woman receives through the nurturance of others may not be completely satisfying, because the act of caring for them also makes tremendous demands on a woman and can deplete her sense of self. In that case, she may well turn to romance reading in an effort to construct a fantasy-world where she is attended, as the heroine is, by a man who reassures her of her special status and unique identity.

The value of the romance may have something to do, then, with the fact that women find it especially difficult to indulge in the restorative experience of visceral regression to an infantile state where the self is cared for perfectly by another. This regression is so difficult precisely because women have been taught to believe that men must be their sole source of pleasure. Although there is nothing biologically lacking in men to make this ideal pleasure unattainable, as Chodorow's theories tell us, their engendering and socialization by the patriarchal family traditionally masks the very traits that would permit them to nurture women in this way. Because they are encouraged to be aggressive, competitive, self-sufficient, and unemotional, men often find sustained attention to the emotional needs of others both unfamiliar and difficult. While the Smithton women only minimally discussed their husbands' abilities to take care of them as they would like, when they commented on their favorite romantic heroes they made it clear that they enjoy imagining themselves being tenderly cared for and solicitously protected by a fictive character who inevitably proves to be spectacularly masculine and unusually nurturant as well.[19]

Indeed, this theme of pleasure recurred constantly in the discussions with the Smithton women. They insisted repeatedly that when they are reading a romance, they feel happy and content. Several commented that they particularly relish moments when they are home alone and can relax in a hot tub or in a favorite chair with a good book. Others admitted that they most like to read in a warm bed late at night. Their association of romances with contentment, pleasure, and good feelings is apparently not unique, for in conducting a market research study, Fawcett discovered that when asked to draw a woman reading a romance, romance readers inevitably depict someone who is exaggeratedly happy.[20]

The Smithton group's insistence that they turn to romances because the experience of reading the novels gives them hope, provides pleasure, and causes contentment raises the unavoidable question of what aspects of the romantic narrative itself could possibly give rise to feelings such as these. How are we to explain, furthermore, the obvious contradiction between this reader emphasis on pleasure and hope, achieved through vicarious appreciation of the ministrations of a tender hero, and the observations of the earlier critics of romances that such books are dominated by men who at least temporarily abuse and hurt the women they purportedly love? In large part, the contradiction arises because the two groups are not reading according to the same interpretive strategies, neither are they reading nor commenting on the same books. Textual analyses like those offered by Douglas, Modleski, and Snitow are based on the common assumption that because romances are formulaic and therefore essentially identical, analysis of a randomly chosen sample will reveal the meaning unfailingly communicated by every example of the genre. This methodological procedure is based on the further assumption that category readers do not themselves perceive variations within the genre, nor do they select their books in a manner significantly different from the random choice of the analyst.

In fact, the Smithton readers do not believe the books are identical, nor do they approve of all the romances they read. They have elaborated a complex distinction between "good" and "bad" romances and they have accordingly experimented with various techniques that they hoped would enable them to identify bad romances before they paid for a book that would only offend them. Some tried to decode titles and cover blurbs by looking for key words serving as clues to the book's tone; others refused to buy romances by authors they didn't recognize; still others read several pages *including the ending* before they bought the book. Now, however, most of the people in the Smithton group have been freed from the need to rely on these inexact predictions because Dot Evans shares their perceptions and evaluations of the category and can alert them to unusually successful romantic fantasies while steering them away from those they call "disgusting perversions."

When the Smithton readers' comments about good and bad romances are combined with the conclusions drawn from an analysis of twenty of their favorite books and an equal number of those they classify as particularly inadequate, an illuminating picture of the fantasy fueling the romance-reading experience develops.[21] To begin with, Dot and her readers will not tolerate any story in which the heroine is seriously abused by men. They find multiple rapes especially distressing and dislike books in which a woman is brutally hurt by a man only to fall desperately in love with him in the last four pages. The Smithton women are also offended by explicit sexual description and scrupulously avoid the work of authors like Rosemary Rogers and Judith Krantz who deal in what they call "perversions" and "promiscuity." They also do not like romances that overtly perpetuate the double standard by excusing the hero's simultaneous involvement with several women. They insist, one reader commented, on "one woman—one man." They also seem to dislike any kind of detailed description of male genitalia, although the women enjoy suggestive descriptions of how the hero is emotionally aroused to an overpowering desire for the heroine. Their preferences seem to confirm Beatrice Faust's argument in *Women, Sex, and Pornography* that women are not interested in the visual display characteristic of male pornography, but prefer process-oriented materials detailing the development of deep emotional connection between two individuals.[22]

According to Dot and her customers, the quality of the *ideal* romantic fantasy is directly dependent on the character of the heroine and the manner in which the hero treats her. The plot, of course, must always focus on a series of obstacles to the final declaration of love between the two principals. However, a good romance involves an unusually bright and determined woman and a man who is spectacularly masculine, but at the same time capable of remarkable empathy and tenderness. Although they enjoy the usual chronicle of misunderstandings and mistakes which inevitably leads to the heroine's belief that the hero intends to harm her, the Smithton readers prefer stories that combine a much-understated version of this continuing antagonism with a picture of a gradually developing love. They most wish to participate in the slow process by which two people become acquainted, explore each other's foibles, wonder about the other's feelings, and eventually "discover" that they are loved by the other.

In conducting an analysis of the plots of the twenty romances listed as "ideal" by the Smithton readers, I was struck by their remarkable similarities in narrative structure. In fact, all twenty of these romances are very tightly organized around the evolving relationship between a single couple composed of a beautiful, defiant, and sexually immature woman and a brooding, handsome man who is also curiously capable of soft, gentle gestures. Although minor foil figures are used in these romances, none of the ideal stories seriously involves either hero or heroine with one of the rival characters.[23] They are employed mainly as contrasts to the more likable and proper central pair or as purely temporary obstacles to the pair's delayed union because one or the other mistakenly suspects the partner of having an affair with the rival. However, because the reader is never permitted to share this mistaken assumption in the ideal romance, she knows all along that the relationship is not as precarious as its participants think it to be. The rest of the narrative in the twenty romances chronicles the gradual crumbling of barriers between these two individuals who are fearful of being used by the other. As their defenses against emotional response fall away and their sexual passion rises inexorably, the typical narrative plunges on until the climactic point at which the hero treats the heroine to some supreme act of tenderness, and she realizes that his apparent emotional indifference was only the mark of his hesitancy about revealing the extent of his love for and dependence upon her.

The Smithton women especially like romances that commence with the early marriage of the hero and heroine for reasons of convenience. Apparently, they do so because they delight in the subsequent, necessary chronicle of the pair's growing awareness that what each took to be indifference or hate is, in reality, unexpressed love and suppressed passion. In such favorite romances as *The Flame and the Flower*, *The Black Lyon*, *Shanna*, and *Made For Each Other*, the heroine begins marriage thinking that she detests and is detested by her spouse. She is thrown into a quandary, however, because her partner's behavior vacillates from indifference, occasional brusqueness, and even cruelty to tenderness and passion. Consequently, the heroine spends most of her time in these romances, as well as in the others comprising this sample, trying to read the hero's behavior as a set of signs expressing his true feelings toward her. The final outcome of the story turns upon a fundamental process of *re*interpretation, whereby she suddenly and clearly sees that the behavior she feared was actually the product of deeply felt passion and a previous hurt. Once she learns to reread his past behavior and thus to excuse him for the suffering he has caused her, she is free to respond warmly to his occasional acts of tenderness. Her response inevitably encourages him to believe in her and finally to treat her as she wishes to be treated. When this reinterpretation process is completed in the twenty ideal romances, the heroine is always tenderly enfolded in the hero's embrace and the reader is permitted to identify with her as she is gently caressed, carefully protected, and verbally praised with words of love.[24] At the climactic moment (pp. 201–2) of

The Sea Treasure, for example, when the hero tells the heroine to put her arms around him, the reader is informed of his gentleness in the following way:

> She put her cold face against his in an attitude of surrender that moved him to unutterable tenderness. He swung her clear of the encroaching water and eased his way up to the next level, with painful slowness. . . . When at last he had finished, he pulled her into his arms and held her against his heart for a moment. . . . Tenderly he lifted her. Carefully he negotiated the last of the treacherous slippery rungs to the mine entrance. Once there, he swung her up into his arms, and walked out into the starlit night.
> The cold air revived her, and she stirred in his arms.
> "Dominic?" she whispered.
> He bent his head and kissed her.
> "Sea Treasure," he whispered.

Passivity, it seems, is at the heart of the romance-reading experience in the sense that the final goal of the most valued romances is the creation of perfect union in which the ideal male, who is masculine and strong, yet nurturant, finally admits his recognition of the intrinsic worth of the heroine. Thereafter, she is required to do nothing more than exist as the center of this paragon's attention. Romantic escape is a temporary but literal denial of the demands these women recognize as an integral part of their roles as nurturing wives and mothers. But it is also a figurative journey to a utopian state of total receptiveness in which the reader, as a consequence of her identification with the heroine, feels herself the passive *object* of someone else's attention and solicitude. The romance reader in effect is permitted the experience of feeling cared for, the sense of having been affectively reconstituted, even if both are lived only vicariously.

Although the ideal romance may thus enable a woman to satisfy vicariously those psychological needs created in her by a patriarchal culture unable to fulfill them, the very centrality of the rhetoric of reinterpretation to the romance suggests also that the reading experience may indeed have some of the unfortunate consequences pointed to by earlier romance critics.[25] Not only is the dynamic of reinterpretation an essential component of the plot of the ideal romance, but it also characterizes the very process of constructing its meaning because the reader is inevitably given more information about the hero's motives than is the heroine herself. Hence, when Ranulf temporarily abuses his young bride in *The Black Lyon,* the reader understands that what appears as inexplicable cruelty to Lyonene, the heroine, is an irrational desire to hurt her because of what his first wife did to him.[26] It is possible that in reinterpreting the hero's behavior before Lyonene does, the Smithton women may be practicing a procedure which is valuable to them precisely because it enables them to reinterpret their own spouse's similar emotional coldness and likely preoccupation with work or sports. In rereading this category of behavior, they reassure themselves that it does not necessarily mean that a woman is not loved. Romance reading, it would seem, can function as a kind of training for the all-too-common task of reinterpreting a spouse's unsettling actions as the signs of passion, devotion, and love.

If the Smithton women are indeed learning reading behaviors that help them to dismiss or justify their husbands' affective distance, this procedure is probably carried out on an unconscious level. In any form of cultural or anthropological analysis in which the subjects of the study cannot reveal all the complexity or covert significance of their behavior, a certain amount of speculation is necessary. The analyst, however, can and should take account of any other observable evidence that might reveal the motives and meanings she is seeking. In this case, the Smithton readers' comments about bad romances are particularly helpful.

In general, bad romances are characterized by one of two things: an unusually cruel hero who subjects the heroine to various kinds of verbal and physical abuse, or a diffuse plot that permits the hero to become involved with other women before he settles upon the heroine. Since the Smithton readers will tolerate complicated sub-plots in some romances if the hero and heroine continue to function as a pair, clearly it is the involvement with other rather than the plot complexity that distresses them. When asked why they disliked these books despite the fact that they all ended happily with the hero converted into the heroine's attentive lover, Dot and her customers replied again and again that they rejected the books precisely because they found them unbelievable. In elaborating, they insisted indignantly that *they* could never forgive the hero's early transgressions and they see no reason why they should be asked to believe that the heroine can. What they are suggesting, then, is that certain kinds of male behavior associated with the stereotype of male machismo can never be forgiven or reread as the signs of love. They are thus not interested *only* in the romance's happy ending. They want to involve themselves in a story that will permit them to enjoy the hero's tenderness *and* to reinterpret his momentary blindness and cool indifference as the marks of a love so intense that he is wary of admitting it. Their delight in both these aspects of the process of romance reading and their deliberate attempt to select books that will include "a gentle hero" and "a slight misunderstanding" suggest that deeply felt needs are the source of their interest in both components of the genre. On the one hand, they long for emotional attention and tender care; on the other, they wish to rehearse the discovery that a man's distance can be explained and excused as his way of expressing love.

It is easy to condemn this latter aspect of romance reading as a reactionary force that reconciles women to a social situation which denies them full development, even as it refuses to accord them the emotional sustenance they require. Yet to identify romances with this conservative moment alone is to miss those other benefits associated with the act of reading as a restorative pastime whose impact on a beleaguered woman is not so simply dismissed. If we are serious about feminist politics and committed to reformulating not only our own lives but those of others, we would do well not to condescend to romance readers as hopeless traditionalists who are recalcitrant in their refusal to acknowledge the emotional costs of patriarchy. We must begin to recognize that romance reading is fueled by dissatisfaction and disaffection, not by perfect contentment with woman's lot. Moreover, we must also understand that some romance readers' experiences are not strictly congruent with the set of ideological propositions that typically legitimate patriarchal marriage. They are characterized, rather, by a sense of longing caused by patriarchal marriage's failure to address all their needs.

In recognizing both the yearning and the fact that its resolution is only a vicarious one not so easily achieved in a real situation, we may find it possible to identify more precisely the very limits of patriarchal ideology's success. Endowed thus with a better understanding of what women want, but often fail to get from the traditional arrangements they consciously support, we may provide ourselves with that very issue whose discussion would reach many more women and potentially raise their consciousness about the particular dangers and failures of patriarchal institutions. By helping romance readers to see why they long for relationality and tenderness and are unlikely to get either in the form they desire if current gender arrangements are continued, we may help to convert their amorphous longing into a focused desire for specific change.

The strategic value of recognizing both the possibility that romance reading may have some positive benefits and that even its more conservative effects actually originate in significant discontent with the institutions the books purport to celebrate becomes even clearer when one looks more carefully at the Smithton readers' feelings about heroine/hero interactions in ideal romances. Those feelings also indicate that small changes are beginning to occur in women's expectations about female and male behavior. Dot and her customers all emphatically insist that the ideal heroine must be intelligent and independent, and they particularly applaud those who are capable of holding their own in repartee with men. In fact, three-fourths of the Smithton women listed both "intelligence" (thirty-three women) and "a sense of humor" (thirty-one women) as being among the three most important characteristics of a romantic heroine. Although "independence" was chosen less often, still, twenty of these readers selected this trait from a list of nine as one of three essential ingredients in the heroine's personality. These readers value romance writers who are adept at rendering verbal dueling because, as one woman explained, "it's very exciting and you never know who's going to come out on top."

Their interest in this characteristic aspect of romantic fiction seems to originate in their desire to identify with a woman who is strong and courageous enough to stand up to an angry man. They remember well favorite heroines and snatches of dialogue read several years before in which those heroines managed momentarily to best their antagonists. Dot and her customers are quite aware that few women can hope to subdue a man physically if he is determined to have his way. As a consequence, they believe it essential for women to develop the ability to use words adroitly if they are to impose their own wills. The Smithton women reserve their greatest scorn for romances with "namby-pamby" heroines and point to Barbara Cartland's women, whom they universally detest, as the perfect example of these. Their repeated insistence on the need for strong and intelligent heroines attests to their wish to dissociate themselves from the stereotype of women as weak, passive, and foolish individuals. Clearly, their longing for competence could be encouraged by showing such women how to acquire and to express it more readily in the world beyond the home.

However, the ideal heroine who temporarily outwits the hero often symbolically "pays for" her transgression later in the same chapter when he treats her brusquely or forces his sexual attention upon her. This narrative may well betoken ambivalence on the part of writers and readers who experience a certain amount of guilt over their desire to identify with a woman who sometimes acts independently and with force. Still, I have placed the "pays for" in quotation marks here because neither the books, nor apparently do the readers, consciously construct the interaction in this particular manner. When questioned closely about such a chronology of events, instead of admitting reservations about the overly aggressive nature of a heroine's behavior, Dot and her customers focused instead on the unjustified nature of the hero's actions. Not only did they remember specific instances of "completely blind" and "stupid" behavior on the part of romantic heroes, but they also often went on at length about such instances, vociferously protesting this sort of mistreatment of an innocent heroine. Given the vehemence of their reaction, it seems possible that the male violence that does occur in romances may actually serve as an opportunity to express anger which is otherwise repressed and ignored.

Although I did not initially question the Smithton women about their attitudes toward the commonplace mistreatment of the heroine, principally because I assumed that they must find it acceptable, the women volunteered in discussions of otherwise good stories that these kinds of scenes make them very angry and indignant. They seem to identify completely with the wronged heroine and vicariously participate in her shock and outrage. When I did wonder aloud about this emotional response to the hero's cruelty, Dot's customers indicated that such actions often lead them to "hate" or "detest" even especially memorable heroes for a short period of time. The scenes may function, then, as a kind of release valve for the pent-up anger and resentment they won't permit themselves in the context of their own social worlds.

However, it is also likely that in freely eliciting feelings of displeasure and even rage, the romance defuses those sentiments in preparation for its later explanation of the behavior that occasioned them in the first place. Having already imaginatively voiced her protest, the reader is emotionally ready to accept the explanation, when it is formally offered, of the hero's offensive treatment of the heroine. Like the heroine herself, she is then in a position to forgive his behavior, because what she learns is that his actions were the signs of his deep interest in her. It is because the ideal hero is always persuaded to express his love with the proper signs that the Smithton women interpret his discovery that he actually loves the heroine as the heroine's triumph. The power, they believe, is all hers because he now recognizes he can't live without her. In actuality, what is going on here, as I have noted before, is that active process of justification whereby the reader is encouraged to excuse male indifference and cruelty if it can be demonstrated that these feelings are also accompanied by feelings of love. The romance may therefore recontain any rebellious feelings or impulses on the part of its heroines or readers precisely because it dramatizes a situation where such feelings prove unnecessary and unwarranted. The reader of the ideal romance closes her book, finally, purged of her discontent and reassured that men can indeed learn how to satisfy a woman's basic need for emotional intensity and nurturant care within traditional marriage.

The reassurance is never wholly successful, however. That reader almost inevitably picks up another romance as soon as she puts her last one down. If we can learn to recognize, then, that the need for this repeated reassurance about the success of patriarchal gender arrangements springs from nagging doubt and continuing resentment, we will have developed a better picture of the complex and contradictory state of mind that characterizes many women who, on the surface, appear to be opposed to any kind of change in female-male relations. Strengthened by such comprehension, we might more successfully formulate explanations, arguments, and appeals that will enable at least some women to understand that their need for romances is a function of their dependent status as women and of their acceptance of love and marriage as the only routes to female fulfillment. If they can be persuaded of this, they may find it within themselves to seek their fulfillment elsewhere, to develop a more varied array of their abilities, and to demand the right to use them in the public sphere ordinarily controlled by men.

Although romances provide their readers with a good deal more than can be delineated here, again, the dynamic surrounding their status as both a figurative and a literal escape from present reality indicates that romance reading may not function as a purely conservative force. In fact, it appears to be a complex form of behavior that allows incremental change in social beliefs at the same time that it restores the claim of traditional institutions to satisfy a woman's most basic needs. It is true, certainly, that the romantic story itself reaffirms the perfection of romance and marriage. But it is equally clear that the constant need for such an assertion derives not from a sense of security and complete faith in the status quo, but from deep dissatisfaction with the meager benefits apportioned to women by the very institutions legitimated in the narrative. When romances are used to deny temporarily the demands of a family, when they are understood as the signs of a woman's ability to do something for herself alone, when they are valued because they provide her with the opportunity to indulge in positive feelings about a heroine and women in general, then their popularity ought to be seen as evidence of an unvoiced protest that important needs are not being properly met. It is the *act* or *event* of romance reading that permits the Smithton woman to reject those extremely taxing duties and expectations she normally shoulders with equanimity. In picking up her book, she asserts her independence from her role, affirms that she has a right to be self-interested for a while, and declares that she deserves pleasure as much as anyone else.

To be sure, this kind of defiance is relatively mild, because the woman need not pit herself against her husband and family over the crucial issues of food preparation, childcare, financial decisions, and so on. But for women who have lived their lives quiescently believing that female self-interest is exactly coterminous with the interest of a husband and children, the ability to reserve time for the self, even if it is to read a romance, is a significant and positive step away from the institutional prison that demands denial and sublimation of female identity. It is unfortunate, of course, that this temporary assertion of independence is made possible only because the manifest content of the novels holds out the promise of eventual satisfaction and fulfillment in the most conventional of terms. As a consequence, the Smithton women materially express their discontent with their restricted social world by indulging in a fantasy that vicariously supplies the pleasure and attention they need, and thereby effectively staves off the necessity of presenting those needs as demands in the real world. Simultaneously, the romance short-circuits the impulse to connect the desire to escape with the institution of marriage or with male intolerance precisely because it demonstrates that a woman like the heroine can admit the truth of the feminist discovery that women *are* intelligent and independent and yet continue to be protected paternally by a man.

At this particular historical moment, then, romance reading seems to permit American women to adopt some of the changing attitudes about gender roles by affirming that those attitudes are compatible with the social institution of marriage as it is presently constituted. This is not to say, however, that its success at papering over this troublesome contradiction is guaranteed to last forever. Perhaps it will not if we begin to admit the extent of romance readers' dissatisfaction and to point out that discontent not only to ourselves, but also to the women who have made the romance business into a multimillion dollar industry. If we do not take up this challenge, we run the risk of conceding the fight and of admitting the impossibility of creating a world where the vicarious pleasure supplied by romance reading would be unnecessary.

NOTES

1. Harlequin Enterprises Limited, Annual Report 1979, 5. Can be obtained from Harlequin Corporate Office, 220 Duncan Mill Road, Don Mills, Ontario, Canada M3B 3J5.

2. Although Harlequin Enterprises, Fawcett Books (CBS Publications), and Silhouette Books (Simon & Schuster) have conducted market research analyses of their prospective audience, none of these companies will disclose any but the most general of their findings. For descriptions of the three studies, see the following articles: on Harlequin, Phyllis Berman, "They Call Us Illegitimate," *Forbes* 121 (6 Mar. 1978): 38; on Fawcett's study, see Daisy Maryles, "Fawcett Launches Romance Imprint with Brand Marketing Techniques," *Publishers Weekly* 216 (3 Sept. 1979): 69–70; on the Silhouette study, see Michiko Kakutani, "New Romance Novels Are Just What Their Readers Ordered," *New York Times*, 11 Aug. 1980, C13.

3. Ann Barr Snitow, "Mass Market Romances: Pornography for Women is Different," *Radical History Review* 20 (Spring/Summer 1979): 150.

4. Ann Douglas, "Soft-Porn Culture," *The New Republic*, 30 Aug. 1980, 25–29; Tania Modleski, "The Disappearing Act: A Study of Harlequin Romances," *Signs* 5 (Spring 1980): 435–48.

5. The complete findings of this study are summarized and interpreted in my forthcoming book, *Reading the Romance: Women, Patriarchy, and Popular Literature*.

6. For a discussion of the lingering influence of New Criticism poetics, see Jane P. Tompkins, "The Reader in History: The Changing Shape of Literary Response," in a volume she also edited, *Reader-Response Criticism: From Formalism to Post-Structuralism* (Baltimore: Johns Hopkins University Press, 1980), 201–26; see also Frank Lentricchia, *After the New Criticism* (Chicago: University of Chicago Press, 1980).

7. Two good collections of essays that survey recent work on the theory of the reader have recently appeared. See the volume edited by Tompkins mentioned in note 6 and Susan Suleiman and Inge Crosman, *The Reader in the Text: Essays on Audience Interpretation* (Princeton: Princeton University Press, 1981).

8. Stanley Fish, *Is There A Text in This Class?: The Authority of Interpretive Communities* (Cambridge: Harvard University Press, 1980), 322. It was Fish's work that persuaded me of the

necessity of investigating what real readers do with texts when the goal of analysis is an explanatory statement about why people read certain kinds of books.

9. I do not believe that attention to the way real readers understand their books and their reading activities obviates the need for further critical probing and interpretation of potential unconscious responses to the texts in question. I also do not believe that an adequate cultural analysis should stop at such an account of their conscious behavior. What careful attention to that conscious response can produce, however, is a more accurate description of the texts to which the women do in fact consciously and unconsciously respond. In possession of such a description, the critic can then subject it to further analysis in an effort to discern the ways in which the text-as-read might also address unconscious needs, desires, and wishes which she, the critic has reason to believe her reader may experience. This procedure is little different from that pursued by an anthropologist whose goals are not merely the description and explanation of a people's behavior, but understanding of it as well. As Clifford Geertz has pointed out, descriptions of cultural behavior "must be cast in terms of the constructions we imagine Berbers, Jews or Frenchmen . . . place upon what they live through, the formulae they use to define what happens to them." Descriptions of romance reading, it might be added, should be no different. See Clifford Geertz, "Thick Description: Toward an Interpretive Theory of Cultures," in his *The Interpretation of Cultures* (New York: Basic, 1973), 14.

10. All information about the community has been taken from the 1970 U.S. Census of the Population *Characteristics of the Population,* U.S. Department of Commerce, Social and Economic Statistics Administration, Bureau of the Census, May 1972. I have rounded off some of the statistics to disguise the identity of the town.

11.

TABLE 1

Select Demographic Data: Customers of Dorothy Evans

Category	Responses	Number	%
Age	(42) Less than 25	2	5
	25–44	26	62
	45–54	12	28
	55 and older	2	5
Marital Status	(40) Single	3	8
	Married	33	82
	Widowed/separated	4	10
Parental Status	(40) Children	35	88
	No children	4	12
Age at Marriage	Mean-19.9		
	Median-19.2		
Educational Level	(40) High school diploma	21	53
	1–3 years of college	10	25
	College degree	8	20
Work Status	(40) Full or part time	18	45
	Child or home care	17	43
Family Income	(38) $14,999 or below	2	5
	15,000–24,999	18	47
	25,000–49,999	14	37
	50,000 +	4	11
Church Attendance	(40) Once or more a week	15	38
	1–3 times per month	8	20
	A few times per year	9	22
	Not in two (2) years	8	20

NOTE: (40) indicates the number of responses per questionnaire category. A total of 42 responses per category is the maximum possible. Percent calculations are all rounded to the nearest whole number.

12. Quoted by Barbara Brotman, "Ah, Romance! Harlequin Has an Affair for Its Readers," *Chicago Tribune,* 2 June 1980. All other details about the Harlequin audience have been taken

from this article. Similar information was also given by Harlequin to Margaret Jensen, whose dissertation, "Women and Romantic Fiction: A Case Study of Harlequin Enterprises, Romances, and Readers" (Ph.D. dissertation, McMaster University, Hamilton, Ontario, 1980), is the only other study I know of to attempt an investigation of romance readers. Because Jensen encountered the same problems in trying to assemble a representative sample, she relied on interviews with randomly selected readers at a used bookstore. However, the similarity of her findings to those in my study indicates that the lack of statistical representativeness in the case of real readers does not necessarily preclude applying those readers' attitudes and opinions more generally to a large portion of the audience for romantic fiction.

13. See Brotman. All other details about the Silhouette audience have been drawn from Brotman's article. The similarity of the Smithton readers to other segments of the romance audience is explored in greater depth in my book. However, the only other available study of romance readers which includes some statistics, Peter H. Mann's *The Romantic Novel: A Survey of Reading Habits* (London: Mills & Boon, 1969), indicates that the British audience for such fiction has included in the past more older women as well as younger, unmarried readers than are represented in my sample. However, Mann's survey raises suspicions because it was sponsored by the company that markets the novels and because its findings are represented in such a polemical form. For an analysis of Mann's work, see Jensen, 389–92.

14. Yankelovich, Skelly and White, Inc., *The 1978 Consumer Research Study on Reading and Bookpurchasing*, prepared for the Book Industry Study Group, October 1978, 122. Unfortunately, it is impossible to determine from the Yankelovich study findings what proportion of the group of romance readers consumed a number similar to that read by the Smithton women. Also, because the interviewers distinguished between gothics and romances on the one hand and historicals on the other, the figures are probably not comparable. Indeed, the average of nine may be low since some of the regular "historical" readers may actually be readers of romances.

15. The Smithton readers are not avid television watchers. Ten of the women, for instance, claimed to watch television less than three hours per week. Fourteen indicated that they watch four to seven hours a week, while eleven claimed eight to fourteen hours of weekly viewing. Only four said they watch an average of fifteen to twenty hours a week, while only one admitted viewing twenty-one or more hours a week. When asked how often they watch soap operas, twenty-four of the Smithton women checked "never," five selected "rarely," seven chose "sometimes," and four checked "often." Two refused to answer the question.

16. The Smithton readers' constant emphasis on the educational value of romances was one of the most interesting aspects of our conversations, and chapter 3 of *Reading the Romance*, discusses it in depth. Although their citation of the instructional value of romances to a college professor interviewer may well be a form of self-justification, the women also provided ample evidence that they do in fact learn and remember facts about geography, historical customs, and dress from the books they read. Their emphasis on this aspect of their reading, I might add, seems to betoken a profound curiosity and longing to know more about the exciting world beyond their suburban homes.

17. For material on housewives' attitudes toward domestic work and their duties as family counselors, see Ann Oakley, *The Sociology of Housework* (New York: Pantheon, 1975) and *Women's Work: The Housewife, Past and Present* (New York: Pantheon, 1975); see also Mirra Komorovsky, *Blue Collar Marriage* (New York: Vintage, 1967) and Helena Znaniecki Lopata, *Occupation: Housewife* (New York: Oxford University Press, 1971).

18. Nancy Chodorow, *The Reproduction of Mothering: Psychoanalysis and the Sociology of Gender* (Berkeley: University of California Press, 1978). I would like to express my thanks to

Sharon O'Brien for first bringing Chodorow's work to my attention and for all those innumerable discussions in which we debated the merits of her theory and its applicability to women's lives, including our own.

19. After developing my argument that the Smithton women are seeking ideal romances which depict the generally tender treatment of the heroine, I discovered Beatrice Faust's *Women, Sex, and Pornography: A Controversial Study* (New York: Macmillan, 1981) in which Faust points out that certain kinds of historical romances tend to portray their heroes as masculine, but emotionally expressive. Although I think Faust's overall argument has many problems, not the least of which is her heavy reliance on hormonal differences to explain variations in female and male sexual preferences, I do agree that some women prefer the detailed description of romantic love and tenderness to the careful anatomical representations characteristic of male pornography.

20. Maryles, 69.

21. Ten of the twenty books in the sample for the ideal romance were drawn from the Smithton group's answers to requests that they list their three favorite romances and authors.

22. See Faust, passim.

23. There are two exceptions to this assertion. Both *The Proud Breed* by Celeste DeBlasis and *The Fulfillment* by LaVyrle Spencer detail the involvement of the principal characters with other individuals. Their treatment of the subject, however, is decidedly different from that typically found in the bad romances. Both of these books are highly unusual in that they begin by detailing the extraordinary depth of the love shared by hero and heroine, who marry early in the story. The rest of each book chronicles the misunderstandings that arise between heroine and hero. In both books the third person narrative always indicates very clearly to the reader that the two are still deeply in love with each other and are acting out of anger, distrust, and insecurity.

24. In the romances considered awful by the Smithton readers, this reinterpretation takes place much later in the story than in the ideal romances. In addition, the behavior that is explained away is more violent, aggressively cruel, and obviously vicious. Although the hero is suddenly transformed by the heroine's reinterpretation of his motives, his tenderness, gentleness, and care are not emphasized in the "failed romances" as they are in their ideal counterparts.

25. Modleski has also argued that "the mystery of male motives" is a crucial concern in all romantic fiction (p. 439). Although she suggests, as I will here, that the process through which male misbehavior is reinterpreted in a more favorable light is a justification or legitimation of such action, she does not specifically connect its centrality in the plot to a reader's need to use such a strategy in her own marriage. While there are similarities between Modleski's analysis and that presented here, she emphasizes the negative, disturbing effects of romance reading on readers. In fact, she claims, the novels "end up actually intensifying conflicts for the reader" (p. 445) and cause women to "reemerge feeling . . . more guilty than ever" (p. 447). While I would admit that romance reading might create unconscious guilt, I think it absolutely essential that any explanation of such behavior take into account the substantial amount of evidence indicating that women not only *enjoy* romance reading, but feel replenished and reconstituted by it as well.

26. Jude Deveraux, *The Black Lyon* (New York: Avon, 1980), 66.

Chapter Fifty-one

From Feminism without Women
Culture and Criticism in a "Postfeminist" Age (1991)

Tania Modleski

Modleski, a prominent literary and cultural critic, here specifically criticizes Radway's methods and conclusions, aligning herself with Snitow: "romances provide women with a common fantasy structure to ensure their continued psychic investment in their oppression." Her own theory of mass-produced romantic fiction can be found in her book, Loving with a Vengeance: Mass-Produced Fantasies for Women *(1982).*

Is the female feminist critic able to give an authentic voice to the women traditionally silenced by patriarchal culture and sometimes even by that culture's sternest dissidents? A widely admired book on women's romances, *Reading the Romance* by Janice Radway, gives an emphatically affirmative answer to both questions. In her study, Radway reports and elaborates on her "ethnographic" researches into a midwestern community of romance readers (called by the fictitious name of Smithton), headed by "Dot," a woman who writes a newsletter evaluating romances each month. Radway's book is both rich in detail and ambitious (interviewing romance readers, giving a history of the paperback industry, considering the texts in the light of Nancy Chodorow's psychoanalytic study *The Reproduction of Mothering*, etc.), and it is not my intention here to conduct a detailed critique of it. Rather, I want to analyze a few of the presuppositions of Radway's ethnographic methodology and in particular to examine the viability for feminist critique of the intimately linked theories of subcultural formations and what has variously been called the acquisition of "literary competence," the accumulation of "cultural capital," or the development of particular "reading formations."[1]

Throughout her study Radway is concerned to justify the superiority of her approach over that taken by the elitist "professors of English," as she calls them, since the latter in her view fail to take into consideration the real women who read romances and who are in the best position to inform scholars about what the women call their reading "habit." According to Radway, there is "no evidence" that we (critics, professors) "know how to read as romance readers do." To support such a position, Radway refers to the work of Stanley Fish, who, she says, first taught her the importance of studying what "real readers do with texts," for meaning, according to Fish, "is constructed from textual materials by a reader who operates not alone and subjectively but according to assumptions and strategies that he or she has adopted by virtue of prior participation in a specific interpretive community," a term that has certain affinities with the more Marxist notion of "subculture."[2] The work of Fish and other theorists of literary competency has in fact appealed strongly to other feminists besides Radway, in part because it provides a way of deconstructing the canon and explaining women's exclusion from this canon and in part because it can help explain how women learn to read the writings of other women. Thus, in a feminist critique of the male literary canon, Annette Kolodny approvingly quotes Murray Krieger's narrative of how people come to understand interpretive conventions and hence to acquire literary competency: "Once one has read his [*sic*] first poem, he turns to his second and to the others that will follow thereafter with an increasing series of preconceptions about the sort of activity in which he is indulging. In matters of literary experience, as in other experiences, one is a virgin but once."[3] But surely, this is a naive account in a post-Althusserian, post-Derridean literary world; for, as the continental thinkers have taught us, often using the same unfortunate metaphorical language, in reading as in writing one is always already a whore.

Given that Radway's "community of romance readers" is, it must be pointed out, an extreme rarity in the world, since reading romances is a perfect example of the serialized activity Jean-Paul Sartre saw as characteristic of mass culture, we need to note that the interpretive conventions enabling us to read romances are not formed in a community or subculture like the one studied by Radway but are, for *most* of us, set in place from birth, that in patriarchal society a female child is born into and simultaneously interpellated by a world where many of the conventions of romance hold powerful sway—in, say, her mother's fantasy life (which in turn shapes her own life at the level of the unconscious), in popular songs and fairy tales, and, later, in novels and movies. These conventions are, then, part of our cultural heritage as women. In short, there is *every* reason to suppose, if we are honest with ourselves, that we know how to read as romance readers do: any woman who has ever responded emotionally to Rhett Butler sweeping Scarlett O'Hara up the stairs knows how to "read" romances (and in fact the Smithton women list *Gone with the Wind* among their all-time favorite novels).

The point here is not only that it is questionable from a moral and political point of view to treat romance readers as if they were natives of Bora-Bora rather than middle-class housewives from somewhere around Kansas (although, of course, ethnographic studies of the natives of Bora-Bora are *also* often morally and politically problematic).[4] The point is also that romances are the property of us all—and not of just white Anglo-Saxon and American women either: Morley's female West Indian and African subjects, we recall, seemed just as avid for mass-produced female fantasies as Kansas housewives, and, of course, Harlequins and other serial romances are translated into dozens of languages. In this regard, the limits of a "subcultural" approach to women's romances ought to be clear, since the popularity of romances is a *cross*-cultural phenomenon, and romances provide women with a common fantasy structure to ensure their continued psychic investment in their oppression.

Moreover, assuming its effectiveness, this fantasy, which promises women complete fulfillment through heterosexual love, ensures the impossibility of women ever *getting together* (as women) to form a "subculture" (if it makes any sense to speak of the majority of the world as a "subculture") and hence to develop a system of values that will effectively challenge and undermine an increasingly hegemonic patriarchal ideology. Because women's experience has been privatized, and because, as Terry Eagleton has argued, criticism belonged to the bourgeois (male) public sphere before it became almost wholly academicized, a woman-oriented criticism could emerge only when feminists began to public-ize and collectively explore their private experience and, through consciousness-raising, to come to terms with the myriad ramifications of feminism's most basic insight, "the personal is political."[5] Located, until recently, on the margins of the academy, the feminist critic has contributed to the forging of a woman's culture based on this insight and has felt herself to be part of a broader movement of women on whose behalf she could sometimes speak because, through consciousness-raising, she in fact *did* speak *to* them—as one of them. Her work is, then, ideally plurivocal, not denying the differences of other women but learning about them through dialogic exchange, rather than through ethnographies that posit an unbridgeable gap between the critic's subjectivity and the subjectivity of "the others."[6]

But because Radway never admits the similarity between herself and the women she studies and, like Fiske and Morley, adopts the pose of the disinterested "scientific researcher," she winds up condescending to the very people she wants to rescue from critical scorn—this despite her claims never to have contradicted the women: "I have always worked first from their conscious statements and beliefs about their behavior, accepted them as given, and then posited additional desires, fears, or concerns that complement rather than contradict those beliefs and assertions" (p. 10). For someone who proceeds to utilize a psychoanalytic methodology in analyzing the texts' appeal to their readers, this is quite an extraordinary claim. It flies in the face of the most basic insights of psychoanalysis—that the unconscious is made up of feelings and desires that the conscious mind finds difficult to tolerate (i.e., the unconscious *contradicts* the conscious mind), and that it is itself, as Freud continually asserted, *characterized* by contradiction. In general, the crucial element missing here is a sense of the various ways a notion of contradiction *must* be brought to bear in any attempt to understand the full complexity of women's relation to culture: contradictions at an intrapsychic level; contradictions between conscious or unconscious fantasies and the discourses that conflict with or discredit these fantasies; and contradictions between competing ideologies and discourses as they are reflected both in popular texts and in the audience's relations to these texts. A recognition that romance readers may be self-contradictory in their attitudes and behavior does not necessarily open up the analyst to the charge of elitism, as Radway seems to fear, *especially* if we are willing to acknowledge how much we ourselves are implicated within those very structures we set out to analyze, how much our own feelings, desires, anxieties, etc., are caught up in contradiction—in short, how much our fantasy lives, for all our cherished feminist ideals, may resemble those of the women we study.

Far from being narcissistic, as it might at first appear, the self-analysis involved in the kind of feminist criticism I would advocate may well provide an antidote to the narcissism I suspect to be at the heart of much reader-oriented popular culture criticism—a criticism which, although claiming a certain objective validity by appealing to the pleasures and tastes of others, often seems to be based on an unspoken syllogism that goes something like this: "I like *Dallas;* I am a feminist; *Dallas* must have progressive potential."[7] It seemed important at one historical moment to emphasize the way "the people" resist mass culture's manipulations. Today, we are in danger of forgetting the crucial fact that like the rest of the world even the cultural analyst may sometimes be a "cultural dupe"—which is, after all, only an ugly way of saying that we exist inside ideology, that we are all victims, down to the very depths of our psyches, of political and cultural domination (even though we are never *only* victims).

All of this is simply to propose a place for the feminist textual critic who recognizes her commonality with other women. Because she is so deeply invested in her methodology, Radway finds it necessary utterly to discredit textual critics—an attack that is curious in light of her decision to accord "Dot," the Smithton community's romance reviewer, great authority. For Dot, it turns out, may be as idiosyncratic in her tastes as any other reader and may in fact have imposed these tastes upon the group as a whole: "Therefore," writes Radway, "while the members of the Smithton group share attitudes about good and bad romances that are similar to Dot's it is impossible to say whether these opinions were formed by Dot or whether she is simply their most articulate advocate" (p. 55). But what, finally, is the *feminist* critic but an articulate advocate of opinions about texts?—opinions which she sometimes shares with other women, and sometimes helps to form.

NOTES

1. For one discussion of literary competence, see Jonathan Culler, *Structuralist Poetics: Structuralism, Linguistics, and the Study of Literature* (Ithaca, N.Y.: Cornell University Press, 1975); and for a very different one stressing interpretive communities, see Stanley Fish, *Is There a Text in This Class?: The Authority of Interpretive Communities* (Cambridge, Mass.: Harvard University Press, 1980). The term "cultural capital" is Bourdieu's. See Pierre Bourdieu, *Distinction: A Social Critique of the Judgment of Taste,* trans. Richard Nice (Cambridge, Mass.: Harvard University Press, 1984). Tony Bennett and Janet Woolacott prefer to speak of "reading formations." See their *Bond and Beyond: The Political Career of a Popular Hero* (London: Methuen, 1987).

2. Janice Radway, *Reading the Romance: Women, Patriarchy, and Popular Literature* (Chapel Hill: University of North Carolina Press, 1984), p. 243n.

3. Annette Kolodny, "Dancing Through the Minefield: Some Observations on the Theory, Practice, and Politics of a Feminist Literary Criticism," in Showalter, ed., *The New Feminist Criticism: Women, Literature, Theory* (New York: Pantheon, 1985), pp. 55–56.

4. The huge body of literature contesting the most basic tenets of classical ethnography is seldom brought to bear self-critically in ethnographic studies of media and mass culture.

5. But for a discussion that challenges Eagleton's pessimism about the "academicization" of literary criticism, see Tony Bennett, "The Prison-House of Criticism," *New Formations* 2 (Summer 1987): 129–44.

6. Recent work on cultural ethnography in general has stressed the point that "culture" is always relational, an inscription of communication processes that exist, historically, *between* subjects in relations of power. See James Clifford, "Introduction: Partial Truths" in *Writing Culture: The Poetics and Politics of Ethnography*, ed. James Clifford and George E. Marcus (Berkeley: University of California Press, 1986), p. 15.

7. So, for example, Ien Ang gathered reader responses to *Dallas* by placing the following notice in the newspaper: "I like watching the TV serial *Dallas*, but often get odd reactions to it. Would anyone like to write and tell me why you like watching it too, or dislike it: I should like to assimilate these reactions in my university thesis." It's interesting to think about what kind of responses she would have elicited had she said she *doesn't* like watching *Dallas*. See Ien Ang, *Watching Dallas: Soap Opera and the Melodramatic Imagination*, trans. Della Cooling (London: Methuen, 1985), p. 10.

Chapter Fifty-two

The Wellsprings of Romance (1989); Let Me Tell You about My Readers (1992)

Ann Maxwell and Jayne Ann Krentz; Diana Palmer

These two articles by Harlequin novelists attempt to justify popular romance fiction by and for women as affirming the value of women (Maxwell and Krentz), providing a necessary "escape" from women's real-life drudgery (Palmer), and not least, offering innocent pleasure. One might see these as their defense against the criticisms of the novelists, literary critics, and sociologists in this part.

The Wellsprings of Romance

Ann Maxwell and Jayne Ann Krentz

What is it about popular fiction that attracts an audience so huge that it requires divisions, subdivisions, and labels in order to cope with it?

Put another way, what is it in popular fiction that makes it popular with those elite among American citizens who are literate enough to read *with* pleasure and imaginative enough to read *for* pleasure?

In large part fiction that is popular owes more to Zoroaster than to Sartre, more to Manes than to Marx, more to Jung than to Freud. Popular fiction is a continuation of and embroidery upon ancient myths and archetypes; it is good against evil, Prometheus against the uncaring gods, Persephone emerging from hell with the seeds of spring in her hands, Adam discovering Eve.

You cannot kill off good myths and legends. Historians continually rewrite the past and we are constantly reshaping our own futures. But our basic myths and legends are immutable. The lessons they teach, the goals they set, and the hope they offer are the wellspring of all that we can and will achieve as human beings.

Strip away the contemporary trappings of any powerful romance or mystery or

Ann Maxwell and Jayne Ann Krentz, "The Wellsprings of Romance," *Romance Writers' Report*, vol. 9, no. 5 (September 1989): 21–23. © 1989 by *Romance Writers' Report*. Reprinted by permission. Diana Palmer, "Let Me Tell You about My Readers," in *Dangerous Men and Adventurous Women: Romance Writers on the Appeal of the Romance*, ed. Jayne Ann Krentz (Philadelphia: University of Pennsylvania Press, 1992), 155–57. Copyright © 1992 by the University of Pennsylvania. Reprinted by permission of the publisher.

horror story or any other piece of genre fiction and you will find at its heart a tale that could be told to and understood by a caveman, a medieval monk, a Renaissance playwright, or a 20th-century corporate executive.

They would all respond to the underlying myth because such myths and legends are timeless.

It is not particularly difficult to analyze the underlying myths of each of the genres. There's no need to get someone with a Ph.D. in English lit to do it for you. Truth is, you'd probably be better off if you didn't get a Ph.D. in English lit to do it. The very fact that you read the genres and get something out of them is all you need to tell you that you have a gut-level understanding of them.

Mysteries, for example, very clearly speak to our need for justice and rational answers in a world where there has always been too little of each. Nobody criticizes the mystery genre for providing pat solutions to crimes that in real life would very likely never be solved. Nobody calls the stories unrealistic and simplistic for that reason, but of course they are. Normal people do not read mysteries and actually believe that in the real world things always work out that neatly. Everyone knows that murders go unsolved every day of the week.

That is not the point. People read mysteries because the myths and legends embedded in them help us maintain our dreams of justice and rational solutions to complex problems. They are morality plays that tell us how things should be and they help us maintain our faith that if we keep working at it, keep struggling, we can achieve at least part of that goal. And where would society be without such goals? If we gave up our hopes and dreams of justice altogether we would very shortly be reduced to violent anarchy.

The same analysis can be done on each genre. Romance is just like any other in that it taps ancient myths and legends. But the unique thing about our genre is that its appeal is primarily to women. That, of course, is what drives all the critics and analysts nuts.

What they don't understand is that women respond to romance stories on an instinctive level because the appeal is to one of our most basic instincts: the need to create the family unit.

Like it or not, women have always had the responsibility for creating the basic family unit, the unit that is the primary socioeconomic unit of civilization itself. That unit begins with the basic bonding of a man and a woman, and every woman knows it.

Given the enormous responsibility that has devolved upon the female of the species, then, is it really any wonder, *any wonder at all*, that women have created myths and legends concerning the formation of that bond? It would be astounding if they had not done so.

Had women chosen to ignore that responsibility five, ten, or fifty thousand years ago, civilization would have gone right down the tubes. But women, by and large, tend to opt for survival, both for themselves and for their families.

No, women do not read romance novels because they actually believe real-life bonds between men and women always work out the way they do in the books. They do not believe this any more than a mystery fan believes all criminals will get caught and punished.

We do not read any of our myths and legends for a reality check. We read them to reinforce our basic survival goals, the goals on which the whole notion of civilization is based.

The point of reading the myths and legends in romance is that the goal of men and women bonding successfully must be kept alive if the human race is to survive. It is as simple as that. Our genre is the literature of human survival. And women are very good at surviving.

No, romance is not a frivolous subject. It is powerful stuff. It has always been with us, altering the destiny of kingdoms and the fates of private individuals. The dark side of romance has caused people to kill and be killed. The bright side has provided others with strength, hope and a reason to live when there seemed to be nothing else worth living for.

Romance focuses on the most fundamental, the most emotionally charged of the legends, the legends of male-female bonding. In doing so, romance clearly reigns supreme among the genres because it has at its heart all the most powerful human emotions and drives.

Love, hate, jealousy, compassion, vengeance, the spirit of self-sacrifice and the spirit of possessiveness and greed, and yes, the thrill of confronting real danger, both physical and emotional, all spring straight from the heart of the romance genre. These are, after all, the forces at work in our myths and legends.

It is worth taking a few minutes to examine some of the most powerful of the romance legends.

Let's take those one at a time and see if we can understand the enduring appeal of these romantic archetypes.

The **Forced Marriage** story: With the exception of the last century or so, daughters have been handed from father to a male chosen *by* the father. The bride's wishes had little or nothing to do with the selection of a lifetime mate. This is still the norm in non-European countries. It isn't hard to understand why women would find a story in which a forced marriage turns out well to be appealing.

As for forced marriages today, they happen all around you. To be pressured into marriage by pregnancy, money or fear of living alone is to enter into a marriage that wasn't freely made.

The **Persephone** story: She's the one who was kidnapped (or swept off her feet, depending on which version you read), carried down to hell, and later miraculously emerged with the seeds of a fruitful life in her hands because Pluto had fallen in love with her. Given the fact that women were rather routinely kidnapped by strangers and forced to make the best of their resulting life, the core of the Persephone myth has a definite allure. Nor has it faded; *The Sheik* finds a new audience with each generation.

The Taming of the Shrew: This romantic myth is particularly piquant, because making the relationship work is the *man's* problem for once, rather than the woman's. In the end the man manages to unite what had been the two warring halves of the woman, her emotions and her razor intelligence. As for the reformed shrew's humble speeches at the end of the play . . . anyone who has read much Shakespeare will suspect that he dropped his quill pen laughing because he knew precisely who did what and with which and to whom the instant the bedroom door closed.

The **Cinderella** story: There's more to this one than the some-day-my-prince-will-come type of wish fulfillment. Cinderella wasn't just sitting around whining and polishing her nails. She was working her little blonde butt off, making the best of an epically bad situation—that of unpaid servant. It was a situation in which unmarried women traditionally found themselves mired. In the end, Cinderella's strength of character is rewarded by a good mate. The message in Cinderella is not that a prince will fall out of the sky if you stand around slack-jawed and empty-handed. The message is that if you work very hard making a go of whatever life you have, you will be rewarded with a better life.

Frankly, it isn't hard to understand why that story has appeal in any time, ancient or modern.

Beauty and the Beast: The message underlying the myth is quite simple: no matter how savage or forbidding the exterior of a male might be, often the ability to love lies beneath; and the right woman can trigger that love.

What kind of women read and enjoy these ancient, ever-new myths of male and female?

Obviously the average romance reader is not a simpleton sitting and spinning on her thumb while waiting for Prince Charming to come rescue her from terminal ennui. Nor is the average romance reader a neurotic looking for a quick romantic fix; she has a sound, organic marriage, knows that bad things happen in the world, and believes in solutions rather than in hand-wringing. She reads romances because they speak to her own, deeply-held beliefs rather than trying to cram other, more trendy, beliefs down her throat.

That's one of the reasons historical romances are enjoying a resurgence today; it is much easier for the author of an historical to use romantic archetypes in their purest form. When writing contemporary romance, the author must often resort to unwieldy or absurd disguises in order to sneak the myth past the editors.

You see, editors are very human. They want to believe they are on the cutting edge of respectable intellectual-political trends, which means that editors are terrified of appearing to put out antifeminist books. They haven't yet discovered a vital truth: ROMANCES AREN'T ANTI-FEMINIST.

No successful contemporary romance writer maintains either publicly or privately that a woman *needs* a man for her life to be complete. A whole lot of women *want* a mate, however, a man who will enhance the quality of her life just as she will enhance the quality of his life. And a whole lot of men want the same thing from their woman, their mate. That's what romances are about, plain and simple—enhancing life, not limiting it.

Until editors get less nervous about the political correctness of contemporary romances, the field will continue to be flooded with books based on two very, very modern myths.

First comes **the househusband** myth: He cooks, cleans, raises kids and does it all with a smile while she goes out and slays dragons. The only difference between this man and a stereotypical 1950s housewife is that he can't get pregnant.

The Alan Alda clone: No matter what a raving bitch the woman is, the man remains sympathetic, supportive, loving and non-judgmental. He is a saint in penny loafers.

Both of these myths have an understandable appeal for women . . . putting sauce on the gander is great fun. However, both of these myths lack an ingredient that is vital to popular fiction: conflict.

A story without conflict or real risk of danger to the heroine is flat and uninteresting. The problem with the new myths in romance fiction is that they lack real gut-level challenge for the heroine.

You don't get much of a challenge for your heroine from a sensitive, understanding, right-thinking modern man who is part therapist, part best-friend, and, yes, mostly female in his thinking processes. He will, of course, be a truly wonderful human being but he is too much like the heroine to provide any real source of conflict in a romance.

Furthermore, this image of the perfect modern man is not realistic in the first place, no matter how much the editors or even we ourselves would like to think it is. A man who does not lose his temper with you? A man who is always sensitive, always deeply in touch with his own emotions and yours? A man who would never growl or snap or sulk or seek vengeance or say he told you so? A man who believes in his heart of hearts that women really should be totally liberated? That they should share in the power that men have always considered theirs by divine right? A man who does not feel deep in his soul that women should look to him for protection and, yes, guidance? A man who does not ultimately like to feel that he is in control of his world and that includes, on some primitive level, his woman?

Give me a break.

You will note that in all the classic myths, the ones that have survived and thus demonstrated real staying power, there is always an element of danger, whether it be physical or emotional, for the heroine; a challenge to be met; a sense of risk. And that sense of danger always emanates directly from the hero. *In all the memorable and powerful romantic myths the heroes always play two roles. They are not only the heroes, they are the villains.*

Tales of romance are essentially tales of strong women taming and gentling that most dangerous of all creatures on earth, the human male.

Those of us who write romance are in the business of recreating ancient legends for modern women. Our craft is as old as the myths and legends themselves. In a very real way we are in charge of keeping a crucial idea alive, the goal of a perfect bond between men and women. What's more, in romance novels we portray that goal of bonding in a strong, positive, powerful manner, one that works toward the survival of the species and of civilization.

We cry out for justice most urgently when we see control of our streets slipping into the hands of violent criminals. So, too, do we most energetically stoke the fires of faith in the ideal of a monogamous, romantic bond when we are faced, as we are today, with threats to the family that include everything from crumbling social structures to a terrifying disease.

The threats we face are not new. They have always been around in one form or another. There has never been a time when men and women bonded perfectly in mutual respect and love and equal sharing of responsibility, just as there has never been a time when the streets were completely safe.

But just as there is hope and some measure of safety on the streets as long as the *ideal* of justice is kept alive, so, too, is there hope for men and women and the human race as long as the *ideal* of the romantic bond between male and female is kept alive.

And that, my sister writers and those of you who read, write, and publish romance novels, is our job.

We are the keepers of the flame.

Let Me Tell You about My Readers

Diana Palmer

It is ironic that romance appeals to almost everyone, but in literature it is something of a ragged stepchild and needs defending. I find it fascinating that the other genres— mystery, horror, science fiction, fantasy, suspense, and western—never have to be justified or explained. Yet romance novels, the revenues from which comprise the bedrock earnings of a large segment of the publishing industry, seem always to stand in need of defense. Critics of the books are legion.

But it is not the critics who matter to me. It is my readers. The women for whom I produce my books are women just like me. Let me tell you about them.

Although I have readers from every walk of life and many of them are much better educated than I ever expect to be, the majority of my readership represents the hard-working labor force. They are women who spend eight grueling hours a day in a garment factory, in front of a classroom, or behind a desk. Most of them are married and have children. Some are divorced or widowed. These hard-working women leave their jobs at the end of the day and pick up their children at day-care centers. They go home to a house that needs cleaning, to dishes that need washing, to meals that have to be prepared. They go home to dirty clothes that must be washed, to organizational tasks that include making sure the kids are bathed and the homework is done.

These women all have one basic thing in common: they know what love is. They live it every day. They sacrifice for their families, they worry, they fuss, but most of them would do it all over again. Family life is as basic a need in some women as life itself.

Romance novels allow these women, who have experienced love and its aftermath, to be many things. They allow them to be virgins again. To be career women. To be debutantes. To be princesses. To live in luxury and even, sometimes, in decadence. The novels allow them to escape the normal cares and woes of life by returning in dreams to a time less filled with responsibilities. Romances allow them to experience all this and more without risking what they already have.

Is fantasy healthy? Does it, as some claim, provide a dangerous escape from problems that are better faced? Some small percentage of any society is susceptible to obsession. Just as some people are addicted to alcohol and drugs, others become addicted to fantasy and withdraw into it to the detriment of their own lives. But for the majority, daydreams can be a very healthy occupation because they enable people to step back from problems that threaten to be overwhelming. They provide breathing room and the opportunity to see obstacles from a safe distance.

My reader mail includes letters from people who have been suicidal, who have suffered serious health problems, who have nursed children with fatal or debilitating defects. These readers tell me that my books and those of other romance authors have helped them get through periods of anguish and grief. In fact, romance novels have many times kept *me* going during the trials and tribulations of my own life. The books do this by providing a brief respite that allows readers to gather their energies so that they can return, refreshed, to face and solve real-life problems. Total escape cannot be healthy. But a breathing space can save one's sanity. Romantic fantasy is a safety valve, a way of letting off steam without boiling any water.

As long as men and women fall in love, romance will continue to thrive. In spite of criticism and ridicule, mockery and disdain, artificial insemination notwithstanding and critics taken into consideration, young girls will secretly dream of young men coming to woo them even if those young girls grow up to become theoretical physicists. Married women will dream of a rich suitor coming to carry them off in a Rolls, a bouquet of roses in one hand, a bottle of champagne in the other, and a promise of deathless passion on his lips. Old women will dream of green meadows and long kisses in the sunshine long after arthritic joints make such pastimes uncomfortable. Cinderella, Beauty and the Beast, and Sleeping Beauty are as eternal as life itself, impervious to reality. Love triumphant with a happy ending. There are so few untarnished things in the real world.

I make no apologies for my choice of vocation. I make no excuses for the type of fiction I choose to write. I produce fantasy for people who need a one-hour escape from reality. I work for the mother of a child with cystic fibrosis who has had to sit up all night alone looking after him. For the wife of a dying paraplegic whose vigil is almost at an end. For the factory worker whose feet hurt. For the teacher who comes home at the end of a trying day to face unswept floors, uncooked meals, and the endless paperwork required of her profession. For the sick woman in the nursing home whose family come to see her once a month. For the farm wife with five children who cheerfully goes about her chores to earn herself a quiet hour in bed when everyone else is asleep. And during that hour she can wear a ball gown instead of an apron, glass slippers instead of faded bedroom shoes.

For all those women, I write books. They are my family, my fans, my friends. I know many of them by name. They write to me and I write back. I remember them in my prayers at night. I never forget that it is because of them that I am privileged to be a successful writer. I owe my career, my livelihood, and my loyalty to them.

I write books for my readers. As long as they continue to read my novels I really don't mind if the world at large ridicules my work or dismisses it as "trash."

I am satisfied as long as that tired factory worker or that worried mother or that elderly woman in a nursing home finds something, anything, in one of my books that makes her life just a little easier or a little happier.

If my work needs a defense, let that be it.

Chapter Fifty-three

Reading Romance, Reading Ourselves (1996)

Beverly Lyon Clark, Karen Gennari Bernier,
Michelle Henneberry-Nassau, Lauren Beth Jenks,
Angie J. Moorman, and Marah Bianca Rhoades

Six women collaborated on this interesting essay, which questions how to make reading the popular romance less a guilty pleasure than "a satisfying experience" for women who are feminists, liberating fantasy that could be "a source of both pleasure and power." Their views reflect an ongoing ambivalence in young people's expectations of romantic love, as well as their uncertain hope that they can "change the power balance."

He bent down over her resting form. He could smell honey and lilacs, her body's natural scents. Her eyes opened, seemed to focus on him, then widened. She looked unsure, not knowing what to expect. He lifted her into his arms.

He could feel her fruits pressing against his hard chest. He crushed her mouth to his, prying her lips apart with his tongue, probing, tasting the soft flesh inside her mouth. She pushed against his chest, struggling to be set free. He held her tighter, kissing deeper and slower. Gradually, her protests subsided. Her arms wound around his neck as her tongue met his in a dance of passion. He groaned deep in his throat. Lowering them both to the couch, he knew that words had no place between them tonight.

In the summer of my thirteenth year I spent a whole week on the beach with a girlfriend reading Harlequins and Silhouettes. We were in honors English and prided ourselves on being fast readers. She could go through two, maybe three, 192-page romances a day. Being a little slower, I could only do one and a half a day. It probably took me longer because I read scenes like the hypothetical one above several times before moving on.

I have a photograph of the two of us from that week. We are sitting side by side in beach chairs. We have on sunglasses that her mother lent us. They are too big for our faces, making us look like girls playing grown-up. We both are reading, oblivious of the fact that our picture is being taken. Now, looking at that photo, I see a young girl very much confused as to why she was feeling what she was feeling between her legs, a young girl who felt privately embarrassed for rereading the sections that referred to breasts and used words like *passion*.

Now, when I look at that picture I wish I could wrest that book away from her hands. (Angie Moorman)[1]

More than one woman who considers herself a feminist has been embarrassed to admit to enjoying romance fiction. Personally, I felt extremely amorous toward my boyfriend immediately after reading one. (Michelle Henneberry)

What is unique about our century is . . . the extent to which love is no longer even deemed worthy of intellectual analysis. Discourses on love have virtually disappeared from our major intellectual enterprises. The interest in love has been relegated almost exclusively to private concerns and popular culture. (Ethel Spector Person, *Dreams of Love and Fateful Encounters* 18)

When I was a teenager I used to read romantic stories in my mother's *Redbooks* and *Good Housekeepings*. I also prided myself—aspiring intellectual that I was—on reading great literature like *Pride and Prejudice* and *Jane Eyre*, but I read and loved them as romance novels. . . .

Notice how I distance myself from mass-market romances—by staking a claim to "high" literature and by projecting my fondness onto the past. All of us coauthors engage at times in distancing strategies, in this essay in the form of a dialogue among participants in classes on "Feminist Criticism," in this collage that will circle around issues of power and desire in reading popular romances. Such a collaborative effort between students and teacher can provide a unique window on the complexities of response to mass culture.

The six of us who have collaborated as coauthors attempt to interrupt the monolithic voice of the academic essay by creating a dialogue that echoes that of the classroom, playing our ideas off those of fellow students, previous commentators, and the fiction itself. This student-centered, cooperative enterprise embodies a pedagogy that we would call feminist.[2] We attempt, further, to piece together a fabric that relies less on the logic of reason and more on the logic of association, a fabric that is less hierarchical, more evocative. Much of what we attempt to communicate is not spelled out but is in the spaces between passages: the reader can listen there for affect, for dissonances and harmonies. For we're not arguing a thesis but rather raising questions, endorsing individual voices, validating differences, attending to process, starting to dismantle the myths of unified subjectivity and of the customary oppositions between high and low culture, between scholarship and teaching, and between student and teacher—even if we never completely dismantle them.[3] (Bev Clark)

. . . the teacher needs to encourage her women students to say what she does not expect them to say and perhaps would rather not hear. (Nina Baym, "The Feminist Teacher of Literature" 75)

Some of the liveliest discussion in the course, the most energized, erupted when we discussed a Harlequin-type romance. (Bev Clark)

The vehement protestations almost knocked my socks off. (Lauren Jenks)

Leslie W. Rabine (166 ff.) seems to be suggesting that Harlequin romances present the possibility of social change to women. I think she is way out in left field. She is wishfully reading an element of social change into this fluffy, sexist, brainwashing garbage. (Lynda Tocci)

Critics like Ann Douglas, JoAnn Castagna, and Robin L. Radespiel would agree with Lynda. Most of us coauthors find ourselves in at least partial agreement—inclined to disdain Harlequins and to see women as victimized. (Bev Clark)

I do not read Harlequins or Silhouettes. I read the historical ones, because then I can rationalize the sexism away—"Well, this *is* the nineteenth century. . . ." (Anonymous student)

Harlequin has become a generic term, like Kleenex or Xerox, but with more negative associations—to the extent that many people pretend to know what they are like without ever having read one. Even critics offering sympathetic readings of women and romance tend to belittle or ignore Harlequins. The Smithton women that Janice Radway studied tended not to like them (*Reading* 56); Carol Thurston is dismissive of the Harlequin Romance and Harlequin Presents series (45n4); Cora Kaplan's sensitive probings of her positive responses focus not on series romance but on a family saga, *The Thorn Birds*.

We coauthors, too, have been guilty of indiscriminately generalizing the ills of society, especially its sexist failings, to Harlequins. In an early draft we went into a long excursus on media images of feminine beauty and indicted Harlequin romances for reinforcing them. Only after reading scores of Harlequins and Silhouettes do we realize that they don't, not particularly. The typical heroine is attractive but not ideally beautiful.

In any case, we here address the rapidly-changing, market-sensitive phenomenon of series romance by focusing on novels published not in the seventies and early eighties, as the most insightful and influential previous critics have (Tania Modleski focused on romances published in 1976; Ann Barr Snitow, on those published in 1977 and 1978; Radway, on those published through 1981; Rabine, on those published through 1984; Thurston, on those published through 1985), but in the late eighties and especially the nineties.[4] And in turning our attention to Harlequins and Sil-houettes rather than the longer, less formulaic historical romances or family sagas—though we continue to be guilty of some distancing maneuvers—we start to explore how the most despised segment of the romance market is addressing women's power and desires. A segment that is also, according to the jacket copy on a 1995 volume in the Harlequin Presents series, the most popular—"The

World's Bestselling Romance Series!"—in this genre that constitutes some forty-six percent of the mass-market paperbacks sold in the United States (Dana Wechsler Linden and Matt Rees, "I'm Hungry" 71). (Bev Clark)

Feminists talk about sisterhood; I do not know how deeply they feel it. The undercurrent throughout feminist criticism of romances is that these scholars and critics know what is right for other women—and oh my, do they feel the "us/them" distinction acutely. (romance writer Kathleen Gilles Seidel, "Judge Me by the Joy I Bring" 172)

Recently critics have begun to situate themselves and their desires more clearly in projects like ours—as Kaplan has in discussing *The Thorn Birds* or as Constance Penley has in discussing the Trekkie slashzines (fanzines that develop the homosexual potential between Kirk and Spock). (Bev Clark)

. . . we're beginning to deconstruct this binary between fantasy and the real and no longer place ourselves as the people who aren't duped by fantasy. (Janice Radway, Response 78)

Not that we students of "Feminist Criticism" manage to position ourselves as romance readers with complete ease. (Bev Clark)

Browsing the book stand in the local grocery story trying to pick from the multitude of "trash" romance novels, I found myself overwhelmingly self-conscious to be purchasing one, and afraid I might even get caught by someone I know. That was only the beginning; after ducking out of the store undiscovered (except by the store clerk) I sheepishly carried the book around for days, doing my best to keep it well hidden. An interesting phenomenon—I was terribly embarrassed that someone might think I was really reading it. Why am I so ashamed of reading this kind of book? (Marah Bianca Rhoades)

I recently walked through a bookstore in the mall and came across a display of romances with a complimentary newsletter entitled *Heart to Heart*. I grabbed one. It contains synopses of new romances: "Devilishly handsome Prince Ryker Triloni kidnaps Jana, telling her it's for her own good . . ."; "Jolie McKibben has the noose around her neck when she is offered a choice: the sheriff can finish the process or she can marry a total stranger who has offered to stand bond for her future good behavior. . . ."

The one character who sounded as if she might have a bit of a feminist in her was also an accessory to a crime and had to fend off feds camped on her doorstep. So, even though she was what one could consider a "strong-walkin' woman," she lived an unbelievable life. What does this imply? Furthermore, it is then revealed that "her only hope of surviving to solve the crisis rests in the hands of the very same Treasury agent who cracked the case and wants her booked!" Hmmm. . . .

Here are a few sample titles in a recommended booklist: *Only By Your Touch, Too Hot to Handle, Mail-Order Temptress, Spinster's Song.* Then there are those that portray deception or force as being romantic: *Tame My Wild Touch, Taming Kate, Sweet Liar, Ravished Bride, Capture My Heart, Traitor's Kiss.* (Lauren Jenks)

The last romance I attempted to read was one of my sister's over six years ago in Butte, Montana. I was bored and thumbing through some books in a bookcase in search of something light to read. My hands closed on a historical romance and I just happened to open it at a section where the woman was tied, spread-eagled (god, I hate that word), to a bed and some ugly, evil man was not only raping her but throwing some kind of stinging lotion on her. I was so disgusted I wanted to put the book down but instead I flipped to the end to see if everything turned out all right. It did. But the happy ending did not erase that vile picture of the rape scene. (Sandra McLeod)

I would like to be raped, but I want it to happen to me exactly as it happened to Cressida in Vice Avenged. *I want a marquis to come to my second-story window at night with a ladder....* (romance fan Helen Hazen, *Endless Rapture* 8)

The plot is the same in each of these novels: a strong, gorgeous man who is initially an adversary of the woman overcomes her aversion to him and they fall in love. This theme creates a situation where she is constantly fighting off his sexual advances because she insists she cannot stand him. She secretly desires him but can't admit it, so the man has to force himself on her for her to accept what she really desires. The problem is that these situations create rapish sexual interactions between the couple. She tells him no, but he knows she means yes (because on some level she really does mean yes) and is forever ignoring her sweet little protests. She tells herself she does not want him while simultaneously allowing him to "have his way." (Marah Bianca Rhodes)

The dark head bent, and he kissed her lingeringly. Her whole body jerked in astonished protest.

He laughed again. There was almost a reckless note in it. Candy stared up at him, frozen. His body moved against hers, explicitly. Candy gasped. She felt the blood rush into her face. In an agony of embarrassment she screwed her eyes tight shut.

What was worse even than the super-cool Justin in this naked fury was the way her body was reacting. Even without kindness or chivalry or any sign of affection, her body responded to him, savouring the harsh caress as if she were a stroked cat. It appalled her. What sort of woman was she? (Sophie Weston, *No Provocation* 118)

I find it disturbing that it takes a marital rape in *No Provocation* to waken Candy sexually (yet exciting too, I'm sorry to admit). Even though the hero Justin "treated her—looked at her—as if she were his enemy" (Weston 117), and leaves her with a bruise on her arm and shoulderblade, Candy becomes starry eyed with love and desire—the opposite of her response to a threatened rape by Armitage, a gangster type who preys on the homeless. Yet that parallel scene brought me up short. I may have been almost seduced by the marital rape, but the near-rape, and especially the overdetermination of Armitage's despicability, reminded me which was the real rape. (Bev Clark)

In a survey reported by Manfred F. DeMartino in 1974, highly intelligent women were asked about their attitudes toward being raped in a nonviolent manner. The following are percentages of women either excited or intrigued by the idea (some responded extremely positively, others had mixed responses, stipulating that the aggressor be attractive or that all guilt or responsibility for pregnancy not be a factor): fifty-four percent of teenagers, forty-four percent of women in their twenties, thirty-nine percent of women in their thirties, thirty-three percent of women in their forties, and twenty percent of women in their fifties responded relatively positively (134). Many, however, did distinguish between fantasy and reality in their responses, and all who had experienced rape first hand responded negatively. (Michelle Henneberry)

Does the percentage decrease with age because these teenage girls are virgins or are used to teenage boys who can't satisfy them anyway? Are the older women less responsive because they have had more sexual encounters and therefore find sex less inviting and dull? (Karen Gennari)

Or might older women channel more energy to areas other than sex—do they have other ambitions? Are they more likely to have experienced rape themselves? Are they more sensitive to the politics of rape?

In a 1985 survey of romance readers undertaken by Carol Thurston, some sixty percent of those polled indicated that they found the portrayal of rape—defined as the heroine having "sex against her will"—exciting (78). More recently, forty-six percent of those polled by Lynda L. Crane found "forcefully aggressive scenes" exciting while thirty-three percent found them unpleasant (267). Recently too the media have given excited attention to works by women that probe the faultlines between sex and violence: Katie Roiphe's concern, in *The Morning After,* that date rape has been over-hyped; Christina Hoff Sommers's defense, in *Who Stole Feminism?* of "mutually pleasurable rough sex" in *Gone with the Wind,* of "the idea that there is nothing wrong with taking pleasure in Scarlett's enraptured submission" (263); Sallie Tisdale's celebration, in *Talk Dirty to Me,* of pornography (which, she explains, is rarely violent). (Bev Clark)

Is there some kind of pleasure in feeling overwhelmed and controlled by a man? This is what I found so upsetting—that yes I think there is something very exciting about that for women—even for myself. (Marah Bianca Rhoades)

Before she even had time to realise what he had in mind, he was tugging her sweatshirt over her head. She opened her mouth to protest, then closed it again. She couldn't stop this—it had been building between them ever since the first time she'd spotted him standing beside her own mare. (Rachel Elliot, *Fantasy of Love* 104)

After growing up with all of these images is it any surprise this is what may excite us, even against our will? (Angie Moorman)

I was finally discovered reading a romance by my liberated eighty-year-old grandmother. After explaining why I was reading it we got to talking about why it is that women find this kind of fantasy exciting. According to my grandmother, women in her day were not allowed to admit to their sexual desires, so they had to be overcome by a man. She told me about some old journals belonging to her mother, found after her mother's death. Her mother wrote about a recurring dream she was having in which she was taken by this gorgeous, strong man who wanted her. She would fight him until her sister would enter the dream and say, "There is nothing you can do, so just enjoy it." She then proceeded to let him have his way with her and did enjoy it, because she did not have to take responsibility for her desires and actions. This apparently was the only way, even in her fantasies, that she could enjoy sex without feeling guilty. Relatively understandable for a woman in the late eighteen hundreds, but I would hope that we have gotten away from that kind of thinking. Perhaps we haven't come as far as I'd like to think. Perhaps this kind of sexual fantasy, and the fantasies portrayed in these romance novels, alleviates the guilt women feel around their own sexuality and sexual desires. (Marah Bianca Rhoades)

Explaining anything to him when he was holding her this way was impossible. Her reasons for being angry were all in a jumble. She almost hoped he would ignore her pleas and continue. Then she could tell her commonsense self that the decision had been out of her hands. (Virginia Hart, *The Perfect Scoundrel* 133)

If a man desires you enough he will overcome you. One of my best friends functions on the premise that she needs to be so appealing that she cannot be resisted by a man. Is she thus implying that sexuality is something for women to be ashamed of? That sexual interaction has to be instigated by the male, and the way a female can take part is by making herself so appealing that he must have her and thus forces himself on her? But, if the woman really wants it (which is why she makes herself so appealing), then of course the man is *not* forcing himself on her. Rape becomes an inoperative term. (Marah Bianca Rhoades)

"This is the first time I've been driven to nearly forcing myself on a woman." His voice was low and harsh as he swung around and stared at her. Laine lay still, emotionally drained. She made no effort to cover herself but merely stared up at him with the eyes of a wounded child. "I can't deal with what you do to me, Laine." (Nora Roberts, *Island of Flowers* 173)

The truth is that a man is not driven to attack one woman in particular because of her charm or anything else. If he attacks, he has a problem with aggression that is directed toward all women. (Michelle Henneberry)

Molly Haskell suggests that we make a clear distinction between real rape and rape fantasies—though admittedly she is addressing private fantasies, not rape as portrayed in romance fiction. She suggests that fantasizing can be a way of gaining control over what is horrendously frightening—that "by envisioning and eroticizing rape, we have gained a psychological ascendancy over it" (94). It may, further, be women who have some control over their lives who fantasize loss of control, passivity, bondage—"a release from the new burdens of independence without . . . having to actually compromise that independence" (96).

The issue of rape has come increasingly to the fore among romance readers. Thurston argues that 1980s erotic series fiction has many fewer rapes than 1970s bodice rippers (106, 78). But then again, she defines rape as "forced sexual intercourse without the consent of and with no pleasure to the woman" (71). I'd be inclined to define rape simply as forced sexual intercourse. Her study seems not to have allowed for what Marah calls "rapish" interactions, in which the threat of force becomes titillating.

It seems to be precisely at the interface between word and deed—between *rape* and *rape*—that the action is: let's not call it rape, but . . . Thurston points, for instance, to the contradiction, in a 1985 Signet flyer on historical romances, between the warning that these "are not stories of rape and pillage" but are "in the tradition of such bestselling authors as . . . Rosemary Rogers" (193). (Bev Clark)

In 1988 I read my first and only Rosemary Rogers novel (I was awaiting a series of tests in a doctor's office and looked for a romance to keep me occupied) and was amazed at the graphic accounts in the book and the frequency with which they occurred. I cannot fathom that flyer's claims. (Karen Gennari)

Romance writers too have become defensive about rape. They stress that outright rapes are disappearing from romances, that in any case the rapes aren't real but fictional. As Daphne Clair writes, "these 'bodice rippers' enable women whose greatest terror is rape to face it safely between the pages of a book, which they know quite clearly has no resemblance to real life but where they can contain and control the experience" (69). In the next paragraph, however, she stresses the continuities between experiences in the book and those in real life: "A few men, nudged by their women, began reading romances to find out how women would really like to be made love to" (69).[5] We don't want "rape," heaven forbid, but whatever you call it, do it to me again. (Bev Clark)

Had Phoebe resisted, he would have released her. Or so Jackson reassured himself afterward. Yet he could never completely convince himself this was true. The passion that ignited within him the instant his mouth closed over hers was like nothing he'd ever known.

But Phoebe didn't resist. There was a split second of something—a sort of shocked stillness—then she seemed to melt against him, her body fitting to his as though it had been created for just that purpose. (Carole Buck, *Sparks* 110)

The Smithton readers that Radway surveyed in her classic study object strongly to the appearance of rape in romance. But they do find some violence acceptable "if it is described sparingly, if it is controlled carefully, or if it is *clearly* traceable to the passion or jealousy of the hero. . . . This curious and artificial distinction that they draw between 'forceful persuasion' and 'true rape' is a function of the very pressing need to know how to deal with the realities of male power and force in day-to-day existence" (*Reading* 76, Radway's italics). Writers have become increasingly adept at finding ways to kindle the excitement presumably sparked by rape without portraying a "real" rape. (Bev Clark)

"Listen, miss," he grated, pointing a threatening finger at her face, "I've had just about enough of you. One more word, and I really will put you over my knee—and I guarantee that you won't sit down for a week!"

"You bully," she spat through clenched teeth. "I hate you."

He laughed in mocking derision. "Do as you're told, or you'll find out just how much I can make you mean that," he warned, and climbed into the car. (Susanne McCarthy, *Satan's Contract* 54, McCarthy's emphasis)

Although romance fiction seems geared toward perpetuating male myths of female character, the majority of these books are written by women. Interestingly enough, it was a female psychologist, Helene Deutsch, who first identified the three character-istics we're struggling with here as the essentials to female personality: narcissism, passivity, and masochism.

Juanita H. Williams summarizes Deutsch's theory by noting that narcissism, in its healthy state, promotes self-worth; in its unhealthy state it leads to an obsession with self, body, fantasy, and identity, resulting in a constant need for affirmation by others. Secondly, the female tendency to be acted upon rather than act is seen as a reflection of the sexual act, man penetrating woman, and is evident even in fantasy life where male fantasies of "real world" ambition contrast female fantasies of narcissistic rela-tionship. Finally, masochism is considered to be the normal condition of women; from the breaking of the hymen to the pain of childbirth, women must seek pleasure and joy through pain. (Michelle Henneberry)

To be the virginal, beautiful, helpless female waiting passively to be overcome by a perfect man who takes her away from the problems in her life to live happily ever after, a man who envelops her and relieves her of the responsibilities of her life—on some level don't we all fantasize about that? Even in me there is some place which wants to be pursued and helpless, to be desired so intensely I do not have to do anything for it. To belong to someone, for in belonging to someone, we no longer have to look out for ourselves but are cared for as a cherished possession. Of course this is not a fully conscious fantasy, and I will scoff at romance novels, but I think the ideology gets at all of us one way or another. (Marah Bianca Rhoades)

Yes, I think that most avid fans of romance fiction still harbor that favorite scenario of Rhett Butler, sweeping Scarlett up in his arms and taking the stairway two steps at a time. Of course, my kind of heroine would still prefer to mount the stairs under her own power. Let Rhett conserve his energy for the main event. But far be it from me to rob American womanhood of this much cherished fantasy. (editor Anne Gisonny, "Category Romance Mini-Course" 195)

I have a friend who always insists that I am a feminist until it comes to opening a door: that is, I want the best of both worlds. I want the benefits of working in a career that any man could have. However, I also expect, or at least hope, that if I am walking with a gentleman, and we enter a building, he will be the one to open the door, and let me proceed ahead of him. Common courtesy, is it not? But why? (Lauren Jenks)

I realize that the contradictions presented in these novels are a direct reflection of the contradictions I find in myself. (Heather I. Braun)

The problem arises when the character's inexperience is seen as an invitation to aggressive sexual advances and later a glossed-over rape, as in *Island of Flowers*: "With no knowledge of seduction, she became a temptress by her very innocence" (Roberts 65). Laine is first attacked by Dillon ("he turned in his seat and captured her") in a small plane, adding to the danger. And love and aggression are shown as interchangeable: "Be grateful, Duchess, that I didn't simply shove you out the door" (18). Almost every "love" scene in this book is dominated by the same aggression, and yet the female character seems to enjoy the encounters. (Michelle Henneberry)

The most damaging "fact" about sex that summer of reading Harlequins taught me was that I was to be acted upon. The men are to be aggressive, persuasively prepared to put her in the mood, regardless of what she wants, often against her better judgment. Inundated with these messages about male/female behavior, I have been kissed, touched, and had sex with when I have been completely unsure if I wanted it. How can you decide any more, after being taught for so long that after a few minutes you will join him in the "mood"? My adolescent summer reading taught me that when the "mood" doesn't hit you after a few minutes, you stand, sit, lie there, and pretend as if it did. Sex was out of my hands. How could I ever enjoy my body sexually when having sex doesn't include me? (Angie Moorman)

Rosalind Coward (42–43) comments that this treatment of female sexuality flows directly from media insistence on the adolescent image. The ideal is an immature body that exudes sexuality but lacks the power of a mature woman. The biggest problem we seem to have with the romance novel is its depiction of the central female character. (Michelle Henneberry)

She went over to the mirror on the inside of the cupboard door and slipped the robe off her shoulder. Yes, unmistakable on the pale skin of arm and shoulderblade was a bruise.
   There was a small sound behind her. Candy turned.

Justin was standing in the doorway. He was holding a mug of coffee.

The aroma wafted across to her. He was looking at the image in the mirror. (Sophie Weston, *No Provocation* 121)

Even when she is on her own the heroine's appearance is described in terms of how she would appear to the man. She may be walking romantically through the garden or on the deck of a boat, or even alone in her room, but she does everything for the invisible eye of the man. Even at her worst she comments on how awful she would feel if he were to catch her in such a compromising position. She is never just herself, she is always the possession of the man, held within the totalizing masculine structure of these books. (Marah Bianca Rhoades)

She flung up her head. The electric tumble of curls danced in the firelight like a halo. She was quite unaware of it. (Sophie Weston, *No Provocation* 52)

Although most series romances have been written from the perspective of the heroine, Thurston's 1982 and 1985 reader surveys reveal that romance readers increasingly want stories that are not "written entirely from the heroine's point of view" (99), stories that explore what the hero thinks and feels. But I think Marah is right to suggest that even when we are privy to the thoughts only of the heroine, we often see her—she often sees herself—from the perspective of the hero. Even when he is raping her. (Bev Clark)

That Justin—cool, self-possessed Justin—could strip her with this cold ferocity was horrible. She had never seen him anything but in control before. He would hate being reduced to this, she knew. There was no trace of his normal courtesy. No chivalry. He treated her—looked at her—as if she were his enemy. As if he despised her. Candy fought back in panic, her mind racing. When he calmed down and looked back on this, he would be appalled, she realized. (Sophie Weston, *No Provocation* 117)

Candy is a character I couldn't even begin to identify with. There is no quality of her personality that pulls me into her or her story. I watch from a distance. (Lauren Jenks)

I think the reader's identification with a romance heroine can only go so far. After all, the heroine herself does not *fantasize* about aggression before it happens; she is subjected to it, she responds to it, she becomes aware of her own sexuality through it, and she reinterprets it. The heroine is usually a sexually naive woman (often to an extreme that no real woman is), and I think a reader's capacity to fantasize about or derive pleasure from the aggression toward the heroine immediately sets her apart from the heroine. (Michelle Henneberry)

Maybe as readers we simultaneously identify with and distance ourselves from the heroine. Kaplan points out, as Laplanche and Pontalis have before her, that fantasy is characterized not by fixed identifications but by "the shifting place of the subject and desubjectification" (129).[6] She was addressing not series romances but family sagas, but the idea also applies to the Harlequins and Silhouettes we've been reading.

Maybe we can even enjoy the portrayal of a rape because of our multiple positioning. In exploring how private rape fantasies may enable reconciliation of conflicting desires, Haskell states, "Because of their subtle and contradictory nature—what seems masochistic being often its antithesis—fantasies cannot be judged by the criteria by which we judge our actions" (98). We can play out in fantasy positions that we would not countenance in life, perhaps gaining pleasure from a representation of rape partly because we can shift the locus of power from the man to the woman (who is doing the fantasizing, after all)—or better yet, because we can simultaneously be both man and woman. (Bev Clark)

I'm currently reading (and I gag to write this) *Chastity's Pirate*, by Naomi Horton. Horton switches subtly back and forth between C. J.'s (heroine's) and Garrett's (hero's) thoughts and frames of mind—it does offer a more satisfying read. Both characters seem more independent somehow. (Lauren Jenks)

I think that, as she identifies with a hero, a woman can become what she takes joy in, can realize the maleness in herself, can experience the sensation of living inside a body suffused with masculine power and grace (adjectives very commonly applied to heroes, including my own), can explore anger and ruthlessness and passion and pride and honor and gentleness and vulnerability: yes, ma'am, all those old romantic clichés. In short, she can be a man. (Laura Kinsale, "The Androgynous Reader" 37, Kinsale's emphasis)

Laura Kinsale, author of historical romances, argues that the reader does not so much identify with the heroine as use her as a placeholder, someone who fills the place of the reader. The characters are internal constructs, the adventure internal too, the resolution an integration of two aspects of the self, hero and heroine. (Bev Clark)

On the other hand, however liberating it may be to enter the male psyche, we are still being asked to view the female character as an object. (Michelle Henneberry)

What sells these books, according to such writers as Kathleen Gilles Seidel (171), Jayne Ann Krentz ("Trying" 107), and Casey Douglas (99), are macho heroes—what some romance writers call alpha males. Crane found that readers were more likely to seek qualities of caring and nurturing in real males than in romance heroes (265). (Bev Clark)

What really interested me about Whittal's *Sunset at Izilwane* was that the heroine turns away from the most egalitarian man in the book—Anthony Phillips—consistently warm, sensitive, and supportive of her needs and feelings. It is the hero Byron, not Tony, who has a problem with a woman being a rancher. He is constantly described as hard, firm, coarse. Frances of course is soft, delicate, feminine. Tony is somewhere in between. He loses Frances to Byron because he is not as hard, mean, and annoying. How could anyone be attracted to a guy who is such a complete asshole? (Lynda Tocci)

. . . the flat truth is that you don't get much of a challenge for a heroine from a sensitive, understanding, right-thinking "modern" man who is part therapist, part best friend, and thoroughly tamed from the start. (Jayne Ann Krentz, "Trying to Tame the Romance" 109)

I have a good friend who always half-jokes about wanting a spouse who will earn the bread and be financially responsible for the couple. This friend just happens to be male. For this reason, I am ashamed to say, I have been guilty of fleetingly thinking of him as being "unmanly."

I could cite other examples from my life where I've bypassed the "straight-and-narrow-good-guy" to take a risk (often ending in dismay) on the "hopeless cause." I think of this as my James Dean Syndrome. Never fails. Dark and dangerous does have its appeal. (Lauren Jenks)

I cannot claim to be fully emancipated from the dream that some enormous man, say six foot six, heavily shouldered and so forth to match, will crush me to his tweeds, look down into my eyes and leave the taste of heaven or the scorch of his passion on my waiting lips. For three weeks I was married to him. (Germaine Greer, *The Female Eunuch* 177)

The romance I responded to most favorably (and I have read no other with a similar story) was one where the man and the woman were best friends that slowly started to realize they were feeling differently toward each other.

Why don't people admit that they like each other until the ends of these novels? (Angie Moorman)

I found the intense dislike between the male and female characters of almost every romance to be melodramatic and extremely unlikely. The two always think that they hate each other and from the beginning must fight their sexual attraction, to discover that they were wrong and that they are really madly and passionately in love.

Can love grow from what is initially a negative base? Dolf Zillmann describes the onset of passionate love, according to the research and theories of E. Walster, as requiring two steps (136–41). The first is an agitation of circumstance that is either positive or negative (most likely negative) and that may come from any source. The second is the labeling of that excitation as passion for another person. A number of experiments are documented to support this idea. A subject is exposed to a dangerous or frightening stimulus and is then approached by an attractive member of the opposite sex; sexual attraction is reported much higher in the agitated subject than in a control. Unfortunately, most of the subjects were men, but it would help my point if we assume that similar results would occur with female subjects.

Zillmann also cites Kenrick and Cialdini, who argue that it is not mislabeling but a decrease in anxiety, after an initial agitation, that fosters love (141–42). Thus if one initially dislikes someone, but the dislike abates, intense feelings of attraction can form.

The romance novel is then the positive or negative stimulus that can be a precursor for love. The abatement of frustration in either the resolution of the plot or, at the very least, a physical end to the reading of such abrasive material, can result in unusually positive feelings. (Michelle Henneberry)

I'm struck by how many of us admit to being influenced, one way or another, by our reading, even to having our ideas of romance shaped by our reading of romances. I think that if someone asked me whether a given story were realistic, I'd say that of course it's just a fantasy. Yet on some other level it would be very real to me, emotionally real.[7] (Bev Clark)

It was nice to read in Radway (*Reading* 61 ff.) that so many women who read romances realize that this is not real life—I am tired of critics suggesting that women who read romances and watch soap operas are idiots who cannot make distinctions between fantasy and reality. (Anonymous student)

Robert Ludlum plots many of his books around bizarre conspiracies.... Stephen King presents us with pets that come back from the dead and little girls who can use mental powers to send buildings up in flames. Anne McCaffrey creates flying dragons.... Most people understand and accept the way in which fantasy works when they sit down to read Ludlum, King, McCaffrey or the others. Furthermore everyone understands that the readers know the difference between real life and fantasy and that they do not expect one to imitate the other. But, for some reason, when it comes to romance novels critics worry about whether the women who read them can tell the difference between what is real and what is not. (Jayne Ann Krentz, "Introduction" 2)

Yet research shows that men who are shown a lot of films that depict violence against women are more apt to commit (or want to commit) violence against women. It should follow that women who read a lot of books that depict romance as simplistically as these do would then expect romance to be this simplistic. As relaxing and amusing as these books can be, sometimes I wonder what influence they are having on me. Then I tell myself it can't be any worse than the message I learned from fairy tales as a child. "The damage is already done ... read on!" (Anonymous student)

Perhaps romances are valuable to the extent that they show us more about ourselves (by helping us to experience and identify our desires), but are not valuable because, as fantasies, they don't tell us more about the world in which these newly identified desires will have to be played out. Everything is personal, nothing is political in these books. (Susan Dearing)

True. Just as this essay is more personal than political. Discussion of romance in "Feminist Criticism" usually turns inward, as the romances encourage us to, to focus on our own desires. Only belatedly do we—mostly white women, mostly feminists, mostly somewhere in the middle class—address how we in turn do violence to others. Only belatedly do we address the racial and class subtexts of these novels. If "subjectivity can be recognized as the place where the operations of power and the possibilities of romance are also played out" (Alison Light, " 'Returning' " 9), we have played out the wider implications of these operations only intermittently. (Bev Clark)

I was surprised that the women in *Sunset at Izilwane* were carefully kept away from doing anything domestic—*housework*. And they had servants! The housework bit appeals to me, and that part of the fantasy seems realistic (as appealing to women). I had some trouble with faithful black servants, though; it really jarred. (Marjorie Crowe)

No Provocation offers a whiff of racist exoticism—in a smoky cellar "an ebony-skinned man danced a flugelhorn through a range of sounds Candy had never even imagined" (Sophie Weston, *No Provocation* 14)—and what I'm tempted to call sexual exoticism, the household help kept in his subordinate place by being, implicitly, gay. *The Perfect Scoundrel* offers up a backcountry Texas town that is surprisingly lily white, even down to the service personnel—no identifiable African Americans, no Latinos. (Bev Clark)

The father's housekeeper in *Island of Flowers* is a strong woman, sort of an earth-mother: she is native Hawaiian and is the keeper of her family's traditions. (Michelle Henneberry)

As Kaplan suggests, mass-market romances often displace sexual taboos onto cultural ones, "the reactionary political and social setting" somehow securing "a privileged space where the most disruptive female fantasy can be 'safely' indulged" (145). Part of the fantasy is that homemaking doesn't have to interfere with love-making. The former gets taken care of by figures that are invisible or conveniently other.

Critics too may indulge in a certain amount of displacement—or of policing to find a scapegoat. Thurston attributes "pink" parties and other "gimmicky promotions" to male publishers out of touch with the majority of their consumers, trying to appeal to "the lower end of the reader demographic scale" (by which she presumably means the less educated and less well off): such an appeal reinforces "the lowbrow (poor taste–poor quality) reputation of the entire romance genre and everyone associated with it" (190, 191). She's guilty, in effect, of doing what she accuses others of doing, only instead of making the cultural association of (low) quality with (female) gender she makes it with (low) class.

Is it significant that those of us who first broached what I'm calling the political are more likely to be in their forties than in their twenties? (Bev Clark)

It's possible—maybe we in our twenties don't have an entire house to clean or a live-in husband or lover to pick up after and we gloss over the parts about housekeepers, etc., because housekeeping is not in our fantasy as something we need to escape from. (Karen Gennari)

This morning I was reading an article in *Ms.* about a young Black woman on welfare raising three children on her own (her abusive husband had left her with no financial support three years ago). This woman was explaining how she felt, trapped, alone with these three young children, without enough money to feed them, and unable to get a job. I started thinking about her reading a romance novel as a form of escape from her life, and wondering whether she would be able to relate enough to the heroines in these novels to find pleasure in reading them. Almost the only young Black women in these novels are domestic helps. Can a poor Black reader imagine herself as the helpless middle-class white woman swept away by the lawyer? If so, what kind of conflict does this create for her in her own life? (Marah Bianca Rhoades)

The one romance reader whom Margaret Ann Jensen interviewed and identified as black is also the one who had the most trouble sorting out fantasy and reality, the one who kept seeking a Harlequin hero in her own life (144, 156). Does an African-American reader of Harlequins need to abdicate reality more completely? Then again, what do we make of Jensen's emphasis on the race of this "abnormal" reader? Is it in keeping with our culture's tendency to embody our sexual faultlines in black actors, from Anita Hill to O. J. Simpson? Even in *Sparks,* the one romance I've read that grants some subjectivity to black characters, the two are confined to a subplot—and it's not the white but the black woman for whom the obstacle to loving commitment is having been a battered woman. (Bev Clark)

Feminine sexuality is . . . the place where the discourses of class difference can be consolidated and those of middle class nationalism ultimately reaffirmed. (Alison Light, "Writing Fictions" 153)

Money is obviously a powerful element in these novels and in women's fantasies. The money, though, never comes from the woman herself. It always comes from the hero, who is wealthy, or if not initially wealthy eventually comes into money. In any case, he is always the provider. In a society where women are trying to gain respect in the workplace, these fantasies undermine their efforts. How can we be struggling for equality in our real lives while fantasizing ourselves out of equal roles? (Marah Bianca Rhoades)

Something about the way Harlequin romances function as products: marketing techniques that keep people buying cosmetics, cars, other consumer goods must be applied to publishing in order to keep readers buying more Harlequins, right? What techniques? Essentially, isn't it a matter of making promises they can't keep? Setting up a desire for something that can never be satisfied so that the buyer will keep on buying, always hoping to be satisfied but never getting what she hoped for? So the H-people have identified a formula that taps into something very strong and deep in women and satisfies it just enough—but never completely—to keep the readers coming back for more. If they ever satisfied the desire completely, the reader would not have to buy another book; she could just go with what she got from the first one. These books offer a satisfaction they can't deliver. (Susan Dearing)

I don't necessarily think they don't satisfy her; I think they're just different enough from her own life. If she found one that directly paralleled her life she would stop buying as she realized that she was living a romance. (Karen Gennari)

Psychoanalysis tells us that wherever there's repetition we need to look beyond the pleasure principle—to something that is not leading to satisfaction, to something that is lacking. (Constance Penley, "Feminism, Psychoanalysis, Popular Culture")

Perhaps instead of not getting satisfaction, the readers enjoyed the experience so much that they choose to go back again and again for more. . . . I sat outside this afternoon, and watched my dog Meghan pursuing her favorite pastime: chasing squirrels. She never catches them, though she'll spend hours stalking. Perfectly happy, she'll bark and wag her tail at the creature while it safely resides in a tree. I often wonder what Meggie would do if she actually caught one. (Lauren Jenks)

I'm inclined to think that the novels are compensating for other lacks, whether the loss of maternal nurturing as Suzanne Juhasz argues or victimization more generally. They may supply a mere bandaid for psychic and societal wounds—yet thereby provide a way of tracing the wounds as well. They "help us to see how it is that we can enter into ideologies of the most oppressive kinds . . . whilst never being fully subsumed or positioned by them" (Alison Light, "Writing" 163).[8] (Bev Clark)

How to liberate the fantasies that women have—fantasies that could be a source of both pleasure and power? How can romance become a part of a feminist revolution? (Susan Dearing)

I unlocked the door to my room. We walked in. I turned on a dim light and he headed for the stereo to select an appropriate tape. As he was deciding, I went to the bed (the only place to really sit in a dorm room) and lay down. The alcohol had made me a little drowsy. I wondered what was going to happen. How far would we go?

I spoke up, "I've never done this before," hoping to get an indication of what to expect. I didn't mean sex. I meant that I had never had someone come back to my room from a party. I didn't know what people did in those situations; I didn't know what I was going to do in that situation.

He sat down on the edge of the bed, looked seriously into my eyes. His thoughts were a mystery to me. A kind smile spread across his face, as he patted the edge of the bed next to him, indicating for me to sit there next to him. "Okay. Let's talk about it." He cared about how my mind was handling what my body was doing.

I instantly felt at ease.

The Harlequins of my summer disintegrated into the dark of the room, floated up to the ceiling and joined the glow-in-the-dark stars stuck to my ceiling. (Angie Moorman)

Maybe we feminists *should* write romances (many of us have said we could easily follow the formula) and address the issues of class, sexuality, and rape-like scenes. We can change the power balance in subtle ways. We can make the romance a satisfying experience—and a true utopia for women. (Karen Gennari)

NOTES

1. The six of us listed as coauthors collaborated on the essay as a whole. We are grateful to the other participants in "Feminist Criticism" cited in the text for permission to quote them as well.

2. See, e.g., Culley, Maher, Treichler.

3. I'm here paraphrasing a statement in another coauthored piece (Clark et al.), which makes a fuller case for such a project and more fully describes the course. In the current project we've attempted to be more egalitarian in both the process and the final product; the positioning of my name as first in the listing of authors is an alphabetical accident.

4. Rabine, for one, notes the "increasingly accelerated process of change" in the romance industry, responding "to new needs of women as a result of recent profound changes in both their domestic and paid labor situations" (166). And perhaps also to fissures between "the mass-production needs of the corporations" and the authors' "quest for creative individuality, for economic independence, and for recognition" (184–85).

5. Hazen, a romance fan, shows a similar vacillation: occasionally she implies that rape is not particularly pathological ("If it is the case that most men are capable of rape, then the act itself cannot be pathological," 15); elsewhere, that one should distinguish between how significant and grand rape can be in myth and literature and how sordid and terrible it generally is in life (73). Or she finds women writers the ones who imagine intriguing possibilities in rape, unlike men: "Men are disgusted by it. They hate it in fact, and they hate it in the imagination" (79). With the exception, of course, of "male intellectual pornographers—de Sade, Flaubert, Baudelaire, Miller, and their kind" (79). Ah yes, Flaubert, that kind.

6. See also Coward: "The 'identification' which the reader or viewer makes is not necessarily with the hero/heroine or star but with the story. It is the anticipation of satisfaction from the story/fantasy that holds our attention, not some identification with a particular character" (203). In terms of Laplanche and Pontalis's analysis, if series romances are secondary elaborations utilizing "ready-made scenarios" rather than "original fantasy," it is still possible to glimpse here the multiplicity of identification more characteristic of "original fantasy," especially given "the profound continuity between the various fantasy scenarios" (see Laplanche and Pontalis 12, 13, 17).

7. See Radway, e.g., *Reading* 187, for discussion of the Smithton women's ambivalence about the reality status of romances.

8. For the classic statement of how mass culture not only reinforces the status quo but also has utopian potential, at least implicitly criticizing the social order, see Jameson.

WORKS CITED

Baym, Nina. "The Feminist Teacher of Literature: Feminist or Teacher?" 1988. *Gender in the Classroom: Power and Pedagogy*. Ed. Susan L. Gabriel and Isaiah Smithson. Urbana: U of Illinois P, 1990. 60–78.

Buck, Carole. *Sparks*. Silhouette Desire. New York: Silhouette, 1993.

Castagna, JoAnn, and Robin L. Radespiel. "Making Rape Romantic: A Study of Rosemary Rogers's 'Steve and Ginny' Novels." *Women and Violence in Literature*. Ed. Katherine Anne Ackley. New York: Garland, 1990. 299–323.

Clair, Daphne. "Sweet Subversiveness." Krentz, *Dangerous Men* 61–71.

Clark, Beverly Lyon, Heather I. Braun, Susan Dearing, Kerry-Beth Garvey, Karen M. Gennari, Becky Hemperly, and Michelle Henneberry. "Giving Voice to Feminist Criticism: A Conversation." *Teaching Contemporary Theory to Undergraduates*. Ed. Dianne F. Sadoff and William E. Cain. New York: Modern Language Assn., 1994. 125–40.

Coward, Rosalind. *Female Desires: How They Are Sought, Bought, and Packaged*. 1984. New York: Grove, 1985.

Crane, Lynda L. "Romance Novel Readers: In Search of Feminist Change?" *Women's Studies* 23 (1994): 257–69.

Culley, Margo. "Anger and Authority in the Introductory Women's Studies Classroom." *Gendered Subjects: The Dynamics of Feminist Teaching*. Ed. Culley and Catherine Portuges. Boston: Routledge, 1985. 209–17.

DeMartino, Manfred F. *Sex and the Intelligent Woman*. New York: Springer, [1974].

Douglas, Ann. "Soft-Porn Culture." *New Republic* 30 Aug. 1980: 25–29.

Douglas, Casey. "Creating the Hero and Heroine." Falk 95–101.

Elliot, Rachel. *Fantasy of Love*. Harlequin Presents. 1990. Toronto: Harlequin, 1991.

Falk, Kathryn, ed. *How to Write a Romance and Get It Published: With Intimate Advice from the World's Most Popular Romantic Writers*. Rev. ed. 1989. New York: Signet, 1990.

Gisonny, Anne. "Category Romance Mini-Course." Falk 182–95.

Greer, Germaine. *The Female Eunuch*. 1970. New York: McGraw-Hill, 1971.

Grossberg, Lawrence, Cary Nelson, and Paula A. Treichler, eds. *Cultural Studies*. New York: Routledge, 1992.

Hart, Virginia. *The Perfect Scoundrel*. Harlequin Romance. Toronto: Harlequin, 1994.

Haskell, Molly. "The 2,000-Year-Old Misunderstanding: Rape Fantasy." *Ms.* Nov. 1976: 84–86, 92–98.

Hazen, Helen. *Endless Rapture: Rape, Romance, and the Female Imagination*. New York: Scribner, 1983.

Horton, Naomi. *Chastity's Pirate*. Silhouette Desire. New York: Silhouette, 1993.

Jameson, Frederic. "Reification and Utopia in Mass Culture." *Social Text* 1 (Winter 1979): 130–48.

Jensen, Margaret Ann. *Love's Sweet Return: The Harlequin Story*. Bowling Green: Bowling Green State UP, 1984.

Juhasz, Suzanne. "Texts to Grow On: Reading Women's Romance Fiction." *Tulsa Studies in Women's Literature* 7 (1988): 239–59.

Kaplan, Cora. "*The Thorn Birds*: Fiction, Fantasy, Femininity." *Sea Changes: Essays on Culture and Feminism*. London: Verso, 1986. 117–46.

Kinsale, Laura. "The Androgynous Reader: Point of View in the Romance." Krentz, *Dangerous Men* 31–43.

Krentz, Jayne Ann, ed. *Dangerous Men and Adventurous Women: Romance Writers on the Appeal of the Romance*. Philadelphia: U of Pennsylvania P, 1992.

———. Introduction. Krentz, *Dangerous Men* 1–9.

———. "Trying to Tame the Romance: Critics and Correctness." Krentz, *Dangerous Men* 107–14.

Laplanche, Jean, and J.-B. Pontalis. "Fantasy and the Origins of Sexuality." *International Journal of Psycho-Analysis* 49.1 (1968): 1–18.

Light, Alison. " 'Returning to Manderley'—Romance Fiction, Female Sexuality and Class." *Feminist Review* 16 (Summer 1984): 7–25.

———. "Writing Fictions: Femininity and the 1950s." *The Progress of Romance: The Politics of Popular Fiction*. Ed. Jean Radford. London: Routledge, 1986. 139–65.

Linden, Dana Wechsler, and Matt Rees. "I'm Hungry. But Not for Food." *Forbes* 6 July 1992: 70–74.

Maher, Frances. "Classroom Pedagogy and the New Scholarship on Women." *Gendered Subjects: The Dynamics of Feminist Teaching*. Ed. Margo Culley and Catherine Portuges. Boston: Routledge, 1985. 29–48.

McCarthy, Susanne. *Satan's Contract*. 1993. Harlequin Presents. Toronto: Harlequin, 1995.

Modleski, Tania. "The Disappearing Act: A Study of Harlequin Romances." *Signs* 5 (1980): 435–48.

Penley, Constance. "Feminism, Psychoanalysis, Popular Culture." Grossberg 579–94.

Person, Ethel Spector. *Dreams of Love and Fateful Encounters: The Power of Romantic Passion*. New York: Norton, 1988.

Rabine, Leslie W. *Reading the Romantic Heroine: Text, History, Ideology*. Ann Arbor: U of Michigan P, 1985.

Radway, Janice A. *Reading the Romance: Women, Patriarchy, and Popular Literature*. Chapel Hill: U of North Carolina P, 1984.

———. Response to Rosalind Brunt. Grossberg 78.

Roberts, Nora. *Island of Flowers*. Silhouette Romance. 1982. Boston: Gregg, 1984.

Roiphe, Katie. *The Morning After: Sex, Fear, and Feminism on Campus*. Boston: Little Brown, 1993.

Seidel, Kathleen Gilles. "Judge Me by the Joy I Bring." Krentz, *Dangerous Men* 159–79.

Snitow, Ann Barr. "Mass Market Romance: Pornography for Women is Different." *Radical History Review* 20 (1979). Rpt. in *Powers of Desire: The Politics of Sexuality*. Ed. Ann Snitow, Christine Stansell, and Sharon Thompson. New York: Monthly Review P, 1983. 245–63.

Sommers, Christina Hoff. *Who Stole Feminism? How Women Have Betrayed Women*. New York: Simon, 1994.

Thurston, Carol. *The Romance Revolution: Erotic Novels for Women and the Quest for a New Sexual Identity*. Urbana: U of Illinois P, 1987.

Tisdale, Sallie. *Talk Dirty to Me: An Intimate Philosophy of Sex*. New York: Doubleday, 1994.

Treichler, Paula A. "Teaching Feminist Theory." *Theory in the Classroom*. Ed. Cary Nelson. Urbana: U of Illinois P, 1986. 57–128.

Weston, Sophie. *No Provocation*. 1992. Harlequin Romance. Toronto: Harlequin, 1993.

Whittal, Yvonne. *Sunset at Izilwane*. 1986. Harlequin Presents. Toronto: Harlequin, 1987.

Williams, Juanita H. *Psychology of Women: Behavior in a Biosocial Context*. New York: Norton, 1977.

Zillmann, Dolf. *Connections Between Sex and Aggression*. Hillsdale, NJ: Erlbaum, 1984.

Chapter Fifty-four

From Constructing Girlhood

Popular Magazines for Girls Growing Up in England,
1920–1950 (1995)

Penny Tinkler

Tinkler examines magazines for British "working girls" as models for courtship and feminine behavior in the first half of the century. Along with television, film, and popular music, mass-circulation women's magazines in the twentieth century continued the role of providing advice, warnings, and paradigmatic descriptions of love once played by sternly "scientific" or religious books such as those excerpted in part 1.

Courting Practice

Romance magazines suggest that girls were tired of the Victorian convention whereby girls remained passive in relations with men. At the same time, they tempered signs of female independence:

> There are a few ultra modern spirits who profess to see no reason why woman should not openly show her inclinations and do her best to win the man to whom her heart has gone out. These urge that it is mere folly for a woman to permit her chance of happiness to pass her by without an effort to retain it, just as it is unworthy of her new-found spirit of independence to meekly pick up the handkerchief when the gentleman deigns to throw it. All of which is very amusing nonsense![1]

Girls were told that it was not their place to initiate contact with the opposite sex be it for platonic or romantic purposes; "it would be forward of you to take the first step. You must not dream of doing such a thing."[2] Once in a relationship girls had to continue to play the waiting game and anxious correspondents who feared their boy was on the retreat were told not to pursue; "listen, no man was ever brought back by running after him. The more you pursue, the further he will fly."[3] Similarly it was not the girl's place to propose. The implication of this was that girls could only indicate their interest in subtle ways, and that their role was limited to one of

From Penny Tinkler, *Constructing Girlhood: Popular Magazines for Girls Growing Up in England, 1920–1950* (Washington, DC: Taylor and Francis, 1995), 137–45. © 1995 by Penny Tinkler. Reprinted by permission.

response. It is ironic that although girls had to secure a husband they were not expected or encouraged to take any positive steps to initiate or maintain a relationship.

Courting custom traditionally bestowed the right to propose on males. Since it was part of the masculine model, a girl emasculated her boy if she took the lead in this matter. The rationalisation of this practice was that,

> No man is too shy to speak when he loves a girl—sooner or later. If you were to speak first, you'd give him a terrible shock. He will never think quite the same of you again— and you'll damage his own self confidence for ever. He will never forget that you thought him such a coward that you could not trust him to do what has always been a man's job. And later on, if you married, when the first rapture had worn off, as sure as I am here, the day would come when the horrible doubt would steel into your mind as to whether he ever intended to propose at all.[4]

This practice emphasised male power, hence a girl's rejection of these norms was perceived as a direct assault on male dominance. "My Pal Peter" described the acceptable limits of female independence such that he accommodated the manners and mores of modern girls without disturbing patriarchal social relations;

> independence is all very well at the right and proper time, but sweetheart this is not the right time. A boy likes to feel himself his girl's protector. A man prides himself on his superior muscular strength, and has no greater delight than when using that strength to save the girl he loves . . . If Dolly learns to leave to the next sweetheart . . . the things she now insists on doing for herself she will advance a good step to the top rung of the ladder that leads to a wedding ring.[5]

In a similar vein *Girls' Favourite* (1927) advised girls "[n]ot to assume a great air of ownership over your fiance. He likes to think that he owns you. It flatters his manly conceit."[6] Male confidence appears to have been incredibly fragile. The fact that girls wanted to and actually did propose, that they desired to initiate and lead in relationships, was antipathetic to the notion of man as hunter and woman as passive hunted. Girls had to be cajoled into passivity and they were encouraged to accept these standards in order to secure a husband.

To simply characterise relationships between men and women as one of power versus powerlessness and activity versus passivity is to miss the complexity of magazine representations. Males were presented as the initiators of relationships but representations also suggest that girls had an active role in manipulating a man through, for example, "playing hard to get." Courtship advice revealed that securing a future husband was a very calculated business; "She must get on pleasant, although not familiar terms with him; make him feel that here is a girl who shares most of his views; let him see that she thinks for herself sometimes; takes an interest in what concerns him, and what goes on in the world."[7] In spite of the representation of men as the initiators of relationships, girls were told that they in fact controlled the level of intimacy. This reasoning excused men from responsibility for their actions and was the prime rationalisation of the sexual double standard; girls and women were made the guardians of public morality and patriarchal standards. Males, in contrast, were not expected to judge the implications of their attentions, they were not able to gauge how far they could go. *As Girls' Friend* explained (1920), "a man is sometimes a little puzzled to know how far he can pay attention of a purely friendly character to girls without leading the recipient to suppose he means more by them than is actually the case."[8] Central to this representation . . . was the notion that there was a fundamental difference between male and female sexuality. The influence accorded to girls in relationships was double-edged and left them responsible for the conduct or misconduct of heterosexual relations. Men, on the other hand, were effectively freed from responsibility and also criticism.

It is difficult to evaluate how far courting etiquette and models of behavior served the interests of girls and women. Boys and men were expected to finance courtship; girls who insisted on paying their own way could be seen as rude. Boys were also expected to show certain courtesies to the female sex; girls who questioned or rejected these practices were castigated. While the courtesies bestowed on girls as part of this etiquette were presented as some of the privileges of being female, they actually imposed constraints on girls. The superficial character of feminine "privilege" was on occasions clearly revealed; take for example this comment from *Every Girl's Paper* (1924):

> Ladies are only considered first by courtesy. Perhaps the man didn't behave in quite a gentlemanly manner, but it was no business of yours to call him to account. He must have thought less of you than you did of him. If you really mean to be a lady you will have to bear many things in silence, that you grumble so much about now.[9]

The "privileges" of the female sex were actually an illusion conferred or retracted at the whim of a man. The ideal of the "lady", for instance, was a device whereby females were constrained into patterns of behaviour which served patriarchal relations and which denied girls the right and the power to counter male abuse of the social standards which enmeshed such ideals. These courtesies were, in fact, more important to the maintenance of masculine identity; through enacting these courtesies men demonstrated and reaffirmed their economic and social power in heterosexual relations.

In return for the compliment a boy bestowed on a girl by asking her out, girls were expected to entertain and please their partner. While males were expected financially to invest in the outing, girls were told to invest themselves in entertaining their male companion. The "girls boys like best" according to an article in *Girls' Favourite* (1922), are those "who will be at all times eager to hear of his prowess at sports or in other directions. There are some girls who find great difficulty in getting away from that fascinating subject of "I," and they are by no means favourites among the male members of the community."[10] *Miss Modern* was similarly concerned with the ornamental and servicing role of girls in relation to boys and advised its readers to "take trouble with those who think you worth knowing. Flatter, listen, chatter, glisten, put on your act to the height of your powers because that's why you're there."[11] Once again female behaviour was referred to as an act necessary to ensnare a future husband.

Courting etiquette of the twenties differed from pre-war days in that it was increasingly acceptable for the modern girl to have a number of male friends before finally marrying. Once she accepted an offer of marriage she was expected to devote all her attentions to her prospective husband (1924):

> It certainly is a little hard on a girl that she should reserve her company for some boy who has not yet given her any definite cause to consider that he is seriously in love with her ... Of course, if she becomes engaged to him that is a different matter. Then he would expect her exclusive attention.[12]

Initially this tolerance of pre-engagement relationships was a response to the demographic imbalance of the 1920s, when girls outnumbered men. In this context, girls could not risk waiting for a boy. This practice, which was well established by the 1930s, also served male interests in allowing them to take the opportunity to court a number of women before finally settling down. This new type of relationship posed problems for girls because it was unclear how they should be managed and interpreted. As Pam explained (1924):

> Gone are the days when girls had to be virtually engaged before they could enjoy a man's companionship. That is all to the good, but the pity is that sometimes girls begin to hope that the nice boy in question is a lover before the idea has entered his own head, or heart. It doesn't do to assume that because he thinks you pretty or has kissed you once or twice that he is making up his mind to devote his life to you. Therefore be kind and friendly, but take his compliments lightly, make no demands on him, leave him free as the wind, and whatever you do don't ask him when he is coming round to call for you again.[13]

Given the prevailing double standard, this new practice meant that girls were increasingly vulnerable to male attentions and abuse.

Flirtation was a recurring topic in working girls' magazines during the early twenties when there was, according to magazines, a "fashion" for it. This was one of the ways in which modern girls could influence relations with men whilst avoiding directive behaviour, which was a male prerogative. Flirts were usually portrayed as somewhat misguided young women who eventually grew out of this stage. Magazines were broadly tolerant of these girls in so far as they were understood to have been borne along by contemporary trends. Girls were warned, however, that flirting was not in their long-term interests; "a reputation for flirting very often keeps men with honest intentions away from you" and "the flirt very often ends up by becoming a lonely old maid."[14] The flirt was sometimes harshly criticised for attempting to exercise power over men; a flirtatious girl was described as cold-hearted and calculating, she led men on "merely for the sake of displaying her power over them."[15] Flirts were also criticised because "through contact with such girls some of our best and truest men have been spoiled."[16] Girls were advised, "Have as many friends as you like, but have them on a fair understanding. A flirt can do incalculable harm, not only to men, but to her own sex. She embitters a man, and he is never the same in his treatment of women."[17] Girls were once again responsible for the ways in which men perceived and treated women. Fiction reinforced this message and conveyed the seriousness of heterosexual relationships; flirts were not good material for a stable and harmonious marriage.

Concern regarding the exercise of female power through flirtation was ironic. Girls were presented as possessing considerable influence over men through their roles as sisters, wives, and mothers, and this was frequently used as a justification for the necessity of female purity in both physical and moral terms. Demonstrations of power were, however, seen as unfeminine because of the threat they posed to male superiority. If women were to exert any influence they had somehow to do so invisibly. Once they overstepped the mark, the fears they provoked could dissuade men from marriage. In the context of the 1920s demographic imbalance such behaviour was portrayed as particularly foolish in that it could seriously exacerbate the already precarious nature of woman's future livelihood. The importance of marriage was also at the heart of the critical stance adopted towards male flirts. Whilst not wishing to inhibit male privilege it was not acceptable for men to ruin a girl's chances of marriage. Preservation of the institution of marriage was of paramount concern in that it secured male interests but also, according to magazines, the future interests of their readers. Within this context magazines were intolerant of men, and also women, who disabled others in the marriage market.

Once engaged, flirtation was forbidden and girls were supposed to be totally loyal. In answer to a reader's enquiry as to whether an engaged girl should flirt, *Polly's Paper* replied: "If she does it is to be hoped that her fiance will discover what she is doing and will jilt her straight away. A girl who cannot keep true to her lover before marriage will make an unfaithful wife afterwards."[18] In this instance, the magazine's response was also shaped by patriotism. During both the First and Second World Wars girls were separated from fiancés for long periods and unlike in peace-time conditions they had the opportunity to mix with other men. In spite of this and the obvious loneliness of many girls, magazines had no sympathy for engaged girls who flirted. Florence, for example, was clearly rebuked in *Polly's Paper* for such behaviour; "I have no patience with girls like you, who become engaged and then, when your boy has to go away from you for a time, find someone else to fill his place and wish to break the engagement."[19] No mention was made of male infidelity in wartime.

Magazines received numerous letters concerning the right age to get engaged and married. Girls were usually advised to wait until they were at least 20 before getting married:

> The heart is never too young to love, but the mind of seventeen is too young to be sure of itself. Real love, like wine, is all the better for keeping, and no girl ever loses a lover worth the having because she is bound to ask him to wait awhile until their love is tested and found genuine.[20]

While 20 was considered a good age for a girl to marry, it was not considered sensible for a boy to consider such a commitment until he was in his mid twenties; before this he was neither emotionally mature or financially stable. Although it was acceptable for a woman to marry a man up to five years her junior, magazines preferred a man to be older than his bride as "Peg's Man Pal" explained: "I believe myself it is far better for the man to be older than the woman, for I also believe in him being the head of the house, not in a bossy, domineering sort of way, but in a steadfast, dependable manner, and this answers best when he is some years older."[21] As this quote illustrates, the age differential was highly significant for gender relations within the home, in particular the husband's authority. Religious differences only emerged as an issue in the *Girls' Own Paper* because of its strong Christian ethos and girls were advised against inter-faith marriages.[22] Class differences were, however, a more commonly depicted obstacle between lovers but one which was confined to the fiction; it is notable though that successful romances either involved a woman with a man from a slightly higher social class or a couple who shared the same social standing.

"Affairs of the Heart"

Love was presented in romance magazines as the most powerful force in a woman's life and readers were repeatedly warned against turning their back on it. While it would be wrong to argue that material conditions and patriarchal social relations were no longer able to uphold the institution of marriage, it is clear that ideological sanctions were crucial to the stability of heterosexual, and more specifically marital, relationships. Love was, moreover, the rationalisation of women's acceptance of marriage and her subordination within it.

Romance fiction relied upon three key scenarios. Firstly there were stories in which the heroine initially fell in love with a villain later to discover her error and transfer her affections to the hero who has been waiting in the wings of the drama. The second scenario focused on the unravelling of misunderstandings which had prevented the hero and heroine from realising their love for each other. The final story-line, which was a transformation narrative, involved a flirtatious and/or tomboyish young woman casting off her modernity in favour of traditional romance culminating in marriage.

A contextual examination of this transformation fiction in romance magazines reveals that editors juggled with what they believed to be a fashion amongst modern girls and what they thought girls should aspire and conform to. An important attraction of the initial independence for the heroine, and from articles we can also assume for the intended reader, was the modernity and freedom it promised from the constraints of patriarchal marriage and motherhood. Audrey Challoner, for example, "believed it was old-fashioned to fall in love and have orange-blossoms and bridesmaids at a wedding, and, to show how up-to-date she was, she left a comfortable home and lived in a tiny flat."[23] Independent or tomboyish behaviour which represented a rejection of patriarchal norms regarding girls' conduct and ambitions, was clearly presented as a desire for the power embodied in masculinity and a rejection of the passive role and inferiority accorded to traditional femininity. Whilst this was acceptable for pre-courting girls depicted in schoolgirl papers, working girls' magazines could not easily accommodate such heroines. In order to persuade the heroine to accept a monogamous heterosexual identity magazine fiction had to show the heroine discovering the error of her ways and voluntarily choosing marriage and motherhood. This usually occurred after some horrendous sexual encounter or rejection. For Audrey Challoner it was the latter:

Eric Mathers has taken you out and given you a good time, and he has only asked for a few kisses in return. Now he has got tired, or perhaps he met somebody else he liked better. So he just means to fade away. He doesn't think he has done anything wrong. This is the modern idea.[24]

Reinforcing the message of non-fiction features, these stories clearly caution readers about the possible dangers of modern ways. The transformation of the heroine was completed, however, only when she fell in love with the hero; indeed, heterosexual love was presented as the primary rationalisation of a girl's acceptance of the constraints of femininity and marriage.

By the close of each story when the heroine had usually found a man whom she loved or would learn to love, she had also undergone a transition. In contrast to her initial depiction as independent, the heroine is finally revealed as child-like and as dependent on the hero for love, protection and tenderness. As Dick explained to Audrey:

My darling, of course it is true that people love each other now just the same as they always will. I love you and I'm going to make you love me. We're going to be engaged, you and I, for just a bit. Then we'll be married . . . Then, according to fairy stories which are a lot truer than some of the rot talked nowadays, we're going to live happily ever afterwards. Do you understand?[25]

In this capacity the hero appears like a father in relation to his child, that is the benevolent patriarch; the hero's masculinity is authoritarian and also protective and in this way it reinforced prevailing notions of relations between the sexes.

Radway argues that women who read romance novels often extract positive reinforcement and pleasure from seemingly restrictive story lines.[26] Magazine fiction contained a range of different features and explicit titles and illustrations which, intentionally or otherwise, framed the fiction in quite specific ways. Whatever pleasures girls extracted from these stories two key skills would probably have been acquired from a regular diet of romance serials. One of the lessons conveyed in fiction, which was reinforced elsewhere in these magazines, concerned the identification of a good man worthy of being a girl's future husband. Heroes tended to be serious and quiet men who worked hard, and although strong they were also restrained. The hero's competitor was, in contrast, frivolous and fun-loving and loved conspicuous consumption as much as he hated work. Bourgeois morality, the work ethic in particular, was at the core of this distinction between the hero and his unworthy competitor; for all the romance in these magazines the message conveyed to girls was that they had to secure a husband who would financially support them. As *Girls' Friend* reminded its readers:

The only love that a woman is justified in putting any faith in is the love that expresses itself in action, . . . when a man really loves a woman he rolls up his sleeves, squares his jaw, and works as he has never worked before . . . The truth is that marriage on nothing a year leads only to happiness in novels. In real life, where people have to eat, and be clothed and have doctors, it is about the shortest known cut to certain misery.[27]

In this way the hero bore a resemblance to the boy-next-door whom readers were encouraged to marry. The main difference between the boy the intended reader was expected to marry and the man portrayed in the fiction was that the latter was forced to display in actions and words the depths of his love for the heroine. In reality, the reader's boyfriend was rarely given the opportunity to demonstrate his feelings so graphically. Magazines suggest, however, that given the same circumstances the reader's "man" would probably behave in the same way.

The second skill which girls were encouraged to learn and use involved interpreting male behaviour in particular ways. Whether this accorded with girls' actual experiences of men is another matter. As Radway argues of modern romances, readers were encouraged to understand male behaviour in certain ways through being privy to the meaning, attributed by the author, to the actions of the hero. These meanings readers were encouraged to transpose on to their own relations with men. In fiction for example, when the hero appeared to punish the heroine, the reader was informed that his behaviour was motivated by pain at the heroine's perceived infidelity or failings; this device subsequently rationalised acts of sexual violence towards women as passion. The hero's violence was also explained as a symptom of his ambivalence towards the heroine as he struggled not to fall in love. It was precisely this reason which, readers were informed, underpinned the actions of Peter when he violently "kissed" Sally: "Down came his hard, contemptuous mouth upon her soft lips. It hurt her. The bruising pressure of their brutal demand was mingled with savage joy."[28] As Radway suggests in her analysis of this "double perspective" in romance novels, "What she [the reader] is encouraged to do is to latch on to whatever expressions of thoughtfulness he might display, no matter how few, and to consider these rather than his obvious and frequent disinterest, as evidence of his true character."[29]

Interwar magazines, like the modern day romances examined by Radway, utilised a double perspective to shore up patriarchal relations. That is, they offered readers an interpretation of male behaviour which was not usually obvious from the actions depicted. Indeed, the importance of love as a device with which to rationalise girls' acceptance of patriarchal relations could only work if they perceived male behaviour in such a way as to read love from it. It was through using this device that magazines rationalised double standards as regards the character of male and female love. The love of a girl or woman was described as deep and permanent. Male love, in contrast, was often shallow, more easily controlled and redirected. This notion of male love . . . stemmed from the belief that men were dominated by their sexual urges rather than any "finer" feelings. Even when a man found his ideal partner, his love was nevertheless different from that of a woman. In reply to Margaret, Peg wrote "There is a little quotation which every girl ought to learn by heart; "Love in man's life plays but a part, 'tis woman's whole existence.' "[30] Peg went on to describe how men continued to need the variety and stimulation of their careers and sports once they were married. This interpretation of male and female love served patriarchal interests in that it rationalised women's total commitment and sacrifice within marriage, and at the same time it justified men's involvement in both the public and private spheres and excused them of any heavy emotional investment in their family and home.

NOTES

1. *Girls' Friend*, 31 January 1920.
2. *Polly's Paper*, 15 December 1919, p. 14.
3. *Peg's Paper*, 29 April 1920, p. 28.
4. *Peg's Paper*, 15 January 1920.
5. *Peg's Paper*, 12 April 1924.
6. *Girls' Favourite*, 12 March 1927, p. 127.
7. *Girls' Friend*, 11 September 1920, p. 387.
8. *Girls' Friend*, 17 April 1920, p. 135.
9. *Every Girls' Paper*, 20 October 1924, p. 42.
10. *Girls' Favourite*, 4 February 1922.
11. *Miss Modern*, May 1940.
12. *Poppy's Paper*, 2 February 1924.
13. *Pam's Paper*, 1 March 1924.
14. *Girls' Friend*, 19 June 1920, p. 243.
15. Ibid.
16. *Girls' Friend*, 24 April 1920, p. 152.
17. *Girls' Friend*, 19 June 1920, p. 243.
18. *Polly's Paper*, No. 2, 1919.
19. *Polly's Paper*, No. 4, 1919.
20. *Girls' Weekly*, 18 February 1922, p. 154.
21. *Peg's Paper*, 29 July 1930, p. 22.
22. *Girls' Own Paper*, October 1945, p. 32.
23. *Peg's Paper*, 11 February 1930, pp. 310–11.
24. Ibid.
25. Ibid.
26. Janice Radway, *Reading the Romance* (Verso, 1987).
27. *Girls' Friend*, 18 September 1920, p. 405. See B. Fowler, *The Alienated Reader* (Harvester Wheatsheaf, 1991), p. 65.
28. *Peg's Paper*, 27 April 1940, pp. 8–10.
29. Radway, (1987), p. 148.
30. *Peg's Paper*, 6 May 1920, p. 30.

Chapter Fifty-five

Reason within Passion
Love in Women's Magazines (1991)

Eva Illouz

Illouz, a sociologist, uses women's magazines to trace the strong association of love with commodity consumption and economic practices in the increasingly materialist world of our own time. She believes that love cannot simply be studied as a product of ideas and culture, but must be viewed as a social practice as well. Her book on this subject is Consuming the Romantic Utopia: Love and the Cultural Contradictions of Capitalism *(1997).*

A well established myth views emotions, romantic love in particular, as irreducible to thought, language and culture. While abundant research has analyzed the social construction of ideas, knowledge and rituals, there has been a stubborn resistance to deconstruct emotion (and more especially romantic love) as a product of social practices.

More recently such deconstructions have been attempted. "Constructionist" social psychologists (Averill, 1985; Gergen & Davis, 1985; Harré, 1986; Lutz, 1986) suggest that emotions are shaped by norms and constraints of social interaction (Hochschild, 1983). Cultural history (Aries, 1973; Flandrin, 1981; Lantz, 1987) shows how seemingly universal emotions such as maternal or romantic love are historically related to demographic fluctuations, family structure, religion, etc. Finally, drawing from Geertz' (1973) hermeneutic view of social action, cultural anthropology (Abu-Lughod, 1986; Feld, 1982; Rosaldo, 1980, 1984) examines how emotions are informed by the meaning systems (or cultural texts) available to social actors.

These paradigms have been critical in promoting the counter-intuitive idea that emotions are social and cultural constructs. But, because they have concentrated on geographically or temporally distant cultures, they have neglected the culture of late capitalism. In an attempt to fill in this gap, this paper analyzes 1) how a seemingly private emotion such as romantic love is shaped by the public discourses of late

Eva Illouz, "Reason within Passion: Love in Women's Magazines," *Critical Studies in Mass Communication,* vol. 8, no. 3 (September 1991): 231–48. © 1991 by the Speech Communication Association. Reprinted by permission of the National Communication Association.

capitalism, and 2) the role mass media play in the "modern" construction of romantic love. Such an inquiry would help us understand how the public sphere interacts with and shapes private emotions.

To start framing the relationship between love and the rather vague concept of "culture of capitalism," I use Weber's idea that Western capitalism is characterized by cognitive and practical rationalization. Cognitive rationalization attempts to comprehend reality by means of "increasingly precise and abstract concepts" (cited in Benhabib, 1986; Weber, 1958). Cognitive rationalization is embodied in scientific inquiry. Practical rationality—which Weber called *zweckrational* or purposive conduct—is the rational assessment of "the probable results of a given act in terms of the calculation of means to an end" (Giddens, 1971, p. 152). Practical rationality has been institutionalized through the market. While the purpose of practical rationality is to maximize profit, the purpose of cognitive rationality is to understand and master Nature through abstract and formal thought.

To analyze how capitalist economic activity (practical rationalization) and institutionalized scientific development (cognitive rationalization)—have affected how love is constructed and talked about, I analyze women's magazines. Women's magazines are especially apt because part of their traditional stock and trade is the codification and interpretation of romantic relationships. Before conducting this analysis, it is first useful to look briefly at the history of the romantic discourse and to note how that history helps frame research questions.

History of Romantic Discourse

According to Singer (1987), there have always been two main antinomic conceptions of love in Western culture: one based on the idea of romantic love per se and the other one based on the idea of interest. The first, he calls the idealist approach, the other the realist.

The romantic or idealist approach has typically stressed elements of self-sacrifice, devotion, suddenness of onset (love at first sight) and the uniqueness of the loved person (Averill, 1985; de Rougemont, 1966; Lantz, 1987). The realist view, on the other hand, has posed that men and women should pair themselves for the sake of economic or other benefits. With the realist view, romantic sentiment is neither absolute nor uncontrollable; it is the outcome of rational assessment (see Soble, 1990). In Weberian terminology, the romantic conception rests on a purely affectual bond, while the realist perspective involves *zweckrationalitat*.

The division between idealist and realist love was especially sharp before the end of the 19th century when marriage was openly motivated by interest (or at least by a rational evaluation of the potential partner) rather than by "romantic" or "idealist" love. In other words, the discursive division between idealist and realist tradition was sustained by an institutional distinction between "interested" marriage and love relationships.

In the middle of 19th century America, marriage underwent significant changes. The "realist" justification of marriage was progressively replaced by an idealist or romantic view of marriage (Lewis, 1983; Rothman, 1984). At least publically, "disinterested" and "gratuitous" love became the more legitimate reason for marriage. Given this history, then, one research issue concerns how contemporary women's magazines treat the idealist and realist traditions of love.

Another transformation concerns the rise of a class of public experts. The emergence of such experts can be traced back to the 1930s when it was believed that "scientific knowledge could improve courtship and marriage" (Bailey, 1988, p. 126). The use of these "scientific" theories has given visibility and legitimacy to sociologists, psychologists, etc., whose function has been to promote procedures of emotional control (Stearns & Stearns, 1988). This scientific discourse progressively widened and now encompasses the para-scientific. Para-scientific discourse is popularized (and often vulgarized) versions of a scientific work that is geared to the public rather than to a community of experts. As such, it may be endowed with less prestige and authority, but it is nevertheless invested with semiotic and institutional marks of competence. Interpersonal relationships—and romantic love in particular—have been increasingly the object of para-scientific scrutiny. Considering scientific discourse on love, then, this study also examines how "scientific" forms of reasoning may affect the construction of romantic love in women's magazines.

Foucault's Perspective on Language and Emotions

To operationalize Weber's general concept of rationalization so that it more specifically applies to the rationalization of romantic love in women's magazines, Foucault's theory of discourse can be quite useful.

Foucault's theory of discourse can easily be extended to the domain of emotions. Discourse theory suggests that our emotions are shaped by the metaphors, the semantic categories and the explanatory rules which characterize a particular field of knowledge. This discursive activity shapes how we organize, communicate our emotions. For discourse theory, language does not "reflect" or "translate" an emotion with a distinct ontological status. In other words, discourse theory suggests that language produces rather than labels emotions.

Foucault suggests that what can be said, thought and felt is regulated by the epistemic rules with which knowledge is produced, organized and validated in a given historical context. Foucault's approach to emotions thus suggests that public definitions of emotions depend on the "regimes of truth" available at a certain historical period, i.e., on the ways knowledge is constructed and validated. In this paper, I will illustrate this idea by examining how romantic discourse is validated through (social) scientific discourse.

Moreover, discourse theory submits that categories of knowledge are categories of power. The entitlement of institutions of discourse to speak, classify, name, and establish the dominant and relevant categories of knowledge is at the heart of symbolic power. The implication of such a view is that emotions are not only cultural but more crucially *political* constructs. This analysis of women's magazines attempts to show how the rationalization of romantic discourse has political implications on the construction of women's subjectivity.

Methods

This study considers all the articles pertaining to love and marriage in *Cosmopolitan* and *Woman* from January through June 1988. These two women's magazines treat romantic relationships more frequently and in greater depth than other magazines which have a more domestic focus (e.g., *Woman's Day, Ladies' Home Journal* and *Goodhousekeeping*), although articles dealing with romantic relations in other women's magazines such as *Self, New Woman,* and *Harper's Bazaar* were also analyzed. In total, 35 articles were considered. Clearly, such sampling is limited and somewhat arbitrary. However, the present analysis is exploratory in the hopes of generating hypotheses on the issues raised in the last section. For such purposes, the sampling was deemed adequate.

For each article, three broad issues are analyzed: 1) the main themes, 2) the metaphors by which romantic love is constructed, 3) the normative logic underlying the romantic discourses.

The theme of an article is provided by what van Dijk calls the macrostructure of a text. According to van Dijk, a macrostructure is "the semantic information that provides . . . overall unity to the discourse" (van Dijk, 1985, p. 116). As van Dijk has amply demonstrated, summaries or leads reflect the macrostructures of a text. In this study, the theme of an article is equivalent to its summary and/or to its lead.

Metaphors are fundamental for the construction of social reality. Using the work of Lakoff (1987), Lakoff and Johnson (1980) and Krippendorff (1989), the paper examines the dominant metaphorical fields within which romantic love is conceptualized. More specifically, metaphors have *logical* entailments; they are embedded with explanatory models of the social world and logical conceptual structures. This study examines if several metaphorical fields (a set of metaphors which have similar logical entailments) coexist in the romantic discourses.

Finally, following Angenot (1982), the analysis considers topoi—the set of assumptions, the normative logic underlying and at the same time exceeding statements about a particular object. Topoi constitute the structured but implicit value-laden (axiological) dimension of discourses. This dimension of discourse is the most difficult to formalize and operationalize because it pertains to tacit assumptions of discourse.

Charting the Heart

Three general rhetorical orientations emerge among the articles. The first, prescriptive articles, gives recipes for attaining a successful relationship, rejuvenating romance in marriage, obtaining a date, etc. The second category, normative articles, involves material on romance standards such as on relationships with forbidden or unsuitable persons (e.g., a boss or a married man). The third category, analytical articles, examines the meaning of love. This category includes polls and popularized sociological or psychological work about love.

Within these rhetorical orientations three main themes can be found: the first concerns the difficulty of finding a mate. When the mate is found, the second problem is to identify whether or not he is suitable. The third problem concerns the difficulty of keeping romance in marriage.

To the first problem, finding a mate, the solution advocated by women's magazines explicitly counters the idea of predestination and instead advises treating mate-seeking much as one would a job search. For example, women's magazines give tips on where one is likely to meet a man (sports clubs, supermarkets, volunteer organizations).

To the second problem of assessing a mate, different solutions are suggested such as "mak[ing] a check list of his assets and defects and see[ing] which one is longer." The idealist conception of love is replaced by a more practical examination of social compatibility. Quizzes are sometimes offered for evaluating compatibility, but most often elaborate discussions draw the boundaries between suitable and unsuitable mates.

Finally, to the third problem (keeping romance), two types of answers are offered: the first involves actually enhancing the romance level and the second is accepting a "new" relationship based on negotiation and occasional conflicts. For example, a magazine might provide several recipes for creating passion (e.g., write love notes and put them on the refrigerator, give unexpected creative presents, prepare a delightful dinner with candles). Such recipes convey one central message: the seeming end of romance is the result of objective practices rather than intrinsic sentiments. Other articles have a more complex strategy; they advocate *psychological* strategies of passion rejuvenation:

> We resist the idea that negotiation and romance cannot coexist . . . Romance and negotiation are not only compatible but necessary in an adult relationship (*New Woman,* February, 1988, p. 45).

When carried further, this logic suggests that romance and marriage do not necessarily coincide.

> . . . Conflicts and even occasional doubts are normal in marriage—especially in the early years, when you must learn to compromise and adjust your own needs and expectations to harmonize with those of your mate. Marriage *means* compromise, conflict, sharing and inevitably surprise (*New Woman,* February, 1988, p. 75).

Thus, when addressing post-marriage disenchantment, these magazines address romance as the ideal while normalizing and legitimizing the absence of marital romance by prescribing alternative models of relationships. In the latter case, it takes a stand against the idealist tradition of love. In this sense, two conflicting models are offered together; the first holds time and routine as the enemies of romance and advocates steps for maintaining intensity and passion. The second model, on the other hand, suggests that realism must be preferred to build long-lasting relationships.

Passion within Reason, Reason within Passion

As indicated, then, broad metaphorical fields for love emerge: love as intense force, love as magic, and love as hard work.

Love as Intense Force

The metaphor of love as an all consuming force is the most familiar. It has been and still is very dominant in the depiction of the first encounter (Rousset, 1981). The metaphor of love as an intense force has several metaphorical sub-fields.

This force may be a *burning* one. For example "there were sparks between them" (*Cosmopolitan*, March, 1988), or this title "Passion: how to ignite, reignite it, make it last" (*Cosmopolitan*, November, 1987). Another force love might be is magnetic, as manifested in "irresistable attraction" or in feelings of being "electrified" (such expressions were found in various issues of the two magazines).

Love as Magic

The metaphor of love as magic may have roots in ancient folk practices, literally employing magic to gain someone's heart (Gillis, 1988). However, in modern discourse, the metaphor of magic simply indicates love's sweeping power. For example: "Truly passionate love can magically transform us into fuller, richer persons" (*Self*, April, 1988, p. 132). Or, "when you stop focusing your attention on your relationship you forget how much you enjoy the magic of love" (*Woman*, April, 1988, p. 26–27).

In the metaphors of love as fire, magnetism or magic, love is always conceived as an autonomous agent, acting with a force of its own, independent of the will or control of the lovers. Grammatically and semantically sentences such as "love struck her heart" suggest love as an entity in itself, detachable from the person and acting on its own. In such ideology, what starts and what keeps love is beyond the conscious and rational understanding of those upon whom it is bestowed. Consequently one can only wait for love to happen; one cannot predict it; one can only be enraptured by it. While these metaphors picture love as an intense force, they may challenge the traditional idealist perspective. For example, an article recommends ingredients to keep love alive: "heroic adventures, secret getaways, the moving bed, dining au naturel [i.e., naked], a picnic in the train, snoozes and snuggles, love notes, sex on the dining-room table" (*Cosmopolitan*, January, 1988). Originality, spontaneity and creativity are promoted here, but these values are what sociologists call "anti-institutional" definitions of the self (Turner, 1976). Analysis of nineteenth century love letters (Gay, 1986; Lystra, 1989) reveals that middle and upper-middle class Victorians abundantly used metaphors of intensity. However, during the Victorian era, these metaphors were always suffused with the vocabulary of devotion, self-sacrifice, fusion and worship of the religious discourse.[1] In contemporary culture, the metaphors of intensity have not only severed their ties with religious discourse, but they reflect a combination of "anti-modernism" and hedonism (Bell, 1976). Here anti-modernism is a complex of anti-institutional values such as spontaneity, quest of an authentic self, creativity and the unconstrained expression of one's emotions (Lears, 1981). These positions contrast with a love bound by the rules of Christian spirituality and devotion, which had characterized the traditional idealist discourse.

Love as Work: The Romantic Ethic and the Spirit of Capitalism

In the work model, effort replaces the magic start, commitment the overwhelming force of passion, relativity the absoluteness of love, and conscious monitoring the spontaneous outburst of passion. For example, one of the most widely used metaphors for relationships is the metaphor of "work." One "works" at a "successful" relationship, "builds it," "lays out its foundations"; the partners are "co-workers" involved in a "team-work"; one wants to "invest" in relationships, get "benefits" out of it, etc. Clearly these metaphors are the language of market exchange transposed to intimate interpersonal relationships:

> As in business or social contract, the parties [of a love relationship] govern themselves by whatever definitions and limits they have agreed on (*Cosmopolitan*, June, 1988, p. 130).

And also:

> Love is a feeling but a relationship is a contract. While falling in love can just happen, a loving relationship requires certain skills in order to be sustained (*Self*, April, 1988, p. 50).

These metaphors have two sets of entailments: the first one is that love is controllable by our thoughts and that, consequently, we are responsible for its success or failure. The second entailment is that love is a commodity responding to the same strategies of market transactions.

In a broad sense, this discourse derives from what Bellah, Madsen, Sullivan, Swidler & Tipton (1985) have called "utilitarian individualism" which contends that the basis of relationships is contractual and must be evaluated in terms of the costs and benefits one exacts from them. A very clear example of such contractual logic is the following:

> No matter how much he loved me, my partner couldn't intuit my needs in some mystical fashion. He had his own needs to worry about. It was up to me to see that my needs were met and the way to do that was to negotiate with him for what I wanted (*New Woman*, February, 1988, p. 45).

The utilitarian premises of this quote are highlighted when contrasted with an organic model of love, also present in women's magazines:

> The very best I-love-you's come with no ifs, or buts attached. They come in the kitchen as well as in the bedroom. They are spontaneous expressions of affection that don't hide silent assumption or demands (*Cosmopolitan*, May, 1988).

The utilitarian form of reasoning suggests that the individual chooses freely his/her relationship from a pool of possible partners. For example, an article in *Self* magazine explains extensively that the process of looking for a man is similar "to the process of looking for a job" to the extent that in order to meet someone, one needs to be decisive and systematic in her search of the "soul mate" (*Self*, 1988). Utilitarianism also promotes independence, autonomy, self-reliance, ability to assert one's personality, needs and aggressiveness.

> Negotiators . . . assume equality and do themselves and their partners the service of stating their needs clearly, hearing out their partners, and compromising with them in those places where the two diverge (*New Woman*, February, 1988, p. 48).

Above all, utilitarian ethos stresses the idea that the relationship is a transaction in which both partners must have an equitable and fruitful exchange:

> . . . love is like a marketplace transaction . . . lovers are content with their relationships to the degree that what they're giving is in line with what they're getting. The weighing of contributions (inputs) to profits (outcomes) can trade off personal attributes such as beauty or personal warmth against power or riches (*Harper's Bazaar*, February, 1988).

The metaphors of business partnerships and transactions have thoroughly pervaded not only the lay(wo)man's common sense of love but also the expert theories of love at work in psychology, sociology and economics. As psychologist D. Goleman put it: "In recent years, the mainstream of psychological research has looked at love almost as if it were a business transaction, a matter of profit and loss" (cited in Frank, 1988, p. 186).

Furthermore, the semantics of "romantic entrepreneurship" uses the same vocabulary which Kohn (1969) found to be characteristic of middle-class values toward work: self-directness, sense of responsibility and self-monitoring. In other words, one may surmise that middle-class women's discourses of romance are characterized by the fact that there is no logico-symbolic disjuncture between their conceptualization of work and romance.

In *The Art of Loving*, Fromm (1956) noticed that the modern ideal of love as a smoothly functioning team was congruent with capitalist ideology; rather than the idealist model of love as organic bond, the modern ideal is based on evaluation of gains and losses. With the idealist model, one is "stricken" or "smitten," but in the modern discursive field, one is responsible for romantic success or failures, one has to "work hard" at a relationship, based on an equitable exchange.

The romantic ethic promoted by these magazines is analogous to that which was instrumental to the formation of the capitalist entrepreneur (Weber, 1958). Weber's work suggests that this ethos promotes an instrumental, rather than affective model by viewing the relationship as a goal to attain through the systematic implementation of controlled and planned procedures. These articles indicate that the language of commodities has provided the lexicon of romantic relationships. The romantic ethic conveyed by women's magazines is fully consistent with the capitalist credo that persons and relationships are given to the same logic of evaluation of costs and profits of business transactions.

These preliminary findings seem to confirm Weber's (1958) and Adorno and Horkheimer's (1972) contention that capitalism is characterized by the penetration of all spheres of life by the culture of capitalism. For Adorno and Horkheimer, the "instrumental reason" has undermined the totality of modern culture. Thus, critical theorists would suggest that the semantic "spillovers" from the economic to the romantic sphere point to a process of what Habermas has called the "colonization of the lifeworld." Lears (1981) suggests that this commodification of the self and of human relationships occurred at the end of the 19th century.

Cultural Contradictions and the Uncertainties of the Heart

These findings leave unexplained the reasons of the tension between "organic" and "contractual" conceptions of love. How can we account for the fact that a relationship, according to these magazines, has to fulfill two contradictory requirements, one affective-gratuitous and one instrumental-utilitarian?

From an anthropological perspective, love-as-an-intense-force relates to an economy of the gift; the contractual conception is capitalistic. The first model is based on the idea of social/economic waste for the sake of an organic bond while the second is based on profitable and equitable exchange. The organic view of love—in opposition to the contractual one—promotes a form of exchange which does not aim at guaranteeing equity or interest. This organic-bond view is antithetical to the utilitarian one.

A traditional, sociological explanation of this contradiction suggests that marriage and romantic love promote different values and that the "intrusion" of love in marriage has created a symbolic contradiction between the values put forth by romantic love (intensity, idealization of the other, interest-free emotion) and the requirements of the institution of marriage (sharing daily life, coping with a less than perfect other, envisioning love in the "long-term," integrating love with the responsibilities of a family and work life, etc.). The problem of the modern synthesis of love and marriage is to merge two incompatible discursive fields, two models of social relationships (one based on intensity and one on continuity) and two incompatible economic rationalities (one of instant gratification, one of long-term investment). This incompatibility translates into

> tensions between . . . partially conflicting conceptions of love and marriage [which] are endemic in our society today (Swidler, 1985, p. 85).

For Swidler, this tension arises as the result of the tension between the need for "spontaneity," "personal intimacy" that are not "anchored in objective patterns of roles and social institutions" (ibid). Although this explanation is sensible, a different line of argument may be offered.

As many historians and sociologists of marriage have now agreed (MacFarlane, 1987; Shorter, 1977; Stone, 1977), the mobilization and mobility of the individual as a productive unit were achieved by the dissolution of communal relationships.

Individualism—both as a social philosophy and as a form of social organization—was central to justify the reorganization of social relationships. Individualism made possible such a reorganization by translating itself in various sentiments, romantic love being undoubtedly the most important of them.[2] Romantic love played a very important role in providing the ideological justifications for realizing the transition from communal to individualist pair-bonding. In other words, the new organization of social relationships entailed by capitalism needed the powerful ideology of romantic love to justify a new process of pair-bonding and legitimize the fact that the community and family were *not* in charge of the marital selection anymore.

On the other hand, the structural organization of capitalist societies makes marriage one of the major channels of reproduction of social classes. As economists of the family would say and contrary to our popular myths, love is rarely socially blind because one of the primary functions of marriage is to reproduce the social order through the organized and structured encounter of social "likes" (Becker, 1981). It follows that modern marriage is caught within a symbolic and practical contradiction: while marriage follows strategies of investment aiming at enhancing one's social position (e.g., "does he make enough money?"; "is he smart enough?"), the ideology of love presents marriage as an "interest free" emotion and bond. The merging of an interest-free love in the market of marriages has created a contradiction endemic to capitalism.

From all the above, it might be concluded that women's magazines (re)produce unconsciously the cultural contradictions of capitalism; however, one of the most original features of women's magazines is that they not only reflect this contradiction but also reflect *upon it*. Far from being unconscious, the contradiction between "ideal romance" and "realist workings of a relationship" is endlessly commented upon and explained. Even more interestingly, women's magazines offer means to manage these contradictions through the implementation of a new epistemology of the self, namely, the "therapeutic ethos."

While individual utilitarianism pointed us to the practical rationalization (*zweck-rational*) of the interpersonal sphere, the therapeutic ethos points us to its cognitive rationalization. By promoting self-reflexive and formal modes of reasoning, the therapeutic ethos instills a "rational" attitude toward the self.

The Science of Love: The Therapeutic Ethos

Bellah, Madsen, Sullivan, Swidler and Tipton (1985), Bellah (1985) and Swidler (1985) have suggested that the therapeutic ethos evolved from the utilitarian individualism which has pervaded American social relationships. However, the therapeutic ethos has an additional dimension of self-knowledge and auto-observation. The therapeutic ethos is a theory of self-knowledge whereas the utilitarian ethos is a way to secure one's interest in interaction.

From my analysis of the articles, the ideology of therapeutic ethos can be said to revolve around the following core propositions:

- Relationships can be divided into "healthy" and "unhealthy."
- The bond that unites a man and a woman is given to study and knowledge, and may be evaluated "professionally" according to objective criteria.
- Given that people can gain the appropriate knowledge, they can control their romantic relationships through work and appropriate strategies.
- Consequently, romantic failure and success depends upon self-knowledge.
- The key to understanding romantic failure lies in early life experience.
- Understanding our past experiences through the appropriate knowledge will lead us to healthy relationships.

The therapeutic ethos functions at two ideological levels: One level legitimizes experts of the psyche and the use of science in interpersonal relations. The second level instills forms of rationality through specific epistemic devices. The therapeutic ethos not only uses and relies heavily on the discursive style and authority of scientific discourses but also imports the very epistemic schemes of social scientific thought within the arena of emotions. The distinction between these two different arguments is very important: The first claim concerns the use of science as a way to assert the symbolic authority of romantic discourses. The second claim is epistemological and concerns the formal logic conveyed by the therapeutic ethos.

The Legitimation of Experts

That the discourse of love is issued by experts relates to what Foucault identified as our cultural tendency to convert everyday statements into *serious speech acts,* i.e., statements which have to undergo procedures of validation controlled and sanctioned by a community of experts. In the magazines' treatment of love, experts are quoted in two main contexts: when the article explains what "starts, keeps and ends love" and when the article prescribes a specific behavior. The prescriptive dimension of the experts' discourse consists in defining the boundaries between normal and patholog-ical relationships. The explanatory dimension on the other hand, provides women with a framework to account for their successes and failures.

The Function of Normalization of the Therapeutic Ethos

Women's magazines refer extensively to the authorized speech of "scientists" (psychologists, MDs or the generic category of "researchers"). In fact, across the 35 articles surveyed, there are 34 references to experts of various categories. Among these 34 experts, 28 are MDs and psychologists, while the remaining 6 are "sociolo-gists," "researchers" and "anthropologists." The reference to the experts is used to unveil and explain what the title of a *Cosmopolitan* article called the "sweet scientific mystery of love" (*Cosmopolitan,* April, 1988). A typical way to introduce an argument is: "In a study. . . ." Moreover, romantic articles rely heavily on statistics and polls to "prove" the validity of their analyses and advice.

Researchers have come up with information and insights gleaned from studies on what attracts us to someone of the opposite sex, how lasting bonds between men and women are forged, how personality and early childhood experience affect our capacity for and success at love (*Cosmopolitan*, June, 1988).

Women's magazines, then, popularize research, but in the magazines, social science is used for normative rather than descriptive purposes. The most important of these normative purposes is defining and prescribing "healthy" behavior; the scientific discourse is used to legitimize a certain vision of normalcy. This function is expressed in ritual phrases such as "it is perfectly normal to," or "while it is healthy to . . ." For example:

> [when a friend of yours dates an ex–boy-friend of yours] it's normal to feel jealous, competitive and left out. . . . The healthy thing is to walk away (*Woman*, February, 1988, p. 16).

The function of normalization converts a moral prescription (good/bad) into simple description validated by semiotic marks of scientific expertise. This normalization of discourse is performed through what has been called "impersonal judgments," i.e., judgments expressed in the impersonal rather than personal form (e.g., "*it* is 'healthy' rather than *I* think it is healthy"). It is also performed through metaphors which make relationships sick or healthy wherein the possible pathology justifies the intervention of experts.

The Explanatory Function of the Therapeutic Ethos

The explanatory function of the therapeutic ethos is at the heart of its symbolic power. Justifications are essential to the ideological arena because they entail different corrective strategies. For example, blaming a romantic failure on male chauvinism, unresolved Oedipal conflicts or the dissolution of human relationships by capitalism will yield very different curative strategies.

Women's magazines—like most psychological textbooks—hold that the cause of "romantic failures" lies in early childhood. Women's magazines suggest that romantic failures point to a personality problem in the woman herself and that her childhood is key in explaining her romantic success or failures. But where Freud's etiology offered a tragic vision of man and woman enslaved by the masked and resistant forces of their unconscious, these magazines promote the idea that one is fully responsible for one's romantic failures. While for Freud the determinism of the unconscious could be overcome only through long and painful analysis, women's magazines promote the view that a woman can easily rise above the patterns of her failures. However, the therapeutic ethos conveys a certain contradiction. On one hand it locates the reason for romantic failures in circumstances beyond the control or awareness of the subject. Because awareness of one's past is difficult to attain, the use of experts becomes necessary and experts thus become the intermediaries between the split parts of our selves. On the other hand, therapeutic ethos fully reinforces the credo of the Protestant ethic—that one is responsible for his/her own (emotional) destiny. Under the rule of the therapeutic ethos, we are all responsible for our romantic welfare.

The historical encounter of the ideology of romantic love and the rise of experts in privatized sections of life has given birth to a paradox: on one hand, marriage (until the end of 19th century relegated to reason, calculation and planning) is now considered the result of irrational and overwhelming force. On the other hand, the use of the expert discourse has made love the object of scientific knowledge and thereby something susceptible to rational procedures of validation.

As previously suggested, the scientization of love occurred during the 1930s during which courses on marriage and courtship were implemented in colleges. (See Bailey, 1988.) According to the actors of the period, modern life threatened the structure and cohesiveness of the family. The basic belief underlying these courses was that scientific expertise could improve courtship and marriage. The voice of these experts became increasingly heard in the larger cultural arena. As Bailey (1988) observed, experts took on the task of advising about love in magazines, advice literature, etc., and women's magazines' use of experts finds its historical roots in the Marriage Education Movement. From this perspective, women's magazines foster neither "irrational" nor "mythical-narrative" forms of thought but rather diluted forms of (social) scientific thought.

Therapeutic Discourse and Forms of Reflexivity

The magazines examined invite women to adopt a proto-scientific attitude toward themselves through a meta-discursive level of discourse, i.e., a level in which discourse explicitly dwells upon its discursive functions. The self-reflexivity conveyed by the therapeutic ethos is brought about not by a specific set of contents (ideological "signifieds") but by formal procedures of thinking.

The Labeling Function. To name and to define are a fundamental stake of the discursive and ideological arena. Calling the physiological response subsequent to our attraction to someone "love at first sight," "sexual desire," "crush," "neurotic enactment of past desires" or "lust" connects us with very different discursive registers. Women's magazines constantly attempt to deconstruct the labels appendant to the concept of romantic love. A typical example is:

> The "go-crazy kind of love," Byrne [a psychologist] contends, is often nothing more than a mad, passionate mislabeling of your emotions (*Harper's Bazaar*, February, 1988, p. 192).

Such discursive strategy parallels cognitive therapies which try to modify their patients' behavior by showing them they have wrongly labelled their emotions. This meta-discursive discussion on the "appropriate" name of one's emotions is likely to increase one's self-conscious awareness of his/her labeling strategies. Labeling strategies are co-terminous with a self-conscious exercise of classification of emotions. The classificatory function of language consists in drawing semantic boundaries between concepts and/or events. Women's magazines self-consciously dwell on this function:

Falling in love on vacation can be hazardous to your heart if you expect to love happily ever after. Romance, on the other hand, can be a delightful adventure that you revel in while it's happening . . . (*New Woman*, August, 1988).

The function of these symbolic boundaries is to construct different shades of emotions by ascribing to each a specific *content*. The construction of a symbolic boundary in fact articulates another boundary, that between "safe" and "hazardous" romantic encounters and conveys elements of middle-class morality:

Passion is more than just sexual desire. It is also characterized by the powerful emotions of love, hate, and rage, of lust, zeal, jealousy and possessiveness. Passion encompasses the myriad expressions of aliveness and intensity in a relationship (*Cosmopolitan*, November, 1987, p. 259).

Or also:

Often the men with whom we have the strongest sexual chemistry are the men with whom we would be the least able to form a compatible marriage (*Woman*, July, 1989, p. 47).

In these examples, the boundary has the function of circumscribing zones of "allowed" and "forbidden" behavior. More importantly, by reflecting on the boundaries between "real" and "ephemeral" feelings, such discussions invite a reflexive posture toward one's self. In fact, women's magazines treat the heart as a text that women have to decipher and interpret correctly:

watch out for anyone who happens to walk into your life when you're having a bad day—that's not love, that's a spillover of feeling from one realm to another (*Woman*, March, 1988).

Thus, women's magazines convey not only a normative content but also a mode of hermeneutic self-reflexivity: Women are advised to interrogate the "true meaning" of their emotions, thus making hermeneutic activity a routine exercise of their romantic self. This hermeneutic activity (i.e., the activity by which women are asked to interrogate the "true" meaning of their feelings) is instrumental in promoting a self-reflexive scientific attitude toward romantic relationships and self in general.

From Self-Analysis to Scientific Analysis. To remedy romantic failures, women's magazines encourage women to adopt a proto-scientific attitude toward their "self." This is achieved through several epistemic devices.

First, women are asked to view themselves as objects of study. Women's magazines suggest that failures in and of themselves do not constitute a problem. Rather, the problem lies in a repeated pattern of failure. For example, in an article dealing with "on falling in love with a man everyone (including you) thinks is wrong for you" (*Woman*, October, 1988), the author—a psychologist—in order to establish whether disapproval of other people is justified, draws the following distinction: "If there's no pattern of going against the tide, I'd feel more confident in the person's judgement" (*Woman*, October, 1988, p. 48). Women are asked to become aware of these repetitions through a process of self-observation and to analyze them in order to remove them. The single variable explaining women's failure is the woman herself, or rather her early childhood. Women are then advised to look for the hidden reasons of their failures in their early relationships.

These elements indicate that women are asked to perform on themselves the operations that define a scientific inquiry: Take human subjects (themselves) as objects of study, identify behavioral patterns, establish correlations, find a causal variable, and unveil the hidden reasons for the behavior.

Moreover, one of the most interesting features of women's magazines is that they offer a discourse which, like many communication studies, denounces the falsity of mass media representations. For example:

> Marriage is not always the romantic fantasy *you see played out in advertisements for honeymoon getaways.* Few, if any, have such an idyllic relation and you should not measure your own marriage against impossibly high standards (*New Woman*, February, 1988, p. 45 [italics added]).

The therapeutic discourse assumes the status of a knowledge that unmasks the illusions produced by mass media. By denouncing the falsity and power of media representations, it invites women to question the cultural sources of their representations. The critical function of women's magazines is most interesting because it suggests that popular culture views itself as illusory knowledge.

This finding indicates that the therapeutic discourse has contributed to formalizing and increasing self-reflexivity which—according to Habermas and many other social analysis—is a distinctive feature of the cognitive rationalization of the life world (Berger, 1973; Lears, 1981; Sennett, 1977).

Love and Rationalization of the Life World

Adorno's and Horkheimer's critical theory rests on the fundamental premise that intersubjective and economic relationships ought to remain in two separate spheres (Kellner, 1989). Habermas (1987) has offered the most compelling elaboration of such an idea. Positing an analytical distinction between the market and the state (what Habermas calls "system integration") and the lifeworld of interpersonal relationships (what Habermas calls "social integration"), Habermas distinguishes between two types of actions: "communicative action" defined as action oriented towards the maintenance of a shared intersubjective framework and "instrumental" action that is aimed at securing one's goals and interests through the implementation of certain means.

Contrary to his predecessors, Habermas is reluctant to equate the negative outcomes of the rationalization of the economic and political spheres ("system rationalization") with the "rationalization of the communicative sphere." Rather, he holds that the rationalization of the communicative sphere—characterized by a decentered view, the differentiation of value spheres and self-reflexivity—is emancipatory and can potentially counter the deficiencies of the system rationalization (Habermas, 1987).

In the context of this study, Habermas' position suggests that, although the semantics of commodity exchange and scientific rationality have penetrated romantic relationships, this rationalization may in fact represent an emancipatory force. Considering the fact that the discourses analyzed here come from women's magazines, the most obvious way to formulate the question of the emancipatory character of the rationalization of love is to know if the rationalization has advanced or hampered feminist politics and if it has reinforced the ascription of women to the sphere of "sentimentality" and "emotions."

Romantic love has traditionally stood as a female quality. As Cancian has showed, romantic love in the US has undergone a process of "feminization," i.e., has come to stand for female worlds and values (Cancian, 1987; Lewis, 1983). "Nineteenth century notions held women as naturally emotional and men as naturally rational" (Lewis, 1983, p. 199). Thus, we should have found women's magazines to convey values and vocabulary associated with "traditional" female values of "irrationality and emotionality." Instead, we find that the lexicon of romantic discourse in women's magazines promotes utilitarian and therapeutic ethos consistent not only with the logic and values of the public sphere but also—and surprisingly—with feminist romantic discourses themselves. As Leach (1981) showed in his study of the feminist discourse of the mid-nineteenth century, feminists countered the "sentimental" discourse of love and advocated a discourse based on rationality and negotiation, both deemed to be necessary conditions to equality. Many of the nineteenth century (and contemporary) feminist discourses about love used the previously noticed utilitarian and contractual outlooks. Thus, the romantic discourse geared to women, far from encouraging an irrational "romantic" view of love, promotes male-connoted attitudes, i.e., stress control, assertiveness and rational forms of thinking. The language of instrumentality, prominent in the male-dominated arena of market exchanges, has been transferred to the "traditionally female" sphere of emotions. This, of course, does not mean that women's magazines as a whole promote feminist politics, but that the semantics of love in women's magazines has undergone important discursive changes.

Many analysts would reject such an evaluation of the rationalization of love. For example, Foucault's perspective would suggest that the incorporation of romantic love into the field of psychological knowledge is inscribed within the larger process of "bio-power," i.e., the increased capacity to control, manage and rationalize life. Bio-power, Foucault contends, uses accounting, statistics, demographics, therapeutics, and other methods to mold individuals into productive self-monitoring subjects who become their own objects of observation and control. Thus, from a Foucaultian view, the encroachment of scientific rationality upon the field of romantic love would make women become their own "panopticon," i.e., would make them examine themselves with the instruments of knowledge and control developed by the modern State so as to produce "disciplined" subjects. However, according to Habermas therapeutic discourse is self-reflexive and emancipatory because it is an instrument of knowledge and self-liberation. Following a Kantian tradition, Habermas believes in the emancipatory power of reason examining its own grounds and suggests that the psychoanalytical discourse—from which the therapeutic discourse sprung—is liberating because it constitutes "self-critique."

The penetration of romantic discourse by the logic of instrumentality is liable to have negative consequences on the woman's subjectivity or "lifeworld": by transferring the language, the rationality and the psychological demands of the public to the private sphere, women may in fact perpetuate a long tradition of "taking care" of romantic relationships. This hypothesis is confirmed in my finding that men less often than women use metaphors of "work," and are more likely than women to view their relationships as play and relaxation (Illouz, 1991). This implies that men and women view their emotional lives according to contradictory discursive logic. Because women are in charge of the emotional labor, they may be at a disadvantage to the extent that they assume a greater share in the relational process than men.

Thus, the practical rationalization of romantic love has an ambivalent political bearing: on one hand it has contributed to framing romantic relationships as an equitable contractual exchange within which women could assert themselves as equal partners. On the other hand, because the rationalization of the romantic discourse has been mostly geared to women, it may have had the effect of consolidating the old idea that women are in charge of emotions and relationships. Moreover, and this is an even more serious concern, the proto-scientific self-reflexivity promoted by the psychological discourse may have—to use one of Weber's most famous expressions— "disenchanted" romantic love by subjecting it to the neutral and dispassionate gaze of a reason aware of itself. Thus, although I have suggested that the encroachment of economic and contractual rationality upon the domain of love was instrumental in providing the ideological grounds for the feminist discourse, I also argue that such an emancipation may have taken its toll: By stressing the same values and forms of reasoning at work in the spheres of market exchanges and science, it may have contributed to extending their power in the communicative and intersubjective domains which, in order to remain meaningful, ought to retain their autonomy from these spheres.

NOTES

1. A 1910 issue of *Woman's Home Companion* provides an example of the interpenetration of religious and amorous discourses: "There is no such thing as true love without reward; for even if one is denied what we call "love returned," there are all the other beautiful rewards that come with loving: the nobler views and higher ideals that love gives one, the joy of serving, the wider sympathy and better understanding, the richer and more complete living" (*Woman's Home Companion*, February, 1910, p. 24). This quote is characteristic of the traditional "idealist" discourse of love which combined motives of selflessness, sacrifice and spiritual elevation with those of love.

2. For example, in her study of nineteenth century love letters, Lystra (1989) showed that the romantic self was instrumental to the formation of an individualist self.

REFERENCES

Abu-Lughod, L. (1986). *Veiled sentiments.* Berkeley: University of California Press.

Adorno, T., & Horkheimer, M. (1972). *Dialectic of enlightenment.* (J. Cumming, Trans.). New York: Herder & Herder.

Angenot, M. (1982). *La parole pamphletaire: Typologie des discours modernes.* Paris: Payot.

Aries, P. (1973). *L'enfant et la vie familiale sous l'ancien regime.* Paris: Le Seuil.

Averill, J. (1985). The social construction of emotion: with special reference to love. In K. J. Gergen and J. Davis (Eds), *The social construction of the person.* New York: Springer Verlag.

Bailey, B. (1988). *From front porch to back seat: Courtship in twentieth century America.* Baltimore: Johns Hopkins University Press.

Becker, G. (1981). *A treatise in the family.* Boston: Harvard University Press.

Bell, D. (1976). *The coming of the post-industrial society.* New York: Basic Books.

Bellah, R. (1985). Individualism and commitment in American life. *Berkeley Journal of Sociology,* 117–141.

Bellah, R., Madsen, R., Sullivan, W., Swidler, A., & Tipton, S. (1985). *Habits of the heart.* Berkeley: University of California Press.

Benhabib, S. (1986). *Critique, norm and utopia.* New York: Columbia University Press.

Berger, P. (1973). *The homeless mind.* New York: Vintage Books.

Cancian, F. (1987). *Love in America: Gender and self development.* Cambridge, UK: Cambridge University Press.

de Rougemont, D. (1966). *Love in the western world* (M. Belgion, Trans.). Greenwich, CT: Fawcett Publishers.

Feld, S. (1982). *Sound and sentiment.* Philadelphia: University of Pennsylvania Press.

Flandrin, J.-L. (1981). *Le sexe et l'occident.* Paris: Le Seuil.

Frank, R. (1988). *Passions within reason: The strategic role of emotions.* New York: Norton and Company.

Fromm, E. (1956). *The art of loving.* New York: Harper and Row.

Gay, P. (1986). *From Victoria to Freud.* New York: Oxford University Press.

Geertz, C. (1973). *The interpretation of cultures.* New York: Basic Books.

Gergen, K. J., & Davis, K. (1985). *The social construction of the person.* New York: Springer Verlag.

Giddens, A. (1971). *Capitalism and social theory.* Cambridge: Cambridge University Press.

Gillis, J. (1988). From ritual to romance: Toward an alternative history of love. In C. Z. Stearns & P. Stearns (Eds), *Emotion and social change.* New York: Holmes and Meier.

Habermas, J. (1987). *Theorie de l'agir communicationnel.* Paris: Fayard.

Harré, R. (1986). *The social construction of emotion.* Oxford: Basil Blackwell.

Hochschild, A. (1983). *The managed heart.* Berkeley: University of California Press.

Illouz, E. (1991). *Consuming the romantic utopia: Introduction to a political economy of love.* Doctoral Dissertation, Philadelphia: University of Pennsylvania.

Kellner, D. (1989). *Critical theory, Marxism, and modernity.* Baltimore: Johns Hopkins University Press.

Kohn, M. (1969). *Class and conformity: A study in values.* Homewood, Ill.: Dorsey Press.

Krippendorff, K. (1989). The power of communication and the communication of power. Paper presented at the 1989 International Communication Association, San Francisco.

Lakoff, G. (1987). *Women, fire and dangerous things.* Chicago: University of Chicago Press.

Lakoff, G., & Johnson, M. (1980). *Metaphors we live by.* Chicago: University of Chicago Press.

Lantz, H. (1987). Romantic love in the pre-modern period: A sociological commentary. *Journal of Social History,* 349–370.

Leach, W. (1981). *True love and perfect union*. New York: Routledge and Kegan Paul.

Lears, J. (1981). *No place of grace*. New York: Basic Books.

Lewis, J. (1983). *The pursuit of happiness*. Cambridge: Cambridge University Press.

Lutz, C. (1986). Emotion, thought and estrangement: Emotion as a cultural category. *Cultural Anthropology, 1*, 287–309.

Lystra, K. (1989). *Searching the heart*. New York: Oxford University Press.

MacFarlane, A. (1987). *The culture of capitalism*. Oxford: Basil Blackwell.

Rosaldo, M. (1980). *Knowledge and passion: Ilongot notions of self and social life*. Cambridge: Cambridge University Press.

Rosaldo, M. (1984). Toward an anthropology of the self and feeling. In R. A. Shweder and R. A. Levine, *Culture theory*. Cambridge: Cambridge University Press.

Rothman, E. (1984). *Hands and hearts*. Cambridge, MA: Harvard University Press.

Rousset, J. (1981). *Leurs yeux se rencontrerent*. Paris: Librairie Jose Corti.

Sennett, R. (1977). *The fall of the public man*. New York: Alfred A. Knopf.

Shorter, E. (1977). *Naissance de la famille moderne*. Paris: Le Seuil.

Singer, I. (1987). *The nature of love*. Chicago: University of Chicago Press.

Soble, A. (1990). *The structure of love*. New Haven: Yale University Press.

Stearns, C. Z., & Stearns, P. (Eds.). (1988). *Emotion and social change*. New York: Holmes and Meier.

Stone, L. (1977). *The family, sex and marriage in England 1500–1800*. Harper Colophon Books.

Swidler, A. (1985). Love and marriage. In Bellah et al., (p. 83–115).

Turner, R. (1976). The real self: From institution to impulse. *American Journal of Sociology, 8*, 989–1016.

van Dijk, T. (1985). Semantic discourse analysis. In T. van Dijk (Ed.), *Handbook of discourse analysis, 2*, pp. 103–136.

Weber, M. (1958). *The Protestant ethic and the spirit of capitalism*. New York: Scribner.

Chapter Fifty-six

From What Does a Kiss Mean?

The Love Comic Formula and the Creation of the Ideal Teen-Age Girl (1975)

Philippe Perebinossoff

This enjoyable article traces the ideal of youthful femininity/masculinity and the way women were supposed to behave in romance through love comics, a genre popular when Perebinossoff wrote this piece in 1975, during the second wave of feminism, and still popular today.

The expressive symbolism of popular and mass art carries with it particular meanings which occur over and over again in a culture only because they feed on certain real social experiences, only because, by reading and responding and assenting to these symbols, even in their fantasy form, we give them a kind of legitimacy. It is not necessary to establish a crude relationship between the number of thriller romances and the rate of pre-marital pregnancies or between the number of love comics and the divorce rate to admit that their existence matters.—Stuart Hall and Paddy Whannel, *The Popular Arts* (London: 1964), pp. 189–90.

Love comic conventions reflect in condensed or capsule form the values popular culture requires of the ideal teen-age girl. Jackie Curtiss, Warhol superstar and author of theatre of the ridiculous plays such as *Heaven Grand in Amber Orbit* and *Vain Victory or the Vicissitudes of the Damned,* says that the reason the title of his memoirs, *Storm of Kisses* or *Forever Rain,* sound like something from a love comic is that he believes that everyone patterns his life along love comic conventions. He adds that he had first thought of composing his memoirs by using selected frames from *Girls' Love* or *Young Romance.*[1]

To deny the possible impact of the love comics' repeated definitions of *LOVE* on a reader's developing identity because love comics are only "entertainment" and not didactic tracts would be just as naive as insisting that one isn't affected or conditioned by repeated viewing of television commercials because one doesn't really pay a great deal of attention to them.

The values perpetuated by love comics are unchanging and the male/female roles are clearly defined. The ideal teen-age girl is physically attractive, fun to be with, and fully dedicated to being a good wife to the man she loves. Marriage is her dream and making that dream a reality is her constant goal. The man is strong and protective.

In love comics men are almost always interested in (a) dating, (b) kissing and (c) subsequently marrying attractive girls. Because of this, girls in the stories enjoy being whistled at and they strive to be attractive to boys. The nicest thing a boy such as Jerry in "I Don't Love You Anymore"* (15) can say to a girl on a movie date is that she is "much prettier than the girl on the screen." It is the girl's duty to be beautiful. As Greg in "Tall Dark and Dangerous" (2) tells Emily, "Concentrate on being beautiful, baby . . . and leave the thinking to me!" The cover of *Falling in Love* (6) equates love with beauty in a headline that reads, "You're young, you're beautiful and you're *Falling in Love*." Cara in "Nothing for Him" (13) sums up the importance of being beautiful when she says, "I know I'm attractive . . . other men want to date me."

Physical attraction is the force that most frequently brings two lovers together. Love comics support the myth of love at first sight and the "stranger" a girl is attracted to "across a crowded room" often turns out to be Mr. Right. In "Love Me Again" (7) Lisa recalls, "I fell in love with Phil from the first moment our eyes met at Elaine's party." She stares at him because he is so handsome and he responds by asking her to dance. In "I Don't Love Him Anymore" (2) Beth notices Ron staring at her "shamelessly" at a party; they are introduced and she says, "It's terribly crowded in here, isn't it, Ron? and warm?" They then adjourn to the privacy of the balcony and are kissing within two frames.

Although a great deal of importance is attached to a girl's being beautiful, the stories often favor the less attractive underdog—the kind of girl who has always had her boyfriends stolen from her by her more attractive and wealthier girlfriend. Incidentally, the "plain" girl often looks just like the "beautiful" one, but the "plain" girl insists that she is not pretty. But the comics root for the underdog and the love of the right man has the power to transform the "plain" girl into a beautiful woman because *he* sees her as beautiful. The man's love makes her beautiful. In "No Chance at Love" (17) Bill says to Pam, "And now I'm going to ask the prettiest girl in the room to dance with me. . . ." Pam assumes that he means he is going to ask her rival in love, Sheila, but he ends up asking her. In the last frame Pam thinks, ". . . as Bill's arms closed around me, I felt prettier than I ever had before—I even felt prettier than Sheila—because at last I had someone who had eyes for me alone!"

In "Game of Love" (25) Gail recalls, "I wasn't the prettiest girl in school . . . but I was very lucky because . . ." after he has won the football game, her boyfriend, Tommy, rejects all the beautiful groupies who are flocking around him and says to

---

*Citations in the text are to the numbered Bibliography.

her, "Hi, prettiest girl in school!" Gail answers, "What's the matter? Lose your glasses?" A man's love makes even a "plain" girl look and feel beautiful.

Clothes play a most important part in a girl's life in love comics and the right clothes can transform a homely career girl into a tantalizing female. For example, in "Let Me Alone" (21) a career-hungry Pamela competes with her co-worker until her boss tells her at a party that although she may be more qualified than her male co-worker, she won't get promoted because she doesn't get along with the people at the office. By this he means that her career-woman's clothes are too drab. He says to her, "You're probably a pretty girl when you're not wearing those business suits or that sack you've got on!" Pamela takes the hint and goes to the powder room and strips down to the sexy hot pants outfit she couldn't resist wearing under her "femme lib" attire. When she returns to the party, her boss exclaims, "Pamela! Like WOW!" and her co-worker is also fascinated by her transformation. In the last frame the two of them are kissing as Pamela thinks, "The moment our lips met . . . I knew! My preoccupation with women's lib had ended . . . I was surrendering!" When Pamela dons a sexy wardrobe, the frustrations which caused her to compete with her male co-worker disappear as her "secret" dream of kissing him becomes a reality. The implication of the story is that only an unattractive girl who cannot capture a man of her own will be content to be a drably dressed career girl and women's liberation advocate.

The right clothes can also be used to great advantage by a clever girl. For example, a revealing bathing suit or nightie, the likes of which Frederick of Hollywood might design, often provide a girl with a tested means of patching up a lover's quarrel. In "Where Is He Tonight" (1) a wife who wants her husband to stay home with her on weekends uses both sexy nighties and skimpy bathing suits to get him "home to stay."

Another characteristic of the ideal girl is that she be fun to be with. Although the comics insist that love is a serious matter, that love is mysteriously ruled by Fate, and that love can cause a girl tremendous anxiety and suffering (symbolized by the girl's pearl-shaped tears that appear on the cover of many comics), a girl needs to be fun to be around if she expects to keep her man. Fun on a date depends on such things as dancing, beach parties, dining at fashionable restaurants, going to the kind of nightclubs that abounded in the films of the thirties, ski trips, yachting, music and driving in fast cars. If the girl does not have fun or provide her escort with a good time, she is in trouble. In "One More Chance" (1) Bonnie worries that her husband will reject her because she's become a party-pooper. In fact, he *tells* her that if she doesn't want to go out to dinner with him, he'll find someone who will. She goes with him, but halfway through the evening complains that she want to go home. She admits, "I don't blame you for being annoyed, Guy! I'm not much fun lately!" As it turns out, however, Bonnie is pregnant, and this makes her party-pooping behavior acceptable.

The stories emphasize that love is an overwhelming passion, but the passion never becomes overtly sexual. Sexual innuendos in the form of underwater kisses and passionate embraces in the moonlight are plentiful, but the ideal unmarried teen-age girl never goes beyond a kiss. A girl may do some comparison shopping and compare one boy's kisses with another's, but she remains pure and sexually inexperienced, the kind of girl Marshall McLuhan observes in Coca-Cola ads: "Her flesh is firm and full, but she is as pure as a soap bubble. She is clean *and* fun loving."[2]

Because the kiss embodies or symbolizes all aspects of love in love comics, it assumes great significance. Being too free with one's kisses is a fatal mistake, but kissing the right person makes "the sky light up and turn topsy-turvy" in "A Kiss for Cinderella" (6). Anne in "The Man of My Dreams" (3) sums up the importance of the kiss when she says to herself while kissing the local hero, "I've been waiting all my life for this moment . . . it's as though I was just born again. . . ." A man's kisses and a man's love revitalize a girl's entire being.

The ideal teen-age girl seeking to be an ideal mate must be willing to make important concessions to the way of life of the man she loves. Giving up a career as a fashion model or secretary is not really a major sacrifice because in the love comic formula one only works *until* one meets the right man. A job is secondary and most often only a means to meet one's "Madison Avenue Prince Charming." In "The Most Wonderful Boy in The World" (9) Joan says to herself upon her arrival in New York City, "I came to New York primarily to find a job . . . but deep, deep down, I had another reason. . . ." This reason is that she heard that all the "greatest guys in the world" live in Greenwich Village. In "Love Isn't a Game" (21) Claudia's father gets her a job in Rome, but Claudia herself says, "I'm not really interested in a *career.*" What she is interested in is the man she met in Rome when she was there on a vacation.

In love comics a job is something one falls back on when there's no man around. Lisa in "Love Me Again" (7) goes back to nursing when she doesn't hear from her boyfriend in the army. She tells herself, "I . . . I've got to do something—to—to— stop thinking about Phil—or I'll just go out of my mind! I guess . . . I could always go back to nursing!" In "Diary of Love" (7) Anne wants to keep working as a secretary "to keep busy" so that she won't think about the boy she loves while he is at sea during a terrible storm.

In most all of the career-versus-love stories I've read, it is rarely considered a possibility that a woman could have both. It is most always an either-or situation. And since career women are presented as sexless machines who wear glasses, love and marriage win out easily. For example, in "Love or Glory" (12) Lisa rejects a brilliant career as a city nurse to return home to marry a young country doctor. She says, "I had more than a career waiting for me in my own home town . . . I had Ben. . . ." It is not considered a possibility that she could work as his nurse or as a nurse in the local hospital. Just as television ads such as the one for Folger's coffee automatically assume that it is the woman's job to make good coffee for her husband, love comics assume that a woman's career is in the home caring for the man she loves.

The woman's "career" at home entails helping her husband get ahead by cooking good dinners for his boss. In "Third Finger, Left Hand" (22) a wife neglects her home duties, and had her mother not cleaned up the house and prepared dinner on the day the husband's boss came over unexpectedly, her husband might have lost out on a big promotion. The wife realizes this as she says, "And if it weren't for mother, everything would've gone wrong! I almost ruined your career!" Her duties in the home are not insignificant and by working together their situation improves and she is rewarded with material luxuries and happy children.

Barbara in "Nobody Kisses a Goddess" (20) proves that she has the makings of a good wife in the following way: Brian, her fiancé, is up for a promotion and she arranges to arrive at the director's dinner early. She flirts with all the "important" men and when Brian arrives, she says to him, "Hush, darling . . . and kiss me! They're all watching!" While they kiss, the executives comment, "By Jove, she kissed him! He must have more to him than we thought!" Brian thus gets the promotion and Barbara establishes herself as a valuable business asset.

Giving up a career in the outside world to dedicate oneself to a career at home may be easy, but other necessary sacrifices can be more difficult. For example, Karen in "For Better or Worse" (25) laments that her husband, Brad, decided to practice medicine in a small town in Maine where he feels he's really needed instead of working in New York City. In the first frame of the story Brad says to her, "Karen, you won't mind being a country doctor's wife, will you?" She doesn't answer him, but thinks to herself, "I *will* mind, Brad! But I don't have much choice!" Once in Maine, Karen objects to the coldness and distance of their neighbors. She tells Brad, "I'm miserable! I've got nothing here! Nothing!" He answers, "You've got me, Karen. You've got a man who loves you very much—" He insists, "my place is here!" and Karen decides to leave him. Shortly before her scheduled departure, however, there is a terrible storm and their house is destroyed by a tornado. As soon as the storm is over all the "unfriendly" neighbors come over to help rebuild the house because the "Doc's a good man." Karen is filled with shame and is forced to acknowledge that her husband had been right all along. Like so many girls in love comics, Karen learns that the man's way is best and that small town values are far superior to mistaken notions about city life.

Often a girl will want her man to give up a dangerous vocation or avocation. In three representative stories, "If You Love Me" (3), "To the Winner" (14) and "Diary of Love" (7) the girls come to realize that they cannot ask their men to give up their life styles. The three girls learn to sacrifice their concerns in favor of the men's wishes. Sally in "If You Love Me" is afraid that she will lose Vic if she forces him to give up his career as a pilot in Viet Nam and concludes, "Vic . . . I want you to be a pilot as long as you want to be one!" Nancy in "To the Winner" wants Jock to stop driving racing cars, but concedes in the end that if he doesn't race, he won't be the same man she loves. In "Diary of Love" Anne remembers all the grief her mother suffered when her father was away at sea, and she asks her boyfriend, Richard, to give up the sea for her. He answers, "You're asking me to give up my life—you're asking me to stop breathing . . . Yes! If I did give it up . . . and we got married . . . you'd find you'd married a DEAD man!" Anne leaves him, but when she finds her mother's diary, she learns that her mother grew to accept—even perhaps to relish—the danger her husband faced and so Anne decides that she too will accept the dangers of the sea because she's learned from her mother's diary that the most important thing in life is love. As ideals, Sally, Nancy and Anne reject their lesser concerns and learn to accept their men's life styles with strength and dignity. The comics thus insist that not *all* women hamper a man's freedom; only the ones who would force a man to give up his life style are guilty. A man raised believing that a man cannot be free unless he rides off into the sunset alone or with a few good buddies need not fear that all women will try to tie him down. Love comic heroines are trained to sacrifice *their* life styles and to accept his.

Because a man's love gives a woman her identity in love comics, it becomes the woman's responsibility to make sure that no "other woman" steals her man, lest she be left alone and selfless. After all, as Laura Penn, "Your Romance Reporter," advises in *Young Romance* (8), "Dating is a very competitive thing." A man becomes a woman's property and any one who interferes is seen as an immediate threat. For example, Donna in "Married in Haste" (14) arrives unexpectedly at her husband's office and finds that his secretary, Abigail Schmidt, is a ravishing beauty. Donna is very upset as she had not considered Abigail a threat because she had presumed that no girl with such a name could be pretty. When Donna gets home, she is so upset that she kicks furniture around and tells herself, "Nobody's going to steal my husband away from me!" Since love comics support the myth that secretaries marry rich bosses, Donna's concern is justified. But Donna has a plan. She organizes a "little blast," i.e., a party, and introduces Abigail to an eligible bachelor. The two of them fall in love immediately. It looks as if they'll be getting married and since married women don't work, Donna's husband comments, "Darn it, honey . . . you may have cost me a secretary!" At this point Donna says to herself, "And saved *me* a husband." The story presents Donna as a "smart chick" and the fact that she guarded her property by getting rid of Abigail upholds this contention.

In "Heartbreak Swinger" (2) girls who are tired of being ignored by men who seem only to have eyes for the "swinger" introduce their rival to a tough man who tames her and subsequently marries her. Once the swinger is out of circulation and therefore no longer a threat, the girls find that they actually *like* her.

One of the things that is most striking about love comics is that all "other" women are presented as threats. Although the comics stress the importance of the family unit, even mothers and sisters cannot be trusted. In "My Mother . . . My Rival" (4) Tina's own mother dances with Tina's boyfriends and in "You've Got to Hang Loose" (24) Jan laments, "My romance with Eric was perfection. Then something came between us—my sister!" Charlotte, Jan's sister, pretends to disapprove of Eric, but in actuality she is out to capture him for herself.

Most often it is one's best girlfriend that one has to fear the most. In "Hate Letters to Wilma" (17) Gail plants seeds of doubt in Wilma's mind about her boyfriend, Norman, so that she can steal him away from her. Through Wilma's period of agony, Gail appears sympathetic to Wilma's dilemma, while in actuality she is the one writing the hateful letters. It is only when Wilma plays at being Nancy Drew that she puts two and two together and finds out that her best friend was out to steal her man.

In "Doctor Heal My Heart" (24) Freda must also play at being an amateur detective in order to prove that her best friend, Vi, is trying to ruin her romance with Rex by making incriminating phone calls. The lessons of both of these stories is that a girl has to be clever and crafty in order to keep her man because when it comes to boyfriends *no* woman can be trusted.

Love comics support the idea that true love exists only when the lovers are isolated from all outside disturbances. Love *means* two people *alone:* the man is the woman's entire world and the man only has eyes for the woman he loves. True love exists in a vacuum, and thus the male friends of the boyfriend or husband are also seen as threats, although to a lesser extent than the woman's envious girlfriends. In "Young in Heart" (14) the younger brother of the groom threatens to ruin Muriel and Doug's marriage until he is sent packing. In "Marry a Swinger" (12) the husband's best friend flirts with Helga until her husband decides that he doesn't like the big-city sophistication that allows men to flirt with other men's wives. He thus rejects city values in favor of Helga's "small town" values.

The ideal man in love comics is often a successful businessman or an athlete or sports car driver. Such a hero is often physically attractive and his good looks and powerful physique frequently cause him to be described as a piece of meat. For example, Vic in "If You Love Me" (3) is deemed a "big hunk of man" and the groovy men who date rich women in "Glamour Girl" (15) are referred to as "handsome hunks of masculinity."

The heroic male proves his love as well as his manhood with his fists. In "Tall Dark and Dangerous" (2) Greg beats up three thugs who insult his new girl friend, Emily. After taking care of the hoods, he says, "After Viet Nam, punks like those don't bother me a bit." Emily is properly impressed. For her, "Greg was quite a guy ... he made other men seem like pantywaists."

The assumption in the comics is that girls like to be fought over and that one tested way a girl can be sure of a boy's love is for him to fight his rivals. Gary realizes this after he beats up Don in "Another Brand of Kisses" (10). Claire, the girl he fought over, says to him after the fight, "Don isn't my boyfriend, Gary ... You are ... if you still want me!" Gary answers, "Want you? What do you think the fight was about?" To the victor go the spoils and Claire's lagging interest in Gary is rekindled because Gary fought for her. Not only did he fight for her, but, what's more important, he won and in so doing proved himself to be the superior man.

Girls, such as Ellie in "Splitsville" (13), encourage boyfriends to fight for them by cheering shouts of encouragement from the sidelines. "Hit him, Greg!" Ellie shouts as Greg beats up a hood who had picked her up after she and Greg had had a lovers' spat. The husband in "Marry a Swinger" (12), whose wife worries that he is not jealous enough of the men who flirt with her, proves his love by protecting her from some thugs. As he hits them, he says, "You're pretty tough with women." Here, as in the romanticized Old West, physical action, i.e., beating up thugs, speaks louder than words to show how a man feels deep down. Poets may write about love, but real men fight for it.

Girls in love comics admire sports heroes. For example, in "The Man of My Dreams" (12) Anne writes, "I met Gordon Ames in my junior year, dear diary ... it was just after he'd won the first big game of the football season almost single-handed." That Gordon carries the team to victory "almost single-handed" sets him apart from the average man.

In "My Mother ... My Rival" (4) Tina, who is anxious to escape from her mother's house because her mother tries to steal her boyfriend to keep herself feeling young, finds that "Allan's car was like our castle!" in that it enables her to escape her mother's sphere of influence. Wheels mean freedom in love comics and the boy with the biggest and fastest car is at a definite advantage when it comes to capturing the affection of the most attractive girl. In "It's A Small World" (13) "Tim Hayden's cycle is Cupid's arrow." In "Treacherous Heart" (5) Gene, a new boy in town, captures the interest of Donna because of his scooter. Their first conversation goes like this: Donna says, "You're new, aren't you? Did I hear you say you've got a bike?" Gene answers, "Yep . . . the Honda is all mine. Want a ride?" As they ride together she thinks, "This is heavenly!" and she asks him to go faster and faster—"I love it!!!" she tells him.

Along with a girl's realization that everything "decent" is to be found in one's home town comes the revelation that the glamorous business executive or sports figure can be far inferior to the dependable, steady—if duller—home town boy. The comics teach their readers to be content with a "dull" home grown boy. The flashy glamorous males the comics *appear* to be idolizing often fail to protect or aid a girl when she is in most need of help. For example, in "Moment of Truth" (23) Nicolette goes sailing with Peter, a stranger she labels her "dream prince," but when a storm hits them at sea and their boat overturns. Peter proves himself to be a coward. He is helpless and whines like a baby. Fortunately, Johnny, Nicolette's boyfriend since childhood, comes to their rescue and Nicolette is thus cured of her temporary fascination with Peter. In the last frame Nicolette writes, "And that night, I saw at last the face of my 'dream Prince'—a face I should have recognized from the very first moment—Johnny's face!"

Penny in "Bad Penny" (23) returns home "sadder and wiser" after two years of living in the "hip" world. It takes her some time to prove to her abandoned boyfriend that she can be depended upon not to run out on him again, but in the end he says to her, "That new position is still waiting for me in the city. But I'd handle it a lot better if I had a wife waiting for me each night when I get home. Will you take the job?" She accepts and says to herself, "I have his love. What more could a woman ask for?"

But even the "dull" boys in love comics have cars and are willing to win fights for the girls they love. For example, Wayne in "He'll Always Need Me" (20) gets tired of watching the girl he's always loved, Eve, make a fool of herself over Billy, who Eve thinks is the "best player on the team," because Wayne realizes that deep down Billy is just a mama's boy. So Wayne beats up Billy and the reward is Eve. The quiet, steady boyfriend wins the big prize. This also happens in "Not For Him Alone" (11) in which a meek Arthur beats up a bearded Don Juan and becomes an "ex-97-pound weakling."

Any man in uniform—and particularly a returning Viet Nam veteran—assumes heroic dimensions in love comics. In "I'm a Woman Now" (5) all the tricks Doris uses to steal a "new girl's" boyfriend are justified because the object of Doris's love is "a real lieutenant in the army, just back from Viet Nam, and handsome in a real rugged sorta way." That he was wounded in action adds greatly to his appeal. Having a man in uniform makes a woman feel proud. Gail in "Game of Love" (25) writes, "I was so proud when Tommy became an Air Corps cadet."

Not only does a girl gain her sense of identity as a woman from the man, but the right man enables her to raise her social standing. He is not lowered to her position; instead, she is raised to his. In the representative "A Kiss for Cinderella" (6) Prince Charming goes to a society ball and falls in love with Cinderella, a poor shop girl who is at the ball only because one of the rich debutantes who had ordered a dress for the ball decides to fly to Rio de Janeiro and gives her the dress. Her low social standing, however, in no way prevents Prince Charming from wanting to marry her. Likewise, the ideal man teaches a girl never to be ashamed of her family. Cecilia in "I Will Be Worthy" (16) keeps her parents hidden away because she is ashamed of them until she finds out that her husband has secretly gone off for the weekend to drink beer and watch the ball game on TV with her father (while her mother is in the kitchen cooking). Her husband feels that her parents are "real" whereas he finds his high-class family and business associates phony.

The ideal man's financial situation is interesting to analyze. In love comics money does not complement love. Rich people are characterized as selfish snobs who prefer idle city sophistication to small town ideals; rich women are presented as being too spoiled to be able to make any sacrifices for a man. In "Glamour Girl" (15) a fashion model comes to realize that her poor boyfriend is worth more than all her dreams of glory as an international model. In the last frame she thinks, "I know it's not wrong to want to be rich—but when you have to give up love for money—you can never enjoy anything. . . ."

In spite of the fact that love and money do not complement one another in love comic theory, a successful union between a man and a woman is usually blessed with material rewards, as in the previously mentioned "Third Finger, Left Hand" (22). In order to have it both ways, a rich boy, who nevertheless has his feet firmly planted on the ground and possesses all of the down home values, will masquerade as poor in order to capture the affection of the girl he loves. For example, in "Never Trust a Sailor" (18) Arnie overhears Nina complaining about the rich boat owners who think they can take advantage of her because they're wealthy and so he pretends to be a deck hand in order to gain her confidence and her love.

In "One More Time" (19) one of the main reasons that Cecile and Mel's early marriage fails is that because he hasn't been to college he isn't able to earn enough money for them to live comfortably. Therefore they separate, but later when he returns *with* his college degree, they get together again and it looks like their second attempt at marriage will be more successful *because* he will be more successful.

Love comics support the status quo. Current topics such as women's liberation, campus revolt, drug abuse, and the Woodstock generation may be introduced into the love stories, but the basic love story formula remains essentially the same. Certainly, girl's clothing styles change and men wear their hair somewhat longer in more recent issues, but the format of the stories does not change; instead the "Now" topics are incorporated into the old formula. In the advice to the lovelorn columns women's liberation is occasionally *mildly* encouraged. For example, Laura Penn gives a girl interested in women's liberation the following advice: "If he [her boyfriend] likes you and respects your ideas, you'll be able to turn his head around and liberate him—but take it gently!" (8). Women's liberation *may* be all right, but it shouldn't cause you to lose your boyfriend. The stories themselves, however, which have as their basis that a man's love is all that is needed to make a woman feel fulfilled, are almost uniformly against the movement. The implications behind the "femme lib" stories is that only women who cannot capture their own men will join the movement. . . .

A fairly recent development associated with the love comic phenomenon is the "classic" love comic. The "classics" are old love stories that are being reprinted to coincide with the current nostalgia trend. The March, 1972, issue of *Young Romance* (8) introduces its "classic" love story, "Footsteps to Heartbreak," in the following way:

> "Thanks for your letters asking for more classic love stories! I guess it's because love hasn't really changed all that much in 20 years. A kiss is still a kiss, and if he makes you cry, it hurts just as much as it did years ago. So here's 'Footsteps to Heartbreak'— exactly as your mother read it and cried when SHE was your age."

In "Heart of Shame" (24), a twenty-year-old "classic," Nancy writes, "I'd left Danville to come to the city hoping for a new exciting life." She falls in love with her boss, and is shocked to find out that he's married. All of her dreams of happiness and success in the city vanish and she returns to her home town where Hal, "a boy I'd known for years," helps her to combat small town gossip about her relationship with a married man.

Writing about the moral creed of the thirties, Louise Tanner observes that the feeling was that " 'The true values are to be found in the small town.' "[3] The same holds true for "classic" love comics as well as for today's love comics. The small town gossips may make it difficult for Nancy to hold her head high, but the values the gossips stringently uphold are the values all love comic heroines must learn to accept if they are going to be successful wives and mothers.

NOTES

1. *New Times,* Vol. 1, No. 1, April 8, 1970, p. 13.
2. Marshall McLuhan, *The Mechanical Bride* (Boston, 1970), p. 118.
3. Louise Tanner, *All the Things We Were* (New York: 1968), p. 81.

BIBLIOGRAPHY

1. *Just Married,* Charlton, 4:84 (April, 1972).
2. *For Lovers Only,* Charlton, 5:64 (April, 1972).
3. *Just Married,* Charlton, 1:65 (June, 1969).
4. *Young Romance,* National, No. 157 (December 1968–January 1969).
5. *Teen-Age Love,* Charlton, 2:60 (September, 1968).
6. *Falling in Love,* National, No. 107 (May, 1969).
7. *Young Romance,* National, 22:179 (February, 1972).
8. *Young Romance,* National, 22:180 (March, 1972).
9. *Falling in Love,* National, 18:130 (March, 1972).

10. *Love and Romance,* Charlton, 2:3 (January, 1972).
11. *Just Married,* Charlton, 1:57 (March, 1968).
12. *Love and Romance,* Charlton, 2:5 (April, 1972).
13. *Teen Confessions,* Charlton, 3:71 (December, 1971).
14. *Just Married,* Charlton, 4:83 (March, 1972).
15. *Falling in Love,* National, 18:128 (January, 1972).
16. *I Love You,* Charlton, 4:96 (March, 1972).
17. *Falling in Love,* National, No. 118 (October, 1970).
18. *Sweethearts,* Charlton, 5:123 (March, 1972).
19. *Love Diary,* Charlton, 4:77 (March, 1972).
20. *Love Diary,* Charlton, 1:64 (January, 1970).
21. *Love and Romance,* Charlton, 2:4 (February, 1972).
22. *Our Love Story,* Marvel, 1:13 (October, 1971).
23. *Young Love,* National, 16:95 (May, 1972).
24. *Young Romance,* National, 22:182 (May, 1972).
25. *Girls' Love,* National, 22:169 (May, 1972).

Chapter Fifty-seven

Endless Love Will Keep Us Together

The Myth of Romantic Love and Contemporary Popular Movie Love Themes (1992)

Crystal Kile

Kile studies the relations of love songs to the movies, two sources of popular romantic myths that form the basis of the powerful culture of romance in America. Films and popular music provide two paradigms of romantic scripts for women, teaching them to be "literate in love," stoking expectations, and providing ideals to which they might aspire.

> People would not fall in love if they had not heard love talked about.
>
> —La Rochefoucauld

> Don't threaten me with love, babe.
>
> —Bessie Smith

"You are nobody until somebody loves you," "Love makes the world go 'round." Don't you want to be in "Puppy Love," "Endless Love," "Love,-exciting-and-new," "Love,-soft-as-an-easy-chair" or "Love-the-one-you're-with"? "Don't you want somebody to love" even though, as the singers tell us, "It hurts to be in love" and "Love Stinks!"? The pervasiveness and the popularity of the theme of romantic love in Western cultural artifacts suggest that the answer is an enthusiastic and emphatic "Yes!!!!" But why?

Little girls' socialization into love begins in the nursery with Barbie brides and Disneyized versions of such tales as "Cinderella." Passing through the rigorous amorous extracurriculars of junior high and high school, expectations colored not

Crystal Kile, "Endless Love Will Keep Us Together: The Myth of Romantic Love and Contemporary Popular Movie Love Themes," in *Popular Culture: An Introductory Text*, ed. Jack Nachbar (Bowling Green, OH: Bowling Green State University Popular Press, 1992), 150–66, © 1992 by Bowling Green State University Popular Press.

just by the romantic experiences of parents, siblings and friends, but also by the pervasive "love offerings" of the various forms of popular culture, the importance of love and romance in our society is perhaps the lesson that adolescents of both sexes learn best. Recent surveys of college students reveal that the "romance culture" that thrives in affiliation with institutions themselves, occupies the center of college life in the minds of the majority of students—especially women. Though important in the lives of both sexes, women, even in the 1990s, remain much more dependent than men on "success" in romantic relationships as a primary source of social identity and validation of social "worth" (Holland and Eisenhardt, especially chapters 11 & 12). While the myth of romantic love means different things to men and women, our culture, especially our popular culture, teaches all of us that love promises much too much to be abandoned lightly.

Succinctly stated, the myth of romantic love in western culture decrees that one only becomes fully "self-actualized"—achieves a full, mature identity and psychic completeness—through choosing a love partner and remaining true to that partner until forces beyond one's control intervene (Harrington and Bielby 131). The search for "true love" is the most important thing in life, for the "true love" relationship promises lifelong companionship, passion and support. Even in the face of the reality of an increased divorce rate during the post–World War II period and a high rate of turnover in "serious" pre-martial and non-marital relationships, we continue to cling to this mythologically central notion that love should be forever. Few couples, even very young ones, begin a relationship, a marriage or decide to cohabitate thinking about divorce or dissolution of the relationship. Instead, we tend to think, "This could be it." To think otherwise would be to step outside the mythologized love ideal in which separation from a lover or loss of a lover is the ultimate tragedy. One of the primary reasons that the film *Ghost* struck such a nerve with movie goers is its assertion that true romantic love is indeed eternal, not just "till death do us part."

Because it is a mode of gendered social organization shrouded in the "mystical" experience of "falling" and "being in love," as inscribed and prescribed by culture myth, what we call "romantic love" is a complex cultural phenomenon. First and foremost, "love" is an emotion. When we speak of cultural myths, we usually conceptualize "myth" as a cultural belief complex based on the *fusion* of emotional and intellectual response to a given subject or cluster of historical events, a fusion that determines our attitudes towards and response to present and future situations. The myth of romantic love, while based *in* Western tradition, is based *on* the liberation of emotion for intellect. As we are initiated into the complex of cultural beliefs about adolescent and adult love relationships, we learn that love into which one "thinks" or "plots" oneself is not "true love." You cannot make a rational decision to be in love. True romantic love is an irrational state into which one falls like a ton of bricks or which strikes one like a bolt of lightning. Love chooses you, not vice versa. Furthermore, the state of "being in love" is constructed in our culture as the ultimate emotional high, the ultimate meeting of human minds and bodies, and the ultimate state of personal fulfillment and bliss. Even in the wake of the so-called sexual revolution, our culture still regards romantic love as the only truly legitimate basis for a sexual relationship outside of or within marriage.

Romantic love and all of the cultural rituals and institutions that are structured by it (e.g., dating, proms, weddings, and, ultimately, the nuclear family) seem so commonsensical and natural to us that it seems strange even to speak of a myth of romantic love. However, upon examining it more closely, the very transparency and centrality of romantic love in our culture demands just such an interrogation and demystification. "Romantic love" is a complex socially constructed ideal, one which seamlessly reproduces itself in our culture from era to era.

The Book of Love (Abridged Version)

Prior to the advent of cheap printing and the rise in literacy rates in European cities that attended the beginning of the Industrial Revolution, romantic love was by and large confined to elite groups in society. Historians generally agree that the "birth of romantic love" occurred during the twelfth century at the southern French court of Eleanor of Aquitaine. "Courtly love," the forerunner of "romantic love," grew out of aristocratic play on the feudal power relationship. As described by Capellanus (c. 1180), in the courtly love ritual a woman, usually married and of higher birth than the knight who courted her, took on the role of "lord," while the knight took on the role of "vassal." He declared his devotion to her, curried her favor in various small ways and did her bidding (Holland and Eisenhardt 93–94).

These "courtly" relationships were sometimes adulterous, but the vast majority remained sexually unconsummated. Sanctioned by Eleanor and perhaps even promoted by her, the ideals and rituals of courtly love spread across Europe, celebrated primarily in the ballads of wandering troubadours who rambled the countryside singing of their "romantic" longing for a particular lady fair and recounting great love stories (Holland and Eisenhardt 93–94; Solomon chapter 6). Most contemporary versions of one of the most popular stories of "courtly love," that of the Lancelot, Queen Guinevere and King Arthur "triangle," usually miss the point that while Arthur and Guinevere were man and wife, only Lancelot and Guinevere were "lovers" in the exalted and idealized "courtly" sense of the word (Solomon 56).

The preponderance of evidence in the historic and literary records of the sixteenth and seventeenth centuries indicates that "romantic love" begins to come out of the aristocratic court and into the popular mainstream during the humanist glow of the Renaissance. For example, Shakespeare brought romantic love to the popular Elizabethan stage, most memorably in *Romeo and Juliet* (c. 1596). Even so, "romantic love" was not fully integrated into culture at this time. We know that in the sixteenth and seventeenth centuries, medicos, churchmen and contemporary wisdom "firmly rejected romantic passion and lust as suitable bases for marriage" (Stone 17). The aim of marriage was the maintenance or enhancement of both kin groups' social positions, and most marriages were arranged by the couples' families. It is widely speculated that Shakespeare himself married for money. Indeed, in terms of Western history, the codification of romantic love as a socially and culturally approved rationale for choice of a life-partner is a fairly recent innovation. It can be traced back only to the continental Romantic movement of the late 18th and early 19th century, and acceptance of the idea of "falling in love" and "marrying for love" was only fully accepted in much of Europe in the early twentieth century.

In early America, the New England Puritan culture of our European forbears was not on the whole as prudish or anti-sexual as popular stereotypes often suggest. Though not overly concerned with the more baroque aspects of "romantic love," Puritans regarded love and compatibility between a man and woman as a legitimate reason for marriage. Their intimate culture was based on a marriage-centered, pro-creative sexual ideal. Though Puritans accepted sex as natural and a comfort to both man and wife, they were not comfortable with any sort of eroticism that could conceivably be linked to paganism, idolatry or atheism. In love, as in all things Puritan, consideration of the heavenly kingdom came first. Ideal love in the domain of marriage "symbolically mirrored [the couple's] love of God" (Stone 16). Though a certain diluted Puritan influence on American love culture remained strong well into the twentieth century, the secularization of love in American culture at the end of the eighteenth and into the nineteenth century generally kept apace with the same European Romantic tendency.

When contemporary Americans think of the dominant middle-class culture of the Victorian Period, we usually think of it as an anti-sexual, repressive culture against which libertine Moderns rose up in revolt. A recent line of historical argument has even argued that the Victorians were the "True Puritans." Actually, though, as in Europe, in America, the nineteenth century is a key point of transition in the life of the myth of romantic love. The seemingly contradictory and oft-remarked-upon high "romanticism" of the Victorian era was at least in part influenced by the extension of the increased importance placed on individualism in western culture during the revolutionary and Romantic periods, and it remains rich imaginary fodder for our contemporary love ideal.

While love and sex remained for the most part antithetical during the Victorian era, it is during the nineteenth century that the institution of marriage became more secularized and based on fulfillment of one partner in the other. Even so, one must remember that though women then exercised greater control over the courtship process than they have in the twentieth century, under the eyes of the law and the churches, they were anything but equal partners in marriage. Long courtships involving an "ordeal of self disclosure" (Seidman 60) were designed to assure the middle class Victorian that he or she was affianced to a truly spiritually, morally and mentally kindred spirit. Only when a couple was so matched, according to the middle-class Victorian regime, could the"beneficent power" of sex be invigorating and uplifting (60). At the same time that the culture insisted on marriage as a control on the deleterious effects of eroticism, on "desensualization" of sex, it mandated that marriage be based on "true love" (60). Popular novels of the era such as those issuing from the "cavalier" school of Sir Walter Scott and the "American Charlotte Brontë" school of nineteenth-century women popular domestic and romance novelists such as Augusta Jane Evans, whose *St. Elmo* (1866) still ranks among the most popular novels ever published in the United States (Nye 28), advocated and perpetuated this "spiritual" romantic ideal. Perhaps more familiarly, one finds an excellent illustration of the Victorian love ideal in Louisa May Alcott's portrayal of the courtships and marriages of Meg and Amy March in *Little Women*.

In the early part of the twentieth century, the meaning and place of sex in relation to love, and therefore the meaning of love itself, began to undergo important changes. Slowly, over the first half of the century, romantic love ceased to be defined in strictly "spiritual" terms, and began to be defined in a way that made it "nearly inseparable from the erotic longings and pleasures of sex" (Seidman 4). This shift in the relationship between sex and love was due in no small part to the increased primacy of the individual in the modern world, the incursion of Freudian psychology into popular consciousness, and the heightened degree of independence from kin and homeplace, as well as increased social mobility that industrial capitalist culture increasingly afforded men, and, to a lesser degree, women. More so than in the Victorian period, "falling in love" represented the bonding of two individuals, and emphasized an increasingly sharp demarcation between the public and private spheres of our culture. Sexual attraction came to be regarded as the underpinnings of love, and thus the basis for lasting relationships (83). As our culture's euphemism of choice for sexual intercourse, "making love," indicates, physical pleasure came to be constructed as a key part of the overall transcendent emotional experience of being in love.

There is no question that from the late 1960s on, graphic, explicit representation and expressions of (hetero)sexuality have pervaded almost every corner of American society, but even at the height of the much-hyped sexual revolution of the sixties and seventies, the myth of romantic love remained central in our cultural discourse. We need only look to the movies to see that this is true. It can be argued that the texts from which the movies were derived are artifacts of the 1950s more than of the 1960s, but *West Side Story* (1961) and *Dr. Zhivago* (1965) were two of the most popular films of the decade. In *The Graduate* (1967), one of the great sixties anti-hero films, recent college graduate Benjamin Braddock is redeemed not through gratuitous sex with Mrs. Robinson, but by the love of Mrs. Robinson's daughter Elaine. In 1968 Franco Zefferelli's *Romeo and Juliet* portrayed the young couple's tragic love in such a way as to resonate with contemporary generational conflict.

The equally tragic *Love Story* (1971), a runaway hit based on Erich Segal's best selling novel, combined the best of the "girl-from-the-wrong-side-of-the-tracks" story and the Romeo and Juliet story into one of the great four-handkerchief movies of all times. When it aired on network television in 1972, 62% of all households watching TV in America that night were tuned in (Whetmore 176). Unlike Romeo and Juliet, Oliver's (Ryan O'Neal) and Jenny's (Ali MacGraw) love defies and over-comes the reprobation of Oliver's wealthy, patrician parents and the financial hard-ship that it incurs. They are becoming fairly well established in their life when Jenny falls ill and dies from a rare form of leukemia. Jenny's last words to Oliver: "Love means never having to say you're sorry." Since "Oliver's" voice-over narration frames the action of the film as an extended flashback ("What can you say about a twenty-five-year old girl who died?"), *Love Story* then becomes a story about the importance of living life to its fullest, about the importance of love to a full life, and about giving oneself over to love whenever and wherever it presents itself. True lovers know no regrets.

As fully exploring one's sexuality became an almost requisite rite of passage/duty for many middle-class Americans and was widely touted as an avenue for self-discovery in American popular culture through the seventies and early eighties, we continued to keep the ideal of romantic love alive. For example, such phenomena as the relationship pattern of pre-marital sexual monogamy nod toward romantic love. If anything, the popularity of traditional weddings, even among couples who have lived together prior to marriage, has increased during the past fifteen years. Even as popular culture representations of romantic love became increasingly sexualized during this period, sex was never wholly de-romanticized. Conversely, even with the much touted "return to romance" that has supposedly more recently accompanied the AIDS epidemic, romantic love has not become wholly de-sexualized. One need only look to the popularity of steamy "supercouple" romance storylines on soap operas or to the "Silhouette Desire" line of romance novels to see that this is the case. One need only turn on the radio or MTV.

Silly Love Songs

Top-40 love songs are intensely powerful and rich mythological nuggets. In them we find in microcosm our culture's ongoing discourse about romantic love. In the typical pop love song, the prescribed brevity of the form combines with the intense emotional affectiveness of music and the constructed emotional ultimacy of romantic love to create an almost orgasmic, ecstatic "perfect love moment" or a moment of "perfect romantic despair" over love. Even in the age of MTV when most popular love songs are packaged and sold to the listener in a highly visual format that often incorporates musical artists' performances within surreal and/or classical narrative frames, love themes from popular movies historically perform better than any other type of love song. One possible explanation for this is that these songs recall the cinematic "perfect moments" that they accompany within richly developed romantic narratives into which the listener has already projected him/herself in the eroticized context of the voyeuristic viewing ritual. The song thus resonates doubly in the "real world," and it resonates more richly on an associative level than do most songs accompanied by specially produced three-minute videos. The explicit co-option of well-loved films into music video, e.g., the use of narrative and visuals that explicitly recall *Rebel Without A Cause* in Paula Abdul's "Rush, Rush" video, as well as the casting of Keanu Reeves in the "James Dean" role, illustrate video artists' and directors' consciousness of the power of immediately recallable cinematic narratives.

Let us now turn to an examination of a series of movie-bound love songs and songs about love that topped the *Billboard* Hot 100 chart during the period 1981–1991. Individually, these songs have launched thousands of wedding receptions, themed thousands of proms and become "our song" for millions of couples. If you regularly listen to adult contemporary or soft-rock radio, chances are that you know all the words to them. Through analysis of these doubly resonant culturally inscribed texts, we can learn not only how the myth of romantic love is constructed and perpetuated in our culture, but about the ways in which the myth of romantic love is tied up in the social construction of our gendered social identities.

> "Say you'll never love another, stand by me all the while"
> "The Ten Commandments of Love"
> —The Moonglows, 1958

During the late summer and early fall of 1981, the theme for *Endless Love,* a Romeo and Julietish tale starring Brooke Shields and Martin Hewitt, topped the charts for nine consecutive weeks, becoming the bestselling single in the history of Motown records. Penned by Lionel Richie and performed by Richie and Diana Ross, it is an almost quintessentially perfect love song. A lovers' ode of absolute devotion to one another, "Endless Love" is on one level a textbook illustration of the fantasy ideal at the heart of the myth of romantic love. At the same time, though, the song hints at a paradox built into the heart of the myth of romantic love, namely, that no love can live up to it.

As they rise and fall, trade phrases and intertwine with and above the lush orchestration, Ross' and Richie's voices literally seem to make love at the same time that they sing of it. The emotional impact of the phrasing and intonations of the singers' delivery combined with the lyrics themselves creates a chimeric impression of this "endless love" as the ultimate merging of the spiritual and the physical. Following the gendered conventions of romantic love, Richie takes on the role of more experienced male lover and makes the overture: "My love, there's only you in my life, the only thing that's right." Ross answers, her voice lightly-spun, high and delicate: "My first love, you're every breath that I take, you're every step I make." Throughout the song they skillfully work trite phrases like "You will always be my endless love," "I'll hold you close in my arms, I can't resist your charms," "I'll be a fool for you," "No one can deny this love I have inside" and "Two hearts that beat as one, our lives have just begun" into a popular masterpiece. Though it would have been easy for this song to slip into absolute banality, the bittersweet-angsty edge of yearning in the intensity of emotion of Richie's and Ross' voices lend "Endless Love" a strangely unrequited quality. In the movie, the young lovers are forcibly separated for years by her parents after Hewitt's character accidentally burns down her family's home. They are reunited, but soon part forever of their own free wills. In the song, this "imperfection" of endless love is left unspoken, but is subtly implied.

In contrast to the abstract perfection of love celebrated and mourned in "Endless Love," the mythic aspect of romantic love celebrated in "Up Where We Belong," the love theme from *An Officer and A Gentleman* (1982) is the power of love to overcome very real adversity. Performed by Joe Cocker and Jennifer Warnes, this song lodged in the top 10 for six weeks during the late fall of 1982, spending three of those weeks at number 1, and went on to win the Academy Award for best song. There is nothing at all ephemeral or sentimental about the song's plodding verses and deliberately swelling and soaring choruses. The implication is that love is an anchor, a security bind between two people, the essence of stability.

More explicitly than in the case of "Endless Love," the lyrics of "Up Where We Belong" encapsulate the plot of the movie that it accompanies. In *An Officer and A Gentleman* a young, working-class man (Richard Gere) and woman (Debra Winger) trapped in dead-end lives try to improve their prospects for success: he by becoming a naval officer, she by latching onto him, or, initially, any naval officer, as a husband. The plot follows the ups and downs of the basic romance formula. In the triumphant climax of the film, their romance apparently over, Gere, in dress whites, in a scene similar to that he would play some eight years later with Julia Roberts at the end of *Pretty Woman,* strides into the factory in which Winger is working, takes her in his arms and carries/leads her out of the factory as "Up Where We Belong" swells in the background and they ride off into the sunset. Life is hard, Joe Cocker sings raspily, "the road is long"; but, sing Warnes and Cocker together, "love lifts us up where we belong . . . far from the world below, up where the clear winds blow." Their voices do not intertwine so much as reinforce one another. In the context of the movie, the song reinforces the ideal of love as a power that will allow the characters to escape painful pasts once and for all, and the idea that success and happiness are functions of love.

> "Woman needs man, and man must have his mate . . ."
> —"As Time Goes By," 1931

The drama of Phil Collins' "Against All Odds," the theme for the 1984 movie of the same name, recalls that of "Up Where We Belong," but stresses more strongly the theme of romantic love and the "possession" of a woman as the source of male identity. In the film, a down-on-his-luck ex-jock (Jeff Bridges) accepts the job of tracking down an ex-teammate's girlfriend (Rachel Ward) who has fled to Mexico. In the music video, which was more popular than the movie, Phil Collins is cast strangely as the repentant lover, a man absolutely howlingly shattered by the departure of his beloved. "You're the only one who really knew me at all," he sings, "Your coming back to me is against all odds, it's the chance I've got to take." This solipsistic psychodrama of male desire and female betrayal (e.g., "I wish that I could make you turn around, Turn around and see me cry") occupied the top ten for ten weeks and rode the top of the charts for three weeks in the Spring of 1984. It was displaced from the number 1 spot by Lionel Richie's "Hello," a similar emotional statement of masculine romantic and sexual desire.

It is important to emphasize the "masculinity" of many popular love songs, especially those connected to popular movies, because all things "romantic" are so often stereotyped as feminine. The predominance of patriarchally-coded masculine address in love songs, especially those from films, presses the question of who possesses the real power in the romantic relationship. The gender relationships illustrated so transparently in movie-related love songs substantiate the argument that although the romance game is a higher stakes affair for women than for men, men still wield emotional and sexual control of the relationship. This is treated unproblematically in most popular artifacts. Phil Collins and Lionel Richie actively speak, seek love, and/or attempt to regain lost love, while contemporary popular women singers like Whitney Houston are relegated to the passive role of "[Wanting] to Dance With Somebody Who Loves Me" or "Saving All My Love For You," of waiting to be activated into love, as it were.

Even though stereotypical representations of women as nymphomaniacal temptresses, obsessive lovers, love objects or "love goddesses" are very popular in the movies and in songs, videos and television shows, there remains in our culture a significant popular taboo on women as romantic instigators. In the popular romance genre, women who are somehow "active" in the pursuit of romance are more often than not portrayed in a three-way relationship in which two women, one of whom usually fails to live up to our dominant culture's ideal of "femininity," battle one another for the love of one man. The message implied in such scenarios is clear: romantic relationships with men are to be valued over all else, especially relationships with other women. Just as in romance novels, soap operas and love songs in general, which to varying degrees flourish in almost wholly female-centered popular subcultures, and as in fairy tales, in movie love songs, the model of traditional gender relations is upheld.

Many love songs sung by men provide an interesting counterpoint to much heterosexual male-directed pornography, the difference being that when romantic love, not sex, is foregrounded in a film or song, men's control of the relationship is depicted as flattering, reassuring or comforting rather than threatening. In John Hughes' teen-cult movie *The Breakfast Club* (1985), Judd Nelson portrays a stereotypical "bad-boy-with-a-heart-of-gold" who, over the course of a Saturday detention, tames one of the high school's "suburban Princesses" (Molly Ringwald) by insinuating himself into the role of her omnipotent, mind-gaming confessor. In a sexually and romantically ambivalent scene at the end of the movie, Ringwald's character gives him one of her diamond-stud earrings to wear. The future of their relationship is left very much up in the air, but the mark that he has left on her is very clear. As Simple Minds sings the hit "love theme" from the movie, "Don't You Forget About Me," a song that hit number one on the charts in early May 1985 and lurked in the Top Ten for eight weeks, the voice of the male singer resonates quite deliberately with the words, actions and motives of Nelson's character. "Don't you try to pretend, It's my feeling we'll win in the end/I won't harm you or touch your defenses: vanity, insecurity," he sings: ". . . Going to take you apart, I'll put us back together at heart." This song is an excellent example of the sort of strong, controlling patriarchal hand that our culture constructs young women to desire and accept unquestioningly. It is an example of how sex and love elide in our dominant heterosexual male culture, and in many mainstream artifacts, and of the way in which men's pursuit of women is softened by the frame of love.

This dynamic is also aptly illustrated in the 1984 "bumbling-stalker" farce, *The Woman in Red*, in which Stevie Wonder's Academy Award–winning song, "I Just Called to Say I Love You," softens the Gene Wilder character's pursuit of "the woman in red" (Kelly Le Brock). Only in such a milieu could truly dark, obsessive songs about love like "Every Breath You Take" (1983) by the Police and "The One I Love" (1987) by R.E.M. be misinterpreted as "love songs" by many listeners and as such go on to become huge hit songs and videos.

The love songs under consideration here reveal that women and men are constructed by our culture to expect very different things from romantic love, and to interpret the myth of romantic love in different ways. In the duets that we have considered thus far, love has been represented as the sublime or fortifying meeting of minds and bodies, but in both cases each voice seemed to agree unproblematically with the other on the defining importance of romantic love. Such is not the case in the two most popular movie love theme duets of the mid-late 1980s: "Almost Paradise" from *Footloose* (1984) and "(I've Had) The Time of My Life" the Academy Award winning song from the *Dirty Dancing* (1987) soundtrack. In both of these songs, it is clear that what each partner has found is that special someone, and that the lovers' implied sexual relationship is fulfilling, but closer examination reveals that the female voices are in love with much more: that she, unlike the male voice, is in love with the magic and fantasy of romantic love itself. In "Almost Paradise," the expectations and needs of the lovers as performed by Ann Wilson and Mike Reno are reconciled to the point that both can agree that they are "knocking on heaven's door" in ecstasy, but the fit is much less comfortable in "I've Had The Time of My Life." The song invites female audiences to negotiate patriarchal restraints on female heterosexual desire by imaginatively constructing themselves in an active-passive sexual-romantic, ultimately very conservative, relationship.

Contextualized by the movie and by the video, the listener-viewer knows that the song "(I've Had) The Time of My Life" refers to a hot summer romance, not an "endless love" situation. Set in the early 1960s in a Catskills resort, *Dirty Dancing* revolves around the passionate infatuation that Baby (Jennifer Grey), a young, upper-middle-class woman, develops for the resort dance instructor, an older, highly experienced man played by Patrick Swayze. Baby's sexual initiation under the skillful touch of Swayze's character is at the heart of this movie, a big summer hit with female audiences. "(I've Had) The Time of My Life" works the same fantasy-dynamic that the plot of the movie does. For female viewer-listeners, it legitimizes a somewhat "illicit" sexual liaison through not love, but by invoking the possibility of love. The voices of the lovers flirt with the notion of romance à la "Endless Love," but sing against one another in passionate challenge and reassurance. "I've been waiting so long, now I've finally found someone to stand by me," moans Bill Medley. Jennifer Warnes corroborates that, "We saw the writing on the wall as we felt this magical fantasy." Though this is a fleeting relationship, Warnes and Medley sing that "this *could* be love," and then go on to sing together that whatever the case, "they've had the time of [their] life." The song is constructed so as to imply absolute mutual consent to the brevity of the affair alluded to here, but leave the window of possibility open for the affair to work out into something more permanent. The overall effect of the song is to finesse the contradiction of love and somewhat casual sex and neatly implicate the male voice into the female-oriented mythic romantic fantasy of *Dirty Dancing*, a fantasy that remains very much within the patriarchally systemized order of gender relationships.

> "I wanna love him So Bad"
> —The Jellybeans, 1964

How, then, do movie love songs sung by women differ from ones sung by men and from "love duets"? The only really popular examples from the time period under consideration are Madonna's "Crazy For You" from the *Vision Quest* soundtrack (1985), and Terri Nunn and Berlin's "Take My Breath Away," the love theme from *Top Gun* (1986). Both films are very male-oriented and action-oriented, and not surprisingly, especially in the case of *Top Gun*, these love themes prove snug ideological fits with the plot and themes of the movies. "Crazy For You" is a straightforward male fantasy of easy female romantic devotion and sexual surrender. Here Madonna does not play on and sweetly subvert the girl-singer, girl-group tradition as she does in the 1989 song and video, "Cherish." "I never wanted anyone like this," she sings sensuously, "You can feel it in my kiss, I'm crazy for you."

"Take My Breath Away," which won the 1986 Oscar for best song, relies much more on the sheer emotional affect of Terri Nunn's undulating voice than on simple "Crazy For You"–type lyrics. To a degree greater than that of any other song discussed here so far, the success of "Take My Breath Away" was also dependent on MTV support of the song's video, a video which pulled almost all of its visuals from the text of "Top Gun." The "Take My Breath Away" video is virtually a condensation of the film's main romance subplot which centers on the relationship between Maverick (Tom Cruise), the top gun of the title, and Charlie (Kelly McGillis), a strictly-business flight performance analyst with a Ph.D. in astrophysics.

As the film opens, Maverick and Charlie are extremely ambivalent toward one another. As the plot unfurls, the audience sees her resistance worn down by his various displays of prowess and charm. Charlie becomes more "feminine," more responsive to him. "Take My Breath Away" accompanies the painstakingly choreographed and edited consummation of their relationship. In the video as in the movie, the audience sees the characters surrender to and consume one another as Nunn sings of the fatedness of the relationship and conjures with her voice the eroticism of the perpetual constant danger that haunts the life of a warrior, and element of the movie's emotional texture celebrated in the Kenny Loggins hit "Danger Zone." To love is to overcome fear. In the lyrics it is actually a second person, her lover, who "turns to [the singer] and say[s] 'Take my breath away,' " but as performed, the singer seems to make the surrender herself, to make this request of a lover. Terri Nunn's voice becomes Charlie's voice.

All of these observations take on added resonance when one considers the hyper-prevalance of phallic and sexual metaphors in *Top Gun*. The intense homosociality of the fighter pilot subculture and of the military in general is foregounded in the film in tandem with the accompanying ideal of predatory male heterosexuality. Charlie is a source of consternation within this microcosm of our dominant culture's "traditional" phallocentric ideal. She is cast not just as a love-object, but as one of the "obstacles" that Maverick must overcome on his dual quest for "Top Gun" glory and for the redemption of his father's name. Sex with Charlie, naturalized within the frame of romantic love, is a critical element in Maverick's recovery of his "manhood" following the ultimate test of his mettle, the crash-death of his best friend. Metaphorically, then, conquering fear is "conquering" the tough woman portrayed by McGillis, taking her breath away. *Top Gun* co-opts a "feminist" character and then deconstructs her using the myth of romantic love as a tool. "Take My Breath Away" takes on the resonances of the whole film and is established as part of a very one-sided, very traditional romantic relationship appropriate to the film's Reagan-era re-romanticizing of the military hero.

Post-Feminist Promises and Courtly Love Redux

Bryan Adams' "(Everything I Do) I Do It For You," the theme from *Robin Hood, Prince of Thieves* (1991) was the bestselling, most popular film-linked love song since "Endless Love," and thus is an appropriate place to begin to conclude this essay. Though it lost its Oscar bid for best song to the theme from *Beauty and the Beast*, ". . . I Do It For You" spent six weeks at number one during the summer and early fall of 1991. It was the most popular love song in America since iconoclastic singer-songwriter Sinead O'Connor topped the charts two summers before with her tortured and aching rendering of the Prince-penned song "Nothing Compares 2 U." While the final shots of the video that accompanied "Nothing Compares 2 U" made slight allusion to *The French Lieutenant's Woman* (1981), a film based on the John Fowles novel in which a woman commits suicide for the sake of her beloved, ". . . I Do It For You," like "Take My Breath Away," had the full force of visuals from a major summer movie with a major male star behind it. *Robin Hood, Prince of Thieves*, of course, had six-hundred years of lore about the vaguely "courtly" relationship of Robin and Maid Marian backing the highly romantic, non-sexual, on-screen relationship between Kevin Costner and Mary Elizabeth Mastrantonio.

As Lionel Richie did with "Endless Love," with "(Everything I Do) I Do It For You," Bryan Adams came up with an almost quintessentially perfect love song, a particularly apt power ballad that captures yet another variety of the pure essence of the myth of romantic love. More than any other song considered here, it plays explicitly on the promise of the "noble lover-saviors" archetype that is erected from early childhood as the core of the women's imaginary romantic play and later romantic fantasy life. In the video of the song, as shots of Adams and his band playing and singing in what appears to be a clearing in a medieval English forest are intercut with heavily edited bits of especially heroic scenes from the film, "Robin Hood," Kevin Costner and Bryan Adams merge into the perfect lover.

This perfect lover is not a strong, silent Lancelot type, but a lover who tells "typical" heterosexual women viewers-listeners what they have been socialized to most want to hear from men. Ironically, since Robin is portrayed here as a dispossessed noble, the "steal-from-the-rich, give-to-the-poor" subtext of the accumulated Robin Hood legend is not foregrounded in the film. Still, it may speak especially clearly to a great number of working women of various classes and feminist stripes. In a similar way, the chaste courtliness of Robin's and Marian's relationship speaks loudly in the age of AIDS. Generous, unselfish, sensuous, brave and articulate, this Robin Hood is the fulfillment of our culture's love promise. Even though women know that the promises "Robin Hood"/Bryan Adams sings are for the most part empty lines, in fantasy they remain very attractive, due in no small part to the fact that the woman addressed in the song is at least nominally in control of the situation. "I would fight for you, lie for you, walk the wire for you," he sings, "there's nothing I want more" than our love. Look into my heart and eyes, then look into your soul, he tells "Marian"/the listener-viewer, then you will see that we are meant for one another: I would give it all up, I would sacrifice my life for you, for our love: "Everything I do, I do it for you." If only Bryan Adams/Robin Hood could close the wage gap between men and women!

Like "Endless Love," like most of the songs that we have discussed here, "(Everything I Do) I Do It For You" quickly became overplayed and tiresome simply because it gives life in words and music to the reality of the yawning gap that exists between "ideal" *romantic* relationships as they work out in popular stories and songs and romantic *relationships* as they exist on a material day to day basis. At the same time, though, heroic songs of devotion, highly erotic songs of romantic surrender, haunting songs about the loss of love, and all of the other possible musical takes on love help insure the seamless cultural reproduction of the myth of romantic love in perpetua.

The songs and films discussed here represent but a mere a drop in the great popular cultural sea of love. Limiting the topic under consideration here to select, very popular movies and movie love themes excluded a number of important issues centered on the myth of romantic love in our culture, but what we find in this limited body of texts is indeed very telling. The most cursory examination of the Top Ten charts reveals that the history of popular love songs in general—not just that of movie love songs—has been and continues to be dominated by men singing about their romantic experiences, their lovers and the ideal of romantic love, and by women who subscribe to this vision. This is a key part of the larger cultural discourse that directs and orders the social existence of women and men in our culture. Even in the 1990s women must conform to the standards of "feminine" behavior, demeanor and attractiveness prescribed by traditional modes of behavior or face social censure and marginalization. While similar standards of "lovability" do exist for men, they are nowhere near as ironclad and restrictive as those demanded of women in our culture. As Paula Kamen reports in her book *Feminist Fatale,* many young women are wary of identifying themselves as "feminist" for fear of "scaring off men." Such is the power of the myth of romantic love.

In what was indeed one of the great chart-weeks ever for the myth of romantic love, the week of May 30, 1964, the top four songs in America according to the *Billboard* Hot 100 charts were The Beatles' "Love Me Do," The Dixie Cups' "Chapel of Love," Mary Wells' "My Guy" and Ray Charles' "Love Me With All Your Heart." As this general discussion of the myth of romantic love and, more particularly, of popular movie love songs of the 1980s and early 1990s has illustrated, few really fundamental changes in our cultural love mythology have taken place since that long-ago, glorious week of radio love. If it has changed at all, the myth of romantic love has evolved in an ameboid manner to encompass and naturalize the increasing rate of divorce and remarriage, and committed non-marital relationship patterns legitimized in American society during the sexual revolution of the sixties and early-seventies and through the eighties. As the descendants of Eleanor of Aquitane and the descendants of her serfs might put it: "Plus ça change, plus reste la même."

WORKS CITED

Bailey, Beth L. *From Front Porch to Back Seat: Courtship in Twentieth-Century America.* Baltimore: Johns Hopkins UP, 1988.

Harrington, C. Lee and Denise D. Bielby. "The Mythology of Modern Love." *The Journal of Popular Culture.* 24(4) Spring 1991: 129–144.

Holland, Dorothy C. and Margaret A. Eisenhardt. *Educated in Romance: Women, Achievement and College Culture.* Chicago: U of Chicago P, 1990.

Kamen, Paula. *Feminist Fatale: Voices from the "twentysomething" generation explore the future of the "Women's Movement."* New York: Donald I. Fine, Inc., 1991.

Nye, Russel. *The Unembarrassed Muse: The Popular Arts In America.* New York: Dial, 1970.

Seidman, Steven. *Romantic Longings: Love In America, 1830–1980.* New York: Routledge, 1991.

Solomon, Robert C. *Love: Emotion, Myth and Metaphor.* Buffalo: Prometheus Books, 1990.

Stone, Lawrence. "Passionate Attachments in the West: A Historical Perspective." In *Passionate Attachments: Thinking About Love,* Willard Gaylin, M.D. and Ethel Person, M.D., eds. New York: Free Press, 1988: 15–26.

Whetmore, Jay. *Mediamerica: Form, Content and Consequence of Mass Communication,* 4th Edition. Belmont, CA: Wadsworth, 1991.

Whitburn, Joel. *Billboard's Top 10 Charts: A Week by Week History of the Hot 100, 1958–1968.* Menomonee Falls, WI: Record Research, Inc., 1988.

DISCOGRAPHY

Adams, Bryan. "(Everything I Do) I Do It For You." *Robin Hood, Prince of Thieves, The Original Motion Picture Soundtrack.* PMG/Morgan Creek CS2959, 1991.

Berlin. "Take My Breath Away." *Top Gun, The Original Motion Picture Soundtrack.* CBS CS40323, 1986.

Cocker, Joe and Jennifer Warnes. "Up Where We Belong." *An Officer and A Gentleman, The Original Motion Picture Soundtrack.* Island CD422842715, 1982.

Collins, Phil. "Against All Odds." *Against All Odds, The Original Motion Picture Soundtrack.* Atlantic CS80152-2, 1984.

Madonna. "Crazy For You." *Vision Quest, The Original Motion Picture Soundtrack.* Geffen CD2-24063, 1985.

Medley, Bill and Jennifer Warnes. "(I've Had) The Time of My Life." *Dirty Dancing, The Original Motion Picture Soundtrack.* RCA CD6408, 1987.

Reno, Mike and Ann Wilson. "Almost Paradise." *Footloose, The Original Motion Picture Soundtrack.* Columbia CD39242, 1984.

Richie, Lionel and Diana Ross. "Endless Love." *Endless Love, The Original Motion Picture Soundtrack.* Mercury CD826277-4, 1981.

Simple Minds. "Don't You Forget About Me." *The Breakfast Club, The Original Motion Picture Soundtrack.* A&M CD3294, 1985.

Chapter Fifty-eight

Seduction and Betrayal: *The Crying Game* Meets *The Bodyguard* (1994); Mock Feminism: *Waiting to Exhale* (1996)

bell hooks

The literary and film critic bell hooks writes vividly of black and white culture, and is an advocate of love as an antidote to racism. Her criticism of Waiting to Exhale *is scathing in its condemnation of the false representation of black women's love lives.*

Seduction and Betrayal: The Crying Game *Meets* The Bodyguard

Hollywood's traditional message about interracial sex has been that it is tragic, that it will not work. Until Spike Lee made *Jungle Fever,* that xenophobic, racist message had been primarily brought to us courtesy of white filmmakers. That message has not changed. When Hollywood sought to do its own version of Coline Serreau's 1989 film, *Mama, There's a Man in Your Bed,* a film about interracial desire where the relationship between a working-class black woman and a privileged white man works, no big white male stars wanted to play the leading role. Though this fact was presented in the news, the reasons were not. No doubt these white men were afraid that they would lose status, invite the wrath of white female moviegoers who do not want to see "their" heroes making it with black girls, or, God forbid, risk being seen as "nigger lovers" in real life. After all, white females constitute a viewing audience that could write thousands of letters protesting love between a white man and a black woman on daytime soaps, letting the networks know that they do not want to see this on little or big screens.

Mama, There's a Man in Your Bed is unique in that it represents interracial love in a complex manner. It raises challenging questions about the difficulties of having a partner who is of a different race and class. It insists that love alone would not enable one to transcend difference if the person in power—in this case the wealthy white man—does not shift his ways of thinking, reconceptualize power, divest of bourgeois attitudes, and so on. As their love develops, the white man is called to interrogate his location, how he thinks about folks who are different, and most importantly how he treats them in everyday life. Since the black woman he loves has children, relatives, and other relationships, he must also learn to engage himself fully with her community. Having worked as a cleaner in his office, she knows his world and how it works. He must learn to understand, appreciate, and value her world. Mutual give-and-take enables their relationship to work—not the stuff of romantic fantasy.

Unlike Hollywood's traditional yet "rare" black female heroine, the black woman in *Mama, There's a Man in Your Bed,* is not an exotic sex kitten, is not a "tragic mulatto." In the French film she is stocky, dressed mostly in everyday working clothes—in no way a "femme fatale." And this fact alone may have made it impossible for any white male "star" to feel comfortable appearing as her partner. By Hollywood standards (and this includes films by black directors), a full-figured, plump, black woman can only play the role of mammy/matron; she can never be the object of desire. Ever willing to cater to the needs of the marketplace, Hollywood may yet do its own version of *Mama, There's a Man in Your Bed* but it is unlikely that it will retain the original's seriousness and complexity of perspective. No doubt it will be another *Sister Act,* where viewers are made to consider just a bit "ridiculous" any black female whose looks do not conform to traditional representations of beauty yet who is or becomes the object of white male desire. The audience must be made to think it is improbable that such a black woman would really be the chosen companion of any desirable white man.

Audiences may ultimately see an American version of *Mama, There's a Man in Your Bed,* as Hollywood has recently discovered once again (as it did during the period when films like *Imitation of Life* and *Pinkie* were big draws) that films which focus on interracial relationships can attract huge audiences and make big bucks. White supremacist attitudes and prejudicial feelings, which have traditionally shaped the desires of white moviegoers, can be exploited by clever marketing; what was once deemed unworthy can become the "hot ticket." Right now, race is the hot issue. In my recent book on race and representation, *Black Looks,* I emphasize that blackness as commodity exploits the taboo subject of race; that this is a cultural moment where white people and the rest of us are being asked by the marketplace to let our prejudices and xenophobia (fear of difference) go, and happily "eat the other."

Two fine examples of this "eating" are the Hollywood film *The Bodyguard* and the independent film *The Crying Game.* Both films highlight relationship that cross boundaries. *The Crying Game* is concerned with exploring the boundaries of race, gender, and nationality, *The Bodyguard* with boundaries of race and class. Within their particular genres, both films have been major box office success. Yet *The Crying Game* received critical acclaim while *The Bodyguard* was overwhelmingly trashed by critics. Magazines such as *Entertainment Weekly* gave grades of "A" to the first film and "D" to the latter. Though it is certainly a better film by artistic standards (superior acting, more complex plot, good screen writing) the elements of *The Crying*

Game that make it work for audiences are more similar to than different from those that make *The Bodyguard* work. The two films are both romances. They both look at "desire" deemed taboo and exploit the theme of love on the edge.

At a time when critical theory and cultural criticism calls us to interrogate politics of locations and issues of race, nationality, and gender, these films usurp this crucial challenge with the message that desire, and not the realm of politics, is the location of reconciliation and redemption. And while both films exploit racialized subject matter, the directors deny the significance of race. Until *The Bodyguard*, American audiences had never seen a Hollywood film where a major white male star chooses a black female lover, yet the publicity for the film insisted that race was not important. Interviewed in an issue of the black magazine *Ebony*, Kevin Costner protested, "I don't think race is an issue here. The film is about a relationship between two people, and it would have been a failure if it became a film about interracial relationships." Similarly, in interviews where Neil Jordan talks about *The Crying Game* he does not racially identify the black female character. She is always "the woman." For example, in an interview with Lawrence Chua in *Bomb* magazine, Jordan says, "Fergus thinks the woman is one thing and he finds out she is something different." Both these assertions expose the extent to which these white males have not interrogated their location or standpoint. Progressive feminist thinkers and cultural critics have continually called attention to the fact that white supremacy allows those who exercise white privilege not to acknowledge the power of race, to behave as though race does not matter, even as they help put in place and maintain spheres of power where racial hierarchies are fixed and absolute.

In both *The Crying Game* and *The Bodyguard* it is the racial identity of the black "female" heroines that gives each movie its radical edge. Long before any viewers of *The Crying Game* know that Dil is a transvestite, they are intrigued by her exoticism, which is marked by racial difference. She/he is not just any old black woman; she embodies the "tragic mulatto" persona that has always been the slot for sexually desirable black female characters of mixed race in Hollywood films. Since most viewers do not know Dil's sexual identity before seeing the film, they are most likely drawn to the movie because of its exploration of race and nationality as the locations of difference. Kevin Costner's insistence that *The Bodyguard* is not about an interracial relationship seems ludicrously arrogant in light of the fact that masses of viewers flocked to see this film because it depicted a relationship between a black woman and a white man, characters portrayed by big stars, Costner and Whitney Houston. Black female spectators (along with many other groups) flocked to see *The Bodyguard* because we were so conscious of the way in which the politics of racism and white supremacy in Hollywood has always blocked the representation of black women as chosen partners for white men. And if this cannot happen, then black females are rarely able to play the female lead in a movie as so often that role means that one will be involved with the male lead.

The characters of Dil (Jaye Davidson) in *The Crying Game* and Rachel Marron (Whitney Houston) in *The Bodyguard* were portrayed unconventionally in that they were the love objects of white men, but they were stereotypically oversexed, sexual initiators, women of experience. Dil is a singer/'ho (the film never really resolves just what the nature of her role as a sex worker is) and Rachel Marron is also a singer/ 'ho. Traditionally, Hollywood's sexual black women are whores or prostitutes, and these two movies don't break with the tradition. Even though Dil works as a hairdresser and Marron makes her money as an entertainer, their lure is in the realm of the sexual. As white racist/sexist stereotypes in mass media representations teach us, scratch the surface of any black woman's sexuality and you find a 'ho—someone who is sexually available, apparently indiscriminate, who is incapable of commitment, someone who is likely to seduce and betray. Neither Dil nor Marron bothers to get to know the white male each falls in love with. In both cases, it is love—or should I say "lust"—at first sight. Both films suggest the feeling of taboo caused by unknowing that actual knowledge of the "other" would destroy sexual mystery, the feeling of taboo caused by unknowing, by the presence of pleasure and danger. Even though Fergus (Stephen Rea) has searched for Dil, she quickly becomes the sexual initiator, servicing him. Similarly, Marron seduces Frank Farmer (Kevin Costner), the bodyguard she has hired. Both films suggest that the sexual allure of these two black females is so intense, that these vulnerable white males lose all will to resist (even when Fergus must face the fact that Dil is not biologically female). During slavery in the United States, white men in government who supported the idea of sending black folks back to Africa gathered petitions warning of the danger of sexual relations between decent white men and licentious black females, asking specifically that the government "remove this temptation from us." They wanted the State to check their lust, lest it get out of hand. Uncontrollable lust between white men and black women is *not* taboo. It becomes taboo only to the extent that such lust leads to the development of a committed relationship.

The Bodyguard assures its audiences that no matter how magical, sexy, or thrilling the love between Rachel Marron and Frank Farmer is, it will not work. And if we dare to imagine that it can, there is always the powerful theme song to remind us that it will not. Even though the song's primary refrain declares "I will always love you," other lyrics suggest that this relationship has been doomed from the start. The parting lover speaks of "bittersweet memories, that is all I am taking with me," then declares, "We both know I am not what you need." Since no explanation is given, audiences can only presume that the unspoken denied subject of race and interracial romance makes this love impossible. Conventionally, then, *The Bodyguard* seduces audiences with the promises of a fulfilling romance between a white male and a black female only then to gaslight us by telling us that relationship is doomed. Such a message can satisfy xenophobic or racist moviegoers who want to be titillated by taboo even as they are comforted by a restoration of the status quo when the film ends. White supremacist viewers can find their own insistence on the danger of racial pollution and race-mixing confirmed by the film, and nationalist black folks who condemn interracial relationships can also be satisfied. The rest of us are left simply wondering why this love cannot be realized.

When we leave the realm of cinema, it is obvious that the dynamics of white supremacist capitalist patriarchy—which has historically represented black females as "undesirable mates" even if they are desirable sex objects, and so rendered it socially unacceptable for powerful white males to seek committed relationships with black women—continue to inform the nature of romantic partnership in our society. What would happen to the future of white supremacist patriarchy if heterosexual white males were choosing to form serious relationships with black females? Clearly, this structure would be undermined. Significantly, *The Bodyguard* reaffirms this message. Frank Farmer is portrayed as a conservative Republican patriarch, a defender of the nation. Once he leaves the black woman "she-devil" who has seduced and enthralled him, he returns to his rightful place as keeper of the nation's patriarchal legacy. In the film, we see him protecting the white male officers of state. These last scenes suggest that loving a black woman would keep him from honoring and protecting the nation.

Ironically, even though *The Crying Game* interrogates the notion of a pure nation by showing that Europe is no longer white, that European citizens are multicultural as well as multicolored, it too suggests via its characterization of Fergus that a white Irishman can sever his ties to nation and his commitment to fighting for national liberation by becoming romantically involved with a black woman. Though Neil Jordan's film, unlike *The Bodyguard,* suggests that this break with national identity can be positive, he does so by suggesting that the national identity one wants to give up is one in which freedom must still be struggle. National identity in England, his film suggests, is not fluid, not static, not so important. In this way, his film deflects the imperialist racism and colonialism of Britain and makes it appear to be the location where everyone can be free, no longer confined to categories. In this mythic universe, fulfillment of desire is presented as the ultimate expression of freedom.

In keeping with a colonizing mind set, with racial stereotypes, the bodies of black men and women become the location, the playing field, where white men work out their conflicts around freedom, their longing for transcendence. In Fergus's eyes, the black male prisoner Jody (Forest Whitaker) embodies the humanity his white comrades have lost. Though a grown man, Jody is childlike, innocent, a neoprimitive. In the interview with Chua, Jordan confirms that he wanted to represent Jody as childlike when he says that in this relationship Fergus "was like the mother." Jody alters the power relationship between himself and Fergus by emotionally seducing him. He represents emotionality and, like Dil (another primitive), is not cut off from his relation to feeling or sensuality. The film highlights the depiction of black males and females as childlike and in need of white parents/protectors. And even though Rea attempts to reverse this representation as the film ends by turning Dil into the caretaker, the one who will nurture Fergus, he reinscribes racial stereotypes through both representations.

Fergus "eats the other" when he consumes Jody's life story, including the mythic narrative that shapes the black man's worldview, and then usurps his place in the affections of Dil. As the film ends, Fergus as white male hero has not only cannibalized Jody, he appropriates Jody's narrative and uses it to declare his possession of Dil. Jordan asserts that "his obsession with the man leads him to reshape her in the image of the guy he's lost." Black bodies, then, are like clay—there to be shaped so that they become anything that the white man wants them to be. They become the embodiment of his desires. This paradigm mirrors that of colonialism. It offers a romanticized image of the white colonizer moving into black territory, occupying it, possessing it in a way that affirms his identity. Fergus never fully acknowledges Dil's race or sex. Like the real-life Costner and Rea, he can make black bodies the site of his political and cultural "radicalism" without having to respect those bodies.

Most critical reviews of *The Crying Game* did not discuss race, and those that did suggested that the power of this film lies in its willingness to insist that race and gender finally do not matter: it's what's inside that counts. Yet this message is undermined by the fact that all the people who are subordinated to white power are black. Even though this film (like *The Bodyguard*) seduces by suggesting that it can be pleasurable to cross boundaries, to accept difference, it does not disrupt conventional representations of power, of subordination and domination. Black people allow white men to remake them in the film. And Dil's transvestism appears to be less radical when she eagerly offers her womanly identity in order to satisfy Fergus without asking him for an explanation. Fergus's actions are clearly paternalistic and patriarchal. Dil gives that Billie Holiday "hush now, don't explain" kind of love that misogynist, sexist men have always longed for. She acts in complicity with Fergus's appropriation of Jody.

Those of us who are charmed by her defiant, bold manner throughout the film are amazed when she suddenly turns into the traditional "little woman," eager to do anything for her man. She is even willing to kill. Her aggression is conveniently targeted at the only "real" woman in the film, Jude, who happens to be white. When Dil assumes a maternal role with Fergus she shifts from the role of 'ho to that of mammy. But when Dil is lured to believe Fergus will be her caretaker, the roles are suddenly reversed. There is nothing radical about Dil's positionality at the film's end. As "black female" taking care of her white man, she embodies a racist/sexist stereotype. As "little woman" nurturing and waiting for her man (let's remember that girlfriend did not faithfully wait for Jody), she embodies a sexist stereotype.

Throughout much of *The Crying Game,* audiences have the opportunity to watch a film that disrupts many of our conventional notions about identity. The British soldier is black. His girlfriend turns out to be a transvestite. Fergus readily abandons his role as IRA freedom fighter (a group that is simplistically portrayed as only terrorist) to become your average working man. In the best sense, much of this film invites us to interrogate the limits of identity politics, showing us the way desire and feelings can disrupt fixed notions of who we are and what we stand for. Yet in the final scenes of the film, Fergus and Dil seem to be primarily concerned with inhabiting sexist gender roles. He reverts to the passive, silent, unemotional, "rational" white man, an identity he sought to escape in the film. And Dil, no longer bold or defiant, is black woman as sex object and nurturer. Suddenly heterosexism and the Dick-and-Jane lifestyle are evoked as ideals—so much for difference and ambiguity. Complex readings of identity are abandoned and everything is back in its place. No wonder, then, that mainstream viewers find this film so acceptable.

In a culture that systematically devalues black womanhood, that sees our presence as meaningful only to the extent that we serve others, it does not seem surprising that audiences would love a film that reinscribes us symbolically in this role. (I say symbolically because the fact that Dil is really a black man suggests that in the best of white supremacist, capitalist patriarchal, imperialist worlds the female presence is not needed.) It can be erased (no need for real black women to exist) or annihilated (let's have the black man brutally murder the white woman, not because she is a fascist terrorist but because she is biologically woman). Because I considered Jude to be first and foremost a fascist, I did not initially see her death as misogynist slaughter. Critically reconsidering the scene in which Jude is murdered, I realized that Dil's rage is directed against her because Jude is biologically female. It cannot be solely that she used the appearance of femininity to entrap Jody, for Dil uses that same means of entrapment. Ultimately, despite magical transgressive moments, there is much in this film that is conservative, even reactionary. Crudely put, it suggests that transvestites hate and want to destroy "real" women; that straight white men want black mammies so badly they invent them; that white men are even willing to vomit up their homophobia and enter a relationship with a black man to get that down-home service only a black female can give; that real homosexual men are brutes who batter; and ultimately that the world would be a better, more peaceful place if we would all forget about articulating race, gender and sexual practice and just become white heterosexual couples who do not play around with changing roles or shifting identity. These reactionary messages correspond with all the conservative messages regarding difference in *The Bodyguard*.

Significantly, the similarities between the two films go unnoticed by those critics who rave about *The Crying Game* and who either trash or ignore *The Bodyguard*. Yet somehow it seems fitting that *The Bodyguard* would be critically rejected in white supremacist capitalist patriarchy. For despite its conventional plot, the representation of blackness in general, and black femaleness in particular, are far more radical than any image in *The Crying Game*. The conventional Hollywood placement of black females in the role of servants is disrupted. In fact, Rachel Marron is wealthy, and Frank Farmer is hired to serve her. However utopian this inversion, it does challenge stereotypical assumptions about race, class, and gender hierarchies. When Frank Farmer acts to fully protect the life of Marron (how many films do we see in the United States where black female life is deemed valuable, worth protecting?) he takes her home to his white father who embraces her with patriarchal care. Again, this representation is a radical break with stereotypical racist norms. It cannot be mere coincidence that a film that makes significant breaks with racist and sexist norms via its representation of black womanhood should be trashed by critics even as another film which reinscribes racist and sexist representations should be extolled as more meaningful. Even though *The Bodyguard* conservatively suggests that interracial relationships are doomed, it remains a film that offers concrete meaningful interventions in the area of race and representation.

People who flocked to see *The Bodyguard*, some of whom saw it many times, cannot simply assume that all the individuals writing reviews were unaware of these interventions. Given the way black life and black womanhood are devalued, the critics may simply have felt that the radical moments in this film should be ignored lest they signal that Hollywood can change—that individuals can create important interventions. The mega-economic success of *The Bodyguard* called attention to the reality that producers, directors, and stars can use their power to make progressive changes in the area of representation, even if, as in the case of Costner, they do not acknowledge the value of these changes.

Despite flaws, both *The Crying Game* and *The Bodyguard* are daring works that evoke much about issues of race and gender, about difference and identity. Unfortunately, both films resolve the tensions of difference, of shifting roles and identity, by affirming the status quo. Both suggest that otherness can be the place where white folks—in both cases white men—work through their troubled identity, their longings for transcendence. In this way they perpetuate white cultural imperialism and colonialism. Though compelling in those moments when they celebrate the possibility of accepting difference, learning from and growing through shifting locations, perspectives, and identities, these films ultimately seduce and betray.

Mock Feminism: Waiting to Exhale

In the past a black film was usually seen as a film by a black filmmaker focusing on some aspect of black life. More recently the "idea" of a "black film" has been appropriated as a way to market films that are basically written and produced by white people as though they in fact represent and offer us—"authentic" blackness. It does not matter that progressive black filmmakers and critics challenge essentialist notions of black authenticity, even going so far as to rethink and interrogate the notion of black film. These groups do not have access to the levels of marketing and publicity that can repackage authentic blackness commodified and sell it as the "real" thing. This was certainly the case with the marketing and publicity for the film *Waiting to Exhale.*

When Kevin Costner produced and starred in the film *The Bodyguard* with Whitney Houston as co-star, the film focused on a black family. No one ever thought to market it as a black film. Indeed, many black people refused to see the film because they were so disgusted by this portrayal of interracial love. No one showed much curiosity about the racial identity of the screenwriters or for that matter, anybody behind the scenes of this film. It was not seen as having any importance, for black women by the white-dominated mass media. Yet *Waiting to Exhale*'s claim to blackness, and black authenticity, is almost as dubious as any such claim being made about *The Bodyguard*. However, that claim could be easily made because a black woman writer wrote the book on which the movie was based. The hiring of a fledgling black director received no critical comment. Everyone behaved as though it was just normal Hollywood practice to offer the directorship of a major big-budget Hollywood film to someone who might not know what they are doing.

The screenplay was written by a white man, but if we are to believe everything we read in newspapers and popular magazines, Terry McMillan assisted with the writing. Of course, having her name tacked onto the writing process was a great way to protect the film from the critique that its "authentic blackness" was somehow undermined by white-male interpretation. Alice Walker had no such luck when her book *The Color Purple* was made into a movie by Steven Spielberg. No one thought this was a black film. And very few viewers were surprised that what we saw on the screen had little relationship to Alice Walker's novel.

Careful publicity and marketing ensured that *Waiting to Exhale* would not be subjected to these critiques; all acts of appropriation were carefully hidden behind the labeling of this film as authentically a black woman's story. Before anyone could become upset that a black woman was not hired to direct the film, McMillan told the world in *Movieland* magazine that those experienced black women directors in Hollywood just were not capable of doing the job. She made the same critique of the black woman writer who was initially hired to write the screenplay. From all accounts (most of them given by the diva herself) it appears that Terry McMillan is the only competent black woman on the Hollywood scene and she just recently arrived.

It's difficult to know what is more disturbing: McMillan's complicity with the various acts of white supremacist capitalist patriarchal cultural appropriation that resulted in a film as lightweight and basically bad as *Waiting to Exhale,* or the public's passive celebratory consumption of this trash as giving the real scoop about black women's lives. Some bad films are at least entertaining. This was just an utterly boring show. That masses of black women could be cajoled by mass media coverage and successful seductive marketing (the primary ploy being that this is the first film ever that four black women have been the major stars of a Hollywood film) to embrace this cultural product was a primary indication that this is not a society where moviegoers are encouraged to think critically about what they see on the screen.

When a film that's basically about the trials and tribulations of four professional heterosexual black women who are willing to do anything to get and keep a man is offered as a "feminist" narrative, it's truly a testament to the power of the mainstream to co-opt progressive social movements and strip them of all political meaning through a series of contemptuous ridiculous representations. Terry McMillan's novel *Waiting to Exhale* was not a feminist book and it was not transformed into a feminist film. It did not even become a film that made use of any of the progressive politics around race and gender that was evoked however casually in the novel itself.

The film *Waiting to Exhale* took the novelistic images of professional black women concerned with issues of racial uplift and gender equality and turned them into a progression of racist, sexist stereotypes that features happy darkies who are all singing, dancing, fucking, and having a merry old time even in the midst of sad times and tragic moments. What we saw on the screen was not black women talking about love or the meaning of partnership and marriage in their lives. We saw four incredibly glamorous women obsessed with getting a man, with status, material success and petty competition with other women (especially white women). In the book one of the women, Gloria, owns a beauty parlor; she is always, always working, which is what happens when you run a small business. In the movie, girlfriend hardly ever works because she is too busy cooking tantalizing meals for the neighbor next door. In this movie food is on her mind and she forgets all about work, except for an occasional phone call to see how everything is going. Let's not forget the truly fictive utopian moment in this film that occurs when Bernie goes to court divorcing her husband and wins tons of money. This is so in the book as well. Funny though, the novel ends with her giving the money away, highlighting her generosity and her politics. McMillan writes: "She also wouldn't have to worry about selling the house now. But Bernadine wasn't taking that fucker off the market. She'd drop the price. And she'd send a nice check to the United Negro College Fund, something she'd always wanted to do. She'd help feed some of those kids in Africa she'd seen on TV at night . . . Maybe she'd send some change to the Urban League and the NAACP and she'd definitely help out some of those programs that BWOTM [Black Women on the MOVE] had been trying to get off the ground for the last hundred years. At the rate she was going, Bernadine had already given away over a million dollars." Definitely not a "material girl." It would have taken only one less scene of pleasure fucking for audiences to have witnessed Bernie writing these checks with a nice voice-over. But, alas, such an image might have ruined the racist, sexist stereotype of black women being hard, angry, and just plain greedy. No doubt the writers of the screenplay felt these "familiar" stereotypes would guarantee the movie its cross-over appeal.

Concurrently, no doubt it helps that crossover appeal to set up stereotypically racist, sexist conflicts between white women and black women (where if we are to believe the logic of the film, the white woman gets "her" black man in the end). Let's remember. In the novel the book is based on, only one black man declares his love for a white woman. The man Bernie meets, the lawyer James, is thinking of divorcing his white wife, who is dying of cancer, but he loyally stays with her until her death, even though he makes it very clear that the love has long since left their marriage. Declaring his undying love for Bernie, James moves across the country to join her, sets up a law practice, and gets involved with "a coalition to stop the liquor board from allowing so many liquor stores in the black community." Well, not in this movie! The screen character James declares undying love for his sick white wife. Check out the difference between the letter he writes in the novel. Here is an excerpt: "I know you probably thought that night was just something frivolous but like I told you before I left, it meant more to me than that. Much more. I buried my wife back in August, and for her sake, I'm glad she's not suffering anymore . . . I want to see you again, Bernadine, and not for another one-nighter, either. If there's any truth to what's known as a 'soul mate,' then you're as close to it as I've ever come . . . I'm not interested in playing games, or starting something I can't finish. I play for keeps, and I'm not some dude just out to have a good time . . . I knew I was in love with you long before we ever turned the key to that hotel room." The image of black masculinity that comes through in this letter is that of a man of integrity who is compassionate, in touch with his feelings, and able to take responsibility for his actions.

In the movie version of *Waiting to Exhale*, no black man involved with a black woman possesses these qualities. In contrast to what happens in the book, in the film, James does not have a one-nighter with Bernie, because he is depicted as utterly devoted to his white wife. Here are relevant passages from the letter he writes to Bernie that audiences hear at the movie: "What I feel for you has never undercut the love I have for my wife. How is that possible? I watch her everyday. So beautiful and brave. I just want to give her everything I've got in me. Every moment. She's hanging on, fighting to be here for me. And when she sleeps, I cry. Over how amazing she is, and how lucky I've been to have her in my life." There may not have been any white women as central characters in this film, but this letter certainly places the dying white wife at the center of things. Completely rewriting the letter that appears in the novel, which only concerns James's love and devotion to Bernie, so that the white wife (dead in the book but brought back to life on-screen) is the recipient of James's love was no doubt another ploy to reach the crossover audience: the masses of white women consumers that might not have been interested in this film if it had really been about black women.

Ultimately, only white women have committed relationships with black men in the film. Not only do these screen images reinforce stereotypes, the screenplay was written in such a way as to actively perpetuate them. Catfights between women, both real and symbolic, were clearly seen by the screenwriters as likely to be more entertaining to moviegoing audiences than the portrayal of a divorced black woman unexpectedly meeting her true love—an honest, caring, responsible, mature, tender, and loving black man who delivers the goods. Black women are portrayed as so shrewish in this film that Lionel's betrayal of Bernie appears to be no more than an act of self-defense. The film suggests that Lionel is merely trying to get away from the black bitch who barges in on him at work and physically attacks his meek and loving white wife. To think that Terry McMillan was one of the screenwriters makes it all the more disheartening. Did she forget that she had written a far more emotionally complex and progressive vision of black female-male relationships in her novel?

While we may all know some over-thirty black women who are desperate to get a man by any means necessary and plenty of young black females who fear that they may never find a man and are willing to be downright foolish in their pursuit of one, the film was so simplistic and denigrating in its characterization of black womanhood that everyone should be outraged to be told that it is "for us." Or worse yet, as a reporter wrote in *Newsweek,* "This is our million man march." Whether you supported the march or not (and I did not, for many of the same reasons I find this film appalling), let's get this straight: We are being told, and are telling ourselves that black men need a political march and black women need a movie. Mind you—not a political film but one where the black female "stars" spend most of their time chainsmoking themselves to death (let's not forget that Gloria did not have enough breath to blow out her birthday candle) and drowning their sorrows in alcohol. No doubt McMillan's knowledge of how many black people die from lung cancer and alcoholism influenced her decision to write useful, unpreachy critiques of these addictions in her novel. In the novel the characters who smoke are trying to stop and Black Women on the Move are fighting to close down liquor stores. None of these actions fulfill racist fantasies. It's no accident that just the opposite images appear on the screen. Smoking is so omnipresent in every scene that many of us were waiting to see a promotional credit for the tobacco industry.

Perhaps the most twisted and perverse aspect of this film is the way it was marketed as being about girlfriend bonding. How about that scene where Robin shares her real-life trauma with Savannah, who is busy looking the other way and simply does not respond. Meaningful girlfriend bonding is not about the codependency that is imaged in this film. At its best *Waiting to Exhale* is a film about black women helping each other to stay stuck. Do we really believe that moment when Savannah rudely disses Kenneth (even though the film has in no way constructed him as a lying cheating dog) to be a moment of profound "feminist" awakening. Suddenly audiences are encouraged to believe that she realizes the dilemmas of being involved with a married man, even one who has filed for a divorce. Why not depict a little mature communication between a black man and a black woman. No doubt that too would not have been entertaining to crossover audiences. Better to give them what they are used to, stereotypical representations of black males as always and only lying, cheating dogs (that is, when they are involved with black women) and professional black women as wild, irrational, castrating bitch goddesses.

Nothing was more depressing than hearing individual black women offering personal testimony that these shallow screen images are "realistic portrayals" of their experience. If this is the world of black gender relations as they know it, no wonder black men and women are in serious crisis. Obviously, it is difficult for many straight black women to find black male partners and/or husbands. Though it is hard to believe that black women as conventionally feminine, beautiful, glamorous, and just plain dumb as the girlfriends in this film can't get men (Bernie has an MBA, helped start the business, but is clueless about everything that concerns money; Robin is willing to have unsafe sex and celebrate an unplanned pregnancy with a partner who may be a drug addict; Gloria, who would rather cook food for her man any day than go to work; Savannah has sex at the drop of a hat, even when she does not want to get involved). In the real world these are the women who have men standing in line.

However, if they and other black women internalize the messages in *Waiting to Exhale* they will come to their senses and see that, according to the film, black men are really undesirable mates for black women. Actually, lots of younger black women, and their over-thirty counterparts, go to see *Waiting to Exhale* to have their worst fears affirmed: that black men are irresponsible and uncaring; that black women, no matter how attractive, will still be hurt and abandoned, and that ultimately they will probably be alone and unloved. Perhaps it feels less like cultural genocide to have these messages of self-loathing and disempowerment brought to them by four beautiful black female "stars."

Black women seeking to learn anything about gender relationships from this film will be more empowered if we identify with the one black female character who rarely speaks. She is the graceful, attractive, brown-skinned lawyer with naturally braided hair who is a professional who knows her job and is also able to bond emotionally with her clients. Not only does she stand for gender justice (the one glimpse of empowering feminist womanhood we see in this film), she achieves that end without ever putting men down or competing with any woman. While we never see her with a male partner, she acts with confident self-esteem and shows fulfillment in a job well done.

The monetary success of a trashy film like *Waiting to Exhale*, with its heavy sentimentality and predicable melodrama shows that Hollywood recognizes that blackness as a commodity can be exploited to bring in the bucks. Dangerously, it also shows that the same old racist/sexist stereotypes can be appropriated and served up to the public in a new and more fashionable disguise. While it serves the financial interests of Hollywood and McMillan's own bank account for her to deflect away from critiques that examine the politics underlying these representations and their behind-the-scenes modes of production by ways of witty assertions that the novel and the film are "forms of entertainment, not anthropological studies," in actuality the creators of this film are as accountable for their work as their predecessors. Significantly, contemporary critiques of racial essentialism completely disrupt the notion that anything a black artist creates is inherently radical, progressive, or more likely to reflect a break with white supremacist representations. It has become most evident that as black artists seek a "crossover" success, the representations they create usually mirror dominant stereotypes. After a barrage of publicity and marketing that encouraged black people, and black women in particular, to see *Waiting to Exhale* as fictive ethnography, McMillan is being more than a bit disingenuous when she suggests that the film should not be seen this way. In her essay, "Who's Doin' the Twist: Notes Toward a Politics of Appropriation," cultural critic Coco Fusco reminds us that we must continually critique this genre in both its pure and impure forms. "Ethnographic cinema, in light of its historical connection to colonialist adventurism, and decades of debate about the ethics of representing documentary subjects, is a genre that demands a special degree of scrutiny." Just because writers and directors are black does not exempt them from scrutiny. The black female who wrote a letter to the *New York Times* calling attention to the way this film impedes the struggle to create new images of blackness on the screen was surely right when she insisted that had everyone involved in the production of this film been white and male, its blatantly racist and sexist standpoints would not have gone unchallenged.

Chapter Fifty-nine

Hooked on a Feeling (1990)

Elayne Rapping

Rapping, a media critic, deplores the new trend of treating romantic "addiction" ("women who love too much") as a kind of disease of the psyche analogous to alcoholism or gambling. She argues that in the popularization of women's feelings as "codependency," the "personal is not political."

Pick an addiction, any addiction. You don't have one? You're hopelessly out of it. According to the current wisdom—or at least the endless list of "experts" who write self-help books, lecture and run workshops for the "addicted generation"—addiction is a nearly universal malady. A recent *Mademoiselle* article on "Addiction Chic" states that "there are an estimated 12 to 15 million people—up from 5 to 8 million in 1976— currently involved in about 500,000 organizations" for people suffering from a mind-boggling array of psychological disorders now characterized as "addictions."

From the well-known Alcoholics Anonymous to the newer groups like Debtors Anonymous, Impotence Anonymous, Sex Addicts Anonymous, Gamblers Anonymous, Depressive Anonymous and Love Addicts Anonymous (sometimes called WWLTM, after Robin Norwood's enormously successful and influential 1985 book, *Women Who Love Too Much*), these groups—their numbers and the kinds of problems they address—are multiplying wildly. Robin Norwood herself, in her recently published second book, *Letters From Women Who Love Too Much*, says "there are over one hundred varieties of Anonymous Programs that exist today." Moreover, she states that, as a psychotherapist, she has "never yet encountered a troubled individual who didn't qualify" for one of these groups.

I became intrigued by this trend because it has touched many people I know and because of its implications for feminism. While Anonymous groups and self-help books proliferate, the most popular of them are the ones about love or relationship addiction, almost all of which implicitly or openly are addressed mainly to women. Go to any B. Dalton or Barnes and Noble and you will be astonished at the number of books with titles like *How to Break Your Addiction to a Person* and *Overcoming Romantic Sexual Addictions*. Why, after all the gains women have made in work and

Elayne Rapping, "Hooked on a Feeling," *Nation*, vol. 250 (March 5, 1990): 316–19. © 1990 by the *Nation*. Reprinted by permission.

public life, are so many still in sexual relationships that hurt so badly they are rushing to buy these books and attend these groups?

One way to get a take on the phenomenon is to look at the blockbusters, the ones that stay for months on the *New York Times* best seller list. Robin Norwood and Melody Beattie are clearly the queens of codependency (the current term for people who stay with abusive, unreliable partners because they are addicted to that dynamic). Norwood's 1985 book and her new follow-up are obvious choices. Not only were and are they best sellers, they have helped create the national network of WWLTM groups. But it is Melody Beattie, whose 1987 *Codependent No More* stayed in the top five of the *Times*'s How-To List for three years and whose recent follow-up, *Beyond Codependency*, is currently number one, who has had the most astonishing success with the genre.

These four books have much in common. Before examining their disturbing implications, it's only fair to point out what is healthy and useful about them. For one thing, they lay out, in plain English and with extensive examples, what is clearly a serious problem for many women and some men. In fact, few women reading these books—whatever their current situation—will fail to feel a shock of recognition at reading Norwood's and Beattie's analyses of heterosexual relationships.

Whether or not Beattie and Norwood realize it, they often present a watered-down version of feminist theories of the dynamics of the traditional family and the pervasive media-generated images of "love," both of which influence the socialization of boys and girls and provide unhealthy models of male/female relationships. Norwood, for example, after giving the tragic case history of "Lisa," comments that "her condition wasn't helped any by the fact that both suffering for love and being addicted to a relationship are romanticized by our culture [and that] very few [media] models exist of people relating as peers in healthy, mature, honest, nonmanipulative and nonexploitative ways."

Beattie's examples more typically describe the results of traditional family conditioning, in which women are the caretakers and rescuers while men, infantilized by a vision of women as the all-powerful but ultimately rejecting mother, retain a great deal of neediness and hostility toward their partners. This elicits, in the woman brought up to care for others and not herself, a deep anxiety and sense of guilt. "Marlyss," for example, is a compulsive caretaker. She "resents how her family and their needs (emotional, physical and sexual) control her life" but, she says, "I feel guilty when I don't do what's asked of me . . . live up to my standards for a wife and mother."

Most *Nation* readers, male and female, will find this pretty obvious. In an urban world, where dinner party conversation addresses the newest theories about sexual and social life, and people talk about their shrinks the way other Americans talk about their grandchildren, this is not exactly headline news. But for many others (and for a lot of us who—no matter what we "know"—are still in relationships that fit the "codependency" model), there is something useful and healing in these books. They do some of what the consciousness-raising movement did twenty years ago: They let us share our deepest, perhaps most shameful pain with people in the same boat, and they provide examples of how others have extricated themselves from similar situations.

Unlike the early women's movement, however, these books do not show how the personal becomes political. Instead, they present addiction as a disease from which one never fully recovers, which only the most vigilant and permanent adherence to the Twelve-Step Program—"working your program," as the lingo has it—can control. I do not wish to discourage people in pain from using these groups or books. For many they are the only available respite from suffering and despair. I am concerned, however, theoretically and politically, with the limitations of what they offer, even when they "work."

The first seven of the twelve steps members of all these groups "work" reek of a kind of religion typified by televangelism. Members must first "admit they are powerless over" the addiction, whatever it is. Then they must come to accept that only "a Power greater than (them)selves" can cure them and make "a decision to turn [their] wills and lives over to the care of God." Beattie and Norwood, both recovering addicts of more than one variety, give heavy personal testimony about the crucial role of surrendering to this very traditional, patriarchal God in their recoveries. Neither is aware of, or interested in, social or political factors that may contribute to their "diseases."

In both cases, their new books—which stress recovery and new beginnings rather than getting out of a bad situation, as their first books did—are far more pushy about accepting one's powerlessness and surrendering one's life to God. Beattie, for example, tells us that she overcame her problems by "trying gratitude." She got down on her knees and "thanked God for each thing I hated about my situation. I forced it, I faked it, I pretended," she says, and "after three or four months, things started to change."

What's wrong with this picture? From a political point of view, just about everything. The passivity, the giving up of one's sense of personal agency, is the antithesis of any belief in the power of political action. Then there's the question of race and class. It's ironic, to say the least, that at a time when drug addiction—of the ordinary street-drug variety—is wreaking havoc in poor communities these books discuss addiction as a primarily middle-class problem. Eating disorders, gambling and overspending, relationship dependency—these are not, surely, the most serious addictions of people living in poverty and/or suffering the effects of systemic racism. They are, however, the obsessions that affect the people who buy self-help books.

Barbara Ehrenreich, in *Fear of Falling*, comments on the national hysteria over drugs. She says that they "symbolize the larger and thoroughly legal consumer culture, with its addictive appeal and harsh consequences for those who cannot keep up. . . ." She is right, but consumerism is not the only aspect of modern life that encourages addictive needs. There is, I think, a link between the problem of street drugs and that of the more psychological, middle-class kinds of addictions the self-help books address. Whether we are heroin addicts or credit card addicts—and the differences are to some extent class-related—we all got that way in the process of growing up and trying to survive in a world that is based on impossible goals and values. It is not just consumerism that induces addictive needs. It is also the fact that we are all, whatever our milieu, taught to be competitive, acquisitive, power-hungry and controlling. But while boys strive to control nature and the public realm, for girls, alas, relationships are still the main arena for playing out power games. Thus the epidemic "addiction" to dysfunctional, unreliable men.

In my perusal of the "love addiction" shelves, I was gratified to find at least two books that seemed to address the larger social context of addictive behavior. The first, written in 1987 by Anne Wilson Schaef, promised more than it delivered. *When Society Becomes an Addict* is an explicitly feminist analysis that is at once insightful, superficial and theoretically murky. Schaef, to her credit, understands that the institutions of society perpetuate addictive behaviors. "The Addictive System operates out of a scarcity model," she says at one point, "a model based on the assumption that there is not enough of anything to go around and that we had better get as much as we can while we can," a perfect description of the 1980s mentality. Unfortunately, her gender-based explanation for why this is so is simplistic, and her suggested solutions are really silly. Schaef sees this society as made up of three Systems: the White Male System (which she equates with the Addictive System); the Reactive Female System, which is the traditional way women have been taught to respond to the White Male System, with total compliance and a willingness to be dominated and abused; and the Emerging Female System, the sole hope for the future of the world. This system is based on theories which depict women, who are socialized to be emotionally caring and sensitive, as inherently superior leaders.

But in real life, women in power—Margaret Thatcher is the obvious example—don't necessarily have these wonderful compassionate qualities. Since Schaef believes they do and will, she proposes a pie-in-the-sky mass therapy movement as a way to change the nation's power structure. Individual men—George Bush and Donald Trump, for example—should, she suggests, deal with their neurotic need for power by voluntarily "feminizing" themselves. Apparently they will be brought to such radical self-transformation by reading Schaef's book.

The most interesting (and ultimately depressing) book I read was Stanton Peele's *Love and Addiction*. Written in 1975, it also makes connections between addictive relationships and the larger social context. Reading it was like waking up in an earlier era—it is filled with the utopian thinking about social change characteristic of the late 1960s and early 1970s. It is also extremely savvy about class and race. It is the only book I read, for example, that analyzes the differences between working-class styles of negotiating relationships and those of the middle class.

What's most impressive about this book is its political conclusions. "The real cure for addiction," says Peele, a social psychologist, "lies in a social change which re-orients our major institutions and the types of experience we have within them . . . [for] we cannot begin to cure it in the absence of a more universal access to our society's resources, and to its political power."

Now that 1960s nostalgia has depoliticized what the 1960s vision, at its politically healthiest, was about, this book was both unsettling and instructive. Returning to Norwood and Beattie, I was even more disturbed by their approach to the very real pain that drives so many people to destructive behavior patterns. They have helped to promote "addiction" as an explanation for personal and social problems and the Twelve-Step Program as the appropriate response. Their success challenges us to take their ideas seriously. Should we, as Beattie recommends, learn to "practice gratitude" for the unbearable circumstances of our lives? Or should we set about changing institutions and power relations? I think we know the answer.

Part VIII

The Experience of Love

It is appropriate to conclude this volume with a sample of current ideas from feminist writers. Jane Rule, writing about her experience as a lesbian, describes the seesawing between power and dependence in both hetero and homosexual relationships and seeks an "ordinary solution." Two authors, Mary Kay Blakely and Mary Gaitskill, published in *Ms.* magazine, have an ironic view of love, while the third, Letty Cottin Pogrebin, also writing in *Ms.*, paints a glowing view of long-enduring love in marriage. While Carolyn Heilbrun urges older women to give up romantic illusions and cultivate other relations, we can see in Barbara Ryan's essay the wish to rescue romantic love for future generations. The French psychoanalyst Luce Irigaray has recently urged much the same idea: love is too good to give away without a struggle; we should reform it so that it does not mean giving away ourselves.

Chapter Sixty

Homophobia and Romantic Love (1981)

Jane Rule

This essay by the fiction writer Jane Rule examines dependency and self-hatred in lesbian relationships, while speculating on whether the origin of lesbian love is the desire to be loved as only women can love.

"Do you mean there are lesbians *here,* in this room?" a young woman asked, horrified. For her the experience of women meeting together once a week, sometimes as many as fifty of them, to break up into small groups and discuss the problems shared by women, had been literally liberating from the sexual pressure she always felt when men were around. That she might have to be on her sexual guard again, this time with women, depressed her badly. A man, reviewing Kate Millett's *Sita* in the *New York Times,* confessed to a depression (the sincerity of which I doubt) because *even* in a lesbian relationship one woman dominated the other emotionally and, more blatantly, sexually. If lesbian sexuality poses all the same problems, while being "a problem" in itself, it is automatically worse. The onus is on the lesbian to prove to heterosexual women and men that her experience is essentially better, if it is to be accepted at all. There is a lot of attractive arrogance, particularly among younger lesbians setting out to do just that, and they have my candid applause for every point they win in the debate. Having grown up in the lesbian silence of the 30s and 40s, having had no sense of community through the 50s, having broken the silence for myself in the early 60s with a gentle and romantic novel, I have developed no skills for that debate, but Adrienne Rich's invitation to enter into a conversation about homophobia in all women, not necessarily in political/feminist terms, but to discover "what's really going on here," calls to my own endless wondering at experience.

If I had been the same age as the young woman who was threatened by the idea of lesbians in the same room, I would perhaps have been angry with her, though when I was her age and a friend of mine expressed the same kind of horror ("What would you do if you ever met a lesbian? I think I'd throw up or faint or die.") I said not a word; and later, in my brooding, neither anger nor any doubt about my silence ever crossed my mind. I felt simply horribly and inevitably alone. Twenty-five years later, I wanted to be instructive, and I think I was gentle and reassuring enough to encourage that young woman to be courteous if not open-minded about experience. I suspect my own sexuality, because of my age and my position as a university teacher, was unreal to her, as I am sure the sexuality of her male teachers even older than I was not. I could not, in good faith, have told her that no lesbian would ever find her attractive and make sexual advances. Most in my generation are timid and circumspect enough to be generally harmless, but lesbians her own age might certainly not only desire her but feel some political zeal in converting her, challenge and bully with as much ego investment as any young male for conquest. Nor, of course, could I have assured any young lesbian that one of her adventuresome heterosexual sisters might not take advantage of her feelings for the experience of it. The young call it "doing numbers" on each other.

I *am* sincerely depressed by how often lesbian relationships are accurate caricatures of heterosexual relationships, though it doesn't surprise me. It's important for Kate Millett to chart accurately what has happened to her, whether anyone is depressed by it or not. It is clear that Kate's obsession with Sita depends on Sita's indifference at this stage in the relationship. The moment Sita relents, offers Kate the sexual security and attention she craves, Kate feels claustrophobic and longs to be free. Over and over again I was reminded of Willa Cather's statement: "Human relationships are the tragic necessity of human life; that they can never be wholly satisfactory, that every ego is half the time greedily seeking them, and half the time pulling away from them."

True. For my much younger self. I was sexually so hungry, humanly so isolated, psychically so traumatized by social judgment that I required of myself a purity of motive so self-sacrificing, a vision of love so redeeming that to be a lover was an annihilation of all the healthy instincts of self-preservation I had. I am still not free of all the phobic reactions that sweet, strong, young self had to resort to in order to stay singularly alive. And though we say over and over again that the young now are not traumatized as we were, I do not really believe that the sexual revolution of the women's movement has reached most nervous systems yet. I was interrupted in the middle of this paragraph by a phone call from a younger friend who said, "My lover, ever since a political fight about tenure at her university eighteen months ago, has vomited every time we have made love, which has been no more than once every two months, and now she's moved into the guest room and says I should make love to anyone else I want." There's the homophobia in ourselves, Adrienne, whether we've known from age eight or only discovered after years of marriage and childbearing that we love each other. No wonder the homophobia in heterosexual men And women is so outrageous to us. Before we confront it in them, never mind that's where we got it, we must understand it in ourselves.

As honestly as I can recall, before I knew any psychological or moral definitions, I turned to women for love because I knew how I wanted to be loved, and I knew only women knew that. From my mother certainly. I had a cherishing father when he was around, but he was rarely around, and so he loved ideas he had made of his children. My mother loved us through our vomitings, broken bones, sulks; listened to our jokes, theories about the world, egomanias, and sorrows. (My father, this day, loves as I think a woman can, but it has taken him seventy-odd years to come to it, and he's rarely gifted.) I did not think then about being loved, though I needed to be. I thought about being loving.

I was not good at it, "half the time greedily seeking . . . half the time pulling away . . ." I could not get clear of the separation of roles, beloved or lover. Like Kate and Sita, I seesawed between senses of power and dependence. Power required too much responsibility. Dependence was too humiliating. In each is the failure to be peer, a failure that is so appalling in the heterosexual model, never mind that some men and women together figure out how to be free of it.

Do we begin by disliking ourselves as women because women are unequally loved? Do we carry that dislike into our love of other women and therefore struggle under a burden: knowing we are worse, we must, therefore, be better? Are we the unclean bitches who must transform ourselves into goddesses? To try to be too good to be true is spiritually so expensive that our failures not only nauseate but destroy numbers of us. I wrote some years ago, "I'd like to try being simply good enough."

It was my lovers who suffered nauseous guilt, not I. They returned to husbands, the church, celibate scholarship. I, instead, found I could not walk down a city street, stand before an audience, eat in front of anyone. I slept, drank, masturbated through days to avoid writing and believed my will to defy those escapes and get back to work would finally kill me. It is not simply a story of the terrible 50s. I hear it all around me now in the "liberated" 70s.

I understand why Bertha Harris wants to insist that lesbians, the only true lesbians, are monsters. She is trying to take our homophobia into her arms and transform herself/us into lovers "bad enough to be true," incestuous, self-centered, addicted, mad. Begin to love there.

I lack the romantic flair, live in too small a community (by choice), have been too long in a central relationship (twenty-three years, by choice). I need more ordinary solutions. Or hopes.

One of my heterosexual friends told me that her lover had said she wasn't a good "wife" to him. She asked him for his definition of a wife. When he had finished telling her, she said, "You're not talking about a wife; you're talking about the mother of a child under six." I am always nervous about the suggestion that, as lesbians, we should mother each other, though I understand that the image comes from our first source of love. Our mothers are also the first source of rejecting power against whom we screamed our dependent rage. As adults, if we cry out for that mother love, the dependent rage inevitably follows, and what is even more disconcerting is that, given total attention and sympathy, we are soon restless to be free, for we aren't any longer children. A young man asked me, in a seminar on Willa Cather, "Don't you think only people of the same sex can have a *real* marriage, not only of the flesh but of the imagination?" "I don't know," I answered, "but what a dreadful thought!" "One flesh" has always struck me as spurious, since each is importantly defined by a sack of skin, and children are not metaphors of union but individuals often made up of gene banks hard to recognize as in any way similar to either parent. "One imagination" is an even more terrifying invasion of the autonomous mind and spirit.

The Greeks treated romantic passion like any other illness, expressed sympathy and a hope for early recovery. Yet we put the state of being in love as the highest good. When I encounter people "entirely in love," I wonder why we couldn't just as well celebrate any delirious fever, say pneumonia, as a state infinitely to be desired. Surely we would be kinder to ourselves and our friends to hope for a cure than to encourage a lifelong ailment, fortunately very rare.

I am not being cynical. The love which Kate Millett describes in *Sita* is finally degrading to both people, patterned as it is on the relationship between a mother and a dependent child. Kate's instinct to get out, to get back to her own work, is her cure. Both the pain of her own dependence and Sita's return to men as lovers strengthen the homophobia in each of them. There can be no lasting delight and nourishment between people when one is always afraid the other will return to "Daddy" with his superior sexual power, the other sure to be suffocated by a possessive child who refuses to grow up and leave home.

I don't think there is any way to root out our homophobia until we also deal with the infantile in romantic love as the weed that it is, choking out the young and real sisterhood that begins to flower among us. We have got to be peers, respecting each other's strengths without dependent envy, sympathetic with each other's weaknesses without cherishing or encouraging them, interdependent by choice, not by terrified necessity.

I love the eroticism among women who like their own bodies, the hard discussion between those who require their own minds, the joy among strong spirits. The young woman who was terrified to be in a room with lesbians learned her fear from men who tried to dominate her. The man depressed at the old pattern of sexual politics, even between two women, was first disillusioned about relationship in heterosexual terms. Each is projecting onto lesbians the basic failure of romantic love between the sexes. If we try to be better at that, we will over and over again feel worse.

Sex is not so much an identity as a language which we have for so long been forbidden to speak that most of us learn only the crudest of its vocabulary and grammar. If we are to get past the pattern of dominance and submission, of possessive greed, we must outgrow love as fever, as "the tragic necessity of human life," and speak in tongues that set us free to be loving equals.

Chapter Sixty-one

The Tender Trap (1988)

Mary Kay Blakely

The popular feminist author Mary Kay Blakely responds here to the claim by the advice book writer Toni Grant that it is "better to be loved than to be right." Compare her rejection of the traditional women's role in love as "impossible . . . for grown women" to Barbara Bross's advice in part 1 and Vivian Gornick's comments on love and the modern world in part 6.

I was still in that fuzzy, post-party fog when I picked up the phone—it was the morning after the bacchanalian, hilarious, affectionate celebration my friends had staged for my 40th birthday. So it took me a few minutes to register the TV producer's urgency when she asked me to cancel my plans for the next Tuesday, travel to New York, and debate Dr. Toni Grant on a national talk show.

"Who is he?" I asked, suppressing a yawn.

"She," the producer said impatiently, "is a psychologist and the author of a new book: *Being a Woman—Fulfilling Your Femininity and Finding Love*. It's getting a *lot* of media attention." I was less than amazed to learn that media hearts were pumping again over another book about women and love, given the tremendous amount of ink poured over women who love too much, not enough, make foolish choices, or love men who hate them. With the possible exception of reshaping women's thighs, there is almost no cause approached more devotedly than straightening out the inept, misguided unsatisfying way women love men.

Dr. Grant's theory is that the Women's Movement did us in by cultivating ambition and assertiveness, in direct collision with male expectations of submission and deference. Women suffer loveless lives, she proposed, because they'd swallowed "the 10 big lies of liberation." The producer suggested it was my duty, presumably as a woman who'd swallowed the lies and survived, to challenge Dr. Grant on live TV. She thought I'd be a sporting opponent to the psychologist's theory that "it's better to be loved than to be right."

I promised her I'd think about it and call her back.

And I *did* think about it, despite a recent vow to swear off all such invitations.

Mary Kay Blakely, "The Tender Trap," *Ms.*, vol. 16 (June 1988): 18–19. © 1988 by Mary Kay Blakely. Reprinted by permission.

"Do you know what you do wrong on talk shows?" a friend calling with an impromptu critique had asked after my last appearance. "You really try to *talk*. Nobody's interested in real conversation at six-thirty A.M.—they're interested in entertainment." I remembered the debates I've had over the last 10 years with outrageous chauvinists and totaled women, serving as foil to any irresponsible idea about women a producer decided to telecast. My friend was right: my passion for women's rights aired as entertainment.

Weighing my plans for Tuesday against contributing my two cents to a debate on whether it's better to be loved or to be right. I declined the invitation. How did I feel, shirking my duty to millions of viewers who would be exposed to Dr. Grant's denigrating advice? Fine.

If the new theory achieves a temporary popularity, it won't be the first or last time women were sold down the river of love. In the desperate search for lasting relationships, women have been persuaded to bundle themselves in Saran Wrap, to express rage silently by flinging cotton balls at their bathroom mirrors, and never, never, to criticize their man. There undoubtedly will be some enthusiasm for Dr. Grant's formula, at least initially, from women who are weary of being right and feeling unloved.

I suspect the weariness is widespread, because last night someone made reference to a scene in the film *Broadcast News*. When the ambitious, idealistic journalist, fully aware that her male boss prefers acquiescent women, challenges him on a decision they both knew was wrong, he responds by attempting to humiliate her: "It must be a terrible burden to be right all the time," he says sarcastically, "Yes," she says, unhumbled. "It is." There was enormous identification with that remark among friends who felt similarly burdened. They would rather not be right, rather not have to push for change. They would rather have things already changed. Yet they continue to carry the burden. Why, when they know as well as Dr. Grant that men have a harder time loving women who challenge them?

It was a question that most of the guests at my 40th-birthday party had answered at some point in their lives. We were long past the first blush of adolescent love, when the desire to be loved dominated the need to be who we were. All of us, I suppose, had faked a kind of lovableness in our youth, by abandoning the complicated parts of ourselves that threatened first bliss. If we could have stopped time, remained in adolescence, we might have continued this pleasantly faked happiness. But buried ambitions or deeply felt beliefs, simmering over time, eventually create heat. It was no longer satisfying to be loved without revealing who we really were. There's an untellable loneliness in being drenched with love directed at someone else.

To suggest love means never having to say you're right is bad advice for teenagers, but it's impossible advice for grown women. It's unimaginable that the wise, thoughtful, witty women at my 40th-birthday party—who've paid heavy dues in their lifetimes to discover who they are—would be more lovable if they stifled the complex or demanding parts of themselves. In fact, it's embarrassing to be known in this group as a two-personality woman, irresolutely stuck between stages of evolution.

Perhaps that is the population Dr. Grant has in mind as her audience—women who present one self to women but another to men. I watched a dramatic example of such chameleonlike behavior at a meeting recently, when a knowledgeable, force-ful, intelligent businesswoman was reduced to a solicitous, indecisive, giggling incom-petent the moment a single man entered the room. Her colleagues blushed for her.

Could the man have felt flattered by her reduction? The ratio at my 40th-birthday party—20 women to three men—suggests there is not a huge population of grown men comfortable with grown women. There are plenty of books by male authors, nostalgic for the good old days when women stifled themselves. Change takes time, as the media are fond of reporting. But for those few men who have ventured out of the territory of adolescent love into the rich frontiers of deeper passions, there seems to be a holding attraction. I saw that, too, on the mature faces of two of the partyers last night.

This man had been in love for nearly a decade with a woman heavily burdened with "being right." Together, they'd swallowed every one of the "big lies" of liberation Dr. Grant mentions in her book—they'd argued about housework, took turns accommodating the moves of two full-blown careers, examined their parenting responsibilities in excruciating detail. Thousands of episodes concerning "who's right" had passed between them, providing each with a thorough, unabridged version of who they were.

They were standing on opposite sides of the room when he caught her eye and, without needing to interrupt her animated conversation, deftly delivered a solidly affectionate, peculiarly intimate smile. There are no shortcuts to that rare smile passing uncoyly between genders—it took this man and woman 40 years and mil-lions of words to earn it. But it gave me goose bumps as I recognized it flashing across the room, that bolt of affection electrified by respect. Here was a woman thoroughly loved precisely because she had risked being right.

Chapter Sixty-two

Modern Romance
A Lesson in Appetite Control (1989)

Mary Gaitskill

The novelist Mary Gaitskill recognizes romance as a "crock" but enjoys it anyway in this amusing personal essay.

At some point between the ages of 13 and 14 I was beset with romance fever. What I mean by that (and what I'll mean for my purposes here) is that excruciating hybrid of hormones and emotions that can, at any time, roar up out of the personal murk in a swollen rose-colored blur and wrap itself around anyone, however inappropriate. It can feel like love but it's different; while love has to do with who and what is being loved, romance can totally ignore such details. Romance has more to do with the person who is doing the feeling; it is the projection of some deeply subjective longing.

Being 14 and in a fever, my romanticism was ready to attach itself to even more than the usually absurd objects—my overweight cross-eyed math teacher, the pouty bleached-blond bad girl sitting in front of me, the dumpy dandruff-encrusted, pasty-faced psychiatrist my parents sent me to. Mainly, though, it pulsated around a large muscular oily boy two grades ahead of me, with whom I had had a few sweaty dates:

My feelings about him were certainly sexual, but, partly because I didn't really know what sex was, these feelings were monstrously dilated and distorted by my equally strong feelings of romance. When I fantasized having sex with him, I didn't picture anything happening below the waist: it was searing eye contact and intense jaw-setting action; there was a thunderstorm raging outside and flowers filling my dimly lit canopied boudoir. Never mind that we could barely hold a conversation; delirious with imaginings I more or less engineered the event, which finally took place on the floor of the garage, and it took several weeks for me to recover from the shocking clash between my fantasy and the actual painful, grunting, odorous occurrence.

Many people have had an experience like this, with various gradations in the gap between the real and the romantic. Some people react by repudiating their romantic

Mary Gaitskill, "Modern Romance: A Lesson in Appetite Control" *Ms.*, vol. 17 (May 1989): 55–56. © 1989 by Liberty Media for Women. Reprinted by permission of *Ms.* magazine.

feelings as lies and illusions—in fact, *The Concise Oxford Dictionary* defines "romance" as "an exaggeration," "a picturesque falsehood," or, as a verb, to "exaggerate or distort the truth, esp. fantastically." Even those adults who describe themselves as romantics tend to append words like "hopeless" to their description as though they know they're being foolish, but that it's a nice kind of foolishness proving how idealistic they are.

At 14, I wasn't about to decide that romance was a crock. My stubborn will to romance simply burrowed underground where it continued to live, finding nurturance in the crevices and claw holds of what was, I'm afraid, a series of seedy and preposterous adolescent experiences. In other words, since I was unable to find romance in the forms I'd been taught by popular culture to expect it—Valentines, flowers, declarations of pure love, gooey theme music that came out of nowhere—I saw it in unconventional places, in those unexpected moments of tenderness and communication that can occur between people in the most superficially unromantic circumstances.

I had, for various complex reasons, learned very little about intimacy and love, about the tension between desire and personal territory, about the space between my needs and the needs of others. All this confusion was exacerbated by the way in which romance was presented to adolescent girls at that time and probably still is: as an inexplicable idealized feeling that you could have for someone you just glimpsed across the room, based mainly on their appearance, a feeling that would end in love and marriage, a feeling that was totally disconnected from and incompatible with anything else in daily life, even sex. It is this disconnection that seems to me the oddest feature of our idea of romance.

Just a few years ago, I had a romantic experience that was very different from my first. I developed an intense crush on a man I worked with, an adorable big-eyed honey who could actually carry on a conversation. The same level of fantasy was in operation as the first time around—except that this time there were no flowers, no thunderstorms, the lights were on full blast and there was major action below, above, and all around the waist. There was only one thing preventing me from luring him into the metaphorical garage; he had a live-in girlfriend.

This situation, which sounds hideously painful, became a sort of epiphany for me. Somehow, in a startling outburst of maturity, I was able to place my romantic feelings in the context of my other feelings for him. I don't mean I suppressed my romantic feelings, or tried to control them—quite the contrary. I allowed them to exist and respected their realness without throwing all of my emotional weight on them. In this way I was able to enjoy my feeling of tenderness for him while allowing space for a gentle, calm, sensitive connection between the truth of who he was and the limits of our relationship.

What I learned from this experience came in mighty handy when, further down the road, I found myself involved with a handsome sexbomb playboy who was a lot of fun but who was clearly not Mr. Right. Although I knew I wasn't in love with him and never would be, I found myself assailed in the night by enormous fanged fantasies of ultimate romantic communion, fantasies in which we performed the most incredible sex acts to the thundering sound track of our equally incredible emotions. None of this had anything to do with what was actually happening between us, but the more I tried to deny my romantic outburst the closer I got to the edge of an obsessional abyss.

Then, on some barely conscious level, I shifted gears. I stopped trying to control and contain my feelings. Instead I simply allowed myself to feel them—to respect their reality in the context of my other feelings for the guy, which ranged from friendship to attraction to disinterest. Throughout the affair, I was able to enjoy my hot romantic feelings for him, and to see him for who he was—which, if you must know, was a charming meatball.

This of course goes against our conventional concept of romance, which is defined as incomprehensible and overwhelming; women, especially, are taught to regard it as a ferocious onset, a feeling that will render them helpless, swooning, and incapable. Whatever turns you on. But remember: to feel helpless and out of control isn't the same thing as being helpless and out of control. Romance is as real as lust, friendship, and love, but it is only part of a shifting spectrum of possible responses. There's nothing wrong with wanting to make out in a flower-filled room while a thunderstorm rages. There's also nothing wrong with wanting to rip off someone's clothes and roll around on the garage floor with them. It's when these feelings don't acknowledge each other that you court disappointment.

By fetishizing romance in the ways that we do, disconnecting it from other feelings and then placing such enormous weight on it, we make it hard for it to flower. For it is only when romance allows for and works with emotional intimacy as well as the power of gut-level sexual passion that all at once, there is loud theme music playing, the flaming sun is setting, you are bursting out of your bodice—or whatever your fantasy is.

Chapter Sixty-three

Endless Love (1997)

Letty Cottin Pogrebin

Pogrebin, a founding editor of Ms. *magazine and author of many books, writes in praise of enduring love through marriage with a man whom she describes as her devoted partner, lover, and closest friend.*

My parents had a miserable marriage. There was no physical violence, but their constant bickering, which often erupted into fierce and frightening quarrels, fell on my ears like blows. Many nights, I monitored their combat, crouched in my bunny pajamas at the top of the stairs, listening to her complaints and self-pity, his rage and ridicule, her accusations of neglect, his slammed doors, the screech of his car tires, the lullaby of her sobs—threnody for a marriage that should never have been. Before it could end in divorce, she got cancer and died. I was 15. I vowed I would never marry.

This December, Bert and I will celebrate our thirty-fourth wedding anniversary. In contrast to my parents' warfare, my relationship with my husband has been the most consistently joyful, least problematic aspect of my life. Ironic, inconceivable, but true. Of course, I haven't escaped my share of personal *mishegaas*—from claustrophobia to Holocaust nightmares—but my marriage is the place where I have always felt at peace, whole, cherished.

It's hard to write about our relationship. I'm afraid of sounding smug when all I am is grateful. Happiness lacks drama. It also arouses suspicion and cynicism. Furthermore, I'm superstitious; I don't wish to tempt the fates. Yet if the silence of people like me allows marriage to be personified by arid unions such as that of my parents, or by abusive spouses on the nightly news—or even by ideologues with a bias against heterosexual matrimony—then maybe it's time to stand up and be counted. So let me say it plainly: I'm a feminist and I've been happily married for more than three decades.

These thoughts are prompted by our summer vacation, a nine-day hike in the Dordogne area of France, just the two of us. To prepare for the journey, we read

Miles Morland's *A Walk Across France,* in which he describes trekking with his wife from the Mediterranean to the Atlantic in 25 days. Before their departure, Morland admits he worried what the two of them would have to talk about.

"How odd," says Bert. "That never worried me." Nor me. Boredom is not something we've experienced in this marriage. As it is, the demands of work, family, and community leave us little time for relaxed conversation, so we looked forward to nine days of uninterrupted "Us."

For six or seven hours a day, we hiked through French forests and farmlands, along tractor paths and country lanes, past fields of sunflowers and twelfth-century churches, and talked about whatever crossed our minds, from the big issues to our bodily functions (which can be a Big Issue when you're out in nature). We canoed, picnicked, wandered through castles and caves, practiced our French, drank countless bottles of Monbazillac, and found one another astonishingly interesting. Wildly unsequential and frankly self-referential, our topics ranged from hiking boots to Hong Kong to Toni Morrison to what we had had for dinner. We talked about the wonders of the Dordogne Valley, managed care, our new grandsons, our aching quads, Benjamin Netanyahu, and the weather. We rejoiced in our physical stamina. Historic sites recalled other places we'd been, recycling us into the spiral of our own history. Silence fell between us as softly as the shadows of the trees. But dialogue shortened the miles, lent the trip its magic, and made me marvel anew at the wellsprings of this long, lovely marriage.

Friederich Nietzsche, of all people, counseled, "When entering in a marriage, one ought to ask oneself: Do you believe you are going to enjoy talking with this [person] up into your old age? Everything else in marriage is transitory."

I take no credit for the fact that the conversation continues. I have no guiding philosophy, no tips for newlyweds, no idea of how anyone else's marriage can be saved. All I know is what I've had—34 years with a devoted partner who is my lover and closest friend. I know how it feels to live with someone whose touch excites, whose counsel calms, whose well-being matters as much as my own. I know that simple contentment is a kind of euphoria, that the familiar can be as intoxicating as the exotic, and that comfort and equality are, over the long haul, greater aphrodisiacs than romanticized power plays. I know how soul-satisfying it is to love someone well and deeply and to be loved for all the right reasons. I know how much more layered life is when everything is shared—sorrow and success, new enthusiasms, old stories, children, grandchildren, friends, memories. I also know that, despite the stereotype of long marriage as state-sanctioned tedium punctuated by acts of patriarchal oppression, the older we get (I'm 58 now, he's 63) the more textured, generous, and pleasurable our relationship has become. We're what's called a good fit.

My 32-year-old daughters, Abigail and Robin, insist I'm being too facile. They don't think it's just luck. They want me to probe deeper; they say there are reasons why a marriage works or doesn't. (They've been married three and four years respectively, so they speak from experience.) As eyewitnesses to our relationship, they believe their father and I made an unconscious decision at the beginning that has determined the course of our marriage. Though we never articulated it, at some deep level, they insist, we decided to ignore the little annoyances, to forgive what could otherwise incense, to be more invested in being happy than in being right. The relationship works without us working at it, they say, because we stay focused on the things we love about each other and don't permit our faults to eclipse those virtues.

"You even excuse him his feminist failings," says Abigail.

"For example?"

"You know you do all the social stuff. You organize the family gatherings, arrange the evenings with friends, buy the birthday presents, send the thank-you notes. He just gets to enjoy it all."

"And when I've asked you about it," puts in Robin, "you say he's inept at those things and if left up to him they wouldn't get done or would get done badly. You notice the discrepancy—theoretically you oppose it—but you've decided it's not worth being bothered about because Dad contributes his own strengths to the relationship. It's more important to you that he's a terrific father, an adoring husband, kind, unself-centered, a great wit, or some such. You've made a bargain to see the good in each other and let the bad stuff bounce off."

"It's bizarre how well you guys tolerate each other's quirks," adds Abigail. "When you're in your workaholic mode, Dad will stay home on a Saturday night with no resentment. And when he forgets to water the plants or call the plumber, you chalk it up to his absentmindedness. You don't have a perfect marriage, but its imperfections are unimportant because neither of you loses sight of the big picture."

According to our daughters, Bert and I are a living, breathing reaction formation—our whole life is a repudiation of our parents' unhappiness (my mother- and father-in-law had serious incompatibility problems too). "Whether you realize it or not," concludes Robin, "you have created a relationship that's as different from your parents' as possible, which is exactly what you both wanted."

There's something surreal about hearing your children deconstruct your marriage. Nevertheless, while their analysis rings bells, it still doesn't explain everything: it doesn't explain why their father and I never tire of one another's company; why we still find each other sexy; why, despite my having greater visibility as a writer than Bert does as a lawyer, he has never been competitive. In fact, he takes more pride in my work than I do.

And he always makes me laugh. When I bitch because the washer and dryer are in constant need of repair, he responds, "Lucky in love, unlucky in appliances." When I praise something he's done, he says, "Honey, you make me feel six feet tall." He *is* six feet tall. When I'm upset because the movie we want to see is sold out, he hugs me and whispers, "At least we have a great marriage."

And we do.

Chapter Sixty-four

From The Last Gift of Time
Life beyond Sixty (1997)

Carolyn G. Heilbrun

Heilbrun, the literary critic and mystery writer (her nom de plume is Amanda Cross), has a fascinatingly unfashionable view: that so far from romance being "the only game in town" for women, middle and old age affords them the freedom to abandon sex and love and cultivate more satisfying relationships, such as friendships.

> [There is] a narrative difficulty which will always be acute: how to attach a heterosexual emotional life to a character whose strength comes from her transcendence of usual sexual roles?
> —Hermione Lee, *Willa Cather: Double Lives*

I cannot quite cure myself of the conviction that if we could discover a word that meant "adventure" and did not mean "romance," we in our late decades would be able to free ourselves from the compulsion always to connect yearning and sex. If an ancient (by American standards) woman finds herself longing for something new, something as yet not found, must that something always be sex or till-death-do-us-part romance? . . .

I have heard women mention their sorrow at having married men they did not love. But in almost every case, it turns out that what is lacking is not only palpitating desire for the husband but also any sense of him as a friend, as someone who can be conversed with readily and often. In *Writing a Woman's Life* I divided men, rather too taxonomically, into lovers and husbands, and I've taken a lot of flak for it. What I neglected to mention is that one may feel overwhelming desire for a man with whom the relationship can "dwindle" (that is, develop) into friendship. It sometimes happens: people do win the lottery. But if obsessive desire and skillful technique are the only basis for the woman's devotion, even that, should she and the man marry, will inevitably become less compelling once it is given full range in the marriage bed. The craving for the sexually skillful lover is almost always abetted by the infrequency of meetings with him. In short, I suggest that the "elderly" leave romance to the young, and welcome friendship. In all the novels . . . —by Cather, Hardy, et al.— which end in the powerful friendship between a man and a woman, the woman has first thrown her hat over the mill at a "romantic" man. This, of course, is an adventure suitable only to the young, or to the aged who wish to suffer forever the plight of unsatisfied sexual passion. Both French's and Lessing's protagonists end up alone, their sane, sensible, intelligent selves, harried but not lost. . . .

Am I able to suggest a substitute, unromantic adventure for women's later life? No, alas, I am not, although I have considered the matter long and hard. I do believe, however, that as we women reach our later years, sex, if it is part of our lives, is a by-product, not the dominant element. Like happiness, or beauty in a work of art, sex after sixty cannot be the object of any undertaking, though it may sometimes be a wonderful and unsought-for result. Whatever the satisfying and as yet culturally endorsed adventure after sixty may be, its necessary element is the sense of something essential and vital having been achieved or discovered or learned. (I *do* wish I could say this in a sexier way.)

Chapter Sixty-five

From Beyond Embarrassment
Feminism and Adult Heterosexual Love (1993)

Barbara Ryan

After briefly reviewing feminist reactions to romance, Ryan tries to theorize the possibility of a feminist "adult heterosexual love": "True, it is a particularly dangerous zone to traverse, much less live in. But this is no reason to pack our bags and leave."

> . . . at least say it. . . . *Love.* There, you can stand up now,
> it didn't kill you. Did it?
>
> —Margaret Atwood

If you advocate feminism, as I do, you spend a lot of time talking about it to the unconverted and listening to their critiques and fears. One common fear is that feminist women cannot allow themselves to love men, or that, if they find themselves falling into this patriarchal "trap," they would earn feminists' scorn for following where their hearts lead.

This anxiety sounds silly when put in these blunt terms, but a moment's reflection shows where people are getting these ideas. If, as feminism tells them, their minds are shaped and skewed by patriarchy, then their affections are probably as unreliable, indeed complicit, in furthering political ends to which feminists must not subscribe. When I try to show these doubters that feminists can and often do establish mutually loving relationships with men, many are surprised. I think that's because the average citizen gets few chances to hear feminists discuss the possibility of adult heterosexual love (AHL). That's an odd reticence when you consider that many, many of us go right on looking for AHL, and many believe that they have found it.

I'm interested in that hesitancy to discuss a topic of great import, not least for its effect on constituents and potential allies. But there are other reasons to reassess our position on AHL. If we do refuse or neglect to do so, it seems to me, we risk mimicry

From Barbara Ryan, "Beyond Embarrassment: Feminism and Adult Heterosexual Love," *Centennial Review*, vol. 37, no. 3 (fall 1993): 471–74, 477–86. © 1993 by the *Centennial Review*. Reprinted by permission.

of a classic masculinist position, that of denying emotions and behaviors that greatly concern many women.

This parallel was brought home to me by, of all things, *Glamour* magazine. In the month I began this article, this popular forum had a good deal to say about adults' intimate relations. "Beyond Sex," ran the headline, "What Pulls a Man Closer?" The answer was prudent silence: "most [men] claimed that nothing turned them off more than verbalizing or dissecting . . . closeness."[1] Well, I thought, if the Average Guy refuses to discuss AHL, then committed feminists should be talking up a storm.

Some fellow travelers have agreed. "One of the central questions that feminist theory needs to discuss," remarks Carol Ann Douglas, "is the question of love as an emotion, an experience—its political, social and theoretical implications for feminism."[2] I agree that it's a central question; what interests me is our silence.[3] This reticence is astounding in a culture obsessed with heterosexuality, cries of male bashing, and women's "natural" bent for love. We see that obsession often enough in daily life: for instance, most gender analysts I know have had, at one time or another, to rebut charges that feminists hate men. We all roll our eyes at this attack: come on, many of us are living with and/or openly loving That Other Gender; don't believe everything you read in the antifeminist media. In fact, though, that's a pretty cheap answer to a real question. As long as feminists don't take a public stand on AHL, even our supporters are likely to feel confused.

They recognize that feminism has much to say about other loves: there's no shortage of information on mother-child, lesbian, and sisterly loves, and even male-male bonding.[4] But there is a shortage of feminist work on the loves propagated at the grocery checkout, even (or especially) when babies are the glue. What has feminism made of Annette and Rebecca "snagging" Warren and Jack with cuddly babies? If, as I believe, most consumers are getting a covert message—Warren really *wanted* to be snagged; babies help men commit themselves to the adult responsibilities they secretly crave in their bachelor days—then the question is how that subtext works for or against feminist goals.

I'd admit, meanwhile, that attention to companionate intimacy is not and should not be feminism's primary political goal. It's clear that worry about AHL is a mark of privilege; coupled intimacy is less pressing a topic than, for instance, economic sufficiency, violence against women, or reproductive rights. Nonetheless, AHL is not a trivial topic: as long ago as 1970, Shulamith Firestone reported that "love, perhaps even more than childbearing, is the pivot of women's oppression today."[5] This being the case, she added that "[a] book on radical feminism that did not deal with love would be a political failure."[6] If this is true, many political failures reside on our shelves and syllabi. Twenty years after Firestone, AHL no longer raises outrage, though there's plenty of evidence that it causes straight feminists shame and avowed embarrassment.

Red faces are interesting in themselves: they suggest that a once public issue has been forced back into private venues redolent of hushed whispers, gossipy "girl talk," and other despised or demonized conversations. This segregation is a mistake, on purely practical grounds: we don't want to indicate, even tacitly, that feminists accept the directives of "Beyond Sex," which amount to telling women to shut up about intimacy if they want to have any. At the same time, feminists' silence on AHL is a moral issue. If we do not manage to bring AHL within feminism's purview, then we agree to denigrate some of straight people's most significant activities.[7]

Besides, I think feminists may utilize AHL with care; if so, it could prove an appealing, established, and useful model of political coalition. AHL, in other words, can be more than a personal goal. It can be a way to think about talking across divides of experience, as well as insight, perspective, what feels "true" or tastes good.

So what causes feminists to suspect or decry AHL? Overzealous binarization seems the likeliest explanation: if the enemy is man, then AHL must be collusion. But surely few are arguing that matters are (or ever have been) so simply sliced along gender lines. Instead, precisely because we now acknowledge layers, feints, gapped identities, and imbricant loyalties, it is more necessary than ever to see what (if anything) AHL offers our cause. If no political agenda or stance is "pure," then AHL is no more or less worthy than other positions feminists could adopt. True, it is a particularly dangerous zone to traverse, much less live in. But this is no reason to pack our bags and leave; indeed, it might only be another mark of privilege to do so.[8] Instead, considering the number of constituents who live in what may be a particularly polluted zone, it is crucial to advocate cleanup, not wholesale abandonment, or the hope of rapture.

This is a nineties viewpoint: in the 1970s, we were more likely to propose sweeping solutions in the name of rigor. "I, personally," wrote Ti-Grace Atkinson in those stormy years, "have taken the position that I will not appear with any man publicly, where it could possibly be interpreted that we were friends."[9] She defended her extreme position as survival tactics: "The price," she wrote, "of clinging to the enemy is your life."[10] Atkinson never represented "the" feminist position: "There is an outrageous thing going on here," responded Anne Koedt, "strictly in terms of pressuring women about their personal lives."[11] But extreme separatism could be (and was) portrayed as feminism *per se,* as if gender differences necessitated gender divides. The consequences of misprision were not always negative: one bright spot was the emergence of openly lesbian feminist activists. The down side, of course, was that many straight women left feminism; in our own day, many have never joined.

When they do sign on as feminists, women who love men may feel insufficiently PC. "I have been living," an AHLing woman wrote to *Ms.* last year, "with an uneasy fear of not being a 'Good Feminist.' "[12] Her worries all but invite caustic critique: this same letter admits that the writer is new to *Ms.* (and to feminism?), evidence that her worries about who should kill kitchen insects may be a toddler's fears. Perhaps, though, such cynicism is antiwoman in this instance. On what grounds shall we ignore her perception that heterosexual union and feminism do not mix? Do they? Was Atkinson wrong? Is rigor outdated? Has something changed so that feminists are now able to love men without worrying that they are falling into a prettified Stockholm syndrome?

No one has addressed these questions seriously: instead, a vaguely "tolerant" attitude gestures at *de gustibus.* In this milieu, our silence represents an appalling timidity and political failure; more to the point, it is a public relations disaster. I don't think feminism has to burble, with Naomi Wolf: "It's time to say you *can* hate sexism and love men."[13] But I do think we have to grapple with a more complex version of her peppy optimism: *can* you really accomplish both aims and if so, are the presumed gains worth the dangers some of us once thought were involved? . . .

Attention to heterosexist privilege (still contested and embryonic) would comprise a major step forward in women's awareness of gender training; so would the lesson that us/them scenarios can be reductionist, lesbophobic, and unproductive. But even if these points were more widely accepted than I think they are, they would not sanction an innocent return to AHL. Questions remain unanswered: "What is love," asked Ti-Grace Atkinson, "but the payoff for the consent to oppression? What is love but need? What is love but fear?"[14] Well, as many of us have found, it may be several things: companionship, religious training, habituated comfort, caring partnership, a moral imperative. All good things, yet none necessarily free of the ugly motivations Atkinson lists. We have far more work to do on addressing her concerns, work that might begin with the admission that many of us enjoy and cultivate AHL. At least say it.

Well, some of you are thinking, who says we do? OK. I must admit that it is embarrassing to write this paper: by doing so, I risk feminist credentials, as well as any claim I might stake to intellectual acuity or social *savoir faire*. For of course my search for AHL may merely be an attempt to rationalize complacency: I expect comments to the effect that I'm justifying, even encouraging, economic dependency and/or emotional security; experiencing co-optation; trying to please a tyrannical Father. All I can tell these critics is that I believe that some women have managed to develop satisfying and feminist AHL relationships, or persuade themselves that they have done so. I would like to give credence to their beliefs and discuss them more widely in feminist venues. Put it this way: must heterosexist privilege call for abnegation? Gayatri Spivak says that the point of having privilege is to use it.

In *On Loving Men* (1980), Jane Lazarre tried to do so. "I am a feminist," she wrote, "who has feared and hated men and who all the while has continued to love them."[15] The source of her fear, and hate, was the belief that AHL caused loss of self: with Beauvoir, Lazarre feared that AHL could prove "poisonous to a woman's autonomy."[16] Few of us would deny this point out of hand; unfortunately, some of Lazarre's other claims are a bit daunting. I'm nonplussed by her certainty that every woman enjoys "the deep pleasure of a penis within her" (she does not even specify that the penis lovers be heterosexual).[17] Adrienne Rich rebuts Lazarre's universalizing with a wry description of "the crude pestle, the blind/ramrod" that makes my straight friends wince but laugh. We know, though, that laughter, like disagreement, must be viewed with some detachment: on no account may learned reactions be permitted to close down our discussion. For instance, we have little reason to dismiss Lazarre's tastes as "mere" false consciousness. It's true that we must question where consent to heterosexual intercourse is constrained by social pressures. But even Catharine MacKinnon, the theorist who has been most helpful in elucidating this crucial point, finds herself, in the nineties, able to appear in public with, indeed, to marry, a man.

Fair enough: MacKinnon is not Atkinson, and she has never argued that heterosexuality is wrong. Nor has she argued, though many have said this of her, that "every fuck is a rape." On the contrary, MacKinnon's engagement suggests that sexual consent can be adjudged, and rightly. More important, for my purposes, her engagement indicates (and no more) that this long-time feminist believes in AHL.

Does her fiancee believe in AHL, too? If he does, I'd be fascinated to learn how he understands that belief in light of his critical interest in psychoanalysis. As is now well known, Jeffrey Masson has deeply problematized central tenets of Freud's discipline, the therapy Irving Yalom calls "love's executioner." If the talking cure really amounts to the death of AHL, it'd be interesting to know if Masson's days in therapy are implicated in his desire to wed. Does he believe in AHL because he experienced psychoanalysis, or despite the days he spent on the executioner's couch?

Leaving aside individual cases, it still seems obvious that one great stumbling block to discussing AHL is the reign of Freud.[18] The great Hermenuet was a product, we know, of a sentimental culture, an ethos widely associated with women's power and the beauties of heterosexual union. Today, largely because of Freud's pathologizing "discoveries," intellectuals have learned to believe that adults' couplings are based on something other than two souls' union: hence Roland Barthes's observation that while everyone educated can talk fluently about sex, few self-styled intellectuals would be caught dead discussing love. Straight feminists are as susceptible to that ideology as anyone else. But we, of course, carry a doubled burden in respect to AHL: if patriarchy is the problem, then why are we joining it, not to mention reproducing it, and building our home lives around the heterosexual pairing on which patriarchy relies?

Caution, then, must be ongoing; at the same time, though, as Patricia Hill Collins points out, "when people reject the world as it is constructed by dominant groups, the power as energy that can flow from a range of love relationships becomes possible."[19] That "range" is crucial: no feminist can advocate one form of adult love as sufficient to all humans. But "love relationships" are also crucial: as Rita Mae Brown and other revolutionaries have noted, "Love is the enemy of unequal social structure. When people really love they become disobedient."[20]

I think that can be true; I also think that it's easier in today's political climate to speak of love when one feels oneself, or one's lovers, to be oppressed. Hence lesbian feminists' willingness to admit their loves; hence support for AHL from many (but not all) black feminists. For June Jordan the question is one of empowerment. "As I think about anyone or any thing," she wrote in 1981, "whether history or literature or my father or political organizations or a poem or a film—as I seek to evaluate the potentiality, the life supportive commitment/possibilities of anyone or any thing, the decisive question is, always, *where is the love?*"[21]

For Jessica Benjamin, in *The Bonds of Love* (1988), it lies in children's identifications with parents. True, she is a hermeneut in the line of Freud. What's interesting about her project, though, is her belief that love does exist, and is in itself beneficial. "Domination," she asserts, "is a *twisting* of the bonds of love" (italics mine); that is, tergiversation distorts an alliance that would otherwise be free of hierarchical play.[22] Working from this premise, Benjamin suggests that revised parenting procedures would increase women's chances of achieving good AHL; interestingly enough, the same revisions would help men love.

In Benjamin's eyes men are as handicapped as women: since, she says, both boys and girls are encouraged to identify with only one parent, both genders usually emerge from childhood emotional cripples, in regard to love. This is an advance, in my view, on Shulamith Firestone's comment that "[m]en can't love."[23] For one thing, it relieves women of the burden of fostering AHL without help from men; for another, it reminds us that women do not, and cannot, provide all emotional answers.

Someone needs to get this point across to Naomi Wolf, who recently claimed to explain "how to love a man and save your feminist soul." The tone grates; so does the message, in part because she never gets around to the all important "how." But the bigger problem is that Wolf has almost nothing to say about AHL: her focus, amidst giggles, is sexual attraction. Well, we know how that works: the problem with biologism, as Joyce Trebilcot pointed out years ago, is that arguments based on "nature" allow straight feminists to exploit unacknowledged privilege.[24] If we stick strictly to AHL, then Wolf offers nothing to counteract Dana Densmore's warning that too easy recuperation of AHL leads many women to

> lavish and dissipate their valuable talents and emotional strength on attempts ... to work things out with lovers so that "love" might be less degrading. And too often all they reap is demoralization, damaged egos, emotional exhaustion.[25]

These cautions are still timely: Catharine MacKinnon has commented on those who "constantly [express] their desire for sexual connection undominated by dominance, unimplicated in the inequality of the sexes, a sexuality of one's own yet with another." The problem, for Densmore and MacKinnon, is "that many people want to believe they already have this more than they want to have it. . . ."[26]

Wolf falls squarely into this postfeminist impasse: ignoring the fact that many feminists don't want to love men, and the interesting proposition that some feminists may *be* men, Wolf praises what she calls "radical heterosexuality" as though the seventies had not happened. Her argument? Simply that she knows how to pick 'em: she tells us that she's especially susceptible to "the oil-stained persona of the labor organizer."[27] Grimy, we see, but still an intellectual: "Men We Love," she promises, "are willing, sooner or later, to read the Books We Love."[28] Gee, really? This would come as news to many fans of Janet Dailey, *Our Bodies, Ourselves,* the NARAL bulletin, and even *Ms.*

In fact, what Wolf seems ominously to advocate is an unacknowledged agenda something like "missionary dating." But, as every evangelical teen magazine warns, it's a risky business to woo the unsaved with Christian *eros.* What happens if the Men We Love, or Have Loved, are *not* willing to read our books—do we, should we, must we, just stop loving them? And if we don't, if we still like having them around, is our AHL, inauthentic, nonfeminist, ignominious?

Even more troubling is Wolf's blithe certainty that feminist women are so strong, in their own minds, that traffic with men poses no real threat to their unshakeable principles. This self-congratulation disguises pernicious nonsense: surely we know, in the nineties, that gender tensions are ongoing. Tracy Chapman gets this right in one mournful sentence: "If you could say the right thing, at the right time, you'd be mine." The trouble she pinpoints here is not just, or primarily, that men have much to learn. It's also that women who want to love men have a lot to learn along with them, a process that can be burdened by assumptions that women just "naturally" understand AHL.

We don't, you know; and we especially don't understand how feminism, AHL, and other loves interact. Some of us admit this: "Shouldn't I have this?" asks Mary-Chapin Carpenter, listing a wealth of leisure, recreation, career success, and personal pleasures. "Shouldn't I have all of this, and passionate kisses?" Well, if you've heard the song, you know that she's not too confident, despite what sounds like an intensely privileged siting on the world she knows. Even Queen Latifah, no shrinking violet, hedges her bets on AHL: "The time is now to mend and be friends."

Janice Raymond agrees: though you will not hear *A Passion for Friends* (1986) on your FM radio, feminists might want to tune in to Raymond's thoughts on female-female friendship. It isn't *When Harry Met Sally,* but something closer to *Thelma and Louise*: Raymond suggests that we rethink women's friendships with each other as an undergirding and "home base" from which to tackle the array of social codes she calls "hetero-reality." Not that Raymond suggests this extrapolation of her thoughts on love—indeed, her most intriguing work is on those women she calls "marriage resisters." Nonetheless, feminist *bricoleurs* might do well to try to combine insights on female-female bonding with new work on AHL.

For with a wider sense of the infinite variety of love and lovers—and a broader understanding of complicity, collusion, and master-slave—today's feminists are unusually well-equipped to rethink AHL as friendship, coalition, intersubjective praxis, cross-cultural bridging, and translation. That is, even if we agree that AHL is a haven supplied by privilege, we may be able to show that it's also, potentially or actually, a laboratory for change. Yes, a nuisance; yes, frequently hard damn work—but, in many cases, a more immediate pleasure and/or benefit than revolutionary programs generally provide. If, as I suspect, pleasure is central to persuasion, then aren't feminists obliged to rethink the diversity of pleasures some still find in AHL?

A feminist AHL, with due attention to power imbalance, gender positioning, and daily struggle, seems an apt model of the dually transformative relationship I think cultural progressives must work on now. Though you know and I know that AHL doesn't always last, we might take that fragility as all the more reason to cherish its strengths. So, please, no hearts and flowers; no "returns to romance," if I can help it.[29] Instead, an AHL that can be visualized as a dialogue trying to double as a cement: that is, a tenuous, resilient, invigorating experience of shared, not always harmonious, commitment to moral ends. One useful model might be a semiprivatized version of Seyla Benhabib's discourse ethics: "a continuous process of conversation in which understanding and misunderstanding, agreement as well as disagreement are intertwined and always at work."[30] It's no picnic and no sinecure: "It is extremely difficult," comments Robin Morgan, "at this moment in history for even the most principled woman and the most principled man to speak the same language."[31] That's OK, though: we're quite accustomed to difficulty, and besides, strained conversations might beat omphaloskeptic self-absorption. Work on AHL, like AHL itself, brims with positive energy for ongoing yet directed social change, as extremist or exclusionary prescriptives too often do not.

To take one example from many, a feminist AHL might help us think through and improve our coalition politics. In the first place, of course, it might help us woo back those straight women who have much to offer feminism, and who are wondering what feminism offers them. On a more abstract level, though, I'm interested in the difficulty of theorizing AHL, and its implications for the concurrent difficulty of joining disparate souls in common cause.

AHL and coalition politics can sound pretty similar: on the latter, Bernice Reagon writes, "I feel as if I'm gonna keel over any minute and die. That is often what it feels like if you're *really* doing coalition work . . . you feel threatened to the core and if you don't, you're not really doing no coalescing."[32] Sounds like earlier comments that AHL is dangerous. But so does the realization that broad and deep systemic change requires co-operation from unknown others. "What *I* really feel is radical," writes Barbara Smith, "is trying to make coalitions with people who are different from you."[33] Some people who are different are straights and lesbians; other people who are different are men and women; and these differences only rest on gender and affectional preferences. If we add the input of race, class, age, etc., then coalition politics looks like Beauvoir's thoughts on authentic love: recognition of the self, the other, the self *as* other, and the rarity of interrelationships with other humans.

To show how this might work, I'll conclude with a love story I find graceful and compelling. It is "The Age of Discretion," and it was written by Simone de Beauvoir.

What I like about this short tale, of a couple in their sixties who negotiate a difficult passage with their only child, is how frankly and easily the couple talks to each other. I know, I know, this is a woman-authored fantasy: nonetheless, it goes a long way toward describing my idea of AHL. It has a lot to do with the way this couple talks: they discuss things; he thinks about the tensions without her prompting; they admit faults; both err. They keep on talking, not necessarily at great length. He takes care of her, and she takes care of him; they get cross, and time passes, and they talk it over, and the relationship emerges strengthened. They are both happier together; both retain rights to disagree, to be autonomous, to get their work done, to work together. Their AHL, in short, is an ongoing conversation in which both lovers speak and listen. The errant child, I should mention, dwindles in significance throughout the story; what this tale describes is a decades-long dyadic sharing constituted in largely verbal terms. Talking, in other words, seems possible and worthwhile; Beauvoir does not promise, or even mention, transcendent bliss.

I really enjoyed this story: I thought it described an AHL feminism could subscribe to. Other models might also be appropriate: I think of Sethe and Paul D., Joseph Shing and Lilith Iyapo, Polly and Piers Hargraves. I like, perhaps most of all, Christopher Tietjens and Valentine Wannop, because I appreciate his comment that marriage is justified by two people's desire to go on speaking with each other.

You may have your own favorites; you may disagree with mine. OK, so let's talk about what comprises a truly feminist AHL. Let's start by at least saying it: *love*. It will not kill us. It may prove dangerous. But facing up to our loves and lovers can only make feminism stronger.

NOTES

1. Thurston Clarke, "Beyond Sex: What Pulls a Man Closer?" *Glamour* (May 1993): 268.

2. Carol Ann Douglas, *Love and Politics: Radical Feminist and Lesbian Theories* (San Francisco: ISM P, 1990) 109. Douglas's work in the archives of feminism has proved invaluable to this study.

3. I foresee that my own silence, on sexuality, will seem perverse. In fact, though, it's intended to steer us away from biologism, a field of study that has always helped us bracket out messy emotions. Such an evasion, in this inquiry, would be illegitimate on the face of it, quite apart from the disservice done AHLing women. But it would also be inappropriate due to our still-recent discovery that desires, like emotions or eating habits, are learned, channelled and controlled. Considering the fact that some couples love through impotency, rape trauma, physical disability, religious observances, and other celibate periods, I think AHL can be discussed apart from "natural" yearnings situated in physiological makeups. In place of biology, then, I'll base my stance on perceptions, particularly some women's perceptions, that they are, or have been, or would like to be in AHL. These perceptions are not the sole property of feminists; far from it. But they are of special interest to a political movement that is devoted to rethinking power relations, privacy, and private power relations.

4. If feminists have detoured interest in AHL into related areas such as child care, parents' gender roles and the nuclear family, there is a "plus": it's high time we wrested so-called family values from the outrageous Right. But the "minus" would have to be that feminists' desire for improved AHL would have been subordinated to their children's supposed needs. This is a scenario we have seen before—she suffered in silence for the sake of her loved ones— and which we cannot allow to substitute for investigations of AHL.

5. Shulamith Firestone, *The Dialectic of Sex: The Case for Feminist Revolution* (New York: Bantam, 1970) 126.

6. Firestone 126. Because Firestone's lack of interest in lesbian and gay loves is well attested, I assume that this "love" refers to AHL, parent-child, and perhaps sibling loves.

7. See Pat Mainardi's comments in "The Marriage Question," *Feminist Revolution,* ed. Redstockings (New York: Random House, 1978) 120–21.

8. I am not arguing that it is "easier" to be a lesbian, but I do think money paves the way here as in other areas. My analogy is really to people living in areas contaminated by hazardous waste: it is usually the poorer families who suffer. Those with money can move away with less financial hardship, a point as true of lesbians as anybody else. Consider, for instance, Martina Navratilova's decision to sell her home in Aspen, and see Cathy McCandless's comment that in gender separatism, as in everything else, "Money can buy you a great deal of distance." McCandless, "Some Thoughts on Racism, Classism and Separatism," *Top Ranking: Racism and Classism in the Lesbian Community,* qtd. in Douglas 256.

9. Ti-Grace Atkinson, "The Political Woman," *Amazon Odyssey* (New York: Links Books, 1974) 91.

10. Atkinson 90.

11. Anne Koedt, "Lesbianism and Feminism," *Radical Feminism,* eds. Anne Koedt, Ellen Levine, and Anita Rapone (New York: Quadrangle Books, 1973) 253.

12. Nancy Victoria Perl, "Letters," *Ms.* (Nov./Dec. 1992): 6.

13. Naomi Wolf, "Radical Heterosexuality . . . or how to love a man and save your feminist soul," *Ms.* (Jul./Aug. 1992): 29.

14. Atkinson, "Vaginal Orgasm: A Mass-Hysterical Response," *Amazon Odyssey* 7.

15. Jane Lazarre, *On Loving Men* (New York: Dial P, 1980) 80.

16. Lazarre 78.

17. Lazarre 79.

18. Julia Kristeva has, of course, tried to rethink this tendency, utilizing love as a new model for the therapeutic relationship. Yet she has little to say about AHL, preferring to focus on mother-child relationships and a sort of psychoanalytic *agape* that cannot afford to select one preferred love object. See, for instance, *The Kristeva Reader,* ed. Toril Moi (New York: Columbia UP, 1986) 238; and Julia Kristeva, *Histories d'amour* (Paris: Denoel P, 1983).

19. Patricia Hill Collins, *Black Feminist Thought: Knowledge, Consciousness, and the Politics of Empowerment* (New York: Routledge, 1990) 182.

20. Rita Mae Brown, "It's All Dixie Cups to Me," *A Plain Brown Rapper* (Baltimore: Diana P, 1976) 198. See also Mary Daly, who praised love's ability to enable the "becoming of new human beings," in *Beyond God the Father: Toward a Philosophy of Women's Liberation* (Boston: Beacon P, 1973) 128.

21. June Jordan, *Civil Wars* (Boston: Beacon P, 1981) 141.

22. See Jessica Benjamin, *The Bonds of Love: Psychoanalysis, Feminism, and the Problem of Domination* (New York: Pantheon, 1988) 219.

23. Firestone 152.

24. Joyce Trebilcot, *Taking Responsibility for Sexuality* (San Francisco: Acacia, 1983) 12.

25. Dana Densmore, "Independence from the Sexual Revolution," *Radical Feminism* 109.

26. Both these quotations come from MacKinnon's afterword to *Feminism Unmodified: Discourses on Life and Law* (Cambridge: Harvard UP, 1987) 217–18.

27. Wolf 30.

28. Wolf 31.

29. Elaine Hoffman Baruch praises what she sees as a return of romantic love in the 1980s; unfortunately, all she bases it on is fear of AIDs and economic straits. This is the sort of pathologizing I have tried to avoid; it may be relevant that the writer works from certain Freudian principles. See her *Women, Love and Power: Literary and Psychoanalytic Perspectives* (1991).

30. Seyla Benhabib, "The Debate over Women and Moral Theory Revisited," *Situating the Self: Gender, Community and Postmodernism in Contemporary Ethics* (New York: Routledge, 1992) 198.

31. Interview with Robin Morgan, *off our backs,* 19:4 (April 1989).

32. Bernice Johnson Reagon, "Coalition Politics: Turning the Century," *Home Girls: A Black Feminist Anthology,* ed. Barbara Smith (Latham, NY: Women of Color P, 1983) 356.

33. Barbara and Beverly Smith, "Across the Kitchen Table: A Sister-to-Sister Dialogue," *This Bridge Called My Back: Writings by Radical Women of Color,* eds. Cherrie Moraga and Gloria Anzaldua (Latham, NY: Women of Color P. 1983) 126.

Index

About the Editor

Susan Ostrov Weisser was born and raised in Brooklyn, New York. Her master's degree in modernist literature is from Northwestern University, and her Ph.D. in the Victorian novel from Columbia University. From 1985 to 1989 she worked on a four-year project, funded by the Spencer Foundation and led by the cognitive psychologist Dr. Jerome Bruner, on the relationship between narrative and selfhood. She is the author of *A Craving Vacancy: Women and Sexual Love in the British Novel, 1740–1880,* and co-editor with Jennifer Fleischner, of *Feminist Nightmares: Women at Odds.*

Dr. Weisser has been a member of the Adelphi University English Department since 1987 and is currently a professor of English there. She also teaches writing part-time at the Gallatin Division of New York University, and is an academic director of the Bard College Clemente Program in the Humanities, a program for low-income students in Harlem. She has three children, Cybèle, Amanda, and Will, and a baby granddaughter, Madeline.